Missing Masterpieces

GERT-RUDOLF FLICK

Missing Masterpieces

LOST WORKS OF ART

1450 – 1900

The British Art *Journal*

IN ASSOCIATION WITH

MERRELL
LONDON • NEWYORK

First published by

The British Art *Journal*
46 Grove Lane
London SE5 8ST

in association with

Merrell Publishers Limited

Head office:
42 Southwark Street
London SE1 1UN

New York office:
49 West 24th Street, 8th floor
New York, NY 10010

www.merrellpublishers.com

First published 2003

Reprinted 2004

A catalogue record for this book is available from the British Library

ISBN 1 85894 197 0

Edited by Robin Simon

Picture research by Philippa Lewis

Index by Carolyn Eardley

Typeset in Adobe Sabon by Alison Guy

Designed by Peter Guy

Printed and bound in China

Contents

To Corinne

Introduction

THIS BOOK was born out of discussions with my friend Mr. Peter Watson. Originally a compendium of all important missing works of art was envisaged, but it soon became clear that such a book was neither feasible nor maybe desirable. I subsequently decided to focus on only about forty famous missing works that could be defined as masterpieces, which would be analysed in detail. That number was subsequently reduced to the twenty-four discussed here.

As I began to research the subject, it soon became clear that many works of art which were listed as missing had either been destroyed or were in fact extant. For example, a painting of *The siege of Gibraltar* in the Milwaukee Art Museum (U.S.A.) was sold recently as by a 'Follower of Joseph Wright of Derby', but has now been firmly identified as the original by Wright of Derby – the very painting that was always thought to be missing. In this case the difficulty in making the correct identification arose from the ruinous state of preservation of the painting, which made a comparison with preparatory drawings hazardous, although not impossible.

This painting, obviously, would not have been eligible for inclusion in the present book. Equally, I did not wish to trace the fate of works which had definitely been destroyed. I wanted to concentrate on works the fate of which remains uncertain, and which might even, conceivably, survive. Indeed, in the course of preparing the book, four masterpieces that I had been researching re-surfaced: a landscape by Canaletto; a mythological subject by Elsheimer; a Gainsborough landscape; and a life-size sculpture by Canova. Another condition for the inclusion of a masterpiece in this account is that there should be substantial visual evidence of its appearance, whether in the form of a preliminary design or some other record such as a copy or engraving. In one instance, where parts of an altarpiece survive and some are missing, the lost elements can be deduced with some certainty from the evidence of their reflection in other, surviving, works.

Works of art and paintings go missing at all times, as the result of changes in taste or neglect. There are also certain periods of history when wars or revolutions force an exceptional number of works of art on to the market, and it is especially in these circumstances that works of art seem more likely to vanish. One such period was around the middle of the seventeenth century, when the English Civil War and the Thirty Years War in Central Europe helped to break up such fabled collections as those of Charles I, Rudolf II, the Earl of Arundel, the Duke of Buckingham and the Duke of Hamilton. Another key period was that of the French Revolution and the Napoleonic Wars, the prolonged after-effects of which continued well into the middle of the nineteenth century. This latter period is especially noticeable for the number of masterpieces that vanish apparently without trace, a phenomenon exacerbated by the marked changes of taste that took place at the time, and which rendered many formerly admired works unfashionable.

As there are many ways in which a work of art can disappear, there are equally many ways in which it can resurface. The unnoticed picture hanging on a landing in a country-house suddenly identified as an important Old Master has become proverbial. It is increasingly rare, but is by no means extinct. Recently, to take a startling case in point, a Cimabue was discovered in just these circumstances. This was so rare indeed that the discovery (now safely in the National Gallery, London) was the first work by the artist ever to be sold at auction.

The most common form of a 'missing' painting, however, is probably the misattributed or the miscatalogued. One often has the notion that a painting would have to change its location before it could go 'missing' but this is not always the case. A painting of *The supper at Emmaus* that has been in the Contarini Chapel of the Church of S. Salvador in Venice since 1534 was only recently discovered to be by Vittorio Carpaccio. The Soprintendenza in Venice had for decades failed to recognise this masterpiece, even though they were specialists in this type of painting and more familiar than anyone with the churches and monuments in their care. Again, a painting of *The seizing of Christ* which used to hang in plain view in a monastery in Ireland, catalogued as Honthorst, was identified by an art historian as a Caravaggio that had been considered lost.

Next to works of art which are physically present but wrongly attributed there are a great number of items which have not been seen for a very long time. Because no-one has seen a particular work of art for decades or centuries, it is often assumed to have perished, but that is often not the case. Canvas and oil paint can take an astonishing amount of punishment before they disintegrate and, as a rule of thumb, it can be stated that paintings often survive better than the buildings in which they are kept.

Finally, I would like to thank those who have helped me with this book, foremost Mr. Robin Simon, editor of *The British Art Journal*, without whom it would not have seen the light of day.

Gert-Rudolf Flick
London
2002

Missing Masterpieces

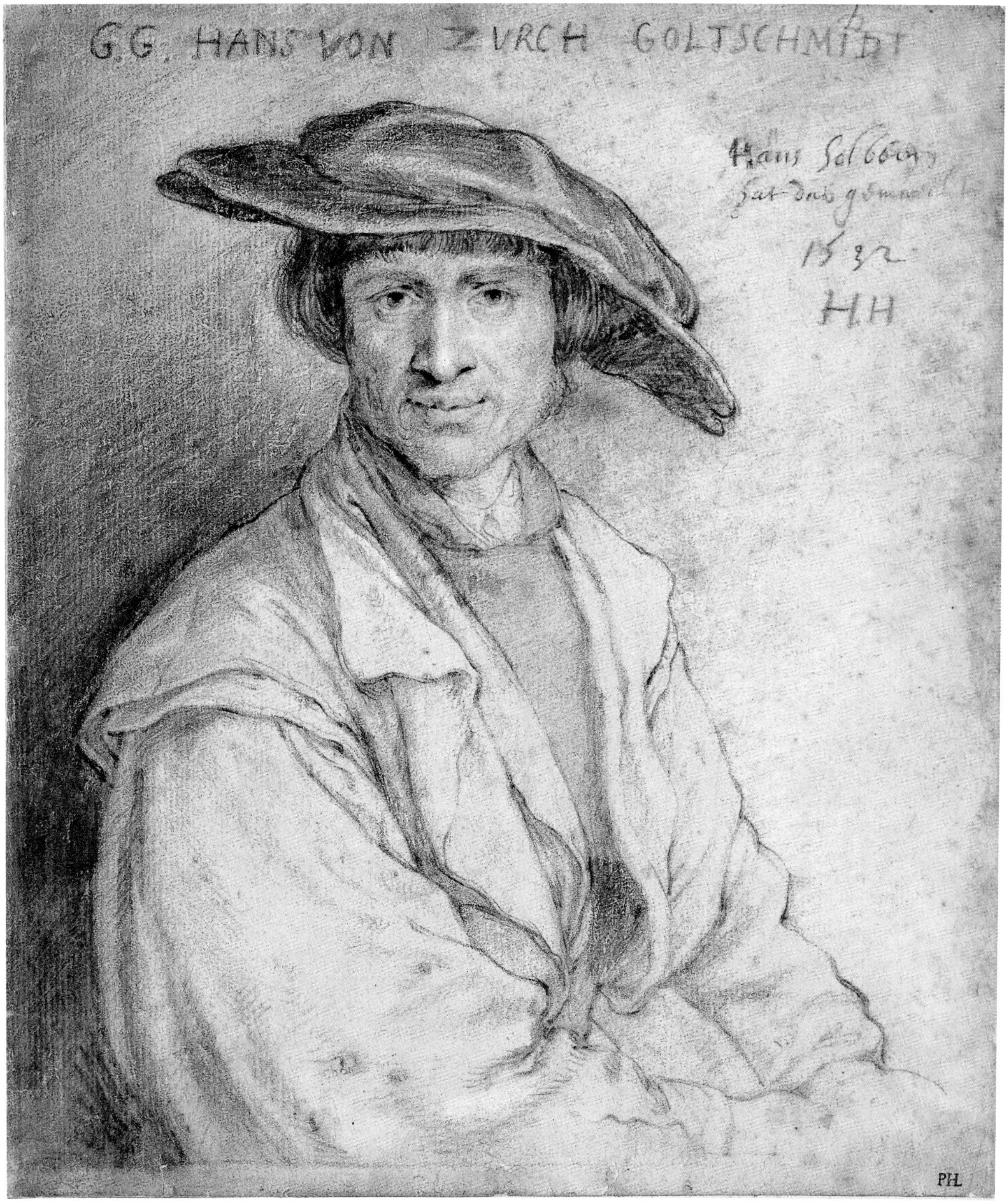

Hans von Zürich by Lucas Vorsterman the Elder (1585-1675), *c.* 1624-8,
after lost portrait by Hans Holbein the Younger (1497/8-1543).
Chalk, 20.5 × 17 cm.
Private collection

Hans Holbein the Younger

1497/8-1543

Hans von Zürich, goldsmith

1532

Oil on paper, laid down on panel
Probably inscribed: '*G.G. HANS VON ZURCH GOLTSCHMIDT /15.32/H.H.*'
Half-length, *c.* 76.2 × 63.5 cm

A painting by Hans Holbein of a goldsmith identified as 'Hans von Zürich' must have been in the collection of the 2nd Earl of Arundel (1586-1646) at quite an early date, when it was copied in a drawing by Lucas Vorsterman the Elder (1595-1675) (private collection). The drawing dates from Vorsterman's employment in Arundel's household, which was between *c.* 1624 and 1628, after he had sought refuge in Arundel's house following a falling-out with Rubens in 1622.[1] Vorsterman's drawing records the inscription on the original, '*G.G. HANS VON ZURCH GOLTSCHMIDT*' on the top line and, below, the date '*15.32*' and Holbein's monogram '*H.H.*'. Immediately above these is apparently a note by Vorsterman, '*Hans holbein hat dn? (?)gema??*', presumably 'Hans Holbein hat diesen gemalt': 'Hans Holbein painted this man'.

The picture was later copied in a pen and ink drawing (Prague, National Gallery) by Wenceslaus Hollar (1607-77) and then etched by him, together with Hendrick van der Borcht, Junior, after the drawing, in 1647.[2] This print provides the first clue to Arundel's ownership, in the legend '*W.Hollar Fecit, 1647, ex Collectione Arundeliana*'. This was the year after Arundel's death in exile in Padua, and Van der Borcht had remained in care of the collection after the Earl's death. The careful identification of the collection in which the original was preserved was due to the fact that the etching was part of a planned publication of the Arundel collection of paintings and drawings in the form of a 'paper museum', a project upon which Van der Borcht, unlike Vorsterman and Hollar (both of whom also worked intermittently on the project), was exclusively employed during the Earl's lifetime.[3] Hollar had been forced to leave London for Antwerp in 1644 and it was only then that he was actually able to finish the work begun in London, and he made prints after works by Van Dyck, Holbein, Elsheimer, Dürer and Leonardo.[4] Hollar's drawing of *Hans von Zürich* carried no inscription, but the etching bears the words '*HANS VON ZURCH GOLTSHMIDT/Hans holbein 1532*'.[5]

The painting, although inherited by the Earl of Arundel's widow, together with most of the Arundel collection, was part of the inheritance disputed by the Earl's heirs. It was last recorded in Paris in the collection of the banker Everhard Jabach IV (1618-96), in his posthumous inventory of 1696, from which we learn that it was a work in oil on paper, laid down on panel:

> Portrait d'un suisse, sur papier, a l'huille, G.G.Hans von Zuricht Goldssmith, grand comme le naturel, colé sur bois, d'Holbeins... 8 liv.[6]

Thomas Howard, 2nd Earl of Arundel and Surrey (1586-1646), was described by George Vertue (1684-1756), the antiquary, as 'the Greatest Collector and lover of

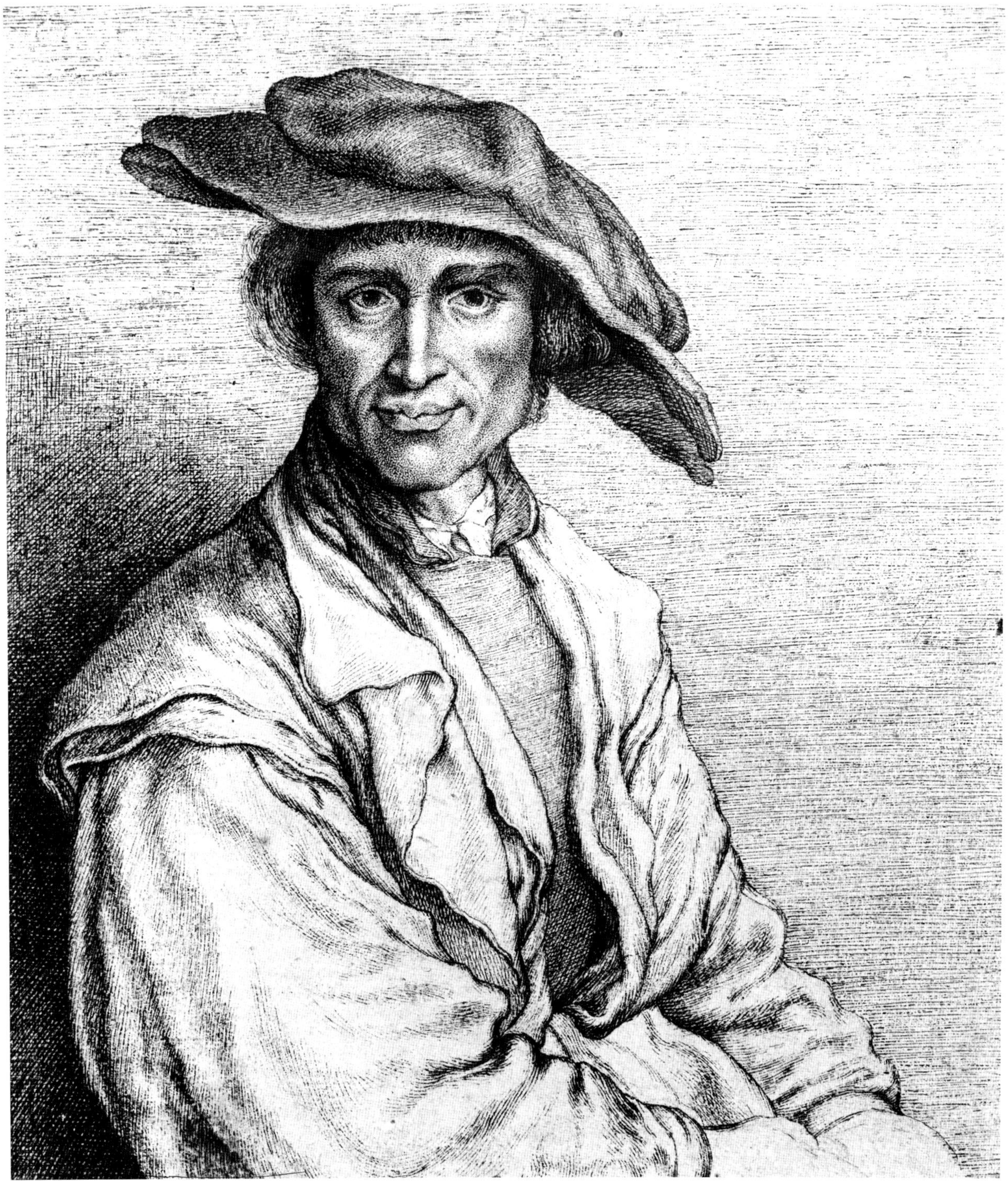

Hans von Zürich, after Vorsterman's drawing after Hans Holbein the Younger, by Wenceslaus Hollar (1607-77).
Pen and bistre, 20.5 × 17.1 cm.
National Gallery, Prague

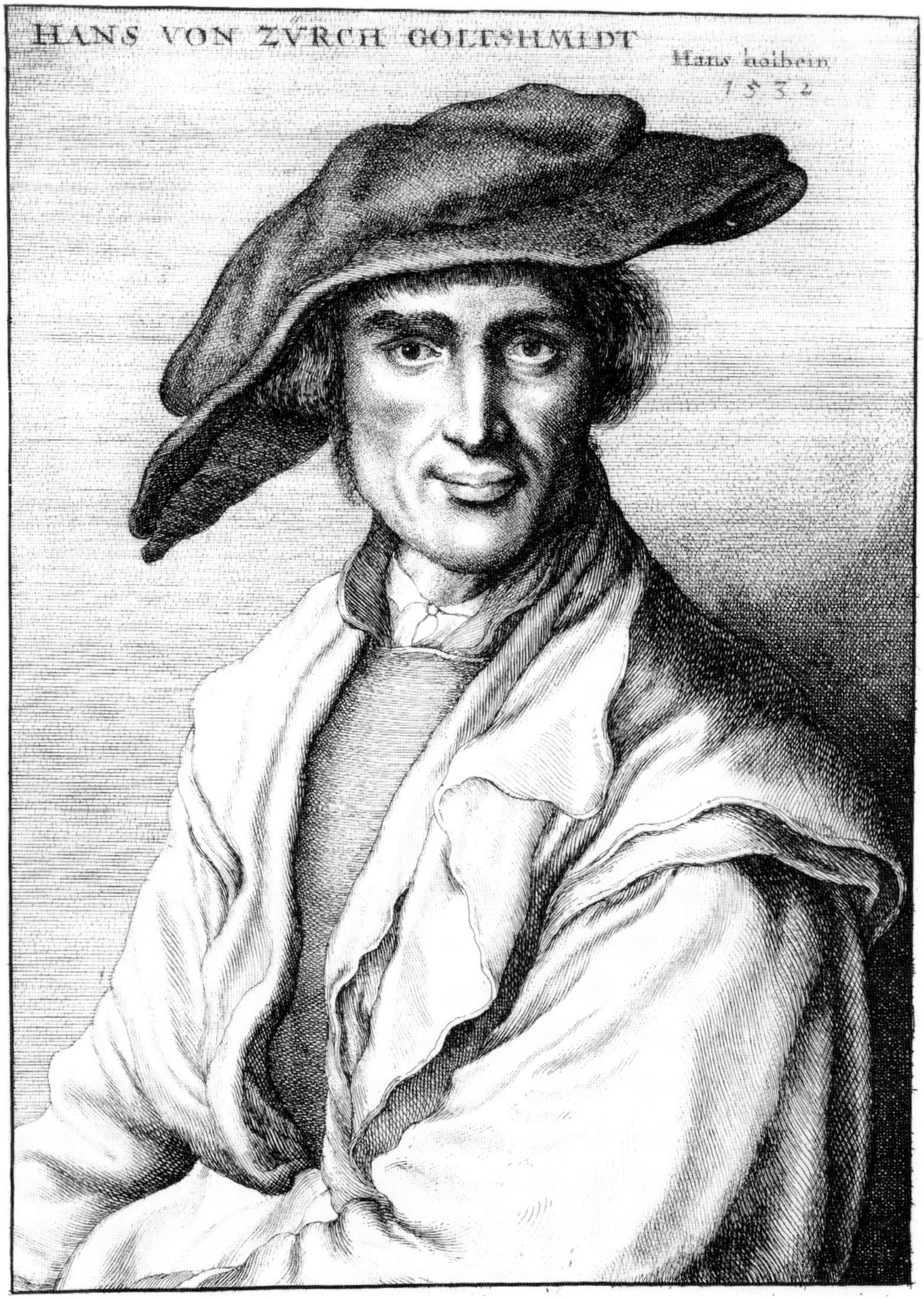

Hans von Zürich, after Hans Holbein the Younger,
by Wenceslaus Hollar with Hendrick van der Borcht, Junior.
Etching, 1647, 20 × 13.1 cm.
British Museum

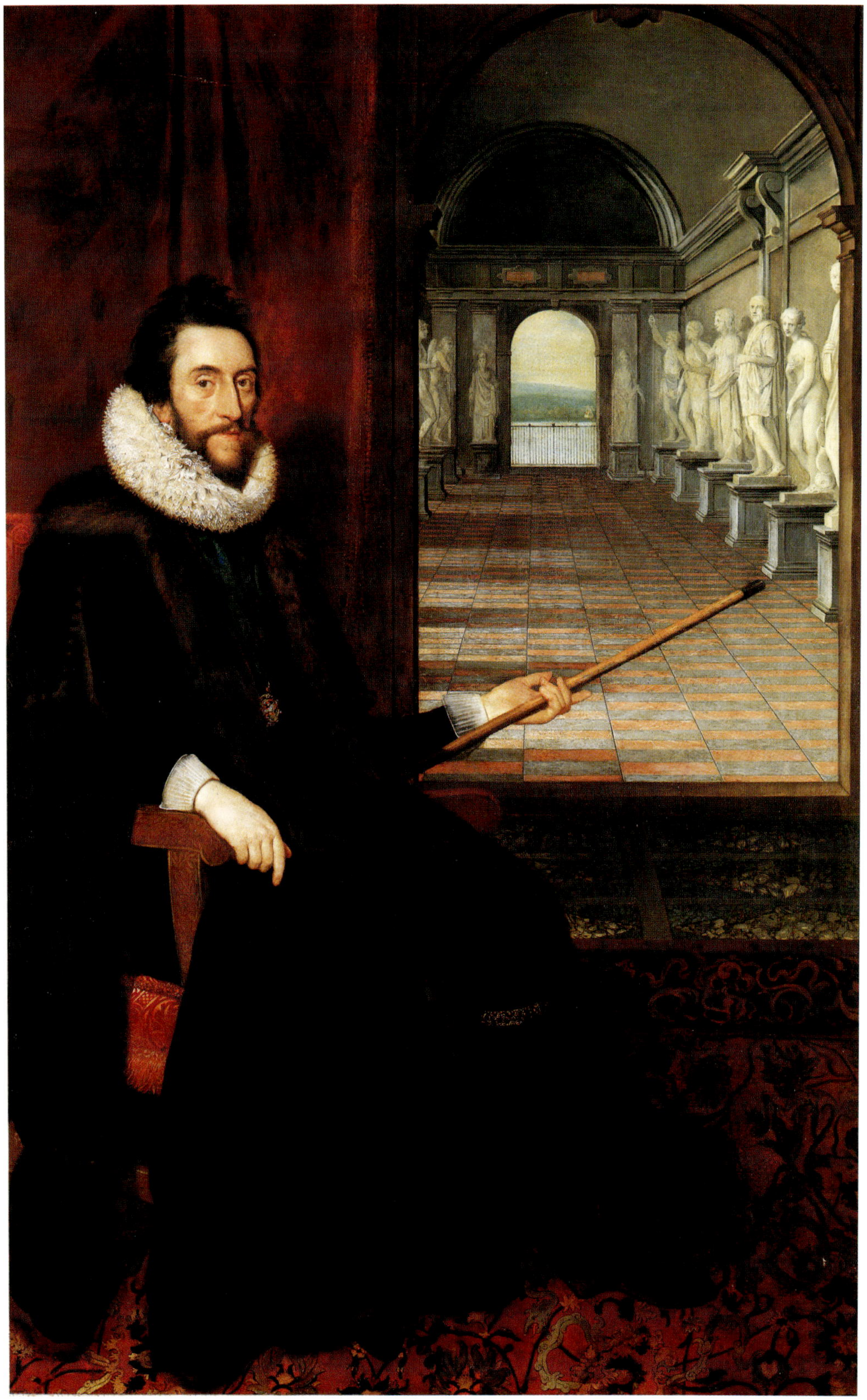

Thomas Howard, 2nd Earl of Arundel by Daniel Mytens (1590-*c.* 1648), *c.* 1618.
Oil on canvas, 207 × 127 cm.
His Grace the Duke of Norfolk, KG, Arundel Castle

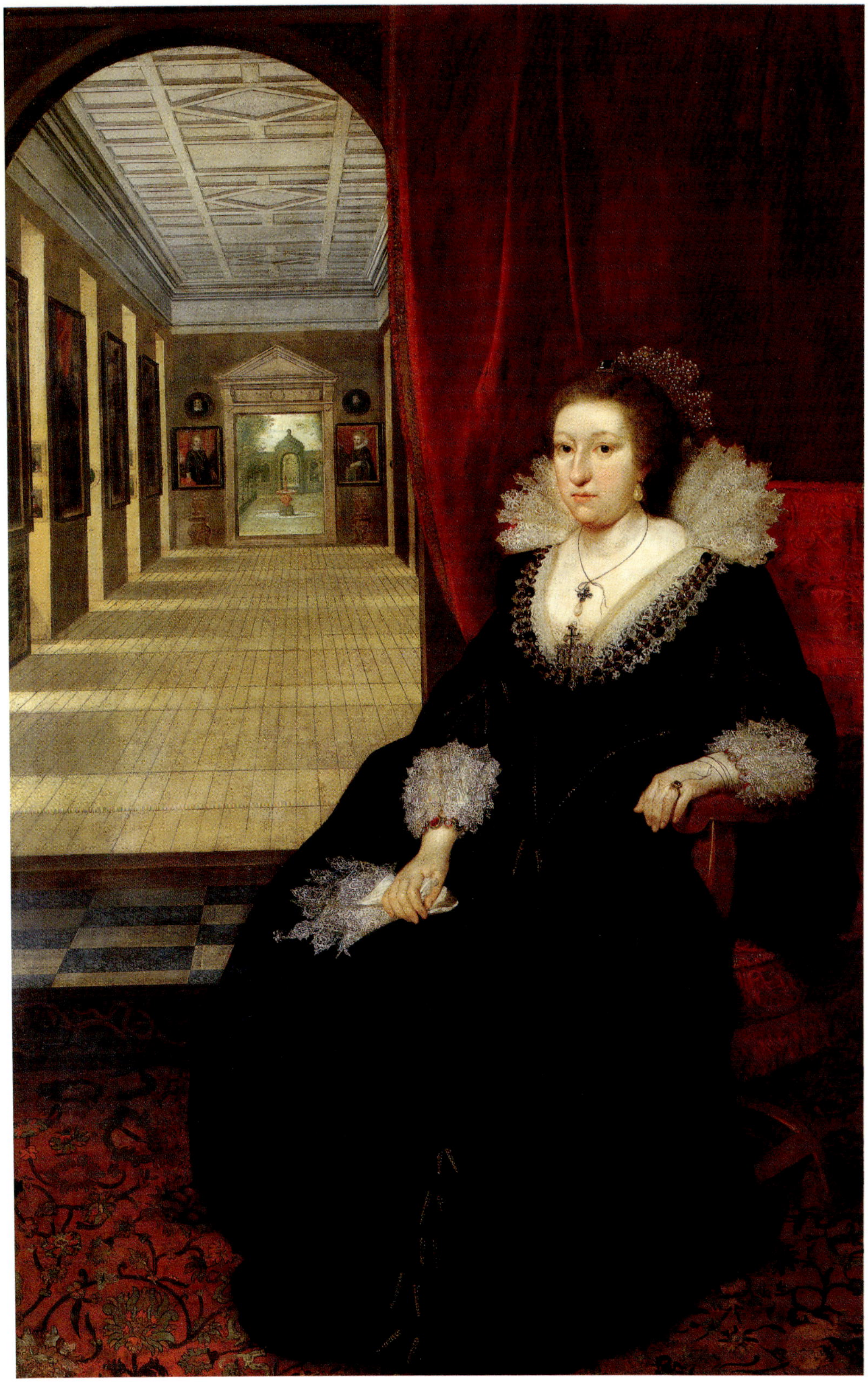

Aletheia Talbot, Countess of Arundel by Daniel Mytens, *c.* 1618.
Oil on canvas, 207 × 127 cm.
His Grace the Duke of Norfolk, KG, Arundel Castle

art of any Nobleman [then] living'.[7] Arundel shared the liking of contemporary collectors such as Charles I and the Duke of Buckingham for Venetian painters, but he had a particular taste for the works of sixteenth-century Northern artists such as Dürer and Holbein, and confessed to 'my foolish curiosity in enquiringe for the peeces of Holbein'.[8] Holbein had worked for Arundel's Howard forebears, and much of Arundel's life was overshadowed by his struggle to restore his family's name and honour, after the disgrace of the execution of his grandfather, the 4th Duke of Norfolk, the death in the Tower of his father St. Philip Howard, and the forfeit of the family's lands and titles.

Some years after the assassination of Buckingham in 1628, Arundel was appointed Lord Steward of the Household in 1640 and created Earl of Norfolk in 1644; but it was not until the Restoration of 1660, fourteen years after Arundel's death, that the family's former dukedom was restored to his grandson, Thomas, even though by that time Thomas was incurably mad.

Despite his difficult character and near-obsession with the status of his family, Arundel is remarkable in the history of collecting and connoisseurship in Britain. Rubens, whom Arundel patronised, described him in glowing terms as 'one of the four evangelists and a supporter of our art'.[9] Other artists he patronised included Van Dyck, Inigo Jones and Daniel Mytens, and he was famously the collector of the 'Arundel Marbles', classical antiquities which he partly acquired himself while on his travels in Italy. Mytens's portrait of *c.* 1618 evokes both Arundel's love of Antiquity and his sense of family history: the Earl is seen gesturing with his Earl Marshal's baton of office towards a splendid (and imaginary) gallery of Antique marbles; while in the companion portrait Lady Arundel, a connoisseur in her own right, is depicted in a picture gallery.[10] Indeed, Arundel's own family finances were not strong, and he was able to indulge his passion for collecting largely through the considerable fortune brought in marriage by his wife, Aletheia Talbot, in 1606. As the heiress of her father, the Earl of Shrewsbury, at his death in 1616 she inherited a further fortune and vast estates in the north of England.

Vorsterman's sojourn in England gives a likely date for the presence of Holbein's *Hans von Zürich* in Arundel's collection, but it is not conclusive. It is important, therefore, to look at the sources of Arundel's famous collection of Holbeins, to assemble which he 'spared neither gold nor silver if anything by Holbein was to be had'.[11] The Fitzalan family's collection, which had been formed by Arundel's great-grandfather, Henry Fitzalan, 12th Earl of Arundel, at Nonsuch Palace, devolved upon his son-in-law, John, 1st Baron Lumley, who added to it. At Lumley's death in 1609, the only surviving representative of the family was his great-nephew, Thomas Howard, 2nd Earl of Arundel, who inherited part of the collection – probably mainly family portraits and Holbeins, including the portrait of *Christina of Denmark, Duchess of Milan* (National Gallery, London) itemised in Lumley's inventory of *Marbles, Pictures and tables in Paynture* taken in 1590. Arundel's brother-in-law, William Herbert, 3rd Earl of Pembroke (1580-1630), enriched the collection, by giving Arundel his 'great booke' of portrait drawings by Holbein (now in the Royal Collection, Windsor Castle).

Arundel also appears to have acquired Holbeins which had been in the collection of Andreas de Loo (d. 1590), a Flemish merchant and spy (possibly of Italian birth) who spent much of his life in London. Karel van Mander describes him as 'an enthusiastic lover of painting... who lived in London and bought all the works of Holbein on which he could lay hands',[12] though whether these were originals or copies is not apparent, nor is it clear exactly which portraits De Loo owned, as his will of 1581 mentions no paintings.

In 1629 Arundel attempted to buy a collection of Holbein's drawings then on sale at The Hague. He wanted to have the drawings on approval as he told Sir Henry Vane, and hoped to have them for £30, '... but rather then fayle as I tolde you, I woulde goe to £50, but never thinke of £100, nor £50 offered without sure to have it. If he would let it come upon security to send it backe, I should be gladde; if not, let it rest'.[13]

Any one of the above routes could have been the means whereby Arundel acquired *Hans von Zürich*, but he could also have purchased it himself on the Continent. He undertook several diplomatic missions during which he seized any opportunities to add to his collection. In 1636, he travelled in state, as Envoy Extraordinary to the Emperor Ferdinand II on behalf of Charles I's nephew, the Elector Charles Louis. Charles Louis was the son of the widowed 'Winter Queen' of Bohemia, but his claim to be reinstated to the Palatinate of the Rhine was rejected. Thus for English interests on the Continent the mission was a failure, but for Arundel, at the height of his art collecting activities, it was a personal triumph. From Cologne onwards he was accompanied by Hollar to record the views, bringing him with him on his eventual return to England. Arundel's embassy arrived back in England from Vienna in December 1637, while the ship containing 'many thousands most excellent pieces of painting and Books which his Lordship gathered in his journey'[14] was delayed by ice in Rotterdam, before arriving safely in January.

As he was travelling, so Arundel acquired paintings: the Bishop of Würzburg gave him a Dürer Madonna (now lost); and at Nuremberg he bought the famous library created by Dürer's friend Willibald Pirckheimer from the then owner, Hans Imhoff. Without either of them realising it, it included originals by Dürer. Writing to Petty from Nuremberg, Arundel did not mention this bargain purchase but instead told him that there was 'not one scrach of Alb: Durer's paintings in oyle to be sold, though it were his Countrye; nor of Holbien, nor any other greate Master. They saye whithin these three or four yeeres greate store of good things have bin carryed out at easy rates; and, not long since, a Lifehever [amateur of art] dyinge, an Italian hath bought and carryed away many of [Dürer's] drawinges'.[15]

Meanwhile, Arundel's son, Lord Maltravers, who was looking after affairs at home, also wrote to Petty, 'My Lord desires that you should endeavor in and about Bassill to gette things of Holben, especially in a house which beelonged to Amor Bacchus [Amerbach]; there beeing a rare dead Christ at length, in oyle, with diverse heads and drawings of Holben and other masters, all now to bee sould. My lord desires that you would buy them and bring them away, or at least the drawings.'[16] It would seem, however, that these works eluded Arundel, as Amerbach's heirs sold the entire collection to Basle city council in 1661.

Arundel and his companions stayed for a week in plague-free Cologne where they visited the churches and cathedral.[17] They passed through again on their return in December 1636 and it is hard to believe that they did not visit the famed Jabach *Kunstkammer*, that of the banker and merchant Everhard Jabach, who died shortly afterwards, and it has been suggested that it was Jabach who introduced Hollar to Arundel.[18] The following year, Jabach's son, also Everhard, visited England, and would, similarly, have studied Arundel's own collection in London, although here the connection is more obvious, for Jabach the Younger is actively advising Arundel. He must be the 'Mr Everard' referred to in letters from

Daniel Mytens to Arundel's secretary, Edward Walker, of February and March 1637. In the first letter Mytens says, '... Mr Everard hath bene at Dorte to see the peece that was said to be of Lionardo, but found it to be onelye a Coppie after Mabuse.' In the second he reports how he and 'Mr Everard' visited Amsterdam to buy paintings and drawings for Arundel which included: '... A man's picture of Holbeen, a foot high. 300 gild. A madona of Albert Durer, aboute the same highte, at 150 gild. A dead man of Albert Durer, in water cullors at 120 gild. A picture of Raphael which is held to be of his hand, but wee hold it not so to be, and is held at 60 gild.'[19] Jabach had a passport from the Cologne authorities of 8 July 1636 'as he intended to travel to the Netherlands', and he went on to visit the London office of the Jabach firm. He was back in Cologne by 14 December 1637.[20] In later years Everhard Jabach was able to take advantage of the misfortunes of Charles I and Arundel to enrich his own collection.

It is difficult to pinpoint among so many possibilites how Arundel acquired *Hans von Zürich*, but the identity of the sitter, too, is elusive. He was a goldsmith, evidently, and the portrait is dated 1532, the year in which Holbein returned to London from Basle after an absence of about four years. On his arrival Holbein relied on the patronage of the German Hanseatic merchants of the London Steelyard, but the portrait of *Hans von Zürich* differs materially from those. First, we know from Jabach's 1696 inventory that it was painted in oil on paper, and not on panel like the Steelyard portraits; secondly, it lacks their domestic setting; and thirdly, it records a man wearing clothes more appropriate to an artisan than a prosperous merchant.

Another example of Holbein's work on paper laid down on panel is the informal portrait of *The artist's family* (Öffentliche Kunstsammlung, Basle) which was painted in Basle, probably in 1528.[21] There is another unusual feature that connects these pictures, as in each case the principal sitters are shown in a 'long' half-length, with hands showing. *The artist's family* is laid down on a standard panel size (confusingly known in English as a 'three-quarter'), 76.2 × 63.5 cm (actually 77 × 64 cm), and it may well be that this was the size of *Hans von Zürich*, a composition which also has an unusually informal appearance. It is the only Holbein portrait in which he employs such a decidedly Italian contrapposto composition, and it has none of the reticence of Holbein's formal portraits, notably those of the members of the Steelyard. These elements and the use of an informal medium suggest that the sitter could have been a friend of the artist, and also that the portrait was painted before Holbein's arrival in England. In 1532, the date of the portrait, until he arrived in London by July of that year, Holbein is likely only to have been in Antwerp for any length of time: he had left Basle in late 1531 (or very early 1532) and lingered in Antwerp en route.[22] Thus, although the sitter was Swiss, there would have been little or no time for Holbein to depict him while in Basle. If the picture was made in Antwerp, then the collection of De Loo, the Antwerp merchant, may have been its first location, where it might subsequently have been purchased by Arundel.

It is likely that Zürich is not the sitter's surname, but simply his birthplace, and so he might thus be found among the goldsmiths of Zürich. Of the various candidates that have been put forward the most plausible is Hans Asper, who was born in Zürich *c.* 1499. He is not, however, recorded as a goldsmith, and there is no evidence of his work before 1531 when he appears as the fully fledged painter of a portrait of Huldrych Zwingli,[23] the religious reformer. It has been suggested that Asper had followed another trade – possibly as a goldsmith – until then, and that

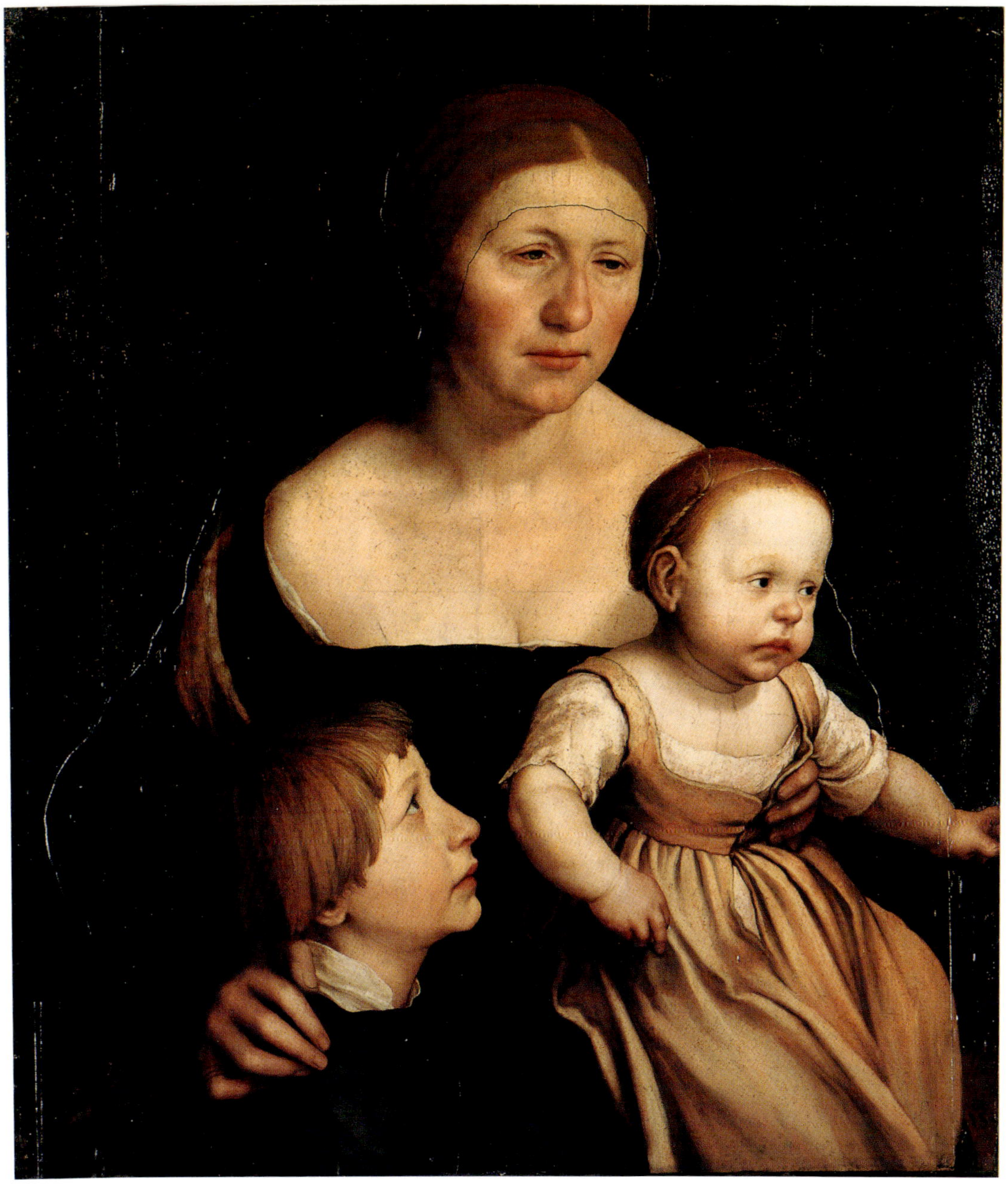

The Artist's Family
by Hans Holbein the Younger,
c. 1528.
Paper laid down on panel,
77 × 64 cm.
Öffentliche Kunstsammlung, Basel, Kunstmuseum

he was even encouraged to paint by Holbein. As a goldsmith living in a protestant country (Basle suffered iconoclastic riots in 1529), he would doubtless have felt the decline in church commissions (much of Holbein's own earlier output in Basle had been religious). Holbein's departure for England left the artistic field open. It seems plausible, given Holbein's skill as a metalwork designer, that if Asper had been a goldsmith, they would have known each other, but there is another connection: Holbein's effectively abandoned wife, Elsbeth Binzenstock, sold the portrait of *The artist's family* to Asper during her lifetime, in 1542. Asper died in 1571 and Elsbeth's portrait was acquired in 1579, through intermediaries, by

Basilius Amerbach (1533-91) of Basle, in whose inventory it appears in 1586.[24] It is tempting to think that if Hans von Zürich and Asper were one and the same, then Amerbach might have bought Asper's portrait too. But no Holbein of Hans von Zürich can be identified in the inventories of the collections formed either by Basilius Amerbach or his father, Bonifacius (1495-1562), who was a friend and patron of Holbein, and had been painted by him in 1519. (He was also the heir and executor of Erasmus.) The Amerbachs' collection was wide-ranging and notable for works by Holbein and for the drawings and models they had bought direct from goldsmiths' workshops. The historical association between Holbein and the Amerbachs would have been particularly appealing to Arundel. As we have seen above, Maltravers had urged Petty to try to buy from the Amerbachs' collection in 1637, unsuccessfully, but the link is tantalising.

In 1641 Arundel and his wife were given the honourable but trying task of accompanying the Queen Mother, Maria de' Medici, to Cologne, where she died on 3 July 1642, reputedly in the house of Everhard Jabach. Arundel began to sell some of his drawings while at Cologne, returned briefly to England before escorting the Queen and Princess Mary to her husband, Prince William of Orange, to the Continent and, having obtained leave to stay abroad for an indefinite period, he resigned his high offices, made a new will and left England for ever in 1642. Although he contributed £54,000 to the Royalist cause, he declined to return to England when summoned and Parliament later sequestered his estates.[25]

The Arundels stayed in The Hague, Amsterdam and Utrecht before settling in Antwerp, where they were joined by most of the collection in 1642/3. (The marbles remained at Arundel House, where they largely survived the Civil War.)[26] The Earl then left for Padua where he settled in 1644, dying there on 4 October 1646. After the Earl's death, the Countess continued to live in Holland, keeping a house at Amersfoort and later living on the 'Cingel' (Singel) in Amsterdam until her own death in 1654.

The dispersal of Arundel's celebrated collection makes depressing reading. Arundel had intended that his collection should be reserved as a family heirloom and an Act of Parliament was passed in 1627 giving him permission to do so. However, in the will he made while waiting at Dover to leave England in September 1641, he left his chattels, houses and revenues from his estates to his wife.[27] In so doing he achieved the opposite of what he intended. Family disputes raged for years and sales denuded the great collection, so that by the end of the century little remained of its former glory.

Arundel's eldest surviving son, Henry Frederick, contested his father's will. Required by his title to live in some state, but with the family's estates sequestered, with Arundel Castle left in ruins by the Civil War, and burdened by his father's debts, he had little choice but to take legal action. His mother complained of Henry's treatment of her: 'He hathe used all meanes to take my due from mee, not suffering mee quietly topossesse any thing that he conceaves may any way be disputable, though it be my inheritance.'[28] Henry pre-deceased her in 1652 and his mentally afflicted son, Thomas, then living in Padua, succeeded to the title as 4th Earl. Thomas's brothers, Henry and Charles Howard, continued to dispute their inheritance, and meanwhile the 2nd Earl of Arundel's own youngest son, William, a Catholic who had married Lady Mary Stafford in 1637 and been created Viscount Stafford in 1640, had much to gain by remaining his mother's favourite. He was always in financial difficulties and when his mother died with-

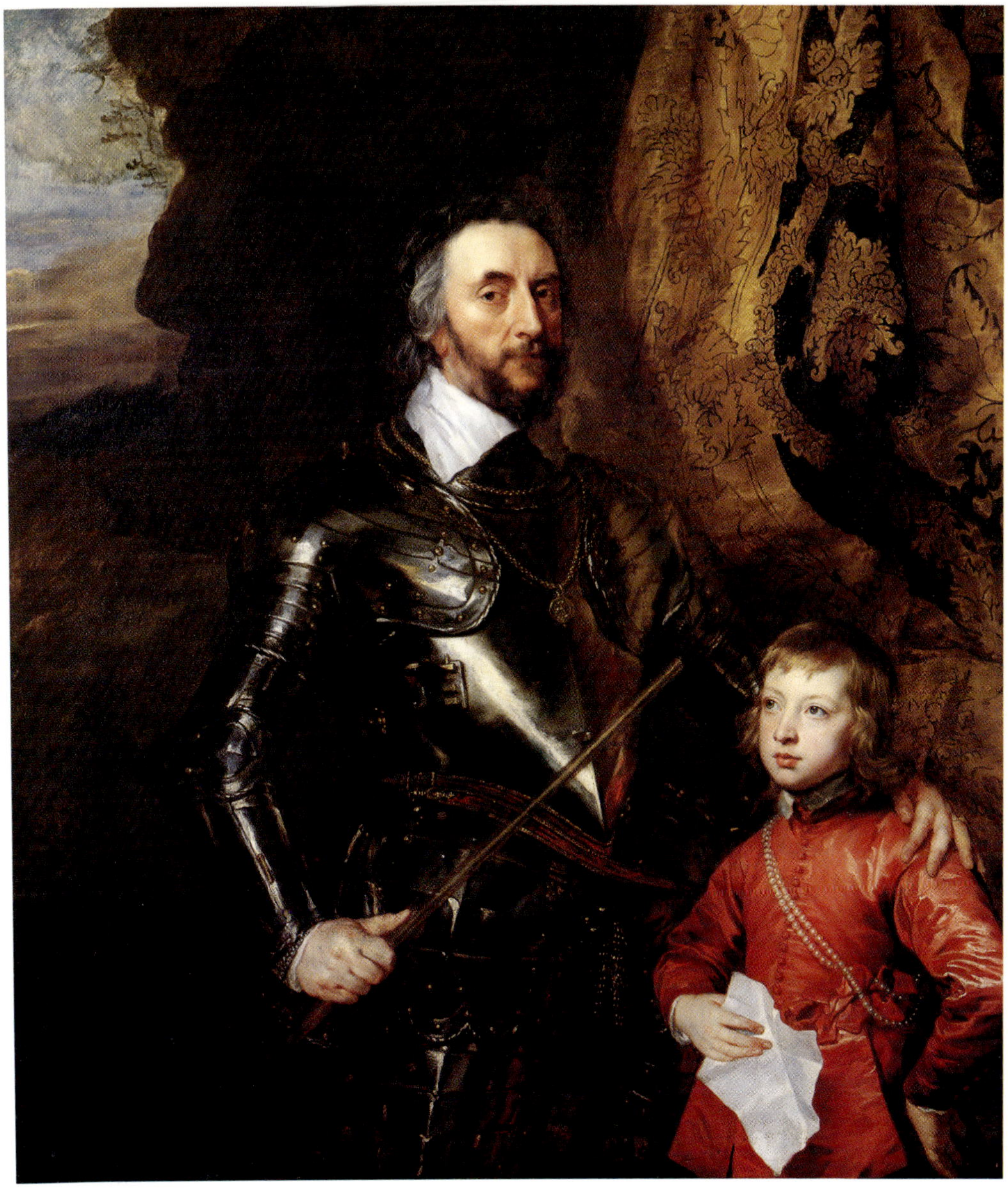

Thomas Howard, 2nd Earl of Arundel with his grandson Thomas, later 5th Duke of Norfolk by Sir Anthony van Dyck (1599-1641), 1635-6.
Oil on canvas, 143 × 120 cm.
His Grace the Duke of Norfolk, KG, Arundel Castle

out a written will on 3 June 1654, Stafford pronounced a nuncupative will, that is, he asserted that an oral will existed in his favour, and immediately set about disposing of works of art and other items.[29]

Stafford's actions met with resistance from the rest of the family. Sir Edward Walker, Arundel's former secretary, was sent out to Amsterdam to block further sales and attempt to effect a settlement. An agreement was somehow struck between William, Viscount Stafford, and the Hon. Charles Howard on 12 June 1654: '... And the said Charles Howard doth herby relinquish all claims and demands unto any of the goods belonging unto the said Countess his grandmother remaining in the Provinces of the low Countries at the time of her death.'[30]

Stafford's English creditors, however, pursued him and in November 1654

Emanuel Halton arrived in Holland as the representative of eleven of them, applying to distrain and hold as security 'all such goods, paintings, cabinets, jewels and other objects located in the house of [Lord Stafford] and the deceased Countess and that they all should be held against judgement and should be inventoried and if necessary confiscated'.[31] The inventory of the Amersfoort house was made in January 1655, although it was only possible to list the seventy works of art hanging on the walls: Stafford and his agent Dirck de Romare took care to conceal several cases of works, the details of which are unknown, behind a locked door. A complete list of the pictures in the Arundel collection was therefore never made, but the fifteen Holbeins listed at Amersfoort included *Hans von Zürich*: 'Holbein... Portret van de goudsmid Hans van Zürich.'[32]

The Amersfoort list was duly used with other estate papers to compile an inventory of goods bequeathed by the Countess and used by the Court of Delegates in the case between Henry Howard, Earl of Arundel, and Lord Stafford. This list of 800 items was drawn up in Amsterdam in some haste and without any system. It is written in Italian, a language with which the Amsterdam estate describers were evidently not entirely familiar. The inventory survives as an incomplete copy of the lost original. It lists over forty works by Holbein, including 'Holbein... Ritratto d'un Orifice Hans von Zurch'.[33] The paintings distrained in Amersfoort were transferred to a third party on 14 February 1655[34] and re-lodged in the house of the Prosecutor General of the Court of Utrecht, Mr Everard van Weede, Lord of Dijkveld and Rateles. In the autumn of 1662 paintings 'belonging to his Excellency Viscount Stafford' were auctioned in Utrecht on Weede's instructions. The auctioneer was the painter Herman Saftleven II (1609-85), whose receipt, issued on 11 October regarding the management of the auction, is the only surviving record of the sale.[35] The paintings sold must have been those taken to Van Weede's house and would thus have included *Hans von Zürich*.

It was no doubt at this 1662 sale in Utrecht that Everhard Jabach bought Holbein's portrait of Hans von Zürich, and he bought at least four other Holbeins.[36] Everhard Jabach IV was the only son of six children, and was born in Cologne. His father, also Everhard, who died in 1636, had established the Jabacher *Kunstkammer*, and Everhard IV was to become both a flamboyant collector and connoisseur as well as a wily dealer. In 1638 he settled in Paris and acted as Cardinal Mazarin's banker, becoming a French citizen in 1647. By the time of the Stafford sale of 1662 Jabach was prosperous enough to have established himself in an impressive hôtel in Paris on the rue Neuve St. Meury where he displayed his prodigious collection.

Like Arundel before him, Jabach allowed artists to study his collection of drawings, but in 1671, however, he came close to bankruptcy and was forced to sell a group of 5,543 drawings and 101 paintings to the Crown. Colbert was merciless in his bargaining, buying the group for a much reduced price, leaving Jabach to declare, 'Consider, in the name of God, that I find myself between the hammer and the anvil, and I have to deal with people who give no quarter.'[37] These sales formed the cornerstone of the French Royal collection. It was probably at this time that Jabach sold four of the Holbeins that he had bought from the Arundel collection, *William Warham*, *Nicholas Kratzer*, *Anne of Cleves* and *Sir Henry Wyatt*, but not, so it would appear, *Hans von Zürich*, since that picture is to be found in his re-formed collection, after Jabach recovered his financial footing. This second collection (including copies of works he had owned previously), is recorded in the inventory compiled after his death on 6 March 1695 and dated

Everhard Jabach IV
by Sir Anthony van Dyck, 1636-7.
Oil on canvas, 113 × 91.5 cm.
State Hermitage Museum, St. Petersburg

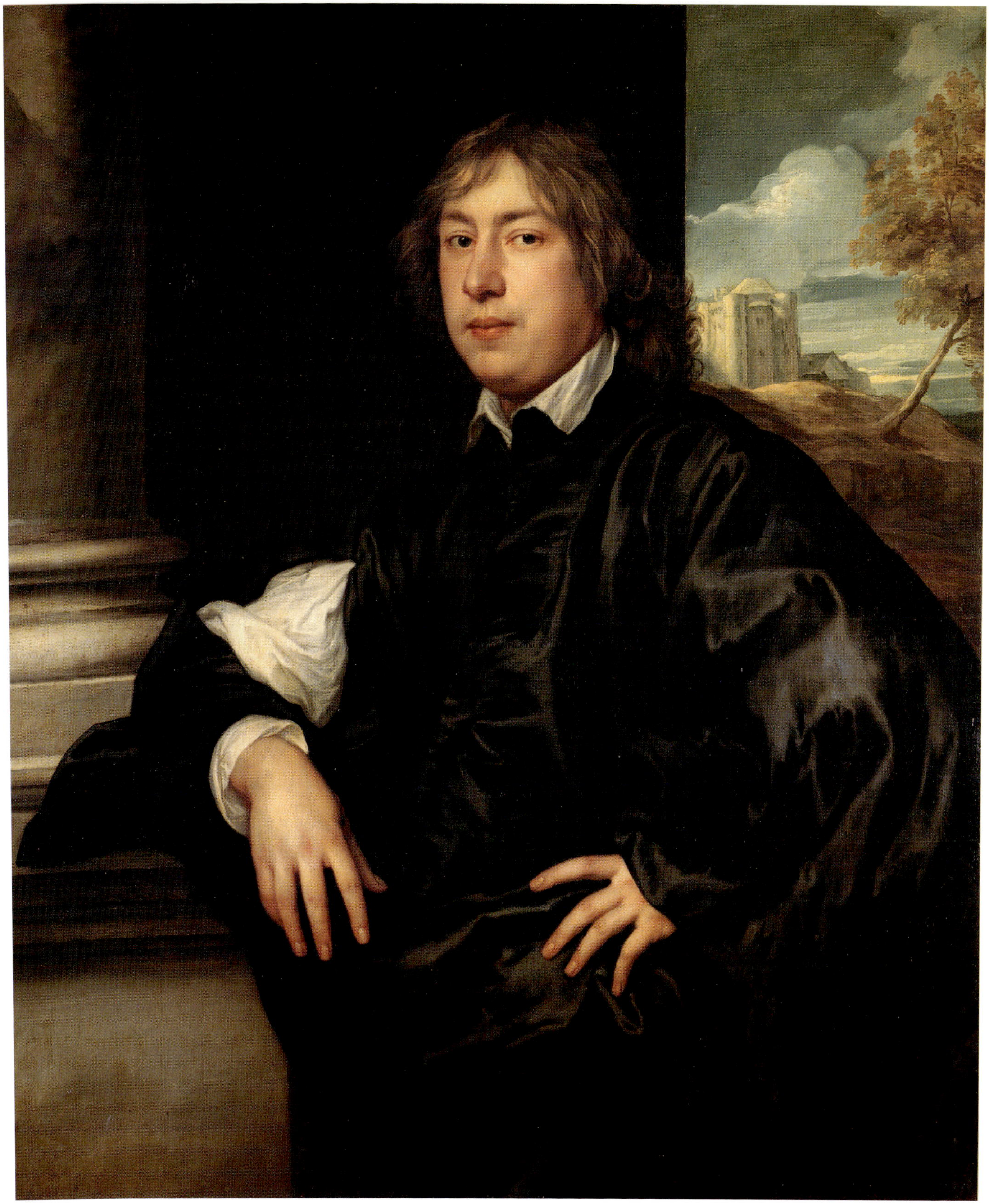

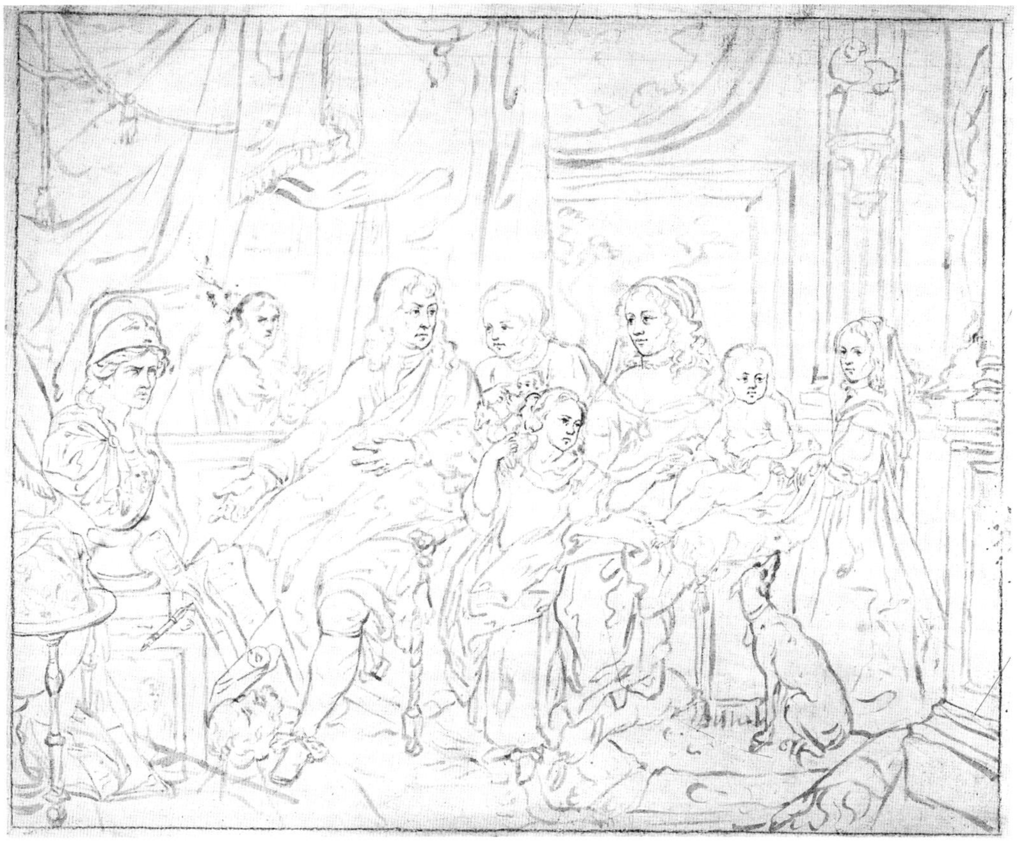

The Jabach family
Drawing by Egidius Mengelberg (1770-1849) after Charles Lebrun (1619-90).
Charcoal, brush and ink on paper, 27.5 × 35 cm.
Wallraf-Richartz-Museum, Cologne

17 July 1696. It is here that the most detailed information available on Holbein's portrait of Hans von Zürich appears:

229. Portrait d'un suisse, sur papier, a l'huille, G.G.Hans von Zuricht Goldssmith, grand comme le naturel, colé sur bois, d'Holbeins... 8 liv.[38]

Four out of Jabach's five children were depicted in a great family portrait by Le Brun of *c.* 1661/2. The eldest, another Everhard, came from Cologne at his father's death (Jabach's wife survived him, to die in 1701) to administer the estate. In the 1696 inventory some items are identified as sold, and a letter from the Everhard heir to his cousin Nikolaus de Groote in Cologne reveals that sales were taking place from the collection after his father's death:

The feasts have somewhat interrupted our sale... I do not know whether we shall start it up again, because it would be so long drawn out and such a hectic business... ; but I think that we would sell the remaining pictures if we felt the need.[39]

No trace can be found of the sale to which Everhard refers, but the great collector Pierre Crozat (?1665-1740) certainly bought many of Jabach's drawings, presumably at this time. Crozat's drawings were catalogued by Pierre-Jean Mariette (1694-1774), with their provenances noted, and then sold in 1741 after Crozat's death. Mariette himself was a principal buyer at that sale and the French Crown bought many of the Italian drawings from him in 1775-6. *Hans von Zürich* does not appear among any of these pictures. The letter of Everhard quoted above goes on to suggest, however, that some of the collection was divided between his siblings. This Everhard died in 1721 in Cologne, having survived his siblings, and he left four sons and a daughter. The eldest of these, again Everhard, lived in the Jabach house on the Stemengasse in Cologne, where his great-grandfather had made his *Kunstkammer*. He then died without children in 1754. Of his brothers, only two, Gerard-Michel and Franz-Anton, appear to have shared their grandfather's interest in art. They both lived in Livorno and were unmarried.

Gerard-Michel Jabach was a friend of Count Antonio-Maria Zanetti, the great Venetian collector, and seems to have been a connoisseur. Drawings which came from Jabach's collection appear in Franz-Anton's sale of 16 October 1753.[40] He was the last of the Jabach line and the name died with him in 1761. His heirs, daughters of his cousin Nikolaus de Groote, also died without children and the Jabach house on the Stemengasse passed to Johan Matthias von Bors, a cousin of the daughters. Goethe visited the house in 1774 and, among other things, reported that the Le Brun portrait of the Jabach family was there.[41] It is through the sale of this painting that we know that remnants of Jabach's collection survived in Cologne.

Von Bors, a collector himself, was a friend of Ferdinand Franz Wallraf (1748-1824) whose collection is now held in the Wallraf-Richartz Museum in Cologne. Through Wallraf, Von Bors met Christian von Mechel (1737-1817), an engraver and art dealer. Von Mechel sold the Le Brun canvas on Von Bors' behalf to Henry Hope (1735-1811), the Dutch banker; while a copy, owned by Jabach's brother-in-law, Heinrich de Groote, is now in Berlin. In a letter written to Wallraf, with all the guile of a dealer, Von Mechel refers to a mysterious portrait:

> I thought I had already asked you or our friend Leykam to send him the portrait from the rubbish or lumber room intended for me in secure packaging. Everything will then go on to Basle. Apropos the lumber. I am sure this can now all be sold; what is there among these pieces that is any good? Are not the two hunting items next to the front door by Weeninx? What other good items are there? A short list with their prices would oblige, or is it being sold licitando? The mass of stuff in the room was standing about and lying around on the floor. There was no opportunity at the time to see it because of the dust and mould.[42]

Von Mechel had engraved and published the works of Holbein in 1780, although without the *Hans von Zürich*. It seems more than likely that, had there been such a work by the master lurking in that dark lumber room, it would have caught his eye, and his letter gives a final poignant glimpse of the remains of a great collection. Any item from that 'lumber room' that might eventually turn up, perhaps even the *Hans von Zürich*, could be identified through Jabach's inventory and the wax seal with which he marked items in his collection, which was engraved with his motto '*VIVIT POST FUNERA VIRTUS*'.

NOTES

1 D. Jaffé *et al.*, 'The Earl and Countess of Arundel: Renaissance Collectors', *Apollo*, August 1996, p. 23, and see ibid., n. 87, citing J. Held, 'Rubens and Vorsterman', *The Art Quarterly*, DCXXII (1969), pp. 111-30.

2 J. Burgheres, *Wenceslaus Hollar, Seventeenth-century Prints from the Museum Boymans-Van Beuningen, Rotterdam*, exh. cat., 1994, no. 89, p. 142, and see n. 63.

3 Jaffé *et al.*, op. cit., pp. 21ff. Vertue recorded that 'The Earl of Arundell had several Gravers constantly at work with a design to make a large volumn of prints of all his pictures drawings & other rarities', 'Vertue Notebooks', I, *Walpole Society*, XVIII (1930), p. 47. Arundel published his collection of Antique inscriptions in John Selden's *Marmora Arundeliana* in 1628.

4 Ibid., p. 23.

5 He omits the 'c' in 'Goltschmidt' and does not record the letters 'G.G.' which do, however, reappear in the record of what is clearly the same picture in the 1696 inventory of Everhard Jabach IV (see below). Vorsterman copied other works by Holbein and certainly in the case of Holbein's *Triumph of Poverty* and *Triumph of Wealth* his correspondence with Arundel about the engraving reveals that Vorsterman took his drawing back to Antwerp with him: letter quoted in Mary F. S. Hervey, *The Life, Correspondence & Collections of Thomas Howard Earl of Arundel*, Cambridge, 1921, op. cit., p. 303. As Hollar made his own drawing while he was in Antwerp, it would have been possible for him to work from the Vorsterman drawing rather than the original painting, as certain features suggest. The original may not have yet been in Antwerp in 1647, although it was certainly there in 1655, when its presence is recorded in an inventory of the Countess of Arundel (see below).

6 Vicomte de Grouchy, 'Everhard Jabach, collectionneur parisien 1695', *Mémoires de la Société de l'Histoire de Paris et de l'Ile-de-France*, vol. XXI, Paris, 1894, pp. 217-92, p. 261. F. Grossman, 'Holbein, Flemish Paintings and Everhard Jabach', *Burlington Magazine*, XCIII (1951), pp. 16-25, p. 20, n. 73.

7 Vertue, quoted in Francis C. Springell, *Connoisseur & Diplomat*, London, 1963, p. 142, n. 47.

8 Letter from Arundel to Sir Dudley Carleton (1573-1632) 17 September 1619, quoted in Hervey, op. cit., pp. 161-2.

9 Quoted in John Martin Robinson, *The Dukes of Norfolk*, Oxford and New York, 1982, p. 97.

10 For Lady Arundel's connoisseurship see: David Howarth, 'The Patronage and Collecting of Aletheia, Countess of Arundel 1606-54', *Journal of the History of Collections*, X, no. 2, 1998, pp. 125-37. The Mytens portraits are on loan from the National Portrait Gallery, London, to Arundel Castle.

11 Hervey, op. cit., p. 256.

12 Karel van Mander, *Het schilder-boeck*, Haarlem, 1603-4, fol. 223a. Vertue also described the De Loo collection in his manuscript concerning Holbein, quoted in Hervey, op. cit., pp. 513-22. The list of the collection appears on p. 518.

13 Letter of 27/17 May 1636, Nuremberg, quoted in Hervey, op. cit., p. 286.

14 Sir William Boswell, ambassador to the Low Countries, writing to Viscount Feilding in Venice 19/29 January 1636/7, quoted in D. Howarth, *Lord Arundel and his Circle*, New Haven and London, 1985, p. 239, n. 15.

15 Quoted in Hervey, op. cit., p. 366.

16 4 August 1637, quoted in Hervey, op. cit., p. 406.

17 See Springell, op. cit., p. 57.

18 Ibid., p. 143.

19 18 February 1637 and 12 March, Hervey, op. cit., pp. 404-5.

20 Grossman, op. cit., pp. 16-25, n. 21.

21 John Rowlands, *Holbein: The Paintings of Hans Holbein the Younger, Complete Edition*, Oxford, 1985, cat. no. 32.

22 Ibid., pp. 77, 81, &c.

23 For a discussion of Asper's work see Lucas Wuthrich, *Zürcher Kunst nach der Reformation. Hans Asper und seine Zeit*, exh. cat., Zürich, Helmhaus, 1981.

24 Rowlands, op. cit., p. 135.

25 For the will of 3 September 1641 see Hervey, op. cit., pp. 459-61, and for the Royalist cause see Hervey, op. cit., pp. 438-9.

26 For a brief discussion of the marbles see D. E. L. Haynes, *The Arundel Marbles*, The Ashmolean Museum, Oxford, 1975.

27 For discussion of the will and dispersal of the collection see F. H. C. Weijtens, *De Arundel-Collectie, Commencement de la Fin, Amersfoort, 1655*, Utrecht, 1971.

28 Countess of Arundel to Lord Andover 14 September 1648, quoted in Robinson, op. cit., p. 118, n. 2.

29 See Weijtens, op. cit., n. 87, for Stafford's

witnesses to the oral will: Van der Borcht, keeper of the Arundel collection, and Francis Junius, the librarian. According to Junius's statement the Countess was no longer in a condition to react with understanding to her son's demands.

30 Weijtens, op. cit., n. 115.

31 Ibid., p. 10.

32 Ibid., n. 133.

33 Mary L. Cox, 'Inventory of the Arundel Collection', *The Burlington Magazine*, XIX (1911), pp. 282-6, 323-5. The Holbein is listed on p. 323. The outcome of the trial was that the oral will was not recognised by the court, but management of the goods left by the Countess and deriving from the Talbot fortune was entrusted to Stafford. Arundel House and its treasures went to the bearer of the title. Tart Hall, the London house which the Countess had built for herself in 1638, went to Stafford, although that too was distrained in 1655 (Weijtens, op. cit., n. 141). No works by Holbein appeared in the Countess's inventory of 1641 of Tart Hall.

34 Except for Rubens's portrait of the Countess, Weijtens, op. cit., nn. 135, 136.

35 Saftleven's sale receipt is in the Fondation Custodia, Institut Néerlandais, Paris.

36 See Grossman, op. cit., for the Jabach Holbeins in the Louvre. A further sale of works, details of which are not known, took place in 1657; and then another in 1684, when the Holbein was not among those paintings sold. Weijtens, op. cit., nn. 140, 151. In the sale of 26 September 1684, 78 paintings were sold, none of which was on the Amersfoort list.

37 For Jabach's dealings with Colbert, see J. Brown, *Kings and Connoisseurs: Collecting Art in Seventeenth-Century Europe*, Princeton, 1995, p. 211.

38 De Grouchy, op. cit., p. 261.

39 'Les festes ont un peu interrompu nostre vente... Je ne sçay sy nous la recommencerons, a cause que cela tirera alla longue et donne une si furieuse occupation... ; mais je cray plus tôt que, pour avencer besoigne, nous partagerons les tableaux restants.' De Grouchy, op. cit., p. 245.

40 *Catalogo della raccolta di celebri disegni che trovansi appresso Francesco Antonio Jabach in Livorno*, De Grouchy, op. cit., p. 246.

41 Johann Wolfgang von Goethe, *Werke*, vol. XXVIII, Weimar, 1890, p. 286.

42 Wilhelm Baumeister, 'On the history of the portrait of the Jabach family by Le Brun', *Wallraf-Richartz Jahrbuch*, vols. III and IV, 1926-7, pp. 211-21.

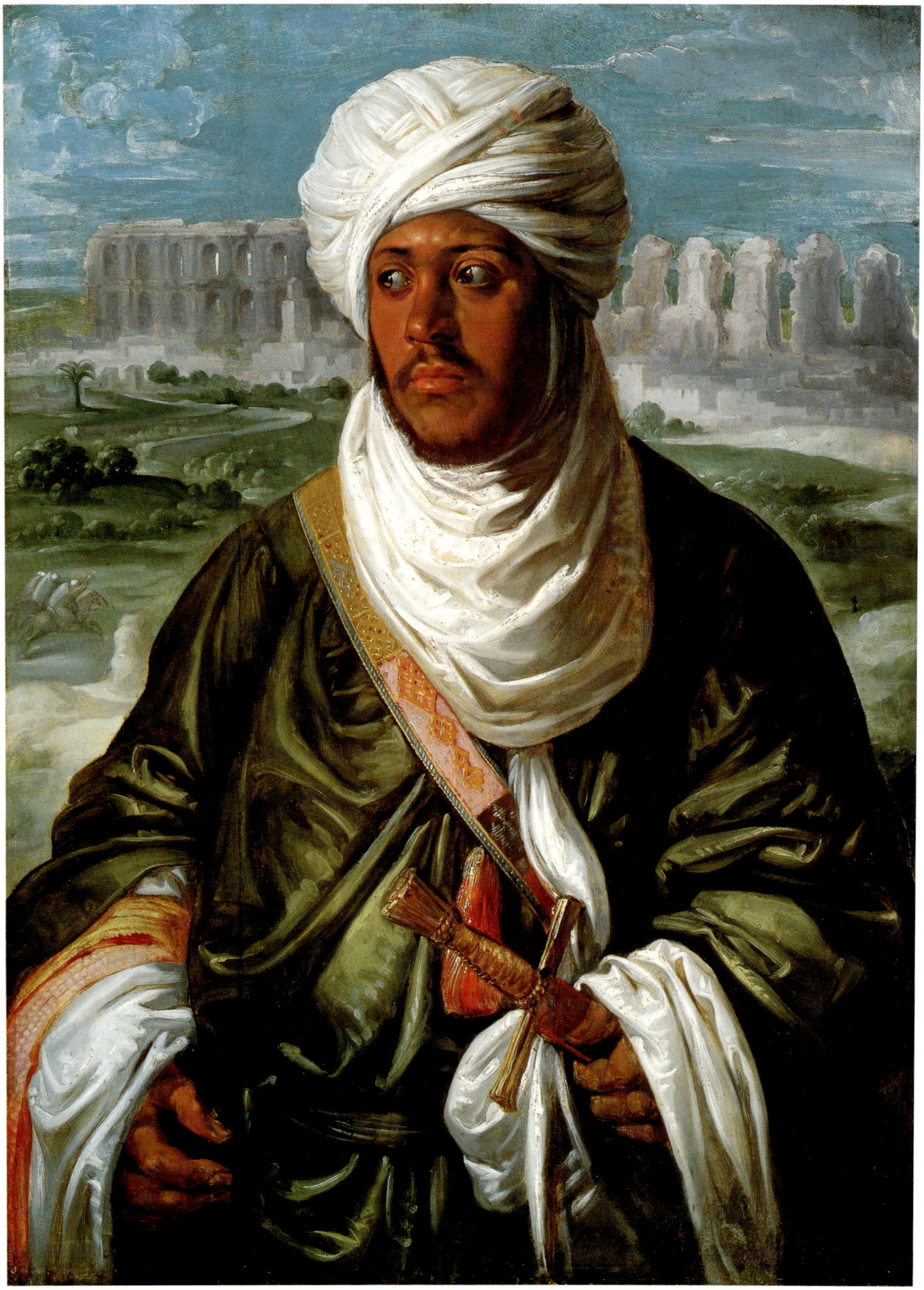

Jan Cornelisz. Vermeyen

1500-59

Portrait of Mulay Ahmad, called 'The King of Tunis'

c. 1535/6

Probably oil on panel
Probably *c.* 76.2 × 63.5 cm

Jan Vermeyen was born in Beverwijk, near Haarlem, in 1500 and was buried in Brussels in 1559. His greatest claim to fame is a series of cartoons for one of the most important tapestry commissions of the sixteenth century: *The Conquest of Tunis*.[1] The importance of tapestry decorations at this time can easily be underestimated today. They were often made to decorate the very grandest royal and imperial apartments and this particular set, woven at vast expense by Willem de Pannemaker in Brussels,[2] was created specifically for a space in one of the royal palaces, as the careful dimensions of each panel indicate.[3] It may perhaps have been the principal room of the Madrid Alcázar, where the series hung in the seventeenth century; or perhaps the royal residence in Toledo.[4]

It is ironic indeed that Vermeyen's lengthy involvement with this most prestigious commission of his life, precisely because it occupied him, one way or another, for so many years, should have contributed to the decline of his artistic reputation. It prevented him from carrying out other commissions which he might reasonably have expected. His career has only been reconstructed in modern times and his achievements rescued from obscurity and mis-attribution. A number of his works have vanished, among them the original eighth and eleventh in the series of the *Conquest of Tunis* tapestries.[5] In addition to these losses, the first and ninth in the series of the original cartoons have also disappeared.

The series was commissioned by the Holy Roman Emperor Charles V (1500-58) who regarded the Tunis campaign of 1535 as among his greatest military achievements, a view shared by some but not all of his contemporaries.[6] The aim of the campaign was primarily the elimination of the feared pirate Khair el-Din, better known as Barbarossa (d. 1546), who had raided the coast of Spain near Valencia in 1529, taking many Christians for slavery. By 1534 Barbarossa had also succeeded in driving Mulay Hasan, the rightful Berber King of Tunis, from his land. Mulay Hasan fled to Spain and pleaded with Charles V to help him reconquer his kingdom. In July 1535 Charles V landed in North Africa with 30,000 men and took Tunis, but Barbarossa escaped to Algeria. The campaign successfully reinstated Mulay Hasan as ruler of Tunis, but his son, Mulay Ahmad, seized power in 1542, effectively overthrowing his father, when Mulay Hasan was on another mission in Europe. On his return to Tunis, Mulay Hasan was given the grim choice by his son of life imprisonment or blinding, and chose the latter.

Vermeyen took part in the Emperor's Tunis campaign from the beginning to the end, and remained in the retinue of the Emperor for years thereafter, finally beginning work on the tapestries themselves in 1546 and finishing in 1550. The delay

Mulay Ahmad.
Copy by Peter Paul Rubens (1577-1642), *c.* 1613-14/20, of a lost portrait by Jan Cornelisz. Vermeyen (1500-59) of *c.* 1535/6.
Oil on panel, 99.7 × 71.5 cm.
Museum of Fine Arts, Boston, M. Theresa B. Hopkins Fund, 40.2

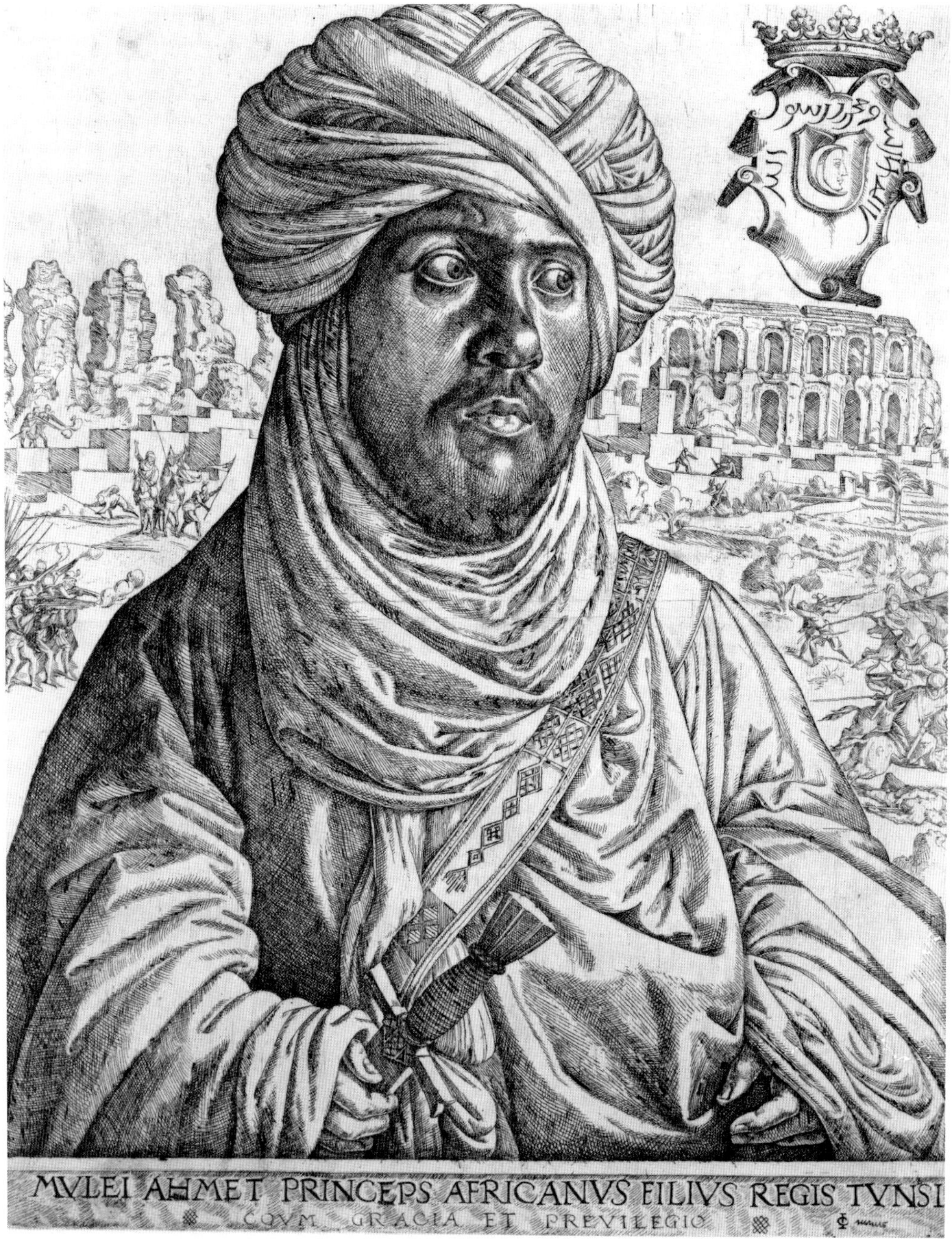

Mulay Ahmad by Jan Cornelisz. Vermeyen, *c.* 1535-6.
Etching, 49.2 × 37.7cm., after lost portrait.
Museum Boymans-van Beuningen, Rotterdam

between the end of the campaign and the commissioning of the tapestries was probably due in part, as Horn suggests,[7] to the fact that the room to house the series still had to be completed.

On 26 May 1536 the Council of Brabant had granted Vermeyen exclusive rights 'to print certain portraits and depictions of the armies of His Royal Majesty and the siege before Tunis... ', a monopoly which was renewed on 19 March 1538. He evidently portrayed both Mulay Hasan and his son in separate portraits, although both the original paintings he made of them are missing. Vermeyen's tall, handsome appearance, and his long beard, from which his nickname 'Barbalonga' was derived, endeared him to the Emperor; and an engraving of the artist bears verses suggesting that the beard reached down to his feet.[8]

Vermeyen's autograph etching of Mulay Ahmad, dating from late 1535 or 1536, must have derived from his own painting of the sitter.[9] This painting has been missing since the middle of the seventeenth century, but was copied by Rubens either in about 1613-14 or around 1620.[10] Rubens's painting itself confirms that there was indeed an original painting by Vermeyen: it is in the reverse sense to Vermeyen's etching, which suggests that Rubens must have had the original painting to work from, a presumption that is confirmed by other details. In his painting, Rubens showed the dagger more correctly beneath the King's left hand,[11] an adjustment which could, of course, have been achieved without reversing the whole composition. Yet otherwise the entire composition – the figure, the landscape background and its architecture – is reversed.

Rubens's splendid portrait of Mulay Ahmad hangs now in the Museum of Fine Arts in Boston.[12] Rubens extended Vermeyen's composition at top and bottom, and the battle scene visible in the background of the etching is replaced by three horsemen. This extension of the composition is consistent with Rubens's preference for a standard size of European portrait close to what is known in Britain as a 'Kit Kat', which measures 91.5 × 71.1 cm, and his portrait of Mulay Ahmad measures 100.3 × 71.1 cm. The 'Kit-Kat' was the size, for example, of Raphael's *Baldassare Castiglione* when in its un-cut-down state, which was how Rubens had seen it in the Gonzaga collection in Mantua, and where he had copied it (Rubens's copy of the *Baldassare Castiglione* is now in the collection of the Courtauld Institute of Art, London).

Although Vermeyen's original painting of Mulay Ahmad is lost, its shape and size, in addition to its composition, can be deduced from the shape of the etching (ignoring the letters) and by reference to Vermeyen's habits as shown in his surviving autograph portraits. It is evident that, in contrast with Rubens, Vermeyen preferred the portrait size known in England (misleadingly) as a 'three-quarter', i.e. 76.2 × 63.5 cm, and it is very probable that the portrait of Mulay Ahmad conformed to this size, as the shape of the etching suggests. The medium and support can also be presumed to have been oil on panel, in accordance with Vermeyen's usual practice.[13]

Some controversy has arisen about the imposing structure in the background of the picture. Peter C. Sutton suggests that the structure is the ruin of 'El Djem in Tunis'.[14] This must be doubted, as El Djem is not in Tunis itself, but about 200 km to the south of the city, and it is highly unlikely that anybody in the expedition of Charles V ever went that far south. The massive ruins are much more likely to represent the old curved Roman aqueduct near the river Medjerda, connecting Zaghwan and Carthage, as suggested by Held,[15] a probability that is further

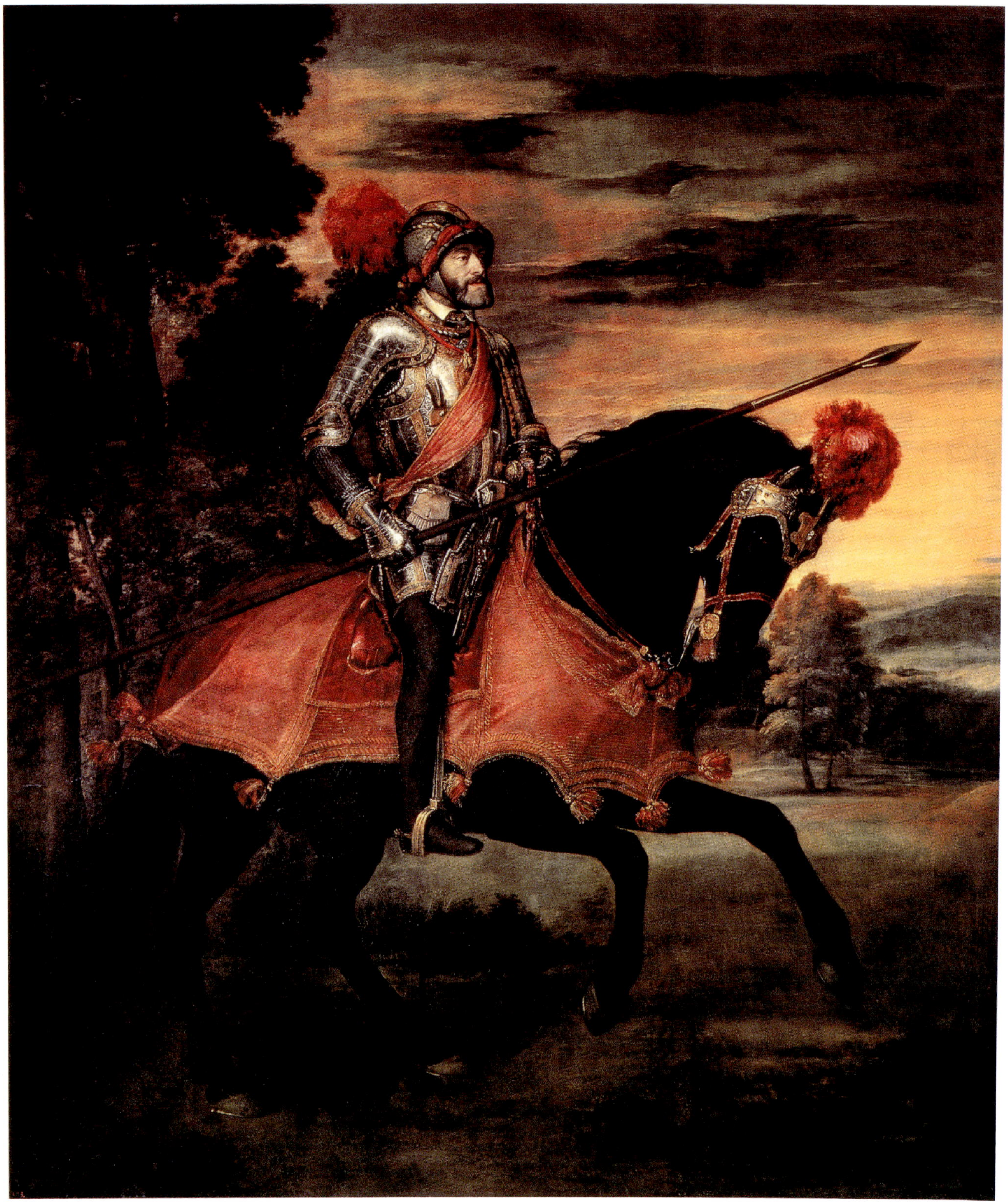

The Emperor Charles V at the Battle of Mühlberg by Titian (Tiziano Vecelli, 1485/90-1576), 1548.
Oil on canvas, 332 × 279 cm.
Museo del Prado, Madrid

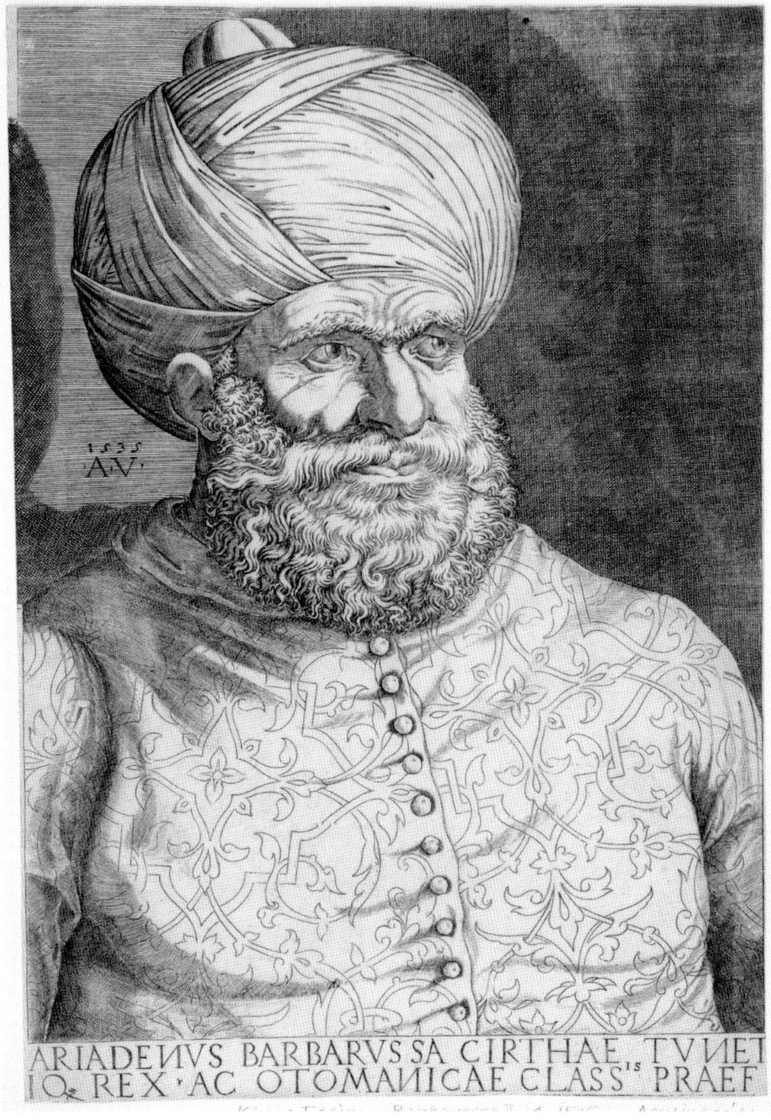

Barbarossa
(Khair el-Din, c. 1465-1546)
by Agostino Veneziano, 1535.
Engraving, 43.5 × 30.5 cm.
Fitzwilliam Museum, Cambridge

strengthened by a closer look at the tapestries in Madrid. The tapestry 'Skirmishes on the Cape of Carthage' shows a curved structure near Tunis (as the title indicates) which comes very close to that depicted by Rubens. The same aqueduct also reappears in the tapestries 'The Fall of Goleta' and 'The Fall of Tunis'.[16]

Rubens's copy of *Mulay Ahmad* remained with him until his death in 1640. So distinctive and powerful a portraitist was Vermeyen, and his works so relatively few in number, that the loss of what was evidently one of his most compelling

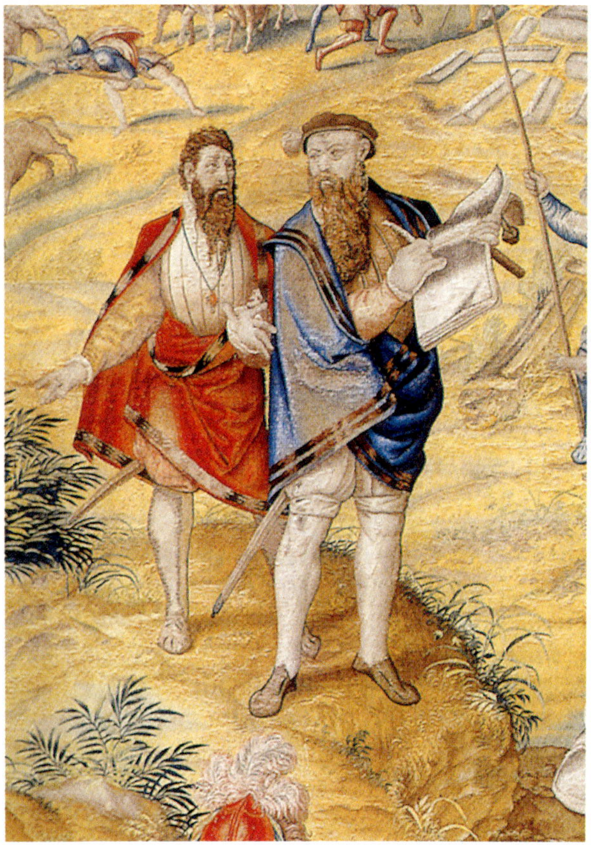

Portrait of Jan Vermeyen and a companion. Detail of Brussels tapestry, 527 × 835 cm., showing 'The Sack of Tunis', from twelve-piece set *The Conquest of Tunis* woven 1549-54 to designs by Jan Vermeyen.
Museo del Patrimonio Nacional, Palacio Real de Madrid

portraits, that of Mulay Ahmad, King of Tunis, is especially poignant. Furthermore, it is characteristic of Vermeyen's historical fate that within eighty or so years of his death both this picture and the related portrait of Mulay Hasan were already passing under the names of different artists in inventories of the seventeenth century. In the inventory of Rubens's estate, for example, the copies he had made after Vermeyen were described as after works by Antonio Mor.[17] It seems clear also that Vermeyen's original portrait of Mulay Ahmad was recorded in 1642 under yet another name, that of Pieter Coecke van Aelst (1502-50), in the inventory following the death of the Antwerp painter and dealer Herman de Neyt. That inventory contains two pictures described as 'Den Moor van Meester van Aelst met Tunis achter' ('the moor by Master van Aelst with Tunis in the background') and 'Den vader vanden voors[chreven] Moor die Keyser Carel te voet valt' ('the father of the said moor, throwing himself at the feet of the

Emperor Charles'), a reference to what was evidently a picture showing Mulay Hasan in supplication before the Emperor.[18]

This mention in the inventory of 1644 is the last certain reference to the portrait of Mulay Ahmad, for in the remaining references to be found in the seventeenth

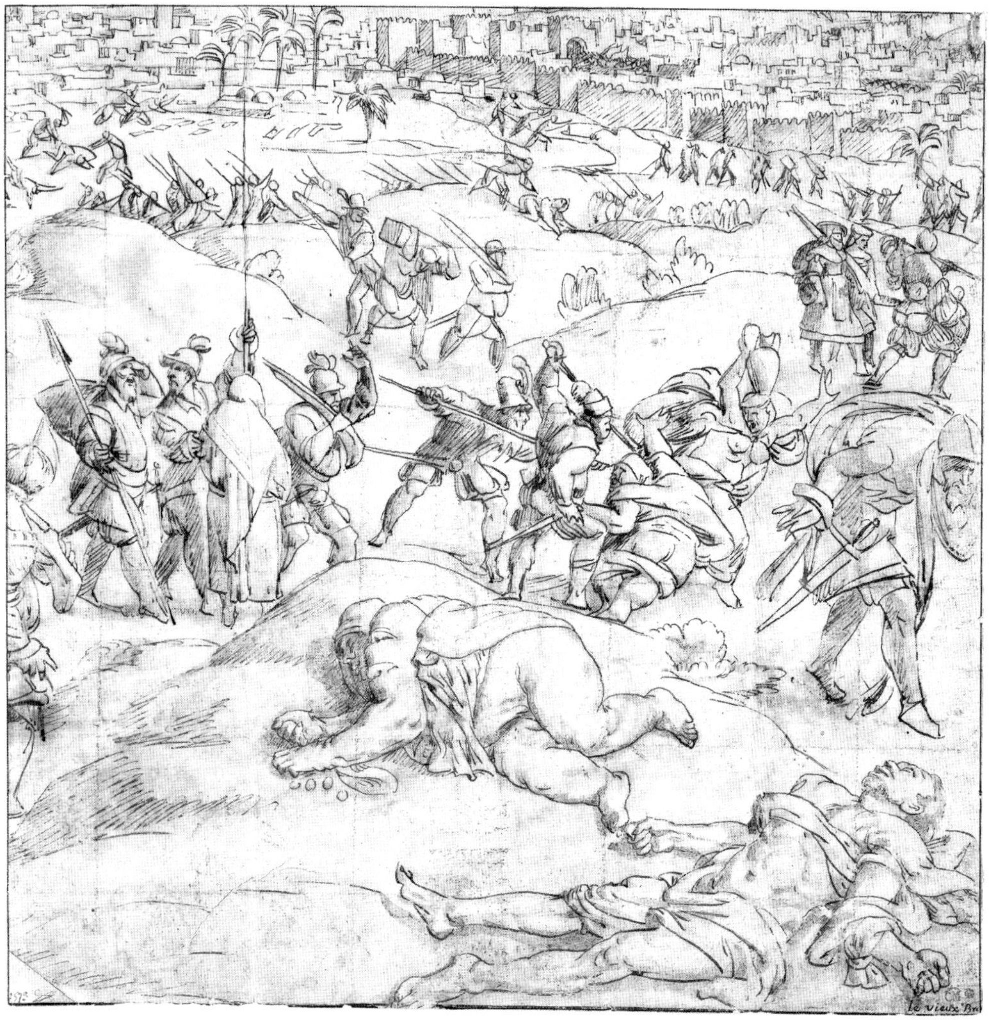

Episode from the Siege of Tunis by Jan Cornelisz. Vermeyen. Pen, brown ink and wash, 35.5 × 34.5 cm. Rijksmuseum, Amsterdam

century it is not clear which 'King of Tunis' is being identified, although paradoxically Vermeyen's authorship resurfaces. One such reference appears in 1644, when the dealer Joan Bocx in Amsterdam confirmed that he had received several pictures for sale from the dealer Mathijs Musson (or Mousson) in Antwerp, including 'nr. 8: Den Conick van Thunes geschildert van meester Hans met den Baert, fl 24' ('the King of Tunis, painted by master Hans with the beard'), which must be a reference to the authorship of Vermeyen.[19] The inventory of David Beckx, drawn up at The Hague on 19 December 1656, contains a reference which correctly identifies Vermeyen as the artist, because one of the forms in which his name is recorded is 'Hans Mayer': '(42) Een contrefeytsel van den coningh van Thunis gedaen bij Hens Mayer.'[20] The 1659 inventory of the estate of the artist

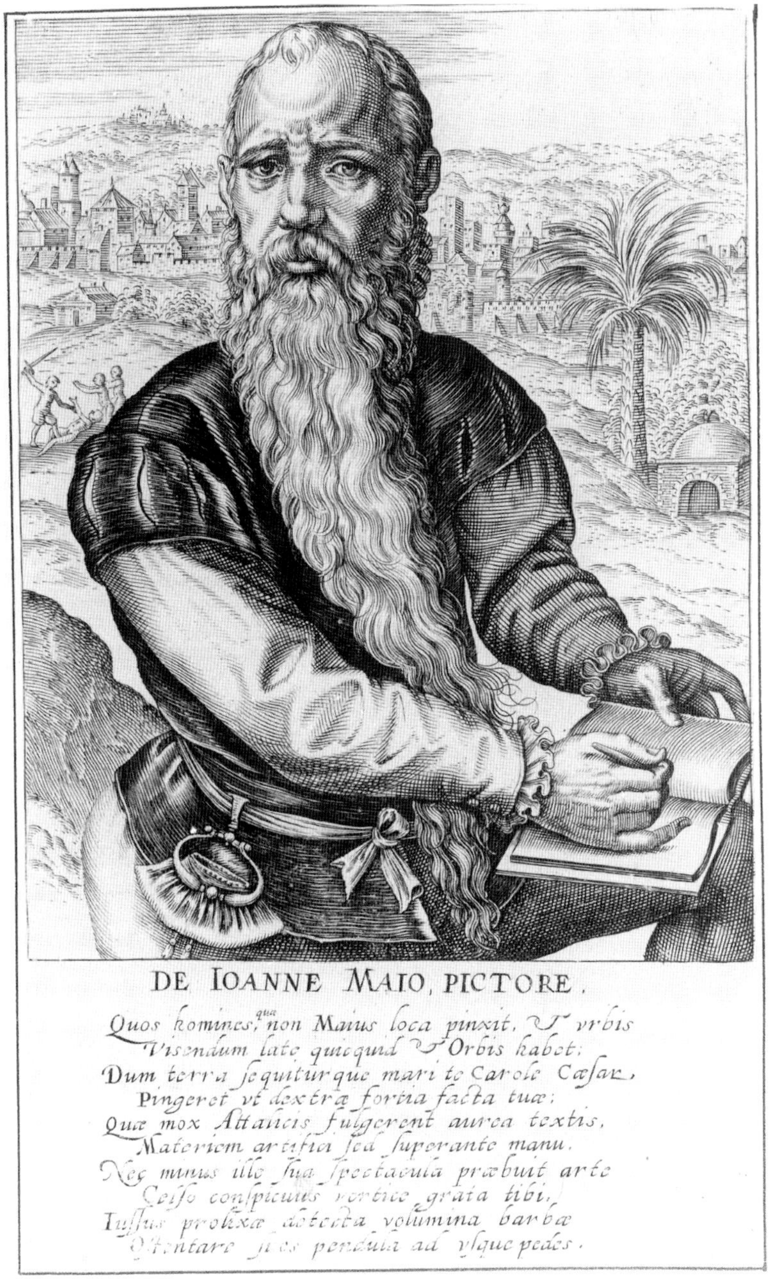

Self-portrait after Jan Cornelisz. Vermeyen ('Barbalonga').
Engraving by Hieronymous Wiericx, 34.5 × 15.5 cm.
Witt Print Collection, Courtauld Institute of Art, London

Frans Snyders (1579-1657), compiled by the same Antwerp dealer Mathijs Musson as mentioned above, notes 'een koeninck van Tuenis Mucleasses 18 gl', where the garbled wording could well indicate 'Mulay Hasan'.[21] The final mention of what might be either picture is in the inventory of the estate of the Antwerp publisher Jan van Meurs, 26-27 October 1659, which contains a work described as 'Item een schilderye den Coninck van Thunes'.[22]

NOTES

1 For a full account of Vermeyen's work and of the relevant literature, see Hendrik J. Horn, *Jan Cornelisz Vermeyen: Painter of Charles V and His Conquest of Tunis*, 2 vols., Doornspijk, 1989.

2 Ibid., pp. 125ff.

3 Ibid., p. 128.

4 Ibid.

5 Because tapestries were usually made for a specific site, they have always been vulnerable to the re-organisation or reconstruction of the palaces for which they were made.

6 Ibid., pp. 112-3, where Horn summarises (p. 113): 'The expedition to Tunis did not meet any long-term political or strategic objective that Charles may have hoped to achieve.'

7 Ibid., p. 116.

8 Ibid., II, pl. A1, woodcut by Hieronymus Wiericx after Vermeyen: '*Jussus prolixae detecta volumiana barbae/Ostentare suos pendula ad usque pedes.*'

9 The etching can be taken to be autograph, Horn, op. cit., p. 20.

10 The earlier date is favoured by Peter C. Sutton, *The Age of Rubens*, exh. cat., Boston, 1993, pp. 235-7, p. 236; the later by Horn, op. cit., pp. 20-21.

11 This point was made by J. Held in 'Rubens' "King of Tunis" and Vermeyen's Portrait of Mulay Ahmad', *Art Quarterly*, III (1940), pp. 173-81; see also J. Held, *Rubens-Studien*, Leipzig, 1987 (see pp. 22-7).

12 See Sutton, op. cit., no. 9, pp. 235-7, where Sutton also discusses the fact that Rubens not only copied the portrait, adding an especially dashing air to the figure, but also re-used the likeness in other compositions of his own.

13 Portraits of 'three-quarter' size and also in oil on panel include Horn, op. cit., cat. nos. A18, A19, A20, and A39, pictures which are all close in date to the missing *Mulay Ahmad*. For portrait sizes see R. Simon, *The Portrait in Britain and America*, London and Boston, 1987, pp. 111-12.

14 Op. cit., following W. G. Constable, 'Rubens in the Museum of Fine Arts, Boston', in *Miscellanea Leo Van Puyvelde*, Brussels, 1949, p. 129.

15 Held, op. cit., 1987, p. 25.

16 See Horn, op. cit., I, p. 356, for the works by Vermeyen which depict the aqueduct, especially the *Micault Triptych* (Horn A106). Although there must be some speculation as to whether the ruins depicted are, rather, those of the arena at Carthage, it seems incontrovertible that the view in *Mulay Ahmad* is essentially of Tunis as shown in the tapestries and the *Micault Triptych*.

17 Nos. 148 and 149, '*Twe portretten van een Koning van Thunis naer Antonius Moro*'. See J. Held, *Rubens-Studien*, p. 22; Constable, op. cit., p. 129; Horn, op. cit., pp. 15ff.; and J. Muller, *Rubens, The Artist as Collector*, Princeton, 1984, p. 121. The implication is that there was also a portrait by Rubens of Mulay Hasan that has disappeared.

18 Mulay Hasan is also depicted in a woodcut of *c.* 1536, half length, after a now-lost image by Vermeyen – see Horn, op. cit., I, p. 19 and A46; and he also appears with his back to the viewer in *A Moorish Banquet*, an etching by Vermeyen, ibid., A50, and see I, pp. 19-20.

19 Held, op. cit., 1987, p. 24.

20 Muller, op. cit., p. 121, n. 3.

21 Ibid.

22 Ibid

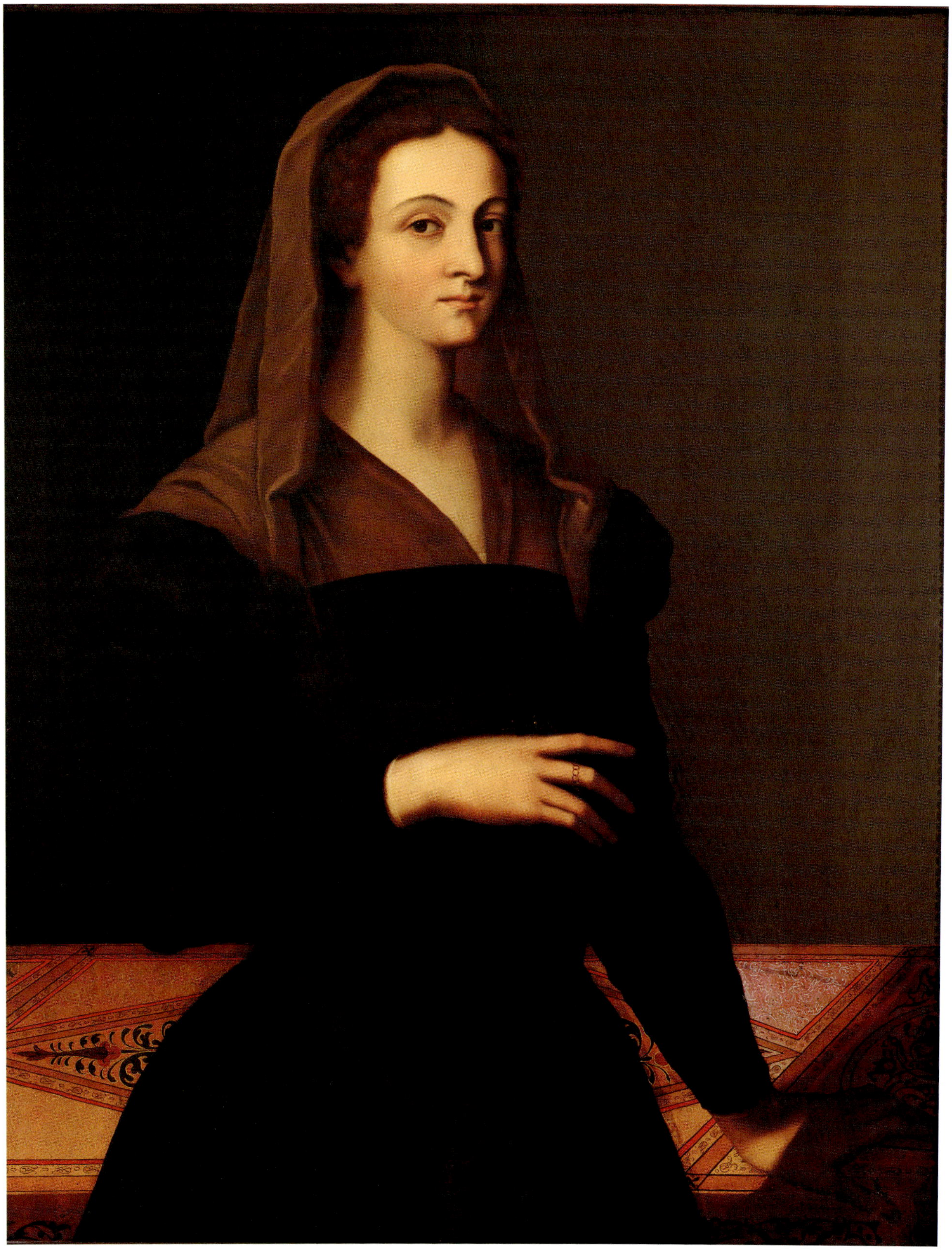

Sebastiano del Piombo

1485/6-1547

Portrait of Giulia Gonzaga

1532

Perhaps oil on canvas, possibly 140 × 110 cm

Sebastiano Luciani, called Sebastiano del Piombo, was born in Venice around 1485, and became a close friend of Michelangelo. After the death of Raphael in 1520, he was one of the leading painters working in Rome and was particularly noted as a portrait painter. Two portraits by him of Giulia Gonzaga (*c.* 1513-66) are documented as having been commissioned, the first and most famous in 1532 by Cardinal Ippolito de' Medici (1511-35), the second in 1547 by Ippolito's cousin Caterina de' Medici, Queen of France (1519-89). Neither survives, although a picture in Wiesbaden Museum, on slate, can be presumed to record the appearance of the lost picture that belonged to Ippolito de' Medici,[1] in which, evidently, she was shown dressed as a widow. Other copies and variants of portraits of Giulia created by Sebastiano are also known.[2]

THE PORTRAIT COMMISSIONED BY IPPOLITO DE' MEDICI

The first reference we have to the commission by Ippolito is a letter from Sebastiano himself to Michelangelo written on 8 June 1532:

> I think I am going to leave Rome tomorrow to go to Fondi to paint a portrait of a lady, I think I shall be there 15 days.[3]

On 15 July Sebastiano wrote to Michelangelo, 'I am now back from Fondi.'[4] Fondi was the home of Giulia Gonzaga, in a castle halfway between Rome and Naples, near Terracina, which she inhabited as the famously beautiful young widow of Vespasiano Colonna, who had died on 12 March 1528. We learn from the 1568 edition of Vasari's *Lives* the detailed circumstances of this commission:

> ... Cardinal Ippolito de' Medici, having become enamoured of Signora Giulia Gonzaga, who was then living at Fondi, that Cardinal sent Sebastiano to that place, accompanied by four light horsemen, to take her portrait; and within a month he finished that portrait, which, being taken from the celestial beauty of that lady by a hand so masterly, proved to be a divine picture. Wherefore, after it had been carried to Rome, the labours of that craftsman were richly rewarded by the Cardinal, who declared that this portrait surpassed by a great measure all those that Sebastiano had ever executed up to that day, as indeed it did; and the work was afterwards sent to King Francis of France, who had it placed in his Palace of Fontainebleau.[5]

Giulia Gonzaga was born into a branch of the ruling family of Mantua. Her father was Ludovico IV Gonzaga, who had married Francesca Fieschi of Genoa in 1497. Her cousin was Federico II Gonzaga, 5th Marquis and 1st Duke of Mantua, who brought the painter and architect Giulio Romano to Mantua. In 1526, at the age of no more than fourteen (if that), Giulia Gonzaga married the crippled Vespasiano Colonna, a widower in his early forties, twenty-seven years her senior,

Giulia Gonzaga as a widow. Copy of lost portrait of 1532 by Sebastiano del Piombo (1485/6-1547). Oil on slate, 110 × 86 cm. Wiesbaden Museum

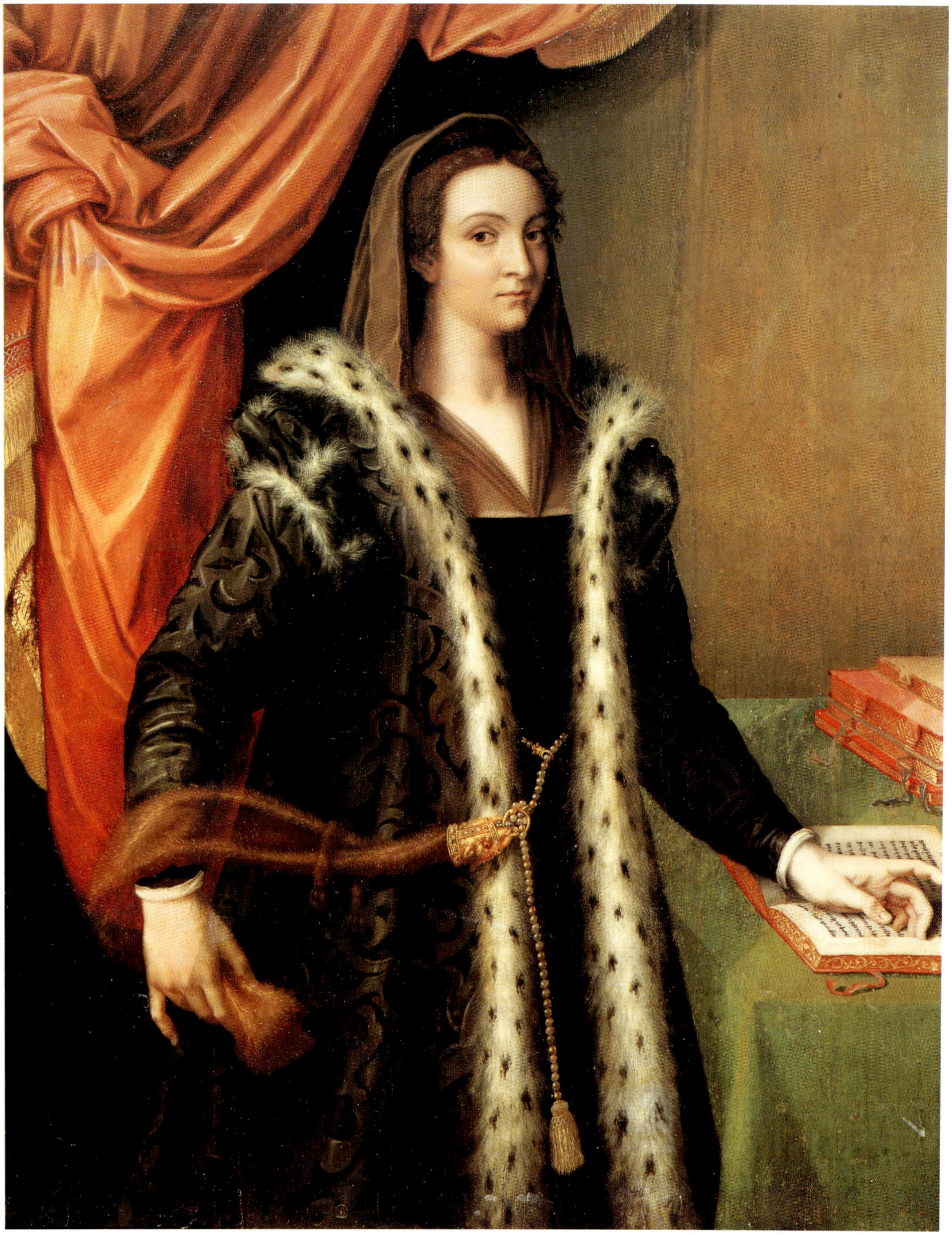

Giulia Gonzaga after Sebastiano del Piombo, perhaps by Cristoforo dell'Altissimo.
Oil on panel, 144 × 111 cm.
Uffizi, Florence

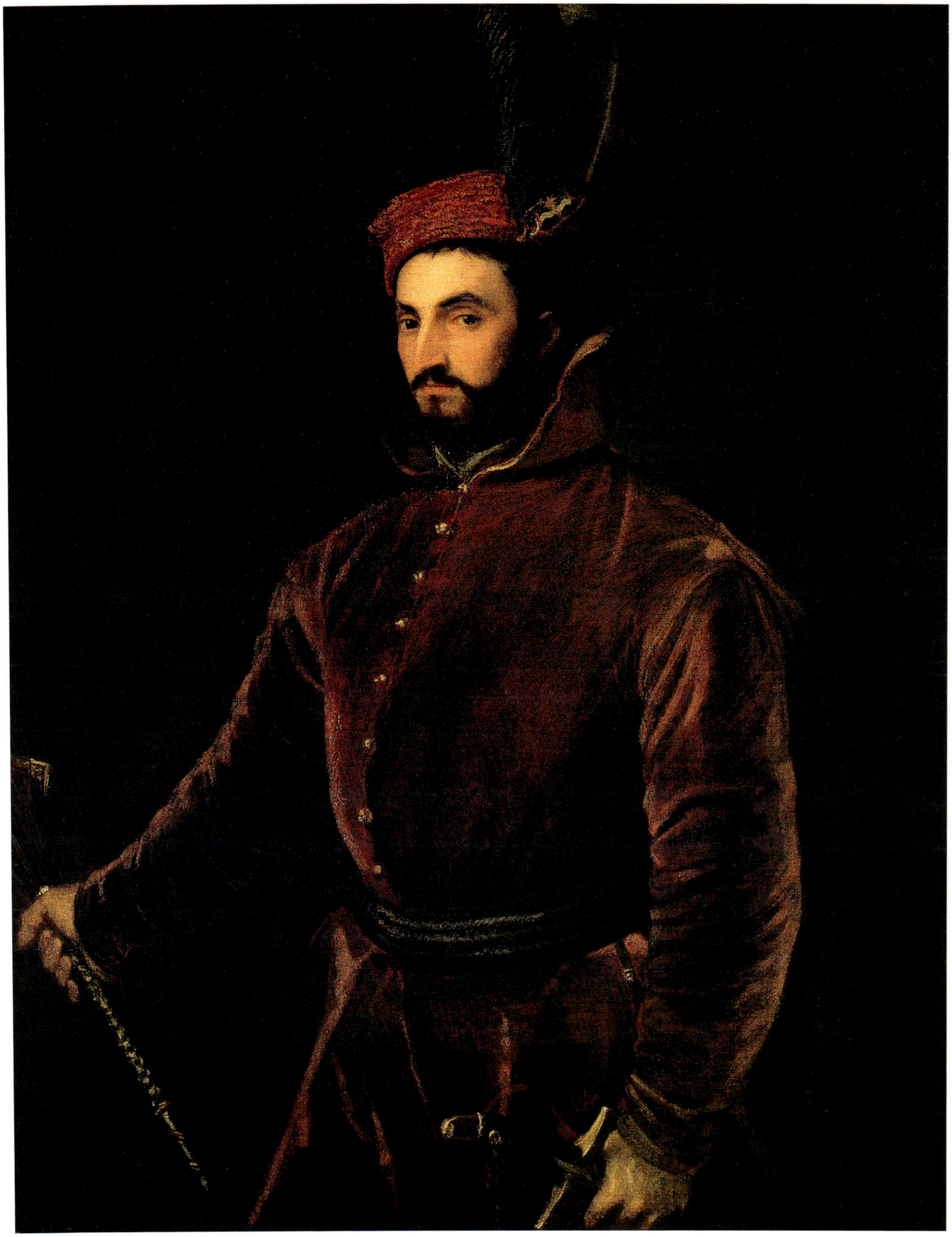

Ippolito de'Medici in Hungarian costume by Titian (Tiziano Vecelli, 1485/90-1576), 1532.
Oil on canvas, 139 × 107 cm.
Pitti Palace, Florence

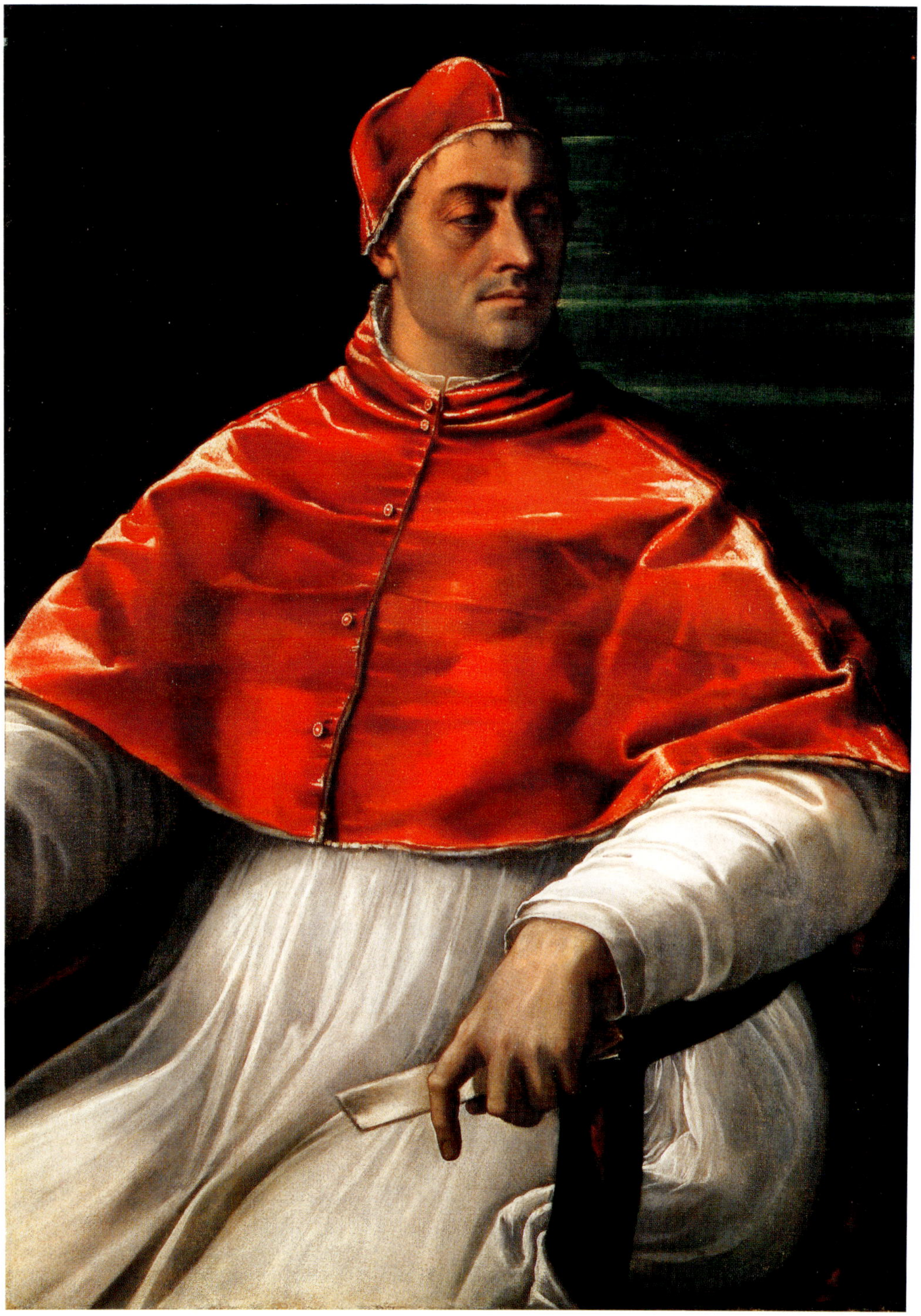

Pope Clement VII
by Sebastiano del Piombo.
Oil on canvas, 145 × 100 cm.
Galleria Nazionale di Capodimonte, Naples

who had one daughter, Isabella, by his first marriage. Vespasiano was a scion of the great Colonna family of Rome, and one of the largest land-owners in the kingdom of Naples. When Vespasiano died he left his property to his wife under certain conditions, and also stated his desire that Isabella was to marry Ippolito de' Medici, the nephew of the Medici Pope, Clement VII.

Ippolito was born in Urbino around 1511, and was the natural son of Giuliano de' Medici, Duke of Nemours (1478-1516), who was the third son of Lorenzo the Magnificent. Lorenzo's brother Giuliano had a natural son, Giulio, who became the second Medici pope as Clement VII. Ippolito was orphaned as a child and taken to Rome by the first Medici pope, his uncle, Leo X (Giovanni, second son of Lorenzo). On 10 January 1529, Clement VII, his father's first cousin, created Ippolito a cardinal and vice-chancellor, and bestowed sufficient benefices upon him to enable him to lead a life of considerable luxury in his Roman palace in Campo Marzio. The desired marriage between Isabella Colonna and Ippolito never took place, however. Instead, Isabella secretly married Ludovico Gonzaga on 26 April 1528, and it was only after his proposed marriage fell through that Ippolito became a cardinal. One reason for Isabella's unexpected marriage may have been the fact that it was at the beginning of 1528 that Ippolito de' Medici first met her youthful and astonishingly beautiful stepmother, Giulia Gonzaga Colonna, at Fondi, when Giulia was barely sixteen and he himself only eighteen or nineteen.

Ippolito and Giulia immediately formed a passionate attachment which was only broken by Ippolito's untimely death at the castle of Itri, near Fondi, seven

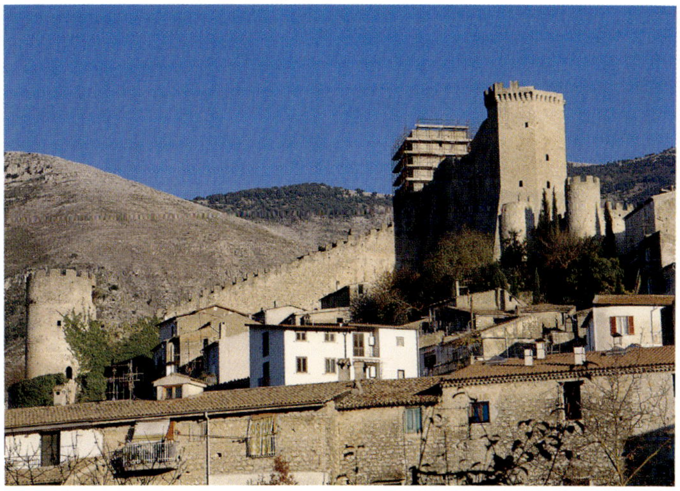

The Castle of Itri near Fondi

years later on 10 August 1535, with Giulia at his bedside. As so often in those times, poisoning was suspected, because Ippolito had been the focus of exiled Florentines in Rome opposed to the rule of his cousin Alessandro de' Medici, who had been made Duke of Florence in 1532 by the Emperor Charles V, the year in which the family returned to power in the city. Ippolito believed himself to have been poisoned by Alessandro, but it seems probable that he died of fever and perhaps the effects of his rather dissolute life.[6] For his own part, it is certain that Ippolito had planned to blow up Alessandro with a gunpowder-filled casket.[7]

Ippolito and Giulia never married, and it is not known for certain whether theirs was a platonic or a consummated sexual relationship, although on balance it is likely that it was indeed platonic. Ippolito was, of course, a cardinal, but he was well known to have been a reluctant one, and his desire to cease to be one was also common knowledge.[8] He had at least one mistress, the famous Venetian courtesan Zaffetta;[9] and when he had his portrait painted twice by Titian it was in lay attire: in armour (in a lost portrait), and in Hungarian costume in 1533 (Pitti Palace, Florence).[10] Ippolito chose Hungarian costume for this latter portrait because he had taken part as papal legate in the campaign of Charles V against the Turks, and he commissioned the portrait of himself by Titian upon his return from Hungary. He also chose to be portrayed in lay dress by Sebastiano.[11] It has been said that Ippolito took the Sebastiano portrait of Giulia with him on his trip to Hungary.[12] This possibility, together with the fact that Sebastiano had to travel to Fondi in order to make the portrait in the first place, suggests that it was upon canvas rather than upon Sebastiano's favoured support of slate.[13]

Ippolito's relationship with Giulia must have been conditioned to a great extent by the status of Giulia on the one hand, especially as a widow, and his cardinalate on the other, together with obstacles placed in the way of Giulia's remarriage by Vespasiano's will. These factors would have precluded anything but the most discreet behaviour, even though their mutual feelings were common knowledge, as a letter swiftly reporting the cardinal's death makes clear:

> Cardinal de' Medici died in Itri on the 10th of this [month of August] at midday, in the manner of a good Christian, and as is done by saints and sinners alike. He was there during his fatal illness in order to be close to Donna Giulia, whom he treated in the most virtuous and courteous way.[14]

Giulia Gonzaga was regarded as one of the greatest beauties of her day, but was also famous for her precocious wisdom and her intellectual and moral qualities. Fondi became a focus for literary figures in the period between Giulia's being widowed in 1528 and her permanent departure for Naples in 1535 following the death of Ippolito.[15] Sebastiano's portrait of her was his 'most widely admired and publicly celebrated portrait of the period after the sack of Rome [in 1527]'.[16] It is testimony to Giulia's great attraction that when in 1534 the famous corsair Barbarossa raided Sperlunga and headed towards Fondi contemporary reports suggested that it was in order to force her into the harem of his master, Suleyman the Magnificent. Romantic though the story is, there is probably as little truth in this legend as in the other rumour of the time that when the Emperor Charles V invaded North Africa in the following year it was to avenge the intended assault upon Giulia's honour.[17]

Her beauty was lauded by many poets of the time, including Ariosto in *Orlando Furioso*:

> Giulia Gonzaga, she that wheresoe'er
> She moves, where'er she turns her lucid eyes,
> Not only is in charms without a peer,
> But seems a goddess lighted from the skies[18]

Sebastiano's portrait, as the definitive image from life of this legendary beauty, became almost as famous as she herself, and it was also praised by several poets, who included Sebastiano's friend Francesco Maria Molza and Giulia's own secretary, Gandolfo Porrini. In his poem, *Stanze sopra il Ritratto della Signora Julia Gonzaga Colonna*, Porrini describes Giulia as dressed in 'habito honesto', that is to say, modest attire, and without the adornment of jewels or rings on her fingers:

> For not only with beauty of thine eyes
> Dost thou enthral and rouse the envy of our age,
> But with wise discourses and lofty thoughts,

The chief adornment of thy breast;
Thence, with such fair spoils embellished,
It has no need of pearls or precious stones,
Just as no other golden chain is needed
To grace still further the beauty of thy throat...
And if no rings bedeck her hallowed hands...[19]

There seems no doubt that this picture is identical with that recorded in a Farnese inventory of 1644, no. 4352, where the sitter is described as a 'widow of the Colonna family', which Giulia indeed was, although the attribution to Titian must be mistaken (it is frequently used in this inventory without any sound basis):

Un quadro in tela con cornice di legno dorata con una Dama Vedova di Casa Colonna, mano di Titiano.[20]

The reason for Giulia's wearing widow's weeds, which, of course, fits with Porrini's poetic description of her, is that her possession of the estates of her late husband Vespasiano was dependent upon her doing so. Vespasiano stipulated as much in his will of 12 March 1528. Giulia was to possess the estates during her lifetime, but only so long as she remained a widow and dressed accordingly. If she married again, she would retain only her dowry and Isabella would become the 'universal heir' of all Vespasiano's estates.[21]

As it turned out, Vespasiano's will could hardly have been more calculated to divide the two young women. Upon her marriage to Ippolito, Isabella would have received a substantial dowry, according to her father's will. Once, however, it had become evident that her marriage with Ippolito was no longer going to take place, it was in Isabella's interests to escape from being merely subjected to her step mother, and so she made her secret marriage into the Gonzaga family.

The presence of Sebastiano's portrait of Giulia in the later Farnese inventory is readily explained: it must have passed into the Farnese family collection upon the death of Ippolito. The Farnese, traditionally opposed to the Medici, and now, from 1534, with a pope of their own upon the throne of St. Peter in the form of Paul III, sequestrated many of Ippolito's possessions as soon as they heard of his death, officially on account of the debts which he owed.[22] Pier Luigi Farnese, the illegitimate son of Paul III, had Ippolito's valuable armour removed, in the middle of the night, from Ippolito's palace in Campo Marzio to the magnificent new Palazzo Farnese (begun by Paul III before his pontificate).[23] The suggestion[24] that Sebastiano's portrait of Giulia Gonzaga (and one of the Titian portraits of Ippolito) went the same way as the armour is strongly borne out by a payment of 5 January 1537 in Paul III's accounts to the silk-weaver Francesco Gucci for '... a green curtain that he has made to cover the portrait of Signora Giulia Gonzaga'.[25]

After its appearance in the Farnese inventory of 1644 the same portrait of Giulia, i.e. the Fondi portrait commissioned by Ippolito, is noted in subsequent Farnese inventories: in 1653 and 1680 (having been transferred to the Palazzo del Giardino, Parma) and again in 1708, 1731 and 1734 (in the Ducal gallery in the Palazzo della Pilotta, Parma). This last date marks the last appearance of the now-missing portrait in the records, and it may well be significant, because 1734 is the year in which Charles Bourbon (1716-88), who had inherited the duchies of Parma, Piacenza and Tuscany in 1731, acceded to the throne of Naples. He subsequently became King of Spain in 1759. The original picture may therefore have been removed from

Parma and made its way, for example, first to Naples and thence to Spain. The taste in art of King Carlo, as he is better known, has not been fully explored, but he was interested in architecture and built the huge royal residence at Caserta, which would, of course, have been in need of furnishing with works of art.

There is some substance to the speculation that the Fondi portrait of Giulia Gonzaga went to Naples, in that a copy of the lost portrait still survives today in the Palazzo Reale at Caserta, a picture presently on loan to the Palazzo Ducale in

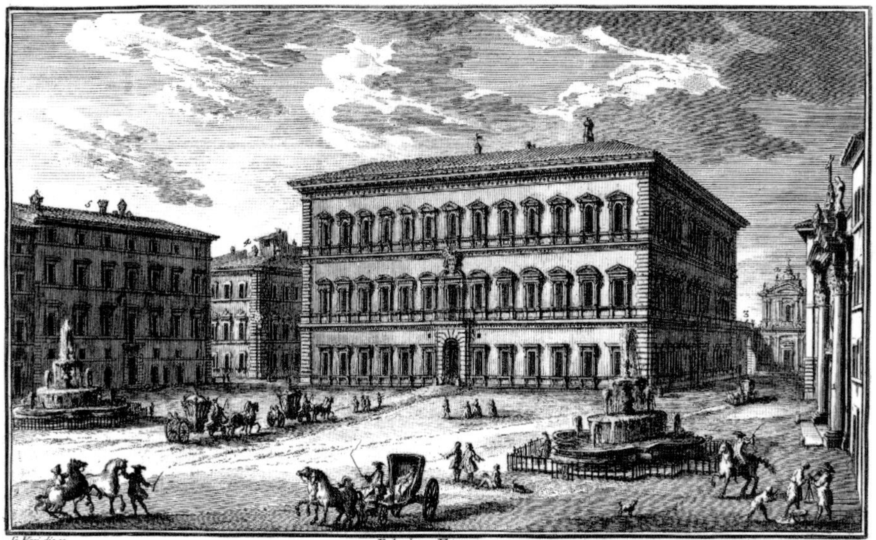

Palazzo Farnese, Rome
from Giuseppe Vasi, *Della Magnificenza di Roma Antica e Moderna*, 1753

Mantua. This particular version of the portrait is probably identical with the picture bequeathed in 1600 to Cardinal Odoardo Farnese (1573-1626), the last member of the Farnese family living in Rome, by Fulvio Orsini (1529-1600),[26] who was a powerful influence upon the patronage of Cardinal Ranuccio Farnese (1530-65) and his brother Cardinal Alessandro Farnese, 'il Gran Cardinale' (1520-89).[27] Unfortunately, many of the records of the Farnese collection which was then formed must have perished when the State Archives in Naples were destroyed during the Second World War.[28]

Orsini also made his own collection, a record of which exists in an inventory copy which he sent to his friend Giovanni Vincenzo Pinelli.[29] It contained a number of paintings by Sebastiano del Piombo, among them two portraits of Pope Clement VII, one showing him with a beard and the other showing him without a beard. There was also the copy of the portrait of Giulia Gonzaga noted above, and the conjunction of these two portraits again suggests that they were thought of as a natural pair, presumably because of their common link with Ippolito de' Medici. Indeed, Fulvio Orsini's inventory also records the presence of a portrait by Sebastiano of Ippolito himself, in lay attire, whether an original or copy:

> Quadretto corniciato di pero tinte, col ritratto d'Ipolito cardinal de' Medici in habito seculare... [30]

The famous portrait of Pope Clement VII without a beard by Sebastiano del

Piombo, from Fulvio Orsini's collection, survives in the Museo e Gallerie Nazionali di Capodimonte in Naples.

THE PORTRAIT COMMISSIONED BY CATERINA DE' MEDICI

This history of the Ippolito/Fondi portrait in the Farnese collections makes it highly unlikely, contrary to what has sometimes been asserted, that the picture was ever given by the Farnese pope, Paul III, to the Queen of France 'after Ippolito's death', in 1541, and the suggestion appears to stem from misunderstanding.[31] It is certain, however, that Caterina de' Medici, when she became Queen of France in 1547, as the wife of Henry II, did order two portraits from Sebastiano, one of which was of Giulia Gonzaga and the other of Pope Clement VII. It seems improbable that Caterina would have needed another portrait of Giulia in 1547 if she had indeed already been sent one by Pope Paul III six years earlier.

It is obvious why Caterina would commission a replica from Sebastiano of one of his portraits of Pope Clement: they were among his most famous portraits and the sitter was one of her most illustrious Medici relations. Indeed, Clement had arranged Caterina's marriage to the young Henry in 1533 – he became heir apparent in 1536 – and even travelled to Marseilles to perform the ceremony. Caterina would also have been aware that her marriage was intended to bring about a reconciliation between France and the papacy.

In contrast, at first sight it is not clear why Caterina should have commissioned a portrait of Giulia Gonzaga, who was still alive. One reason would have been that the portrait, like its subject, was so celebrated. That was ample justification at the time for the commissioning of a replica from the artist. But there were, perhaps, more compelling personal reasons. The original portrait was commissioned by Caterina's second cousin Ippolito in 1532, at which point Caterina was still only about thirteen years old and, although she was the sister of Alessandro, the cousin with whom Ippolito was at odds, the moving attachment of the two lovers may have made an early impression upon Caterina as it certainly did upon Italy generally.

Documents survive which confirm that Caterina commissioned the portraits in question, and that they were duly delivered to her in France, following the death of Sebastiano in 1547. In August of that year Cardinal Alessandro Farnese wrote to the papal nuncio in the French court:

> The Queen wrote some time ago to Fra Sebastiano del Piombo that he should make and send the portrait of Pope Clement, and that of Signora Giulia Gonzaga, both of which he made with every care, but the poor chap did not have time to send them before he died.[32]

The reply from France was written on 30 September,[33] and the French ambassador in Rome then duly arranged for the dispatch of these two portraits of Pope Clement and of Giulia.[34] Both of them appear after Sebastiano's death in an inventory of his household goods dated 25 June 1547. There were two paintings of Pope Clement VII, one on canvas and one on slate, and one painting of Giulia Gonzaga, probably on slate.[35] Their presence in the French royal collection is recorded in a garbled note by Père Dan in 1642, where he notes the presence of a portrait of Clement VII and one of his 'sister' (Clement did not have a sister).[36] Subsequently, the same two paintings, described as on slate, can be found in a list of the paintings at the French royal palace of Fontainebleau compiled in 1692.[37] There is no further record of either picture.

Notes

1 M. Hirst, *Sebastiano del Piombo*, Oxford, 1981, p. 116, pl. 150. See also pls. 151, 152, for two further types of portraits of the same sitter.

2 See L. Dussler, *Sebastiano del Piombo*, Basel, 1942, pp. 116-20, and Hirst, op. cit., pp. 114-19. Another portrait showing Giulia as a widow, also a copy, is in the Palazzo Reale, Caserta – see below.

3 'Credo dimane partirmi da Roma et andar insino a Fondi a retrarre una signiora, et credo starò 15 zorni.' G. Poggi, P. Barocchi, and R. Ristori, *Il Carteggio di Michelangelo*, 5 vols., Florence, 1973, III, p. 408.

4 Ibid., p. 419.

5 G. Vasari, *Lives of the Painters, Sculptors and Architects*, 2 vols. (Everyman Library), London, 1996, II, p. 148. The original runs: '...essendo il cardinale Ippolito de' Medici innamorato della Signora Giulia Gonzaga, la quale allora dimorava a Fondi, mandò il detto cardinale in quel luogo Sebastiano accompaganato da quattro cavai leggieri a ritrarla; et egli in termine d'un mese fece quel ritratto, il quale venendo dalle celesti bellezze di quella signora e da così dotta mano, riuscì una pittura divina; onde portata a Roma, furono grandemente riconosciute le fatiche di quell' artefice dal cardinale, che conobbe questo ritratto, come veramente era, passare di gran lunga quanti mai n' aveva fatti Sebastiano insino a quel giorno. Il qual ritratto fu poi mandato al re Francesco in Francia, che lo fe' porre nel suo luogo di Fontanableò.' Vasari, *Le Vite...* , R. Bettarini and P. Barocchi, ed., 6 vols., Florence, 1996– , V, p. 97.

6 See S. A. Nulli, *Giulia Gonzaga*, Milan, 1938, pp. 29, 35, 36; M. Hollingsworth, *Patronage in Sixteenth-century Italy*, London, 1996, p. 251.

7 See Hollingsworth, loc. cit.

8 Hirst, op. cit., p. 114, n. 105.

9 See, for example, Nulli, op. cit.

10 H. Wethey, *The Paintings of Titian,* 3 vols., 1969-75, II, *Portraits*, cat. 66, p. 119, pl. 65.

11 Hirst., op. cit., p. 114; see below.

12 M. Oliva, *Giulia Gonzaga Colonna tra Rinascimento e Controriforma*, Mursia, 1985, p. 297.

13 See below and n. 34.

14 '... il cardinale de' Medici morì in Istri alli 10 di questo [mesa d'agosto] a mezzo dì, da buon cristiano, come fanno li peccatori et fedeli. Gli fu men dura la morte per esser vicino a donna Giulia, la quale gli usò assai virtuose cortesie.' Paolo Giovio to the Bishop of Faenza, Nulli, op. cit., pp. 35-6.

15 Nulli, op. cit., pp. 22ff.

16 Ibid., p. 115.

17 Discussed by Nulli, op. cit. pp. 24ff.

18 Ludovico Ariosto, *Orlando Furioso*, Venice, 1550, canto 46, VIII: 'Giulia Gonzaga, che dovunque il piede/Volge e dovunque i sereni occhi gira,/Non pur ogn'altra di beltà le cede/Ma, come scesa dal ciel, Dea l'ammira.' Translated by William Stewart Rose, London, 1831.

19 'Perchè non sol co'begli occhi legaste/E faceste geloso il secol nostro;/Ma, con saggi discorsi e voglie caste,/Ch'è la parte miglior del petto vostro;/E di si bella spoglia indi l'orneste,/Che bisogno non ha di perle, o d'ostro:/Come ancho uopo non v'è d'altro monile/... E se sparse di gemme hor no portate/Le santissime man...'. See E. H. Ramsden, 'Concerning a "lost" Portrait of a Lady', *Come, Take this Lute, A Quest for Identities in Italian Renaissance Portraiture*, 1983, ch. 5, pp. 156-7. The relevant poems by Molza and Porrini are in P. Serassi, ed., *Delle Poesie Volgari e Latine di F. M. Molza*, Bergamo, 1747, I, pp. 135-61, with a mistaken attribution of the Porrini poem to Molza. See Hirst, op. cit., p. 116, n. 116.

20 See Bertrand Jestaz, *Le Palais Farnèse III, 3, L'inventaire du Palais et des Propriétés Farnèse à Rome en 1644*, Ecole Française de Rome, 1994.

21 Nulli, op. cit., pp. 18-19: '... servando lo abito de védua, et in evento che si maritasse, che se piglia la dote sua, et Isabella resti erede universale tanto del Stato di Campagna quanto del Regno at di Apruzio, o non li parta vivente mia mogliere in abito [di vedova] come di sopra de la obedienza sua.'

22 'Sotto nome di spoglie': Benedetto Varchi, *Storia Fiorentina*, Florence, edn. 1838-41, vol. III, p. 329.

23 Ibid.

24 Oliva, op. cit., p. 205.

25 L. Dorez, *La Cour du pape Paul III*, 2 vols., Paris, 1932, II, p. 100: 'Et più scudi ventitre b. settant' otto pagati a Maestro Francesco Gucci, setaiolo, per lo prezzo di uno cortinaggio di taffeta verde che ha fatto per coprire lo ritratto della Signora Giulia Gonzaga. Scudi 23.b.78.'

26 See 'Inventario dei Beni di Fulvio Orsini' published by P. de Nolhac, 'Une galerie de peinture au XVIe siècle. La collection de

Fulvio Orsini', *Gazette des Beaux-Arts*, 1884, pp. 427-36. The painting is listed as no. 16. C. Robertson, 'Osservazioni sul mecenatismo del cardinale Odoardo Farnese', in *I Farnese: Arte e collezionismo. Studi*, Milan, 1995. See also Ramsden, op. cit., p. 136 and n. 6.

27 C. Robertson, *Il Gran Cardinale: Alessandro Farnese, Patron of the Arts*, New Haven and London, 1992.

28 *Der Glanz der Farnese*, exh. cat., Munich, 1995, p. 47.

29 The document is in the Biblioteca Ambrosiana, Milan. Cf. n. 26 above.

30 Hirst, op. cit., p. 114, pl. 149.

31 Hirst, p. 116, and n. 111, citing Dorez, op. cit., I, p. 276. Dorez says that it was 'offered' to the Queen of France in 1541, but there is no reason why the then Queen of France should have been interested in having a portrait of Giulia, even if one had eventually been sent. Equally, Caterina de' Medici, whom we know actually commissioned such a portrait, only became Queen in 1547. Hirst states, 'We know from a remark of Vasari's that after Ippolito's death... the Fondi portrait was given to the French queen as a present.' Vasari never says this, and the misunderstanding presumably stems from Vasari's having mentioned the 'present Queen of France' and an unfinished portrait of her by Sebastiano in the sentence immediately preceding his reference to the Ippolito portrait of Giulia, which he states was 'afterwards sent to King Francis'. This too may be a mistake: the statement does not appear in the 1550 edition of the *Lives*, but only in the 1568 edition, an amendment which must have been based upon Vasari's information from Primaticcio, who would have been aware of a portrait by Sebastiano in the royal collection (Caterina was still alive). The only other possibility is that there was another version of the Fondi portrait sent to Francis I, Henry II's father, in 1541. Francis I was a serious patron and collector, who had been in close touch with Ippolito de' Medici in his lifetime, and 1541 was a year in which the Farnese Pope was making efforts to heal relations with France: his grandson went to the French court with his tutor on 10 August that year, and a present might have been made at the time. This is highly speculative, however, and G. Drei, *I Farnese: Grandezza e Decadenza di una Dinastia Italiana*, Rome, 1954, p. 30, even assumes that the ten-year-old boy was sent as a sort of symbolic hostage to the French king. It is difficult to see why a Farnese pope should ever send the King of France the portrait of a beautiful Gonzaga loved by a Medici whom he himself had evidently disliked, and whose goods he had plundered.

32 'La Regina scrisse già a Fra Bastiano del Piombo che li facesse et mandasse il ritratto di Papa Clemente, et quello della Sra. Julia Gonzaga, quali egli fece con ogni diligensa bellisimi ma il poverino non hebbi tempo di mandarli prima che morisse.' Hirst, op. cit., pp. 115-16.

33 M. Hirst, 'Sebastiano del Piombo's *Pietà* for the Commendador Mayor', *Burlington Magazine*, CXIV (1972), pp. 585ff., pp. 592ff.

34 F. and B. Gasparoni, ed., *Arti e Lettere*, Rome, 1865, ii, Appendix, p. 69.

35 M. Hirst, *Sebastiano del Piombo*, Oxford, 1981, p. 155. It is likely that Sebastiano's usual procedure was first to paint a portrait upon canvas and only subsequently upon slate. As noted above, the original Fondi portrait is more likely to have been painted upon canvas.

36 Père P. Dan, *Le trésor des merveilles de la maison royale de Fontainebleu*, Paris, 1642. Dan also states that the pictures were sent by Clement to King Henry II, which is impossible, since Clement died in 1534 and Henry only became King in 1547. The date of Clement's death also rules out entirely any possibility that it might be the Fondi portrait that is being referred to here, since it was Ippolito's treasured possession, and he did not die until 1535. Hirst interprets this reference in Dan as indicating Sebastiano's portrait of the Pope's niece, i.e. Caterina de' Medici: op. cit., p.119, n. 125.

37 D'Estrechy, *Inventaire des Tableaux du Roy restez au Cabinet des Peintures du château de Fontainebleau*.

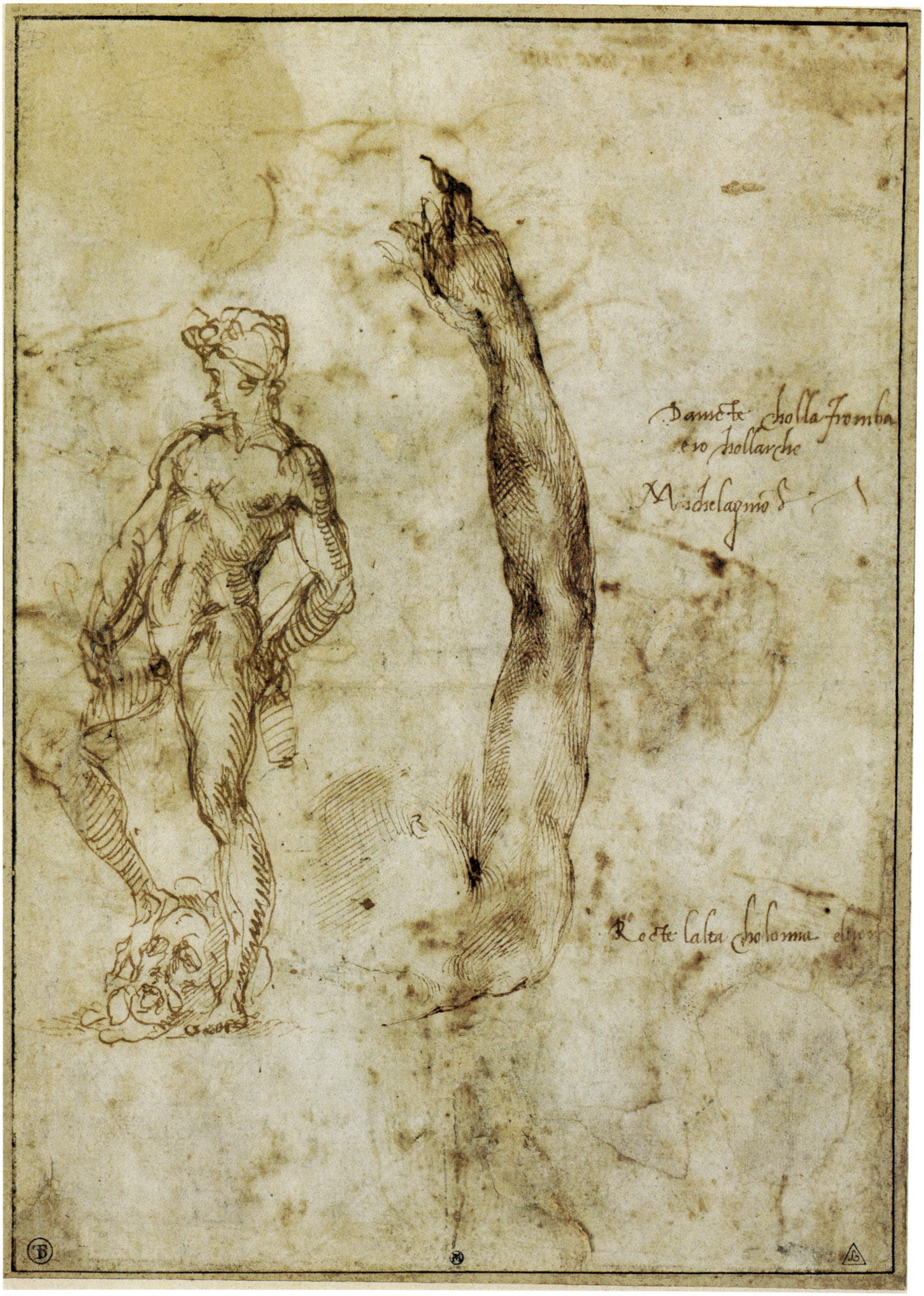
Dauicte cholla fromba
e io chollarche
Michelagnio
Rocte lalta cholonna

Michelangelo Buonarroti

1475-1564

David

1502-3

Bronze
Height: 131.5 cm or 176 cm

The bronze sculptures of David by Donatello and Verrocchio are today among the most familiar images of the Italian Renaissance. Indeed, they are rivalled only by the marble *David* of Michelangelo (Accademia, Florence). There was once, however, another remarkable bronze *David*, directly inspired by the Donatello, and created by none other than 'the divine' Michelangelo. It was so famous in its day that it was celebrated in an address at Michelangelo's funeral, even though it had been created some sixty years before. But it has been missing since the end of the eighteenth century.

In both the first and second editions of his *Vite*, Vasari states that the statue was commissioned for Piero Soderini, *Gonfaloniere* of the Republic of Florence.[1] Although Soderini was much involved in trying to get the sculpture finished, it is evident from a letter which the Florentine ambassadors wrote from France that it was commissioned by the Signoria from Michelangelo as a present for Pierre de Rohan (1451-1513), Sieur de Gié, later Duc de Nemours and Maréchal de France. He was a member of 'Le Conseil Royal', the twelve-member body of advisers closest to the King of France, and his wish to receive a bronze figure of a David is reported in this letter, dated 22 June 1501:

> The Maréchal de Gié indeed seems fond of the city and has vigorously pleaded with us to write to the Signoria that he desires you to cast a bronze figure of a David for him like the one which is in the courtyard of the Signoria and that he will pay you the costs. But let us truly believe that he means what he says and that a present will be given as trust. We see he is fond of the city. We leave this to the Signoria's decision.[2]

Pierre de Rohan's request must have referred to the bronze sculpture of David which Donatello had executed in the 1450s.[3] Pierre de Rohan was the military commander under the French king, Charles VIII, during his invasion of Italy. During the course of the campaign the French had briefly occupied Florence, from 17-28 November 1494, and Charles VIII had taken up residence in the Palazzo Medici.[4] At this time Donatello's *David* stood in the courtyard of the same Palazzo, where De Rohan must have seen it. The ambassadors' letter was written in June 1501, by which time Donatello's work had been transferred to the Palazzo Vecchio, seat of the Signoria (on 29 December 1495).[5] The Signoria took De Rohan's wish very seriously, a fact that can be explained through a closer look at the political situation of Florence at the time and its relationship to France.

In November 1494 Pisa rebelled and asserted its independence from Florence which, for economic and strategic reasons, wished to keep the city under its control. During Charles VIII's campaign in Italy members of his 'Conseil Royal', in

Study for lost bronze *David* (1502-3) and arm of David by Michelangelo Buonarroti (1475-1564), *c.* 1502.
Pen and ink, 26.5 × 18.4 cm.
Musée du Louvre, Paris

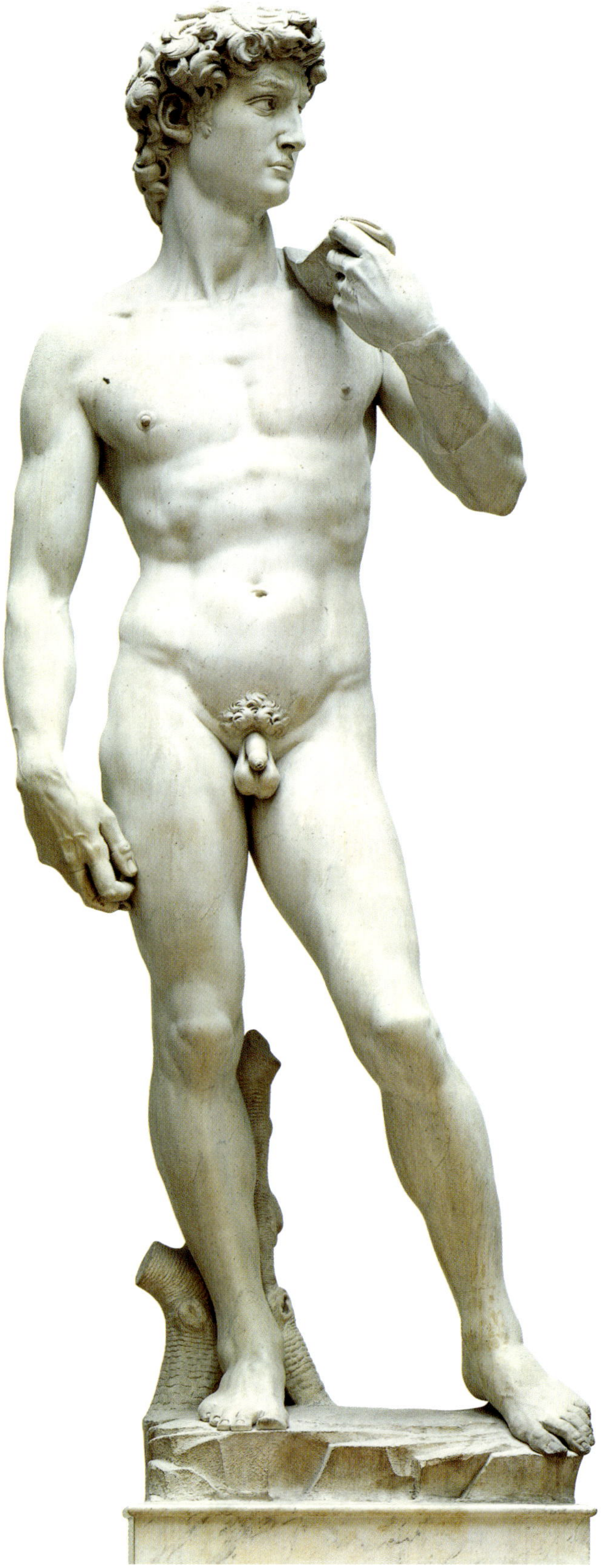

which Pierre de Rohan played a prominent part, discussed the possible return of Pisa to Florence. The King made no decision at the time but Pierre de Rohan had argued in favour of Florence.[6] De Rohan's pro-Florentine stance is explicitly documented in the ambassadors' letter of 1501 and explains why the Signoria felt it wise to oblige him. In fact, in June 1501 the city was being freshly advised by new ambassadors whom it had thought expedient to send to France in the preceding month. The new French King, Louis XII (Charles VIII died in 1498), had become infuriated with the attempts of Florence to form an alliance with Spain in its aim of regaining control of Pisa, and the ambassadors had also taken a *douceur* to the French King of 20,000 *fiorini*.

After more than a year had passed, the Signoria decided to give the commission for the bronze *David* to Michelangelo and thus a contract was drawn up on 12 August 1502. The contract specifies that the subject was to be a *David* and that it was destined for Pierre de Rohan, although no mention is made there of his preferred prototype.[7] The medium was to be bronze and 'two-and-a-quarter bracchi' in height, i.e. around 131.5 cm, not quite life-size ('alti bracchiis duobus et uno quarto alterius bracchi in circha, bronzi').

It was stipulated that Michelangelo had six months to execute his work but he did not complete the commission within the time, not least because, immediately after the contract for the bronze *David* was signed, Michelangelo contracted with the Opera del Duomo, on 16 August, to create his huge marble *David* which was later to be erected in front of the Signoria. He began work on the marble *David* on 13 September and it was almost finished ('quasi finita') on 25 January 1504. He thus worked on the bronze and the marble over the same period of time. According to a document of 31 December 1502 the artist had by then received the greater part of his remuneration for the bronze statue, while another payment reported in a document dated 10 October 1503 indicates that the work had been cast. Nevertheless, it evidently remained rough, and not 'finished', meaning that the surface working had not yet been carried out, as a letter from Soderini of 30 June 1508 makes clear ('resta rozzo': 'it is still rough').[8]

Pierre de Rohan's fortunes changed in early 1504 when he fell out of favour with Louis XII's wife, Anne de Bretagne, was accused of embezzlement and banished from Court.[9] With De Rohan gone, Florence now found itself needing a new contact at the French court. To this end the Signoria, through their ambassador Francesco Pandolfini, decided to approach Louis XII's new finance minister, Florimond Robertet.[10] Robertet was aware of the Republic's predicament. He was also passionately interested in the arts, and it seemed that he could be turned into someone who was favourably inclined towards Florentine interests. Above all, he was one of Louis XII's closest advisers. A letter written by Pandolfini from Genoa on 28 April 1507 confirms Robertet's favourable inclination towards a solution of the continuing problem of Pisa.[11] In a document of 22 August 1508, Soderini confirms that the *David* was to be finished and sent to Robertet.[12] Robertet was too cautious to reveal in advance exactly what he would do in exchange for Florence, but by June 1509 the Republic had finally been able to regain Pisa. Robertet had played a key part and had received the *David* early in that year. The statue had left Livorno for France by 26 December 1508, having been finished ('rinettata') by Benedetto da Rovezzano, because Michelangelo had gone to Rome.[13]

A clue to the missing sculpture's appearance can be gleaned from Ascanio Condivi's book *Vita di Michelangelo Buonarroti*, first published in 1553. It was written

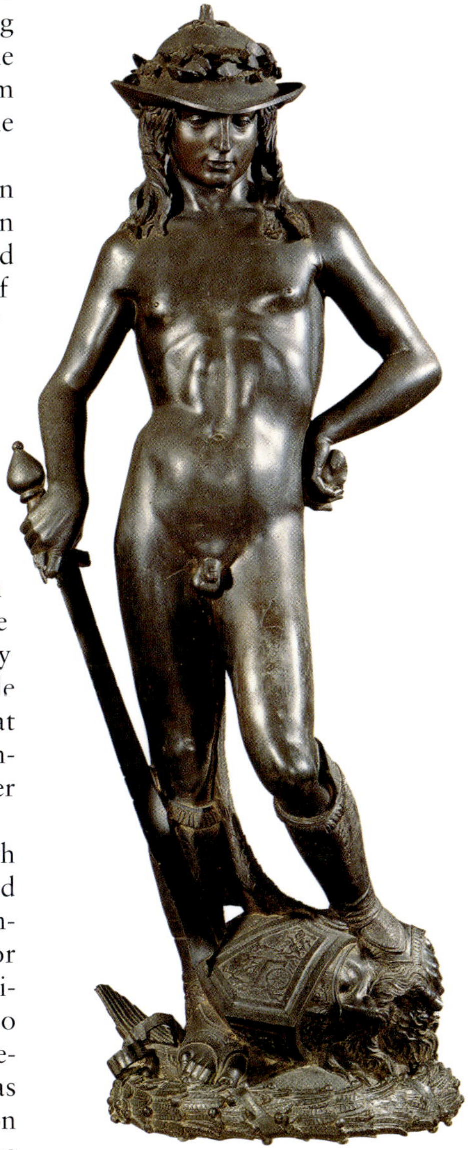

David by Donatello (*c.* 1386-1466), 1430s-'50s.
Bronze, ht. 158.2 cm.
Museo Nazionale del Bargello, Florence

David by Michelangelo 1502-4.
Marble, ht. 409 cm.
Accademia, Florence

directly under Michelangelo's influence and so, although Condivi never saw the bronze itself, his description can be presumed to be accurate. He reported that the sculpture represented David standing over Goliath, which in subject conforms with the Donatello, where the head of Goliath is under David's left foot (in the Verrocchio, in contrast, the head is merely between the feet):

> ... doppo il Gigante [i.e. the marble *David*] ricercato da Piero Soderini suo grande amico gittò di bronzo una statua grande al naturale, che fu mandato in Francia, e similmente un David con Golia sotto. Quel che si vede nel mezzo della corte del palazzo de' Signori è di mano di Donatello uomo in tal arte eccellente molto di Michelagnolo lodato.[14] ('... after the Giant, having been sought out by his great friend Piero Soderini, he cast in bronze a statue, life size, that was sent to France, and which was likewise a David [but with] Goliath beneath. The one which can be seen in the middle of the courtyard of the Palazzo della Signoria is from the hand of Donatello a man excellent in that art and much praised by Michelangelo.')

The description is confirmed in the eulogy delivered at Michelangelo's funeral by the humanist Benedetto Varchi (1503-65), where he refers to the sculpture:

> Un Davitte, il quale ha Golia sotto i piedi, nontanto a imitazioni, quanto a concorrenza di quello, che era nel cortile del Palagio de Signori di mano di Donatello, molto ammirato e commendato da lui.[15] ('A David, who has Goliath beneath his feet, not so much in imitation of as in conformity with that which was in the courtyard of the Palazzo of the Signoria by the hand of Donatello, much admired and commended by him [Michelangelo].')

Varchi, equally, can never have seen Michelangelo's sculpture, and he evidently drew upon Condivi's biography, but there is every reason to suppose that he was perfectly well informed about these details.

An autograph drawing by Michelangelo at the Louvre has long since been identified as a study for the bronze *David*.[16] Several extant statuettes have also been proposed as related to Michelangelo's bronze figure, for example, a bronze statuette in the Louvre; a wax figure in the Victoria & Albert Museum; and a copy of a modello in the Casa Buonarroti. None, however, of these statuettes is definitely by Michelangelo, whereas the drawing in the Louvre is inscribed and signed by his own hand:

> Davicte cholla fromba
> e io chollarco
> Michelagniolo.

This has been translated as:

> David with his sling
> and I with my bow
> Michelangelo.[17]

The drawing indeed shows Goliath very much beneath the feet (or, to be precise, one foot) of the David. Although it is the right foot rather than the left as in the Donatello, careful examination suggests that Michelangelo's first lines otherwise followed the Donatello closely. For example, the right arm was originally more in the position of that in the Donatello, with the upper arm subsumed within the profile of the upper body and the lower arm protruding beyond it. The left arm also was originally higher up and against the hip, more like that in the Donatello, while the right hand, again like that in the Donatello, holds a sword the outlines of which can just be made out. The extraordinarily large eye-sockets of the Goliath

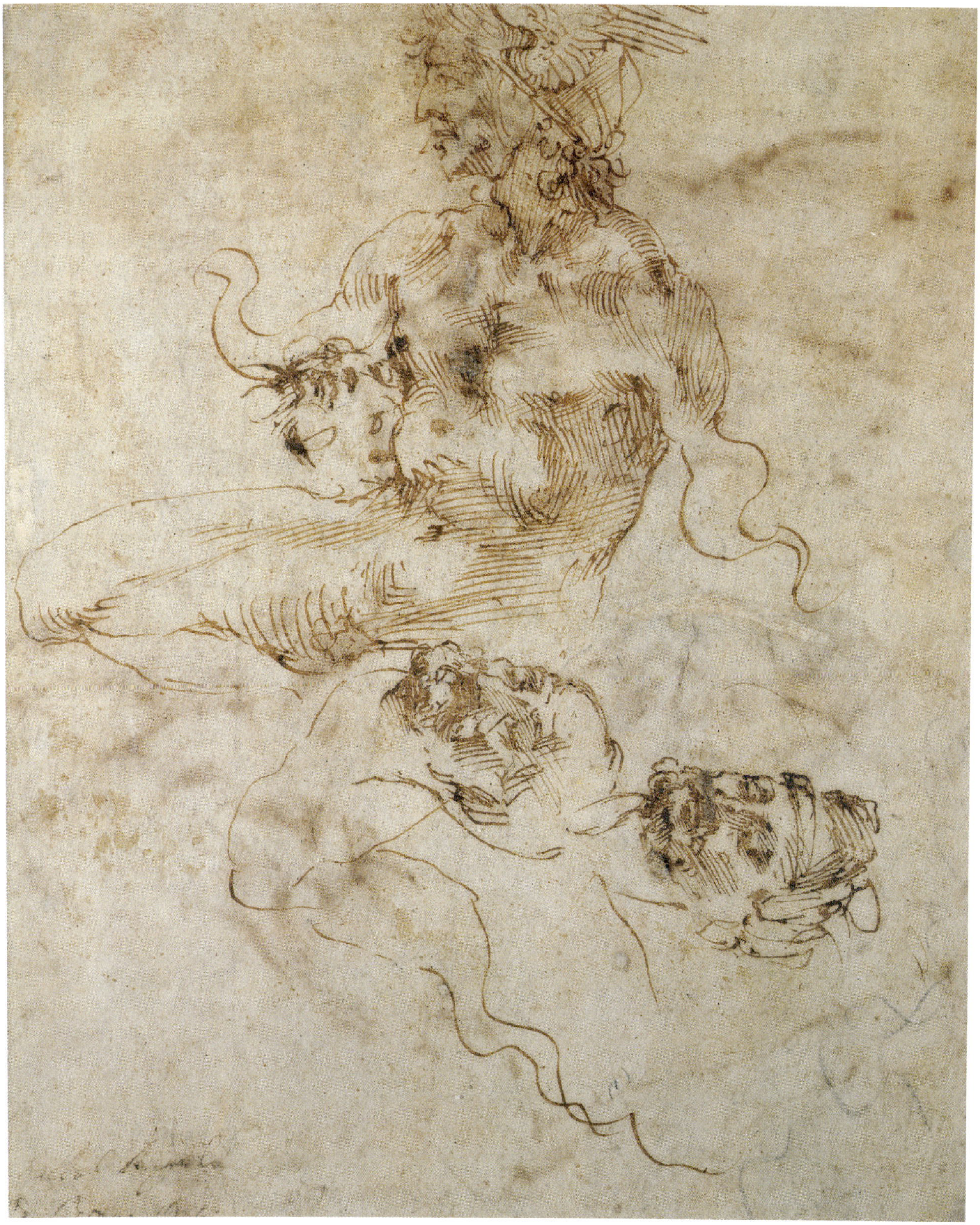

Study of a triton and three heads by Michelangelo.
Pen and ink, 24.4. × 19.4 cm.
Ashmolean Museum, Oxford

head also seem to reflect this feature of Donatello's sculpture, the study of which by Michelangelo can perhaps be identified again in similar heads in another drawing of this period (*Triton and three heads*, Ashmolean Museum, Oxford).

Another visual clue about the appearance of the missing sculpture is to be found in a stucco relief by Rosso Fiorentino of a *Young Warrior* in the Galerie François Ier at Fontainebleau. The direction of the head in the stucco follows that of the Louvre drawing, and the left hand also conforms with that drawing. The bronze *David*, at the time that Rosso was working in France, was not far from Fontainebleau, where Rosso probably saw it. It has reasonably been observed that the only difference between the pose of the Fontainebleau stucco and the drawing – and hence, by inference, the missing sculpture – is the right foot which, in the Rosso stucco , is no longer raised over a head of Goliath, and rests on the ground.[18]

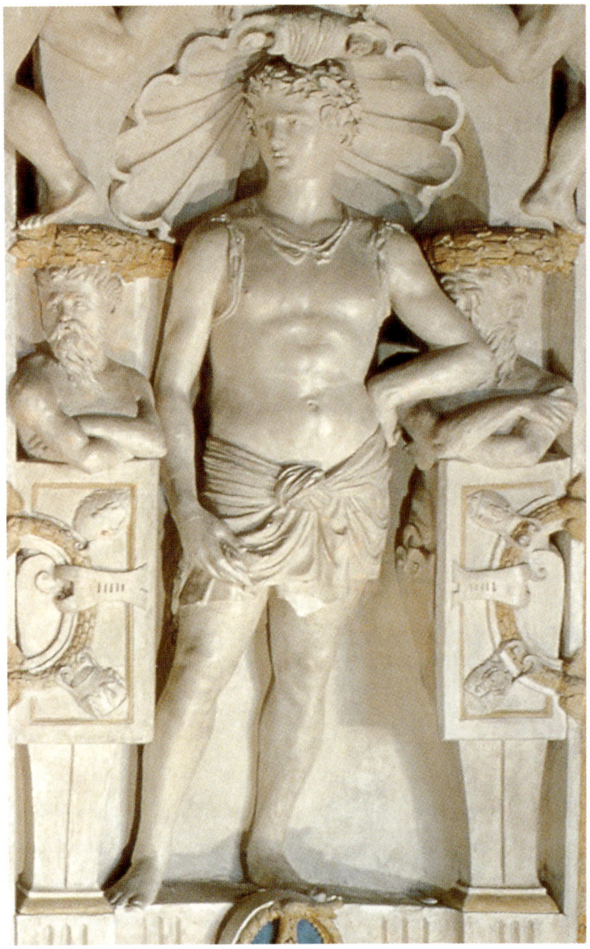

Young warrior.
Stucco relief by Rosso Fiorentino (1494-1540) in the palace of Fontainebleau

When the sculpture arrived in France at the beginning of 1509 it was placed in Robertet's palace in Blois, the Hôtel d'Alluye in rue Saint Honoré, because the construction of his château at Bury, where the sculpture is later documented, was not begun before 1511-14. It was then installed at Bury, and appears in two engravings of Bury in Jacques Androuet Du Cerceau's famous book *Les plus*

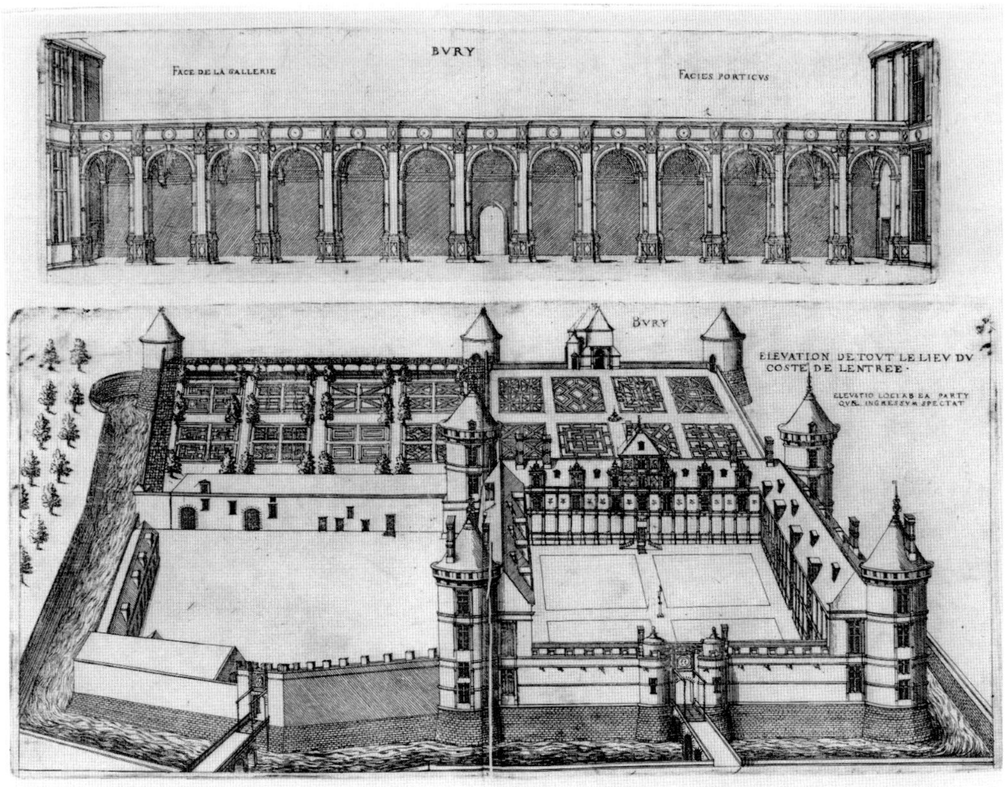

Château de Bury from the entrance side. Engraving by Jacques Androuet Du Cerceau (*c.* 1515-*c.* 1590) from *Les plus excellents bastiments de France*, 1576-9

excellents bastiments de France (1576-9, vol. II, ff. 124, 125). Du Cerceau does not describe the objects at Bury but Michelangelo's sculpture is visible in the middle of the courtyard, standing on a column. Although the representation is too small for its detailed appearance to be apparent, it does seem to conform in its profile with the Louvre drawing, with one leg bent at the knee, especially in Du Cerceau's elevation as seen from the entrance side. Michelangelo's masterpiece was the first thing that the visitor saw when entering the château across the drawbridge. It was framed by the gateway, and seen in profile directly in front of the doorway of the main house, which was on the far side of the courtyard.

The sculpture is then mentioned in a description of Bury in Jodocus Sincerus' *Itinerarium Galliae* first published in 1616 and again, for example, in 1627:

> ... a citadel... , magnificent and large. In the columned area is placed an image of King David in bronze valued at a high price: which is said to have been taken to that place from Rome almost a century ago.[19]

In fact, shortly after Florimond Robertet's death in 1527, the sculpture had already been recorded at Bury, in an inventory of 4 August 1532, compiled by his widow, which lists the 'David' as:

> Finalement et trionphamment nostre beau grand David, qui est au milieu de ce chasteau.[20] ('Lastly, and triumphantly, our beautiful large David, which is in the middle of this château.')

The original of this inventory is not known but it was published as a transcription by Henri Chesneau in his biography of Charles, Marquis de Rostaing, in 1650.

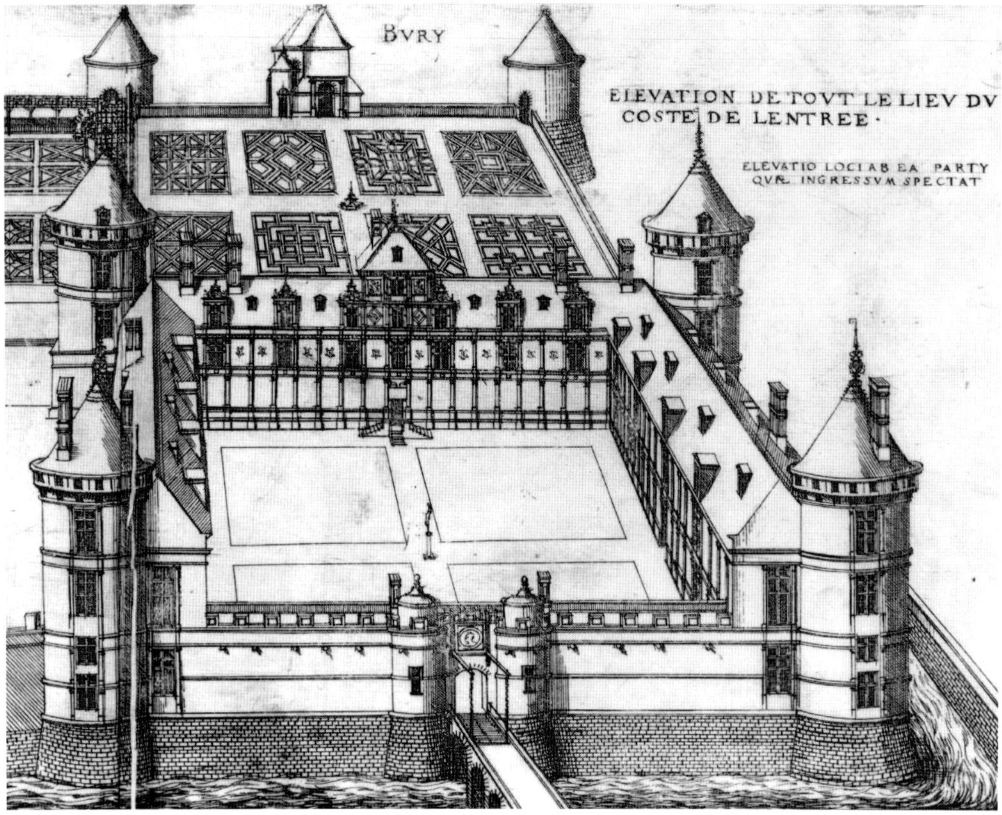

Detail of *Château de Bury from the entrance side* showing Michelangelo's bronze *David*

The rest of the book is so embellished as to have raised doubts about its authenticity,[21] but there is every possibility that Chesneau based his book on inventories that have since vanished, and indeed Chesneau was actually employed by the Marquis de Rostaing.[22] The account is also significant in that it wistfully reports that the sculpture had been removed from Bury:

> Autrefois dans cet endroict mesme
> il y avait un beau David,
> mait tout-a-coup l'on le ravit
> a cause de son prix exstresme
> et emporta-t-on ce grand Roy
> dans le chasteau de Villeroy
> oú l'on en fait un si grand comptre
> que chaque sculpteur va disant
> qu'il vaut sa grosseur d'or pesant
> tant il est d'une heureuse fonte.[23]

The reason was that the Neufville de Villeroy, who had acquired Bury from the descendants of Florimond de Robertet, took the sculpture to their Château de Villeroy, near Mennecy. There are some indications as to when it might have happened. For example, when the Italian collector and connoisseur Cassiano dal Pozzo visited the château of Villeroy in 1625 he makes no mention of having seen a sculpture by Michelangelo, and so it cannot have arrived there by that date. In 1633, however, the Villeroy family sold Bury to Charles, Marquis de Rostaing – but evidently without the Michelangelo bronze, the removal of which Chesneau laments.[24] Later accounts of Villeroy confirm that the *David* was to be seen there and no longer at Bury. Antoine Nicholas Dezallier d'Argenville published a guide book in 1755 which includes a description of the terrace of Villeroy:

La troisième terrasse est au dessus du Château & du parterre. Une belle allée vous conduit à une demi-lune, où est elevée une colonne antique, de marbre blanc veiné, dont les volutes du chapiteau sont formées par quatres cornes de belier. (Il y a aussi quatre mascarons au lieu de roses) Cette colonne porte une figure de bronze d'un homme tenant un ceste.[25] ('[The third terrace is above the Château and the parterre. A beautiful 'allée' leads you to a half-moon, where there is erected an antique column, of white veined marble, the volutes of the capital of which are formed of four rams' horns. (There are also four mascarons in place of roses [both terms referring to decorative architectural features].) This column bears a bronze figure of a man holding a sling.')

The French word 'ceste' meant a leather strap or belt, and so presumably indicates a sling in this case,[26] if Dezallier d'Argenville is indeed referring to Michelangelo's *David*. Furthermore, this record of its appearance accords with what can be made out in Du Cerceau's views of the courtyard at Bury, where the sculpture originally stood: it is clearly set upon a column, the capital of which, under magnification, has protuberances that might even be meant for rams' horns. It was apparently upon a column, with the Florentine *stemma* upon its base, when first taken to Robertet's house in Blois in 1508/9.[27]

It is remarkable, of course, that no reference is made to Michelangelo, but evidently by the eighteenth century the connection between the sculpture and its creator had been lost. This might also be the reason why the French collector, writer and connoisseur Pierre-Jean Mariette (1694-1774) reported that Michelangelo's famous bronze sculpture of David was no longer to be found in France.[28]

The last of the Villeroy family, Gabriel-Louis François de Neufville-Villeroy (born 1731), Comte de Sault, later Marquis and finally Duc de Villeroy, was guillotined on 28 April 1794 at the height of the Terror of the French Revolution. Before his death an inventory was drawn up on 12 October 1793 ('21st of the first month of year II of the French Republic') by 'Sergent, député a la Convention Nationale, Lemonnier, Moreau, Gueron, maire [i.e. the mayor mentioned in the document below], Pater et Bellanger':

On this day… we, the members of the Monuments Committee appointed by law, went to the house of Citizen Villeroy in the local authority of Mennecy in the company of the Citizen Mayor and two of his municipal officials. We visited all the premises of this house, guided by the porters and caretakers since Citizen Villeroy was not present. In an outbuilding ['une remise'], we found the following items:

1) a figure in bronze of David having just slain Goliath…

[here follow another 9 items and items in the main hall of the château]

… All these objects mentioned belonged to the said Citizen Neufville Villeroy, but after his death they should belong to the Republic in view of the fact that his natural heirs are assumed to have left the country. We have taken them under the protection of the Nation to prevent their suffering any attack or damage while they are [still] enjoyed in usufruct by the said Citizen Villeroy, wherefore we require the municipality of Mennecy to watch their conservation carefully and to see to it that they are not destroyed, or conceivably sold by Citizen Neufville, without their having warned us, the Monuments Committee, since we have identified the said works as of value to the Republic.[29]

The National Archives in France contain another document, of 25 November 1794 ('25 *brumaire* of the year III of the Revolution'), signed by two functionaries,

Dardel and Jolain, which lists a number of bronze sculptures at Villeroy, and describes a figure of David as:

> ... une figure répresentant un David qui foule aux pieds la tête de Goliath d'environ 5 pieds et demi, de proportion assez belle [qui] parait être de Jean Boulogne ou de son école.[30] ('A figure representing a David who crushes the head of Goliath under his feet, of about five 'pieds' and a half, of rather fine proportions, appearing to be by Giambologna or his school.')

The description is significant in revealing that the head of Goliath was being 'crushed' beneath the feet of the David, because that is the implication of the Louvre drawing, where the right foot of the David is shown on top of the head of Goliath, actually pressing on his right eye, and almost clawing at it, a touch of brutal realism that suggests Michelangelo's originality in his reponse to a given model.

The size of the sculpture ('d'environ 5 pieds et demi') would amount to approximately 1.76m. It does not appear to correspond to Michelangelo's contract of 1502, which stipulates a height of 1.3m. The difference could readily be explained by a simple mistake or the inclusion in the measurements of the base (i.e. the capital of the column) of the statue, but it should be recalled that Condivi described the statue as 'life size' ('grande al naturale'), and it has been suggested that Michelangelo made it larger than the contract stipulated.[31] The Revolutionary officials add an interesting comment to the effect that all the statues they list are in good condition and would serve equally for the decoration of 'the Museum' or the 'National Garden' ('Toutes ses statues sont en bon état et peuvent servir soit à décorer le Museum soit à embellir le Jardin National').[32]

We know from the October 1793 document quoted above that the destruction of works of art at Villeroy was confined to the burning on 13 October 1793, together with a certain amount of singing and dancing, of paintings of the former kings of France and of the Bourbon family ('these pictures will be burned on this day after vespers'); to the destruction of an equestrian statue of Louis XIV ('which will be smashed up this day before the local inhabitants') and of a plaster bust of Louis XVI ('which will also be smashed'); while all traces of the fleurs-de lys, 'a feature of this *commune*', were to be erased.[33] The 1794 record reveals that Michelangelo's *David* had not been destroyed during the preceding period and, on the contrary, that the officials had a better use for it in mind. By this latter date the Terror had passed its height, with the execution of its chief architect, Robespierre, on 28 July 1794.

Since, unlike its last known owner, Michelangelo's bronze had survived until this date, its chances of now remaining intact would, if anything, have been enhanced. Villeroy itself swiftly reverted to the legal heirs (unlike the rest of the property of the late Gabriel-Louis-François de Neufville-Villeroy); but it seems possible that the statue had left the estate by this date, together with the other works that had been identified as being of special interest to the Republic. If it had not, it is unlikely to have remained there for much longer, because the estate changed hands, and was subsequently broken up.

The sequestration of the estate of Villeroy was lifted at the petition of Marie-Anne-Thérèse-Philippine de Montmorency, widow of Charles-Joseph de Boufflers, on behalf of herself and the two other heirs, as soon as October 1795.[34] On 16 October 1796, however, Villeroy was sold to Antoine-François-Pierre la

Fontaine-Grandcourt for Ffr1.03m, whose activities, and those of the next owner, can only now be described as 'asset-stripping'. Grandcourt intended to have the contents of the estate sold from 4 December 1796 onwards at public auction, although the auction was postponed. The property was then bought by a certain Pierre Boignes (or Boynes) on 4 August 1804. In 1811 Boignes demolished the château and most of its outbuildings, selling the materials for more than he had paid for the entire estate.[35]

In recent times, the Mayor of Mennecy and the local authority celebrated the gift to them by the Levitt-France company of the sad remains of this once splendid château. Ultimately, the loss of this great 'stately home' was the result of Gabriel Neufville-Villeroy's denunciation to Fouquier-Tinville by the citizens of Mennecy ('dénonciation des citoyens menneçois') on 19 April 1794.[36] On 21 July 1972, when their descendants, the present-day citizens of Mennecy, celebrated the creation of a modern 'culture park' on the devasted estate of Villeroy, only a few outbuildings of the historic château remained. There is no way of knowing whether it was one of these ('une remise') that once sheltered Mennecy's greatest 'cultural asset', Michelangelo's fabled *David*, before its discovery by the Monuments Committee of the Revolution in October 1793. What is certain is that the sculpture has not been seen since it was recorded in those chillingly matter-of-fact documents drawn up at the height of the revolutionary period.

NOTES

1 For an English translation (1568 edition) see G. Vasari, *Lives of the Painters, Sculptors and Architects*, 2 vols. (Everyman Library), London, 1996, II, p. 655. The 1550 and 1568 editions of *Le Vite...* are printed together in R. Bettarini and P. Barocchi, ed., 6 vols., Florence, 1966–, see vol. VI, p. 21.

2 '[...] El Maricial de Gié in verità mostra essere afezionato alla città et chon ghrande istanzia ci a preghato che noi schrivamo alle Signorie vostre che 'llui desiderebbe che se gli faciessi gittare una fighura di bronzo d'uno Davitte chome quello ch'è nella chorte delle Signorie Vostre et che lui pagherà la spesa. Ma chrediamo bene che 'llo dicha chon animo gne ne sia fatto uno presente chome fiducie. Noi lo vegiamo afezionato alla citta. Rimettiamociene alla diliberazione che ne faranno le Signorie Vostre.' See L. Gatti, '"Delle cose de' pictori et Sculptori si può mal promettere cosa certa"; la diplomazia Fiorentina presso la corte del Re di Francia e il David bronzeo di Michelangelo Buonarroti' in *Mélanges de l'école Française de Rome: Italie et Mediterranée*, vol. 106, 2, 1994, pp. 433-72, p. 440, and *passim* for information on the historical background and the relevant documents for this commission.

3 See, for example, A. Parronchi, *Opere giovanili di Michelangelo*, Florence, 1968, vol. I, p. 153; Charles de Tolnay, *The youth of Michelangelo*, Princeton, 1943, p. 205; and M. Hirst in *L'officina della maniera: varietà e fierezza nell'arte fiorentina del Cinquecento fra le due repubbliche (1494-1530)*, exh. cat., Florence (Uffizi), 1994, cat. 23, p. 118.

4 See [L. Landucci], J. del Badia, ed., *Diario Fiorentino dal 1450 al 1516, di L. Landucci continuato da un anonimo fino al 1542... con annotazioni da Iodoco del Badia*, Florence, 1883, p. 80.

5 The other bronze sculpture of a David, by Verrocchio, had been in the Palazzo Vecchio since 1476, and De Rohan probably also knew it as well, but the statue in the courtyard, to which the ambassadors refer, may be assumed to have been that by Donatello. It has been asserted that at some point the Verrocchio took its place for a period of time (F. Caglioti, 'Il *David* bronzeo di Michelangelo (e Benedetto da Rovezzano): il problema dei pagamenti',

in F. Caglioti *et al.*, *Ad Alessandro Conti (1946-1994)*, Pisa, 1996, pp. 94-5, although there appear subsequently to have been difficulties in substantiating this argument. The visual evidence, especially the Louvre drawing discussed here (see below), points towards the Donatello as Michelangelo's model and not the Verrocchio. The two sculptures are quite different in appearance: Donatello's is nude, Verrocchio's clothed (they are also of different heights, with Donatello's standing at 158 cm, Verrocchio's at 122 cm), and Michelangelo's bronze *David* was nude, like Donatello's. For the date of the transferral of the Donatello to the Palazzo della Signoria see F. Caglioti, 'Donatello, i Medici e Gentile de' Becchi: un po' d'ordine intorno alla Giuditta (e al 'David') in Via Larga – III', *Prospettiva*, 80 (October 1995), pp. 15-58, p. 19, where a document quoted on p. 22 suggests that it was still there on 22 May 1498 (see also pp. 26-7).

6 Yvonne Labande-Mailfert, *Charles VIII et son milieu (1470-1498)*, Paris, 1975, p. 385. In 1499 he had already received from the Signoria seven Roman heads and two bronze busts that had belonged (perhaps significantly) to Lorenzo de' Medici: J. Cox-Rearick, *The Collection of Francis I*, New York, 1996, p. 76.

7 The contract is reprinted in Caglioti, op. cit., 1996, doc. 2; Gatti, op. cit., pp. 457-8.

8 For these details see respectively Gatti, op. cit., p. 442; Caglioti, op. cit., 1996, p. 113; Gatti, op. cit., pp. 444, 448.

9 See Labande-Mailfert, op. cit., p. 514.

10 See C.-A. Mayer and D. Bentley-Cranch, *Florimond Robertet (?-1527): Homme d'Etat français*, Paris, 1994.

11 See A. Desjardons, *Ambassade diplomatique de la France avec la Toscane*, 6 vols., Paris, 1869-86, II (1861), p. 243: 'Robertet ha un animo pronto verso le Signorie Vostre'. Robertet's support of the Florentine position was not unconditional.

12 Gatti, op. cit., pp. 449-50 and n. 74.

13 [G. Gaye], J. W. Gaye, ed., *Carteggio inedito d'artisti dei secoli XIV, XV, XVI pubblicato ed illustrato con documenti pure inediti dal dott. G. Gaye*, 3 vols., Florence, 1839-40, II, p. 106. Gatti, op. cit., pp. 450-1 ff.

14 Ascanio Condivi, *Vita di Michelangelo Buonarroti*, ed. G. Nencioni, with contributions by M. Hirst and C. Elam, Florence, 1998, p. 22.

15 Benedetto Varchi, *Orazione Funerale di M. Benedetto Varchi. Fatta, e recitata da Lui pubblicamente nell'essequie di Michelangelo Buonarroti in Firenze, nella chiese di San Lorenzo*, Florence, 1564, p. 29, cf. Caglioti, op. cit., 1996, p. 97; Gatti, op. cit., p. 456.

16 Musée du Louvre, Cabinet des Dessins, no. 714 recto. The relationship between the drawing and the bronze sculpture was first proposed by M. Reiset, 'Un bronze de Michel-Ange', in *Athenaeum française*, 1853, cf. Gatti op. cit., pp. 433, 469. See also, for example, S. Levine, 'Michelangelo's marble David and the lost bronze David: the drawings', *Artibus et Historiae*, 9, 1984, pp. 91-120; L. Dussler, *Die Zeichnungen des Michelangelo: kritischer Katalog*, 2 vols., Berlin, 1959, I, p. 134, no. 213.

17 C. Seymour, *Michelangelo's David: A Search for Identity*, Pittsburgh, 1967, p. 7, who points out that the 'bow' is a play upon the sculptor's use of a bow-drill.

18 For the above observations on the relationship between the bronze *David* and the stucco, see G. Répaci-Courtois, 'A propos du David en bronze de Michel-Ange', *La Revue du Louvre et des Musées*, 1976, pp. 250-54, figs. 225-30. For the dating of the stucco see S. Pressouyre, 'Les Stucs', in *La Galerie François Ier à Fontainebleau, Revue de l'Art*, 16-17, 1972, p. 27. Répaci-Courtois also observes that the right arm fully worked up on the same sheet as the drawing for the bronze *David* may be seen as a finished version of the right arm of the bronze rather than, as is so often assumed, the marble. Since, in the design of the whole group, this arm is a pentimento, and is then separately worked up, it is likely to represent the final shape of this feature on Michelangelo's lost sculpture.

19 '... arcem 3 leucis distantem. magnificam & amplam. In medio areae columnae imposita est imago Regis Davidis aereae, magni pretij aestimata: quae Româ iam ferè ante seculum eò translato traditur.' And see Gatti, op. cit., p. 465.

20 F. Grésy, 'Inventaire des objets d'art composant la succession de Florimond Robertet', in *Mémoires de la Société Imperiale des Antiquaires de France*, ser. 3, X, 1868, p. 58.

21 Mayer and Bentley-Cranch, op. cit., p. 114; but see Clifford M. Brown, '"Une nostre-Dame de pitié... de la main du grand Miquel-Ange"; A lost painting attributed to Michelangelo in the 1532 inventory of the Château de Bury', in *Bibliothèque d'Humanisme et Renaissance*, 53 (1981), pp. 159-63, p. 161.

22 Gatti, op. cit., p. 466.

23 Quoted by Grésy, op. cit., p. 64. Chesneau's book seems to exist only in one elusive

copy: ibid., p. 2. The lines might be translated (allowing for a slight obscurity towards the end):
'Formerly, even in this very place
There was a beautiful David
But all at once he was taken away
Because of his great value
And this great King was brought
To the château of Villeroy
Where he is held in such high esteem
That every sculptor is forced to say
That he is as much worth his weight in gold
As he is happy in the casting.'

24 These points are made by Gatti, op. cit., p. 466, who observes that it can be assumed that the sculpture had been removed by this date, even if later editions of guide books, presumably repeating unchecked information, report the figure as still being at Bury in 1649 and 1699. See also J. Nouaillac, *Villeroy, Secrétaire d'Etat et Ministre*, Paris, 1909, p. 285.

25 A.N. Dezallier d'Argenville, *Voyage Pittoresque des Environs de Paris ou Description des Maisons Royales, Châteaux et autres Lieux de Plaisance, situés a quinze lieues aux environs de cette ville*, Paris, 1755, p. 251.

26 Gatti, op. cit., p. 468.

27 Cox-Rearick, op. cit., p. 76; Gatti, op. cit., pp. 462-3.

28 P. J. Mariette, *Abecedario*, ed. P. de Chennevières and A. de Montaiglon, 6 vols., Paris, 1851-60, I, p. 217.

29 Translated from J. Judith, *Mennecy, son Histoire, sa Vie*, 1973, p. 93. Villeroy was in hiding part of this time, or vainly protesting his republican sympathies. He was finally sentenced to death by the notorious Fouquier-Tinville on 27 April 1794 and guillotined the following day.

30 Archives Nationales, Paris, sometimes incorrectly cited in the literature. The correct reference is to F/17/1197 (dossier 2, sous-dossier 14). Our thanks are due to Florence Charvaud of the Centre d'accueil et de recherche des Archives nationales.

31 Condivi, op. cit., p. 22. See Hirst, op. cit., p. 118; Gatti, op. cit., p. 463; Cox-Rearick, op. cit., p. 463, n. 192.

32 See Répaci-Courtois, op. cit., p. 254, n. 11.

33 Judith, op. cit., pp. 94-5.

34 Ibid., pp. 152-3.

35 Ibid., pp. 16, 19 (Boignes did not live at the château, but at 9 rue Neuve-Saint-Gilles, Paris). See also P. Blanchot *et al.*, *Mennecy sous la Révolution ou la Révolution de Jean Michel*, Le Mée-sur-Seine, 1989, p. 257.

36 Ibid., pp. 217ff.

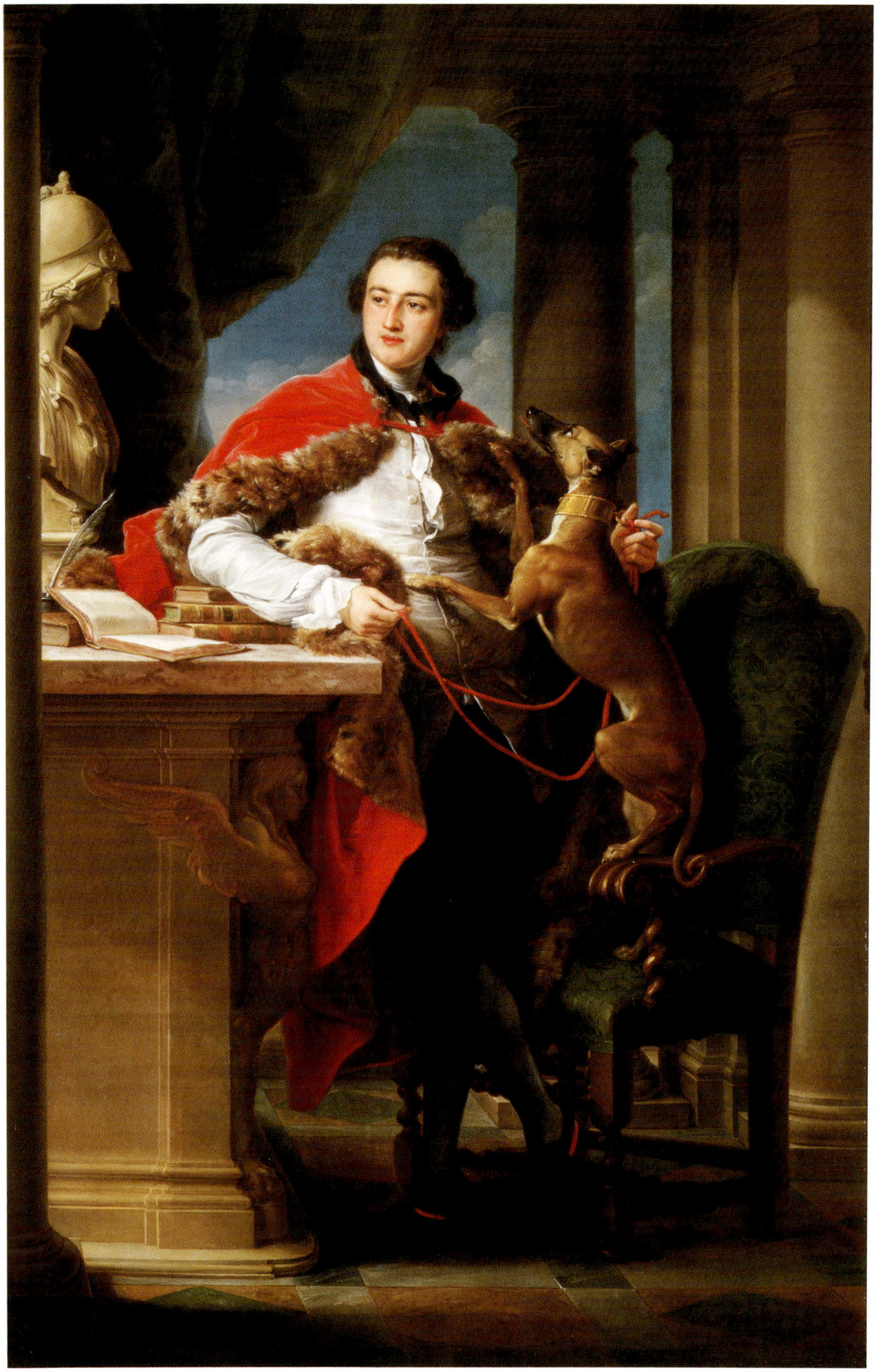

Pompeo Batoni

1708-87

Hector's farewell to Andromache

1758-60

Oil on canvas
c. 274 × 396 cm

Gavin Hamilton

1723-98

Andromache bewailing the death of Hector

1758

Oil on canvas
c. 274 × 396 cm

Hector's farewell to Andromache by Pompeo Batoni and *Andromache bewailing the death of Hector* by Gavin Hamilton formed a remarkable double commission by the young Charles Compton, 7th Earl of Northampton (1737-63), while he was in Rome on the Grand Tour, but both pictures have been missing since the last quarter of the eighteenth century. On 5 April 1758 'Mr Compton' (he succeeded his uncle to the title later that year) was reported by the artist John Parker as having commissioned from Gavin Hamilton a very large history picture.[1] This was *Andromache bewailing the death of Hector*, the subject of which was taken from the *Iliad*. The picture, which was exhibited at the Society of Artists in 1762, was completed by the summer of 1760,[2] as emerges in a letter of the Abbé Grant to Sir James Grant of Grant, Rome, of 31 May 1760. In the same correspondence, 22 October 1760, the Abbé refers to it as 'the best piece of modern painting I have ever seen'.[3] It is also mentioned favourably by Winckelmann in a letter to Wilhelm Musel-Stosch of 3 January 1761, and he goes on to describe the Batoni, although in rather less favourable terms:

> The latest in the arts concerns two paintings for Lord Compton. One is by an English painter, Hamilton, and depicts the body of Hector lying stretched out on a bed with his mother, Andromache, and other ladies of the Trojan royal house weeping over him. The composition is good and the figures are drawn with some expertise and taste. The heads are almost Grecian in their conception and their attitudes show the calm that the ancients sought, but the colours are hard, unattractive, coarse and somehow lacking in power; this will deter those who cannot look beyond the colouring from searching for and finding the good points. The other is by Pompeo Battoni and shows Hector leaving Troy for the last time, bidding farewell to Andromache, who is trying to hold him back, asking him not to risk his life for the sake of their married love and the love of their only son, who is being held by his nurse; the child is afraid of the plumes on Hector's helmet and is cowering back in the nurse's arms. This painting is only good in its colours, which have the gay and reflective quality of Rubens' school, but it does not have the masculine tone of Raphael,

Charles Compton, 7th Earl of Northampton by Pompeo Batoni (1708-87), 1758.
Oil on canvas, 235.3 × 149.3 cm.
Fitzwilliam Museum, Cambridge

Titian and their schools. Nevertheless, the picture will be successful for those who do not know much about painting. The drawing is faultless, but the figures lack above all the Homeric spirit which they incorporate. It further seems that the painter had help in his original design from a young Frenchman from the Academy, who has helped him out of his biggest problems, and that he has continued in this manner to complete the work. The action of the figures is exaggerated. Andromache is overjoyed like a Fury, and Hector makes a movement like a pupil of Marcel, the instructor at the *Mode-Gratie,* and the ideas for the heads are not very noble. Andromache resembles a hundred plain faces which can be seen not only in Rome and Florence but anywhere south of the Alps. Hector, who was a young prince, is depicted as a soldier from the Thirty Years War, haggard and thin. The architecture does not correspond to the time, and the whole matter is not understood by the painter. If you want to repeat this criticism, I ask you not to use my name, because Batoni wants to be my friend, and he is an honest man.[4]

Both pictures were recorded in an inventory of Lord Northampton's house in Grosvenor Square, two months after his death of tuberculosis at Lyons on 18 October 1763, together with the (surviving) full-length portrait of the Earl by Batoni. Listed as hanging in the Dining Room are 'The Earl of Northampton whole length by Pompeo Battoni, a large Historical Picture of Hector taking leave of Andromacha [*sic*] in a very rich large [cancelled] carv'd [inserted] and gilt Frame by Ditto...' In The Back Parlour was 'a large Historical Picture of the Death of Hector in a carved and gilt frame'[5]

Both pictures were sold off at some point in 1773, the year before Northampton's successor, the 8th Earl of Northampton, was finally declared bankrupt, the Hamilton fetching rather more than the Batoni, as reported by Father John Thorpe, SJ (1726-92) to Lord Arundell on 1 January 1774. Winckelmann had preferred Hamilton's approach to Greek subjects to Batoni's, but Father Thorpe's opinion was the reverse:

If he [Batoni] was man of a more exalted and generous spirit, it must sure have hurt him soarly when one of his largest and best pictures 'the parting of Hector from Andromache' for which Ld. Northampton gladly paid £300 was sold again in London for seventy Guineas, while the companion of it, an inferior picture by Hamilton sold for something more.[6]

Both the Batoni and the Hamilton had evidently been inherited by Northampton's infant daughter, Lady Elizabeth Compton, who was born in 1760, their fate being controlled by her guardian, her grandmother – and Northampton's mother-in-law – the Dowager Duchess of Beaufort.[7] Their existence was noted by Walpole in his *Anecdotes*, composed during the 1760s, citing their presence in Northampton's house and in that of the Duchess of Beaufort. No trace of either picture has been found since Father Thorpe's report of their disposal, a sale which must have been undertaken by the Dowager Duchess.[8] The loss of the two pictures amounts to a substantial lacuna in the material available for an informed account of the early stages of the development of neoclassical taste.

BATONI'S *HECTOR'S FAREWELL TO ANDROMACHE*

Charles Compton, 7th Earl of Northampton, had been born in Lisbon on 22 July 1737, where his father had been appointed *chargé d'affaires* in 1728. The family returned to England in 1745. Some time after completing his studies at Christ Church, Oxford, Compton left on a Grand Tour of Italy (as noted above),[9] and was recorded as being in Padua by 23 June 1757. Throughout his Tour he bought valuable pieces, commissioned important works of art, and met influential people, such as the architect Robert Adam,[10] with whom he discussed new plans for Castle Ashby, his house in Northamptonshire. While in Rome in April 1758 he commissioned a large full-length portrait of himself by Batoni (237.5 × 148.6 cm) which is now in the Fitzwilliam Museum, Cambridge.

Although commissioning a portrait by Batoni was standard practice for Grand Tourists in Rome, the commissioning of a history painting from him was more unusual. The exact size of *Hector's farewell to Andromache* is unknown but since the painting was a companion piece to Gavin Hamilton's *Andromache bewailing the death of Hector*, which was about 9′ by 13′ (about 274 × 396 cm), the Batoni was presumably of similar proportions. The picture has been missing since it was last referred to, as noted above, on 1 January 1774, but the appearance of the composition is recorded in a squared-up signed drawing in the Musée des Beaux-Arts in Besançon (D1028), where there are also two signed preparatory drawings: one a study of soldiers (D1029), and one of a woman (D2259).[11]

In addition to Winckelmann's mentioning the picture in the letter quoted above, it was also referred to by Sir Thomas Robinson, the diplomat and ambassador to Spain (1738-86), later Lord Grantham. He wrote about it, while referring to a similar composition by Anton Mengs, in a yet more critical way, in a letter to his father from Rome dated 9 August 1760:

> As to the Historical Picture of Hector & Andromache, I shall only make one Distinction between them without entering into a detailed Account of them. Which is, that Menx [Anton Mengs] has drawn Hector Andromache & Astyanax within the Walls of Troy, while Battoni's is il Signor Ettore, la Signora Andromache, & il fammillo Astyanax on the Theatre in the Haymarket. This last picture however is doing for my Ld. Northampton.[12]

It would appear that both the Batoni and the Hamilton had been commissioned in early 1758, because the artist John Parker, who was resident in Rome, referred to the Hamilton in a letter to Lord Charlemont of 5 April that year, reporting that 'Mr Compton' had 'ordered a large history piece to Mr Hamilton', adding (as Ingamells observes, 'characteristically') 'and had he seen my work I flatter myself I should have been employed too.'[13] In December 1758, when Charles Compton was in Florence, he received the news of his uncle's death, and his own succession to the earldom of Northampton. He returned to London by April 1759 and on 13 September of the same year married Lady Anne Somerset, daughter of the 4th Duke of Beaufort. They had a daughter, Elizabeth, who was born on 25 June 1760. In all probability the Batoni had arrived in London by 1762, because its companion by Hamilton was exhibited at the Society of Artists in that year and the two pictures would have been sent from Italy at the same time.

The fate of the Batoni is entwined with unfortunate developments in the Northampton family. Northampton became a close friend to the young King George III, and was subsequently appointed Ambassador Extraordinary and Plenipotentiary to Venice. This appointment was announced on 16 May 1761, but the credentials were not issued until 26 August 1762, whereupon the couple set off from London, leaving their child in the care of Anne's mother, the Duchess of Beaufort. During their journey to Italy, or perhaps whilst still in London, the Northamptons both contracted tuberculosis, from which Anne died on 18 May 1763. Charles, who was hardly fit for diplomatic ceremonies, left Venice but died

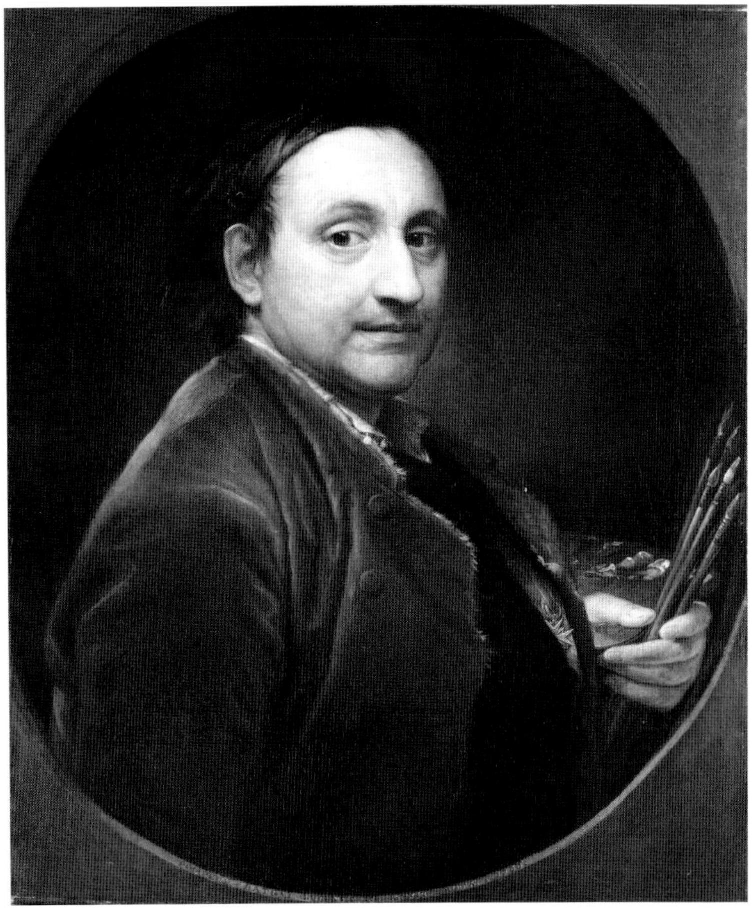

Self-portrait
by Pompeo Batoni (1708-87).
Oil on canvas, 58 × 56 cm.
Bayerische Staatsgemäldesammlungen, Munich

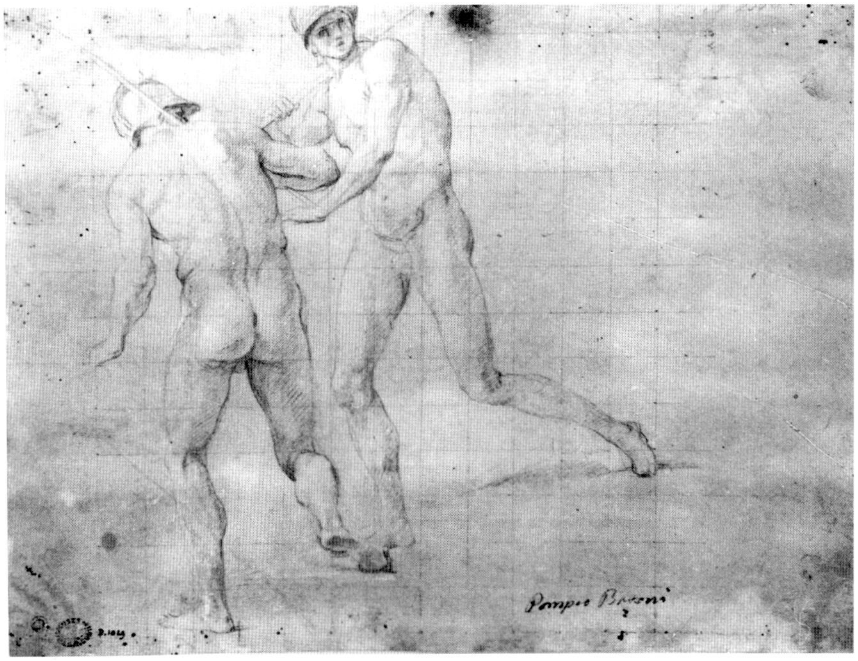

Study for lost painting
(*Hector's farewell to Andromache*)
by Pompeo Batoni.
Red chalk heightened with white chalk, 22.3 × 28.4 cm.
Musée des Beaux-arts et d'Archéologie, Besançon

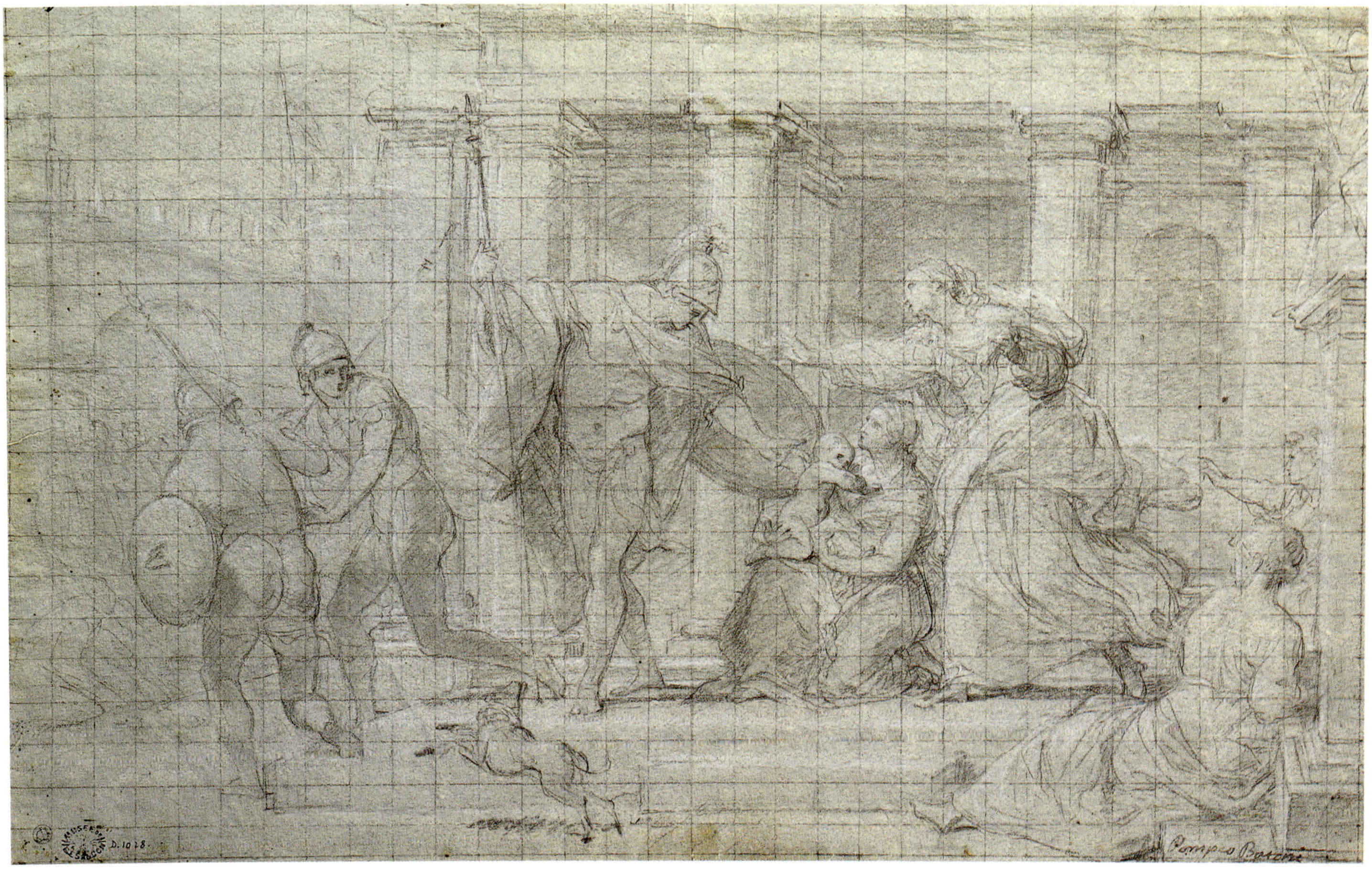

Hector's farewell to Andromache.
Design by Pompeo Batoni for lost painting.
Black chalk heightened with white chalk, 24.8 × 38 cm.
Musée des Beaux-arts et d'Archéologie, Besançon

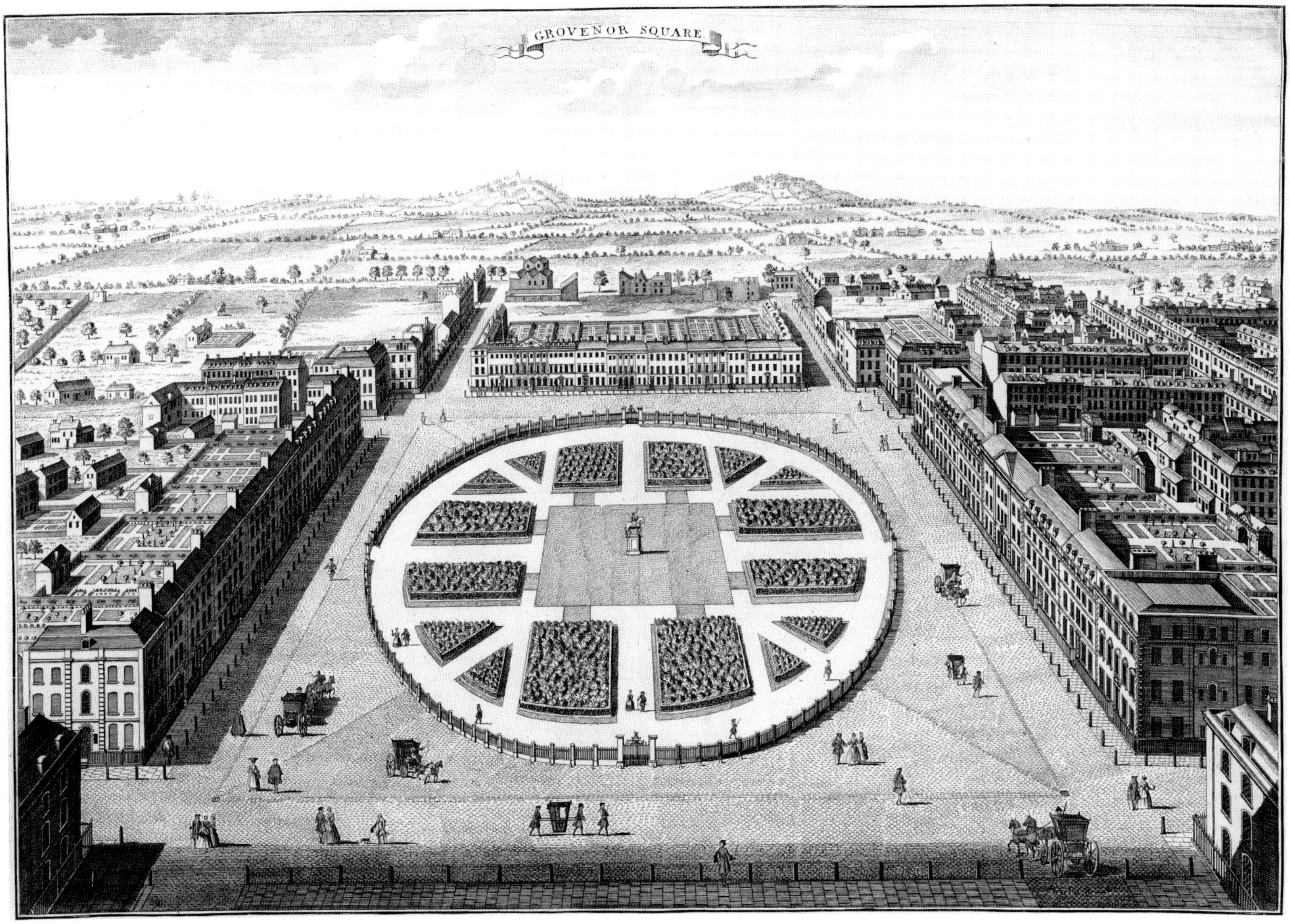

Grosvenor Square
in the eighteenth century.
Anonymous engraving, 1754.
Guildhall Library, London

on 18 October the same year, in Lyons, whereupon his younger brother, Spencer, succeeded to the title as the 8th Earl.[14]

The posthumous inventory then made has been quoted above, but Horace Walpole also refers to Batoni's *Hector* and to the portrait of the 7th Earl, in his *Anecdotes*, which he began on 1 January 1760. At the beginning of his section on Pompeo Batoni, Walpole reports:

The duchess dowager of Beaufort has a very large picture of Hector leaving Andromache by Pompeio, very faintly coloured, and a whole length by him of her son-in-law the earl of Northampton.[15]

In the final section on the artist he writes:

At the house of the late Earl of Northampton in Grosvenor-square is his portrait whole length with a large greyhound; the earl in a crimson velvet cloak with furs, by Pompeio Battoni. The earl died in Italy, and left an only daughter, by his wife (who died there also daughter of Noel duke of Beaufort). In the same house a very large picture of Hector and Andromache, indifferent, by the same Pompeio.[16]

It is clear that Walpole is recording the same two pictures by Batoni but at the two different addresses in which they were kept at different times. The first reference is to the Duchess's house in Berkeley Square, where she looked after her granddaughter Lady Elizabeth Compton; the second reference must refer back to an earlier date, when the pictures were still in the Earl's house at Grosvenor Square. Under the terms of the 7th Earl's will, he made separate and ample

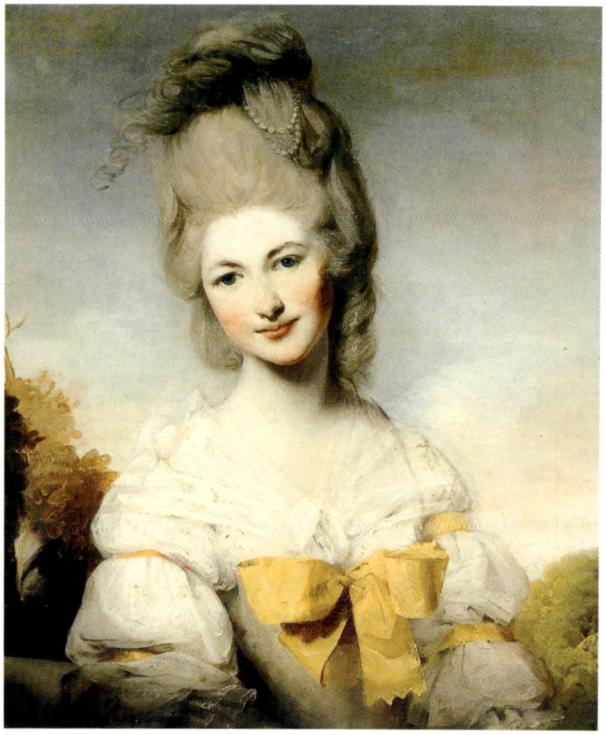

Lady Elizabeth Compton
by the Revd. Matthew William Peters (1742-1814).
Oil on canvas, 76.2 × 63.2 cm

provision for his brother commensurate with the 'rank and dignity' of an earl, but left everything else to his daughter, whose grandmother the Dowager Duchess of Beaufort was named as guardian, and to whom administration of the will was granted.

The will was proved 6 December 1763 (i.e. at the same time that the inventory of the Grosvenor Square house referred to above was taken) and 'administration with the will... of all and singular the Goods Chattels and Credits of the Right Honourable Charles late earl of Northampton deceased' – save for that part of the will which referred to the bequest to his brother from his personal estate – 'was granted to the most Noble Elizabeth Duchess Dowager of Beaufort the natural lawful Grandmother and next of kin and Curatrix or Guardian lawfully assigned to the Right Honourable Lady Elizabeth Compton spinster an infant the natural and lawful daughter and only child of the said deceased for the use and benefit of the said infant and until she shall attain the age of twenty-one years she having been first sworn duly to administer for that no other Executor or any other Residuary legatee is named in the said will.'

The will does not specify individual paintings, but it is clear from the subsequent records that paintings were included among the 'Goods [and] Chattels' that went in the first instance into the care of the Dowager Duchess of Beaufort and were then inherited by Lady Elizabeth at the age of twenty-one. This explains why the Batoni was recorded by Walpole as at the Duchess's house: from 1764-8 the Duchess lived at 7 Grosvenor Square, the late Earl's house, where she initially moved in order to look after her little granddaughter. The pictures then went, including the Batonis and the Hamilton, together with the eight-year-old Lady Elizabeth, to the Duchess's house in Berkeley Square until Lady Elizabeth's marriage into the Cavendish family in February 1782.[17]

Lady Elizabeth certainly kept the Batoni full-length portrait of her father, as it later appeared as Cavendish property; and a list of pictures, probably dating from 1781, and thus immediately preceding her marriage, was made at the Berkeley Square house where Lady Betty (as she was known) had been living with her grandmother. Some of the pictures appear to have Lady Betty's initials beside them, clarifying her ownership.

The brief descriptions in this list, often giving no name of the artist, make it difficult to identify individual paintings, but Batoni's *Hector's farewell* is not in evidence, nor does it appear in any subsequent inventory at the Northampton seat of Castle Ashby. The reason, evidently, is that it had been disposed of by this date, as the Dowager Duchess was entitled to do under the terms of the will, and as is clear from Father Thorpe's letter quoted above, dated 1 January 1774.

The Duchess's reasons for selling off the Batoni and the Hamilton can now only be guessed at, although the proceeds would certainly have been for the benefit of her granddaughter. The 8th Earl, however, who had financial difficulties from early on, finally went bankrupt in 1774 through having supported an unsuccessful political candidate, in one of the bitterest and most expensive contests in parliamentary history, which was estimated to have cost £160,000, and his chattels were sold by auction at Castle Ashby over five days in September 1774. After the auction, the Earl lived in Switzerland, where he died.

HAMILTON'S *ANDROMACHE BEWAILING THE DEATH OF HECTOR*

The history painter and portraitist Gavin Hamilton, who spent most of his career in Rome, was immensely influential in the growth of neo-classical taste in Europe. He not only moved in the same circles as Winckelmann and Mengs but was the intimate friend of, and a formative influence upon, the great sculptor Antonio Canova. The young Jacques-Louis David, in Rome in 1780, drew upon Hamilton's compositions. Between 1782 and 1784 Hamilton was busy on the most substantial decoration of its time in Rome, eight large-scale decorative canvases for the Stanza d'Elena in the Villa Borghese, on the theme of Paris and Helen, five of which are still *in situ*. From about 1769 onwards, Hamilton became one of the most important archaeologists then working, and he was accompanied upon his digs by, among others, Giovanni Battista Piranesi. Hamilton was also a dealer on a scale that can rarely have been matched, a fact closely connected with his archaeological excavations, and he played a part in a number of the most famous discoveries of the eighteenth century.

His career also reflects the importance of himself and his fellow Scots of the Enlightenment in the birth of neo-classicism, and indeed, the Scots formed the largest national group at the Academy in Rome after the Italians.[18] Robert Adam, for example, met Hamilton in Rome in 1757,[19] and had himself been discussing architectural projects with the future 7th Earl of Northampton in Padua in June 1757.[20] *Hector's Farewell*, a subject also painted by Hamilton *c.*1769, is the title of a poem by the exiled Jacobite poet William Hamilton of Bangour, whose portrait Hamilton painted (Scottish National Portrait Gallery), a poem which itself marks a turning-point in the translation of Homeric epic into English. Hamilton also knew the Scottish painter Allan Ramsay, who spent much of the latter part of his life on a project to find the site of Horace's Sabine Villa.

Hamilton first went to Rome in the mid-1740s, perhaps as early as 1744 but certainly by 1748, and it has been speculated that he had some Jacobite connections, in addition to his portrayal of William Hamilton who was exiled in France from 1746 until his death in 1754.[21] He trained in Rome with the painter Agostino Masucci who had himself worked for the Jacobite court and who is traditionally the painter of the high altarpiece of the Scottish church in Rome, S.Andrea degli Scozzesi.[22] Hamilton had been born at Murdieston House, Lanark, into a well-connected and well-to-do family, and studied humanities at the University of Glasgow. After training with Masucci, he returned to London by July 1751, and practised there as a portrait painter, returning to Italy in 1756, where, with at least one visit thereafter to Scotland, he remained.[23]

It is in Scotland also that specific studies of Greek and Roman literature had been taking place which would directly have influenced Hamilton and therefore the course of neo-classicism in Europe.[24] One author was Robert Wood (1717?-71), who has been called 'the principal instigator of English Hellenism',[25] one of the subjects of Hamilton's *Wood and Dawkins discovering Palmyra*. It was probably Wood who recommended Hamilton to the Duke of Bridgewater in 1758 for the first of the two versions of *The anger of Achilles*. Wood himself published privately in 1767 his *Essay on the Original genius of Homer* (published London, 1769), when Hamilton was well into the Homeric series of paintings which he called 'my great plan for life'. Hamilton was also the friend of James Stuart, Nicholas Revett and Matthew Brettingham, in whose company in 1748 he went by foot on a six-week visit to Naples. It has been suggested that it was Hamilton who actually suggested the trip to Greece, on which he originally planned to go, which led to the ground-breaking publication of Stuart and Revett's *Antiquities of Athens* (from 1762 onwards).[26]

Several of Hamilton's most substantial history pictures, devoted to heroic Greek and Roman themes, which were usually of a massive size, are now lost. Many were published in engraved form during his lifetime by Domenico Cunego at Hamilton's expense, and this includes five out of the sequence of six Homeric paintings. The canvases measured on average 9′ × 13′(about 274 × 396 cm) and one of them was *Andromache bewailing the death of Hector*. Although the original painting has been lost, its appearance is recorded in one of Cunego's engravings. Each of Cunego's engravings which can still be compared with a surviving painting is in the same sense as the original and that was evidently the case with *Andromache bewailing*, because the composition also survives in the form of a pen and brown ink drawing by Hamilton, which is in the same sense as the engraving. The sketch is one of a pair with *Achilles mourning the dead Patroclus*, and the pair was sold

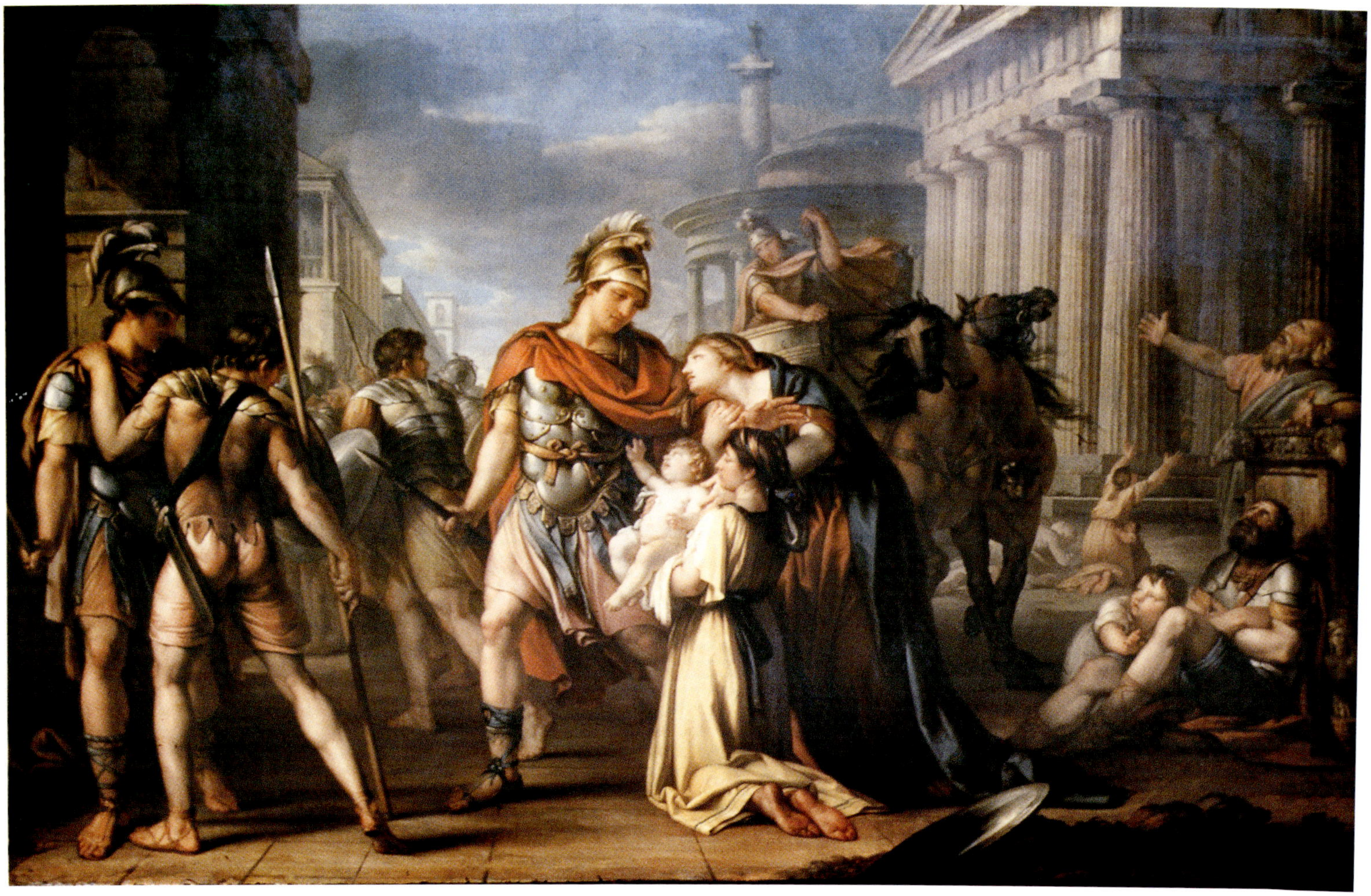

Hector's farewell to Andromache
by Gavin Hamilton
(1723-98) *c.* 1769.
Oil on canvas, 315 × 395.5 cm.
Hunterian Art Gallery,
University of Glasgow

in Rome on 11 June 1973 (Livia, lot no. 3). They are now in the Yale Center for British Art. The fact that these drawings survived as a pair in Rome reflects the fact that these two scenes were the first two to be executed by Hamilton consciously as part of his projected set of six engravings after the *Iliad* of Homer, even though the two scenes are separated chronologically within the series. There is also a *modello* of the composition in the National Gallery of Scotland (oil, 64.2 × 98.5 cm).

While so many of Hamilton's original works have vanished, the pictures and antiquities which he acquired for re-sale, among them Leonardo da Vinci's *Virgin of the rocks* (National Gallery, London) the *Townley Marbles* (British Museum) and the *Warwick Vase* (Burrell Collection, Glasgow) are recognised as some of the greatest works of art in European collections. Yet other spectacular antiquities, including several that were part of the great collection of Lord Shelburne which Hamilton created, are now in collections in the United States of America.[27]

Andromache bewailing the death of Hector is one of the five Homeric subjects by Hamilton that were engraved by Domenico Cunego between 1764 and 1778. While it initially formed a pair with Batoni's *Hector's farewell to Andromache* for Lord Northampton, Hamilton later painted the Batoni subject himself, a work

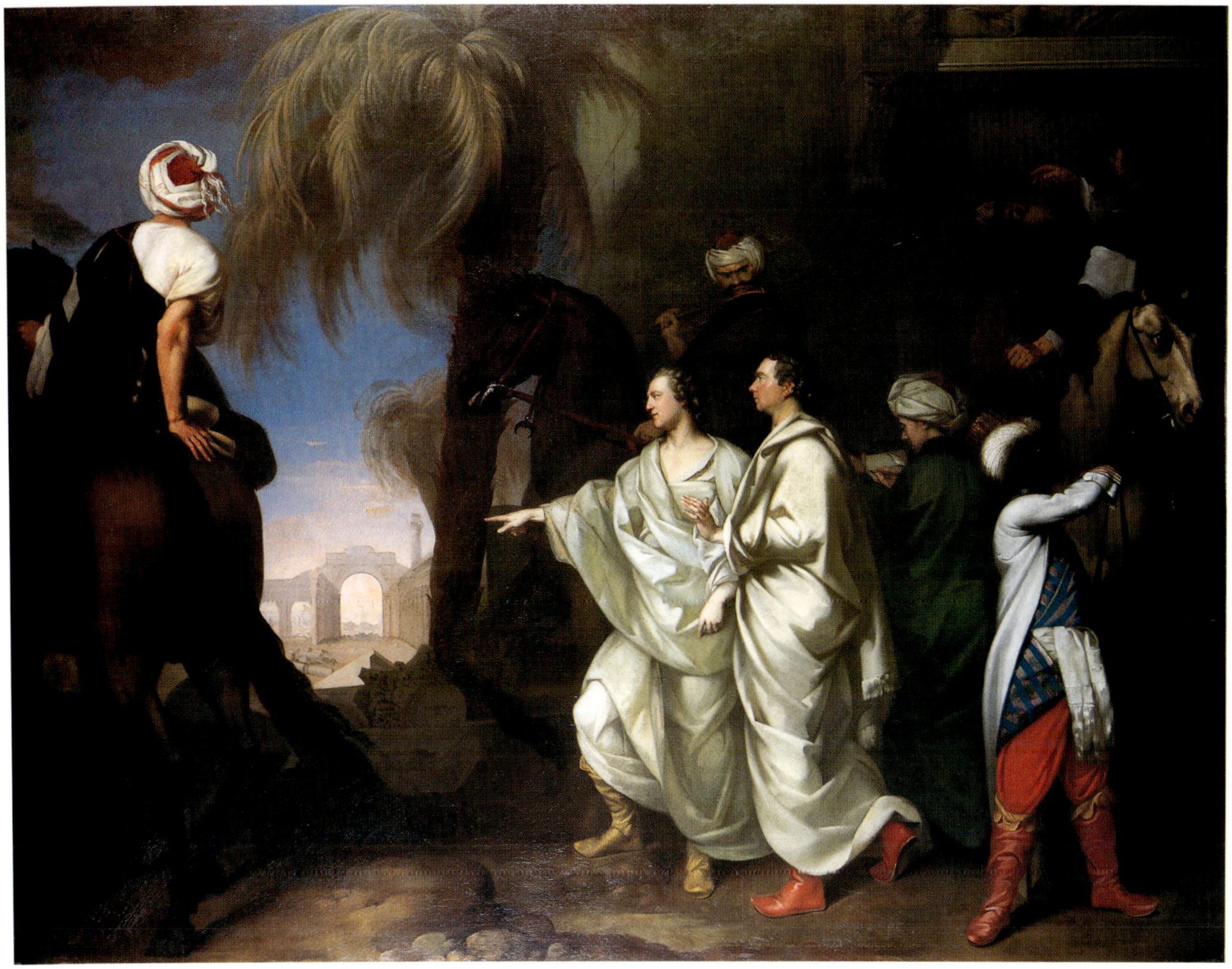

which was acquired by the 8th Duke of Hamilton in *c.* 1776 and which survives in the Hunterian Museum, Glasgow, although it is the only episode in Hamilton's sequence of six Homeric subjects which was not engraved by Cunego between 1764-78.[28] The other Homeric paintings by Hamilton that are at present untraced include *Priam pleading with Achilles for the body of Hector* (commissioned by Luke Gardiner, 1771) and *Achilles dragging the body of Hector round the walls of Troy*, commissioned by Francis, Lord Tavistock, and painted 1762-5, and subsequently in the Duke of Bedford's collection at Arniston. This painting was sold by the family as early as 1767, since the subject so closely recalled the early death through a riding accident of Tavistock in that year.[29] One of two versions of *The anger of Achilles for the loss of Briseis* – that commissioned by Francis Egerton, 3rd Duke of Bridgewater, by 1758 – is also missing, although the other, for the 2nd Viscount Palmerston, survives (Broadlands; exhibited at the RA 1770, but engraved in Rome in 1769). This latter painting was undertaken by Hamilton in 1766, as a replacement, so far as Hamilton's own scheme for a set of engravings of the series was concerned, for the earlier Bridgewater commission of the same subject (for whatever reason). In a letter of the previous year, 1765, to

Wood and Dawkins discovering Palmyra by Gavin Hamilton.
Oil on canvas, 309.9 × 388.6 cm.
National Gallery of Scotland, Edinburgh

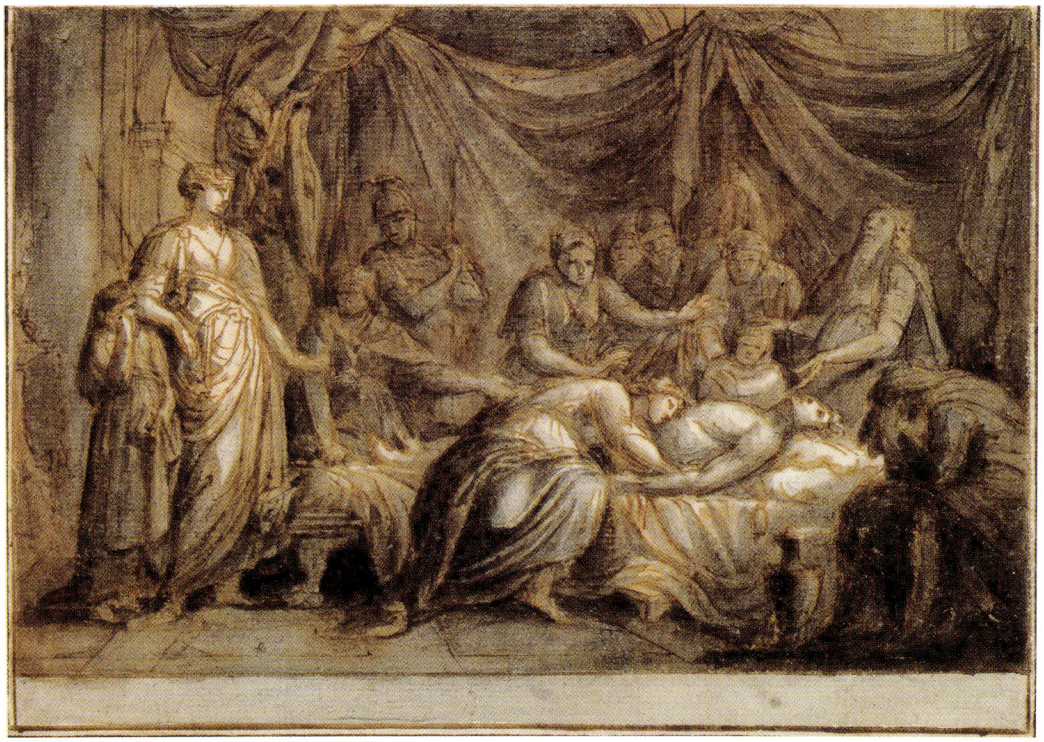

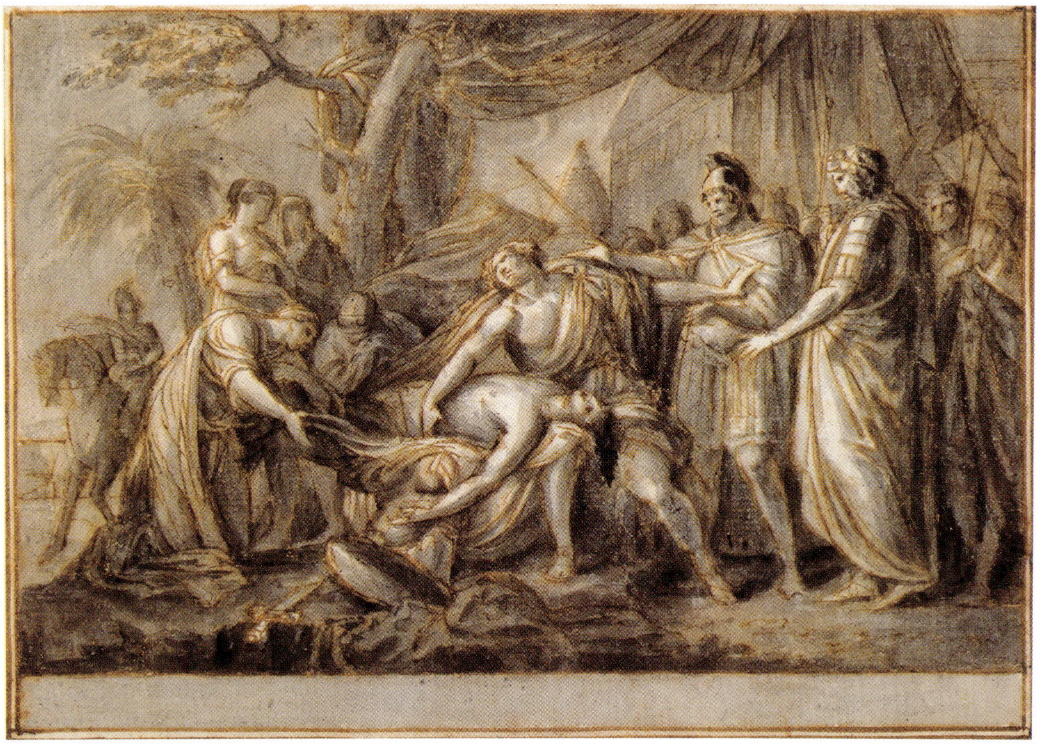

Andromache bewailing the death of Hector.
Design by Gavin Hamilton for lost painting of 1758.
Pen and brown ink, 14 × 21 cm. Yale Center for British Art, New Haven

Achilles mourning the dead Patroclus. Design by Gavin Hamilton.
Pen and brown ink, 14 × 21 cm. Yale Center for British Art, New Haven

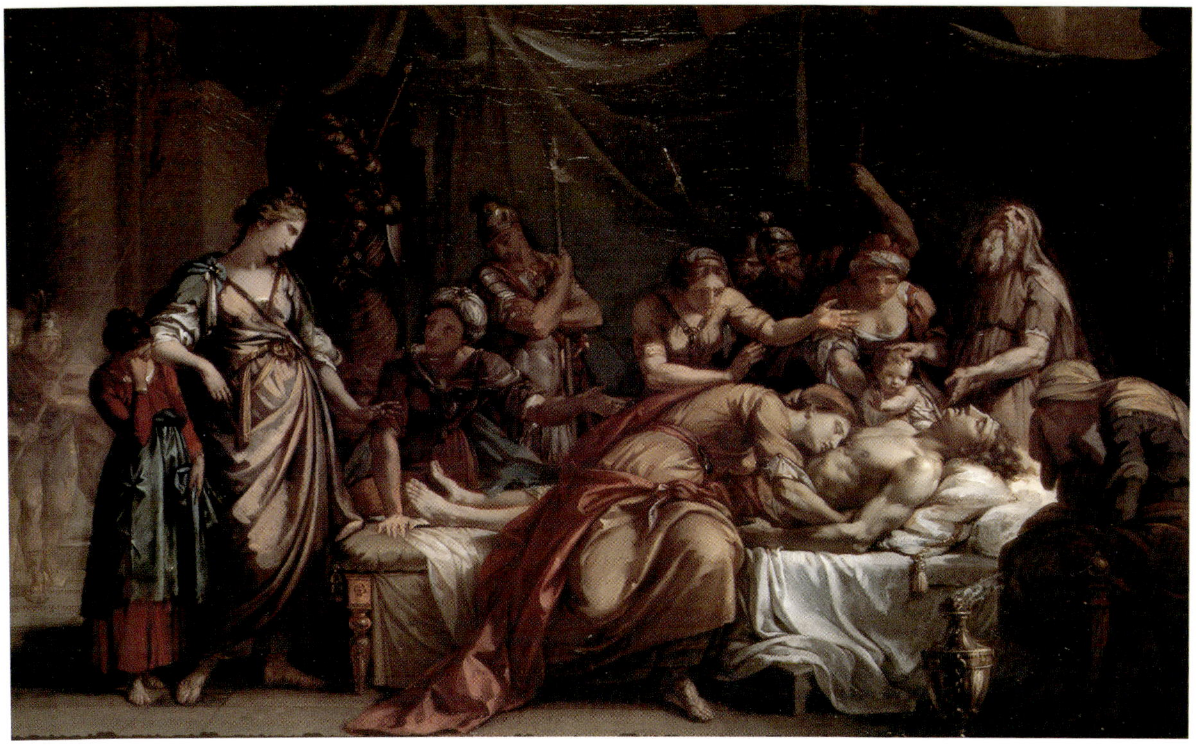

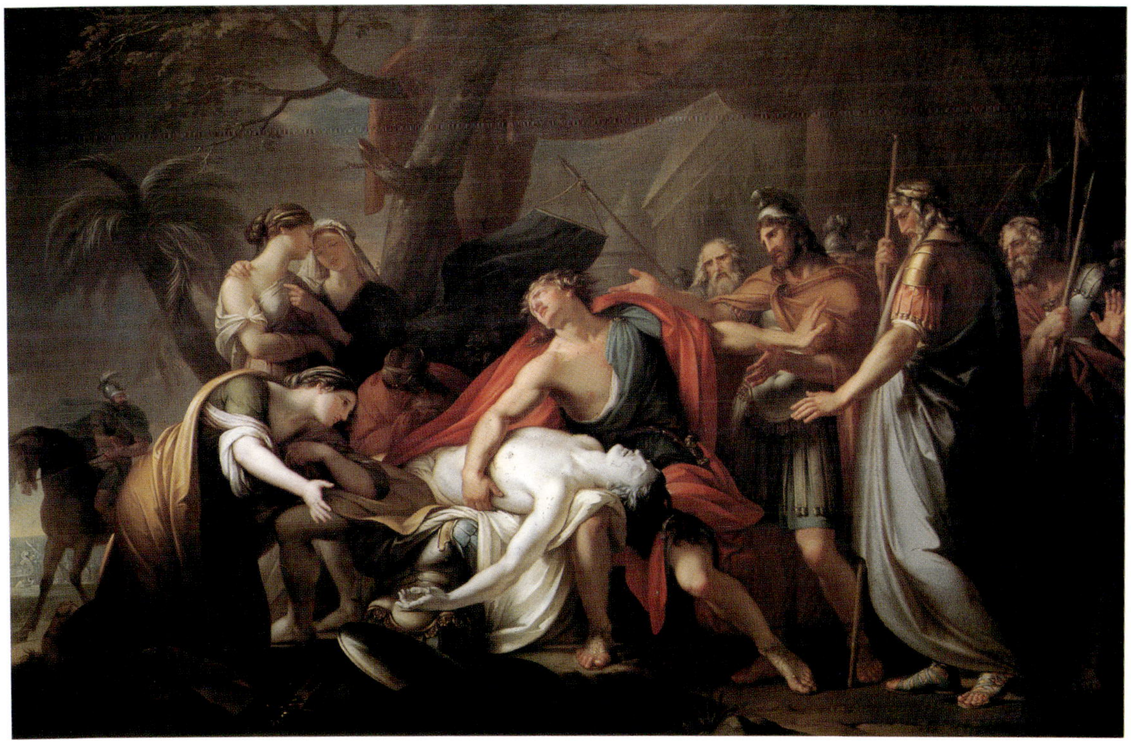

Andromache bewailing the death of Hector. Modello by Gavin Hamilton for lost painting.
Oil, 64.2 × 98.5 cm. National Gallery of Scotland, Edinburgh

Achilles mourning the dead Patroclus by Gavin Hamilton.
Oil on canvas, 274 × 396 cm. National Gallery of Scotland, Edinburgh

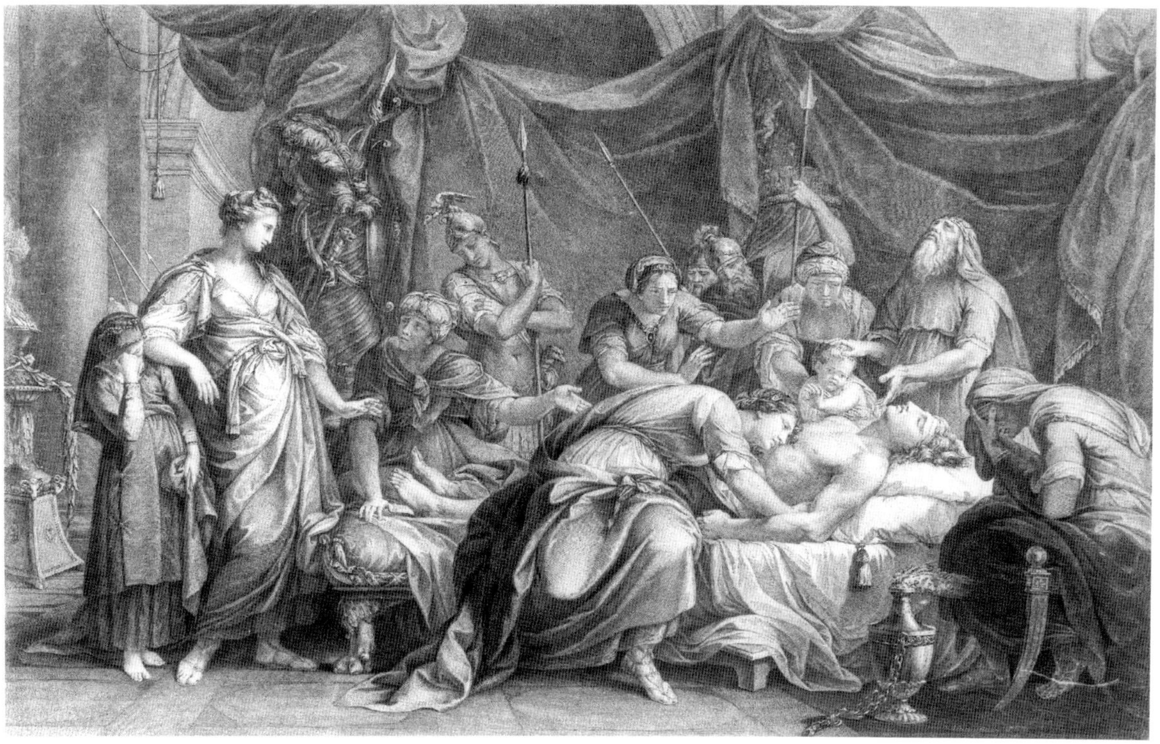

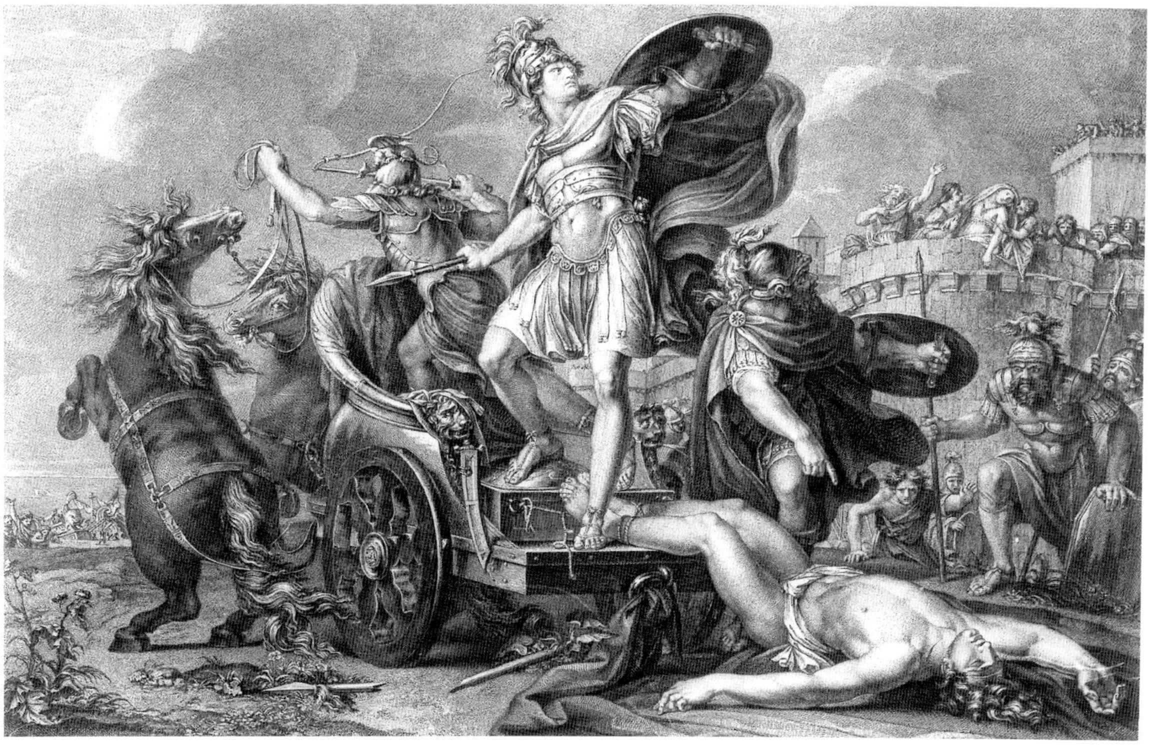

Andromache bewailing the death of Hector.
Engraving by Domenico Cunego after lost painting by Gavin Hamilton

Achilles vents his rage on Hector.
Engraving by Domenico Cunego after Gavin Hamilton

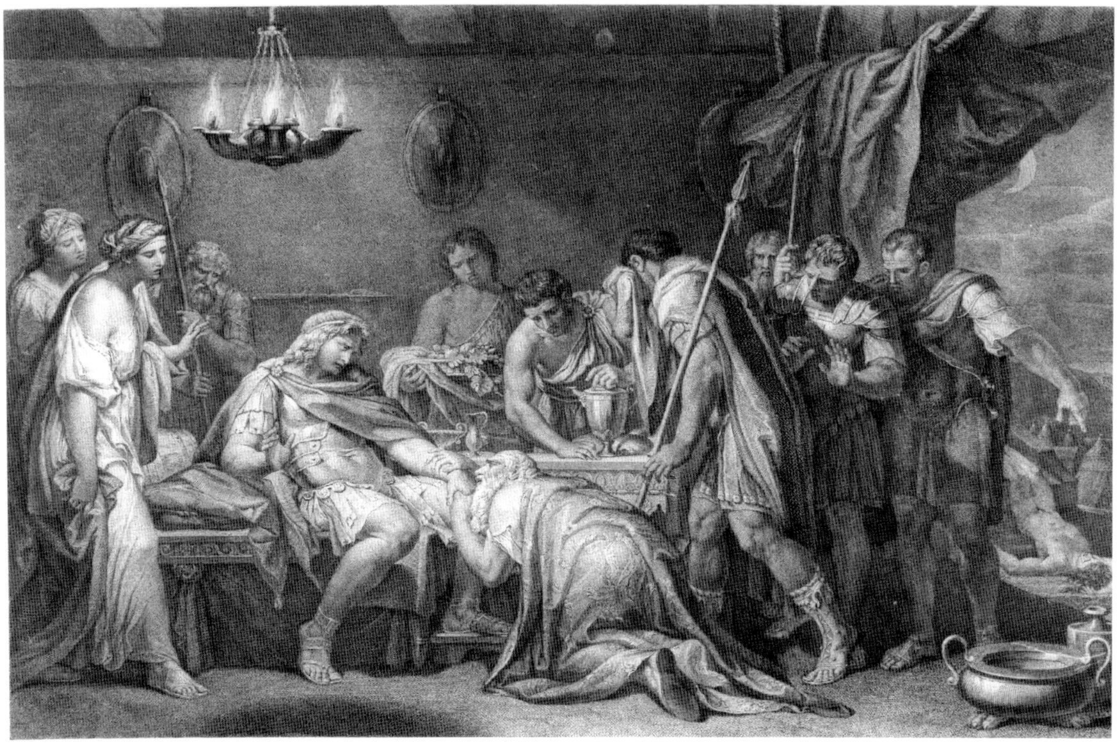

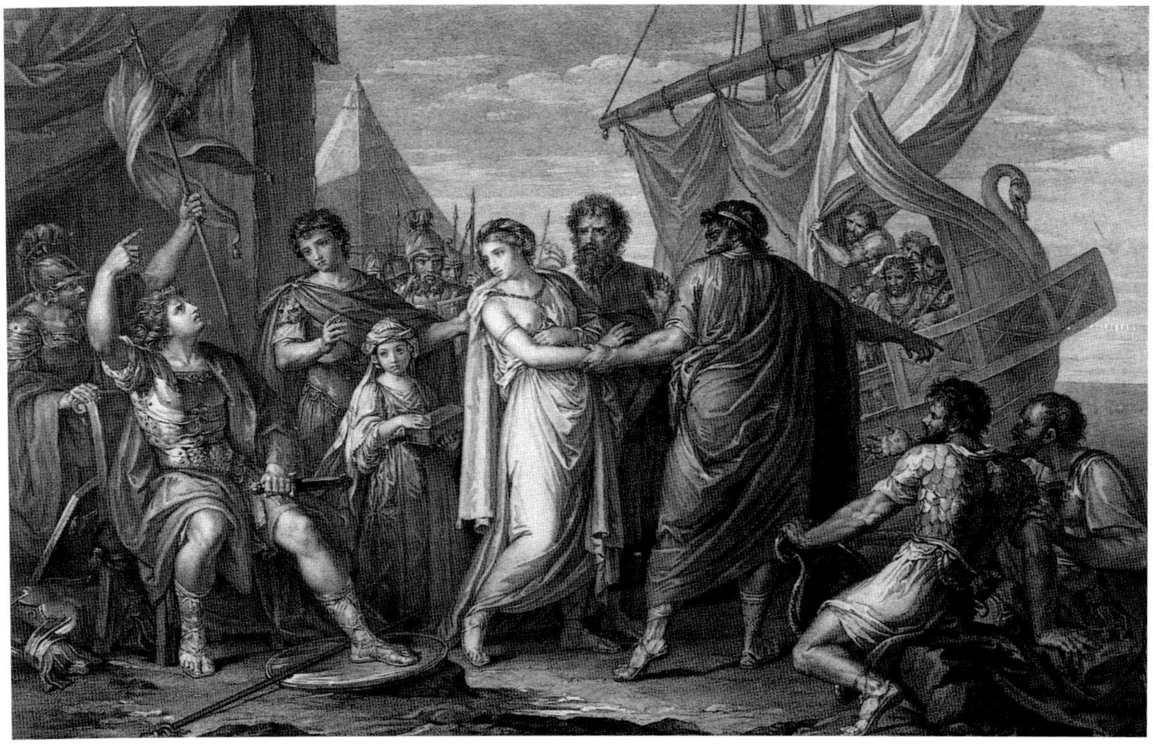

Priam redeems the dead body of Hector.
Engraving by Domenico Cunego after Gavin Hamilton

The anger of Achilles for the loss of Briseis.
Engraving by Domenico Cunego after Gavin Hamilton

Lord Palmerston, Hamilton referred to *Andromache bewailing the death of Hector*:

I should be glad to know what your Lordship thinks of the print of Andromache bewailing the Death of Hector: it is the first of a set of six prints I intend to publish from Homer, and consequently I am anxious about the success of it.[30]

In a letter of 1768 it is clear that Hamilton has not yet finished *The anger of Achilles*, and also that he has now certainly discounted the early Bridgewater commission of the subject as belonging to the Homeric set, because he refers to three pictures as finished, mentioning 'the three other subjects to be done to complete the set', the three completed being *Andromache bewailing the death of Hector*, *Achilles mourning Patroclus* (for Sir James Grant, commissioned 1760, completed 1763)[31] and *Achilles dragging the body of Hector round the walls of Troy*. *The anger of Achilles* was followed by *Priam pleading for the body of Hector* (noted above, and commissioned in 1771, from which it is again clear that the order of execution did not follow the narrative of the *Iliad*) and *Hector's farewell to Andromache*.

Hamilton also painted Roman subjects but some of these are also lost, including *Agrippina weeping over the ashes of Germanicus*, painted for Lord Ossory (exhibited RA 1769); and two paintings after Milton's poems *Il Penseroso* and *L'Allegro*, created for William Wedell (engraved by Cunego 1768) have also vanished.

Quite apart from the question of changing taste, with such losses from Hamilton's oeuvre it is hardly surprising that his reputation declined, although it has recovered somewhat, and such undoubted – and also massive – masterpieces as *Wood and Dawkins discovering Palmyra* (National Gallery of Scotland) have recently begun to receive greater appreciation. Yet Hamilton's reputation was high in his own day, and not only as a painter: he was much admired as a learned figure both in Roman and wider European society. He was admitted to the Accademia di S.Luca in 1761 and also to the exclusive literary association of the Arcadians.[32] By 1767 John Aikman of the Ross wrote of him:

Mr Gavin Hamilton ... is what the Italians call the Premiero and we call the Principal, in the Academy of painting at Rome... He is a sweet-blooded gentleman, and being the most renowned of all the History Painters of this age is highly-respected at Rome.[33]

NOTES

1 J. Ingamells, *A Dictionary of British and Irish Travellers in Italy 1701-1800*, New Haven and London, 1997, p. 713. See also P. McKay, 'A Patron of Promise: Charles, 7th Earl of Northampton' in *Northamptonshire Past and Present (Journal of the Northamptonshire Record Society)*, vol. VIII, no. 4 (Northampton, 1992).

2 Noted in the fullest account of Hamilton, Duncan Macmillan, *Scottish Painting; The Golden Age*, exh. cat., London and Edinburgh, 1986, pp. 32-3; see especially 'the Epic Age', pp. 31-41, pl. 23, cat. 36, although Macmillan does not mention the commissioning in the first instance by the 3rd Duke of Bridgewater of *The anger of Achilles*, which was actually the first of the Homeric series to have been devised, even if it was never completed or was lost early on. This would have been the logical first scene for Hamilton to have chosen when he started his series of six Homeric scenes, since it is the first in order of appearance in the *Iliad* – see Macmillan, p. 38. The Bridgewater commission was evidently in hand by 1 March 1758, Ingamells, op. cit., p. 125, citing Lyte letters, MSS (1 March 1758). See also D. & F. Irwin, *Scottish Painters at Home and Abroad 1700-1900*, 1975, p. 102 and n. 23.

3 Macmillan, op. cit., pp. 32-3, and nn. 6, 7, citing Seafield Papers, Register House, Edinburgh, GD 248/177/1, and E.K. Waterhouse, 'The British Contribution to the Neo-Classical Style of Painting', *Proceedings of the British Academy*, XL (1954), pp. 67, 69.

4 Irwin, op. cit., p. 102, and n. 23, and A.M. Clark, ed. E.P. Bowron, *Pompeo Batoni: Complete Catalogue*, New York and Oxford, 1985, p. 277 (original German, from Winckelmann, *Briefe*, vol. II, pp. 111-12).

5 The extracts from the inventory have been kindly supplied by Charles Noble, Assistant Keeper of Collections, Chatsworth.

6 Father Thorpe to Lord Arundell in a letter dated 1 January 1774. Cf. Clark/ Bowron, op. cit., p. 277; Ingamells, op. cit. pp. 939-42.

7 See below.

8 See below.

9 Ingamells, op. cit., pp. 713-14.

10 McKay, op. cit., p. 263.

11 Clark/ Bowron, op. cit: see cat. nos. 222, D45, D46, D48, and pl. 210 (the squared-up drawing).

12 G. Beard, 'Batoni and Mengs', *Leeds Art Calendar*, no. 44, 1960, pp. 23-4.

13 Ingamells, op. cit., p. 713.

14 McKay, op. cit., p. 272.

15 Horace Walpole, *Anecdotes of Painting in England... volume the fifth and last*, ed. F. W. Hilles and P. B. Daghlian, 1937 pp. 18-20. The Dowager Duchess of Beaufort lived in 7 Grosvenor Square, 1764-8 (*Survey of London*).

16 Walpole, loc. cit.

17 She married George Augustus Henry Cavendish, Lord George Cavendish, third son of 4th Duke of Devonshire. He became Earl of Burlington in 1831 (*The Complete Peerage*).

18 Macmillan, op. cit., p. 33.

19 Ingamells, op. cit., pp. 447-8

20 Ibid., p. 713.

21 Macmillan, op. cit., p. 32; Ingamells, op. cit., p. 447.

22 Ingamells, loc. cit.

23 Ibid.

24 Macmillan, op. cit., pp. 31ff.

25 Ingamells, op. cit., p. 1016.

26 Ibid., p. 447.

27 Ibid., p. 450.

28 Ibid., p. 448.

29 Ibid., p. 929.

30 Macmillan, op. cit., p. 38.

31 Ibid., p. 33.

32 P. J. M. McEwan, *Dictionary of Scottish Art & Architecture*, Woodbridge, 1994, p. 259.

33 Macmillan, op. cit., p. 33.

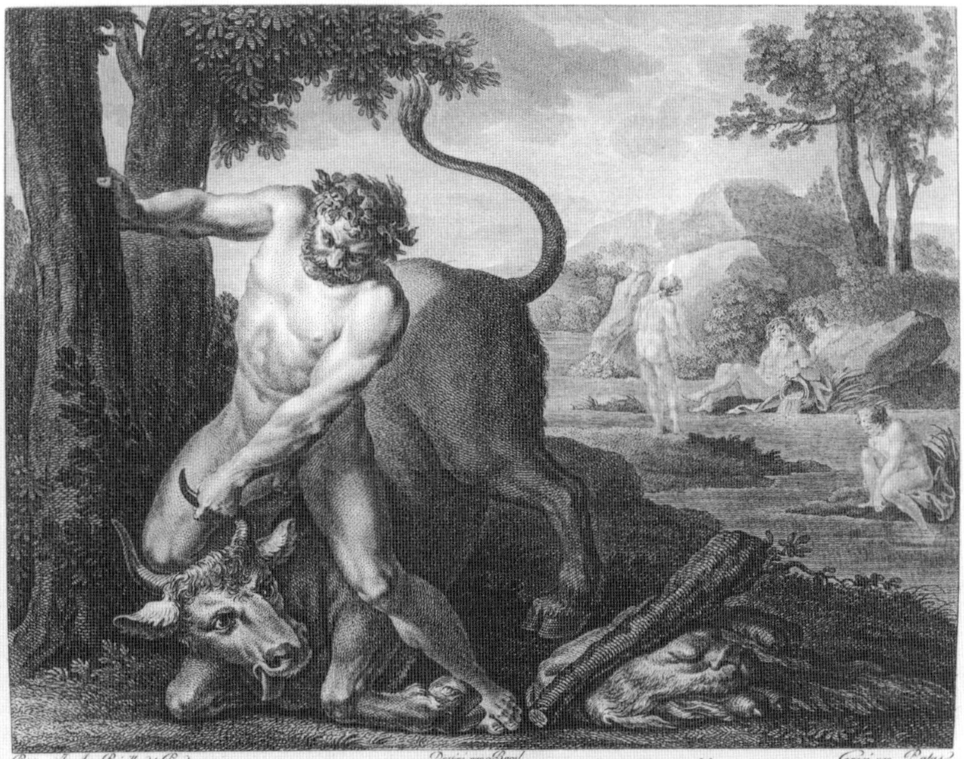

Peint par J. A. Regillo dit Pordenon. *Dessiné par Borel.* *Gravé par Patas.*

HERCULE ET ACHELOÜS.

De la Galerie de S. A. S. Monseigneur le Duc d'Orléans.

A.P. D.R.

ÉCOLE VENITIENNE.

IIE TABLEAU DE JEAN ANTOINE REGILLO.

DIT PORDENON.

Peint fur Toile, ayant de hauteur 6 Pieds 1 Pouce, fur 7 Pieds 1 Pouce de large.

Dejanire, fille d'Oenée étant recherchée en mariage par un grand nombre de Héros, son Pere la promit à celui qui vaincroit les autres. Hercule et Acheloüs, qui prétendoient à ce beau prix, combatirent l'un contre l'autre. Acheloüs fut vaincu malgré tous ses efforts: il prit ensuite la forme d'un Serpent, sous la quelle il fut encore défait; enfin celle d'un Taureau, sous la quelle il ne réussit pas mieux. Hercule l'ayant terrassé lui arracha une Corne et le contraignit d'aller se cacher dans le fleuve Thoas, qui fut depuis appellé Acheloüs: il doña à son vainqueur la Corne d'Amalthée, ou la Corne d'abondance pour ravoir la sienne.

Les Ouvrages de Pordenon sont fort recherchés des Connoisseurs. La beauté du Coloris, un Style grand et noble, un bon gout de Dessin et une grande facilité d'exécution les firent souvant préférer à ceux du Titien. Cette préférence, comme on le sçait, ne fut jamais l'effet du caprice ni de la mode si l'on considere que le Titien lui même ne pouvoit voir sans émotion et sans une jalousie extrême les Ouvrages et les Succès d'un si célèbre rival.

Quoi que le Sujet de ce Tableau soit assez ingrat, on y reconnoit un grand caractère de Dessin et un Coloris d'une grande force; mais à côté des beautés que l'on y remarque, on y apperçoit l'empreinte d'un Pinceau étranger et téméraire qui n'a pu parvenir à faire disparoître les dommages du tems.

Pordenone

c. 1483-1539

Hercules and Achelous

c. 1535

Oil on canvas
c. 200 × 240 cm

Giovanni Antonio de' Sacchis, known as Giovanni Antonio da Pordenone, was born in about 1483 in Pordenone in the Italian region of Friuli. Around 1535 he executed two paintings which were certainly later treated as pendants, *Hercules and Achelous* and *Milo of Croton attacked by wild beasts*, and they appear to have been designed as such. They had similar, even identical, measurements and related subject-matter, in each case a man wrestling with a wild animal or animals, and their compositions are arranged in such a way as to complement each other. The two pictures are of particular interest for their having passed through so many of the most distinguished European collections.

One of these two paintings, however, *Hercules and Achelous*, has not been seen since the latter part of the nineteenth century, although its appearance is recorded in two different engravings: by Patas in Jacques Couché's catalogue of the Orléans collection (that of the Duc d'Orléans called 'Philippe Egalité') published 1786-1808;[1] and, in the same sense as the Patas, by Gaetano(?) Venzo (d. 1843), where the landscape background is extended on all sides.[2] The other painting, *Milo of Croton attacked by wild beasts*, survives in the David and Alfred Smart Museum at the University of Chicago.

In the Greek myth of the Labours of Hercules the hero eventually triumphs against great odds over evil forces. A typical image of Hercules is the *Farnese Hercules*, an Antique sculpture discovered in 1540 and now in the Museo Nazionale Archeologico in Naples. It shows the two main attributes of Hercules, his club and a lion's skin which he won by slaying the Nemean lion – one of the Labours. The story of Hercules' fight with the river god Achelous is told in Ovid's *Metamorphoses* IX. Hercules and the river god Achelous were rivals for the hand of Deianira, the daughter of the river god Oemeneus, who are probably to be identified with two of the figures in the background of Pordenone's composition. During the fight Achelous transformed himself first into a snake and then into a bull, whereupon Hercules finally overcame him by breaking off his horn.

The measurements of both paintings were recorded in 1689 when they were in the collection of Queen Christina of Sweden (who died in that year), the *Hercules* being given as 8.5 × 9.5 '*palmi*', which closely compares with the 8.25 × 9.5 *palmi* recorded of the *Milo*.[3] The two paintings subsequently entered the collection of Philippe, Duc d'Orléans (d. 1723), in 1721. They were catalogued in that collection in 1727 by Du Bois de Saint Gelais and recorded as being on canvas and identical in size: 6 *pied* 1 *pouce* × 7 *pied* 1 *pouce*.[4]

The earliest record of them is in an inventory of 1648, when they were in the famous collection of Gian Vincenzo Imperiale (1582-1648) in Genoa, where the

Hercules and Achelous.
Engraving by Patas after lost painting of c. 1535 by Giovanni Antonio de' Sacchis, called Il Pordenone (c. 1483-1539).
Published in J. Couché, *Galerie du Palais Royal gravée d'après les tableaux des différentes Ecoles qui la composent*, Paris, 1786-1808

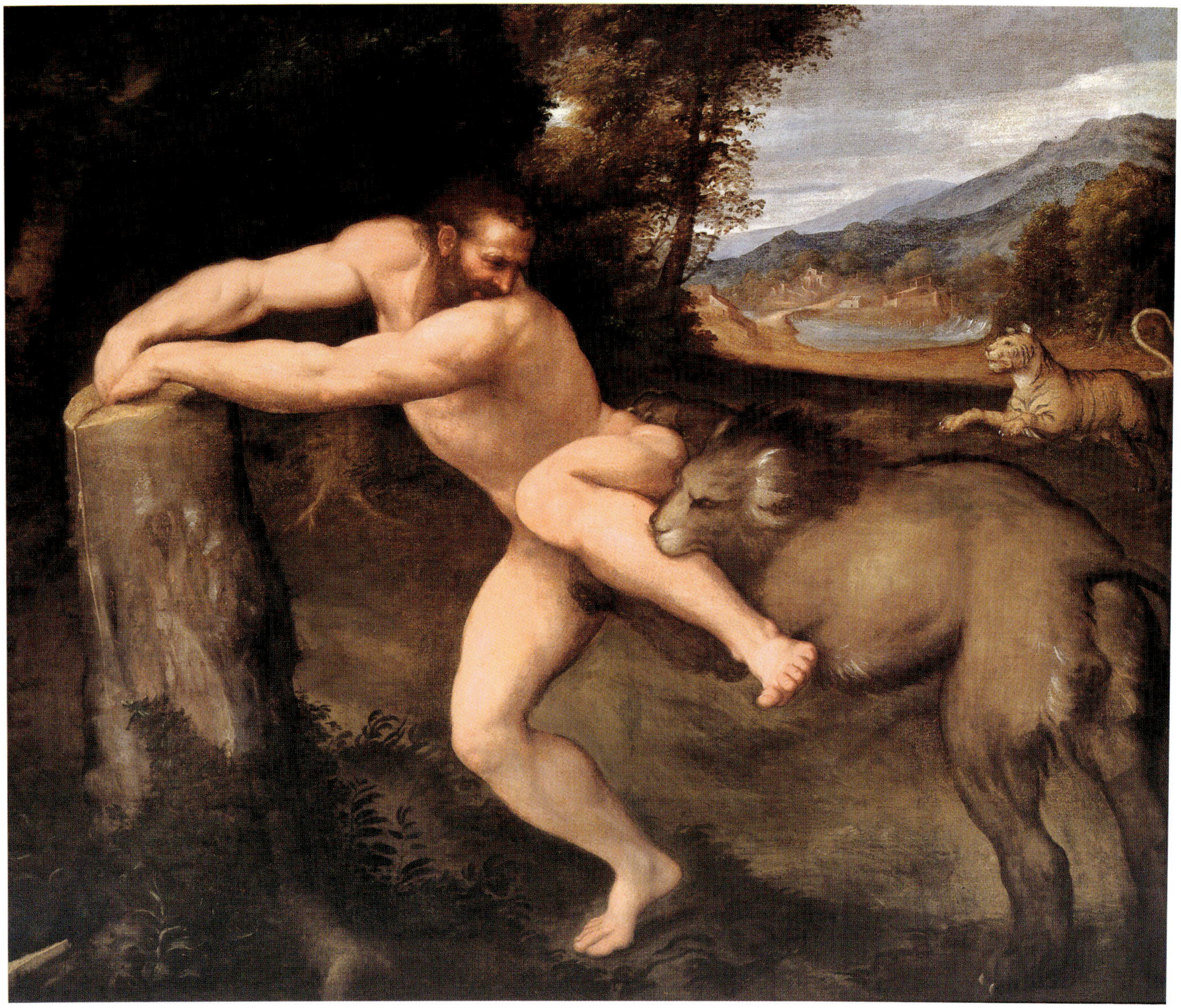

Milo of Croton being attacked by wild beasts by Pordenone, 1534-6.
Oil on canvas, 204.5 × 238.1 cm.
The David and Alfred Smart Museum of Art, University of Chicago, purchase, the Cochrane-Woods Collection 1975.31

Hercules appears with an attribution to Luca Cambiaso. It is, however, listed immediately after the *Milo*, which is properly given to Pordenone, and the two pictures are again recorded as identical in size, 8 × 9.5 *palmi*.[5] They were also framed in identical fashion, in the carved and gilded Genoese frames which Imperiale had had made for this collection, and which are described as such in the Queen Christina inventory.[6] In that inventory, the two pictures were both attributed to Pordenone, but although the pictures appear together in other inventories, evidently as pendants, the *Hercules* was attributed to another artist as early as 1648, as noted above. This latter attribution, to Luca Cambiaso, was repeated in an intervening inventory, that of Francesco Maria Balbi, in 1665, who acquired fifty-nine pictures from Imperiale's heir Francesco Maria Imperiale at a sale on 25 August in that year. This list, of the pictures Balbi bought, was drawn up on 2 September 1665 and records the two pictures one after the other: 'Milone del Pordenone/Ercole del Cambiaso'.[7]

Queen Christina had evidently been interested in the Imperiale collection for some little time before this date, and she lost no time in having an emissary contact Balbi with a view to buying some of his pictures.[8] She showed herself chiefly interested in more or less Venetian works, but also based her selection on the choice previously made by the painters Giovanni Benedetto Castiglione, called 'il Grecchetto' (1610?-1665?), and Domenico Fiasella, called 'il Sarzana' (1589-1669), both of whom had known Gian Vincenzo Imperiale well, and who had been engaged together especially with Grecchetto's brother Salvatore Castiglione (*c.* 1622?-after 1676) in trying to sell part of the collection to Carlo Gonzaga II, Duke of Mantua.[9]

Grecchetto and Sarzana had selected thirty-seven works for the Duke from Gian Vincenzo Imperiale's collection, and it is noticeable that only one of the two paintings by Pordenone, the *Milo*, appears on the list of this selection which Grecchetto sent to the Duke of Mantua's Chancellor, Conte Carlo Bulgarini, on 22 October 1661.[10] Grecchetto also wrote to the Duke himself the same day, stressing the need to move swiftly, because the Imperiale heir, Francesco Maria, needed money and was also agitated over a feud with his brother, Giovanni Battista (who had not been left any works of art). He noted that there were many other 'marble statues and other pictures which because of the lack of time I have not been able to list as I said I would. However, the essential point consists in laying hands on the 37 listed pieces'. If the Duke acquired specifically these thirty-seven works, Grecchetto asserts, he would create a gallery without equal in Italy, and one fit to recapture the vanished glories of the great Gonzaga collection – which had been sold in 1627-8.[11]

This last remark was a telling touch, since to re-establish a great Gonzaga collection was precisely the aim of Carlo II; but it was not to be. For various reasons, partly the price demanded by Francesco Maria Imperiale, who had also hoped sell more of the works in one go, the lengthy negotiations did not succeed. On 2 March 1664, for example, the pictures chosen eighteen months earlier had still not been sent to Mantua, and the sale finally lapsed with the death of the Duke in 1665.[12] The pictures were then formally put up for sale, a move which required the assent of the Genoese Senate, and Balbi was able to acquire fifty-nine of them. Queen Christina then bought forty of these in 1667, among them, evidently, the *Hercules* as well as the *Milo*. In fact, she somehow or other also acquired at least three other works from the Imperiale collection, including the portrait of Gian Vincenzo Imperiale by Van Dyck, perhaps by negotiating simultaneously with the Imperiale heir directly.[13]

Gian Vincenzo Imperiale, being both a collector and a patron of the arts, seems likely to have bought the pictures rather than to have inherited them, although his source for them remains obscure. His father Gian Giacomo, a Doge of Genoa, was not noted for having a distinguished art collection but Gian Vincenzo's collecting, in contrast, was lauded by Grecchetto, who specifically states that he had acquired his pictures himself over a long period of time:

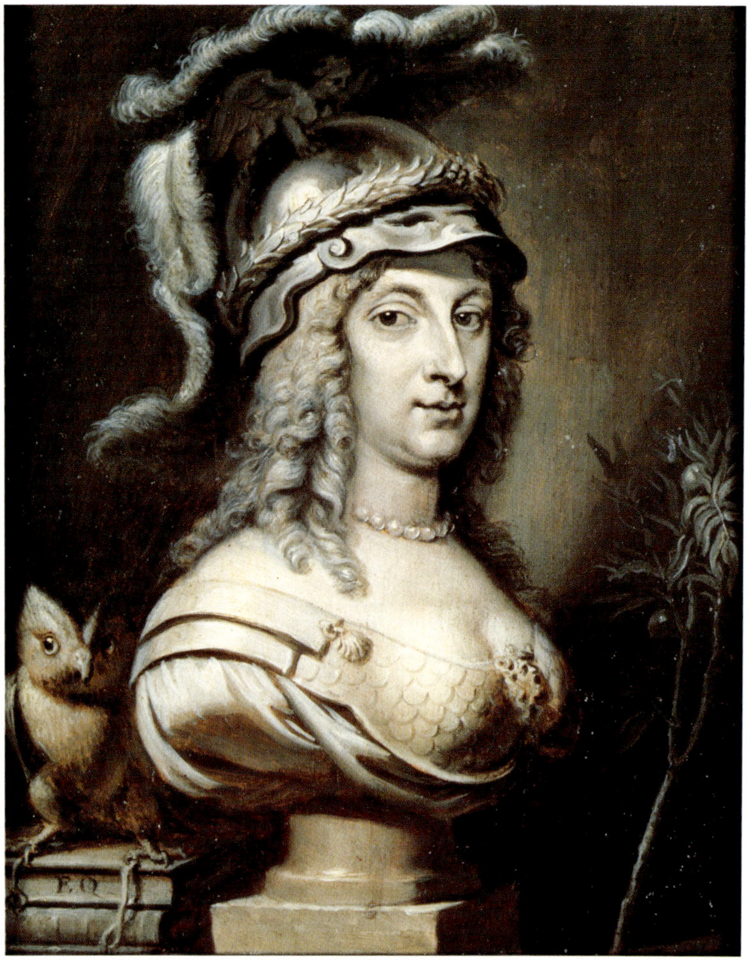

Allegorical portrait of Queen Christina of Sweden.
Musée de la Chartreuse, Douai

Basta il dire che questa e raccolta fatta con lungo corso d'anni da Giovanni Vincenzo Imperiale, cavaliere eminente in lettere, opulente in oro et quello che piu l'onora di ottimo gusto nella pittura. ('Suffice it to say that this is a collection made over many years by Giovanni Vincenzo Imperiale, a gentleman eminent in letters, of great wealth and, what is more, of the finest taste in painting.')

He then adds, with a distaste that he reveals elsewhere in his correspondence:

Tutto all'opposito del presente Francesco Maria suo figlio. ('All very much the opposite of this son of his, Francesco Maria.')

Gian Vincenzo had indeed been a remarkable collector and patron. He was, for example, in 1601-3, one of the very first in Italy to commission work from Rubens, at the time of Rubens's visit to Italy, when he himself, Gian Vincenzo,

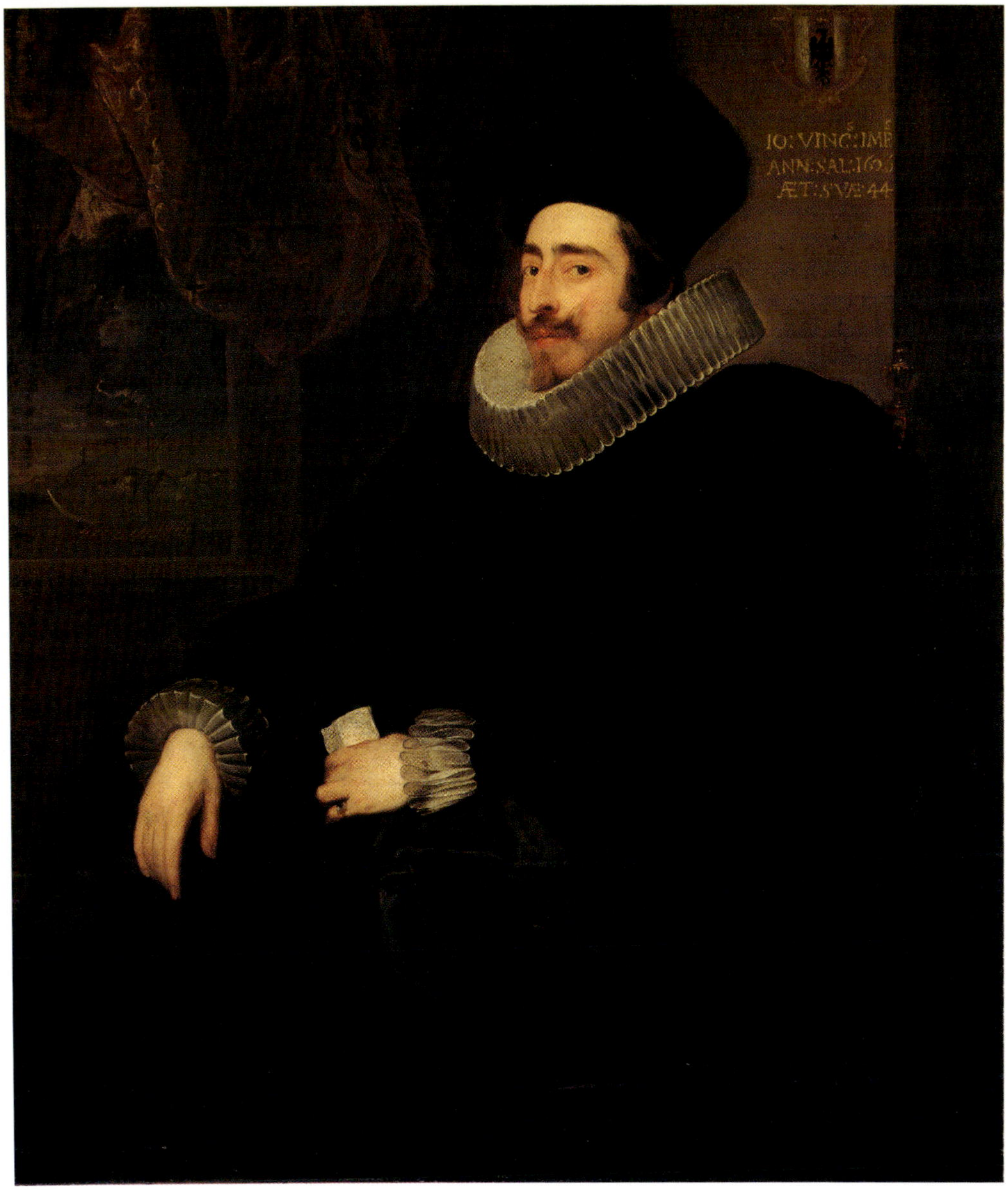

was barely twenty years old. He subsequently had himself painted at least twice by Van Dyck (full length, Brussels; three-quarter length, National Gallery of Art, Washington, DC); and his second wife, Brigida Spinola, is herself recorded in one of Rubens's most celebrated portraits of an Italian sitter (National Gallery of Art, Washington, DC).

Gian Vincenzo Imperiale (1582-1648) by Anthony van Dyck (1599-1641), 1626.
Oil on canvas, 127 × 105 cm.
National Gallery of Art, Washington, DC, Widener Collection

Following the record of the two pendant pictures by Pordenone in the Imperiale collection, their history can be traced quite clearly until the nineteenth century and, in the case of the *Milo*, up to the present day. When Queen Christina died in Rome on 19 April 1689, she left her entire picture collection to her long-time friend, Cardinal Decio Azzolino, who survived her by only a couple of months. Azzolino's heir was his nephew, the Marchese Pompeo Azzolino, who sold the collection to Prince Livio Odescalchi, the nephew of Pope Innocent XI. Prince

Livio Odescalchi was a soldier, the commander of the papal forces and a passionate art lover. Enriched by his family connection to the Pope, he was able to acquire the Queen Christina/Cardinal Azzolino pictures and immediately the Odescalchi collection ranked amongst the most important in Rome. When Livio Odescalchi died childless in 1713 – he had remained a bachelor all his life – the collection passed to two relatives, his nephew Livio Baldassare Odescalchi and Cardinal Benedetto Odescalchi, who wanted to sell the collection.

Livio Odescalchi had enlarged the collection considerably and added thousands of drawings to it, and only a few buyers in Europe could afford a collection of this importance. The coffers of Louis XIV of France, for example, were empty from numerous wars but a possible buyer emerged in the person of his nephew Philippe d'Orléans (1674-1723), the son of the King's brother ('Monsieur'). During his uncle's lifetime, Orléans was not given any important political or military commissions precisely because of his close relation to the Crown, and instead he turned his interest to artistic, cultural and intellectual matters, and occasional outbursts of notorious intemperance.[14] On Louis XIV's death in 1715, however, Orléans, *faute de mieux*, became Regent, for Louis XV was only a child of six, although the actual upbringing of the little King was carefully placed in more sober hands. Despite his scandalous private life under the Regency, Orléans proved himself faithful to the Crown, while continuing to add to his already considerable art collection.

His collecting activities brought him into contact with Pierre Crozat (1665-1740), a rich banker,'*amateur et curieux*' in art.[15] Crozat arrived in Rome in November 1714 with a brief from Philippe to acquire the Odescalchi pictures, and he spent the first six months familiarising himself with the pictures and the personalities of the sellers. Despite Crozat's efforts, the sale progressed slowly, as the Odescalchi insisted on a very high price. Finally, eight years after the negotiations had begun, the paintings were sold to the Duc d'Orléans in 1721, and duly appeared in the catalogue prepared by Du Bois de Saint Gelais in 1727.

On the death of the Regent in 1723, the paintings went to his son Louis, who sold some, especially nudes, which he thought offensive: he even attacked Correggio's *Io* with a knife.[16] The collection passed in turn to his son Louis-Philippe, a collector of medals and gems. Finally, the collection reached Louis Philippe Joseph, 5th Duke of Orléans (1747-93), 'Philippe Egalité', who in 1787 sold the gem collection to Catherine of Russia. In the same year, with a second, larger, sale in view, he commissioned a survey of his pictures, which then numbered 479. Philippe Egalité was not interested in art but in politics and gambling, and despite his immense wealth, he was constantly in debt, meanwhile harbouring the idea that he could become King or Regent after the deposition of his cousin Louis XVI. For this subversive purpose he corrupted a large part of the political establishment in France, which cost him an additionally great sum of money, and he sided with the Revolution – hence 'Egalité'. He himself, however, was executed shortly after the King in 1793.

Before his death, the sales of his pictures had progressed, beginning in 1791. The Dutch and Flemish pictures went to Thomas Moore Slade, acting on behalf of Lord Kinnaird and others; the French and Italian works went to the Belgian banker Viscount Edouard de Walckiers (or Walquiers) of Brussels, a man as politically subversive as Orléans. Walckiers almost immediately – without waiting for the shipment of the canvases – sold the collection on to a relative, the banker

Comte Laborde de Méréville. The *Hercules and Achelous* and the *Milo* were among those paintings.

The Dutch and Flemish paintings were sold off in London in April 1793. By 1798 Laborde de Méréville had sold the French and Italian works to Jeremias

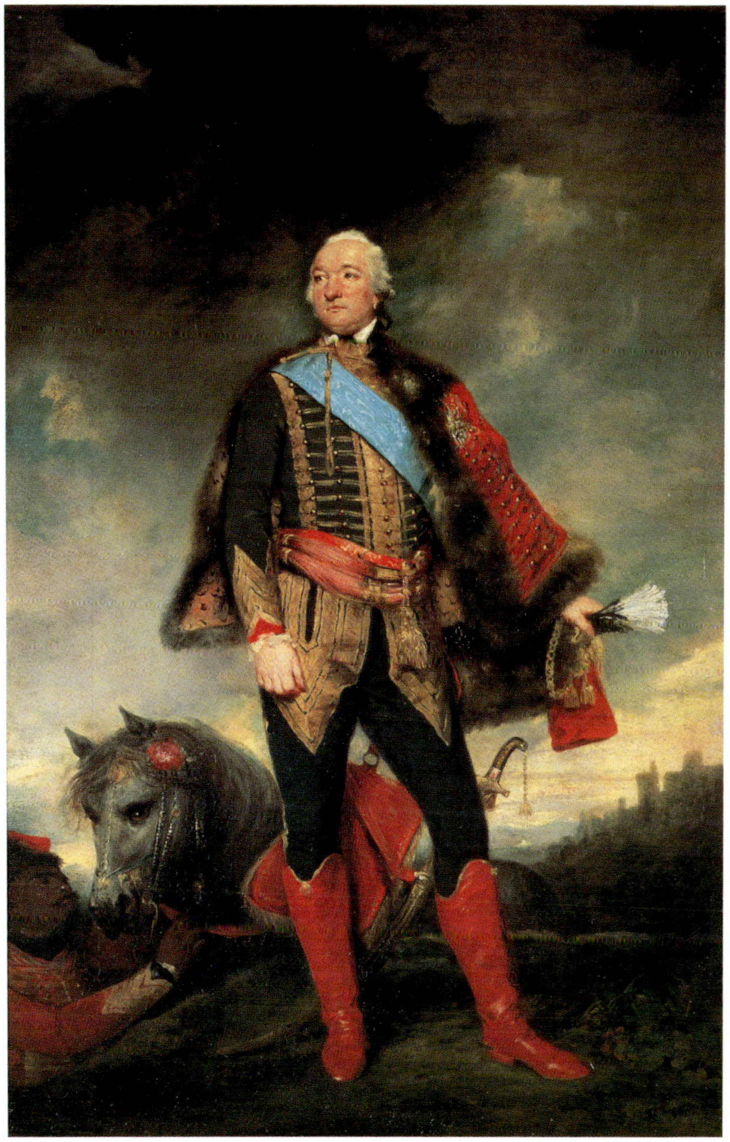

Louis Philippe Joseph, Duc de Chartres and Duc d'Orléans, called Philippe Egalité (1747-93)
after a portrait of 1785
by Sir Joshua Reynolds (1723-92),
perhaps by Richard Evans
(1784-1871), *c.* 1831.
Oil on canvas, 67 × 43 cm.
Musée Condé, Chantilly

Harman, an English banker and merchant, for £40,000.[17] The dealer Michael Bryan, acting on behalf of a syndicate of English aristocrats headed by the Duke of Bridgewater, bought the collection from Harman for £43,500.[18] He then conducted a sale at 'Mr Bryan's Gallery, No. 88 Pall Mall', which lasted from 26 December 1798 until 31 July 1799. The pictures that were on view in this sale in London sold very slowly and some not at all, and at the sale as such the members of the Bridgewater syndicate finally paid out £48,228 but only took £34,617. The important aspect of the operation from their point of view was that they had previously chosen outstanding works for their own collections.[19]

In 1800, when the 'rump' of the Orléans collection began to be sold at Christie's (a further sale, by Coxe, Burrel, & Foster, took place in 1802-3), *Hercules and Achelous* and *Milo* were sold to John Bligh, 4th Earl of Darnley (1767-1831),

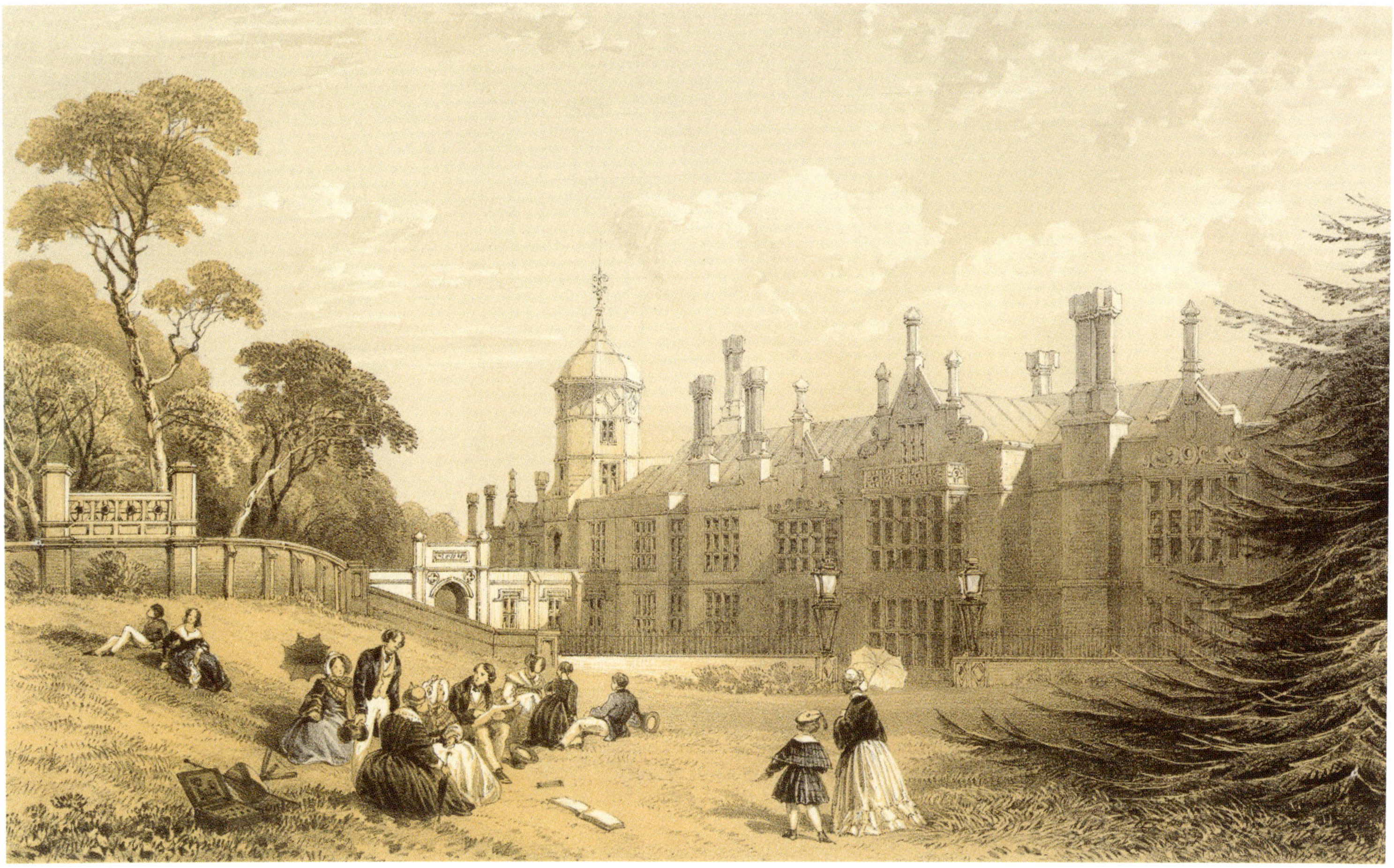

Cobham Hall, seat of the Darnley family

from S.C.Hall, *The Baronial Halls and Picturesque Edifices of England*, 1848

who had already bought several Venetian paintings from the Orléans collection, and they went to the Darnley family home of Cobham Hall. Both pictures were listed there in 1824 by William Buchanan in his record of works which had entered England after the French Revolution.[20] The two pictures continued to remain together at Cobham, where Waagen mentions them in 1854.[21]

At this point, the commonly accepted sequence of the provenance needs to be revised in the light of new, hitherto unpublished, evidence, which also introduces into the history a distinguished collector whose achievement has been underestimated. It is usually held that the *Milo* and the *Hercules* reappeared as contiguous lots in the sale of Mr.R.P.Roupell on 25 June 1887, as lots 82 and 83 respectively.[22] The *Milo* can be traced further, and was in the Honourable Society of Lincoln's Inn sale at Sotheby's on 18 December 1946 (lot 91) which reads:

The property of the Honourable Society of Lincoln's Inn
No 91 Giorgione
Milo of Croton torn by lions
80″×98″
From the collection of Queen Christina of Sweden
From the collection of the Regent Philippe, Duc d'Orleans
See Dubois De Saint Gelais, 'Description des tableaux du Palais Royal', 1737 [=1727]
From the collection of the Earl of Darnley, Cobham Hall.
From the collection of R. P. Roupell Esq.

It was this clue in the entry to a provenance of the *Milo* from the collection of Robert Prioleau Roupell (1798-1886) that apparently led Waterhouse to assume that both the pictures were the unidentified contiguous lots in the posthumous Roupell sale at Christie's of 25 June 1887:

Rubens School
82 A Legendary Subject – unstrained
83 The Companion [to the above].

In fact, these lots cannot have been either of the pictures in question because, as the records of Lincoln's Inn reveal, Roupell had already donated the *Milo* to Lincoln's Inn on 6 June 1870. The same record in the Inn's 'Black Book' contains a careful note from Roupell explaining how he came to acquire the work,[23] which was at the time of the sale of works of art from the Darnley collection, a sale which took place on 12 July 1862. Roupell, of whose collection seven pictures are now in the National Gallery, London (including Giovanni Bellini's *Blood of the Redeemer*), maintained the attribution to Giorgione that the *Milo* had borne in the Darnley and Orléans collections. He makes no reference to the *Hercules*, however, which had also appeared in that sale, and it seems clear that he did not buy it. Nor, since both these lots were, in fact, 'bought in' at Christie's, was the *Hercules* bought by anyone else; and this Darnley sale is, therefore, the last record of Pordenone's *Hercules*:

Pordenone
90 Hercules killing Achelous. From the Orleans Gallery...
Giorgione, Ascribed to
93 Milo of Crotona torn by lions. From the Orleans Gallery.[24]

At the Lincoln's Inn sale of 1946, the *Milo* is recorded as bought by 'Edge', and the records of Lincoln's Inn show that the Inn received an astonishing £500 for it. It was subsequently sold at Sotheby's on 21 March 1973, lot 51 ('Giovanni Antonio de Lodesanis, called Il Pordenone. Milo of Croton Attacked by Wild Beasts. 80¼″ × 97¼″, 204cm × 247cm') where it was bought by the London art dealer Christopher Gibbs; it was then bought by the Smart Museum, Chicago, from Gibbs in 1975.

NOTES

1 J. Couché, *Galerie du Palais Royal gravée d'après les tableaux des différentes Ecoles qui la composent...* , 3 vols., Paris, 1786-1808.

2 Charles E. Cohen, *The Art of Giovanni Antonio da Pordenone: Between Dialect and Language*, 2 vols., Cambridge, 1996, II, p. 708.

3 G. Campori, *Raccolta di cataloghi ed inventarii inediti*, Modena, 1870, publishes the 1689 *post-mortem* inventory of Queen Christina's collection: *Hercules*, p. 370; *Milo*, p. 373. See E. K. Waterhouse, 'Queen Christina's Italian Pictures in England' *in Queen Christina of Sweden, Documents and Studies*, Stockholm, 1966, pp. 372-5, p. 374, nos. 32, 33, citing Olof Granberg, *Drottning Kristinas Tavelgalleri på Stockholms slott och i Rom*, Stockholm, 1896, who published all the surviving inventories of the collection of Queen Christina. The measurements of the two pictures in question are given by Waterhouse as 82 × 98½″.

4 One 'pied' is about one English foot plus three-quarters of an inch and the 'pouce' approximately one inch. Du Bois de Saint-Gelais, *Description des tableaux du Palais Royal*, Paris, 1727, see Cohen, op. cit., p. 707. *Hercules and Achelous* is cat. 78 in Cohen (vol. II), pls. 653-4 (copies); see pp. 423, 456 (nn. 155, 158), 491, 492, 704, 705, 706, 707-9. Cohen points out that the Patas is likely to be the more accurate record of the missing painting. The *Milo* is cat. 77 (vol. II), pls. 644-7, colour pl. 31; see pp. 363, 370, 423-5, 455 (nn. 150, 151), 456 (nn. 152, 153, 155060), 491, 492, 663, 675, 701, 703-7, 708, 709, 722, 741, 742. For a discussion of the frescoes of similar subjects on the Palazzo Rorario in Pordenone see, e.g., pp. 705-6; it seems clear that any fresco was of *Milo* and that there was no accompanying *Hercules*.

5 See R. Martinoni, *Gian Vincenzo Imperiale, politico, letterato e collezionista genovese del Seicento*, Padua, 1983, p. 234: in the inventory the *Milo* is no. 90 and the *Hercules* no. 91; the *Milo* is valued at 500 '*scudi d'argento*' (and as such was one of the two most expensive items, the other being a Veronese), the *Hercules* at 300 *scudi*.

6 Ibid., pp. 247, 299-300. Martinoni quotes the descriptions of the two pictures as they appear in Du Bois de Saint Gelais, op. cit. at n. 4 above, and in the 1689 *post-mortem* inventory of Queen Christina's collection: see pp. 299-300.

7 Ibid., p. 219. In view of the fact that this attribution to a Genoese artist appears as early as 1648, and that the *Hercules* appears regularly to have been valued at a lower rate than the *Milo*, there is the faint possibility that it had been painted by Cambiaso to match Pordenone's *Milo*. Cohen, op. cit., sets out the argument in favour of the attribution to Pordenone of *Hercules and Achelous* on pp. 708-9.

8 Ibid., pp. 220ff.

9 Ibid., pp. 213ff. The intriguing correspondence between the Duke of Mantua, the Duke of Mantua's Chancellor and the Duke's agents in Genoa, the two Castiglione brothers and their colleague Il Sarzana, is in *Fonti per la Storia della Pittura, I-III, Serie Documentaria*, 'Lettere e Altri Documenti intorno alla Storia dell Pittura. Giovanni Benedetto Castiglione detto il Grecchetto. Giovanni Francesco Castiglione. Salvatore Castiglione', Genoa, 1971-5 [Part III, Monzambona], vol. I, pp. 55ff.

10 Ibid., pp. 54-6.

11 Ibid., pp. 57-8.

12 Martinoni, op. cit., pp. 213ff.

13 Ibid., p. 221. The pictures that she did not acquire from Balbi remained in the Balbi house where they were recorded in the nineteenth century.

14 For his life see, for example, C. Revitt, *The Man who would be King: The Life of Philippe d' Orléans, Regent of France*, London, 1997.

15 During the seventeenth century the word '*collectioneur*' was not used in France and persons with Crozat's intentions and aspirations were called *amateurs* or *curieux* (equivalent to 'connoisseur')

16 The pieces of the painting were collected and repaired, with a replacement head by Prud'hon. Louis died in the monastery of Sainte-Geneviève, Paris, in 1752. Revitt, op. cit., pp. 289, n. 325.

17 For the sequence of events in the sale of the Orléans collection, see, for example, Jordana Pomeroy, 'The Orléans Collection: its impact on the British art world', *Apollo*, February 1997, pp. 26 ff.; D. Sutton, 'The Orléans Collection', *Apollo*, May 1984, pp. 362 ff. See also F. Haskell, *The Ephemeral Museum: Old Master Paintings and the Art Exhibition*, 2000.

18 See the 'memo of Agreement between Francis, Duke of Bridgewater, Frederick,

Earl of Carlisle, and George Earl Gower Sutherland', file J14/27, Castle Howard Archives (cited by Pomeroy, p. 31, n. 5: the reference is to George, Earl Gower, who subsequently became Marquis of Stafford and finally 1st Duke of Sutherland).

19 Pomeroy, op. cit., p. 30.

20 William Buchanan, *Memoirs of Painting with a Chronological List of the Importation of Pictures by the Great Masters into England since the French Revolution*, 1824, 2 vols., see vol. I. The *Milo* and the *Hercules* are respectively p. 126, p. 128. See also Hugh Brigstocke, *William Buchanan and the Nineteenth-Century Art Trade* [London], 1982.

21 G. F. Waagen, *Treasures of Art in Great Britain*, 3 vols., London, 1854, III (repeating Buchanan), *Hercules*, p. 19: the *Milo* is mentioned on the same page.

22 See Waterhouse, op. cit., p. 374 (nos. 23, 33).

23 Thanks are due to the Librarian of Lincoln's Inn for kindly furnishing this information.

24 The sale records show a reserve of 25 guineas against the *Hercules*, with a bid of just £1.15; the *Milo* carried a reserve of 20 guineas with a final bid of £10.15. Roupell therefore bought the picture after the actual sale

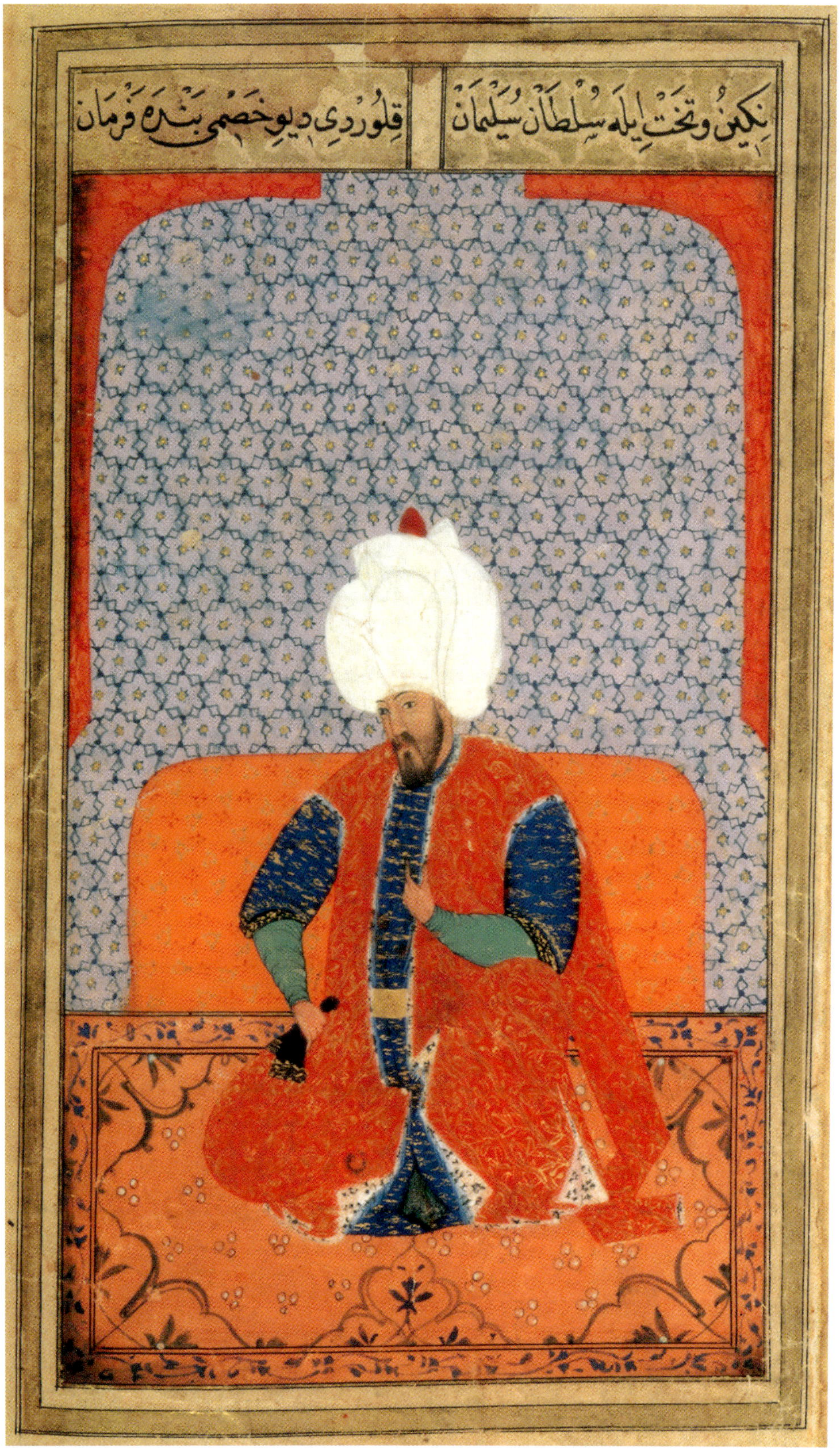
نكين وتخت ايله سلطان سليمان
قلوردى ديو خصمى بنده فرمان

Titian (Tiziano Vecelli)

c. 1485/90-1576

Suleyman the Magnificent

Probably oil on canvas
Gonzaga version, dimensions not known
Della Rovere version, *c.* 107 × 90 cm

Roxelana, wife of Suleyman

Probably oil on canvas
c. 98 × 76 cm

SULEYMAN THE MAGNIFICENT

Suleyman I, known as Suleyman the Magnificent, was born in 1494 in Trebizond, where his father Selim I had his court. He ascended the throne in 1520 and under his rule the Ottoman Empire expanded to its greatest extent. He died in 1566. Suleyman was the single greatest political and military threat to Europe during most of his reign and the forces that should have opposed his incessant pressures upon Europe – he laid siege to Vienna in 1529, for example – the Holy Roman Empire (the Habsburgs), the Papacy and the Kingdom of France (the Valois), were at odds with each other when not positively at war, and unable to present a united front. Indeed, Francis I, King of France, was at one time actually allied to Suleyman rather than with the rest of Europe against him.

Venice joined an alliance with the Pope and the Holy Roman Emperor Charles V against the Turks in 1538, and it is in the period 1537-9 that we find references to two separate portraits of Suleyman being created by Titian, the greatest painter in Venice. One of these portraits was painted for the Duke of Mantua and the other for the Duke of Urbino. The latter commission also included portraits of Charles V and Francis I, and Titian also painted a portrait of Pope Paul III (1534-49). Paul III usually attempted to remain neutral between France and the Empire, or at least to perform a balancing act between the great European powers. Only Titian, however, might be said to have been successfully neutral, for in due course he painted all the principal actors on the international stage, friend and foe alike. The commissioning of portraits of Suleyman raises interesting questions about the demand and supply of 'celebrity' portraits at this time. Titian's portraits of Suleyman, however, for both Mantua and Urbino, have disappeared.

These two portraits are recorded in the Gonzaga collection in Mantua and in the Della Rovere collection at the Duke of Urbino's court in Pesaro, respectively. They were commissioned within a very short time of each other by brothers-in-law, Federico Gonzaga, Duke of Mantua, and (probably) Francesco Maria della Rovere, Duke of Urbino, who was married to Federico's sister, Eleonora Gonzaga. Both portraits seem still to have been in existence around 1630. One disappeared

Suleyman the Magnificent.
Persian miniature, 25 × 15.5 cm (page).
British Library, MS. Add. 7880, fol. 73v

at the time of the sale of the Gonzaga collection in 1626-7; the other at the time of the transference of the Della Rovere collections to Florence as part of the inheritance of Vittoria della Rovere in 1631.

The Gonzaga/Mantua paintings almost all went to England when Charles I acquired them in 1627. In an inventory of the Gonzaga collection of 1627 the (presumed) portrait of Suleyman is mentioned, identified as 'Un quadro dipintovi sopra il ritrato di Selim re de' Turchi con corniche bianca L.30', where the reference to 'Selim' can be taken to have been mistaken. Not all the Gonzaga pictures went to London, however, for some were deliberately held back by Daniel Nys, the King's agent, and his associates, for their private purposes. It would seem that this portrait, with a modest price, and doubtful identification, was one of those not selected to go to into the collection of Charles I, and no further trace of it exists.

There is a 1631 inventory of the Della Rovere pictures, and it includes a painting of 'Soliman II' that can safely be identified with Titian's portrait of Suleyman I.[1] As mentioned above, the inventory is connected with the move of the Della Rovere pictures to Florence, and so it is in Florence that one might think to look for any further trace of this lost portrait of Suleyman. Other Titian pictures, with a similar provenance, especially examples that had belonged to Francesco Maria della Rovere, including the portraits of himself and his wife, of *'La Bella'*, and *The Venus of Urbino* (bought by Francesco's successor, Guidobaldo II), are all in Florence today. But there may have been less interest in what one might term the more 'political' portraits by Titian noted by Vasari in the 'guardaroba' at Pesaro as follows:

> There are in the guardaroba of the same Duke, by the hand of Tiziano... the portraits of Charles V, King Francis as a young man, Duke Guidobaldo II, Sixtus IV, Pope Julius II, Paul III... and Suleiman Emperor of the Turks, which portraits, I say, are by the hand of Tiziano, and most beautiful.[2]

Of those which Vasari mentions, *Sixtus IV*, *Julius II*, and *Paul III* appear to be in Florence today, while other pictures which *may* be identical with items in the Urbino collection are scattered elsewhere. Of the *Suleyman* there is no sign after 1631.

A curious aspect of these lost portraits of Suleyman is that Titian can never actually have seen his subject and there are numerous other instances of this practice on the part of the artist, including, for example, the portraits of the Popes Julius II and Sixtus IV noted by Vasari in Pesaro: the first was after Raphael and the second probably after a medal.[3]

THE GONZAGA PORTRAIT

The portrait of Suleyman that came into the possession of Federico Gonzaga was evidently a replica of a portrait of the 'Great Turk' that Titian had already made in 1538. An exchange of letters between Federico and his agent in Venice, Benedetto Agnello, shows that, while Federico had evinced interest in having a portrait of 'The Turk' as early as 2 March 1537, it proved no easy matter.[4] Federico was anxious that the portrait should be an accurate likeness, but when they tried to get the loan of a portrait from which to copy it was unexpectedly refused by the 'brute' ('bestia') who owned it.[5] Negotiations dragged on well into

Self-portrait after Titian (Tiziano Vecelli, *c.* 1485/90-1576). Engraving by Giovanni Brito, 1550. British Museum

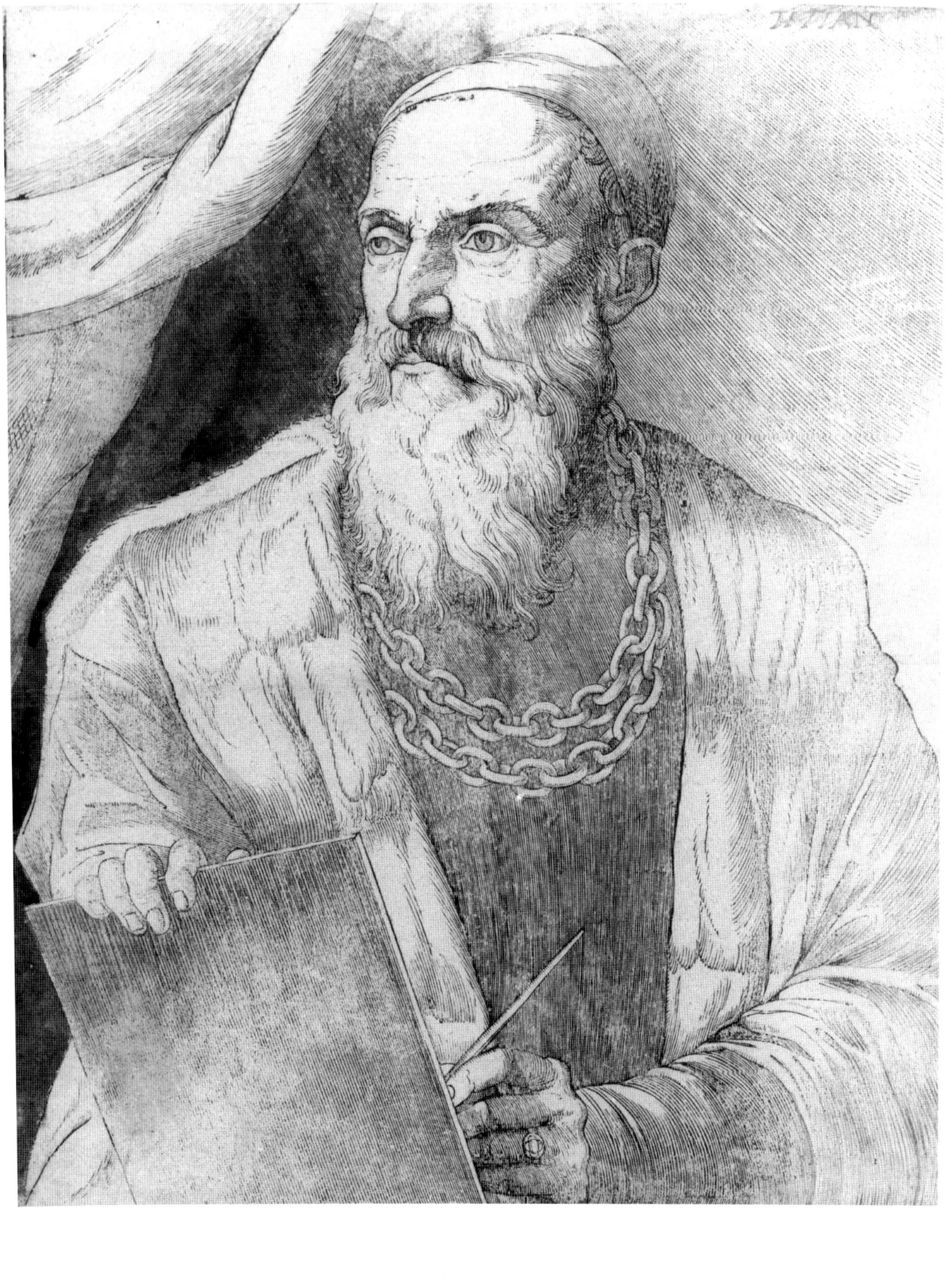

the following year, until the time came when Agnello reported on 23 August 1538 that Titian had now completed a portrait of 'the Turk', only as another commission, and that he had managed to obtain a likeness from a medal and 'from another portrait'. Agnello says that Titian is willing to do a version swiftly for Federico, and Federico replies on 27 August that Agnello should tell Titian that he would be glad to have such a portrait. Incidentally, the reference in the letters of 3 and 18 September (set out below) to 'emperors' refers to portraits of Roman emperors which Federico had already commissioned, but which he was still waiting for, even though the correspondence about them stretches back to 3 September 1537, when Titian was promising to deliver them within eight days. The procrastination was characteristic of Titian. The letters about the proposed replica of a portrait of Suleyman are as follows:

23 August 1538 (Benedetto Agnello to Federigo Gonzaga)
Because on previous occasions Your Excellency has shown interest in having a portrait of the Turkish gentleman, I thought I should tell you that Maestro Titian has now made such a likeness, taken, if I am not mistaken, from a medallion and another portrait which is said by many who have been to Constantinople to be very similar to the life, and it seems to be the very Turk in the flesh and that, if Your Excellency should desire a copy of it, I can report that Maestro Titian has said that he will do it immediately.

27 August 1538 (Federigo Gonzaga to Benedetto Agnello)
Be sure to press Titian for our paintings and also ask him on our behalf to do a portrait of the Turk, as he has offered to do, which I would be delighted to take.

3 September 1538 (Benedetto Agnello to Federigo Gonzaga)
I have given Maestro Titian to understand the intentions expressed by Your Excellency concerning the Emperors and the portrait of the Turk; he tells me that he will not fail.

18 September 1538 (Benedetto Agnello to Federigo Gonzaga)
Maestro Titian is getting on very well with the portrait of the Turk, and he also holds out hopes of soon finishing the paintings of the Emperors, but I suspect that it may take longer than he says.

20 September 1538 (Federigo Gonzaga to Benedetto Agnello)
We would like to have the portrait of the Turk which Titian is doing soon, so keep pressing him for it.[6]

THE DELLA ROVERE PORTRAIT

The Della Rovere portrait of Suleyman is generally assumed to have been commissioned by Guidobaldo II della Rovere, and to be later in date than the Gonzaga portrait. In fact, there is no direct evidence to support this assumption, which presumably springs from the fact that the first mention of the picture is in a letter of 20 June 1539 from Leonardi, Ambassador of Guidobaldo II in Venice, to the Duke:

I went to Titian's house yesterday, as all week he has been saying that he would have finished those three pictures of Caesar [i.e. the Holy Roman Emperor, Charles V], of France [i.e. the King of France, François I] and the Turk, which I consider to be very beautiful indeed.[7]

When Vasari mentions all three of these portraits among the other pictures and portraits in the 'guardaroba' of the Duke in Pesaro, he does not state who commissioned them. Although Guidobaldo was indeed a patron of Titian, so was his predecessor, Francesco Maria della Rovere, and the latter is a more likely person to have commissioned a portrait of Suleyman in the first instance. The reason is that on 31 January 1538 Francesco Maria was appointed commander-in chief of the forces of the alliance against Suleyman mentioned above, which was formed by the Emperor Charles V, the Pope, and Venice. Francesco Maria had already been given a house in Venice by the Venetian state on 1 December 1537, and on 8 February Venice formally joined the league, that is, shortly after Francesco had formally taken command.

Francesco's commissioning a portrait of Suleyman, in addition to those portraits of Charles V, Francis I and Paul III which were also recorded in Pesaro, may have marked his appointment as commander-in chief. Such a commission was directly related to the tradition of collecting images of 'uomini illustri', portraits of famous men, past and present, formed regardless of whether or not the individuals in question were on the same 'side' or not, politically or militarily, as the person who commissioned the pictures.[8]

When Francesco Maria took up his appointment at the start of 1538, he was already a keen patron of Titian. In 1536 he had commissioned portraits of himself and of his wife Eleonora Gonzaga, portraits which arrived in Pesaro in April 1538. At the same time, in 1536, he had also acquired from Titian the *Girl in a blue dress* ('*La Bella*', Pitti, Florence). In 1532 he had commissioned three pictures from Titian, a *Christ*, a *Hannibal* and a night *Nativity*. The *Hannibal* sufficiently suggests his interest in assembling portraits of 'uomini illustri', and Vasari records an intaglio of Hannibal in the ducal guardaroba at Pesaro.[9]

Guidobaldo II, however, succeeded Francesco abruptly following the latter's unexpected death on 22 October 1538. At this juncture, earlier portrait commissions of Francesco's would, in the nature of things, still be outstanding. They would have remained uncompleted, or uncollected, at the artist's studio. The length of time between the commissioning of Francesco Maria's own portrait in 1536 and its delivery in April 1538 is quite normal for a Titian commission, and rather shorter than was the case in many other instances. If Francesco Maria did indeed commission in 1538 the three portraits mentioned in 1539, they would not normally have been delivered before the year following that of the commission, and so the letter of 20 June 1539 could be seen as reporting an enquiry after them on behalf of Francesco Maria's successor, and not necessarily as referring to a commission by Guidobaldo himself.

THE SEQUENCE OF THE COMMISSIONS

Taking all the above factors into account, a rather different sequence from that generally assumed can be proposed. On 23 August 1538, as we have seen above, Agnello tells Federico Gonzaga that Titian has already done a portrait of the Turk. Agnello's reference could be to a portrait of Suleyman that was indeed started but not yet finished. The picture certainly intended for Della Rovere was reported as still not quite finished on 20 June 1539, and nor were the two portraits mentioned together with it, those of Charles V and of Francis I. These three portraits, as already noted, make sense as a 'set', and specifically if commissioned by Francesco della Rovere in 1538. All three were later noted by Vasari in a 'political' group of portraits in the 'guardaroba' at Pesaro, which included three popes, one of whom, Paul III, was the key person at the time of Francesco Maria's appointment.

It is possible that Francesco Maria's brother-in-law Federico Gonzaga commissioned a portrait of Suleyman in the middle of 1538 *after* Titian had started on a similar commission for Francesco Maria. There is also evidence that Federico was indeed aware (as one would suppose to have been the case) of Titian's working for his brother-in-law, and that this work could interfere with his own requests for pictures. When Agnello writes to Federico Gonzaga on 18 September 1538, for example, about the likelihood of Titian's finishing the pictures of the emperors and of Suleyman, he concludes by saying that he thinks it will all take longer than Titian says, '... la causa e che il signor Duca d'Urbino lo mena seco a Pesaro, ove S.E., dice di voler andar questa settimano ad ogni modo'.[10]

When Agnello saw the portrait of Suleyman in August 1538, it was evidently still in the artist's studio, and Agnello states clearly that Titian has *just* made a portrait of Suleyman: '... ho voluto dire che M.Ticiano hora n'ha fatto uno cavato' ('I wanted to report that Messer Tiziano has now made a likeness'). Word had evidently got around about it, since people had already commented on its being true to life. It had not yet, however, been sold nor been delivered to whomever might have commissioned it. If it were indeed part of one commission of three related portraits from Francesco della Rovere, it might well not have been delivered before the other two – and within two months of this first mention of the Suleyman portrait Francesco Maria was dead.[11]

TITIAN'S SURVIVING PORTRAIT OF SULEYMAN

One of Titian's portraits of Suleyman still exists, but only as a portrait within a larger composition featuring other contemporary portraits, namely, *Ecce Homo* (Kunsthistorischesmuseum, Vienna, inv. no. 73), dated 1543. Here the turbanned Suleyman can be seen in profile at the right hand side, upon a horse, alongside a man in armour, also upon a horse, who can be identified as Alfonso d'Avalos, Marchese del Vasto, whom Titian separately portrayed (*Portrait with a page*, Axa Collection, on loan to the Louvre, *c.*1533; *The allocution of the Marchese del Vasto*, Prado, Madrid, 1540). In front and to the left of them can be seen the figure of the octogenarian Doge Pietro Lando. The reasons for this conjunction of portraits is that the Doge had concluded a peace with the Turks in 1540. The Marchese in turn had fought a victorious expedition against the Turks at Tunis in 1535; was the Emperor's governor at Milan, 1538-46 (when he died); and had attended the coronation of Doge Pietro Lando in 1539. The picture was commissioned by the Flemish merchant resident in Venice, Giovanni d'Anna (Van Haanen). [12]

Suleyman is shown in this portrayal in profile to the left, with moustache, no beard, but with a face sufficiently lined to suggest his correct age at the time (forty-nine or so). It seems possible that this image is connected with an equestrian portrait by Titian (perhaps a preparatory painting) recorded as having been seen, in Titian's house, by Nicolò Barbarigo, who wrote from Constantinople to the Signoria of Venice on 20 September 1578 to that effect:

> Io vidi altre volte nella casa di titiano, fra le relequie delle sue pitture, un ritratto di Solimano a cavallo in una tela vecchia e negletta, che si potra haver facilmente, et intendo che e molto simile.[13]

It seems probable, in view of the closeness in dates, that the missing portraits

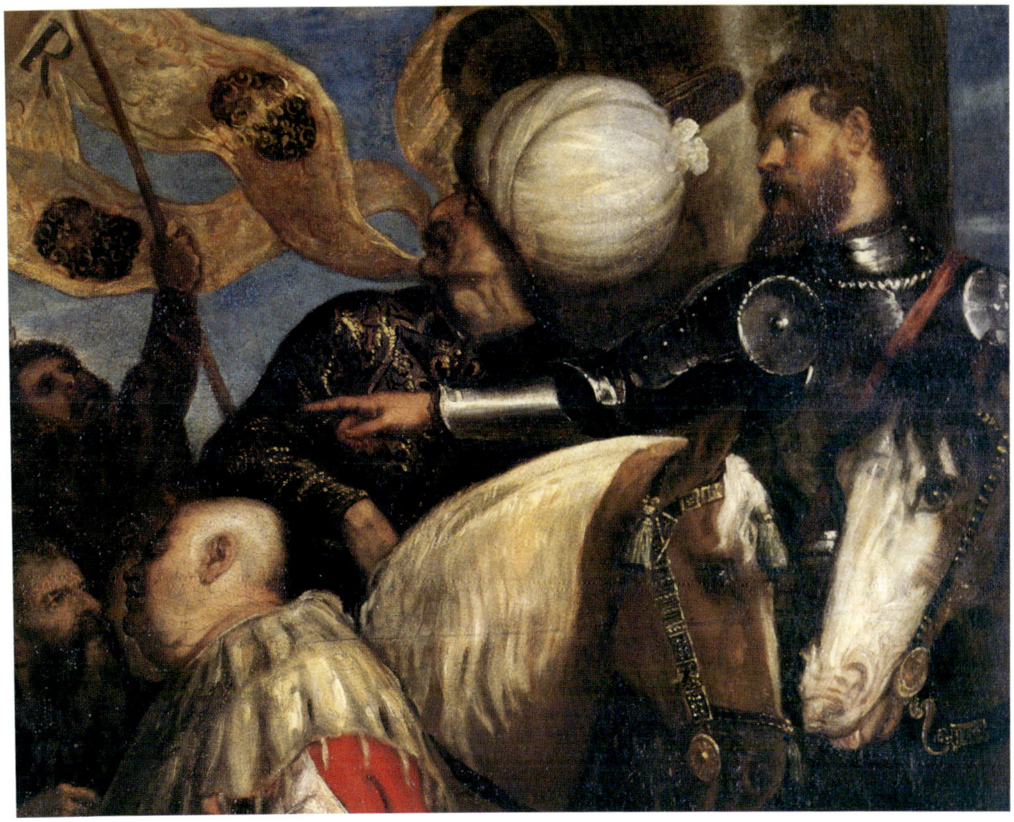

Detail of *Ecce Homo* by Titian, 1543, showing profile portrait of Suleyman the Magnificent. Oil on canvas, 242 × 361 cm. Kunsthistorischesmuseum, Vienna

would have shown Suleyman much as he appears in the *Ecce Homo*. Titian might conceivably have 'aged' his subject between the two dates, i.e. 1538/9 and 1543, but in the *Ecce Homo* Suleyman also appears in profile, which accords with the statement of Agnello in 1538 that Titian had created his likeness by reference to a medal in the first place – because medals usually show features in profile – as well as to another painting.[14] Indeed, the extraordinary twisting pose of Suleyman in *Ecce Homo* suggests that Titian was unwilling to compromise the accuracy of a likeness derived from an authentic medal profile by extrapolating a three-quarter view. At the same time, there is a pleasing consonance between the *Ecce Homo* portrait and a Matteo Pagani woodcut of Suleyman published in Venice in *c.* 1550, the only significant difference being the later addition of a beard.[15]

A medal ascribed to Alfonso Cittadella ('Lombardi') could conceivably be that referred to by Agnello as having provided the model for Titian's first portrait of Suleyman. It shows the turbanned head of a young man and bears the cast inscription '*SOLYMAN IMP TUR*',[16] and Alfonso evidently knew Titian well.[17] Donati identified the prototype on which both the medal and related engravings were based as a woodcut, Cod. Chigiano G.II.39, Bibl. Vaticana, vol. IX, fol. 155, which survives as an illustration inserted into the section of Sigismondo Tizio's *Historiae Senenses* covering the years 1520-25.[18] This source, however, only accounts for an early image of Suleyman as he appeared around 1520, and not for Titian's portrayal of him in maturity, and so Titian's subsequent recorded consulting of 'another painting' evidently came into play in order to create the lost portraits.

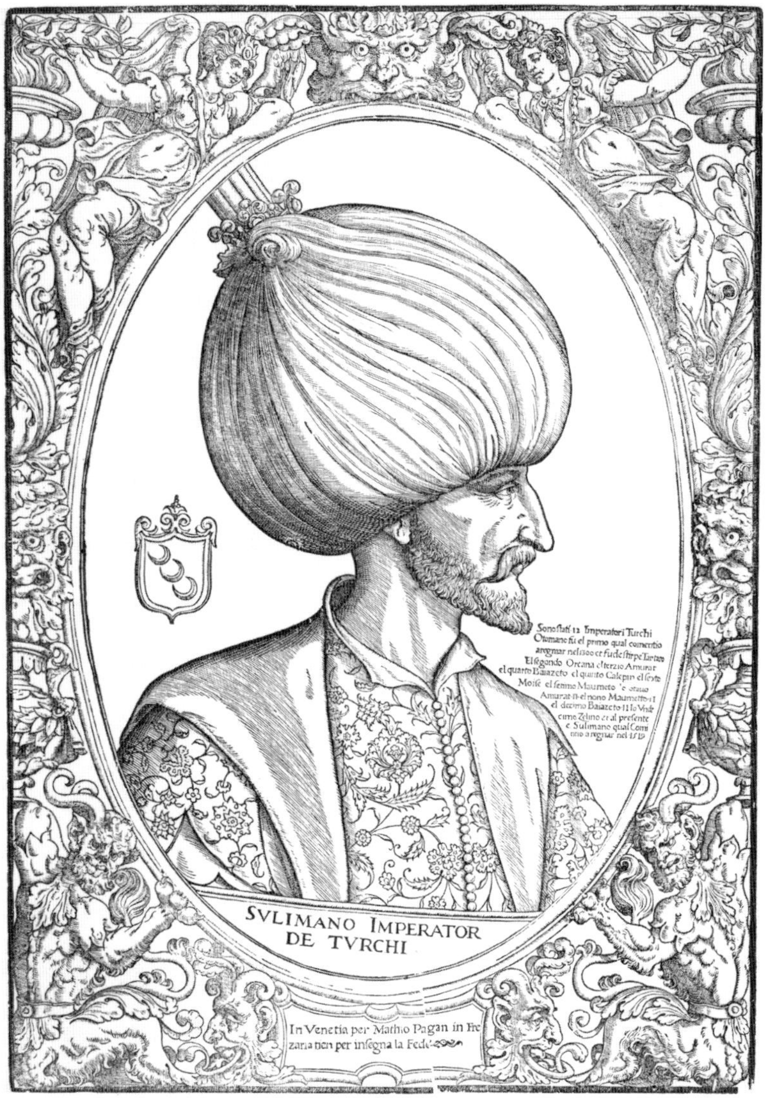

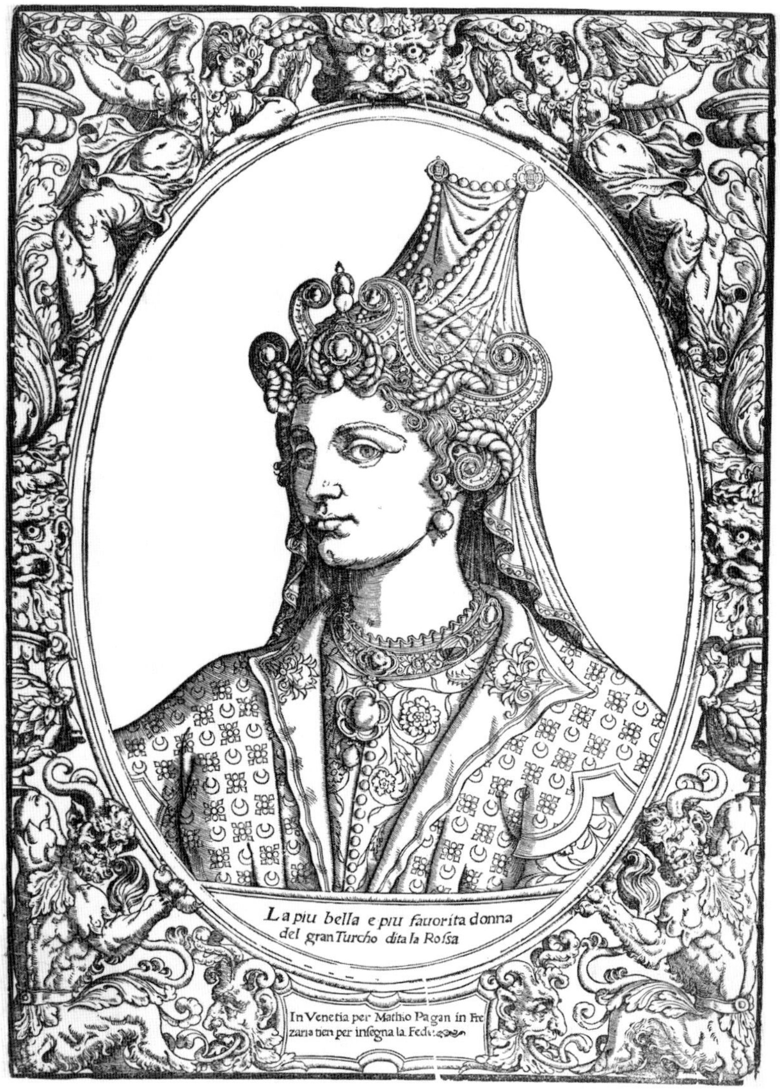

Suleyman the Magnificent.
Anonymous woodcut published by Mathio Pagani, Venice, *c.* 1550, 52.5 × 36.1 cm.
British Museum

Roxelana.
Anonymous woodcut published by Mathio Pagani, Venice, *c.* 1550, 51.9 × 35.8 cm.
British Museum

ANOTHER LOST PORTRAIT OF SULEYMAN BY TITIAN

In addition to the two recorded pictures discussed above, there was evidently at least one other individual portrait by Titian of Suleyman. It is described in a letter of Bishop Ippolito Capilupi to Cardinal Ercole Gonzaga of 8 March at some point before 1563 (the year of the Cardinal's death) to the effect that he was sending 'a small picture with a portrait of the Turk by Titian':

To the Cardinal of Mantua

In the last few days Titian has given me a small picture which is a portrait of the Turk, done by his hand, and has asked me to be so good as to send it to your Excellency. I had it dispatched to Ambassador Tridapale for this purpose, and I believe that he should have received it by now. The same Maestro Titian desires that your Excellency should do him the favour of intervening with the Marquess of Pescara either by letters or by word of mouth if your Excellency comes to Trent, as it is said that you will do, for him to ensure that in Milan Titian's annual pension of 200 scudi is paid, which Charles V of happy

memory gave him; it is now two or three years since he last received anything from this pension. I know that your Excellency loves Maestro Titian for his virtues and for the services which he has performed, which merit this favour from your courtesy without any other reason, but nevertheless it will also be a singular favour to me and will demonstrate to Titian that I have been of service to him with you in this transaction as the good friend that I am to him. I humbly kiss the hand of your Excellency.
Venice, 8 March 1569 [*sic*] [19]

It is possible that the appearance at least of this picture is recorded in a picture formerly in the Marinucci collection in Rome, which was sold at Christie's 24 March 1961 and bought by Agnew's (for £7,350). This latter picture measures $28\frac{1}{2} \times 24$ inches (about 72×61 cm), which is close to the standard canvas size for a bust-length portrait (as this is) of around 30×25 inches. It is not certain that the Bishop would definitely refer to such a picture as 'small', although that may be the implication of similar contemporary references. Since the bishop's letter was prompted by his direct meeting with Titian, the authorship of the portrait he describes cannot be in doubt, and his correspondent, Cardinal Ercole Gonzaga, was himself very familiar both with Titian's work (he was himself one of Titian's patrons) and with the collection at Mantua: he was the brother of Federico (and of Eleonora, of course) and was twice regent at the Mantuan court.[20]

The *ex* Marinucci portrait, which is not accepted as autograph by Wethey,[21] is closest to the Vatican Library woodcut of Suleyman referred to above: the collar and the pattern on the robe and the buttons all appear to reflect an element in the print. As Donati observed, the image it offers of Suleyman shows him as he appeared in about 1520; most significantly, however, it does not reflect Titian's style of about 1538 and cannot therefore reflect the appearance of either of the two principal missing portraits, from the Gonzaga and Della Rovere collections.

There is another portrait, in a Titianesque style, of Suleyman (Budapest, Nemzeti Museum, Historiche Bildergalerie, no. 438), which Wethey also identifies as not autograph.[22] It is sufficiently close, however, to the Titian style of portraiture for it to be taken into account. It is close to the Pagani woodcut of *c.* 1550, but in the reverse sense: the buttons, the collar and the over-garment, and the head-dress, all connect the two images. It is possible that Pagani's woodcut follows, if not this exact painting, then the original, and it is also possible that this missing original was by Titian. It also seems possible that Pagani's woodcut is intended to show Suleyman as slightly older than he appears in the Budapest canvas. The Budapest picture, however, is most unlikely to record the appearance of either the Gonzaga or the Urbino portrait, because it shows Suleyman with a beard, as does Pagani's woodcut. In 1543, however, just four or five years after the earlier two portraits of *c.* 1538, Titian showed Suleyman in the Vienna *Ecce Homo* not with a beard but only with a moustache. It is known that the older Suleyman had a beard,[23] and Titian would not have reversed this development.

ROXELANA, WIFE OF SULEYMAN THE MAGNIFICENT

Roxelana is the name by which Hürrem Sultan, the wife of Suleyman, was known in the West. He was devoted to her, and his feelings for her 'affected his actions deeply'.[24] It was not in fact usual for the Sultans to take legal wives, but Roxelana, who had been presented to Suleyman as a slave concubine, so captured his affections that she successfully insisted upon his first freeing her and then marrying

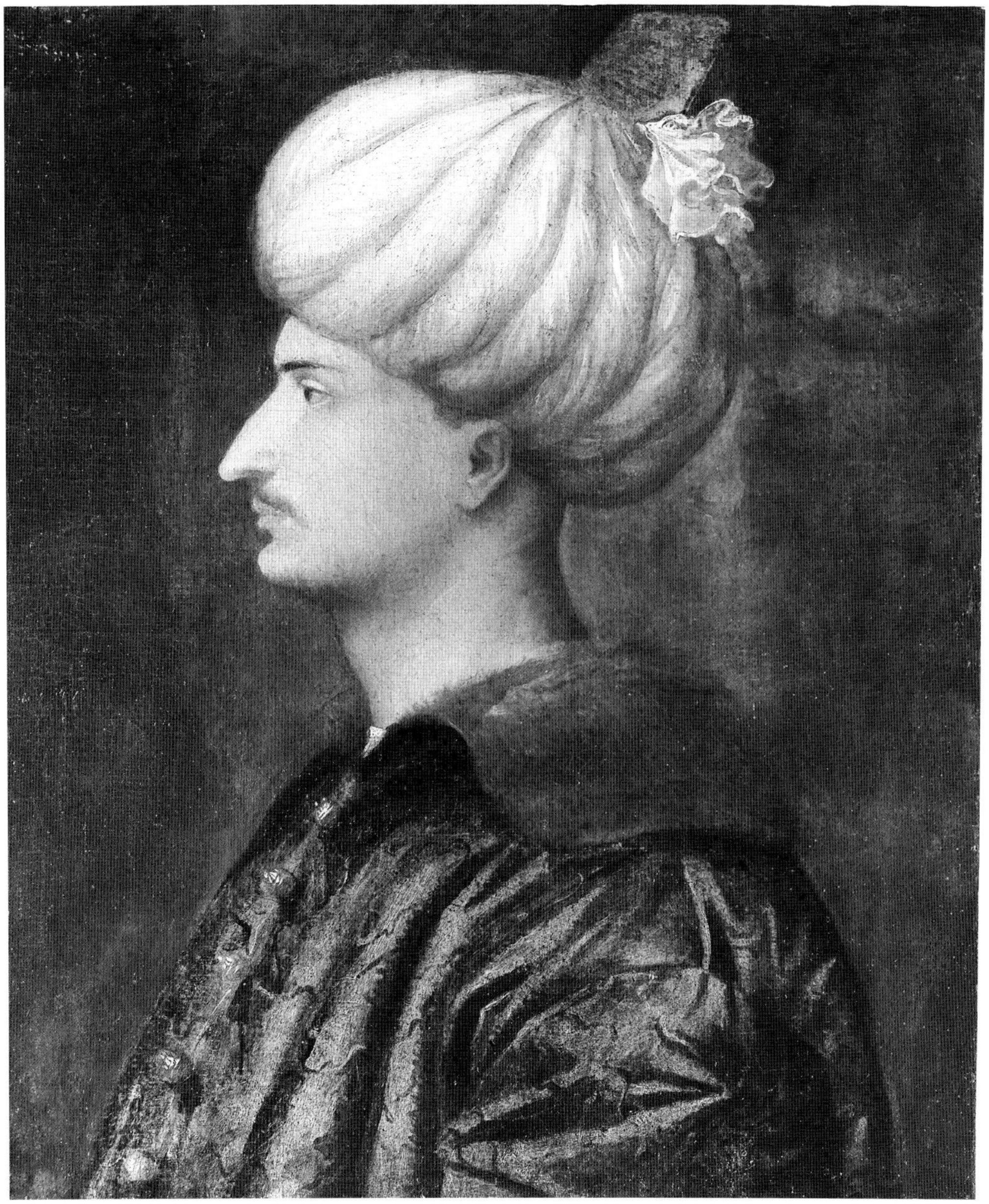

Suleyman the Magnificent, probably after Titian.
Oil on canvas, 72 × 61 cm.
Formerly in the Marinucci collection, Rome

her, by refusing him her favours until he did so. By 1526 she had borne him four sons and one daughter.

Vasari[25] records that Titian created a portrait of 'La Rossa', as she was also known, probably on account of her colouring as a 'Russian' or, more probably, a Ruthenian. Vasari notes, in the house 'at Venice' of the Danish sculptor Cattaneo, portraits by Titian, among others, of '... Rossa, wife of the Grand Turk, at the age of sixteen, and of Cameria, her daughter, with the most beautiful dresses and adornments'. The sculptor, 'our Danese' as Vasari calls him, was a close personal friend of Vasari[26] and helped him in research for the *Lives*, and so this information should be taken seriously. There are problems with this account, however, in

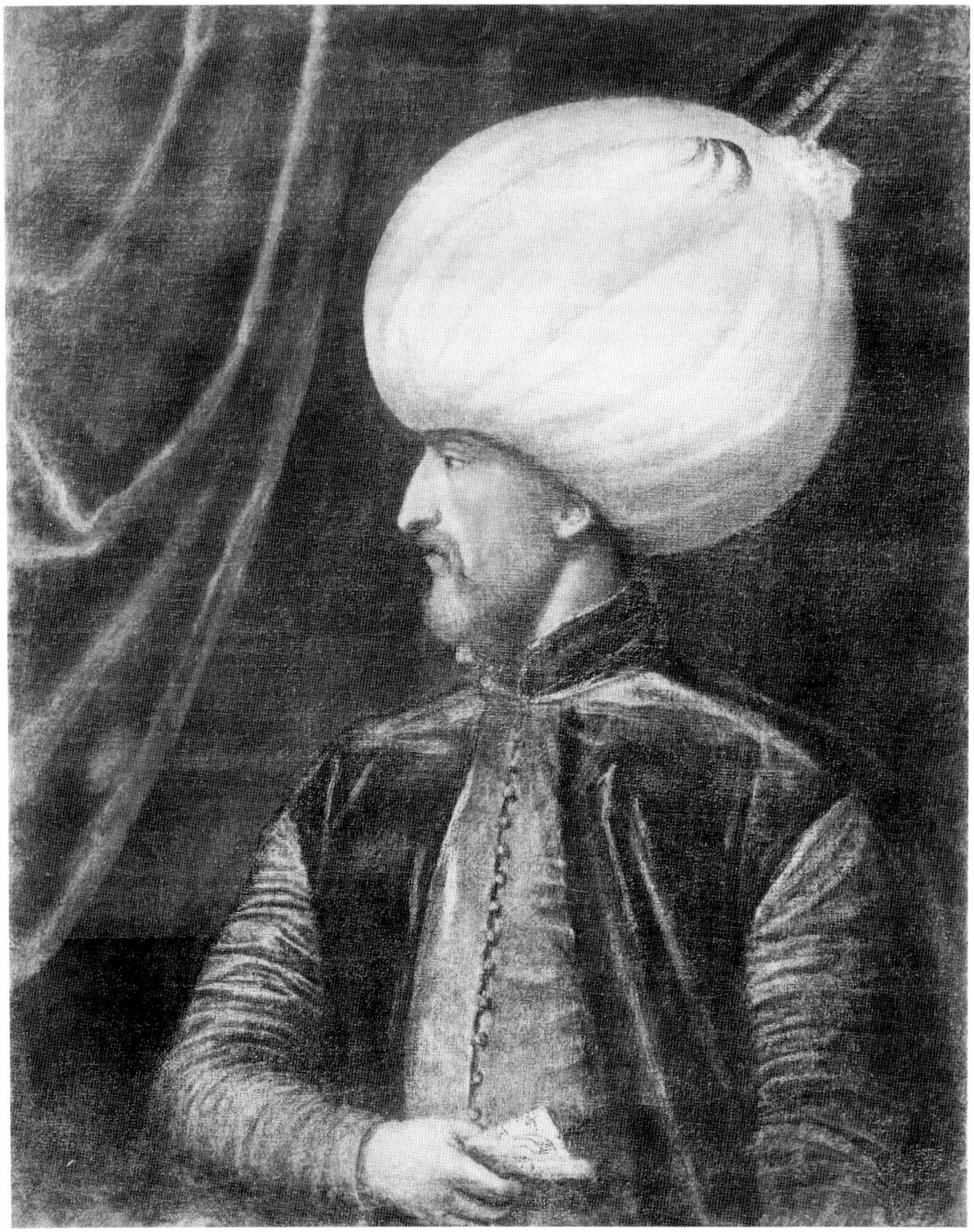

Suleyman the Magnificent after Titian.
Oil on canvas.
Nemzeti Museum, Budapest

that Roxelana's only daughter was called Mihrimah,[27] although that may not be an insuperable problem, given the strangeness to Italians of Turkish names and problems of orthography and transliteration.

It has been assumed that the portrait showed Roxelana with her baby in arms.[28] Since Roxelana herself is reported as only sixteen at the time the portrait was made, that is a reasonable supposition. There is no necessity to suppose, however, that Titian created his portrait at the same time. Throughout his career, Titian painted portraits after earlier records of people he sometimes never saw. There is a Matteo Pagani woodcut of Roxelana of about 1550, the pendant to the woodcut of Suleyman, which bears the inscription: *'La piu bella e piu favorita donna del gran Turcho dita Rossa*'. This too is an historical document rather than a contemporary representation, because by this date Roxelana would have been about forty-six whereas the woodcut shows a young woman.

There is a painting in Sarasota (John and Mable Ringling Museum) which appears to show the same sitter, and this latter picture, measuring 98 × 76 cm, is the best candidate for the lost portrait of Roxelana by Titian. The features are close to those of the sitter in the Pagani woodcut, but there appears to be general agreement that the picture is not an autograph work by Titian.[29] A detail of particular interest in it, however, is the presence of a marten at the sitter's hand[30] because comparison can be made with the presence of a marten-fur muff with gold and jewelled head in the portrait by Titian of Eleonora Gonzaga dated to autumn/winter 1536-7.[31] This jewelled muff was an accessory 'reserved for women of high lineage',[32] and so its use in the Sarasota picture suggests that the sitter was of high rank.[33]

The Sarasota picture is in the same sense as the Pagani woodcut, which would normally indicate that the painting is after the print. Print-makers were, however, perfectly capable of making a print in the same sense as a painting. And the pendant portrait of Suleyman published at the same time would also have had to be taken into account in presenting the image of Roxelana. What argues against a strict relationship between the Sarasota image and the woodcut is the considerable difference in the costume, where there is far more difference than is apparent between, for example, the *Suleyman* painting in Budapest and the related print.[34] The head-dress is markedly different between painting and print, for the print appears to show a distinct type in the details of its summit: the front of it is 'four-horned', which is apparently authentic in type.[35] The possibility is that a lost Titian (?) original may have inspired the woodcut, a painting which included distinctly Turkish features, but it is impossible to say whether that was the case.

Titian himself announced, in a letter of 11 October 1552 to Philip of Spain, that he was sending him two 'small' pictures, one of which was a 'Queen of Persia'.[36] The assumption is that this would have been a portrait of Roxelana, but the Sarasota picture discussed above, for example, in so far as its style can be directly related to that of Titian himself, does not look like a Titian of *c.* 1552, and so must be ruled out, and the picture that Titian sent to Spain must be considered lost. Hope, however, has suggested that the missing picture was probably not even a particular portrait, but 'was presumably one of those paintings of pretty girls in elaborate costume already so familiar from his [Titian's] oeuvre'. [37] Certainly, there was not much distinction made at the time between 'Persia' and 'Turkey', as a letter of 3 August 1559 from García Hernández to Philip II shows. In it Hernández says that he will send a small picture of by Titian of 'una Turca o Persiana hecho a su fantasia'. [38] In Spain Ponz saw a 'Sultana', in the palace of the Conde de Chinchón at Villaviciosa.[39] In a letter of 29 January 1569 Nicolò Stoppio, an agent of the Duke of Bavaria in Venice, told J.J.Fugger that Jacopo Strada had witheld a beautiful 'Pomona' by Titian for himself and had sent the Duke of Bavaria a much less handsome portrait by Titian of a 'Persian lady'.[40]

There was a Venetian fascination with all things to do with 'the Great Turk', which evidently included a taste for pictures of attractive young women in exotic dress, and so a number of associated works or copies exist from the general circle of Titian, and several of them have been put forward as possible portraits of Roxelana. Some are related quite closely to the Sarasota type; some of them, however, carry the name of Caterina Cornaro, partly because they exhibit wheels, Saint Catherine's

Roxelana, wife of Suleyman, sometimes attributed to Titian.
Oil on canvas, 97.8 × 76.2 cm.
John and Mable Ringling Museum, Sarasota, Florida

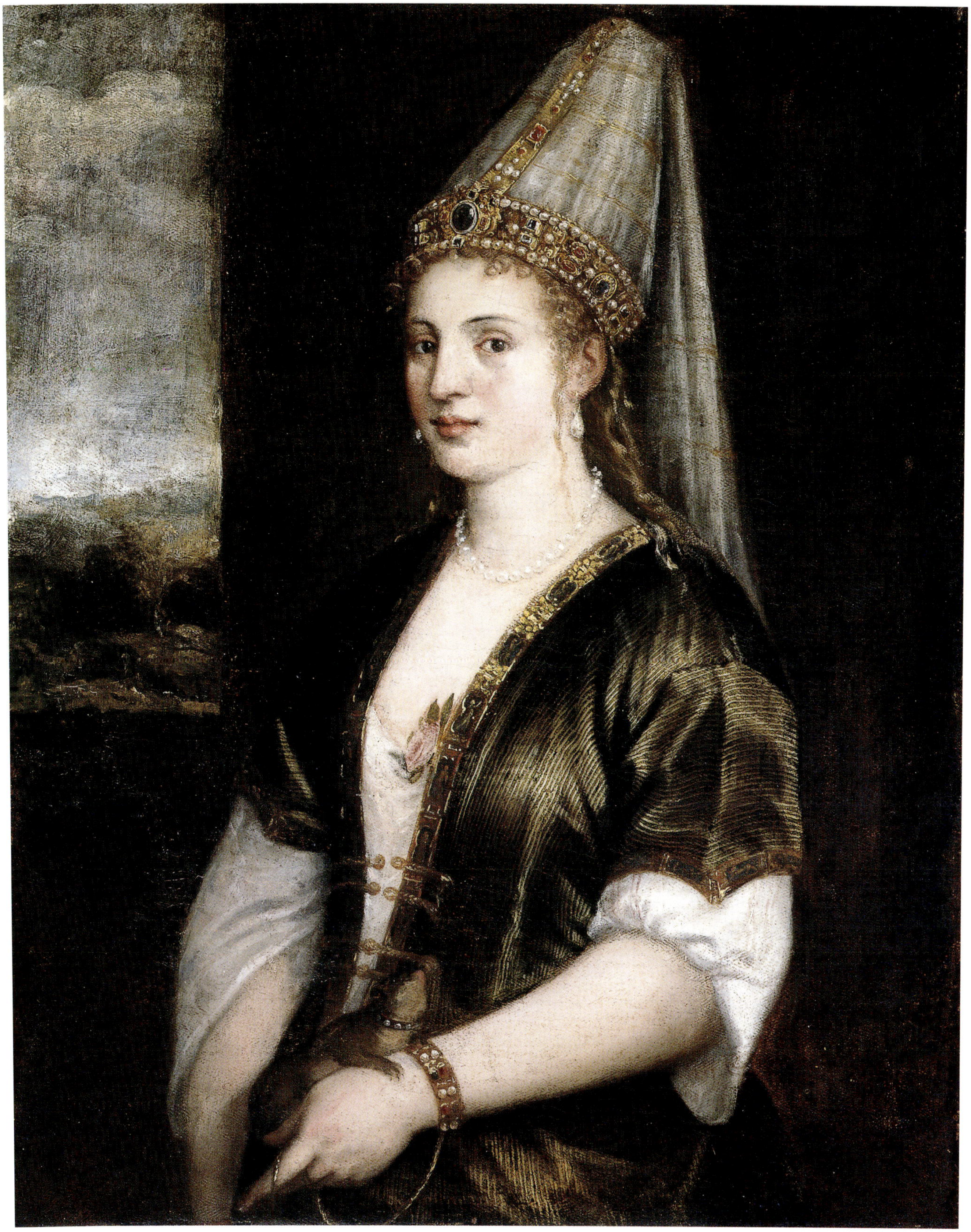

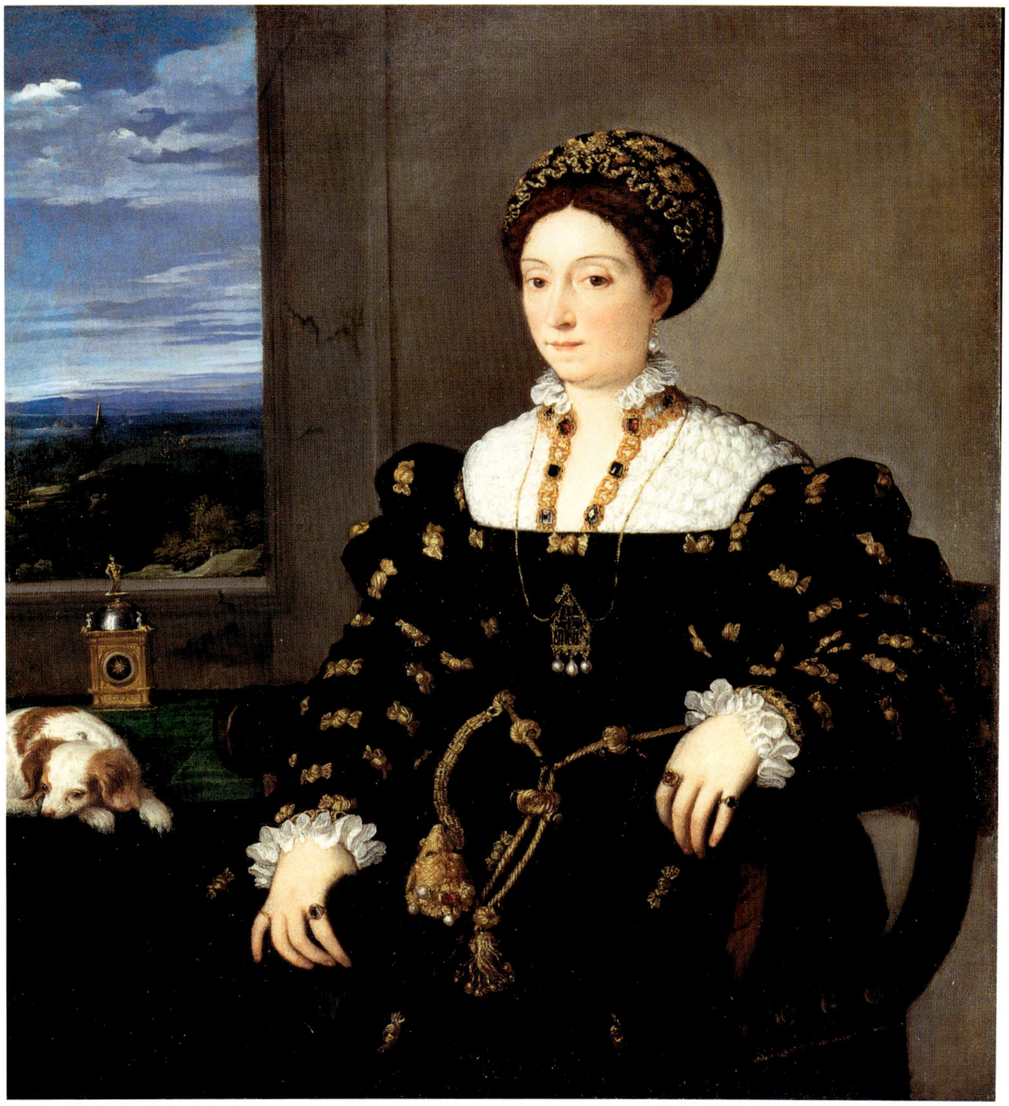

Eleonora Gonzaga by Titian.
Oil on canvas, 114 × 103 cm.
Uffizi, Florence

Portrait of a young woman in Turkish costume as St. Catherine, called 'Cameria, daughter of Suleyman the Magnificent, as St. Catherine', after Titian.
Oil on canvas, 102.5 × 76.5 cm.
Courtauld Institute of Art, London, Prince's Gate Collection

attribute of martydom. This group includes the so-called 'Cameria' in the Courtauld Institute collection (the name which Vasari wrongly gives to Roxelana's daughter), which ought not on this account (its inclusion of a Christian symbol) to be of a Turkish subject.[41] Yet the head-dress in this picture is undeniably Turkish in its 'horned' appearance, and resembles that in the Pagani woodcut.

The explanation for this confusing and conflicting iconography may be as Wethey states: that the wheel here, as in other related examples, was added later. One reason for this addition of a catherine wheel would have been the enduring Venetian fascination with the legend of Caterina Cornaro: a suitably exotic female image, of whatever kind, needed only the addition of this particular attribute to make such an identification likely. Certainly, such portraits, with the additions made to them, have further confused the record of what Hernández vaguely referred to as images of 'una Turca o Persiana', and still no authentic version of Titian's lost portrait of Roxelana is known.

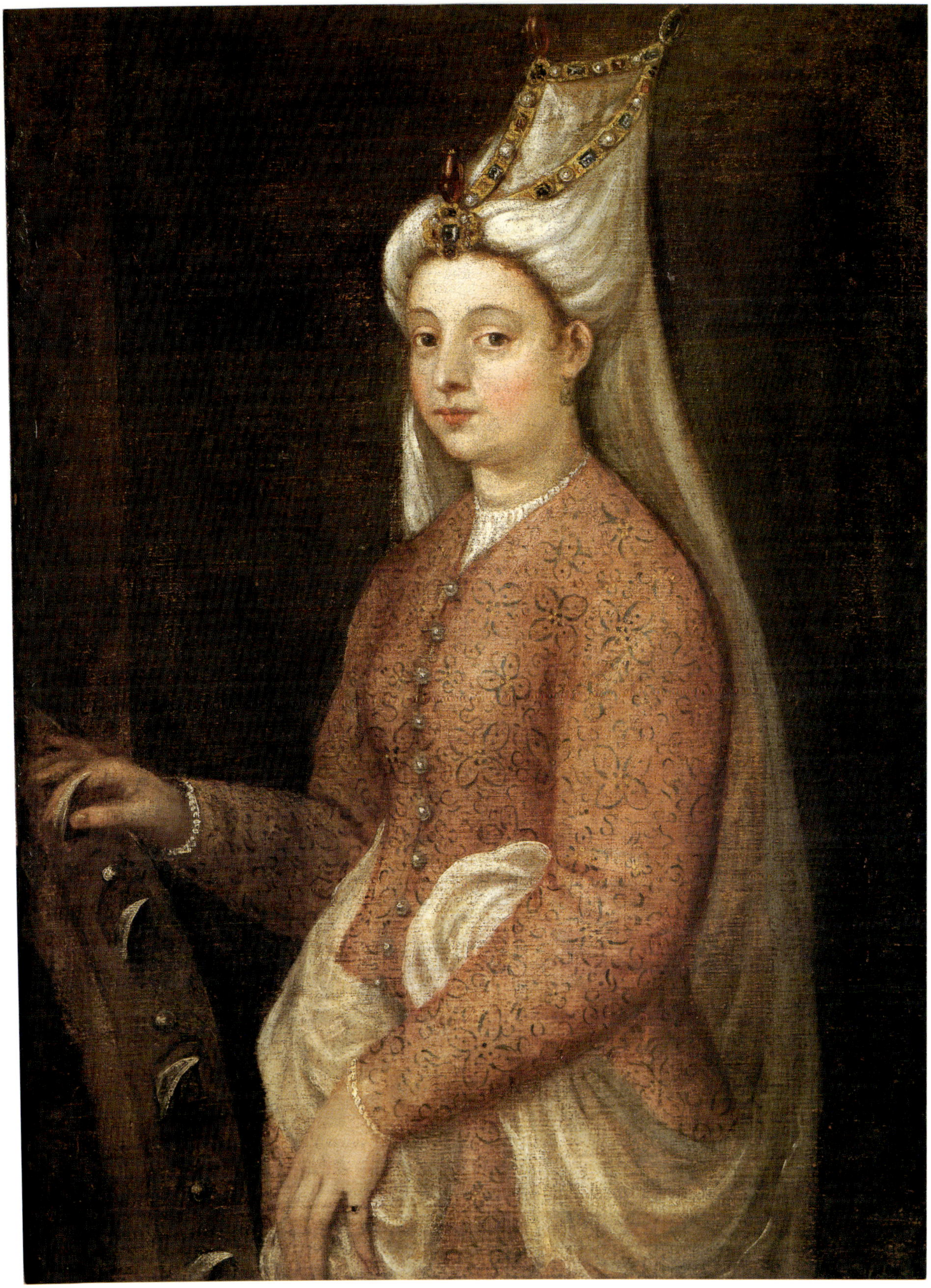

NOTES

1 G. Gronau, 'Die Kunstbestrebungen der Herzöge von Urbino', *Jahrbuch d. Kgl. Preuss. Kunstsammlungen*, XXV, 1904, p. 10.

2 G. Vasari, *Lives of the Painters, Sculptors and Architects*, 2 vols. (Everyman Library), London, 1996, II, pp. 789-80.

3 *Tiziano nelle gallerie Fiorentine*, exh. cat., Florence, 1978, '1631: L'eredità di Vittoria della Rovere', pp. 93ff., cat. nos. 31, 32, respectively, and cat. 36 for *Paul III* mentioned above. In view of the fact that Titian is reported to have painted his portrait of Suleyman in *c.* 1538 by referring, in part, to a medal, it is interesting to note that Titian painted, at Aretino's request, a profile portrait in 1538 of Francis I after a medal made by Cellini in France in 1537. The first sighting of the portrait of Francis I now in the Louvre, identified as this picture, is in 1653 in the inventory of the collection of Cardinal Mazarin. The Urbino portrait, according to Vasari, specifically showed the King when young, as this one does, so much so that this picture has also been dated rather to *c.* 1530, when the King was 36 (Hourticq, cited *Le Siècle de Titien*, exh. cat., Paris, 1993, p. 579). The Urbino collection picture has been identified with the version in the collection of Maurice de Coppet, Lausanne, which measures 107 × 90 cm (H. Wethey, *The Paintings of Titian*, 3 vols., 1969-75 II, *Portraits*, cat. 38), and these are the probable dimensions of the Della Rovere portrait of Suleyman.

4 The whole correspondence can be found in D. Bodart, *Tiziano e Federico II Gonzaga: Storia di un rapporto di committenza*, Rome, 1998, pp. 150ff.

5 Agnello to Federico Gonzaga, 5 May 1537, Bodart, op. cit., p. 309.

6 23 August 1538: 'Perche altre volte V.E. cercava di havere un ritratto del signor Turco, ho voluto dirli che M. Ticiano hora n'ha fatto uno cavato se non me inganno da una medaglia et da un altro ritratto, qual si dice di molti che sono stati a Constantinopoli esser tanto simile al naturale, che pare il medesimo Turco vivo, per volendone V.E. uno la me ne fara dar aviso che M. Ticiano ha detto che lo fara subito' (see Bodart, op. cit., pp. 321ff., no. 292). 27 August 1538: 'Non mancate di sollicitar presso a Tiziano li nostri quadri, et di più pregatilo per nostra a farne un retratto del Tirco, come il se vi ha offerto di fare, che l'havremo gratissimo' (ibid., no. 293). 3 September 1538: 'Ho fatti intendere a M. Ticiano quanto la E.V. m'ha fatta scrivere delli Imperatori e del ritratto del Turco; egli dice che non mancarà' (ibid., no. 294). 18 September 1538: 'M. Ticiano ha in bonissimo essere il ritratto del Turco, et da speranza de finir anche presto li quadri di Imperatori, ma dubito che la cosa andrà più in longo di quel che egli dice' (ibid., no. 296). 20 September 1538: 'Ni seria grato d'aver presto il ritratto del Turco che fa Tiziano, e però sollicitatelo.' (ibid., no. 297). J. A. Crowe & G. B. Calvacaselle, *Life and Times of Titian*, 2 vols., London, 1877, II, pp. 498-9.

7 'Fui Hyeri da titiano, il quale per tutta questa settemana dice che harà finito quei tre quadri di cesare, francia e il turcho, che a mio giudicio sono molti belli.' Quoted in L. Donati, 'Due immagini ignote di Solimano I (1494-1566)', *Studi orientalistici in onore di Giorgio Levi della Vida*, Rome, 1956, vol. I, pp. 219-33, p. 219. The assumption about Guidobaldo's responsibility for the commission was made by Von Hadeln, in his edition of Ridolfi, glossing Ridolfi's reference to Titian's having made a portrait of Suleyman; and it was also made by Gronau, who adds in the *Charles V* and *Francis I* as part of the same supposed commission of Guidobaldo. It does seem clear, from the context of the Leonardi letter, and from the contemporary circumstances, that the three would indeed have formed part of the same commission, although not necessarily from Guidobaldo II. For the Von Hadeln, Ridolfi, and Gronau references, see Donati, op. cit., p. 219, and nn. 2, 3.

8 Vasari makes this point and refers back to the habit in classical times. A major text which served as a model or inspiration was Petrarch's *De Viris Illustribus*, completed in Padua in 1375. Federico's commissioning from Titian the famous 'emperors'(although the series included Julius Caesar), referred to in the correspondence above, was in the same tradition.

9 Vasari, loc. cit.

10 Crowe & Calvacaselle, loc. cit.

11 This line of thought argues against the comments of Donati who asserts that this picture was the first of *three* such portraits of Suleyman; that it is identical with the *ex* Marinucci portrait (see below); that this latter portrait is by Titian (Wethey does not accept it); and that it would have

been made in about 1520. Donati, op. cit., p. 221. The wording of Agnello's letter does not allow for this interpretation.

12 Wethey, op. cit., I, *The Religious Pictures*, pl. 91, cat. 21, pp. 79ff.

13 Wethey, op. cit., II, *Portraits*, p. 204, citing Brunetti, 1935, p. 123; see also Donati, op. cit., p. 4, n. 5, citing T. Bertele, *Il palazzo degli ambasciatori di Venezia a Constantinopoli*, Bologna, 1932, p. 72, n. 40. 'I saw on other occasions in Titian's house, among the remnants of his pictures, a portrait of Suleyman on a horse in an old and neglected canvas that could be easily obtained, and which I believe is a very good likeness.' An equestrian portrayal of Suleyman also exists in a Venetian woodcut of *c.* 1563 but in it he is shown as a young man, and this particular aspect must therefore have been taken from an earlier representation: J. M. Rogers & R. M. Ward, *Suleyman the Magnificent*, exh. cat., British Museum, 1988, no. 3, see p. 50.

14 Titian painted a portrait of Francis I of France after a medal by Cellini. See n. 2 above.

15 Rogers & Ward, op. cit., no. 4a, p. 51 (ill.), BM 1878.7-13. 4164.

16 L. Planiscig, *Die Estensische Kunstsammlung, I*, Vienna, 1919, no. 385, pl. 16.

17 There is a curious story in Vasari (op. cit., I, pp. 863-4) concerning portraits of Charles V by both Alfonso and Titian in strange circumstances in Bologna in 1532-3.

18 Donati, op. cit., p. 226, fig. 2.

19 M. Gualandi, *Nuova raccolta di lettere*, 3 vols., Bologna, 1844-56, III, p. 20. Ippolito Capilupi was born in 1511; he wrote poetry in Latin and Italian and translated from Greek and Latin. Gualandi's transcription must be in error about the year: he gives 1569, but the Cardinal died in 1563. It is significant, for the purposes of the history of the Gonzaga pictures, that Cardinal Ercole was regent for the seven-year-old 2nd Duke of Mantua, following Federico's death in 1540, and then again from 1550 for the 3rd Duke, following the death at 17 of the 2nd Duke.

20 Vasari, loc. cit., records that Titian had painted the Cardinal's portrait.

21 Wethey, op. cit., II, *Portraits*, pp. 190ff., esp. L-27/1, p. 204.

22 Ibid., pp. 190ff.

23 Rogers & Ward, op. cit., pp. 46ff.

24 Rogers & Ward, op. cit., 1988, p. 16.

25 Op. cit., II, p. 796.

26 Ibid., p. 50.

27 See BM cat. p. 16.

28 Donati, op. cit., p. 223.

29 Wethey, op. cit., II, *Portraits*, L-28, p. 205.

30 Not a weasel, as Wethey states, Wethey, loc. cit.

31 *Titian Prince of Painters*, exh. cat., Venice/Washington 1990-1, pp. 220-4.

32 Ibid., p. 222.

33 The portrait of Eleonora assumes additional importance in this context, in view of the circumstances which suggest that it was her husband, Francesco Maria della Rovere, who commissioned Titian's portrait of Suleyman for the court of Urbino at Pesaro (see above).

34 See above.

35 Rogers & Ward, op. cit., cat. 4b, p. 51.

36 Wethey, loc. cit.

37 C. Hope, *Titian*, London, 1980, p. 125.

38 Crowe & Calvacaselle, op. cit., II, pp. 277, 515.

39 A. Ponz, *Viage de España* (13 vols., Madrid, 1776-84), edn. Madrid, 1947, VI, p. 561; see Wethey, loc. cit.

40 Wethey, loc. cit.

41 Wethey, op. cit., II, *Portraits*, L-2, p. 190, pl. 269

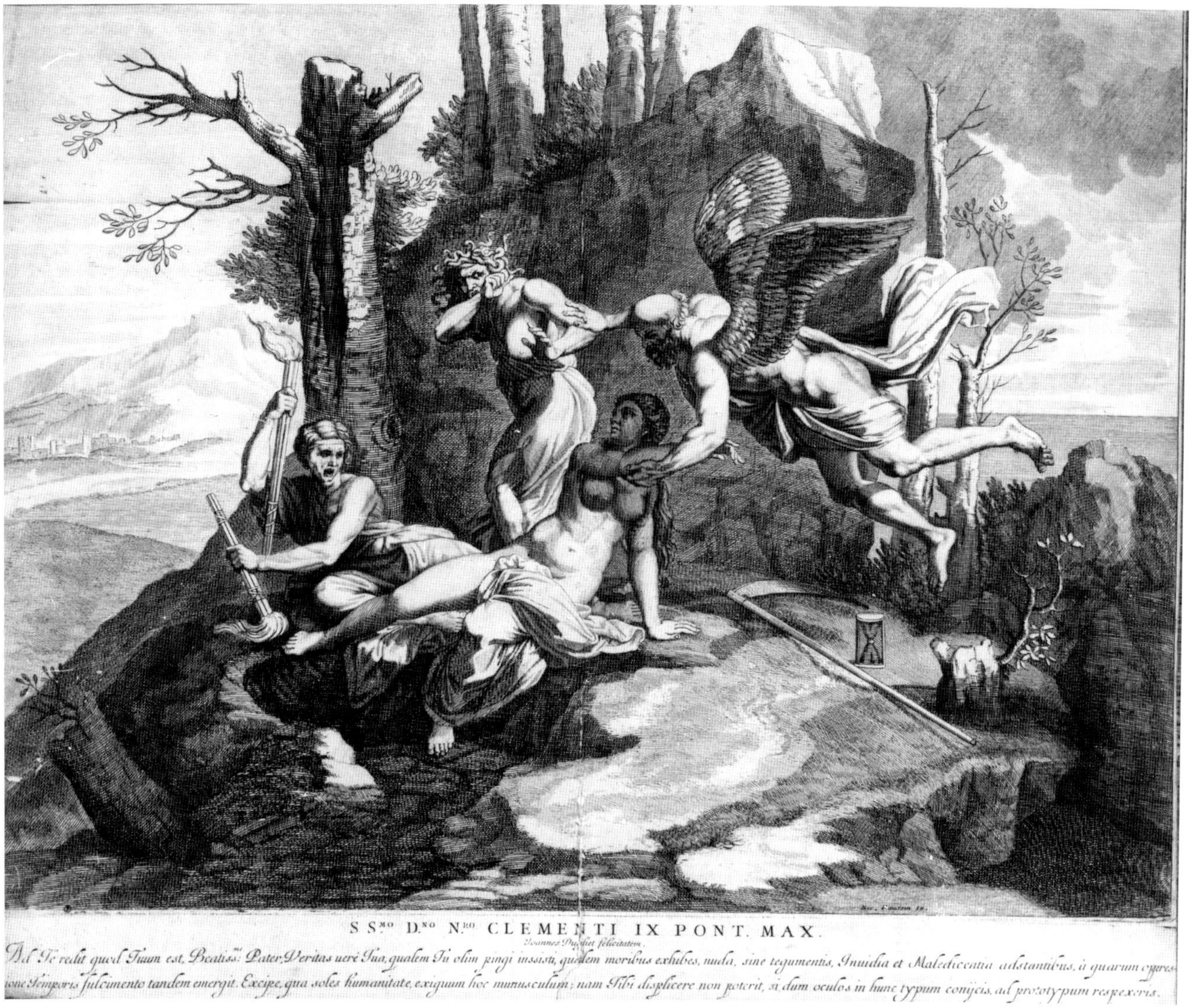

Time saving Truth from Envy and Discord.
Engraving by Etienne Baudet (1638-1711) and Jean Dughet (1614-76), *c.* 1667-9,
after lost painting by Nicolas Poussin
(1594-1665) of *c.* 1638-40.
Witt Print Collection, Courtauld Institute of Art, London

Nicolas Poussin

1594-1665

Time saving Truth from Envy and Discord

Oil on canvas
Dimensions unknown

Time saving Truth from Envy and Discord was painted in about 1638-40 for Giulio Rospigliosi (1600-79), later titular Archbishop of Tarsus and papal nuncio to Spain (1644), Cardinal (1657), and finally Pope (Clement IX, 1667-9). He also suggested the theme.[1] It subsequently passed into the Rospigliosi-Pallavicini collection but vanished from the records after 1806, although its appearance is known from engravings, copies, and a drawing. There is a reference to the painting in 1853 which might imply that it was then still in existence.[2] The principal engraving (in reverse) was published by Poussin's brother-in-law Jean Dughet, 1667-9, and bears a dedication to Pope Clement IX (Rospigliosi). A circular version of the subject, differing in composition, was made for Cardinal Richelieu in 1641, and the meaning of the allegory

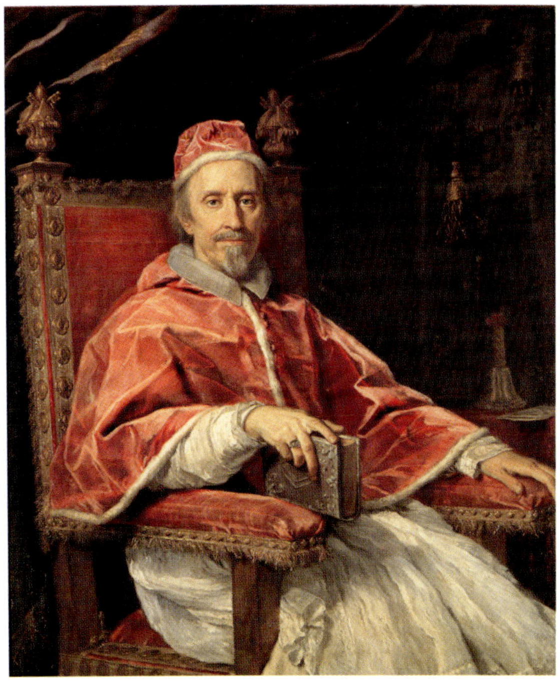

Pope Clement IX
by Carlo Maratta
(1625-1713), 1669.
Oil on canvas, 145 × 118 cm.
Pinacoteca Vaticana

has been the subject of an extended study by Saxl.[3] The theme was a popular one in the seventeenth century, and suggests that Time 'is the deliverer of Truth from persecution and oppression and in the end brings honour and reputation'.[4]

Giulio Rospigliosi was both learned and creative and wrote religious and classical allegorical dramas for the circle of Cardinal Francesco Barberini (the Palazzo

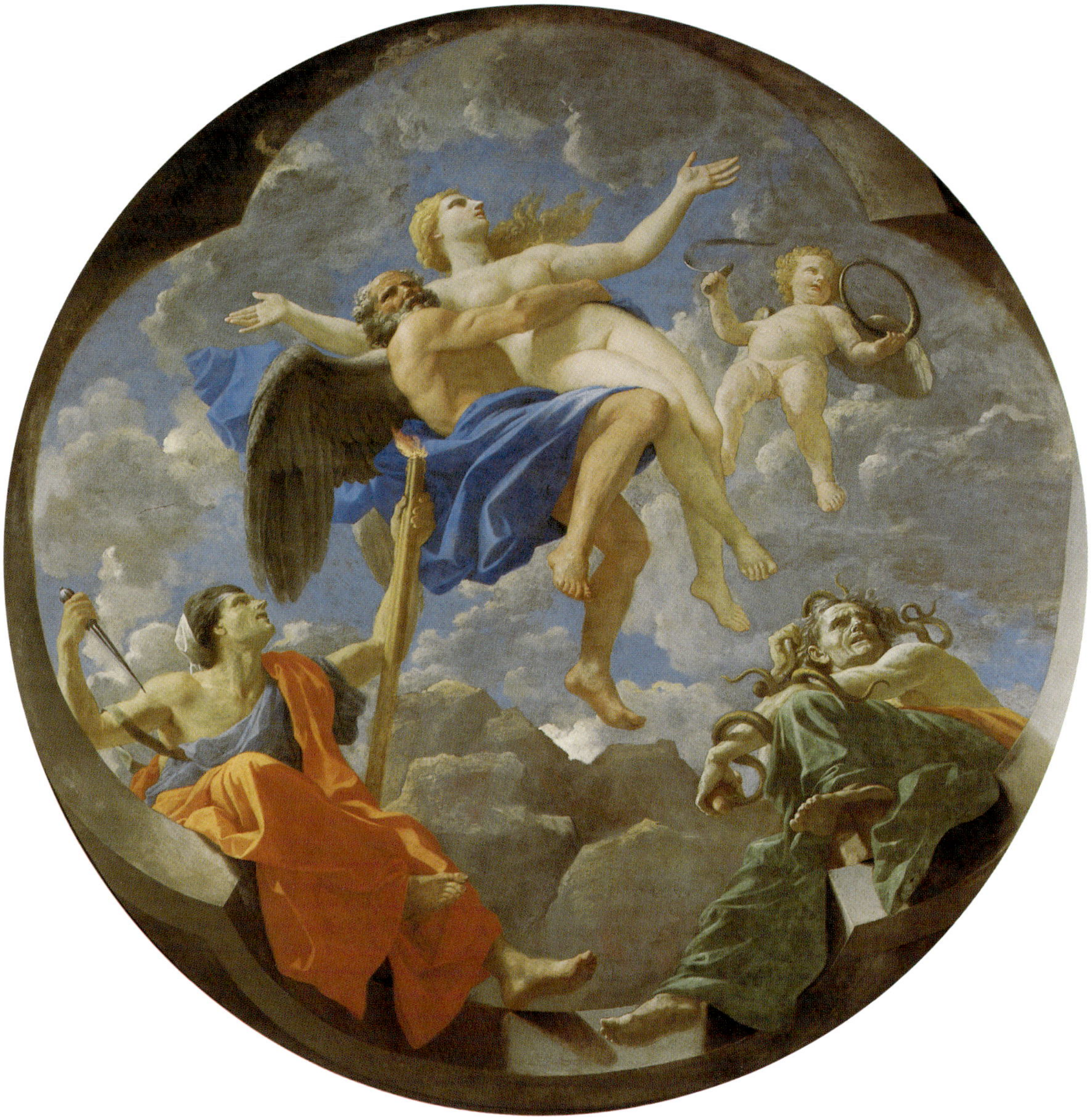

Time saving Truth from Envy and Discord by Nicolas Poussin. Oil on canvas, diam. 297 cm. Musée du Louvre, Paris

Barberini had its own theatre), which were often set to music.[5] These works included *Chi soffre speri*, which Milton heard on its first performance in Rome on 27 February 1639, a work with which Rospigliosi, it has been claimed, created the comic opera. Rospigliosi accompanied Cardinal Barberini on his legations to France and Spain, which would have brought him into close contact with Poussin's patron Cassiano dal Pozzo. There is a consonance of thought between Rospigliosi's works and the subject-matter of the Poussin paintings he commissioned, as there is also, for example, with the *Sacraments* that were being created at the same time for Dal Pozzo.[6] Rospigliosi, who is credited with having discovered the legend 'Et in Arcadia Ego', itself the subject of one of Poussin's most celebrated compositions, was a confessed admirer of the artist. He is recorded as having lamented the fact that Poussin had died before he became Pope, when he might properly have been able to employ his genius.

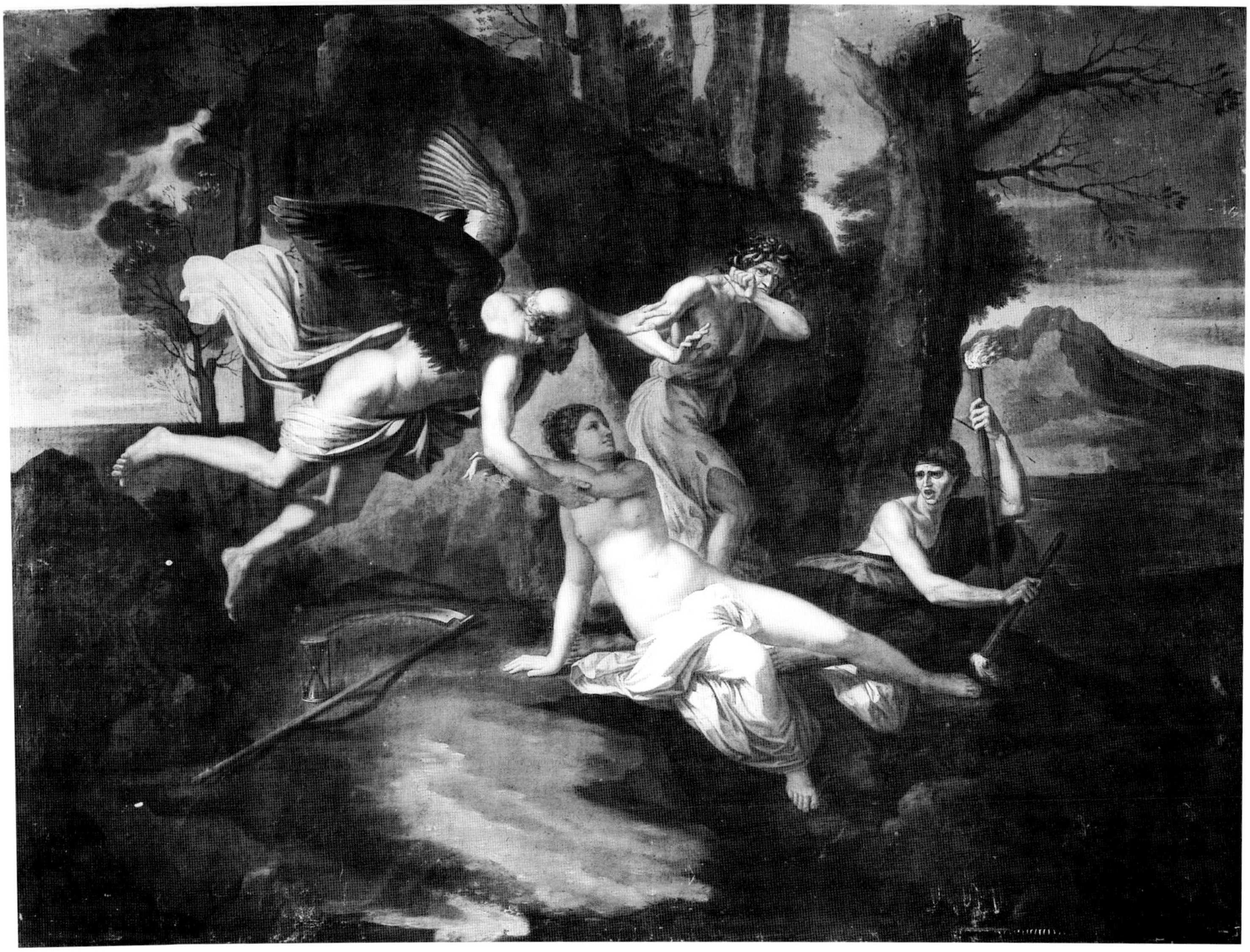

Time saving Truth from Envy and Discord.
Copy of lost painting by Nicolas Poussin.
Oil on canvas, 73.5 × 99 cm.
Private collection (Sotheby's, London, 1 May 1970, lot 152)

Time saving Truth from Envy and Discord shares much of its interesting history with one of Poussin's best-known pictures, *A dance to the music of Time* (Wallace Collection, London). Both were commissioned by Rospigliosi, and in both cases it was Rospigliosi who suggested the theme.[7] Blunt considered that *Time saving Truth* should be dated to 1638-40 and *A dance...* to around 1639-40.[8] This dating would agree with the circumstances of the commissioning of the two paintings and their common theme of Time. *Time saving Truth...* remained in the Palazzo Rospigliosi, where *A dance...* was also housed (and not in the adjoining Pallavicini collection – see below), until its disappearance after 1806.[9]

Poussin went to Paris in 1640-2 and before he left Rome, that is, at about the same time as the commissioning of the two paintings already mentioned, Rospigliosi apparently also commissioned from Poussin a *Rest on the flight into Egypt*, a painting that was specifically in the Rospigliosi collection but

Time saving Truth from Envy and Discord
by Nicolas Poussin (1594-1665).
Initial design for lost painting.
Pen and bistre over black chalk,
11.9 × 15 cm.
The Royal Collection, © 2001
Her Majesty Queen Elizabeth II

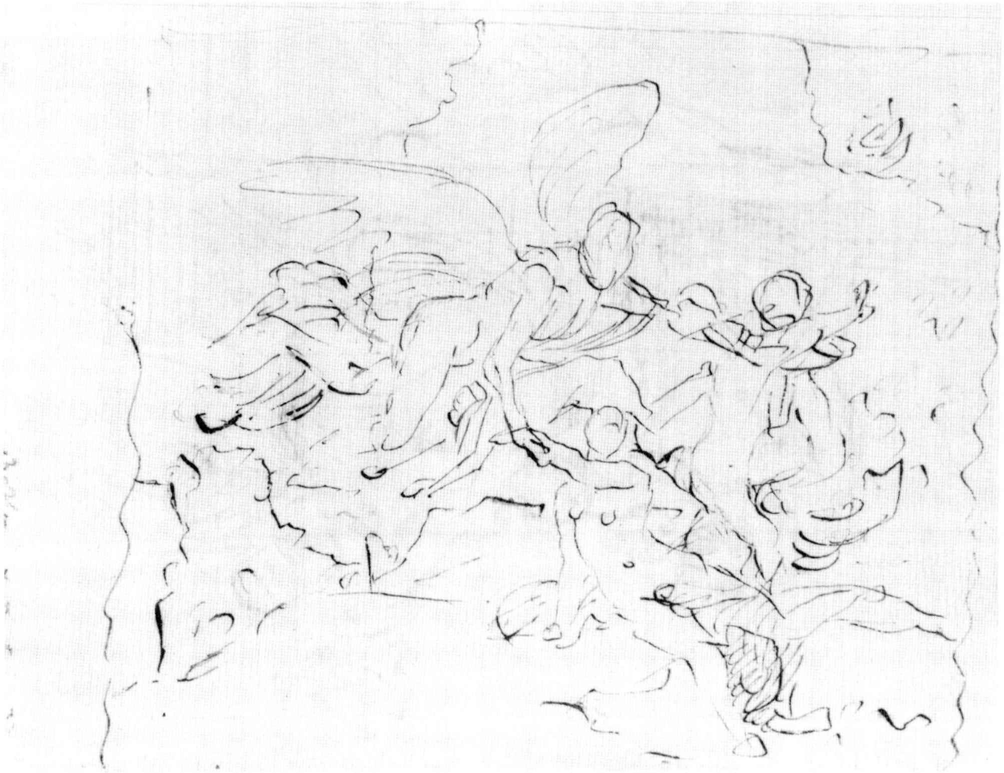

which has also been lost, being known only from engravings.[10]

At one point in time, both *Time saving Truth...* and *A dance...* (and presumably the *Rest on the flight into Egypt*) came to Palazzo Barberini, between 1674 and 1694, where the Pope who commissioned them had enjoyed his theatrical successes. The reason is that at this time the Palazzo Barberini was let to Cardinal Lazzaro Pallavicini (1602-80), whose ambitions for his Genoese family had led him in 1670, in the year after he had been created Cardinal by Clement IX, to unite his niece, Camilla Maria Pallavicini (1645-1710), in marriage to Giovanni Battista Rospigliosi (1646-1722), the nephew of the same Pope.[11]

The subsequent curious history of the family's collection begins at this point, and turns on Lazzaro Pallavicini's determination that through Camilla Maria, who was the only child of his brother Stefano (1608-87), the name of Pallavicini should be perpetuated, in the form of a new, Roman, branch of the family. To this end, he contrived a most complex scheme of inheritance, essentially keeping separate within the walls of the same palace the Pallavicini and Rospigliosi branches of the family, and their respective art collections, the Pallavicini part of which comprised works that he had inherited and acquired, together with those of his brother Stefano.[12] The palace, which the family bought in 1704, was on the Quirinale, and is still occupied today by the Pallavicini family and the Pallavicini gallery of pictures. The Rospigliosi collection, however, together with their part of the palace, was sold off in 1931-2. This odd history has a bearing on the possible fate of the missing picture – or indeed pictures – by Poussin.

Lazzaro Pallavicini's inheritance arrangement provided that, if the Rospigliosi had only a single male child (always remembering that Camilla Maria Pallavicini

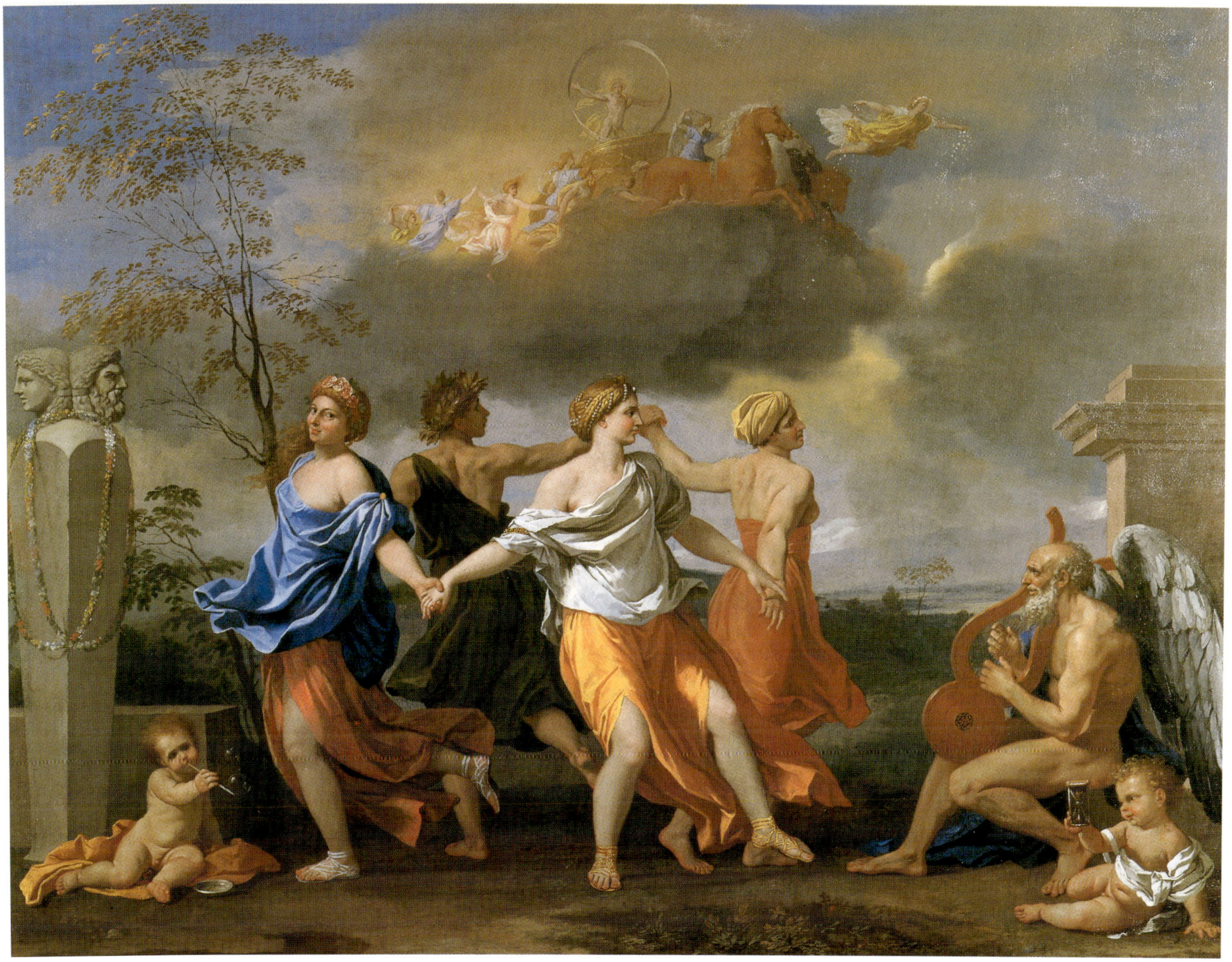

A dance to the music of Time by Nicolas Poussin.
Oil on canvas, 82.5 × 104 cm.
The Wallace Collection, London

was married to Giovanni Battista Rospigliosi), then he would take, on inheriting, also the name of Pallavicini, together with all the possessions. If and when a second male child appeared, however, the elder would take the name of Rospigliosi alone and the younger would take the name of Pallavicini alone, the latter inheriting that part of the family's possessions identified by Lazzaro Pallavicini in his will of 2 October 1679, the year before his death, and which essentially constitutes the nucleus of the collection today.[13] The elder son would own the Rospigliosi inheritance.

This is what happened to begin with, for Camilla Maria and Giovanni Battista had two male children, the first being Domenico Clemente Rospigliosi (d. 1752) and the second Niccolò Maria Pallavicini (d. 1759). The will of Camilla Maria of 11 September 1710[14] identifies as beneficiaries her two sons, in the form

'Domenico Clemente Rospigliosi' and 'Nicola Maria Pallavicini'. The Lazzaro Pallavicini will of 1679 identifying the Pallavicini inheritance operated specifically in favour of Niccolò Maria, and so the inventory of 1713 of the 'guardarobba e palazzo' of Camilla Maria's husband was therefore intended to specify the Rospigliosi collection in his possession. On his death in 1722, the Rospigliosi collection duly went to their elder son Domenico Clemente Rospigliosi, and the Pallavicini collection to the younger son, Niccolò Maria Pallavicini.

The division thus achieved was, however, short-lived, despite the promising existence of a Rospigliosi and a Pallavicini heir, because of subsequent lack of sufficient heirs on both sides. Niccolò Maria Pallavicini, who had married Vittoria Altieri, died without issue in 1759. His Pallavicini heritage therefore passed to his nephew, Giovanni Battista (Pallavicini), the younger son of his brother Domenico Clemente Rospigliosi. The elder of Domenico Clemente's sons, Camillo (Rospigliosi), had inherited the Rospigliosi collection upon his father's death in 1752, but he died in 1769,[15] and so Giovanni Battista Pallavicini consequently took the name of Rospigliosi-Pallavicini. He then died in 1784, and although he and his wife Eleonora Caffarelli had produced two sons, one of them, Luigi, had died before reaching maturity. The elder of these brothers, Giuseppe, therefore became the sole heir, bearing both names again, as Giuseppe Rospigliosi-Pallavicini (d. 1832) and holding both collections. He in turn had a single son, Giulio Cesare Rospigliosi-Pallavicini (b. 1781), whose marriage to Margherita Colonna ultimately led to the division of the double inheritance, for their marriage produced two sons, Clemente Rospigliosi and Francesco Pallavicini. The family collections descended separately from this point on, until the Rospigliosi collection was dispersed, at first secretly and then in two public sales in 1931 and 1932. Even at this stage the Pallavicini attempted to re-unite the two collections, but the sales took place despite their offer to purchase the entire Rospigliosi collection at any price.[16]

When the Rospigliosi moved into their palace on the Quirinale in 1704, it was decided that the Rospigliosi branch would occupy the ground floor and the second floor; the Pallavicini would take the first floor and the first two terraces of the garden. The Pallavicini collection, as noted above, occupies the same space now as then, namely, the large rooms of the first floor and the rooms to the sides of the Summer House of Aurora, which contains the famous fresco of *Aurora* by Guido Reni.

Camilla Maria, who arranged all this with her husband, added to the family's collection as a whole, taking great care in some, but not all, cases, that any additions should be divided equally between the two sections of it.[17] For example, of four 'Battles' by Cristiano Reder, she made sure that two went to the Pallavicini and two to the Rospigliosi. The same was sometimes also true of pictures that had specifically derived from the Rospigliosi line. Thus, drawings by Bernini and by Claude, which apparently came from the estate of the Rospigliosi Pope, Clement IX, were divided up. Landscapes certainly commissioned by Clement IX from Claude, namely the *Landscape with shepherds* of *c.* 1637 and *Landscape with Mercury and Aglauros* of 1643, both went, under the system of fair shares, not to the Rospigliosi side but to the Pallavicini (where they remain). A painting that originally came from the Pallavicini, Batoni's *Vision of St. Philip Neri* of *c.* 1733-4, which was commissioned by Niccolò Maria Pallavicini (a 'religiosissimo cavaliere') for the chapel of his palace in Frascati, was ultimately sold by Prince Gerolamo Rospigliosi in 1931, and so had evidently been assigned to that part of the family.[18] That sale also saw the dispersal of the relevant part of the Colonna paintings which had arrived in the family with the marriage of Giulio Cesare Rospigliosi-Pallavicini to Margherita Colonna in the nineteenth century. Following the custom, these had been dutifully divided between the two collections in their separate galleries, about seventy to each side.[19]

Poussin's *Time saving Truth from Envy and Discord* and *A dance to the music of Time* were in the Rospigliosi collection rather than the Pallavicini, the first, according to Blunt until 'around 1800', the second until 'after 1800',[20] and Blunt further states that the latter was 'bought from the palace by Cardinal Fesch'.[21] The actual year was 1806 when three Poussins (the other being the *Rest on the flight into Egypt*) were recorded as having been acquired by the Cardinal from the Rospigliosi collection.[22] At this time, as we have seen, the two collections were under one owner, Giuseppe Rospigliosi-Pallavicini. These particular sales of pictures apparently took place from the Rospigliosi collection only. The reason, probably, was that the Pallavicini pictures could not be sold, since they were held in trust specifically for a Pallavicini heir under the arrangement created by Lazzaro Pallavicini in 1679.

The reasons for Giuseppe's having to sell around 1806 are not known, but they must have been pressing, for only a decade later, in 1816, he embarked on additions to the family collections of works of art which have been described as 'of exceptional importance'.[23] That he sold the Rospigliosi Poussins in the early years of the century is, however, suggestive, for members of the Roman nobility had come under intense financial pressure during this period from the successive French and Neapolitan invasions which took place from late 1797 until the overthrow of Napoleon.[24] From the moment Napoleon first reached Rome in 1797, countless works of art were taken away to France; and with the subsequent establishment, under France, of the 'Roman Republic', heavy taxes were imposed. During these difficult times, 1806 was a period of relative calm, because Pope Pius VII had negotiated the Concordat of 1801, which guaranteed a certain degree of autonomy. It was not until 1808 that French troops finally re-invaded Rome with the aim of overthrowing the temporal power of the Papacy, and it was in the immediately following years that the greatest financial hardships were felt. Perhaps Giuseppe Rospigliosi in 1806, for whatever motive, merely wished to accommodate Cardinal Fesch's evident desire to build up his art collection.

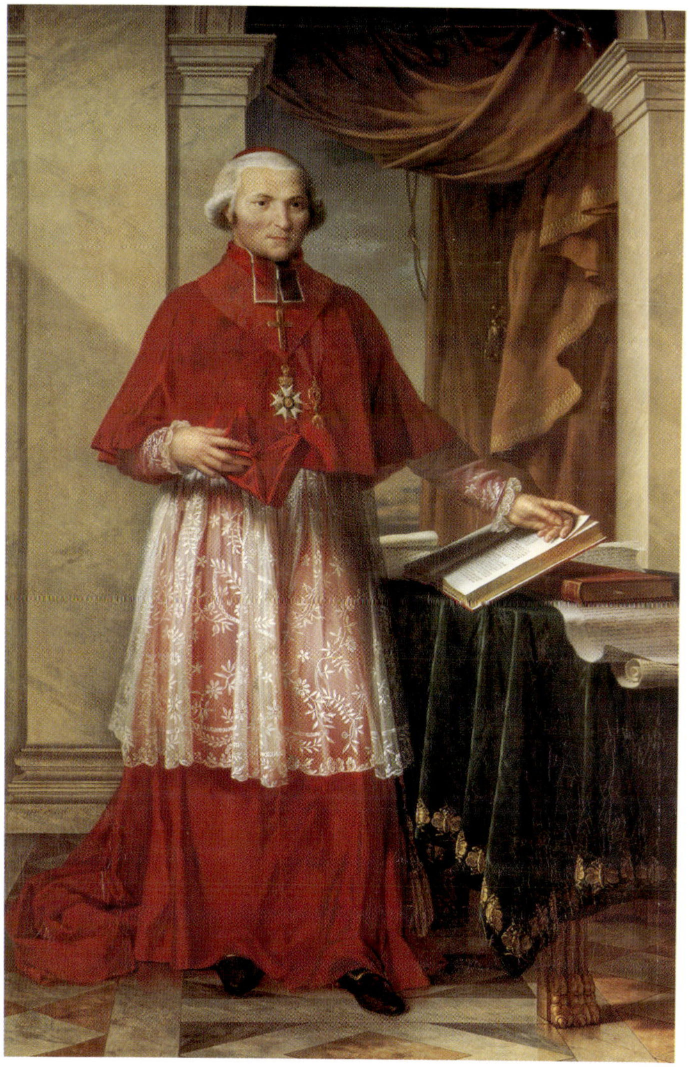

Cardinal Fesch
by Charles Meynier (1768-1832).
Oil on canvas.
Château de Versailles

Joseph, Cardinal Fesch (1763-1839), Napoleon's 'uncle', was in fact linked to Napoleon because his father had married Napoleon's widowed mother Letizia as his second wife. After the fall of Napoleon she came to live in Rome with the Cardinal.

The Cardinal had a passion for Poussin in particular, and the inventory at his death in 1839 lists no fewer than seventy-eight paintings as 'Poussin'. His collection was distributed between three palaces: Palazzo Falconieri at 1 via Giulia; Palazzo Ricci, at 147 via Giulia (in this century the home of Mario Praz); and 'Palazzo detto Madama Letizia' (i.e. the house assigned to Napoleon's mother).[25]

Two of the identifiable works by Poussin in the Fesch collection are *A dance to the music of Time* and the now-missing *Rest on the flight into Egypt* mentioned above, which Giulio Rospigliosi had commissioned from the artist. The latter was listed in the summary 1841 catalogue of the Fesch collection (no. 1053) and was also recorded there as having come from the Rospigliosi collection.[26] *A dance...* was again described at some length in the pre-sale catalogue of the Fesch collection in 1844.[27] It was bought by Lord Hertford at the Fesch sale of 1845, but *Time saving Truth...* , its 'companion', cannot be identified in any of these records after 1806.

Oddly, however, both are mentioned in the same context shortly after the Fesch sale, when they are mentioned together by Jean Victor Cousin in a commentary on Poussin pictures which had entered English collections. The context does not necessarily imply that Cousin believed *Time saving Truth...* had gone to England:

> Sometimes even sacred or profane history is insufficient for him [Poussin]: he invents, he uses his imagination, he has recourse to moral and philosophical allegory. It is there perhaps that he is at his most original, and that his thought unfolds in all its liberty and loftiness. *Arcadia* is a lesson in high philosophy in the form of an idyll. *The Testament of Eudamidas* portrays the sublime confidence of friendship. *Time plucking Truth from the clutches of Envy and Discord*, the *Dance of Human Life*, are the celebrated models of this genre.[28]

NOTES

1 G.P.Bellori, *Le Vite de' pittori, scultori ed architetti moderni...* Rome, 1672, p. 448. Maratta's portrait of Pope Clement IX is in the Hermitage, St Petersburg.

2 A.Blunt, *Nicholas Poussin, The A.W.Mellon Lectures in Fine Art, 1958, National Gallery of Art, Washington, D.C.*, 3 vols., New York and London, 1967, 'A Critical Catalogue', cat. no. 123, pp. 83-4. The drawing is in the Royal Collection, W.Friedlaender and A.Blunt, *The Drawings of Nicholas Poussin. A Catalogue Raisonné*, 5 vols., London, 1939-74, II, p. 25, no. 150. Blunt lists five copies of the painting. For the 1853 reference, see n. 28 below.

3 F.Saxl, 'Veritas filia Temporis' in *Philosophy and History. Essays presented to E.Cassirer*, R.Klibansky, H.J.Paton, ed., Oxford, 1936, pp. 197-222, see esp. pp. 212-15. This circular version is in the Musée du Louvre, Paris, inv. 735; see Blunt, op. cit., catalogue vol., no. 122, p. 83.

4 Saxl, op. cit., p. 202.

5 See Blunt, op. cit., text vol., pp. 153ff.

6 Ibid; see p. 155 for the *Sacraments*.

7 The allegory of *A dance...* has also been the subject of study: see E.Panofsky, 'Et in Arcadia Ego', in *Philosophy and History. Essays presented to E.Cassirer*, op. cit., pp. 222-54, esp. pp. 241ff.; and see Blunt, op. cit., catalogue vol., cat. no. 121, pp. 82-3. For the history of *A dance...* and other Poussin commissions of Rospigliosi, together with an account of his character and achievements in the arts, see R.Beresford, *A Dance to the Music of Time*, exh. cat., Wallace Collection, London, 1995.

8 Blunt, catalogue vol., nos. 121, 123, pp. 82-4.

9 See inventory of Giovanni Battista Rospigliosi of 26 June 1713 published by F.Zeri, *La Galleria Pallavicini*, Florence, 1959, pp. 299-330: (p. 310) no. 297 (*Time saving Truth*), and (p. 319) no. 512 (*A Dance...*); *Rest on the flight into Egypt* is (p. 302) no. 302; Andrea Manazzale, *Rome*

et ses environs. Dernière edition augmentée et corrigée par l'antiquaire, 2 vols., Rome, 1802, I, p. 127. The date of 1806 is that of the acquisition of three Poussins from the Rospigliosi collection by Cardinal Fesch – see below – confirmed by a letter of the Director of the French Academy in Rome, Suvée, to Cardinal Fesch of 31 December 1806: *Correspondance des Directeurs de l'Académie de France à Rome, nouvelle série, II, Directorat de Suvée 1795-1807*, II, 1984, p. 902, cited by Beresford, op. cit., p. 63, 'Aftermath', n. 2.

10 Blunt, op. cit., text vol., p. 154, and see n. 99. Zeri, inventory of 1713, loc. cit., p. 310, no. 302. Andreas Andresen, *Nicolaus Poussin, Verzeichniss der nach seinen Gemälden gefertigten gleichzeitingen und spätern Kupferstiche*, Leipzig, 1863, abridged and illus. French trans. by Georges Wildenstein, *Gazette des Beaux-Arts*, 1962, II, pp. 139ff. The *Rest on the flight to Egypt* was last seen by the then Director of the National Gallery, London, Sir Charles Eastlake, in a collection in Marseilles in 1864: see Beresford, op. cit., p. 21 and n. 42, and, for other works by Poussin owned by Rospigliosi, pp. 20-21.

11 Zeri, op. cit., p. 11.

12 They included, for example, the thirteen panels by Rubens, *Christ and the Apostles*: the family's patronage of and friendship with Rubens dated back to their native city of Genoa in the early years of the century (see Zeri, op. cit.). Another art-loving member of the family was Niccolò Maria Pallavicini (1650-1714), the illegitimate son of Carlo Pallavicini (d. 1668, brother of Lazzaro and Stefano), famously the friend of Carlo Maratti. He was in close touch with Camilla Maria, for example, but his important art collection was dispersed outside the Rospigliosi-Pallavicini; see S. Rudolph, *Niccolò Maria Pallavicini: L'ascesa al Tempio della Virtù attraverso il Mecenatisimo*, Rome, 1995.

13 See Zeri, op. cit., introduction, pp. 9-21; the 1679 Pallavicini will is published on pp. 291-8.

14 Getty Provenance Index I-733.

15 For references to *A dance to the music of Time* in the 1769 inventory following Camillo's death see Beresford, op. cit., pp. 65, 71.

16 Ibid., pp. 20-21. The 'few miserable traces' of the Rospigliosi collection left on the second floor of the palace have passed, Zeri states, to the Italian Federation of Agricultural Societies.

17 See Zeri, introduction, loc. cit., *passim*, and especially p. 15.

18 A.M. Clark, ed. E.P. Bowron, *Pompeo Batoni: Complete Catalogue*, New York and Oxford, 1985, cat. no. 3, pp. 210-1, sold Guido Tavazzi, Rome, 20 December 1932, lot 784. Two landscapes by Batoni (ibid., cat. nos. 18, 19) which were also disposed of at the same sales (these were sold Guido Tavazzi, Rome, 2 May 1931, lot 403, and 15 December, lot 371, respectively), may, in contrast, have originated with a commission from Domenico Clemente Rospigliosi, since one of them shows the castle of Zagarolo, a duchy which the Rospigliosi acquired from the Ludovisi.

19 Zeri, loc. cit.

20 Blunt, op. cit., catalogue vol., respectively p. 83 and p. 81.

21 Ibid., p. 81.

22 Beresford, op. cit., see n. 9 above; and see also Getty Provenance Index I-1833.

23 Zeri, loc. cit.

24 See, for example, the account in Christopher Hibbert, *Rome, Portrait of a City*, 1985, pp. 227ff.

25 Getty Provenance Index I-1833.

26 Blunt, op. cit., catalogue vol. no. 62, pp. 44-5, referring to *Catalogue des tableaux composant la Galerie de feu son Eminence le cardinal Fesch, Rome, 1841, Salviucci et Fils.*

27 Commissaire-expert du Musée Royal du Louvre, *Galerie de feu S.E. le cardinal Fesch ancien archévèque de Lyon, etc. ou catalogue raisonné des tableaux de cette galerie* [sale catalogue], Rome, 1844, pp. 60-3, quoted by Beresford, op. cit., pp. 66, 72.

28 J.V. Cousin, 'De divers tableaux du Poussin qui sont en Angleterre et particulièrement de l'Inspiration du Poète, *Archives de l'Art français*, III (1853-5), p. 17. In his last paragraph Cousin makes a point of thanking the owners of collections of engravings after Poussin which he had consulted, and so the references cannot conclusively be taken to refer to his knowledge of the painting in each case.

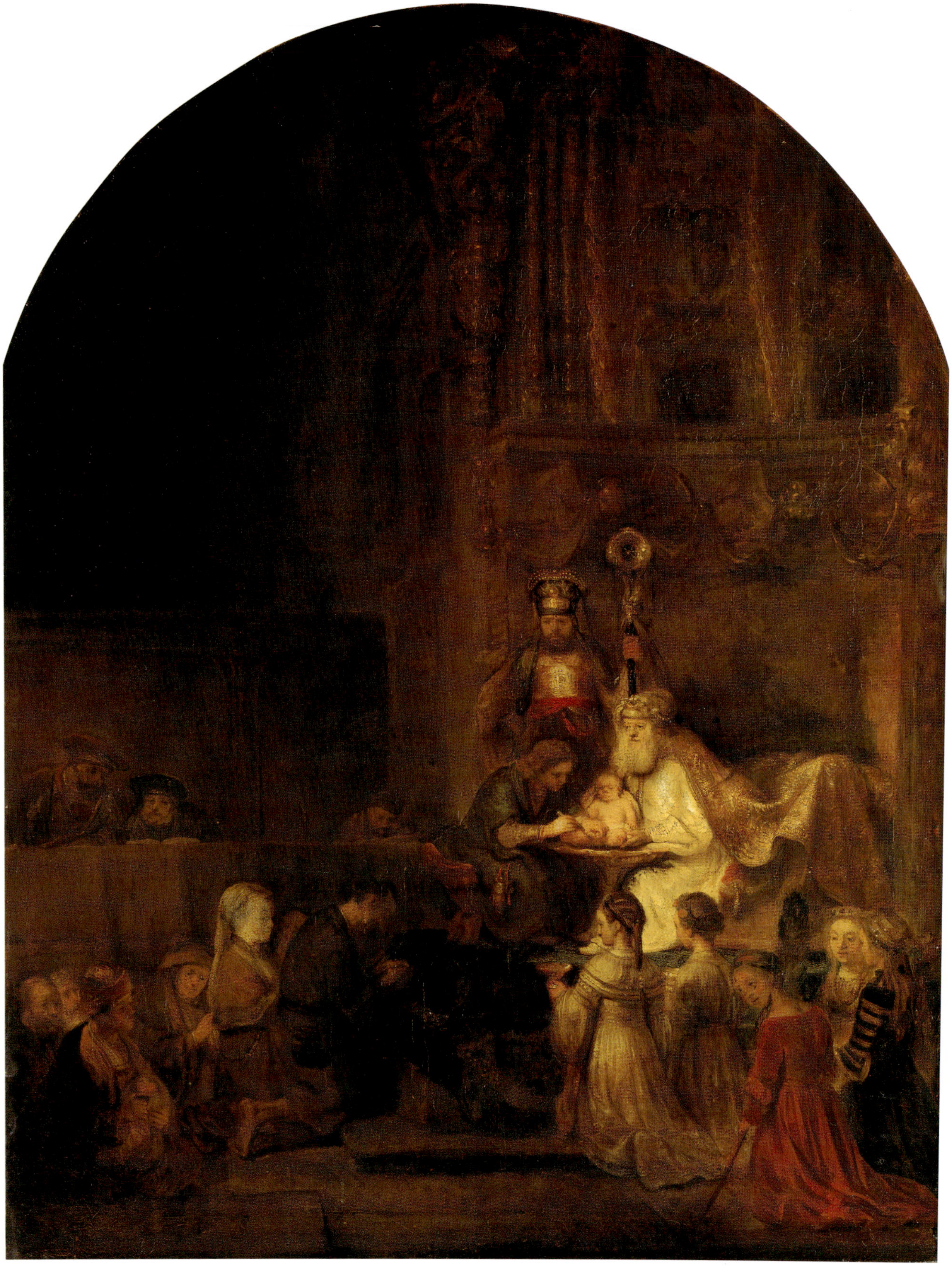

Rembrandt Harmensz. van Rijn

1606-69

The Circumcision

1646

Oil on canvas
c. 98 × 73 cm

Rembrandt painted the *Circumcision* in 1646, together with a *Nativity* (*Adoration of the shepherds*). They were the last two of seven paintings purchased or commissioned by the Stadtholder of the Northern Netherlands, Prince Frederik Hendrik of Orange, for his palace in Noordeinde, The Hague. The first five pictures are of scenes from the *Passion of Christ* and form a coherent group which was probably displayed in a specific location within the Oude Houf (Old Court). Rembrandt was evidently familiar with the 'gallery' in the palace for he refers to it in one of his seven letters connected with the project addressed to the Stadtholder's secretary, the distinguished scholar and man of letters Constantijn Huygens.[1] Huygens had recently written of Rembrandt's art in the most flattering terms in his autobiography of about 1631. Of *Judas returning the thirty pieces of silver* (now in a private collection in England) Huygens wrote:

> It can withstand comparison with anything ever made in Italy, or for that matter with everything beautiful and admirable that had been preserved since the earliest antiquity.[2]

The *Passion* series itself consists of five paintings which were executed by Rembrandt variously between about 1632 and 1639,[3] and all these pictures survive in the Alte Pinakothek, Munich. On 29 November 1646, Rembrandt was paid for a *Nativity* and *Circumcision*. The *Nativity* survives with the *Passion* series in Munich, but the *Circumcision* was lost at some point in the eighteenth century. All seven pictures were recorded in the inventory of the Stadtholder's widow, Amalia von Solms, of 20 March 1668, and described as 'in the Court in the Noordeinde':

> Seven paintings made by Rembrandt, all with black frames,
> oval at the top and with gilt carved leaves all round:
> The first being the nativity of our Lord Jesus Christ.
> The second the circumcision.
> The third the crucifixion.
> The fourth the descent from the cross.
> The fifth the entombment.
> The sixth the resurrection.
> The seventh the ascension of our Lord Jesus Christ.[4]

Amalia von Solms died in 1675 and it is not known 'how and precisely when [the series] entered the collection of Johann Wilhelm (Jan Wellem), Elector Palatine, in Düsseldorf, before 1716'.[5] Although they had appeared in the 1668 inventory, they were not in the 'Disposition Book' of Amalia of 1 January 1673, nor in the deed of the division of her estate dated 1676 drawn up after her death the previous

The Circumcision.
Copy of *c.* 1646 after lost original by Rembrandt Harmensz. van Rijn (1606-69).
Oil on canvas, 98 × 73 cm.
Herzog Anton-Ulrich Museum, Brunswick

year, and so they did not, presumably, go to any of her and the Stadtholder's four daughters.[6] It has been suggested that they may have passed into the collection of Amalia's grandson, Prince Willem III, better known as William III 'of Orange', King of England 1688-1702.[7] The next certain fact, however, is that all seven pictures were recorded in 1719 as having been in the collection of Johann Wilhelm, Elector Palatine (r. 1690-1716), when the *Nativity* (*Adoration*) and *Circumcision* were described as:

> No. 86. Die Geburt mit 11 Figuren
> N. 87. Die Beschneidung mit 19 Fig.[8]

The collection was moved several times: in 1758 to Mannheim (returning in 1764); 1794 to Glückstad (for some ten years); and before 1805 to Kirchheimbolanden. In 1806 it was moved to Munich as part of the collections of the Wittelsbach family, where it was included in the Pinakothek founded by King Ludwig I which opened in 1836.[9] The *Circumcision* was not, however, mentioned in a restorer's report of 1756, which concerned the remedial action that had been taken to repair damage caused to the *Passion* series and the *Nativity* for reasons that are not known. The painting of the *Circumcision* must therefore, presumably, already have disappeared or have been in too bad a state to be repaired.[10]

In 1778 the collection in the Electoral Gallery at Düsseldorf was engraved and published, and the six remaining paintings in the group – the five *Passion* scenes and the *Nativity* – are shown on the walls of the gallery in the prints that record the 'hang'. These six are also recorded in the catalogue accompanying the prints, but the *Circumcision* is neither engraved nor catalogued in this publication.[11]

The appearance of the *Circumcision* is, however, recorded in a copy, probably a 'workshop replica' (Herzog Anton-Ulrich Museum, Brunswick).[12] This copy – or replica – like the *Nativity*, conforms in shape, with an arched top, and in its similar size to the pictures in the *Passion* series. Clearly, however, these two pictures do not form part of the same narrative as the other five, since they are part of the *Infancy of Christ* story. Nor does the scale of the setting and the figures in the *Circumcision* accord with that of any of the other six pictures, a fact that has been interpreted as evidence of Rembrandt's inconsistency, the result of haste or carelessness on the part of the artist. The high opinion which Rembrandt had of his own work in these commissions, however, as shown in the letters, and the high price which he requested for all of them, does not accord with this assessment, even though Rembrandt's phraseology has, equally, been dismissed as courtly flattery or mere extravagance of language.[13]

In support of the argument that Rembrandt was less than fully dedicated to his work on the *Passion* series the poor condition of two of them in particular, the *Resurrection* and *Entombment*, has been reported as further evidence of haste on the part of the artist.[14] Rembrandt, however, must certainly have intended to produce something suitably extraordinary for the Stadtholder, a patron who would have been of prime importance for an ambitious artist in that country at that time. Rembrandt's letter of 12 January 1639 is specifically about these two pictures, the *Resurrection* and *Entombment*, and he stresses, in a phrase that has caused much controversy over its exact meaning, that he had 'finished [them] with studious application... for in these two pictures the greatest and most natural emotion ("die natuereelste beweechgekickheijt") has been expressed, which is the main reason why they have taken so long to execute'.

Furthermore, had the Stadtholder not been satisfied with his *Passion* series, he would hardly have commissioned in 1646 two more paintings from Rembrandt. Not only that, but for both the *Nativity* and the *Circumcision* the Stadtholder paid Rembrandt precisely double the previous rate he had allowed him:[15]

His Highness orders his treasurer and Paymaster General Willem Ketting de Jong to pay to N. Rembrant, painter of Amsterdam, the sum of two thousand four hundred Carolus guilder, for having made in the service of His Highness and delivered two paintings, the one the nativity and the other the circumcision of Christ, and therefore... 2400:0:0 The Hague, this 29 November 1646.[16]

Presumably, only the death of Prince Frederik Hendrik on 14 March 1647 prevented his further patronage of Rembrandt and, as we have seen, the principal reason for the poor condition of these paintings is that they were somehow damaged in the eighteenth century, whereupon they had to be restored. The restorer's words added in an inscription on the *Resurrection* – '*Rimbrand Creavit me. P. H. Brinckmann resuscitavit Te/1755*' – are therefore evidence of a heartfelt response to the accident that had taken place, rather than a criticism of Rembrandt's original workmanship.[17]

It is important to note that Rembrandt had earlier taken care to insert a prominent self-portrait in the second picture which he had made for the *Passion* series, the *Elevation of the Cross*. The point here is that, although it was the second to be painted, it was the first to be viewed in the narrative sequence, which would have been an especially prominent place in which to show a self-portrait as a piece of publicity. The artist's presence within the picture also reflected, however, a sound theological approach related to contemporary interpretations of the subject as bearing on the question of individual sin that 'crucifies our Lord afresh'.[18]

Although the *Elevation of the Cross* is the first picture in the narrative, it seems that it was not the first to be painted, which must have been the *Descent from the Cross*. This is different from the other pictures in the series in being on panel, and the shape of its top does not exactly conform to that of the other works, which are on canvas. It appears that Rembrandt had first painted this picture, partly in emulation of Rubens, an artist in whom both Huygens and the Stadtholder were very interested, but whom they failed to attract to the The Hague. The composition is closely related to Rubens's famous *Descent from the Cross* in Antwerp Cathedral (but then in St. Walburga, Antwerp), which Rembrandt would have known from the engraving by Lucas Vorsterman of 1620. Huygens had specifically referred to Rubens in his autobiography in the context of his discussion of Rembrandt's art (and that of his rival Jan Lievens).

As it happens, Rembrandt had already included a self-portrait in this painting of the *Descent from the Cross*, but more obscurely.[19] It would seem that he therefore took the opportunity presented by the second picture, the *Elevation of the Cross*, which appears initially to have been commissioned by Huygens as a pendant to the *Descent*, to make his presence more obvious. Judging from Rembrandt's subsequent letters to Huygens, it was the Stadtholder himself who then commissioned the three remaining *Passion* scenes from Rembrandt:

[February 1636]
... I hope that your lordship will please inform His Excellency that I am very diligently engaged in completing as quickly as possible the three Passion pictures which His Excellency himself commissioned me to do: an Entombment, and a Resurrection and an Ascension

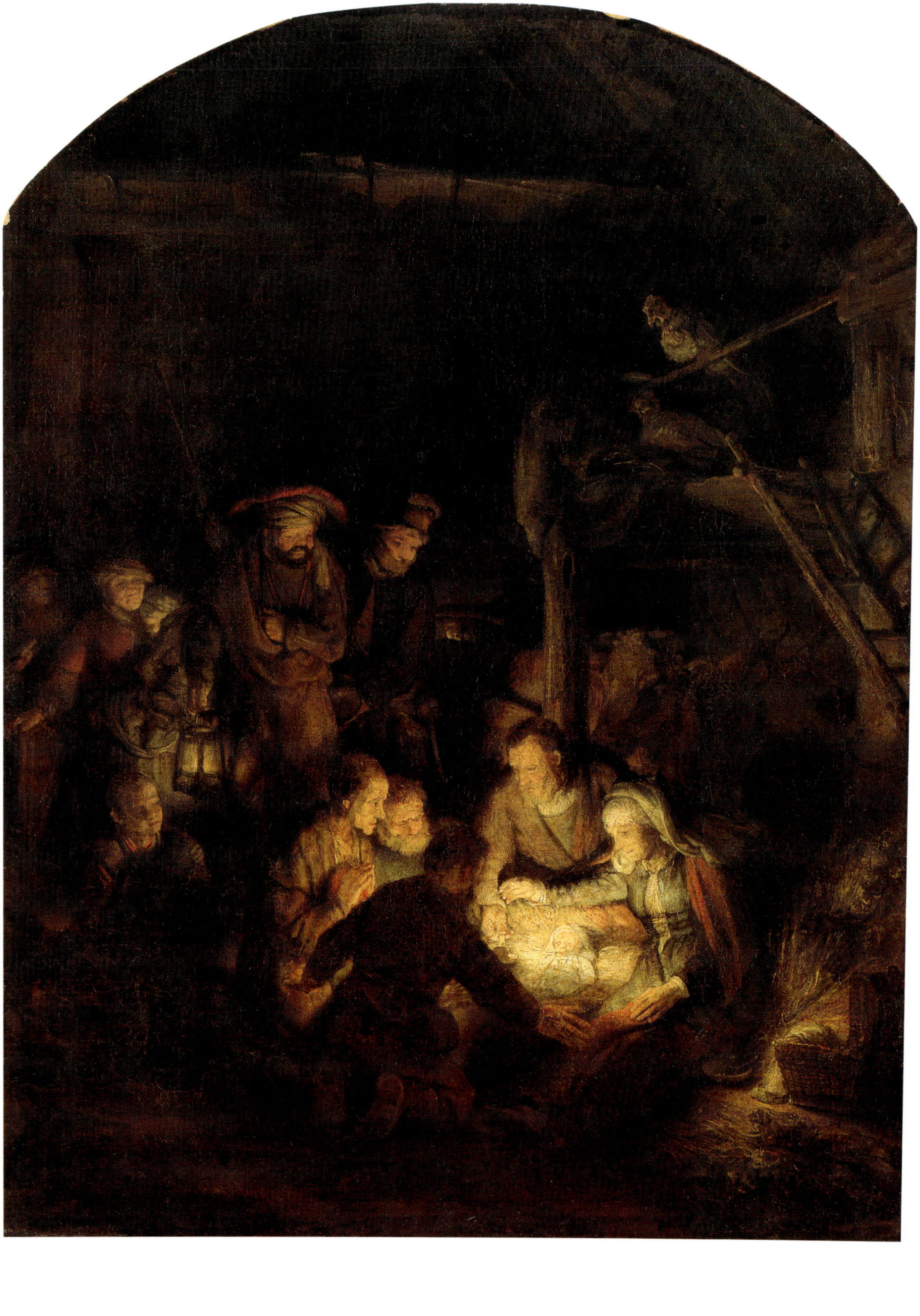

of Christ. Of these three aforementioned pictures one has been completed, namely Christ ascending to Heaven, and the other two are more than half done. And should it please His Excellency to receive this finished piece at once or the three of them together, I pray you my lord to let me know.[20]

The inclusion of this self-portrait in the first picture of the *Passion* series also suggests that Rembrandt would indeed have been careful to ensure the quality of the other images, as the correspondence appears to confirm. After the letter quoted above, Huygens in fact asked Rembrandt to come to The Hague in order to inspect *in situ* the first three pictures of the *Passion* series that he had delivered while he prepared to finish the remaining two which he describes in the letter as 'more than half done'. The third picture that he completed was, of course, also the first of the three pictures newly commissioned by the Stadtholder in order to create a *Passion* series, developed from the two pendants already in his possession. Furthermore, it was not the next scene in the narrative sequence that Rembrandt had finished at this stage, but the last, the *Ascension*.

Such apparent inconsistencies can be detected in many aspects of the creation of this group of seven paintings, and the scale and nature of the *Ascension* have also been identified as further evidence of Rembrandt's lack of care in creating them.[21] It has been acutely observed, however, that these peculiarities concerning the *Ascension* are probably not the result of carelessness but rather the reverse, and that there were good reasons for painting the *Ascension* at this stage. According to this line of thinking, the *Ascension* looks the way it does precisely because it was designed to appear not at the end of a sequence but in the middle of a group of five, which thus formed a pleasing whole from the point of view of overall composition and rhythm.[22] Indeed, one might go further and suggest that the *Ascension* was actually hung above the other four, which could have been in pairs below and to either side of it: an arrangement around a doorway suggests itself. Both Rembrandt and Huygens were naturally concerned to see the *Ascension* in place in order to judge that the whole group would indeed 'fit' before the artist proceeded, as eventually he did, to complete the series with the *Entombent* and *Resurrection*. In his second letter to Huygens of February or March 1636, Rembrandt wrote:

... I shall follow anon to see how the picture [i.e. the *Ascension*] accords with the rest.[23]

On his visits to the palace in The Hague, Rembrandt would also have become familiar with the other works of art on view; and, after all, he had painted Maurits, the brother of Constantin Huygens, in 1632 (Hamburger Kunsthalle, Hamburg), and had portrayed the wife of the Stadtholder, Amalia von Solms (Musée Jacquemart-Andrée, Paris), in the same year. The Stadtholder's collection of pictures in 1632 already included two and probably three pictures by Rembrandt.[24]

The presence of these other works by Rembrandt, and of one of them in particular, may itself go some way towards explaining the apparent oddities in the composition of the *Circumcision* noted above. One of the early Rembrandt paintings in the Stadtholder's collection was a *Presentation in the Temple* (*Simeon in the Temple*), which is almost certainly that in the Mauritshuis, The Hague, and dated 1631.

The main objection, aesthetically, to the lost *Circumcision* is that the scale of its figures especially is so at odds with the rest of the 'series'. Yet it should be recalled that it does not actually form part of the same narrative as the *Passion*, even though shaped to conform with those pictures, being framed in the same way, and

The Nativity by Rembrandt, 1646.
Oil on canvas, 97 × 71.3 cm.
Alte Pinakothek, Munich

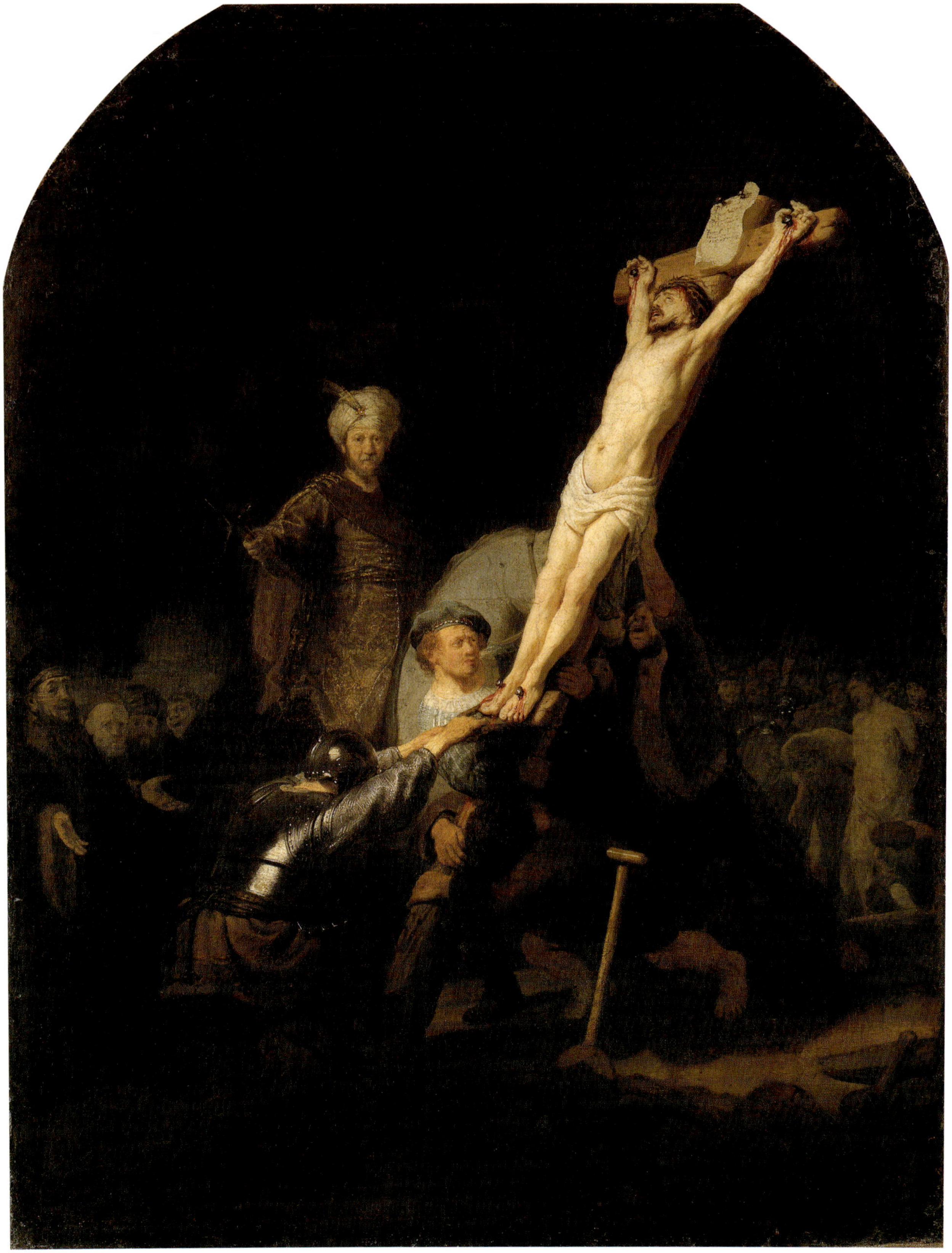

Elevation of the Cross by Rembrandt, *c.* 1633.
Oil on canvas, 96.2 × 72.2 cm.
Alte Pinakothek, Munich

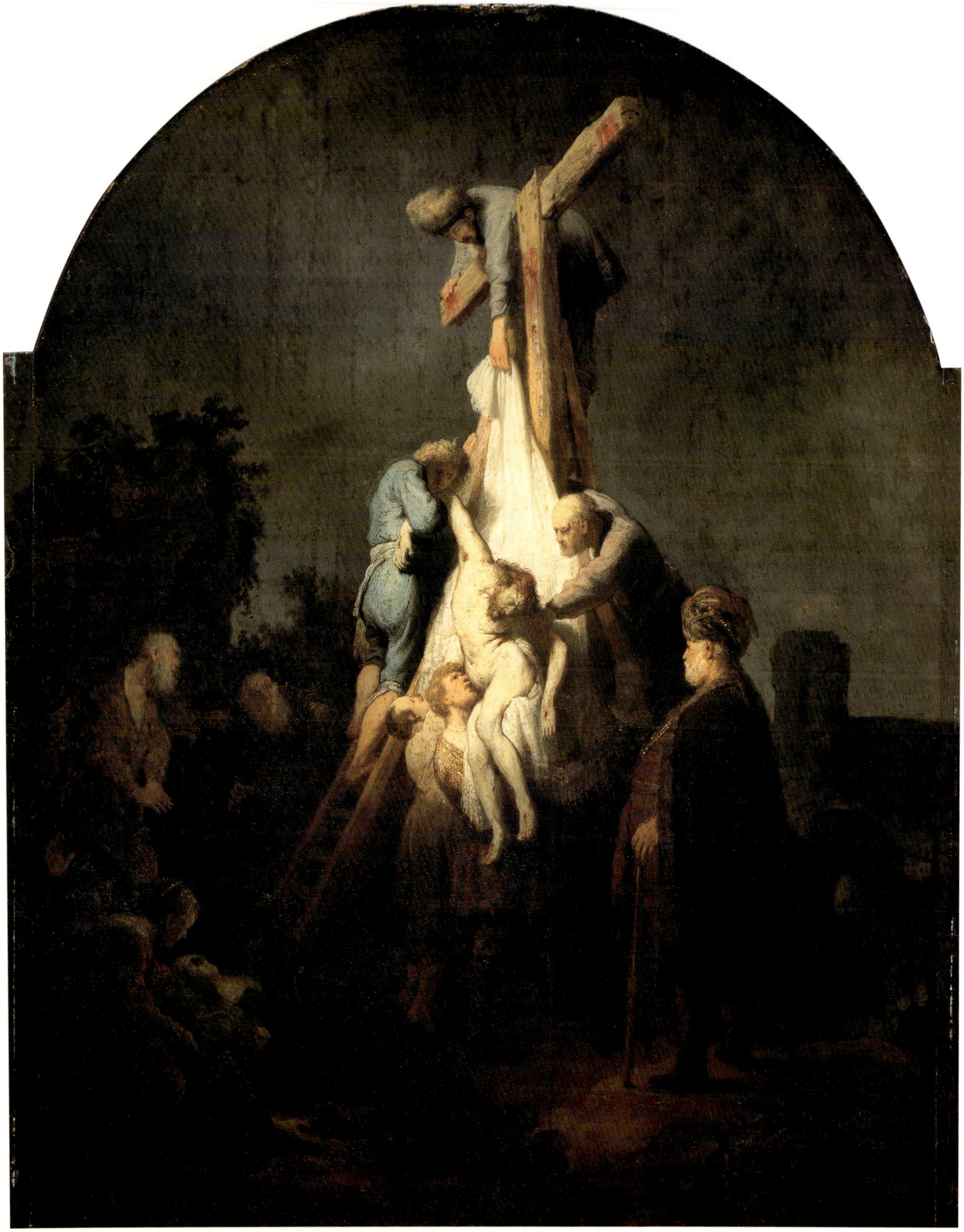

Descent from the Cross by Rembrandt, *c.* 1633.
Oil on panel, 89.4 × 65.2 cm.
Alte Pinakothek, Munich

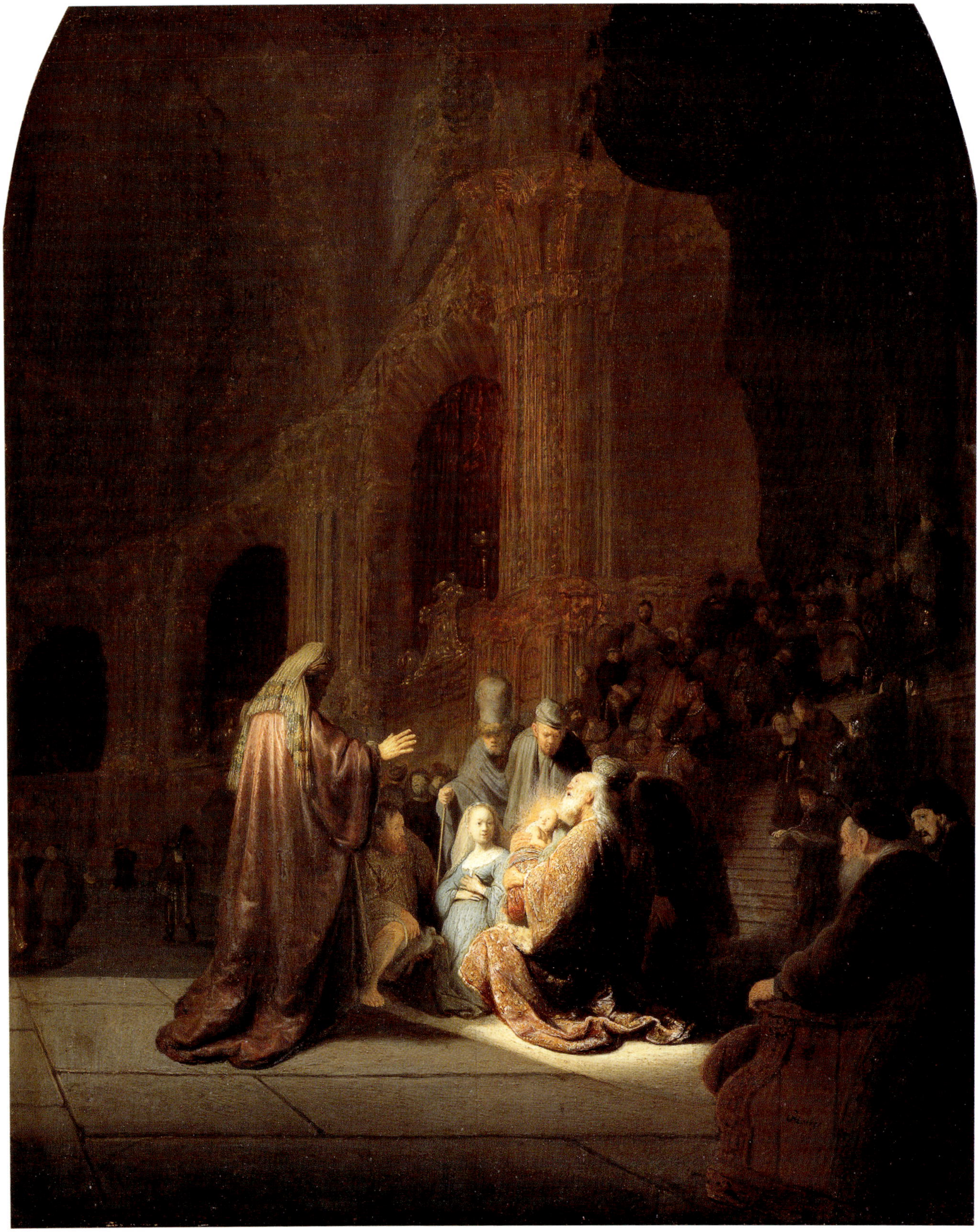

The presentation in the Temple (Simeon in the Temple) by Rembrandt, 1631.
Oil on canvas, 60.9 × 47.8 cm.
Mauritshuis, The Hague

of the same size. The setting of the *Circumcision*, in the Temple, and the small scale of the figures set well back in the picture space, do, however, accord closely with the 1631 *Presentation in the Temple*. It may be that, far from representing an uncharacteristic muddle on the part of Rembrandt, the artist was being careful to make the *Circumcision* fit, in its setting within the Temple, with the picture of the *Presentation* which, of course, he knew the Stadtholder to possess. Both these scenes were traditionally shown in Dutch art as taking place in the Temple and, earlier in his career, around 1630, Rembrandt had etched the circumcision, and had shown the scene as taking place within the Temple. Rembrandt later changed the setting, in his etching of 1654 and painting of 1662 (National Gallery of Art, Washington, DC), to the textually more correct notion of showing the circumcision taking place within the Stable, at the same time making the iconography more specifically Christian.[25]

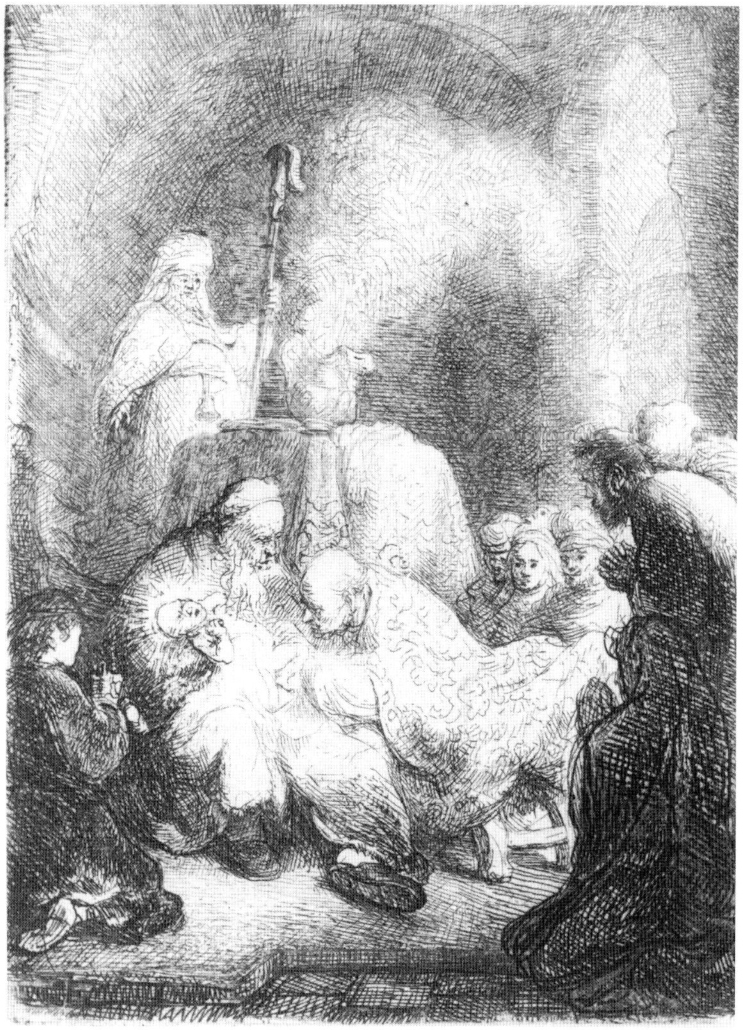

The Circumcision (in the Temple) by Rembrandt, *c.* 1630. Etching, 8.8 × 6.4 cm

The Stadtholder's *Nativity*, in contrast with the *Circumcision*, does accord more in scale of the figures, as well as in size and shape, with the *Passion* series.

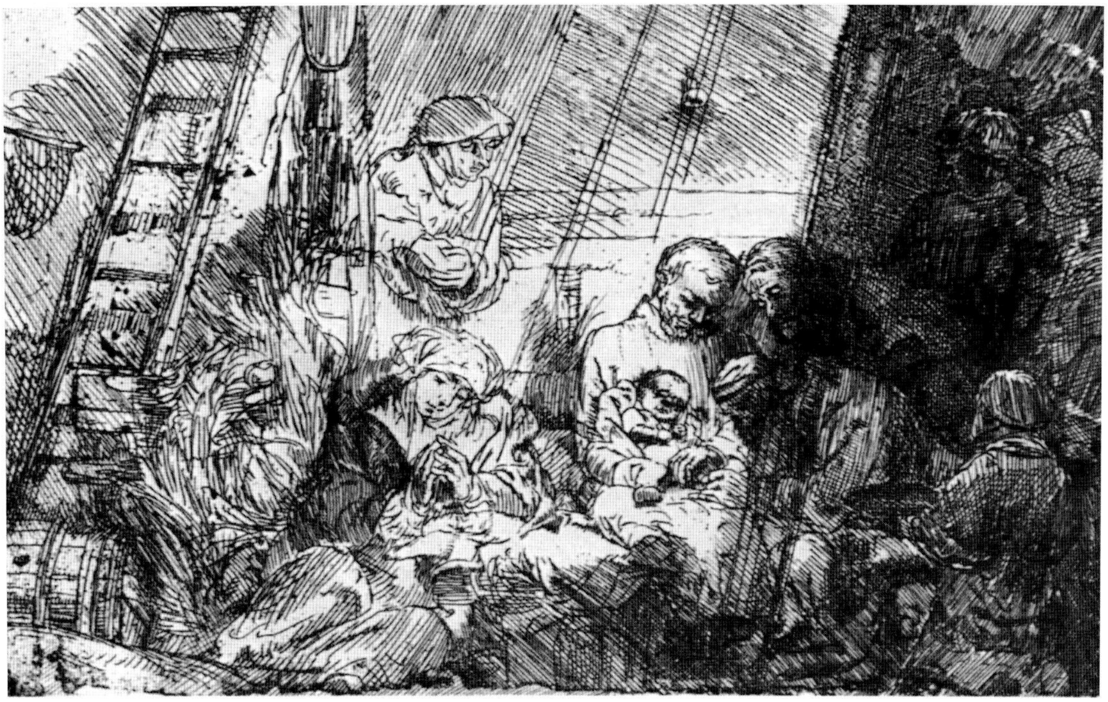

The Circumcision (in the Stable) by Rembrandt, 1654.
Etching, 9.4 × 14.5 cm.
Sotheby's, 29 June 1987 (249)

So far as the original arrangement of all these pictures within the Stadtholder's gallery is concerned, we may surmise that some sort of compromise was forced upon artist and patron alike in order to fit the new pictures into an overall 'hang'. With this in mind, it is important to stress that the *Nativity*, *Circumcision* and *Presentation*, in that order, form a correct and coherent narrative sequence in themselves of the *Infancy of Christ*, but that two of them were shaped and framed to accord with the previously completed *Passion*.

After he had painted the *Circumcision* in these unusual and particular circumstances for the Stadtholder, Rembrandt, as noted above, etched the subject in 1654, but this time using the setting of the Stable. This Stable is remarkably like that employed in his painting of the *Nativity* for the Stadtholder, and Rembrandt adopted the same setting in the still later painting of the *Circumcision* which he made for the Amsterdam collector and art dealer Lodewik van Ludick.[26]

NOTES

1 H. Gerson, *Seven Letters by Rembrandt* [translated into English by Yda D. Ovink], The Hague, 1961; *The Rembrandt Documents*, compiled by W.L. Strauss and M. van der Meulen…, New York, 1979, pp. 126ff. G. Schwarz, *Rembrandt: His life, His Paintings* [1984], London, 1991, p. 107, notes that another letter, of 1662, survives but only in Italian translation.

2 Translated in Schwarz, op. cit., pp. 73-6, p. 74.

3 The five paintings of the *Passion* series are assessed in J. Bruyn, B. Haak, S. H. Levie, P. J. J. van Thiel and E. van de Wetering, *A Corpus of Rembrandt Paintings. By the Stichtung Foundation Rembrandt Project*, The Hague, 1982– [three volumes, up to 1642]: *Descent from the Cross* [vol. II], A65, pp. 276ff.; *Raising of the Cross* [vol. II], A 69, pp. 311ff.; *Ascension* [vol. III], A118 pp. 202ff.; *Entombment* [vol. III], A 126, pp. 271ff.; *Resurrection* [vol. III],

A127 pp. 280ff. Hereafter *Corpus*.

4 Quoted in C. Brown, J. Kelch & P. van Thiel, *Rembrandt: the Master & his Workshop – Paintings*, exh. cat., National Gallery, London, New Haven and London, 1992, p. 156. See *The Rembrandt Documents*, op. cit. The *Corpus*, op. cit., has a full account of the provenance under A 65 (vol. II). It is evident that Rembrandt had to supply the ebony frames and it is likely that the gilded leaves were a later addition: *Corpus*, vol. II, pp. 285-6.

5 Brown *et al.*, op. cit., p. 156.

6 *Corpus*, pp. 285ff.

7 Ibid.

8 Ibid: '[G. J. Karsch] *Gründliche* Specification *derer vortrefflichen und unschatzbaren Gemählden… , In der Galerie der Churfürstl.* Residenz zu Düsseldorf… '.

9 Brown *et al.*, op. cit., p. 156.

10 The restoration in question had recently been undertaken by the court painter to the Elector Palatine Carl Theodor (r. 1742-99) in Mannheim, Philipp Hieronymus Brinckmann (1709-61) – at which time he inscribed the *Resurrection* with the date 1755 – who wrote to Carl Heinrich von Heinecken in Dresden on 30 March 1756: '… ich möchte wunschen Sie seheten unsere Rimbrand wie sie jetzt Seindt ich habe alle 6 wieder in guten standt gebracht. Die auferstehung Christi habe die Mahlerey von seinem alten Tuch herunter genommen und auf ein Brett gemacht, und so dasz auch nicht dass mindeste ryssel oder sprüngel ersehen.' *Corpus*, vol. II, p. 286.

11 *La Galerie Electorale de Dusseldorff ou Catalogue Raisonné et Figuré de ses Tableaux… par Chretien de Mechel &c*, Basel, 1778. The six Rembrandt paintings are cat. nos. 214-9 and see pls. XVI, XVII.

12 Arthur K. Wheelock, Jr., *Dutch Paintings of the Seventeenth Century, The Collections of the National Gallery of Art* [Washington, DC], Washington, 1995, under cat. no. 1942.9.60 (656), pp. 270-76, p. 274, n. 6.

13 For example, Schwarz, op. cit., p. 117.

14 Ibid. Schwarz's record of a conversation (ibid., p. 117) with the modern conservator of the *Entombment* only confirms that the picture is in poor condition, and not that it was badly painted in the first place. A sympathetic discussion of the Passion series is S. Schama, *Rembrandt's Eyes*, 1999, pp. 435ff.: he does not agree with Schwarz's assessment.

15 Rembrandt had been given 600 guilders for each of the *Passion* series but had hoped for more. The payments are discussed in *Corpus*, vol. II, pp. 284-5.

16 *Corpus*, vol. II, p. 285.

17 'Rembrandt created me. P. H. Brinckmann brought thee back to life/1755'. See Schwarz, p. 117, where he takes a negative view of this evidence and of Rembrandt's proceedings.

18 See H. Perry Chapman, *Rembrandt's Self-Portraits: A Study in Seventeenth-Century Identity*, Princeton, 1990, pp. 108ff. He quotes (p. 112-3) a poem by Jacobus Revius, 'He Bore Our Griefs', first identified by Tümpel as a telling contemporary literary parallel: C. Tümpel, *Rembrandt*, Amsterdam, 1986, p. 136.

19 Chapman, op. cit., pp. 108ff. Chapman, p. 110, also summarizes the arguments for dating the sequence of painting.

20 Schwarz, op. cit., p. 107.

21 For example, ibid., p. 113.

22 E. Kai Sass, *Comments on Rembrandt's Passion Paintings and Constantijn Huygens's Iconography*, Copenhagen, 1971, pp. 36-8.

23 *Corpus*, vol. II, p. 285. Rembrandt's harmonizing of the *Ascension* with the preceding pictures and those to follow is discussed, ibid., vol. III, pp. 206-7.

24 Inventory of August 1632, which also indicates that none of the *Passion* series was yet there: see e.g., Chapman, op. cit., p. 109.

25 See Wheelock, op. cit., cat. no. 1942.9.60 (656), pp. 270-76, pp. 272-3.

26 Wheelock, op. cit., and illus. p. 271. It is possible that Rembrandt was responsible also for an early etching of the subject in *c.* 1625/6 where the setting is also within the Temple, but the attribution is uncertain, see Brown *et al.*, op. cit. (*Drawings and Etchings*), pp. 161-2, illus. p. 162.

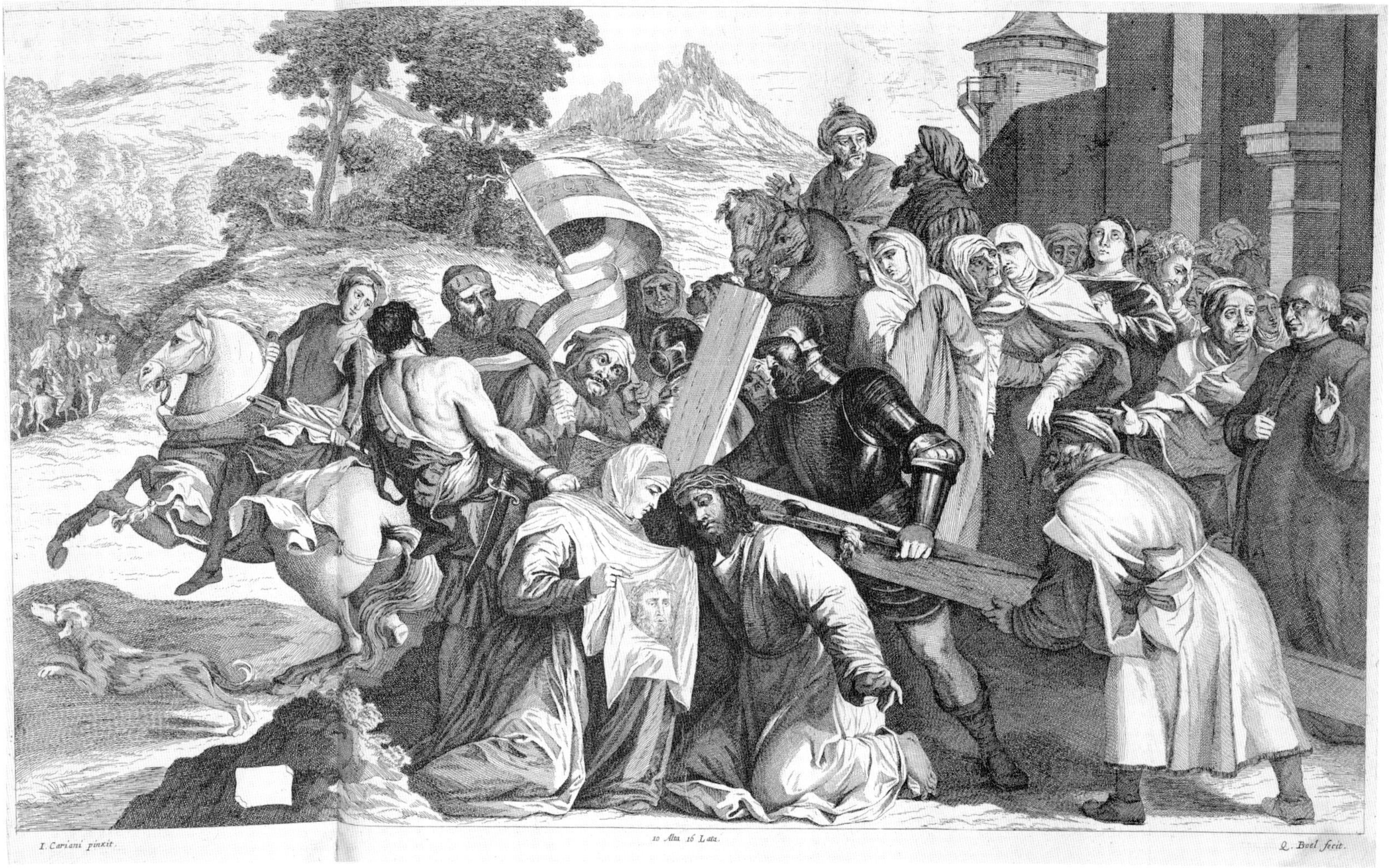

Christ carrying the Cross, with St Veronica.
Etching by Quirin Boel published in *Theatrum Pictorium*, Antwerp, 1658, after lost painting of 1535-40 by Giovanni Busi, called Cariani (*c.* 1485-after 1547)

Giovanni Busi, called Cariani

c. 1485-after 1547

Christ carrying the Cross, with St. Veronica

1535-40

Oil on canvas
c. 208 × 312 cm with frame

Christ carrying the Cross, with St Veronica is first mentioned in the correspondence between James, 3rd Marquess and 1st Duke of Hamilton (1606-49), and his brother-in-law, Basil, Viscount Feilding (1608-75), later 2nd Earl of Denbigh.[1] It appears thereafter in a series of inventories and pictorial records, having entered the famous collection of Archduke Leopold Wilhelm, who became Governor of the Spanish Netherlands in 1646. He died in 1662, and passed the painting together with many others to his nephew Emperor Leopold I (1640-1705) but *Christ carrying the Cross* is last heard of in 1702, and no trace of it has subsequently been found.

Feilding, a connoisseur and diplomat, was appointed Ambassador Extraordinary to Venice on 14 September 1634, where he remained until 1638. In 1636 Hamilton began forming a major picture collection, and Feilding was in an ideal position to help him by negotiating the purchase of important pictures and collections which came on to the market in Venice. The surviving correspondence between Feilding and Hamilton, from the autumn of 1635 until the summer of 1638, constitutes a detailed record of Hamilton's purchases during that period.[2]

Hamilton's motives in building up a collection on this lavish scale requires little explanation: his closeness to the King – he succeeded to the position of his uncle, the 1st Duke of Buckingham, within the royal household, as Master of the Horse – evidently had much to do with it. Clarendon believed that during the 1630s Hamilton 'had the greatest power over the affection of the king of any man at that time'.[3] Hamilton certainly informed Charles on several occasions of works of art that were for sale, for example, on 11/21 March 1636: 'I have tould the King thatt ye wrytt to me of ane rare pictur thatt was att Venis, he is desyrous to knoe the storie, and whatt bignes itt is of and the prys.'[4] One of his secrets was that, 'unlike Arundel, he knew well the king's tastes, co-operated in acquiring for Charles what he most coveted and was generous in his gifts to the king'.[5] The desire to form an important art collection on the part of a principal courtier to Charles I, for whom art was such a passion, would arise naturally. Hamilton's collecting can be understood as part of the normal way in which rivals for royal favour might attempt to reinforce their positions and gain an advantage over others.[6]

Hamilton's collecting appears to have been limited to the years leading up to the first Civil War of 1642-6. During the uneasy peace that followed, Hamilton was entrusted with the command of the Scots, with whom the King had made a desperate and secret alliance. Hamilton's incompetent generalship allowed Cromwell to win the second Civil War. He was captured at the bitterly fought Battle of Preston of 1648, and executed shortly after the King in 1649.

In a letter of 1 May 1637 Feilding mentioned to Hamilton that the great collection

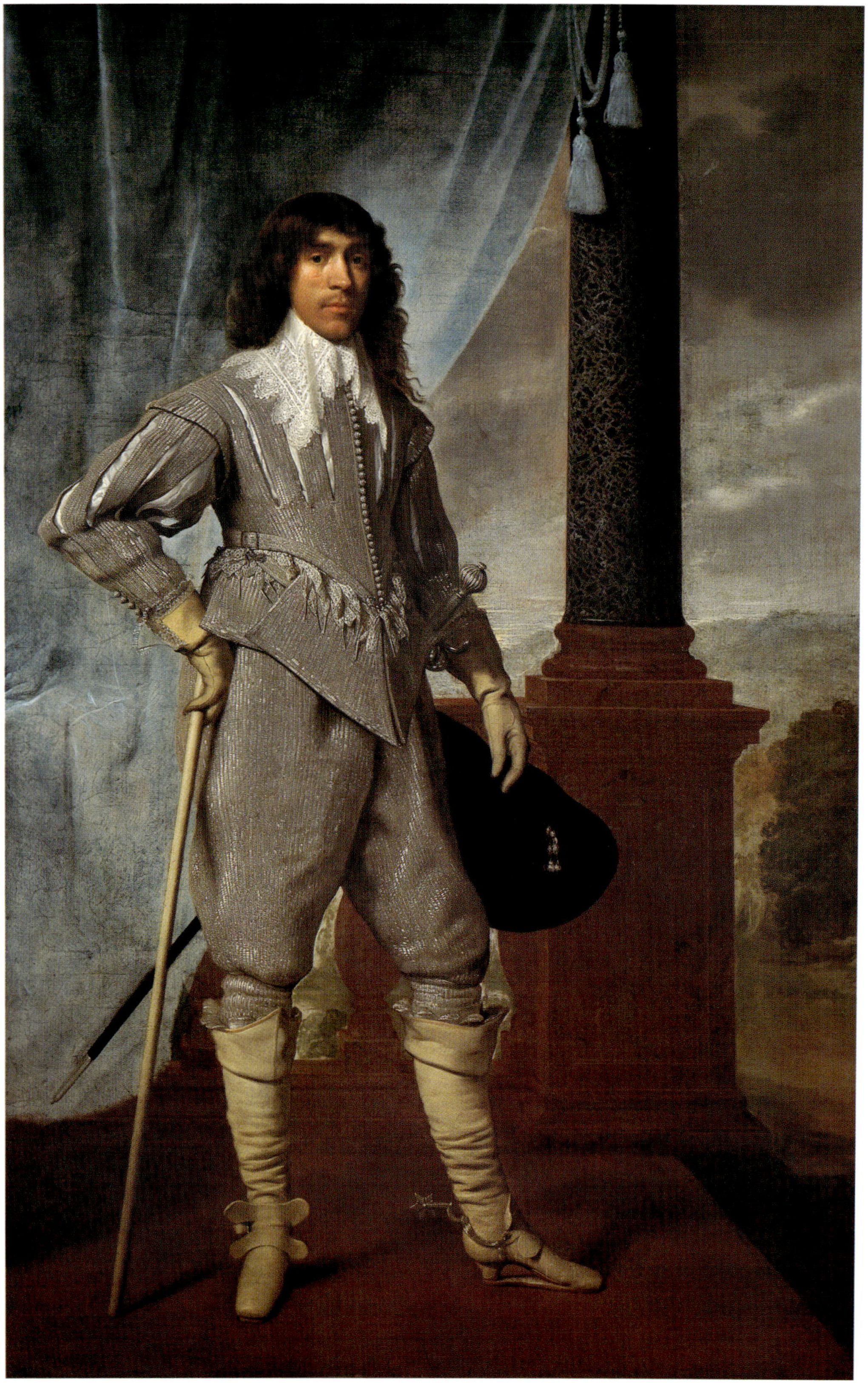

James, 3rd Marquess and 1st Duke of Hamilton (1606-49) by Daniel Mytens (1590-1647), 1629.
Oil on canvas, 220.9 × 140.9 cm.
Scottish National Portrait Gallery, Edinburgh

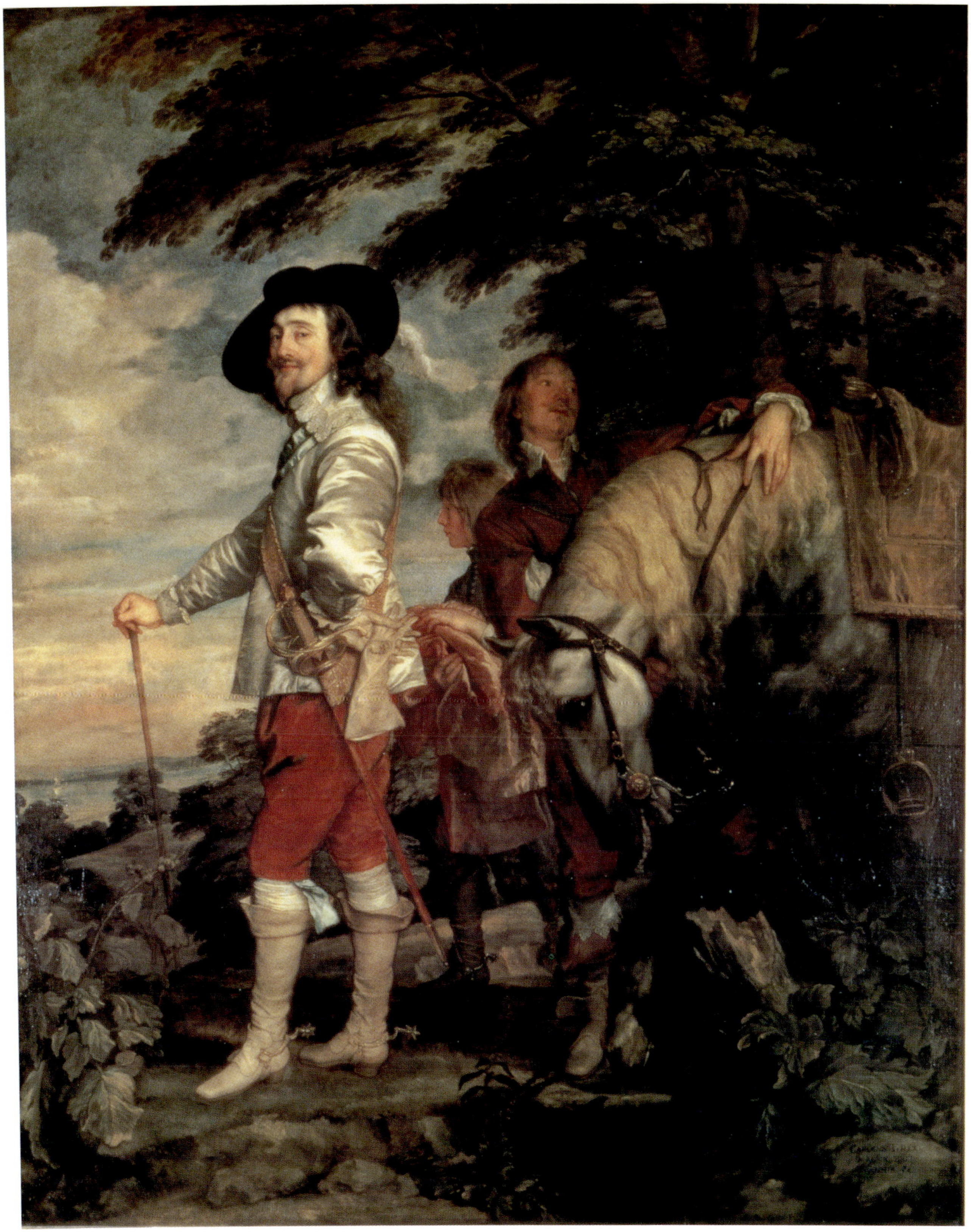

Charles I à la chasse by Sir Anthony van Dyck (1599-1641), *c.* 1635.
Oil on canvas, 272 × 212 cm.
Musée du Louvre, Paris

of the merchant Bartolommeo della Nave was available for '... m/20 Ducketts but I am told by a friend that they may be bought down to m/2 pound sterling, and if they could be had at that price your lo.p will not meet hereafter with so many excellent peeces, nor att so easy a rate'.[7] Della Nave's collection was famed for its Titians, highly praised by contemporaries, and had already attracted the attention of Charles I and the 2nd Earl of Arundel, and other connoisseurs in England and elsewhere. Hamilton's letter of 7/17 July 1637 reveals that, in seeking to acquire the Della Nave collection, he was at first acting on behalf of the King who

> ... is so extremely takine ther with as he hes persuaded me to by them all, and for thatt end hes furnished me with munnis, so, brother, I have undertakin that they shall all cume into Ingland, booth pictures and statues, out of which he is to make choyes of whatt he lykes, and to repay me whatt they coost if I heave a mynd to turne marchand.[8]

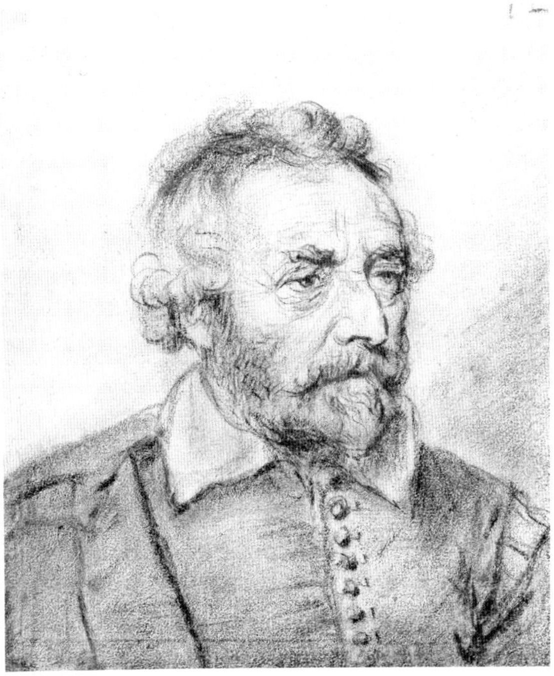

Thomas Howard, 2nd Earl of Arundel by Jan Lievens (1607-1674), *c.*1643. Black and red chalk, 18 × 14 cm. Kupferstichkabinett, Staatliche Museen zu Berlin

By the time, however, that Feilding had finally negotiated a price of 15,000 ducats in late 1638, the King was in no financial position to buy the collection, and so Hamilton acquired it. Before negotiating the Della Nave purchase, Feilding had written to Hamilton from Venice on 10/20 March 1636:

> I have sent you a list of some I am bargaining for you and the price the owner holds that att wch not withstanding I hope to bring down to 7 or 8 hundred Ducketts at the most wch I am sure you will be well satisfied with because I know by the comments of the most skilful of that art to be orginalls except that of Titian.[9]

The list to which Feilding refers survives and among the 35 paintings mentioned is:

> A great peece of Cariani: divers esteeme that picture to be of Georgons hand, who was Cariani's scholar, but excell'd him.[10]

Hamilton replied from St James's on 8/18 April 1636 saying that he believed the price (80 ducats)[11] expensive but that he was 'much in looufe with pictures'.[12]

Several inventories or lists were made of Hamilton's collection,[13] ranging over the period from 1636, when he was first making major purchases, to 1649, when he was executed and some of his collection was sold. It is not known for which of his houses the inventories were made, or whether or how the collection was split between his various houses, although the Cariani was hung in the 'Lower Gallery' of one of them.[14] The most detailed description of the missing Cariani is in Inventory No. 15, which is thought to be the earliest inventory that has survived, since it is does not include pictures from the Della Nave collection, which were bought in 1638 and arrived in 1639:

> 32: A picture of our Saviour bearinge his crosse St Veronica offerringe him a Towell, 3 men on horsebacke, 20ty other figures of men and women besydes little figures of men and horses afarre of – with a landschape of Johannes: Cariano.[15]

For most of the pictures on this list a description is given, with a space at the end left blank for the artist's name. In the case of some pictures, the name has been added, in a different hand. The Cariani is one of few pictures, however, which has the artist's name included in the same hand as the description and presumably indicates that the work was signed.

The picture appears again in 'A Catalogue of my Lord Marquesses pictures' (inventory No. 5) which can be dated to before 12 April 1643, the date upon which the Marquess was created Duke of Hamilton. Six hundred pictures were listed as in forty-four cases, and the Cariani, in case 23 (with three other pictures), is described as 'Christ carring his Cross Johanes Cariani.' Inventory No. 6 (probably the first version, of which No. 5 is a clearer copy) has again in case 23 'A great piece of Johnis Cariani of Chr: Karring of his crosse'.[16] On 27 March 1643, before Hamilton was created Duke, Parliament, which badly needed money to finance its military campaign, had passed an order to sequestrate the estates of Royalists. Hamilton had his collection of pictures and English possessions seized, and they were given into the custody of Feilding who, unlike his brother-in-law, was a parliamentarian. The list might therefore have been made at this time, when the collection was being packed prior to being sent to Feilding.

On 20 March 1647-8, a notice was issued from the Parliament of Scotland in Edinburgh to the Lords and Commons of England, 'praying that certain pictures and other property of the Duke of Hamilton... May be re-delivered to his grace in consideration of the great suffringe of the said Duke both in his person and fortune since ye beginning of these comotions'.[17] It seems likely, however, that this request was never granted, and only a small number of pictures was documented as being back with the Duke's family after his death.[18]

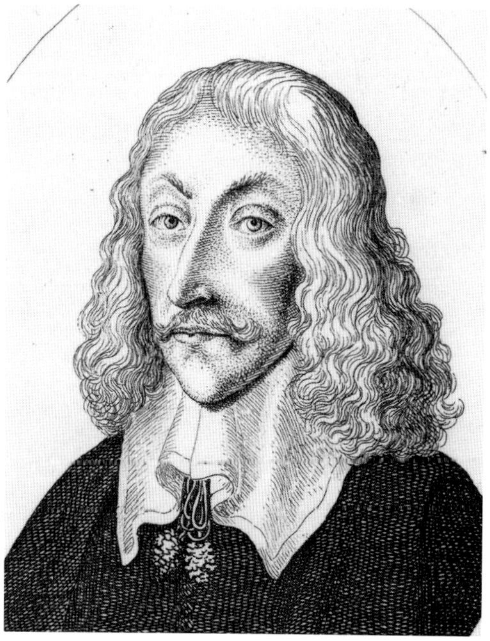

Basil Feilding, 2nd Earl of Denbigh (1608-1675).
Engraving published by William Richardson in 1811

A further list of Hamilton's pictures refers to King Charles as deceased, and it must therefore have been drawn up after January 1649, but whether it predates Hamilton's own execution on 9 March 1649 is not known. The list is compiled in French and is of particular interest since it includes dimensions. It could possibly be a list of pictures for sale from the Duke's collection and may have been made specifically for the Archduke Leopold Wilhelm, into whose collection the picture is known to have passed, and it has been suggested that it could have even been compiled by the Archduke's agents.[19] The Cariani appears as No. 175: 'Jean Coriani Nostre Seigneur portant le Croix, h. 9 la. 13'.[20]

Shortly after Hamilton's death on 9 March 1649 moves were made to sell some of the collection in the Netherlands, although only part of the story of how they were taken out of England, and by whom, is now clear. The Duke's heir was his brother William, who escaped to Holland with at least part of the collection.[21] If Feilding's custody of the pictures was still effective, he was certainly well qualified to know about potential buyers, and to arrange their sale. There are other examples of collections being protected for royalist heirs by sympathetic parliamentarians. One such instance was that of the 2nd Duke of Buckingham, who had been born in the very year of his father's assassination in 1628. The estates he was to inherit were sequestered by Parliament at an early stage of the Civil War, but the Duke was able to regain control of the art collection in October 1647 and immediately sent most of it abroad for safety.[22]

In the case of Hamilton's works of art, many of them swiftly passed into the possession of the Archduke Leopold Wilhelm, because by 19 April, a little over a month after Hamilton's death, a passport was issued to Archduke Leopold by 'the States General of the United Netherlands' authorising him for 'the export of paintings and gallery exhibits from the United Netherlands to Brussels free of carriage

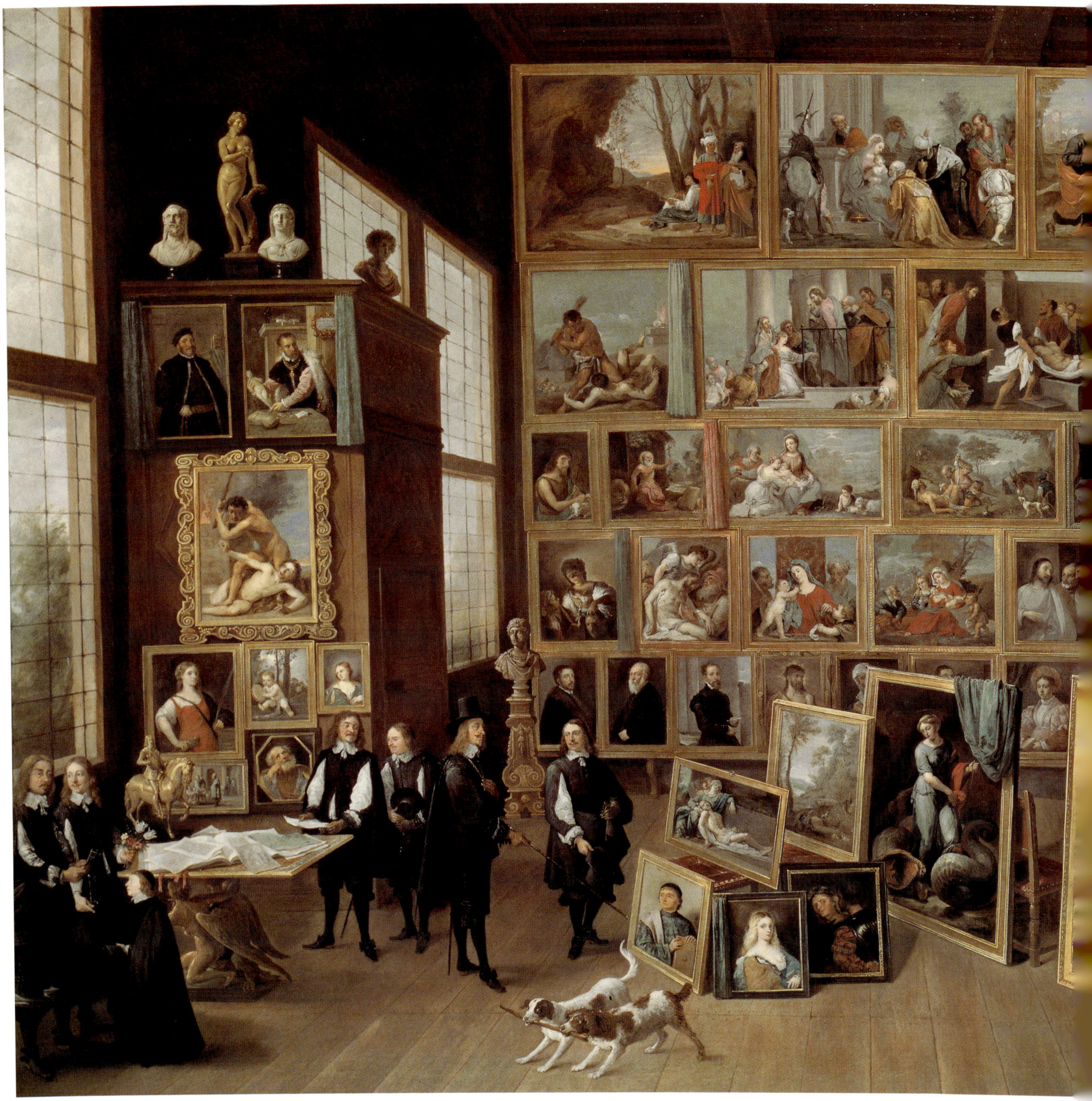

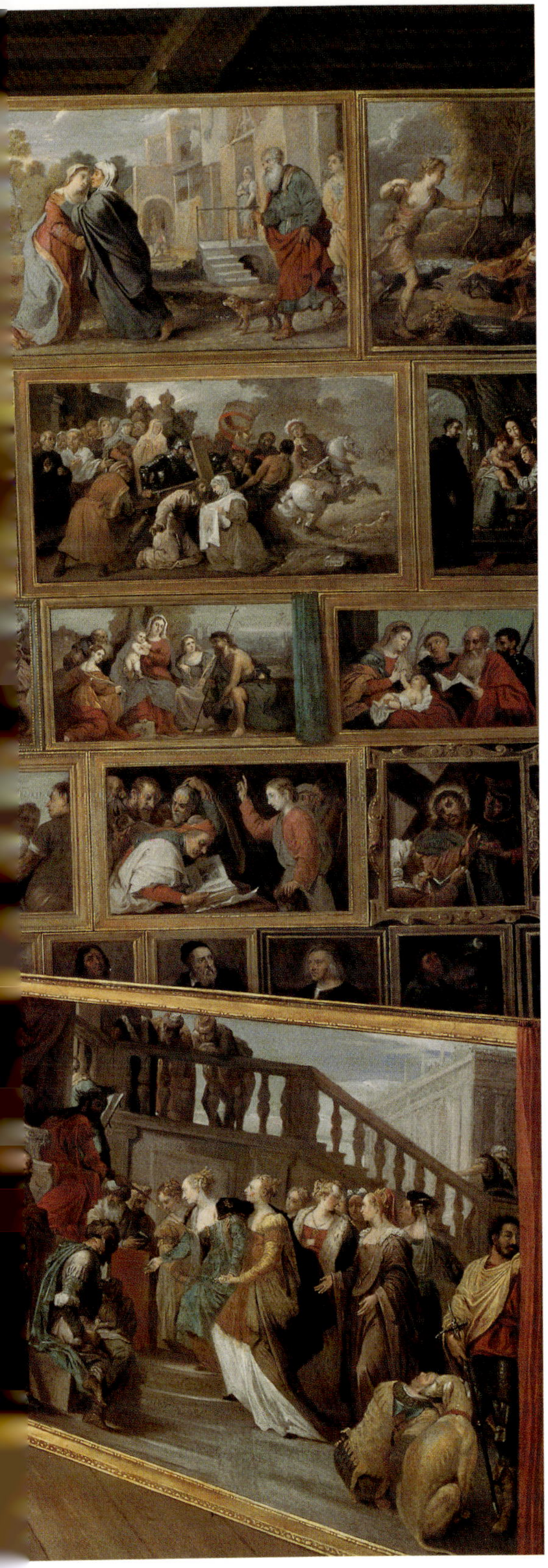

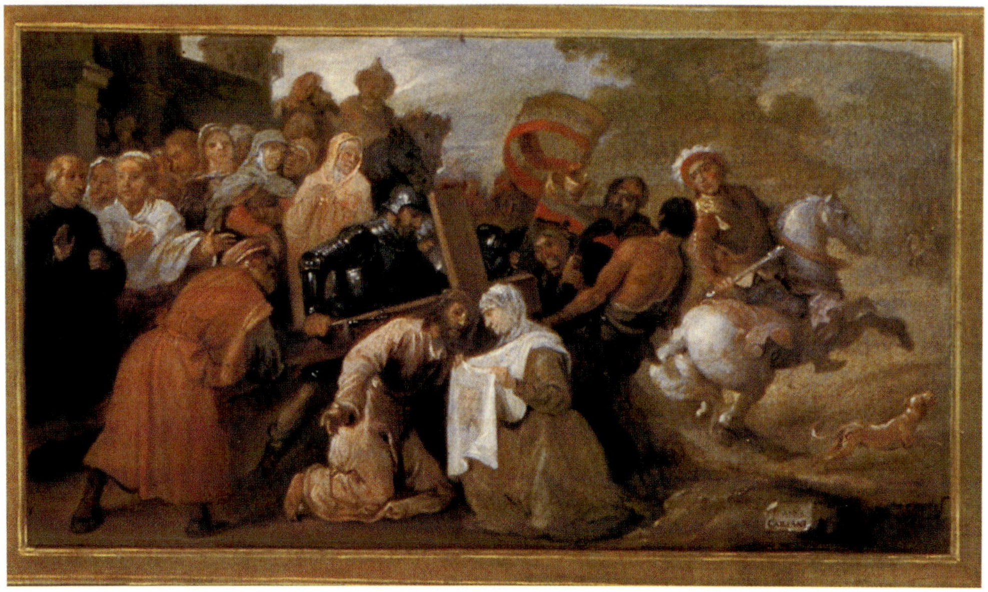

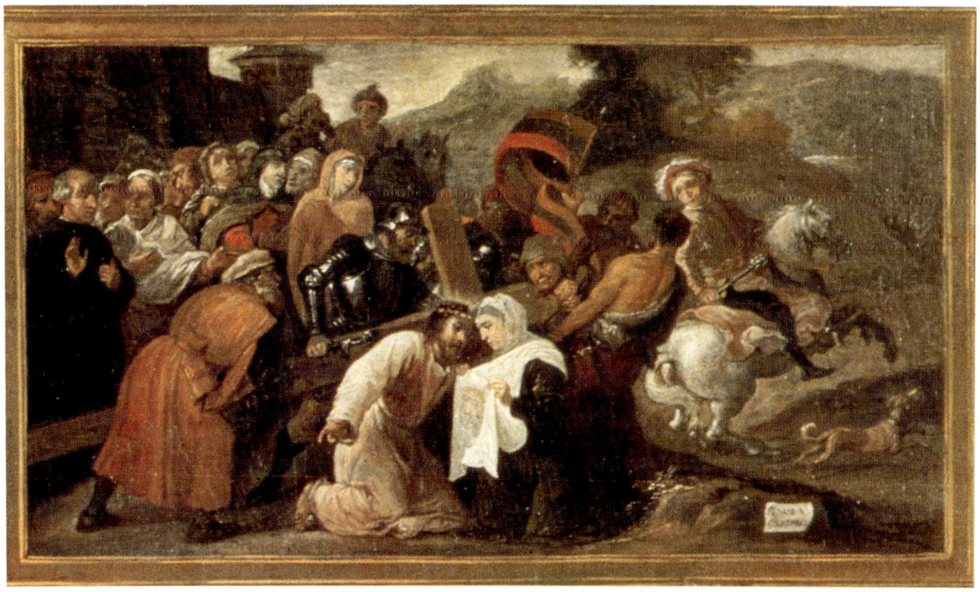

The Archduke Leopold Wilhelm in his picture gallery.
by David Teniers the Younger (1610-90), 1651.
Oil on canvas, 123 × 163 cm. Kunsthistorischesmuseum, Vienna

Detail of Vienna version of *The Archduke Leopold Wilhelm in his picture gallery* by David Teniers the Younger in 1651 showing the lost Cariani

Detail of Petworth version of *The Archduke Leopold Wilhelm in his picture gallery* by David Teniers the Younger showing the lost Cariani (see p.142)

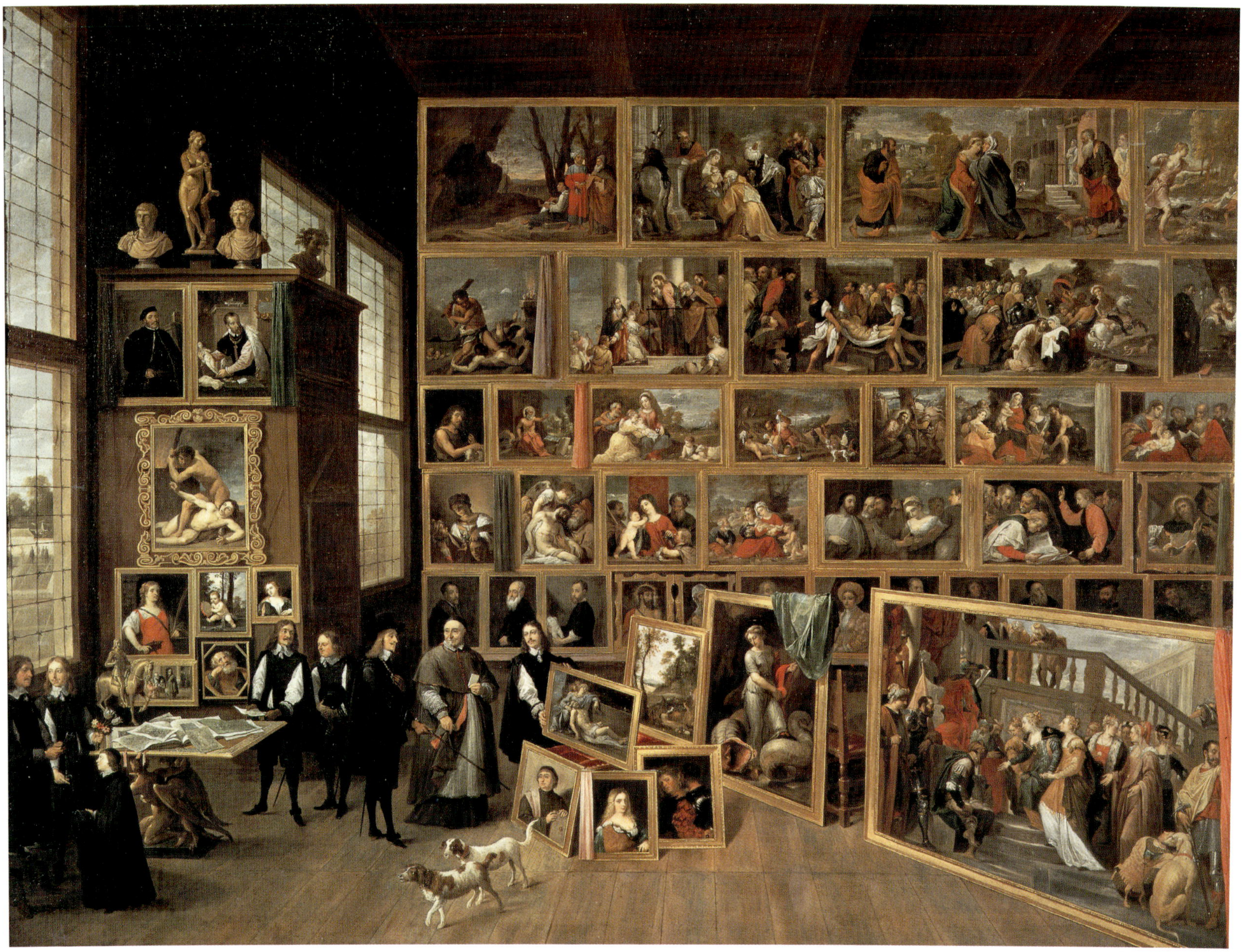

The Archduke Leopold Wilhelm in his picture gallery
by David Teniers the Younger.
Oil on canvas, 127 × 163 cm.
Petworth House, Sussex, The National Trust

charges and without being required to pay any duties thereon'.[23] Eighty paintings and other objects and works of art from the late Duke's collection are listed, all the paintings being from the Della Nave collection. The Cariani was therefore not among them, but evidently came to the Archduke along with the many other paintings he subsequently acquired from the Hamilton collection.

The Cariani was bought at an early stage in this process, however, because by 1651 David Teniers the Younger, appointed court painter to the Archduke, and director of his collections in that year, included it, along with other Hamilton pictures, in a 'Gallery Picture' showing the pick of the Archduke's collection. This composition is quite an early example of a genre where individual collections are recorded in the form of a conceit that imagines them to be crowded into one conveniently designed gallery interior. In practice, it is almost certain that none of the interiors which we see in such paintings records the actual hang and disposition of a collection, or even a particular room in any particular building. The inclusion of a suitable selection of interested parties – painters, dealers and the owner himself – reflects the artificiality of the device, and in this painting Teniers depicted himself showing the Archduke around the recently acquired Italian paintings, supposedly gathered together in his gallery in Brussels.

The Gallery of the Archduke Leopold exists in two principal versions (although other variants are known), in the Kunsthistorisches Museum, Vienna, and in Petworth House, Sussex, which are identical in size and format, although with some minor variations among the subordinate details, and the Petworth version is signed and dated 1651.[24] Cariani's *Christ carrying the Cross* appears in both versions, on the back wall, towards the right-hand side of the second tier of pictures.

The extraordinarily rapid building of a major international collection of works of art by Hamilton was surpassed by the activities of Archduke Leopold Wilhelm, who only began collecting pictures after his appointment as Governor of the Spanish Netherlands in 1646. By 1649 or so he had built up an astonishing collection of around 617 Italian and 885 northern pictures.[25] He was buying at an especially auspicious time because he was able to benefit so much from the current dispersal of the great English collections, including that of the King in addition to Hamilton's.

In 1656 Archduke Leopold moved to Vienna, taking his collection with him, and Teniers made small oil copies of individual paintings in the collection, most of which were finished in the same year.[26] Some 243 of these sketches of the Italian paintings were published as prints, by different print-makers, as an album in the *Theatrum Pictorium* which was first published in Antwerp in 1658 and again in 1684 when the plates were numbered. The lost Cariani is not among the small oil copies of Teniers, and so, apart from the 'gallery pictures', its appearance is chiefly known from the print in *Theatrum*, where it is No. 166.

It was etched for the *Theatrum* by Quirin Boel, one of a Flemish family of engravers, and beneath the image are the measurements '*10 alta 16 lata*'.[27] It is one of only a few large prints which have been folded into the book, probably indicating the size of the original work. A blank cartouche (in later editions carrying the words 'I. Cariani Pinxit') on the left side of the print indicates where the painting was signed, a device which, while unusual in Cariani's *oeuvre,* is not unknown, and the signature can be discerned in both the Petworth and Vienna 'gallery pictures'. The presence of a signature is also suggested by the description in a detailed inventory of the Archduke's collection of the same period as the engraving, drawn up in 1659 by Jan van der Baren (1615-86/7), director of the Archduke's collection in Vienna. The Cariani appears as no. 89 and is described as:

> A large piece of oil painting on linen showing Christ being led off [?] to be crucified, surrounded by a large crowd and with St Veronica kneeling by Him with His train [?]. At the bottom left there is small box with the words 'Joannes Cariani'... In a gilded frame with ox eyes [?], 10 hands high and 15 hands and 4 fingers wide... An original by the said Joannes Cariani.[28]

In Vienna, the Archduke's collection, which was by this date very large, was hung in the Stallburg, the former stables of the Hofburg Palace. It comprised some 517

Italian paintings and 888 German and Dutch works, as well as 542 sculptures and 343 drawings.[29]

When Archduke Leopold Wilhelm died in 1662 he bequeathed his collection of paintings to his nephew Emperor Leopold I (1640-1705), who moved it, together with other Habsburg art treasures, to another part of the Hofburg. In 1702, Folner's 'Short readable account... ' ('Kurz lesenswurduge Erinnerung... ') gave a description of paintings in the Imperial, Spiritual and Temporal Treasuries, and the Cariani appears among them, 'in the second hall, known as the Roman Room', as no. 6, 'a beautiful work by Giovanni Cariani' ('*Ein schones Stucke von Johann Cariani*').[30] Also in this room was a *Story of Lazarus* by 'Bordenau', presumably indicating Pordenone, which was among forty-four paintings mentioned in a letter of 1732 from Johann Martin Rausch, Imperial Court Painter, to the Buildings Clerk of the Bohemian Court as being sent to Prague, but wrongly described at that stage as 'No. 7 A Burial of Christ, by Cariani. (?)' ('Nr. 7 Eine Grablegung Christi, von Cariani. (?)'). It had been shown hanging immediately next to the Cariani in both versions of the Teniers 'gallery picture' (Vienna; Petworth) and for some reason a mistake was made in its attribution in this letter. This is the last mention of Cariani's name in connection with the collection and there is no mention at all of his painting of *Christ carrying the Cross, with St. Veronica* either in this list or in any subsequent inventories.

It is not easy to imagine what might have happened to the painting, although it seems that it had already gone missing or been otherwise disposed of by 1720. In that year, Ferdinand R. Storffer was commissioned by Leopold I's successor, the Emperor Charles VI (1685-1740), to make a painted inventory of the Imperial Collection, as exhibited in the Stallburg. The collection was engraved and published in three volumes (the other two being published in 1730 and 1733) and they show the paintings arranged within the wall decoration of the rooms. These illustrations show that some paintings had been cut or added to in order to fit the carved and gilded panelling, which suggests a possible fate for the Cariani. But Cariani's *Christ carrying the Cross* does not appear in this inventory, and nor is the painting shown in the *Theatrum Artis Pictoriae*, an inventory of engravings of paintings made from 1728-33 by Prenner. The Prodromus inventory of 1735 contains all but four of the 243 pictures from Archduke Leopold's collection engraved in Teniers' *Theatrum Pictorium*, and the Cariani is one of the four that is not included.[31]

Many of the paintings which were part of Archduke Leopold's collection, and which had come from the 1st Duke of Hamilton, remained in the Imperial Collection. Some, such as the Pordenone, were sent to Prague or to Budapest, but many stayed in Vienna and form the basis of the Kunsthistorisches Museum. No further reference is made to the Cariani after 1702, except the erroneous attribution to the Pordenone in the letter of 1732. It is possible that it was cut down in order to fit into a hanging scheme, and its attribution lost at that stage.

NOTES

1 Hamilton was created 1st Duke in 1643 in which year Feilding succeeded his father as 2nd Earl of Denbigh.

2 Paul Shakeshaft, 'Documents for the history of Collecting: I. The Correspondence of Hamilton and Feilding', *Burlington Magazine*, CXXVIII (February 1986), pp. 114-32 (hereafter Shakeshaft). The double dating

of some of the correspondence quoted is the consequence of Feilding's occasional use of the Gregorian Calendar and Hamilton's use of the English Calendar.

3 Quoted by K. Sharpe, *The Personal Rule of Charles I*, New Haven and London, 1992, p. 166.

4 Shakeshaft, p. 123 (Warwick CRO, Feilding MS C1/59).

5 Sharpe, op. cit., pp. 166-7.

6 See Shakeshaft, for example, p. 115, and pp. 116-7, for Hamilton's 'loathing' of that great collector the Earl of Arundel. In this he had partly inherited the antagonism between the 1st Duke of Buckingham and the Howard family. See D.H. Willson, *King James VI and I*, London, 1956, pp. 394ff.

7 Ibid., p. 124 (SRO GD 406/1/9589). The 'm' indicates thousands.

8 Shakeshaft, p. 125 (Warwick CRO Feilding MS C1/82).

9 Ibid., p. 123 (SRO GD 406/1/9543).

10 Shakeshaft, p. 123. n. 3, and p. 131, Appendix II (NRA (S) Ham.MS M4/5).

11 Ibid., and see n. 45.

12 Shakeshaft, p. 123 (Warwick CRO Feilding MS. CI/70).

13 K. Garas, 'Die Entstehung der Galerie des Erzherzogs Leopold Wilhelm', *Jahrbuch der Kunstsammlungen in Wien*, N.F., XXVII (1967), pp. 39-80. E.K. Waterhouse, 'Paintings from Venice for Seventeenth Century England', *Italian Studies*, VII (1952), pp. 1-23. See also R.K. Marshall, *The house of Hamilton in its Anglo-Scottish setting in the Seventeenth Century: with a calendar of the correspondence in the Hamilton Archives at Lennoxlove, to 1712*, Ph.D., Edinburgh University, 1970.

14 NRA (S) Ham. MS. M4/17. In addition to the Hamilton estate in Scotland, at some stage during the 1630s Hamilton lived at Wallingford House, Charing Cross, formerly the residence of the 1st Duke of Buckingham. His wife, sister of Feilding and niece of Buckingham, died there on 10 May 1638. There was an order for sequestration on the house dated 13 April 1649, following Hamilton's execution, and it is probable that the picture hung there in the 'Lower Gallery'. The Duke had also built a house in Cheyne Walk, Chelsea, next to the Manor House, from about 1639. In 1653 this too was seized by Parliament. See *Survey of London*.

15 Garas, op. cit., p. 46.

16 Ibid., p. 47.

17 We are most grateful to Dr Rosalind Marshall for this information. See *The Royal Commission on Historical Manuscripts*, Fourth Report, part 1, p. 274.

18 Waterhouse, op. cit., p. 7.

19 Shakeshaft, p. 130, n. 32.

20 NRA (S) Ham. MS. M4/40, inscribed on the box in modern times '*inventory of pictures in the Collection of Archduke Leopold Wilhelm, which are now in the Vienna Gallery – Late 17th century*', although it seems clear from some of the phrasing of the manuscript that originally it must have been drawn up within a short time of the execution of Charles I. See Garas, op. cit., p. 79.

21 J. Brown, *Kings and Connoisseurs: Collecting Art in Seventeenth-century Europe*, Princeton, 1995, p. 161.

22 Ibid., pp. 160-1

23 J. van der Waals, *Der Printschat van Michiel Hinloopen*, Amsterdam, 1988, pp. 204-5.

24 Peter C. Sutton *et al.*, *The Age of Rubens*, exh. cat., Boston, 1993, no. 124, pp. 576-8.

25 Garas, op. cit., p. 42; Brown, op. cit., p. 162.

26 These sketches were later dispersed. Many entered British collections, including 120 which went to Blenheim Palace whence they were sold in 1886: *The Age of Rubens*, op. cit., p. 586. Others were lent from Harewood House ('Executors of the late Princesss Royal') to the 'Cabinet pictures by David Teniers' exhibition at Kenwood House, 1973.

27 See, for example, R. Pallucchini and F. Rossi, *Cariani*, Milan, 1983, no. 32, p. 118 and fig. 107.

28 'Ein grosses Stuckh von ohlfarb auf Leinwath warin die Ausffinhrung zur Creutzigung, dabei viel volch, bei ihme khniedt die heli Veronica mit dam Scweistuech, undten auf der linckhen Seithen ist ein zettel, drauff geschrieben: Johannes Cariani... In einer vergulden Ramen mit Oxenaugen, 10 Spann hoch und 15 span 4 finger brait... Original von obgemelten Joanne Cariani.' Transcribed by Adolf Berger in *Jahrbuch der Kunsthistorischen Sammlungen des allerhochsten Kaiserhauses*, I, 1883, p. XCI.

29 Garas, op. cit., p. 1.

30 A. Ritter von Perger, 'Studien zur Geschichte der K.K. Gemäldegalerie im Belvedere zu Wien', *Berichte und Mittheilungen des Alterthums-vereines zu Wien*, VII (1864), pp. 102-68, p. 132.

31 K. Garas, 'Das Schicksal der Sammlungen der Erzherzogs Leopold Wilhelm', *Jahrbuch der Kunsthistorischen Sammlungen in Wien*, 64 (1968), pp. 181-278.

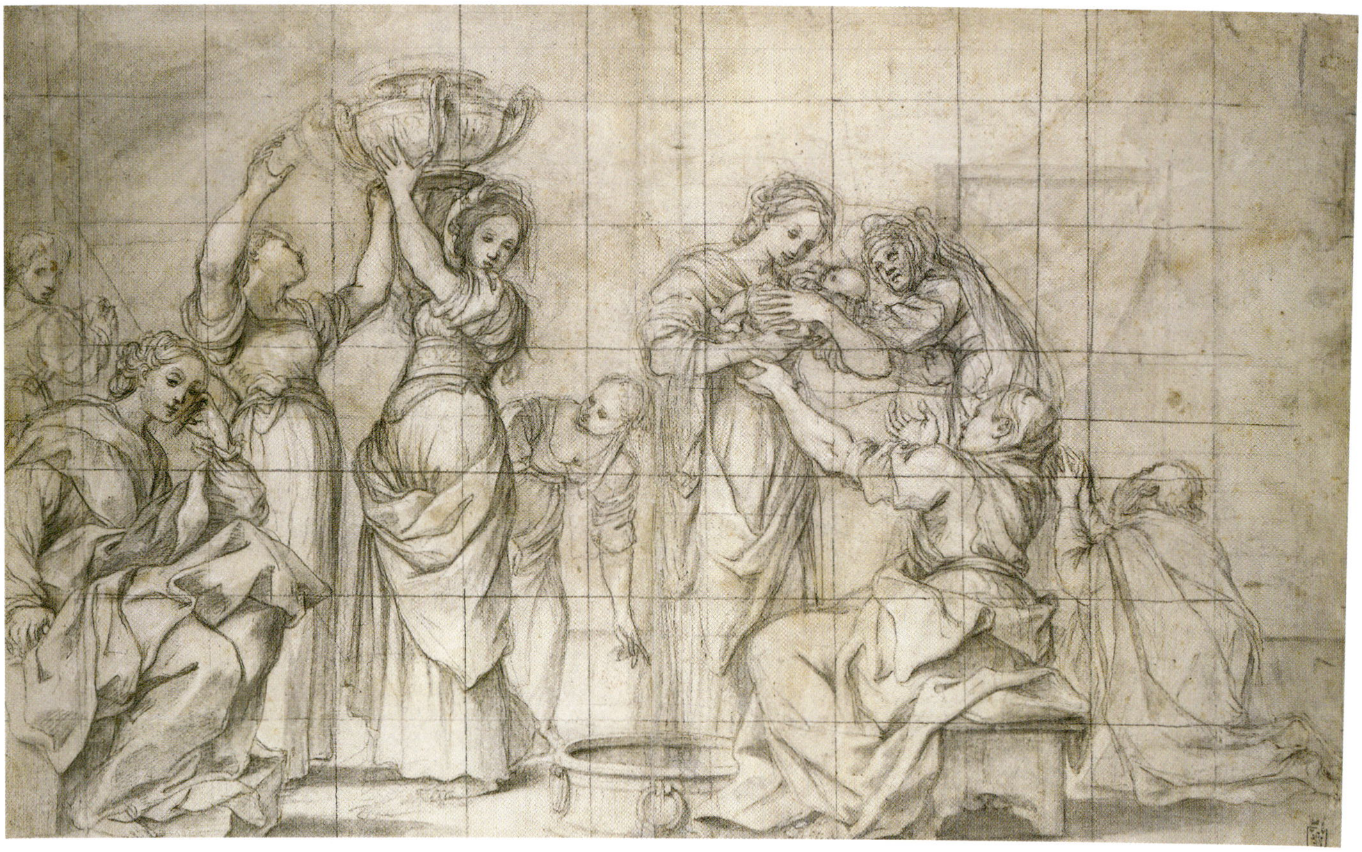

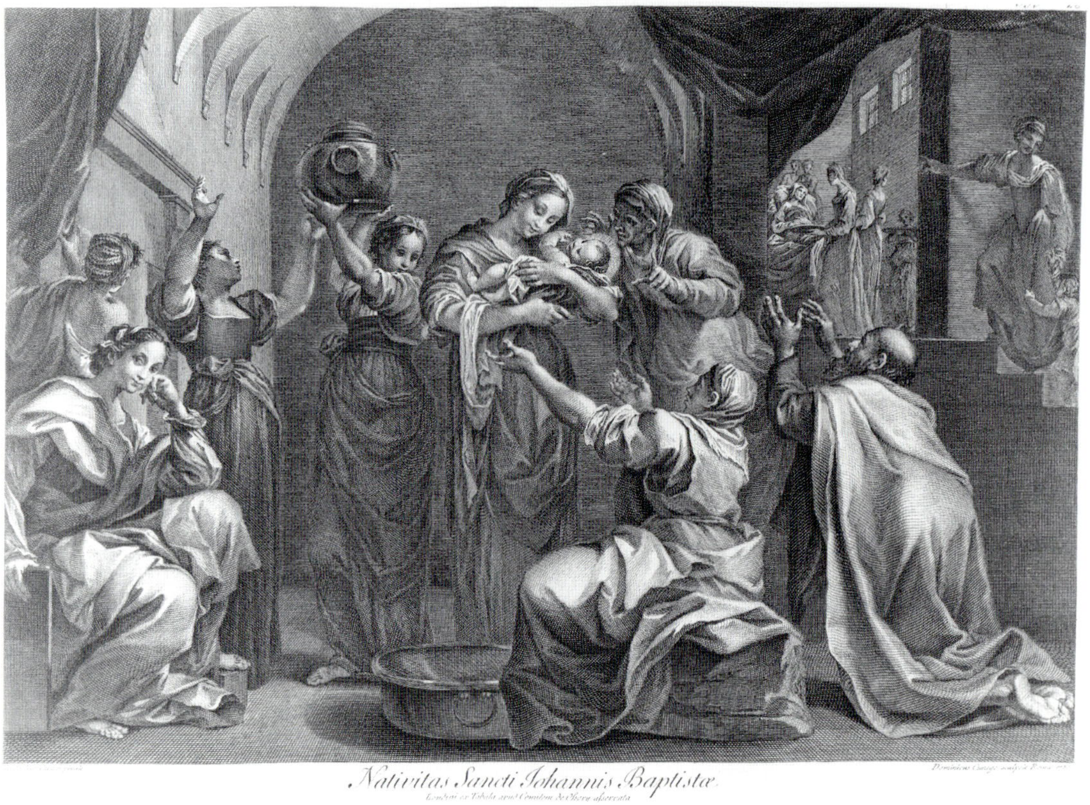
Nativitas Sancti Johannis Baptistæ

Lodovico Carracci

1555-1619

The birth of St. John the Baptist

c. 1590

Probably oil on canvas
Life size

Gavin Hamilton (1723-98), painter, archaeologist and art dealer, wrote from Rome on 27 September 1769 to John FitzPatrick, 2nd Earl of Upper Ossory (1745-1818):

I mentioned in my last [letter] the idea I had form'd of making your Lordship a collection of one agreeable picture of each good master, which in time I flatter myself may be formd without any great expence & shall allwise have that plan in view...[1]

This letter was one of many Hamilton wrote to the Earl from Rome in which he described paintings and antiquities that he had acquired, or hoped to acquire, and which he recommended Ossory should buy. The Earl's family seat, Ampthill Park, Bedfordshire, a late-seventeenth-century house, was being altered and added to by Sir William Chambers during the late 1760s and early 1770s, and Ossory was buying works of art to fill it. In an earlier letter, dated 23 May 1767, Hamilton had commented, 'I am well acquainted with your Lordship's taste & know how difficult it is to please you.' Some three years later, on 6 March 1770, he wrote:

... you desire me to send you something of the school of Raffael or the Caracci's, I have therefore taken the liberty to send you a very fine picture of Ludovico Caracci representing *The Birth of St. John the Baptist* consisting of six or seven figures as large near as the life. It is in his first stile that's to say a mixture of Correggio & Tintorett & was the first picture that got him any credit in Bologna, I had it out of the Bonfilioli collection where it has been allwise much esteemed, the St Zacheria on one side of the picture returning thanks to heaven for the birth of his son & the Sibilla Cumea on the other, are remarkable fine figures, the picture however has grown black as most of his pictures are, being painted up at once on a dark grownd, it is boldly painted tho not high finished & the chief merit of the picture is the simplicity of the composition & justness of expression, in a word it is more a fine picture than a pleasing one.

He charged 807 *scudi* for the picture and all expenses.

The picture has been missing since its last probable record in the early nineteenth century, but its appearance is known from its inclusion by Hamilton in his *Schola Italica Picturae*, a volume of engravings of Italian paintings from the sixteenth and seventeenth centuries which he published (without a text) in Rome in 1773. The inscription under the engraving translates as 'The birth of St. John the Baptist; from the picture kept at the house of Lord Ossory, London',[2] and states that it was painted by '*Ludovicus Caracci* 'and engraved by Domenico Cunego in Rome in 1769. In addition, there is a further record of the composition in the form of Lodovico Carracci's own preparatory drawing for the painting, squared for transfer (Ashmolean Museum, Oxford).[3]

The famous Bonfiglioli collection, from where Hamilton tells Lord Ossory the picture came, was particularly renowned for its drawings, and the Carracci family[4]

The birth of St. John the Baptist by Lodovico Carracci (1555-1619). Preparatory drawing, 35.6 × 56.7 cm, for lost painting.
Ashmolean Museum, Oxford

The birth of St. John the Baptist. Engraving, 1769, by Domenico Cunego, after lost painting by Lodovico Carracci.
Published in Gavin Hamilton's *Schola Italica Picturae*, 1773

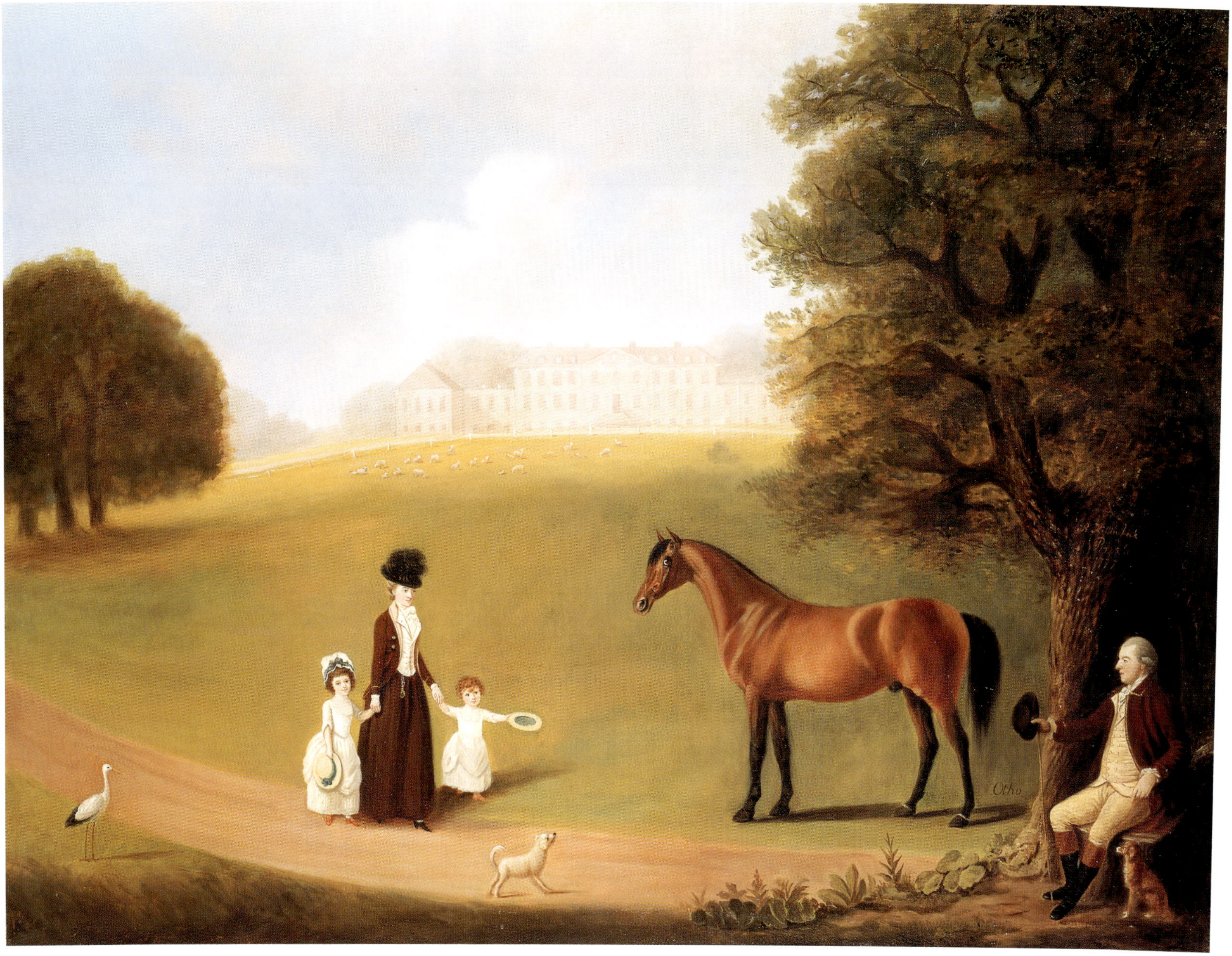

The Earl and Countess of Ossory and their children at Ampthill by Benjamin Killingbeck (*fl.* 1763-89), 1777.
Oil on canvas.
Private collection

Self-portrait by Gavin Hamilton (1723-98).
Black chalk, 53.3 × 43.2 cm.
Scottish National Portrait Gallery, Edinburgh

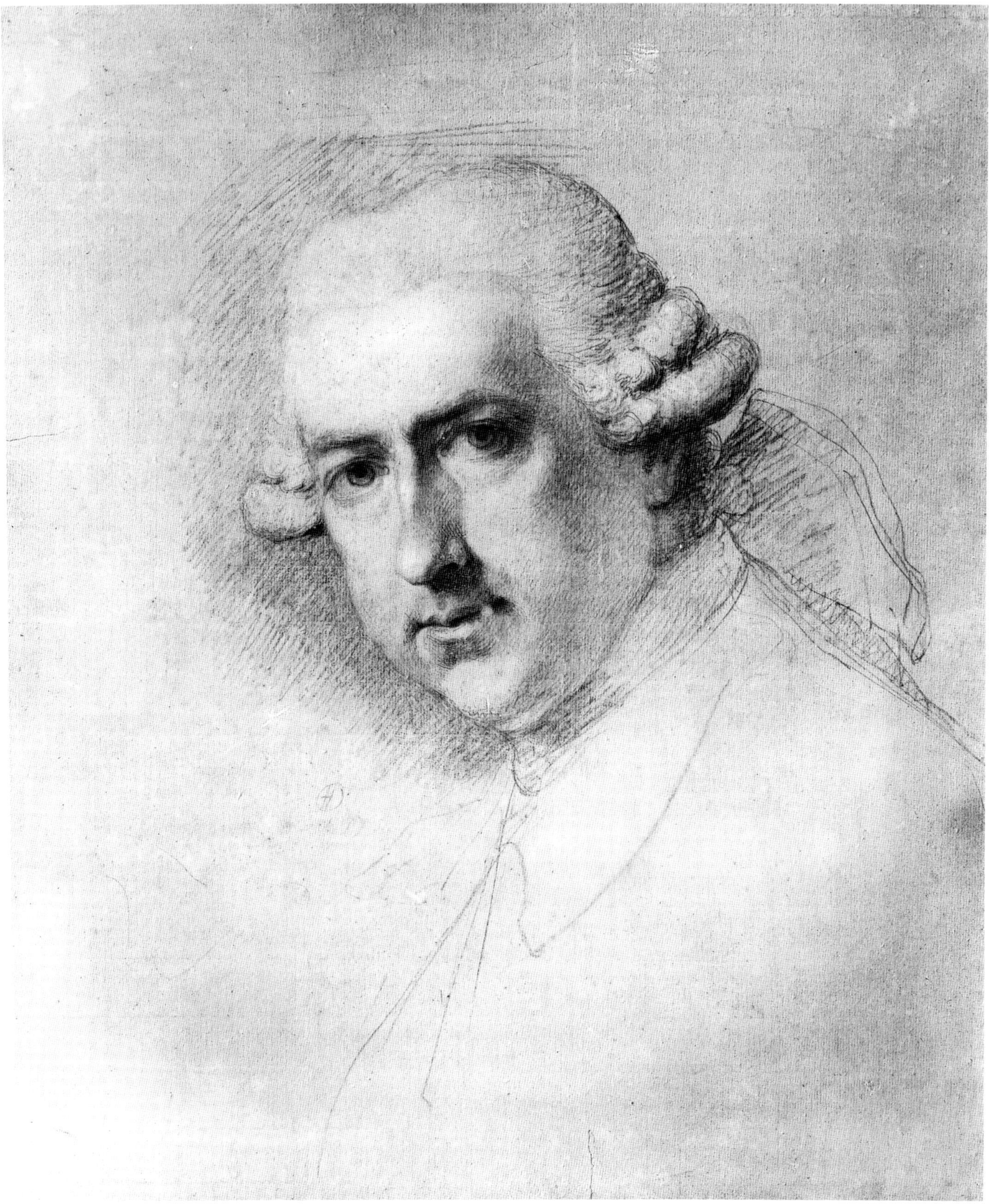

was well represented in the collection. The large painting which Hamilton acquired was mentioned in an inventory of 1757 of the pictures in the 'Galleria Bonfiglioli' :

Quattro quadri grandi, la nascita di S. Gio. Battista, la B. V. Assunta, la coronazione della B.V.. e la Presentazione al tempio, del Pisanelli.[5]

There was a drawing by Lodovico Carracci of the same subject also recorded in the inventory,[6] but this must have been upright in format rather than landscape, since it is known that it was created for another version of the subject, an altarpiece which survives in the Pinacoteca Nazionale, Bologna.[7]

The painting of the *Birth of the Baptist* is not among the few mentioned by Jonathan Richardson the Younger (1694-1771) when he visited the Palazzo Bonfiglioli during his tour of Italy in 1721, but he was only able to see the framed drawings and a few pictures, as '.... Signor Bonfiglioli .... [was] out of Town'.[8]

Gavin Hamilton must have acquired the painting soon after its mention in the Bonfiglioli inventory of 1757. A document dated 1 March 1770 states that 'Gavino Amilton' exported three pictures from the Papal State, one of which was 'of the school of Carracci',[9] and this must refer to the *Birth of St. John the Baptist*, which Hamilton's letter of 6 March 1770 to Lord Ossory mentions ('I have... taken the liberty to send...'). There was evidently some delay because on 27 April 1770 Hamilton tells him, 'I have inclosed a bill of loading for the pictures mentioned in my last which are shipd on board one of the best ships in the Leghorn trade & hope will sail soon.'

As no inventory of Ampthill or of Lord Ossory's other properties in London or Ireland exists, it is not known where the picture went or, indeed, whether Ossory decided to keep the Carracci once he had seen it. Given, however, that Gavin Hamilton's *Schola Italica Picturae* of 1773 was in some sense a catalogue of pictures that had passed or were passing through his hands, it would have been odd to describe Ossory as the owner of the Carracci if he had declined it.

John FitzPatrick, 2nd Earl of Upper Ossory, had travelled to Italy during the latter part of 1763 and 1764. It was probably during his Grand Tour that his interest in paintings and works of art developed, and that he first started to commission and buy pieces in order to form a collection.[10] Edward Gibbon, who met him in Florence on 31 August 1764, stated that, although he considered him immature, the young Earl did have a great affection for pictures.[11] Horace Walpole, on the other hand, thought Ossory 'one of the most sensible amiable young men I ever saw'.[12] Walpole already knew the future Lady Ossory,[13] and corresponded with her over a period of almost thirty years (1769-97). On 14 December 1771 he wrote:

If Lord Ossory has a mind to enrich Ampthill, Mr Hamilton [Sir William Hamilton] has brought over a charming Correggio, and a collection of Tuscan vases, idols, amulets, javelins and casques of bronze, necklaces and earrings of gold from Herculaneum, Pompeii and Sicily, sacrificing instruments, dice of amber, ivory, agate, etc. in short enough antiquity to fill your whole gallery at least.[14]

Lord Ossory collected assiduously, and his transformation of Ampthill was described at the turn of the century in glowing terms:

The birth of St. John the Baptist by Lodovico Carracci, *c.* 1604. Oil on canvas, 420 × 268 cm. Pinacoteca Nazionale, Bologna

The present mansion is a very superb edifice, with wings, and a flight of steps leading into the hall. It contains a valuable collection of paintings by old and modern masters; such as Julia [*sic*] Romano, Palma, Rubens, Vandyck, Caracci, Rembrandt, Teniers, Cuyp,

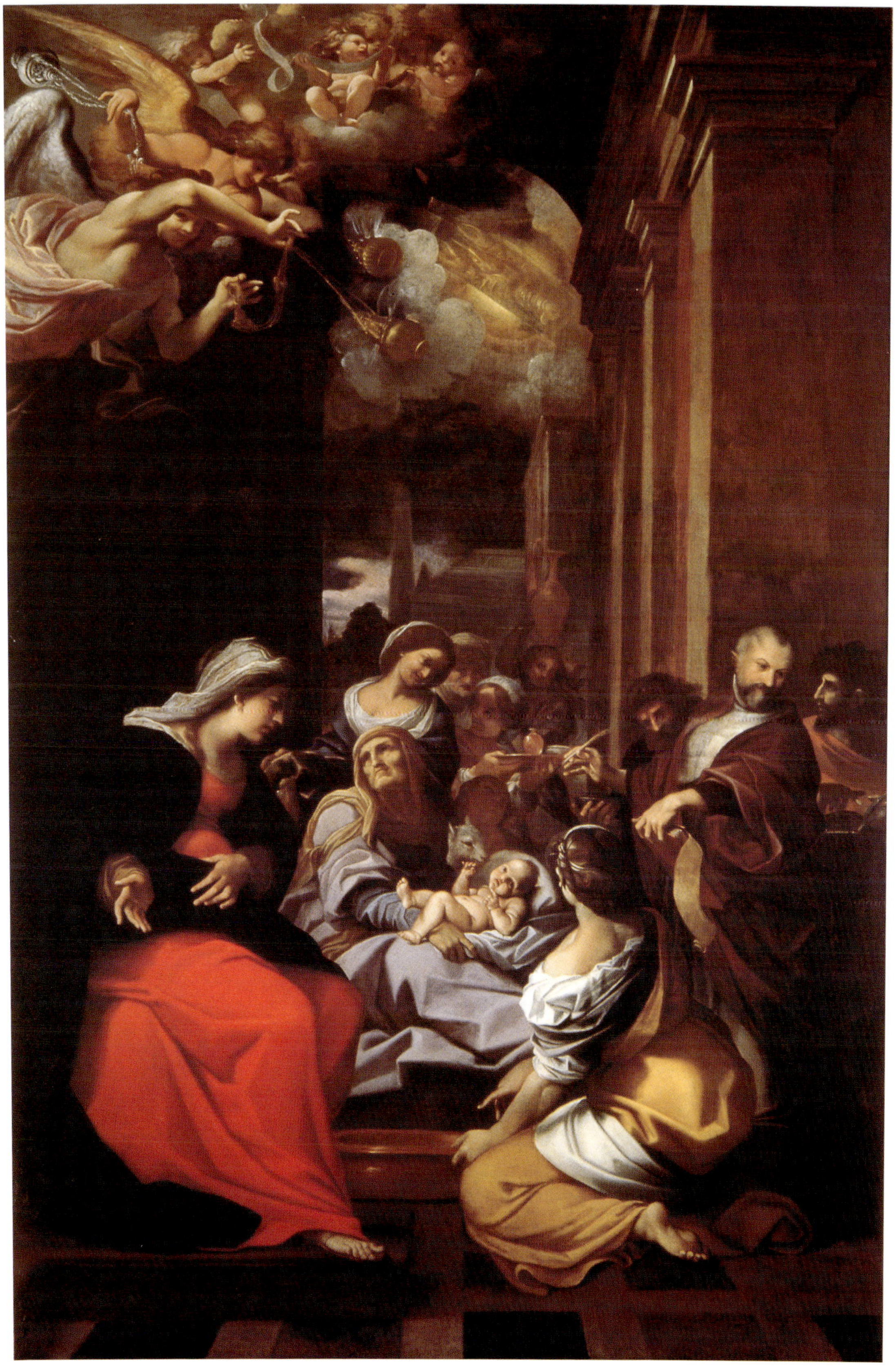

Loutherbourg, Gainsborough, Stubbs, Sir Joshua Reynolds, &c. a handsome library, and a museum of natural history. Among the pieces of Sir Joshua are several family pictures; also portraits of himself, Garrick, Sterne, &c.[15]

The list of painters includes Carracci but, as the title of the picture is not given, it cannot be absolutely certain that it was the *Birth of St. John the Baptist*. Both before and after the date that this account was published, 1801, there were several sales associated with Lord Ossory, but, again, the Carracci does not appear in any of them. In 1775 Mr Christie held a sale of 'The Rich and Genuine Household Furniture, some Pictures etc' of Lord Ossory at his house in Lower Brook Street on the corner of Grosvenor Square. In the same year the Ossorys moved to a new London address in Grosvenor Place, a move which was presumably the reason for the sale. The 21 pictures entered for sale included a painting by Gavin Hamilton, *The death of Hector,* and several Old Master paintings, but the *Birth of St. John the Baptist* was not among them.

The 2nd Earl of Upper Ossory died at Ampthill in 1818, and, as he had no legitimate son, Ampthill was left to his nephew Lord Holland together with 'all the useful furniture to enable him to inhabit it without much expense... '.[16] He left property and jewels to his two legitimate daughters, Lady Ann and Lady Gertrude FitzPatrick, and further bequests to his illegitimate children, but there are only a few mentions of individual pictures, and the Carracci *Birth of the Baptist* is not among them. The Irish estates were left to John and Richard Wilson, his illegitimate sons, who were to assume the name and arms of FitzPatrick.

On 8 April 1819 a sale was held at Christie's of 'A small part of the very choice Collection of Italian, French, Flemish and Dutch Pictures of the Earl of Upper Ossory, Dec. Brought from his Lordship's late Country Residence... '. The contents included several works by Sir Joshua Reynolds, and a picture by Gavin Hamilton, but there was no picture by Lodovico Carracci among the Italian works. The following year, on 14 June, a further sale of Lord Ossory's collection was held by Evans, the auctioneers, but it contained only drawings and prints and no paintings.

Lord Holland died in 1840, and in 1842 his widow, who much preferred living at Holland House, London, rather than in the country at Ampthill,[17] sold the house to a neighbour, the Duke of Bedford. Shortly afterwards, 'Three truck-loads of furniture and pictures were reported in April to have arrived at Holland House from Ampthill'[18] and in May Christie's held a large sale of 'The Collection of Pictures by Italian, French, Dutch and English Masters of The Earl of Upper Ossory, Decd. Removed from Ampthill Park'. Although 24 years after the death of Ossory, this sale, together with the earlier ones, gives a useful indication of the range of Lord Ossory's picture collection, in the absence of any inventory. Some pictures still remained in the family, and the Carracci may have been among them.

To complicate the story a little, a work by Lodovico Carracci entitled *The Birth of St. John* had appeared on 4 June 1812 (lot 33) at the auctioneer Peter Coxe of London in a sale of paintings only, on behalf of 'Two Foreign Gentlemen; and A Gentleman'. The work failed to sell and was 'bought in' at £12,[19] but on 28 April 1813 the same auctioneer, Peter Coxe, listed (lot 91) a '*Caracci, Birth of Saint John*', and it is likely that this is the same work as that in the previous sale. On this occasion it was sold for £8.18.6.[20] An annotated catalogue of this latter auction gives the measurements of the work as 15 inches high by 20 inches wide.[21] This work cannot be the oil painting, with its 'six or seven figures as large near as the life' but, judging from its size and price, it could well be the drawing now in the Ashmolean, the preparatory study for the lost painting, which bears the collector's mark of Sir Thomas Lawrence (1769-1830).[22]

There is, however, a possible clue to the history of the missing painting, subsequent to its presence in the Ossory collection. In 1825, Ferdinando Belvisi, an amateur art historian, had published in Bologna his *Elogio Storico del Pittore Lodovico Caracci* in which he listed oil paintings, 'brought to my attention after careful research'.[23] Belvisi started his list in Bologna, his home town, and he then lists works by Lodovico Carracci in other Italian cities, before moving on to Germany and France. Finally, in England he mentions two collections in London which contain pictures by Lodovico Carracci, one of them being a 'Nascita di S. Gio. Battista' in the 'Stanze del Sig. Giovanni Udny'. It is not known when Belvisi saw this painting nor, crucially, over how many years he had been compiling his notes, but this entry does none the less prompt some speculations about the fate of the missing picture.

The outstanding collectors in the Udny family were John (1727-1800), British Consul in Venice (1761-76) and in Leghorn (1776-*c.* 1798), and his brother Robert (1722-1802). John Udny was also a dealer in paintings, both originals and copies, and regularly sent pictures back to his brother in London.[24] In 1762 he had bought drawings from the Sagredo collection in Venice, and in 1763 he sold some of the drawings which had come from the Bonfiglioli collection (via Sagredo)[25] to the 4th Duke of Marlborough. Robert Udny, who died just two years after John, wanted the collection to be kept together after his death, and in his will he had given the Royal Academy the opportunity to obtain it. This offer is recorded in the Council Minutes on 30 March and 10 April 1802,[26] but it was not taken up, and the collection was subsequently dispersed at several sales.

The first such sale was held in 1802 at Christie's and was entitled 'The Valuable Collection of Italian, French, Flemish and Dutch Pictures, late the property of John Udny, Esquire, Deceased, selected by him with great Taste and Judgement, and at an infinite Expence [*sic*], during a Residence of Thirty Years as British Consul at VENICE and LEGHORN'. There was a further sale at Christie's on 18 and 19 May 1804, which was described as

> The Entire Collection of Pictures Belonging to Robert Udny Esq, deceased, ... comprising Chef d'Oeuvres of great masters and obtained out of the Cabinets of, among others, The King of Naples at Capo di Monte, The Duke of Salviati, Cardinal Aldobrandini, Prince Chigi, Signor Taddeo Taddeo and D. Livio Odescalchi, and the Duke of Braschiano.

The sale included 'A Holy Family: small figures; by Ludovico Caracci: a beautiful composition, and finely executed on board', but both this description and the size (13 inches by 17 inches) preclude it from being the missing *Birth of St. John the Baptist*. According to the annotated catalogue, there was an Udny (unidentified) who bought a few lots at this sale. There was also a six-day sale held by Philipe and Scott of the 'Entire Cabinet of Robert Udny, Esq comprising the Capital Collection of Drawings, by the Greatest Masters, chiefly of the Italian Schools, ... ' beginning on 4 May 1803. Among the drawings by Lodovico Carracci was a *Nativity of the Virgin* in grisaille (Day 2, lot 135) and an engraving by 'Luigi' Cunego of a *Nativity*, after Lodovico Carracci (Day 5, lot 555). Neither of these can have been the missing painting.

There was, however, another 'Giovanni' Udny – John Robert, the son of the Consul, who was born at Leghorn in 1779, and died in 1861. This 'Giovanni'

Udny had succeeded to the Udny estates in Scotland and as Laird of Udny on the death of his uncle, Robert, in 1802.[27] He had made his career in the Army, retiring in 1812, and in 1825, the date of Belvisi's publication, he is recorded as residing at 44 Grosvenor Street and Udny Castle, Aberdeenshire. There was therefore a 'Sig. Giovanni Udny' living in London at the time Belvisi published his *Elogio*, and he might well have owned the large painting by Lodovico Carracci.

Some of the 2nd Earl of Upper Ossory's collection had remained with the family at least until the twentieth century,[28] but if Belvisi's account is accurate, and there is no reason to doubt it, the Udnys might have acquired the picture directly from the 2nd Earl, whom they could have met in Italy. The Udny brothers certainly owned large numbers of Carracci drawings, including many which had been in the Bonfiglioli collection. The missing painting could have remained in John Robert Udny's possession long enough for Belvisi to record it in his publication of 1825. Since then, however, the painting has not been seen.

NOTES

1 The principal source for the quotations below is National Library of Ireland, NLI MS 8012 (iii). The MS spelling has been retained.

2 '*Nativitas sancti Johannis Baptistae; Londini ex tabula apud comitem de Ossory Asservata*'.

3 *The birth of St. John the Baptist* is on the *recto*; there are two studies of legs on the *verso*. The drawing, which measures 35.6 × 56.7 cm, was acquired by the Ashmolean at Sotheby's on 11 July 1972, lot 6. C. Robertson and C. Whistler, *Drawings by the Carracci from British Collections*, exh. cat., 1996/7, no. 5. G. Feigenbaum, *Lodovico Carracci: A Study of His Late Career and a Catalogue of his Paintings*, Ph.D. Diss., Princeton, 1984; idem, 'Catalogo dei dipinti', in Clare Robertson, ed., *Lodovico Carracci*, exh. cat., Bologna, 1993, no. 57, p. 123; idem, 'Drawing and Collaboration in the Carracci Academy', in *Essays in Honor of Irving Lavin on his Sixtieth Birthday*, M. Lavin, ed., New York, 1990. Malvasia's seventeenth-century biography of the Carracci is reprinted with notes in Anne Sumerscale, *Malvasia and the Carracci*, Pennsylvania, 2000, see esp. pp. 248-9 (n. 365) and pp. 312, 324.

4 Lodovico Carracci and his cousins, Agostino (1557-1602) and Annibale (*c.* 1560 - 1609).

5 'Four large paintings, the Birth of St. John the Baptist, the Assumption of the Blessed Virgin, the Coronation of the Blessed Virgin, and the Presentation in the Temple by Pisanello.' Published by G. Campori, *Raccolta di cataloghi ed inventarii inediti*, Modena, 1870, p. 616.

6 Ibid., p. 618.

7 Inv. 463. From an inscription on the back of this work we know that this painting was placed on the altar of the Church of S. Giovanni Battista on 17 June 1604. Malvasia (1616-93), the Carraccis' seventeenth-century biographer, recounts a story about a commission Lodovico Carracci received for a painting of *The Birth of St. John the Baptist* for the high altar. While Carracci was trying to negotiate a higher rate for the work, Guido Reni produced a magnificent drawing and offered to do the altarpiece 'for half the price'. Carracci, however, finally secured the commission, and Malvasia stated that Reni's drawing 'now hangs in the library of the Bonfiglioli Gallery, as does the other one done by Ludovico'. C. C. Malvasia, *La Felsina pittrice: Vite de' pittori bolognesi*, 2 vols., Bologna, 1678, II, p. 12. In 1696 on the death of 'ecc.mo S. Doctore Silvestro Bonfiglioli of Casa Grande, via Galleria in the Parish of San Benedetto', an inventory was made by a notary. It does not list the painting but does include the drawing: 'un disegno con la nascita di S. Gio. Battista di Lodco Carazzi in cornice, e cassetta dorata e suo vetro'.

8 *An account of some of the sculptures, bas-reliefs, drawings and pictures in Italy*, 1722. Richardson listed the upright drawing of the *Nativity of St. John the Baptist* by Lodovico Carracci as being in the Bonfiglioli collection although, unlike Malvasia, he does not specify that it was hanging in the library. Shortly after Richardson

visited the collection, the drawings were sold to the Venetian nobleman Zaccaria Sagredo (1653-1729), a prestigious collector, 'for 3,000 zecchini'. Sagredo was forced to sell the collection in 1743, when it was bought by Joseph ('Consul') Smith (*c.* 1674-1770).

9 Antonio Bertolotti, 'Esportazione di oggetti di Belli Arti da Roma nel secolo XVIII', F. Gori, *Archivio Storico Artistico Archeologico e Letteraio della Città e provincia di Roma*, vol. IV [1880], p. 86.

10 It was probably while in Rome that he met Gavin Hamilton, and subsequently embarked on forming a collection.

11 *Gibbon's journey from Geneva to Rome. His Journal from 20 April to 2 October 1764*, Georges A. Bonnard, ed., *c.* 1961.

12 J. Ingamells, *A Dictionary of British and Irish Travellers in Italy 1701-1800*, New Haven and London, 1997.

13 Lord Ossory married the estranged wife of the 3rd Duke of Grafton in 1769. They had two daughters, who both died unmarried. After the death of Lady Ossory in 1804, Lord Ossory had a liaison with Mrs Elizabeth Wilson, and by her had three children.

14 W. S. Lewis *et al.*, ed., *Horace Walpole's Correspondence*, 48 vols., 1937-83, XXXII, p. 70.

15 John Britton and Edward Wedlake Brayley, *The Beauties of England and Wales...*, I, 1801, p. 65. Lord Ossory was a friend of Reynolds, and under the terms of Reynolds' will he was to have first choice of any picture. He chose the *Venus and Cupid* (now in a private collection in the USA). The portrait of Sterne mentioned here is that now in the National Portrait Gallery, London.

16 The son of Ossory's sister, Lady Mary. Lord Ossory's will was dated 15 July 1817, and proved 16 May 1818: Bedfordshire Record office, RO31/16.

17 'The Holland Estate, 1818-1842', Bedfordshire Record Office.

18 Lord Ilchester, *Chronicles of Holland House, 1820-1900*, 1937, p. 306. We are grateful to Dr C. J. Wright of the British Library for drawing attention to this text.

19 B. Frederickson, *The Index of paintings sold in the British Isles during the nineteenth century*, vol. 3 (Getty Provenance Index), London, New York, Paris, 1993, p. 258, as '£8.18'

20 Annotated sale catalogue in the Rijksprentenkabinet, Amsterdam: '£18.8.6'.

21 Frederickson, op. cit., p. 245.

22 In 1835 his collection was sold. In 1836 the Earl of Ellesmere acquired 150 drawings by the Carracci that had come from the estate of Lawrence, among them the drawing now in the Ashmolean Museum.

23 F. Belvisi, *Elogio Storico del Pittore Lodovico Caracci*, Bologna, 1825, p. 51.

24 For John Udny see Ingamells, op. cit.

25 See n. 8 above.

26 Information kindly communicated by Mr. Andrew Potter of the RA Library (letter of 29 June 1999).

27 Information kindly supplied by Aberdeen City Council (material on the Udnys written by Mary Fraser).

28 On Friday 18 July 1924, a century after the 2nd Earl of Upper Ossory's death, a further sale connected with him was held at Christie's. One of the Earl's illegitimate sons, John Wilson, who had been left his father's Irish estates, Grantstown Manor and Lisduff in Queen's County (*The Complete Peerage*, 1913), had been created Lord Castletown of Upper Ossory in 1869, and it was his son, the 2nd Lord Castletown (d. 1937), who consigned the pictures for sale. Among the pictures were *Archbishop Laud* by Van Dyck and *Venus and Cupid* by Sir Joshua Reynolds. The catalogue quotes from Reynolds' will: 'I desire the Earl of Ossory [2nd Earl] would accept of some picture of my own painting, that he takes his choice of those of my painting, which shall be unsold at my death.' See n. 15 above.

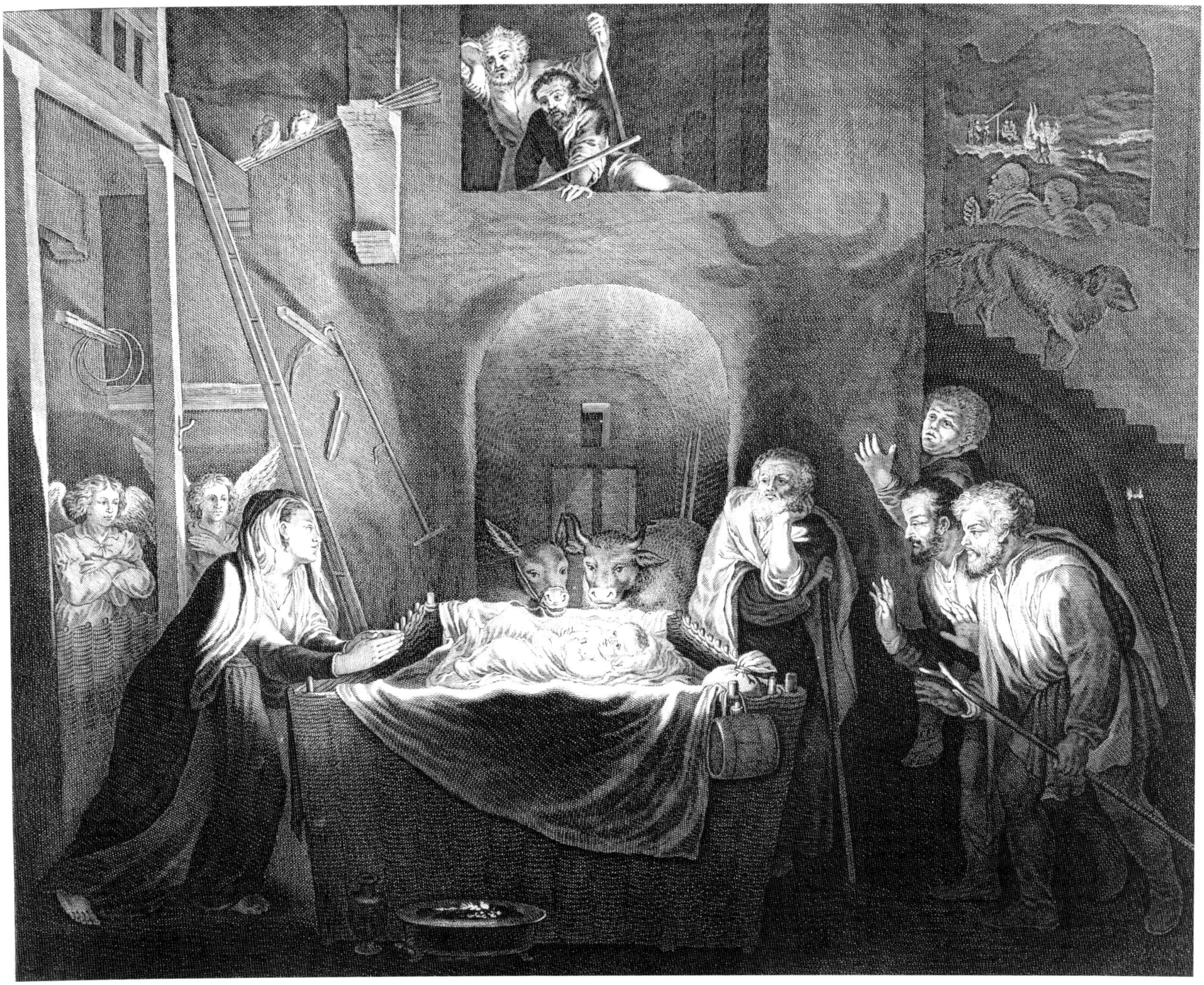

Night Nativity.
Engraving, 1655-8, by Jeremias Falck (*c.* 1610-77),
after lost painting by Lorenzo Lotto (*c.* 1480-1556/7)

Lorenzo Lotto

c. 1480-1556/7

Night Nativity

c. 1527-9

Oil on canvas
Dimensions unknown

In the first half of the seventeenth century two brothers, Gerard (1599-1658) and Jan Reynst (1601-46), formed a large collection of paintings and Antique sculptures. Jan, a successful commodities merchant, lived mainly in Venice from 1625 and acquired most of the Venetian paintings which the brothers owned, many of which had come from the collection of Andrea Vendramin after his death in 1629.[1] Jan was advised in his purchases by the Flemish painter and dealer 'Niccolò Renieri' (Nicolas Régnier, 1591-1667), and he concentrated on the outstanding artists who were working in Venice in the early years of the sixteenth century: Giorgione, Titian, Palma Vecchio, Pordenone and Lorenzo Lotto.

In 1642 Gerard inherited the residue of the collection formed by his grandfather Jan Nicquet (1539-1608) which had been expanded by his uncle, Jacques Nicquet (1573-1642). Some of that collection had been acquired in Venice where the Nicquets had an office from 1593.[2] The Reynst brothers displayed their collection principally in their house on the Keizergracht in Amsterdam, although part of it was shown in Jan's house in Venice.

In 1648 Carlo Ridolfi (1594-1658), artist and biographer, dedicated the first part of *Le Maraviglie dell'Arte* to the Reynst brothers:

> *A gl'Illustrissimi Signori Fratelli Reinst,* IL CAVALIER GIOVANNI SIG.DI NIEL, E *Commissario appresso la Maestà Christianissima per li Potentissimi Stati delle Prouincie Vnite,* E GERARDO SENATORE D'AMSTERDAMO.[3]

The title page, which Ridolfi designed, bears the Reynst coat of arms, and in the book he praises the brothers' collection and identifies various works they owned. In his life of Lorenzo Lotto, Ridolfi mentions a night *Nativity* scene:

> While Lorenzo was staying in Venice, he was working on various paintings at the same time, including the birth of Christ, feigning the action at night-time, with the Angels around the crib and the Virgin Mary illuminated by the brightness which pours from the Baby, a very unusual Painting, it is now in the house of Mr. Jan Reynst, a Dutch gentleman in Amsterdam.[4]

This painting is now missing and is known only through an engraving, probably in reverse, by Jeremias Falck (*c.* 1610-77), of 1655-8.

It is not known when the painting was acquired by the Reynst brothers. It does not appear to be listed in Jacques Nicquet's inventory of 1642,[5] for example, although the artist's name is not specified in the case of many of the paintings (most of which were landscapes), and there is no record of Jan Reynst's acquiring it in Venice.

Lotto was born in Venice in about 1480, but spent many years away from the city painting altarpieces and portraits in Bergamo and in the Marches. He was,

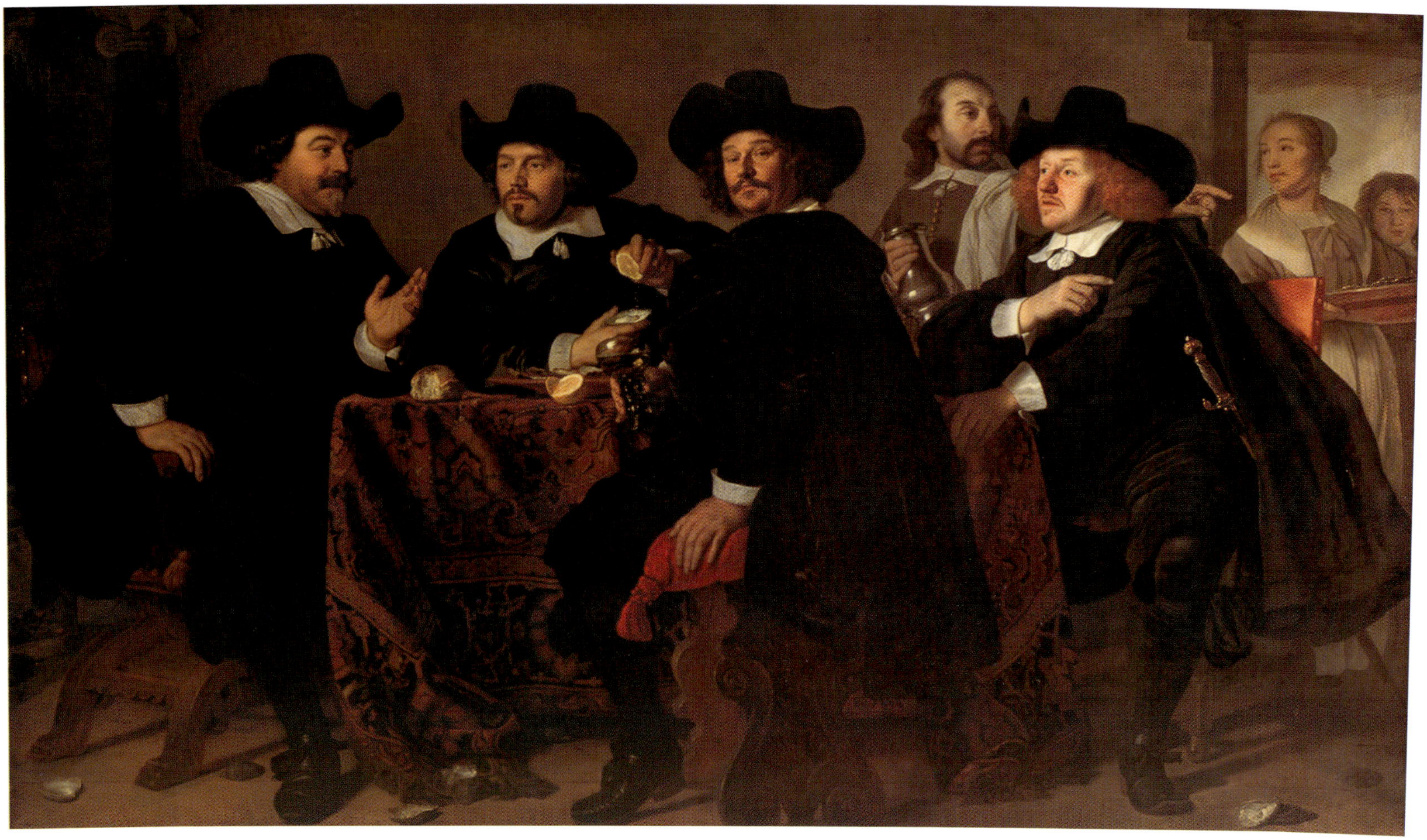

The Governors of the Kloveniersdoelen by Bartholomeus van der Helst (1613-70), 1655 (Gerard Reynst at front of the table, holding a glass of wine).
Oil on canvas, 173 × 283 cm.
Historisch Museum, Amsterdam

however, based in Venice 1525-32, and again in 1540-42. According to Ridolfi's account quoted above, the missing Reynst *Nativity* was painted in Venice, and comparison between the Falck engraving and other Venetian works of the 1520s, such as the *St. Nicolas of Bari Altarpiece* (1527-29) in Santa Maria dei Carmini in Venice, suggests a possible date of 1527-29 for the missing work.[6] Lotto's life and works are comparatively well documented. Forty letters written by him between 1524-39 have been preserved, but none appears to mention the *Nativity*. A personal account book, *Il Libro de Spese diverse,* also survives, and it documents three pictures of a night *Nativity*, but the dates covered in the accounts, 1538-56, preclude any of these being the missing painting.[7]

Giorgio Vasari (1511-74), in his life of Lorenzo Lotto, written a century before Ridolfi, had also referred to a night *Nativity*:

> And in the house of Tommaso da Empoli, a Florentine [who lived in Venice] there is a picture of the Nativity of Christ, painted as an effect of night, which is one of great beauty, particularly because the splendour of Christ is seen to illuminate the picture in a marvellous manner; and there is the Madonna kneeling, with a portrait of Messer Marco Loredano in a full-length figure that is adoring Christ.[8]

At first sight, it might seem that this painting is unlikely to be the same as the Reynst picture[9] because in the Falck engraving the Virgin appears to be stooping rather than kneeling, but the gesture of her hands clasped in prayer suggests that she is in the act of genuflecting – kneeling with only one knee bent – which might accord with Vasari's description. There would remain the question of whether one of the figures at the right could represent Marco Loredan. There are precedents for members of noble families during the Italian renaissance having been represented in the role of a shepherd, and it was an appropriate position for a donor (which Loredan must have been in this instance). The two figures at the right are carefully individualised, one white-haired, the other dark and also younger in appearance.

There can be no certainty, however, that Tommaso da Empoli's painting and that later recorded in the Reynst collection were one and the same,[10] and there are other versions of a night *Nativity* by Lotto either recorded or surviving. Marcantonio Michiel (*c.* 1484-1552), a contemporary of Vasari, for example, also mentioned a night *Nativity* – 'The Nativity, with the Child lighting all the picture... ' – which, instead of belonging to Tommaso da Empoli was in 'the House of Messer Leonino Brambato' in Bergamo.[11]

Jan Reynst died in Venice on 22 July 1646, shortly before the publication of Ridolfi's book.[12] His brother, Gerard, as his universal heir, probably shipped the majority of the paintings from Venice to Amsterdam soon after Jan's death,[13] although six or seven pictures remained in Venice, where they are recorded in the collection of Niccolò Renieri.[14] The Reynst Cabinet in Amsterdam was celebrated during the seventeenth century, and many visitors commented on it. Melchior Fokkens in 1662 described the house as

> ... one of the most excellent houses in Amsterdam, in view of its valuable paintings and other extremely exquisite curiosities, and it is estimated that these foreign valuables should be valued at three tonnes of gold or more and not less... like a royal palace inside...[15]

In 1650 the art dealer, Michel Le Blon (1587-1658) wrote to Queen Christina of Sweden that the magistrates of Amsterdam were eager to buy some of Gerard

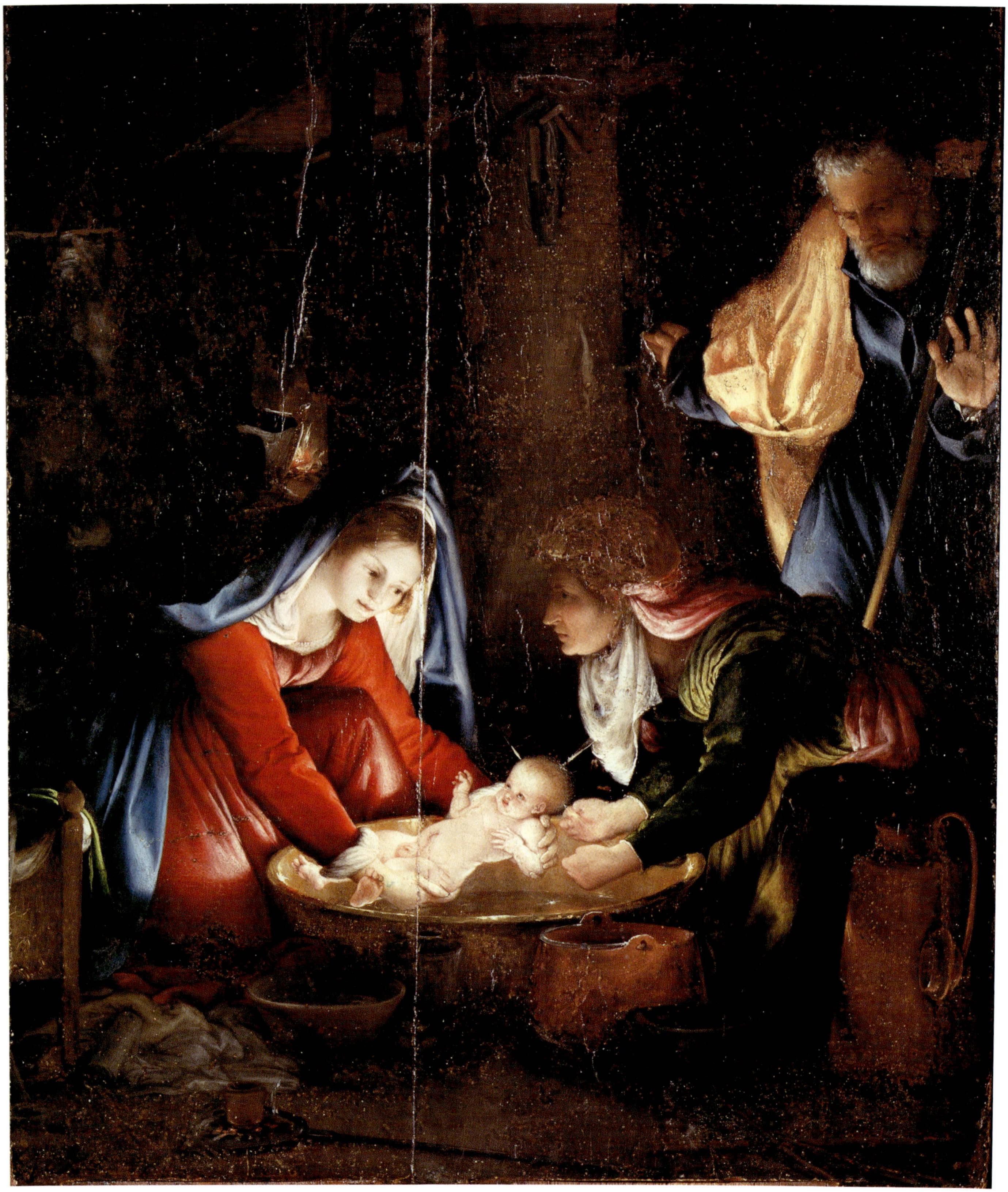

Night Nativity by Lorenzo Lotto, 1521.
Oil on panel, 55 × 65.7 cm.
Pinacoteca Nazionale, Siena

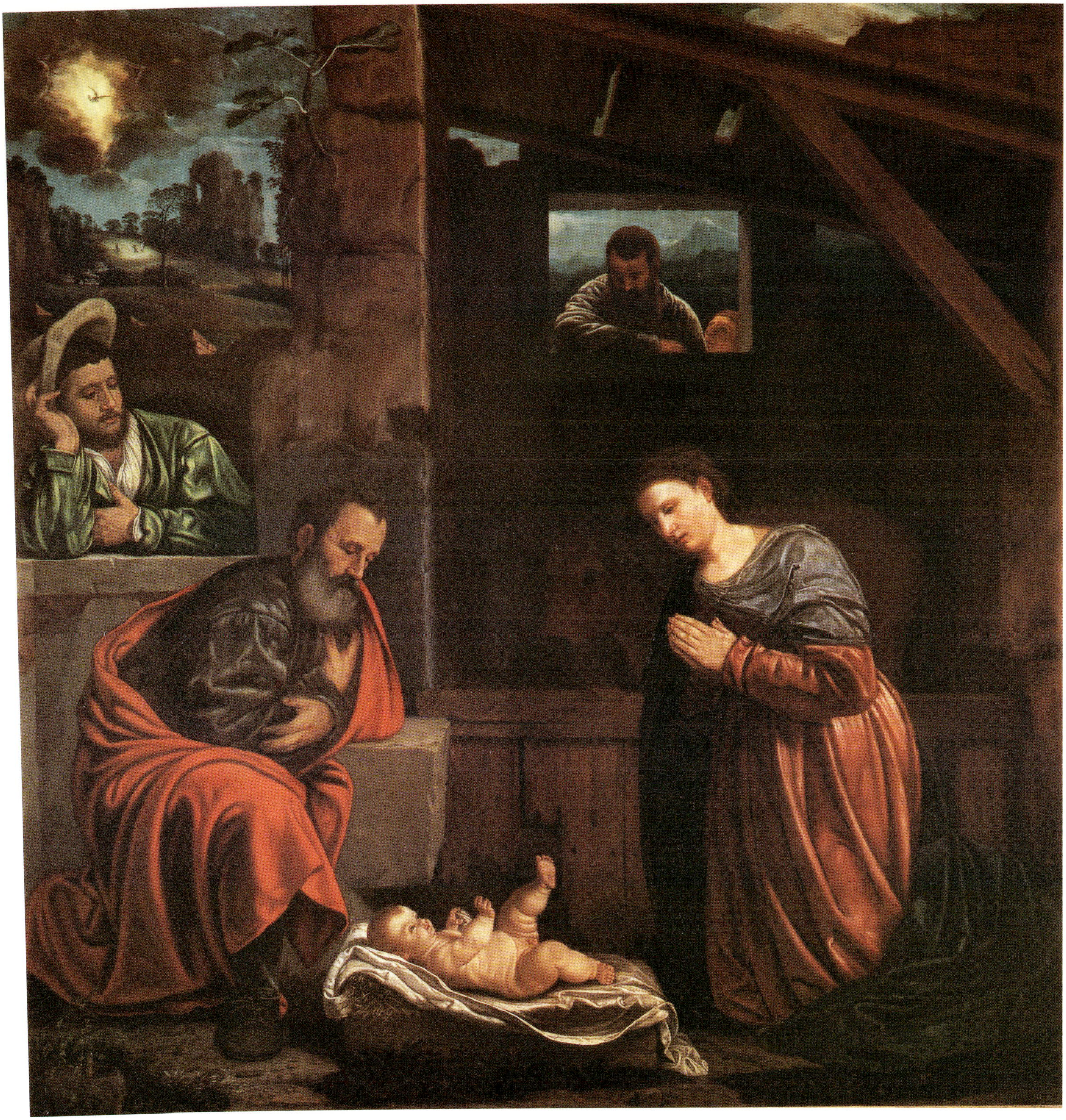

Night Nativity by Gian Girolamo Savoldo (1480?-1548).
Oil on panel, 192 × 180 cm.
Pinacoteca Civica Tosio Martinengo, Brescia

Reynst's Antique sculpture for their new town hall. He then went on to suggest that she should buy the pieces herself.[16]

In about 1655 Gerard Reynst commissioned a number of artists to make engravings after paintings and sculpture in the collection. Thirty-three pictures in a collection estimated to total around 200 were engraved by the time of Gerard Reynst's death by drowning in Amsterdam in 1658, as were 110 Antique sculptures.[17] They were published after his death in two separate volumes in the late 1660s, the paintings in *Variarum Imaginum... Caelaturae* and the sculptures in *Signorum Veterum Icones per D.Gherardum Reynst... , Collectae...* None of the pictures engraved had come from the Vendramin collection,[18] but most were by Italian painters.

Lotto's *Night Nativity* was included in the *Caelaturae* but, although the pictures were originally engraved without letters or numbers, in the standard, lettered, edition, copies of which differ from each other in some respects, it appeared as catalogue no. 18, pl. 18, inscribed as after a painting by Veronese: 'P.Caliari pinx.'.[19] The engraving, as noted above, was made by Jeremias Falck, a Pole, who had arrived in Amsterdam from Copenhagen in about 1655.[20] According to Falck himself, he was paid 2,600 guilders for his work for Reynst – a considerable sum for an engraver at that time. Work on the engravings ceased after Gerard's death, and Falck wrote in a letter of 10-20 December 1658:

> ... there was hope of having turned another 1000 guilders from him, if the fine gentleman [Reynst] had not so unfortunately died, which is to be lamented, since in this city there are not many such connoisseurs to be found.[21]

After Gerard Reynst's death, his widow Anna became his sole heir, and she added a title page to the thirty-four plates of the *Caelaturae*,[22] the original Latin of which can be translated as follows:

> Engravings of various subjects painted by most famous artists, presented in most elegant plates. These pictures are partly with the widow of Gerard Reynst, who during his life was a senator and magistrate of his city, and partly they were sent to Charles II, King of England, as a gift from the most powerful states of Holland and West Friesland. In Amsterdam.[23]

The reference here to Charles II concerns the 'Dutch gift'. In 1660 the Council of the Provinces of Holland and West Friesland had decided to make a substantial gift to the newly restored King of England. In a letter of 2 September 1660 the Council wrote:

> We have been told for sure that... His Majesty is not very interested in modern masters but has a particular delight in ancient pieces and Italian masters. And, since in the Cabinet of the widow of Reynst some such pieces are to be found, we request that Your Excellency may endeavour to enter into negotiations with the above-mentioned widow and to arrange for the transfer of these objects for a proper price.[24]

Later that month, on 27 September 1660, Simon Van Hoorn, who was advised in the selection by the art dealer Gerrit Uylenburgh (*c.* 1626-*c.* 1690) and the sculptor Artus Quellinus (1609-88), reported that he had purchased twenty-four paintings and twelve Antique sculptures 'which are all the best and most interesting in the opinion of the connoisseurs who understand the art of painting... ', and that Anna Reynst was to receive 40,000 guilders.[25]

The Dutch Gift was accompanied to England by Ludwig van Nassau and Simon van Hoorn, Mayor of Amsterdam, who was a close friend of the late Gerard

Reynst.[26] The event was recorded in a poem written by J. V. Vondel and dedicated to Van Hoorn:

> STUART, their champion, with delight
> Hears silent canvas and marble speak
> And knows the excellence of each work
> That charms judicious eyes and hearts;
> All products of Italian art
> Receive due honour from the King
> And from the wisdom of his Delphic voice.[27]

The Dutch Gift arrived in England at the beginning of November 1660 and was put on exhibition in the Banqueting House, Whitehall:

> And yesterday the Lords Ambassadors from the States of the United Provinces, presented to his *Majesty* in the Banqueting House at Whitehall, an extraordinary crimson embroider'd velvet Bed, Cloth of State, Chaires and Stooles suitable, worth very many Thousands of pounds, and also an excellent Collection of Pictures of the most Famous, Auncient and Moderne Masters, with a great number of Statues of white Marble of excellent Sculpture: and to day these Lords Ambassadors had Audience, wherein His *Majesty* heartily thank'd them for so worthy a Present, and express'd his willingness to enter into a neerer Alliance with them.[28]

The 'Lords Ambassadors', Van Nassau and Van Hoorn, themselves recorded the reactions of the King in a letter:

> ... the paintings and statues... were seen by the King and the entire court, by all the grandees of England and by almost all the foreign Ministers and were admired by them all and considered to be one of the finest gifts that could even have been made to a Prince. The King himself took great delight in the works, studying each piece with great curiosity and commenting on them.[29]

There is unfortunately no extant list of the pictures bought from the Reynst collection, nor of all the pictures that comprised the Dutch Gift. Denis Mahon has identified paintings in several Royal inventories, in particular those of Charles II, as from the Dutch Gift, but Lorenzo Lotto's *Night Nativity* is not among them.[30]

If Lotto's *Night Nativity* was not selected as part of the Dutch Gift, it might well have stayed in the Reynst collection for a few more years, and the collection remained celebrated even after the twenty-four paintings and twelve sculptures had gone to England. One distinguished visitor was Cosimo III de' Medici, Grand Duke of Tuscany, who on Tuesday, 3 January 1668, recorded his impressions of the Reynst house:

> ... they have a good collection of old paintings and by the best masters of Lombardy, the remnant of a great collection bought by their forebears in Venice from the Vendramin. In addition to the pictures one can also see statues and marbles, both Roman and Greek, and a quantity of medals, among them some coins of great antiquity, something truly to be valued highly for its rarity.[31]

Just a few years after this visit, Anna Reynst (d. 1671) sold some, or all, of the collection at auction in Amsterdam. Constantijn Huygens wrote to his brother on 29 May 1670, 'Our Bisschop... is in Amsterdam where the very celebrated Cabinet of the Reynst is presently being sold... '[32] and it appears that Gerrit Uylenburgh, who had advised on the selection of the Dutch Gift, was involved in the sale.[33] He, at any rate, probably acquired works at around this time from the collection and in the following summer (1671) Uylenburgh, who employed copyists

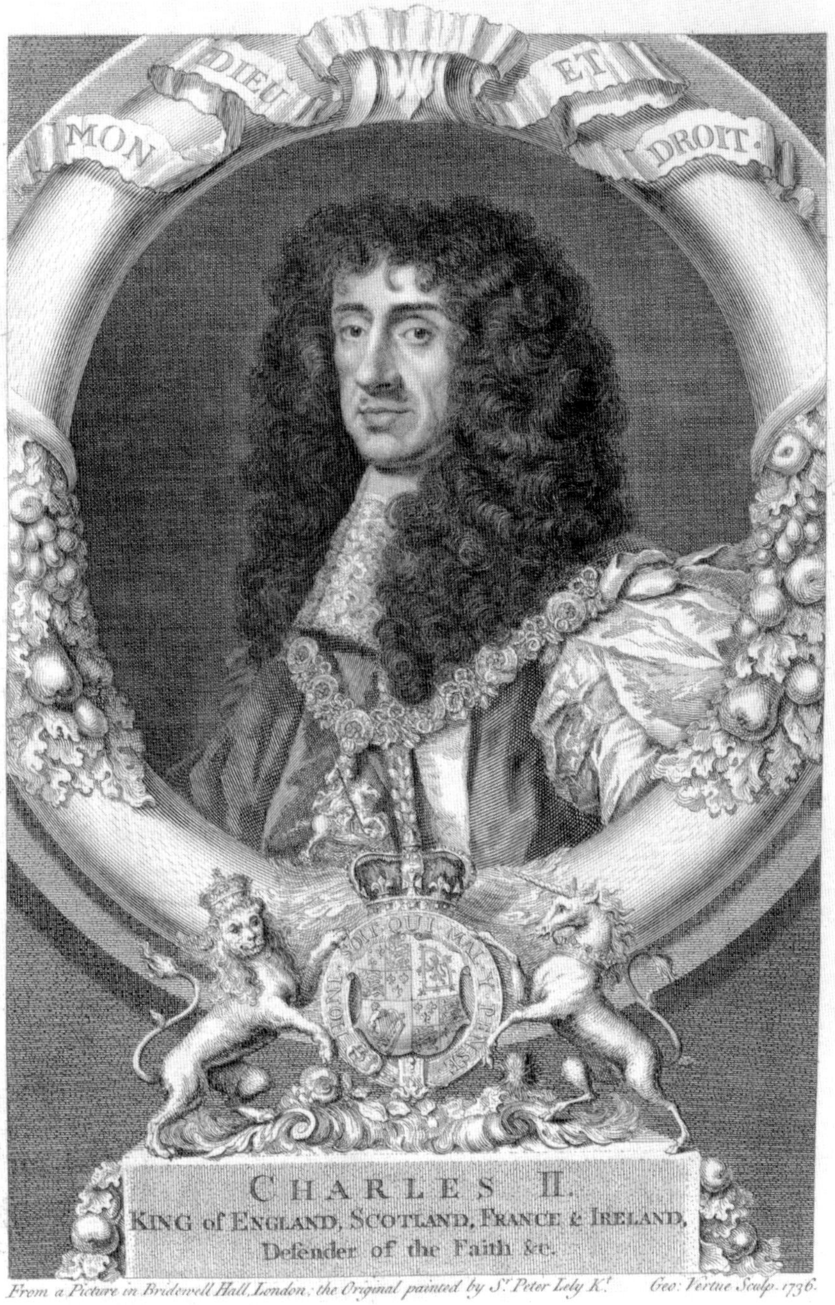

Charles II (1630-85).
Engraving by George Vertue (1684-1756), 1736, after a painting by Sir Peter Lely (1618-89).
Private collection

to work for him, attempted to sell thirteen Italian paintings, which were said to have been in the Reynst collection, to the Elector of Brandenburg. This resulted in a protracted and well-documented controversy, as it was claimed that twelve of the paintings were only copies of original Old Master paintings.[34] Lotto's *Night Nativity* was not among those offered to the Elector.[35]

In around 1675, partly as a result of this saga, Uylenburgh was declared bankrupt, and an inventory was made of the possessions in his house on the Nieuwe Keizersgracht.[36] He had a particular interest in Italian paintings, and had imported many Italian works to Amsterdam. The list reflects this, although, after the *débâcle* with the Elector, there is no certainty that some of those listed might not have been copies. The list does not appear to contain the Lotto, although some of the paintings are anonymous and the descriptions brief. An auction was held of his pictures, and shortly afterwards he went to England, where he remained for the rest of his life. In 1676 Charles II put him in charge of the pictures in the royal collection, perhaps as a reward for his involvement in the Dutch Gift.[37]

Gerard and Anna Reynst's son, Joan (1636-95), inherited his family's interest in art, and travelled to Italy in 1675 partly to buy pictures, but it is not known whether he was actually left any of the celebrated collection. In 1671 he bought a large house in Amsterdam (incorporating the famous clandestine Roman Catholic church of Onze Lieve Heer van Solder, and now the Museum Amstelkring), where a picture attributed to Andrea Schiavone, *Presentation in the Temple*, which had been in the Reynst collection, was already hanging.[38]

Only one other former Reynst picture is known to be still in Holland, having been acquired by none other than the collector Jan Six (1618-1700), subject of one of Rembrandt's most famous portraits and an Amsterdam contemporary of the Reynst brothers.[39] He probably acquired *The dance of naked children* by Palma Giovane indirectly from the collection, presumably after it had been offered by Uylenburgh to the Elector. No other Reynst pictures included in the *Caelaturae* remain in the Netherlands, although a substantial number of those in the Dutch Gift are still in the Royal Collection in Britain.

There remains the faint possibility that Lotto's *Night Nativity* passed with other *ex* Reynst pictures to Nicolaes Anthonis Flinck (1646-1723), the son of Rembrandt's pupil Govaert Flinck. His collection was housed in Rotterdam, and although his tastes lay chiefly in the direction of drawings,[40] Houbraken recorded that it contained 'masterpieces by Italian Old masters such as Titian, Palma Vecchio... Carracci, Guido... ', but there is no mention of the *Night Nativity* by Lotto, and its fate is unknown.

NOTES

1 The brothers also acquired an important collection of antiquities from the same collection. For a comprehensive list of Vendramin's collection see Anne-Marie S. Logan, *The 'Cabinet' of the Brothers Gerard and Jan Reynst*, Amsterdam, Oxford and New York, 1979, pp. 171-4.

2 Jacques Nicquet went bankrupt in 1621 and probably had to sell some of his collection. The 1642 inventory of Jacques Nicquet's collection is in Logan, op. cit., pp. 248-68.

3 'To the most illustrious brothers Reynst, the Cavalier Giovanni, Lord of Niel and Commissioner to his most Christian Majesty for the most Powerful States of the United

Provinces, and Gerard, Senator of Amsterdam'. C. Ridolfi, *Le Maraviglie dell'Arte* (1648), 2nd edn., Padua, 1835, 2 vols.; see D. von Hadeln, ed., 2 vols., Berlin, 1914-24.

4 'Trattendosi Lorenzo in Venetia, lavoro parimente opere diverse, e tra quelle la nascita di Cristo, fingendo l'attione du notte tempo, con Angeli intorno al Presepe in compagnia della vergine Madre illuminati da splendori, che escono dal bambino, rarissima Pittura, hor é nelle case del Signor Giovanni Reinst Gentil'huomo Olandese in Amsterdamo.' Hadeln, ed., op. cit., p. 145.

5 See n. 2 above.

6 P. Humfrey, *Lorenzo Lotto*, New Haven and London, 1997, pp. 98-100.

7 *Libro di Spese Diverse (1538-1556)*, P. Zampetti, ed., Florence, 1969. In contrast, it is possible to date two other paintings of this subject much earlier, to 1521, on the basis of style. One, which has been cut down, is in the Pinacoteca Nazionale in Siena. The other exists in the form of a copy in the Accademia, Venice. See Humfrey, op. cit., pls. 61, 66.

8 Vasari, *Lives...* (Everyman Library), 2 vols., London, 1996, I, p. 947. R. Bettarini and P. Barocchi, ed., *Le Vite...* , 6 vols., Florence, 1996–, vol. IV, p. 552: '... et in casa Tommaso da Empoli Fiorentino è un quadro d'una Natività di Cristo finta in una notte, che è bellissimo, massimamente perchè vi si vede che lo splendore di Cristo con bella maniera illumina quella pittura, dove é la Madonna ginocchioni, et in una figura intera che adora Cristo, ritratto messer Marco Loredano.'

9 Vasari, *Lives...* , op. cit., vol. II, p. 470, states that Tommaso also had a night *Nativity* by Gian Girolamo Savoldo ['Bresciano']: 'In the house of Tommaso da Empoli at Venice is a Nativity of Christ, a very lovely effect of night, and there are some other similar works of fantasy, in which he was a master.' It is possible, however, that Vasari was on this occasion mistakenly recording Lorenzo Lotto's *Night Nativity* as being by Savoldo (Humfrey, op. cit., p. 101), although it is also possible that Tommaso da Empoli could have owned night *Nativity* paintings by both Lotto and Savoldo. We also know from Lotto's account book that Tommaso had commissioned him to paint a portrait of his wife, Marietta Novella, in September 1541.

10 Humfrey, op. cit., p. 98, argues that they are not. One of his reasons is that 'according to Vasari, Tommaso's picture contained the full-length, kneeling figure of the patrician Marco Loredan – whereas the two shepherds on the right of the Falck engraving are both stooping rather than kneeling...' But Vasari does not say that Loredan is kneeling, rather, that the Virgin is kneeling: '... dove é la Madonna ginocchioni, et in una figura intera che adora Cristo ritratto messer Marco Loredano.'

11 *The Anonimo [Marcantonio Michiel]: notes on pictures and works of art in Italy made by an anonymous writer in the sixteenth century*, translated by P. Mussi, ed. G. C. Williamson, London, 1903, p. 81 (based on the Italian edition of 1884 with notes by Dr. Frizzoni, but first published as *Notizia d'opere di disegno... scritta da un anonimo...* , Jacopo Morelli, ed., Bassano, 1880). This is the picture now in the Pinacoteca Tosio Martinengo, Brescia; illus. Humfrey, op. cit., pl. 135, p. 133.

12 Logan, op. cit., pp. 240-41, has compiled a list of paintings in his collection, based not on an inventory but on citations by Ridolfi, which may or may not constitute the entire collection.

13 Logan, op. cit., p. 35.

14 S. Savini Branca, *Il collezionismo veneziano del '600*, Padua, 1964, p. 269, states that Niccolò Renieri bought these pictures from Jan, and identifies them.

15 For the original text, see Logan, op. cit., p. 36. According to Conte Carlo Cesare Malvasia (1616-93), who may have got his information from Niccolò Renieri, the brothers' collection also included drawings by the Carracci: C. C. Malvasia, *La Felsina pittrice: Vite de' pittori bolognesi*, 2 vols., Bologna, 1678, p. 467.

16 Logan, op. cit., p. 89. Neither negotiation succeeded.

17 Ibid., pp. 38, 39. Since Falck had been expecting to do further work on these engravings (see below) it seems that the project would have been more extensive but was brought to an abrupt halt by Gerard Reynst's sudden death. As no inventory survives of the collection, these engravings are now the main source of information about it.

18 Ibid., p. 39.

19 For the publishing history of the *Caelaturae* see Logan, op. cit., esp. pp. 39ff. and n. 4.

20 Falck was in Amsterdam 1655-7. See J. C. Block, *Jeremias Falck, sein Leben und seine Werke*, Danzig, Leipzig and Vienna, 1890.

21 Block, op. cit., p. 11, quoted in F. Lugt, 'Italiaanische kunstwerken in Nederlandsche verzamelingen van vroeger tijden',

Oud Holland, LIII (1936), p. 116, n. 40.

22 Thirty-four plates because one of the paintings was engraved twice.

23 See Logan, op. cit., p. 38 and n. 1.

24 Logan, op. cit., pp. 77ff. An often repeated suggestion that Reynst had bought from the Commonwealth Sale of Charles I's collection after his execution in 1649 originated with George Vertue, but Denis Mahon has been unable to identify any of the pictures in the Reynst collection with those at the Commonwealth Sale. See Denis Mahon, 'Notes on the "Dutch Gift" to Charles II: I', *Burlington Magazine*, XCI (November 1949), pp. 303-5, p. 303, n. 10; idem, parts II (loc. cit., pp. 349-50) and III, loc. cit., XCII (1950), pp. 12-18.

25 Logan, loc. cit.

26 Gerard Reynst and Simon van Hoorn are shown together in a portrait group by Bartholomeus van der Helst of 1655, *The Four Governors of the Kloveniersdoelen* (Historisch Museum, Amsterdam): illus. Logan, op. cit., p. 23.

27 Eighth verse of ten-verse poem. See original in Logan, op. cit., p. 76 and fig. 4.

28 *Mercurius Publicus*, 8-15 November 1660 and *Parliamentary Intelligencer*, 12-19 November 1660, quoted in Logan, op. cit., p. 81. See Mahon, op. cit., p. 305.

29 For original see Logan, op, cit., no. 96, p. 83.

30 Mahon, op. cit., passim. A Guercino that was part of the gift, *Semiramis receiving news of the revolt of Babylon*, is not recorded in any of the royal inventories and Mahon located it in the collection of the Dukes of Grafton, descendants of the King's mistress, Barbara Villiers, Viscountess Castlemaine. Presumably, the picture was a gift from the King to his mistress and, since not all the paintings in the Dutch Gift have been identified, it must remain a possibility that the *Night Nativity* was among them and that it passed out of the royal collection in a similar way.

31 '... anno una buona raccolta di pitture antiche e de' migliori maestri di Lombardia, residuo di un gran gabbinetto comprato da'loro antenati in Venezia del Vandramino, et oltre alle pitture si viddero alcune statue e marmi greci e latini con quantità di medaglie, tra le quali alcuni coni, delle più antiche, cosa in vero per la rarità stimabilissima.' Logan, op. cit., p. 67.

32 Logan, op. cit , p. 90. The reference is to Jan de Bisschop: see J.G. van Gelder, 'Jan de Bisschop', *Oud Holland*, LXXXXVI (1971), pp. 218-9 and letter in App. VI, 15.

33 Logan, op. cit., p. 91.

34 Ibid., pp. 91-7.

35 Logan, op. cit., p. 91, gives a description of the attempted sale. No Lotto (or even a Veronese) was included in the list of pictures to be appraised by a panel of artists in Amsterdam in 1672.

36 A. Bredius, *Kunstler Inventare: Urkunden zur Geschichte der Holländischen Kunst des XVIten, XVIIten, und XVIIIten Jahrhunderts*, The Hague, 1915-22, vol. V, pp. 1660-84.

37 Mahon, op. cit., I, p. 304, n.19.

38 See *Dictionary of Art*. It had been installed in 1663. The picture has now been cleaned and, according to the Director of the Museum (verbal communication), it is believed it to be a copy, possibly by Uylenburgh.

39 His collection, augmented by his descendants, is now on public view in the Six House in Amsterdam.

40 The Duke of Devonshire bought 500 drawings from the collection the year after Flinck's death, many of which are still at Chatsworth. See *Dictionary of Art*. Some fifty paintings were included in the sale following the death of Flinck's third and last child in 1754.

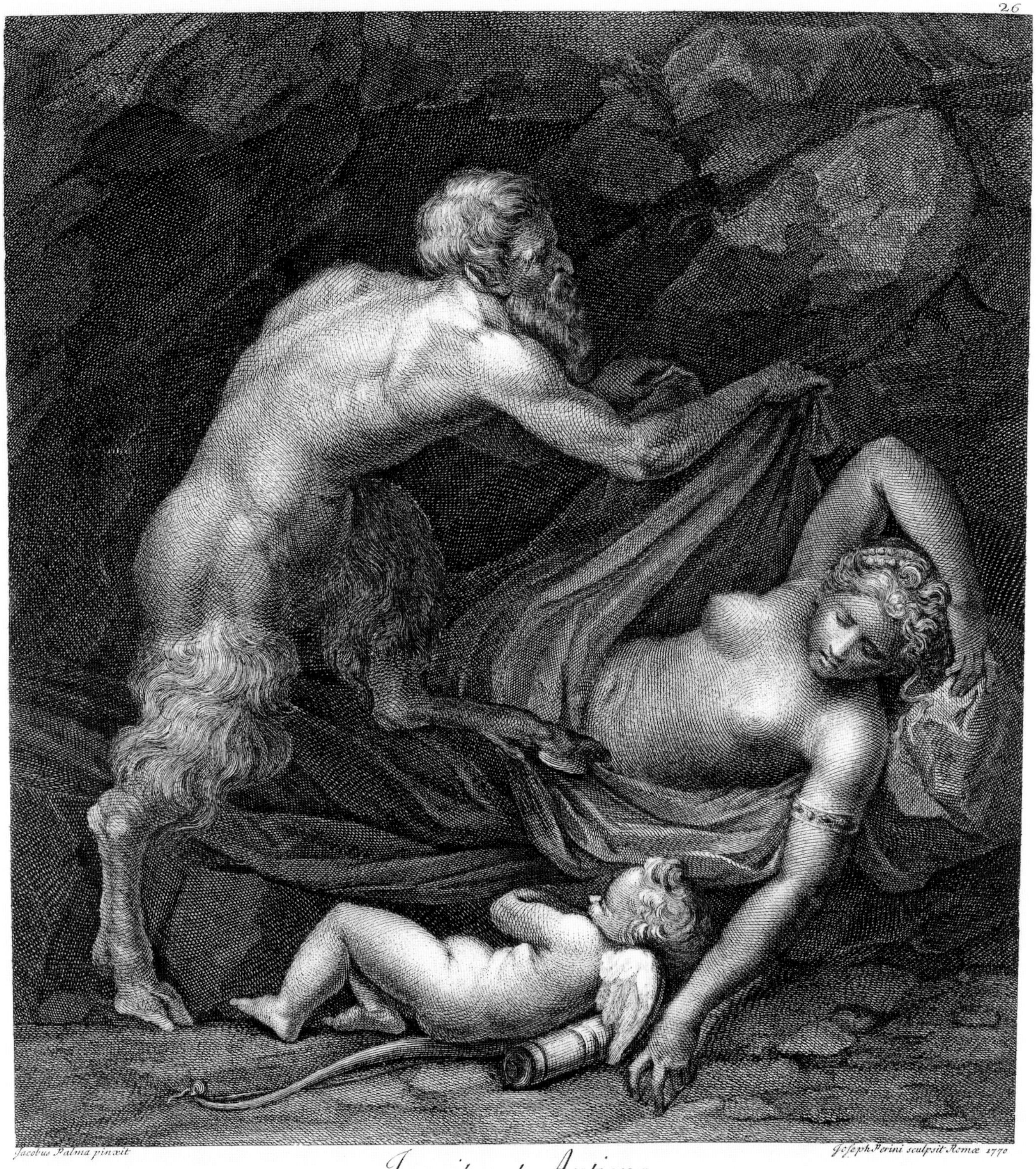

Jacobus Palma pinxit. Joseph Perini sculpsit Romæ 1770

Juppiter et Antiopa

Ex Tabula in Ædibus Principis Pio Romæ afservata

Schola Italica.

Palma Giovane

c. 1548-1628

Jupiter and Antiope or '*A Satyr admiring a sleeping Venus*'

Oil on canvas, 'chiaroscuro' (grisaille)
c. 138 × 115 cm

Gavin Hamilton's *Schola Italica Picturae* published in 1773 includes an engraving made by Joseph Perini (1748-after 1795) of a *Jupiter and Antiope* (as '*Juppiter et Antiopa*') by Palma Giovane. Hamilton's volume was a collection of forty engravings of sixteenth- and seventeenth-century Italian paintings either in collections and churches in Rome or which Hamilton, painter, archaeologist and dealer, had sold or wished to sell. While, therefore, the *Schola* was a serious attempt to offer a visual history of the Italian School, it also functioned as an advertisement for Hamilton's activities as a dealer.

The inscription states that the engraving of *Jupiter and Antiope* is 'from the picture kept in the house of Prince Pio in Rome'.[1] The picture has been identified as that appearing in an inventory of 1 March 1689, taken at the death of Cardinal Carlo Francesco Pio di Savoia (1622-89), attributed to Dosso Dossi; and again, but now unattributed, as a painting appearing in an inventory of the collection of Cardinal's nephew and heir, Prince Francesco Pio di Savoia, of 23 March 1724.[2] The painting has been missing since its appearance in a number of sales in London in the first part of the nineteenth century.

Cardinal Carlo Francesco, the first recorded owner of the picture, was the head of what was a prominent Ferrarese family. He moved the family to Rome in 1650, and was made a Cardinal under Pope Innocent X in 1654. In 1655, as Bishop of Ferrara, he welcomed Queen Christina of Sweden to that city. He resigned his see and returned to Rome in 1662, afterwards becoming Cardinal Protector of the (Hapsburg) Empire.[3] In 1664 the Cardinal's house and collection was described by Bellori:

> In the palace of His Eminence [there are] various rooms decorated with the rarest pictures: [including] two life-size Venuses by Titian... with a good library.[4]

The collection was known for its works by sixteenth-century Venetian and Ferrarese painters, including Dosso Dossi, and in the 1689 inventory, which carries the attribution to Dosso, the *Jupiter and Antiope* is recorded as measuring 'alto palmi 6, largo 5' (about 138 × 115cm).[5] In December 1697 the Cardinal's nephew and heir, Prince Francesco Pio di Savoia, is recorded as lending 138 works to one of the exhibitions that was held regularly in the cloisters of the Roman church of S Salvatore in Lauro.[6] This had become a prestigious event, and a great social occasion. The Prince agreed to lend to the exhibition at his own expense, but only on condition he should be the sole lender, although in the event some other works were shown in the upper gallery of the cloister.[7] It is not known whether the Palma Giovane was among the Venetian Old Masters shown from the Prince's

Jupiter and Antiope after Palma Giovane (*c.* 1548-1628). Engraving by Joseph Perini for Gavin Hamilton's *Schola Italica Picturae*, 1773. British Museum

collection, a selection which included paintings by Bellini, Tintoretto and Veronese.

The Palma Giovane remained in the family's collection, and it appears in an inventory of Prince Francesco Pio di Savoia dated 23 March 1724 as 'nello stanzolino presso la sud a. 8.a. stanze'. It was listed as no. 225, and although no artist is given, it is described in some detail, even though the subject is identified in a different way: 'Un quadro di una Venere… , et un Satiro con un Amoretto in terra, in tela con cornice dorata, alto palmi 9 largo palmi 7 in circa.'[8] The way in which the picture is described leaves no doubt that it is the same picture. The absence of a firm identification of the subject as Jupiter and Antiope is understandable, because classical myth tells how Antiope, a princess of Thebes, was loved by Jupiter (Zeus) in the shape of a satyr, to whom she bore twin sons. In this picture, the sleeping Antiope is accompanied (as is sometimes the case) by a Cupid lying on the floor, a figure also associated with Venus. The measurements given differ slightly from those in the earlier inventory, but can be accounted for by the fact that they include the frame, which is mentioned in the description.

Having published the painting in an engraving of 1770, and described it as in the Pio collection, by 1777 Hamilton had evidently acquired at least one painting from the same source, because on 13 March that year he was able to write to the Marquess of Lansdowne:

> I have got in my possession an old copy of the famous picture of Titian at Venice representing St Peter Martyr. If your lordship can find a place for such a large work in the end of your library, you shall have it for £100… It comes out of the collection of Prince Pio, who died lately in Spain.[9]

The Prince, Giberto Pio di Savoia, Cardinal Carlo Francesco's great-nephew, had indeed just died in Spain, where the family had moved in mid-century, and with him the male line ceased.[10] The family's move gave rise to one of the stranger episodes in the history of collecting. Because of increasing fears about the loss of family collections and works of art from Rome, the Vatican had imposed a ban on their export. On this occasion, Prospero Lambertini, Pope Benedict XIV (r. 1740-58), went further. In 1750 he not only refused Prince Giberto permission to take the collection out of Rome, but also issued a compulsory order of purchase. His purpose was to join it with the Sacchetti collection, which he had acquired through a mutually agreed sale two years before, in order to create the Pinacoteca Capitolina, and he finally bought 128 of the Pio pictures.[11]

The *Jupiter and Antiope* was not one of these pictures, and it not only remained with the Pio family but also, from the evidence of the inscription on the engraving, remained in Rome, although whether that was because the papal ban remained in force is not known. The ban on exports was frequently circumvented by dealers such as Hamilton, sometimes by falsifying attributions or by other more obvious methods of smuggling. Indeed, Sir Joshua Reynolds was proud of having arranged for Poussin's *Seven Sacraments* to be smuggled out of the Papal States, and exhibited them at the Royal Academy.[12] Whatever the precise situation where the *Jupiter and Antiope* was concerned, Hamilton's publication of the engraving appears at least to have been effective in achieving a sale, for the picture was acquired by the 'picture-mad'[13] William (later Sir William) Hamilton (1730-1803), envoy to Naples from 1764 and Minister Plenipotentiary from 1767. It is possible that the fact that the picture was only to travel as far as Naples

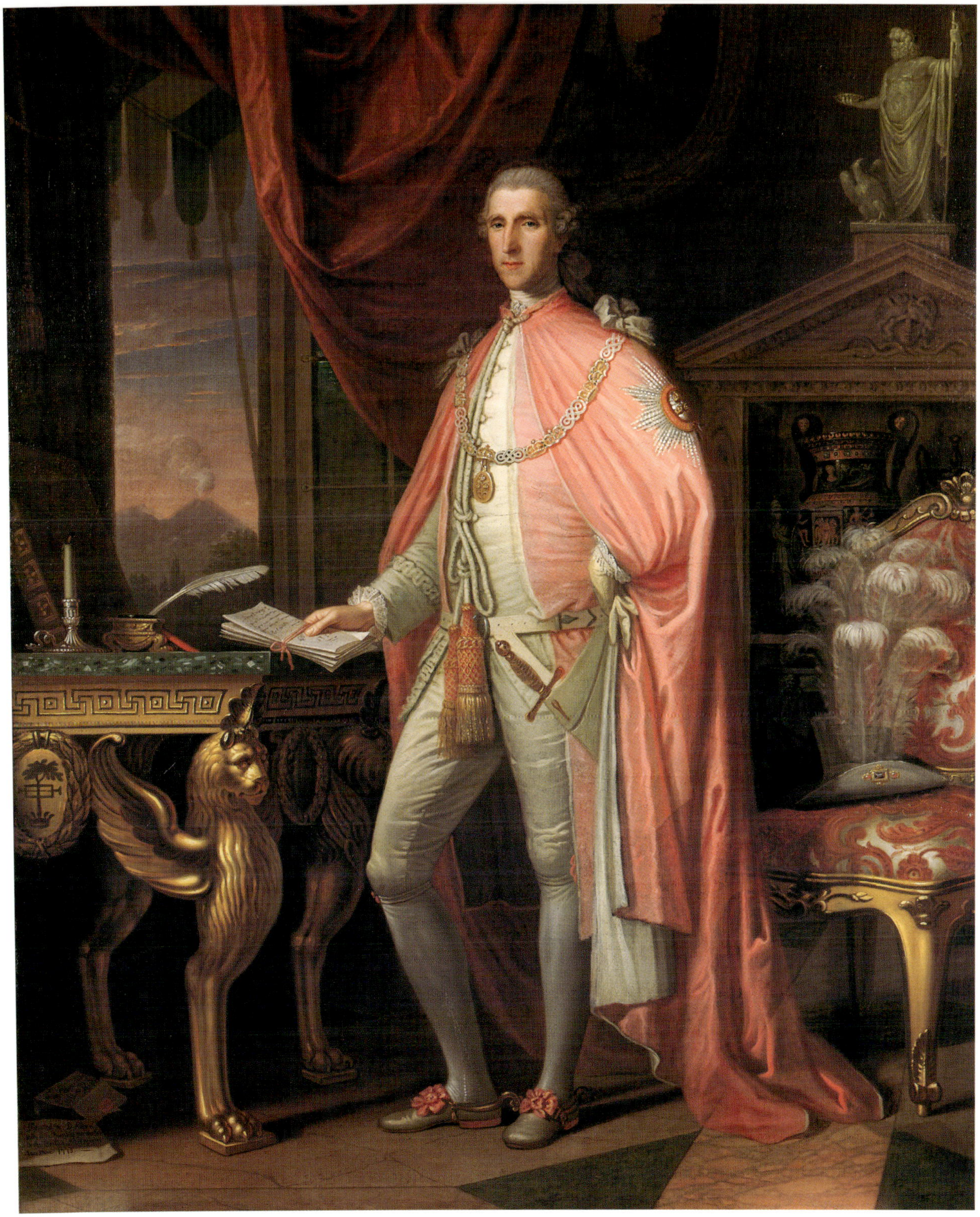

Sir William Hamilton by David Allan (1744-96), 1775.
Oil on canvas, 228 × 181.2 cm.
Trustees of the National Portrait Gallery, London

may have eased its export from Rome but, in practice, Hamilton, his partners and rivals, such as Thomas Jenkins (1722-98), seldom if ever had any difficulty in arranging for both paintings and antiquities to go abroad, although it could be expensive and complicated in terms of bribes and other inducements to officials.

William Hamilton had already formed, as reported by Horace Walpole on 8 June 1764, 'a good collection of pictures, which he sold by auction in 1761... ',[14] and was now adding to his second such collection during his stay in Naples. Having never made the grand tour, William and his first wife, Catherine, visited Rome in 1768, where they were shown round by the German art historian Johann Joachim Winckelmann (1717-68) and the British dealer and architect James Byres (1734-1817). He had probably already met Gavin Hamilton before this visit, but they were life-long friends: he bought paintings and objects from him over a long period of time, and he owned a bust of Gavin Hamilton by the Irish sculptor Christopher Hewetson (Hunterian Collection, University of Glasgow).[15]

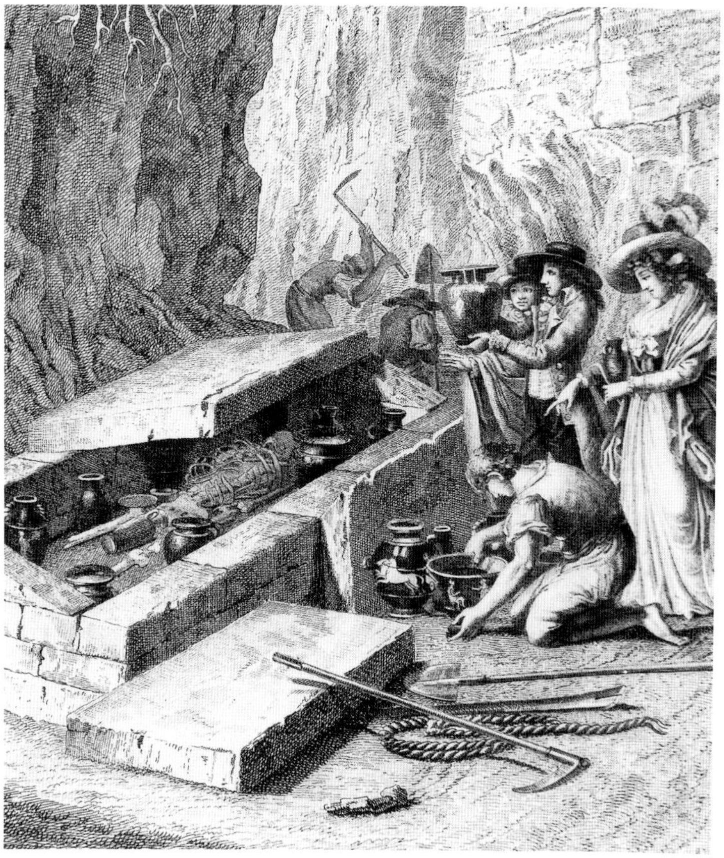

Excavating a classical tomb at Nola, 1790.
Engraving after Christopher Kniep (1748-1825).
Frontispiece to vol. I of J. H. W. Tischbein, *Collection of Engravings from Ancient Vases Discovered in the Kingdom of the Two Sicilies between 1789-90, 1793-after 1803*

William Hamilton was an insatiable collector. In addition to being 'picture-mad', he created, successively, two important collections of antiquities while in Naples. Some of the objects he acquired directly from the excavations which were taking place nearby at Pompeii and Herculaneum, and in 1766, having already begun collecting, he acquired the Porcinari collection of Greek vases. By 1771 his collection contained '175 terracottas, over 600 bronzes and 6,000 coins, ivories, glass and gems, and 730 vases. This first collection was catalogued by the mysterious Baron d'Hancarville, although the tale of its publication, which lasted from 1767 until 1796, is a saga in its own right,[16] and it was sold to the British Museum for £8,400 in 1772, in which year William was knighted.

Following this sale, Sir William started to build a second collection of antiquities, which was also eventually published,[17] and he acquired outstanding pieces such as the Warwick Vase (Burrell Collection, Glasgow), which he bought from Gavin Hamilton, and the Portland Vase, which he bought from James Byres (British Museum).

Sir William's main residence in Naples was the Palazzo Sessa, and it was here that most of his collections were housed. Contemporary accounts tell of Sir

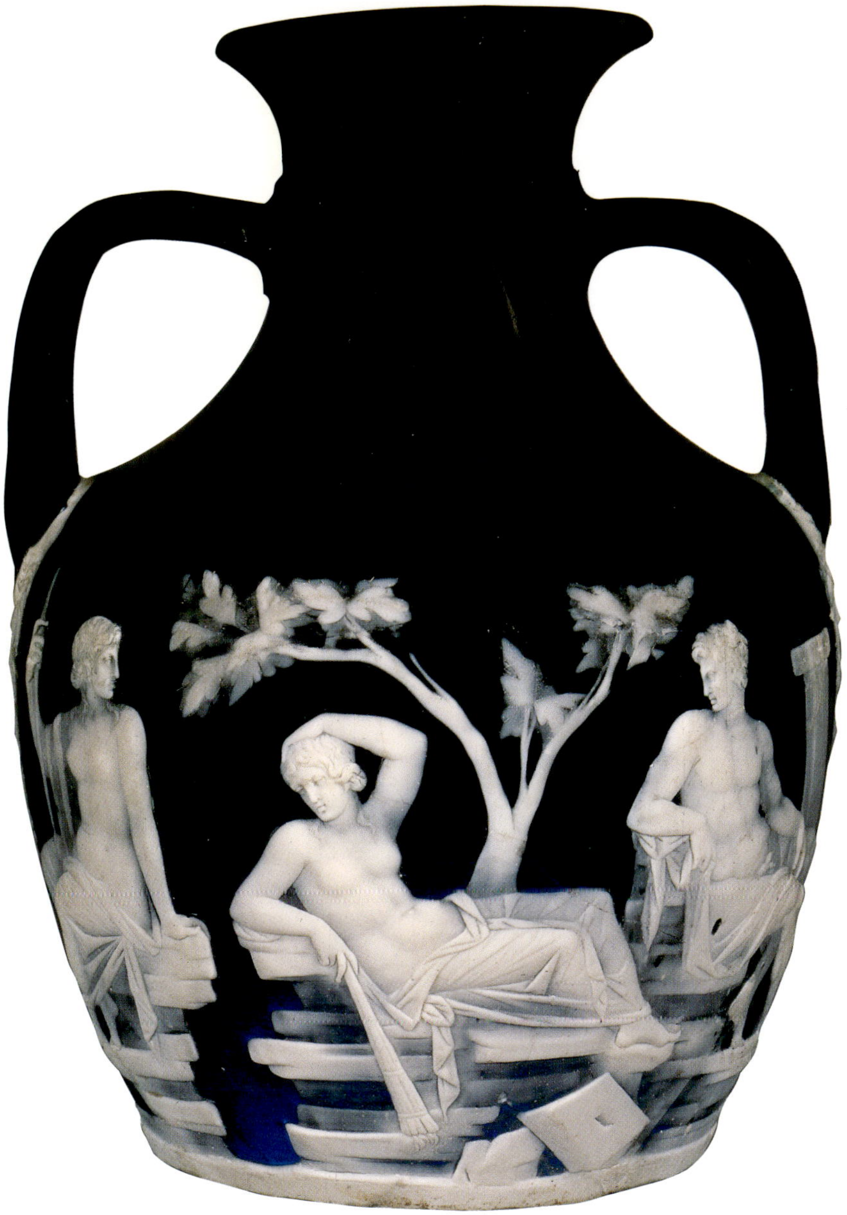

The Portland Vase,
Roman, 1st century BC. Glass.
British Museum

William showing his collection of antiquities and paintings to his many visitors. Charles Burney, who was travelling in Italy in 1770, wrote:

Mr. H. took me in to his study to shew me his charming Coreggio – the subject is a naked Venus[18] who has taken Cupid's bow from him... 'tis a wonderful fine picture... After this Etruscan vases and other antiquities of the highest antiquity and value, other curiosities, both natural and artificial, curious books etc – then went up stairs to tea, where we found, a Neapolitan prince and princess – 2 or 3 ambassadors, Lord Fortrose, the French consul, with a number of English etc.[19]

In 1785, James Byres slily referred to quite another kind of acquisition of Sir

William's, Emma Hart, who was to become the famous Lady Hamilton and lover of Lord Nelson:

> [Sir William] has lately got a piece of modernity from England, which I am afraid will fatigue and exhaust him more than all the volcanoes and antiquities in the Kingdom of Naples.[20]

Sir Willam's nephew Charles Greville had needed to distance himself from Emma, who had been his mistress, and so persuaded his uncle to take her over. Sir William promised his nephew that he would 'hobble in and out of this pleasant

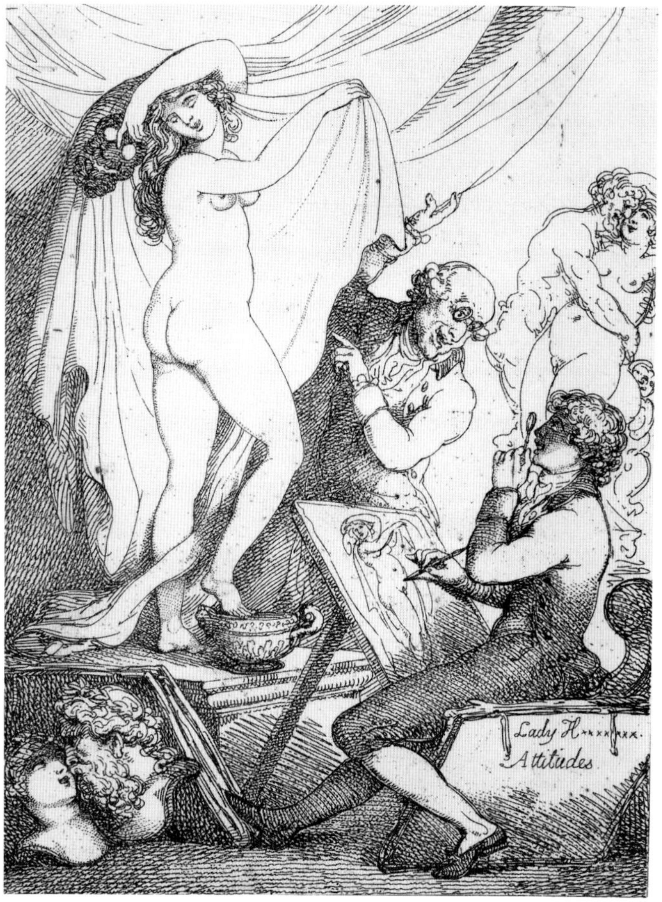

*'Lady H******* Attitudes'* by Thomas Rowlandson (1756-1827), 1790s.
Etching, 23.8 × 17 cm.
British Museum

scrape as decently as I can', and agreed to have her to stay in Naples. Gavin Hamilton was ready to assist on this occasion also, and travelled with Emma and her mother from England as far as Rome.

Sir William fell wildly in love with the twenty-one-year-old girl and she was soon performing her peculiar dances for him and his guests. In the 1780s Goethe wrote about Emma's 'Attitudes' in which, dressed in a Greek costume:

> ... [she] lets down her hair and, with a few shawls, gives so much variety to her poses, gestures, expressions, etc., that the spectator can hardly believe his eyes... The old knight idolizes her and is quite enthusiastic about everything she does. In her he has found all the antiquities, all the profiles of Sicilian coins, even the Apollo Belvedere.[21]

Hamilton made Emma his second wife (his first having died in 1782) in 1791, whereupon Walpole made a similarly sardonic observation: '[He has] actually married his gallery of statues.'[22]

By the early 1790s, however, the French army was threatening what Goethe described as 'Naples… a paradise [where] everyone lives in a state of intoxicated self-forgetfulness',[23] although it was not only the French who were to disrupt Hamilton's contented life: in September 1793, Horatio Nelson anchored in the Bay of Naples and met Emma Hamilton for the first time.

In 1798 the French invaded Rome, and Naples became ever more vulnerable. Sir William grew increasingly concerned about the safety of his collections, and compiled a 'Catalogue of my pictures July 14th 1798'.[24] He listed his collection in the Palazzo Sessa room by room, sometimes adding measurements and comments by the descriptions. Hanging in the Gallery was the *Jupiter and Antiope*, although described as 'A Venus cupid & Satyr in oil Chiaro Scuro by young Palma'. It is the first hint that the painting was in 'chiaroscuro', which probably means that it was in grisaille. There were two Galleries on the *piano nobile* of the Palazzo Sessa, and these grand rooms were where Sir William hung the 'finest Old Master and copies of others, along with the Flemish paintings'.[25] This was the part of the collection that most visitors to the *palazzo* were shown.

Later that same year Hamilton ordered his collection to be packed under the supervision of James Clark, who had formerly copied paintings for him and acted as his agent. The nineteen cases which were to be sent away were documented in 'A Catalogue of Pictures, Marbles, Bronzes etc. The property of The Right Honble. Sir William Hamilton, K.B. &c. &c. &c. Packed at Naples in Octr. Novr. & Decr. 1798 Under the Direction of Sir William's much obliged and most obedient humble Servant James Clark'.[26] In Case No. 12, listed as item 4, is the Palma Giovane *Jupiter and Antiope*:

> Palma Giovani,
> A Satyr raptuously admiring a sleeping Venus – Cupid presiding.
> In Chiaro Oscuro.

The measurements are given as 'Height: … 5 3' and 'Breadth or Length… 4 6'. The measurements of this, as of all the pictures, are in Neapolitan *palmi* and *once*, as Clark carefully noted in his list and as annotated by Sir William, and they nearly accord with those given in the Pio di Savoia inventory of 1689, 'alto palmi 6, largo 5'. The collection was eventually packed and ready to be shipped to England in 1800.

In November 1798 King Ferdinand tried to take Rome from the French. The attempt was unsuccessful, and the Royal Family, accompanied by servants, courtiers and close friends, including Sir William and Lady Hamilton, were subsequently forced to flee Naples for Palermo. In the few days before setting sail on Nelson's ship, the *Vanguard*, the Queen organised for her plate and jewellery to be packed and sent to Emma, before being taken discreetly on board ship.[27] Sir William was having to leave Naples after thirty-four years living in the city, and Emma reported to Lord Greville that they had '… left everything at Naples but the vases & best pictures, 3 houses elegantly furnished, all our horses & 6 or 7 carriages'.[28]

There were fierce storms on the voyage to Sicily. The party suffered much discomfort, and the King and Queen's six-year-old son unexpectedly died on the journey. Later in the same month Sir William suffered his own great misfortune

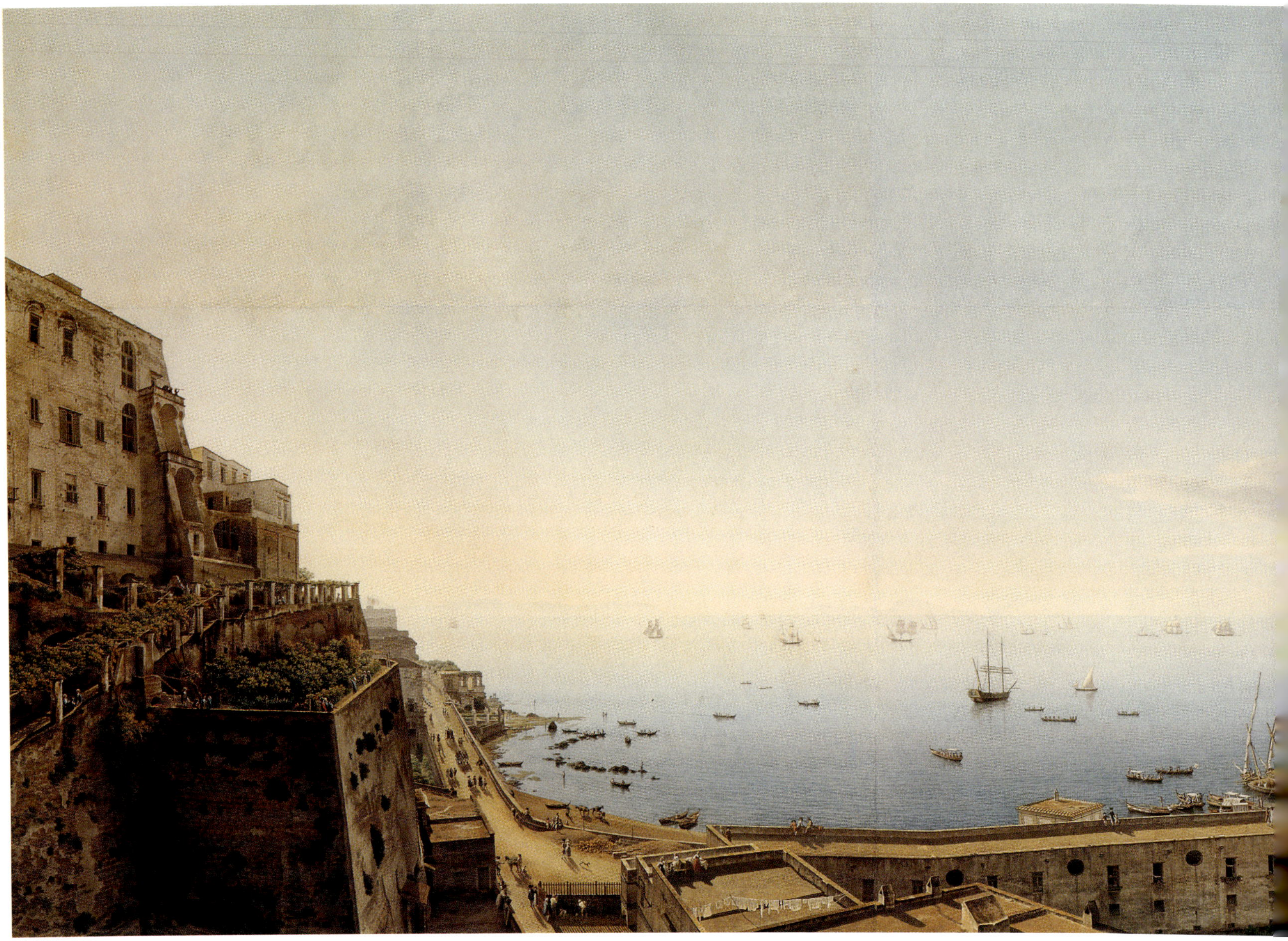

View of the Bay of Naples from the Palazzo Sessa
by Giovanni Battista Lusieri (1755-1821), 1791.
Pen, ink, gouache and watercolour on paper, 102 × 272 cm.
The J. Paul Getty Museum, Los Angeles

when the *Colossus*, which was transporting his collection of vases back to England, sank off the Scilly Isles.[29] A year later, on 25 December 1800, he wrote in a letter to Richard Worsley:

> ... six large cases of my vases and antiquities you may have heard went down in the Colossus – Lord Nelson our good friend saved all my pictures on board the Foudroyant [Nelson's flagship] and are all in London but not yet unpacked.[30]

Before this, in the same letter, Hamilton had bemoaned his financial state, and the part the British Government had played in his predicament by not paying some of the expenses he had incurred during his posting to Naples. The Hamiltons had returned to England the previous month, but now Sir William, precisely because of his financial problems, was forced to sell some of his picture collection. Some

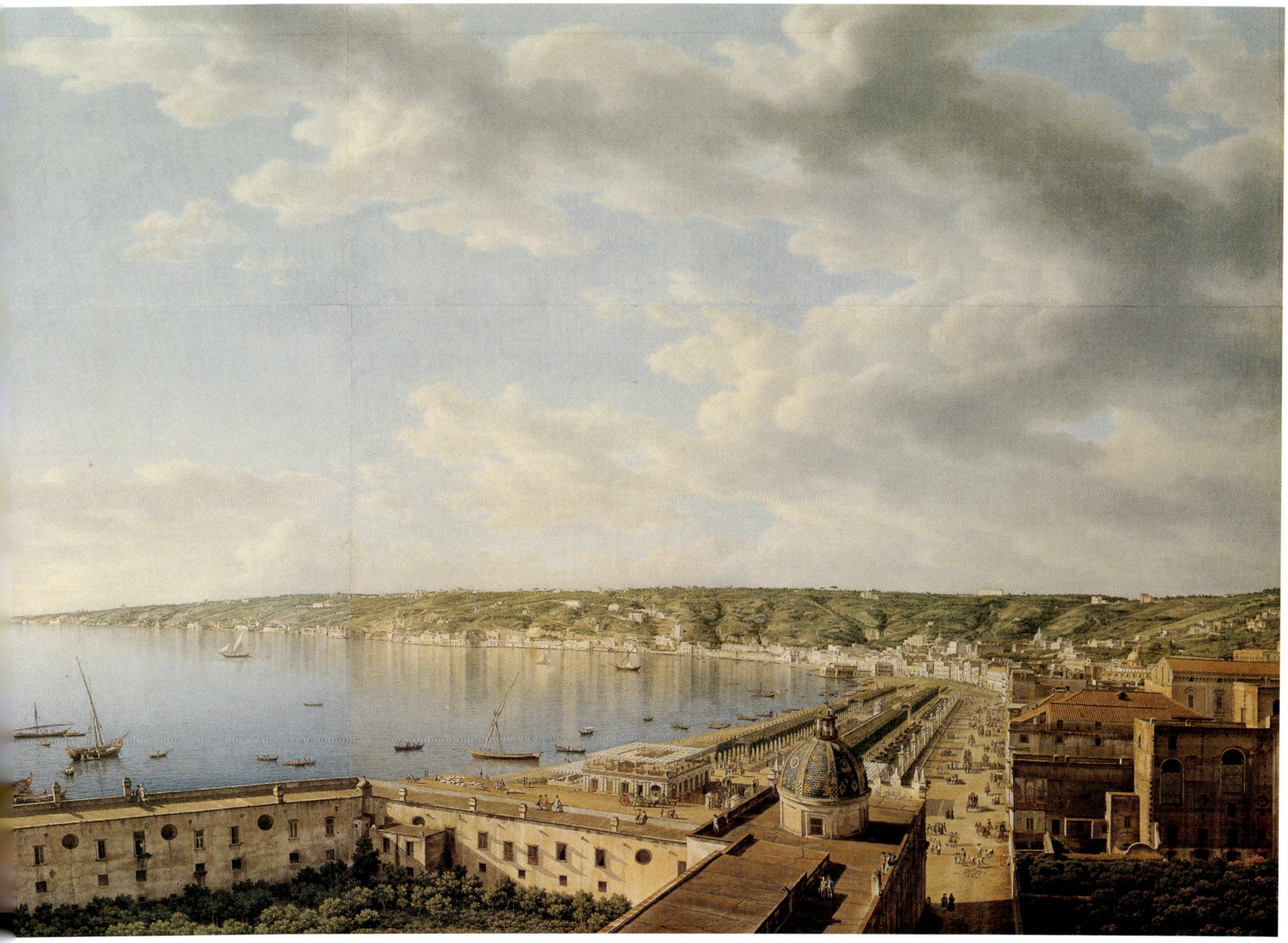

150 pictures were entered in a sale at Christie's on 27 and 28 March, and in a further sale on 17 and 18 April 1801.

These two sales attracted much comment, although it was not always entirely complimentary. Joseph Farington in his diary entry for Wednesday 25 March 1801, records, 'Sir Wm. Hamilton's sale of pictures I went to with C & Mrs Offley. – A very indifferent collection.'[31] William Buchanan was similarly dismissive, although he did qualify his comments:

> Although the collection of Sir William Hamilton contained very few pictures of price or of consequence, yet it might be deemed unpardonable to pass over unnoticed a collection which belonged to so distinguished a connoisseur, in all objects connected with virtù.[32]

He added that 'it was formed at a period before the capital works of the great masters were separated from the walls of those palaces which they had so long adorned, and when copies of these, or works of a second-rate class only, could be procured'.[33]

Despite these occasionally low opinions of Sir William's paintings, the March sale made the more than respectable figure of £5,025.13s, despite the fact that several pictures did not reach their reserve price. The Palma Giovane was included in the first day of the March sale, as lot 55, and was described in the catalogue as:

> A Satyr admiring a Sleeping Venus, Cupid presiding, in Chiaro-Scuro. This picture was in the Collection of Great Italian Masters, published by Gavin Hamilton at Rome.

Added in the margin in pencil: '*In the Collection of Prince Pio, at Rome, and was engraved.*' Written in pencil beside the description in the auctioneer's copy of the catalogue is the figure '*11.11.0.*'[34] No buyer's name is noted, although this catalogue does include some buyers' names beside other lots, and so it might appear that picture did not sell and was 'bought in'. None the less, it is probable that it did sell, as its appearance in sales over the next few years would seem to confirm.

On 2 March 1809 the painting was again was put up for sale, but this time at Phillips, as lot 42, by 'A Gentleman of known Taste and Judgement' who had collected pictures 'from various Cabinets on the Continent, and enlarged [his collection] during the last Ten Years by Additions from various Collections'. Added in pencil beside the description of lot 42 ('Palma. Venus and Satyr in Chiaroscuro engraved in Scola [sic] Italica') is '*5.10*' (i.e. £5.10s), but the buyer is again not recorded. On 31 January 1811, however, when the same painting is included in a sale at Mr Harry Phillips ('Palma. A sleeping Nymph surprised by a Satyr, engraved in the Scuola [*sic*] Italica'), the title page of the catalogue states that Mr. Richard Davies, who was a jeweller, was the seller for the day, and lot 52 – the Palma Giovane *Jupiter and Antiope* – has the figure '*£7.17.6*' added beside it. Evidently, it did not sell, because when, on 22 March 1814, the picture was again put up for sale at Phillips (lot 180), as 'Palma, Venus Cupid and Satyr (Chiaro Scuro)', the seller on the title page was again Richard Davies. It was again bought in, with '*£14.14*' inscribed in pencil beside the lot description.

The picture next appears at Christie's on Tuesday 30 March 1824. The sale on this occasion was principally made up of pictures from the collection of Sir William Temple, but also included 'A Few Fine Specimens of Italian Masters, Lately Consigned from Italy'. Lot 17 was entered as 'Palma... A sleeping Nymph with a Cupid and Satyr'. Added in pencil in the auctioneer's copy of the catalogue is, on the left, '*Sir A.C.*'. At the end of the description is pencilled the instruction '*to go*', i.e. that there was no reserve on the picture and that it was to be sold at whatever price offered. The initials here refer to the seller, Sir Alexander Creighton of Harley Street, who was the ex-physician to the Imperial family at St. Petersburg, and who bought many items from Christie's between 1824-1836.[35] The buyer is recorded as 'Taylor' and the hammer price was £4.4. This is the last time that the Palma Giovane is known to have been sold, and the picture is not recorded again after this date.

NOTES

1 '*Ex Tabula in Aedibus Principis Pio Romae asservata*'.
2 I. Jenkins and K. Sloan, *Vases and Volcanoes*, exh. cat., London, 1996, p. 276, information supplied by Burton Frederickson of the Getty Provenance Index.
3 *The Dictionary of Art*.
4 'Nel Palazzo di Son Eminenza diverse camere ornate di pitture rarissime: due Veneri al naturale di Titiano,... Con una buona libreria... ', G.P. Bellori, *Nota Delli Musei, Librerie, Galerie, et Ornamenti di Statue e Pitture ne'Palazzi, nelle café, e ne'Giardini di Roma*, 1664.
5 'Six *palmi* high by five wide'. Information courtesy of Burton Frederickson.
6 F. Haskell, 'Art Exhibitions in XVII Century Rome', *Biblioteca dell'Archivum Romanicum. Studi Secenteschi*, vol. 1, 1960, see pp. 116ff.
7 Ibid., p. 117. G. de Marchi, *Mostre di Quadri a S. Salvatore in Lauro (1682-1725)*, Rome, 1987.
8 'A painting of a Venus... and a Satyr, with a Cupid on the ground, on canvas with a gilded frame, about 9 *palmi* high by 7 *palmi* wide.' J. Bentini, ed., *Quadri Rinomatissimi – Il Collezionismo dei Pio di Savoia*, 1994, p. 124.
9 S. Guarino, '"Qualche Quadro per Nostro Servizio": i dipinti Pio di Savoia inventariati, venduti e dispersi', in Bentini, op. cit., p. 104.
10 Ibid. Prince Giberto's heir was his sister Isabella, married to a Spanish nobleman.
11 Ibid.
12 M. Postle, 'Driven by Passion', *The Royal Academy Magazine*, no. 45, Winter 1994, pp. 34-5.
13 Horace Walpole quoted in Jenkins and Sloan, op. cit., p. 75.
14 *Anecdotes of Painting*, F.W. Hilles and P.B. Daghlian, ed., vol. V, 1937, pp. 228-9.
15 Jenkins and Sloan, op. cit., pp. 276-7.
16 See, for example, J.Ingamells, *A Dictionary of British and Irish Travellers in Italy 1701-1800*, New Haven and London, 1997, p. 454.
17 J.H.W. Tischbein, *Collection of Engravings from Ancient Vases Discovered in the Kingdom of the Two Sicilies between 1789-90*, 5 vols., Naples, 1793–.
18 Now attributed to Cambiaso: Ingamells, loc. cit.
19 Charles Burney, *Music, Men and Manners in France and Italy*, 1770, p. 195.
20 Ingamells, op. cit., p. 456.
21 Quoted in Flora Fraser, *Beloved Emma*, 1986, p. 121.
22 Quoted in Ingamells, op. cit., p. 457.
23 Fraser, op. cit., p. 126.
24 British Library, Add. MS 41,200, ff. 121-8.
25 Jenkins and Sloan, op. cit., p. 85.
26 Fitzwilliam Museum, Cambridge, Percival Bequest MSS, in B. Fothergill, *Sir William Hamilton, Envoy Extraordinary*, 1969, p. 427. N. Ramage, 'A list of Sir William Hamilton's property', *Burlington Magazine*, XCCCI (October 1989), pp. 704-6.
27 Fraser, op. cit., p. 228.
28 Ibid., p. 230.
29 Two-thirds of the vases were eventually salvaged, and sold to Thomas Hope in 1801 (see *Dictionary of Art*).
30 Brinsley Ford Archive, Paul Mellon Centre, London, Sir William Hamilton folder, letter from Worsley MSS 55 (Lincolnshire Record Office).
31 K. Garlick and A. Macintyre, ed., *The Diary of Joseph Farington*, London, 1978-84, 16 vols., IV, p. 1527.
32 William Buchanan, *Memoirs of Painting*, 2 vols., 1824, II, p. 73.
33 Quoted in Jenkins and Sloan, op. cit., p. 75.
34 Sale catalogue in National Art Library, Victoria & Albert Museum, London.
35 We are grateful to Francis Russell of Christie's for this information.

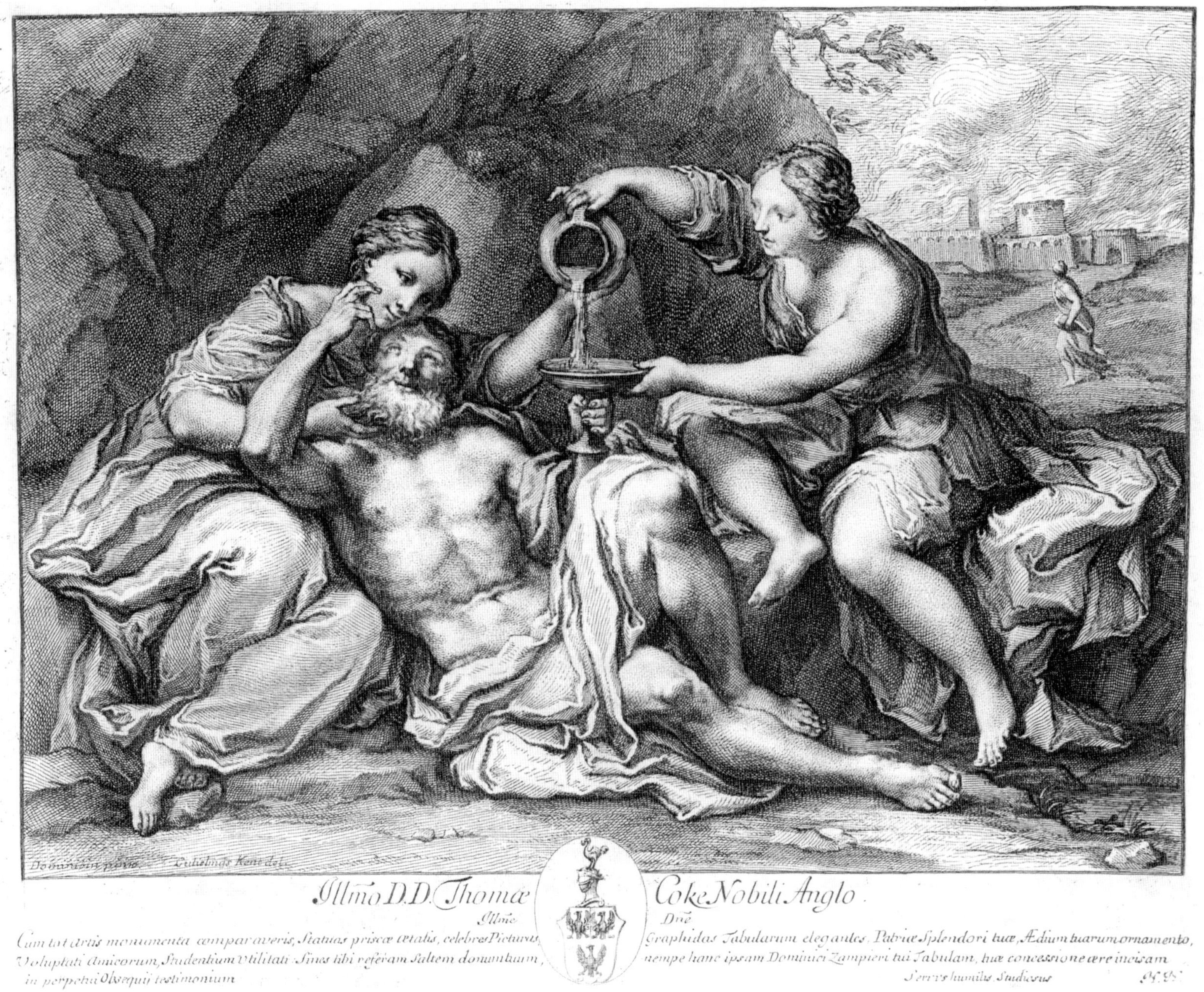

Lot and his daughters.
Engraving by Jakob Frey (1681-1752), *c.* 1618, after a drawing by Willam Kent (1685-1748)
of a painting by Domenichino (Domenico Zampieri, 1581-1641).
Witt Print Collection, Courtauld Institute of Art, London

Domenico Zampieri, known as Domenichino

1581-1641

Lot and his daughters

1630

Oil on canvas
Possibly 190.4 × 251.6 cm

Thomas Coke (1697-1759), 1st Earl of Leicester, was one of the great English collectors, patrons and connoisseurs of the eighteenth century. At the age of fifteen he embarked on a four-year Grand Tour (1713-17), accompanied by his tutor Dr. Thomas Hobart (d. 1728). He spent most of his time in Italy, where he developed his taste and love of the arts. In 1714, he wrote from Rome to his grandfather that he had become 'a perfect virtuoso, and a great lover of pictures'.[1] Coke's acquisitions were meticulously recorded in an account book that was kept by his valet Edward Jarrett,[2] and they included a painting by Domenichino, *Lot and his daughters*, which has since disappeared.[3] The composition is recorded in an engraving that can be dated to about 1718, carrying a dedication to Thomas Coke, and the picture can also be traced in the inventories of the Coke family.

The composition is also known from a drawing for it by Domenichino himself (Royal Collection), which shows it to have been, like the painting in the Coke collection, 'landscape' in shape, i.e. wider that it was high.[4] The same picture can, in all probability, be traced back to seventeenth-century records, one of them dating to the time of Domenichino. The story is complicated by the fact that Domenichino evidently painted the same subject in at least one other version, also recorded in engravings, but which was 'portrait' in format (i.e. higher than it was wide).

On June 25 1718 the following payment appears in Edward Jarrett's account book:

Sent to Mr Kent at Rome:
A cupid by Guido Reni & Lot by Domenichino 400 Roman Crowns.

This means that 'Mr Kent', William Kent (1685-1748), was being paid 400 Roman crowns for the two pictures supplied. Only a few months later, on 15 November 1718, Kent told another patron of his successful transactions, 'Mr Coke had a fine picture of Domenichino and another of Carlo Marrat & a very large one of Giuseppe Chiari,'[5] and it is reasonable to suppose that this Domenichino was the same *Lot and his daughters* for which he had been paid in June.

William Kent was to become one of the most influential architects and designers in the history of British art, but at this time he was an unknown young man with his career still to make. He arrived in Italy in 1709 and had been in Rome since 1710.[6] While in Rome he was supplementing his income by functioning as an agent and dealer, acting as a go-between with the Italians and visiting 'milordi' from England.

The fact that Kent mentions the three artists Domenichino, Carlo Maratta (or 'Maratti', 1625-1713) and Giuseppe Chiari (1654-1727) in the same sentence is no

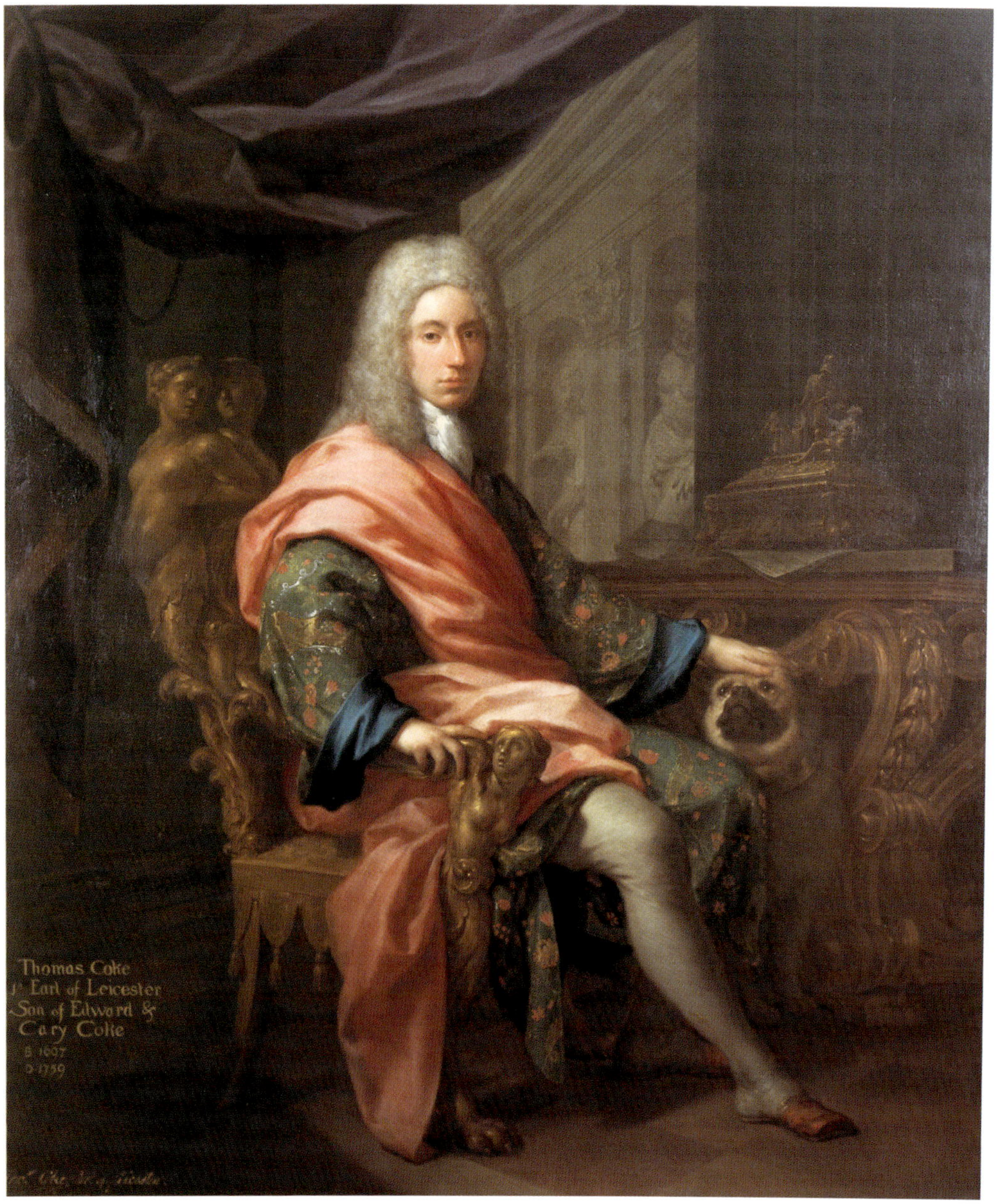

Thomas Coke, 1st Earl of Leicester (1697-1759),
by Francesco Trevisani (1656-1746).
Oil on canvas.
Collection of the Earl of Leicester, Holkham Hall, Norfolk

coincidence. Kent was himself a pupil of Chiari; Chiari had been taught by Maratta; and Maratta was a serious collector of works by Domenichino. No record of a *Lot and his daughters* by Domenichino is to be found in Maratta's extensive inventory of 1712, or in that of his wife of 1711,[7] but there is a further link between Kent and Maratta. The crucial record of the appearance of the Coke Domenichino, *Lot and his daughters*, is an engraving made by Jakob Frey (1681-1752), a Swiss engraver who lived in Rome, who had been very much assisted by Carlo Maratta when he settled in the city in 1702.[8] Frey also purchased Maratta's important copper-engraving business after he died.

The dedication on Frey's engraving implies that the original painting is in the possession of Thomas Coke:

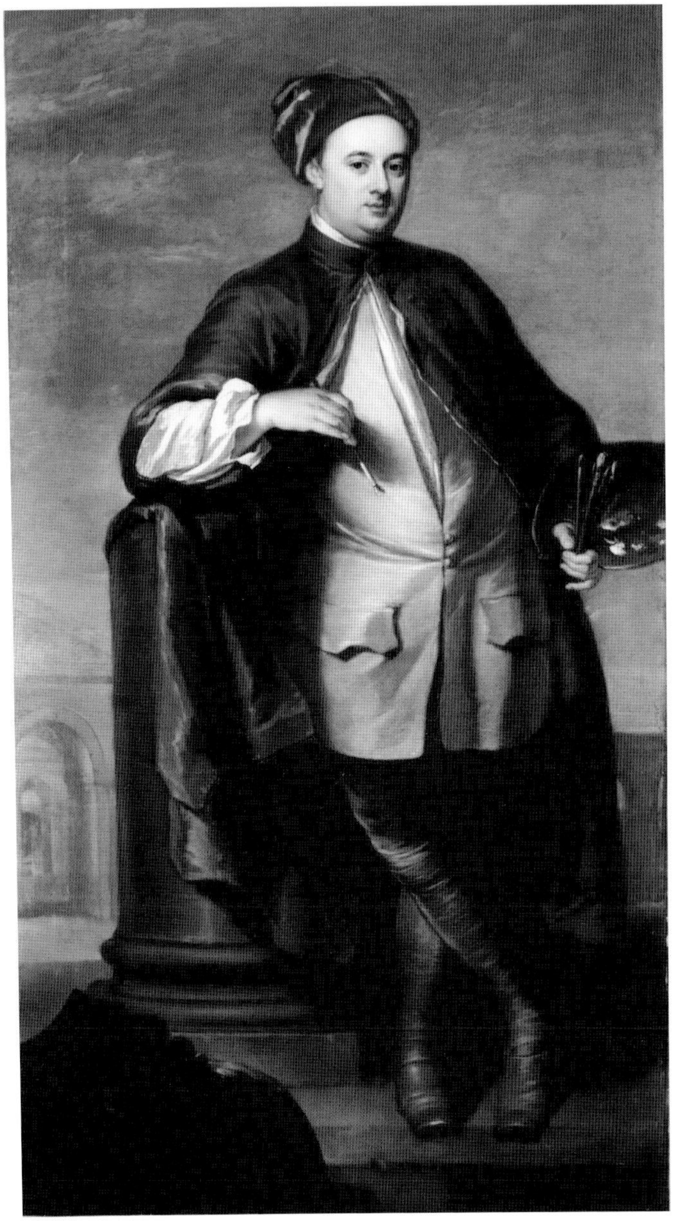

William Kent (1685-1748)
by William Aikman (1682-1731),
c. 1723.
Oil on canvas, 197 × 104 cm.
Sotheby's, London, 15 November 1989 (32)

Jllmõ D. D. Thomae Coke Nobili Anglo / Jllme Dne / Cum tot artis monumenta comparaveris, Statuas priscae Aetatis, celebres Picturas, Graphidas Tabularum elegantes, Patriae Splendori tuae, Aedium tuarum ornamento, / Voluptati Amicorum, Studentium Utilitati: Sines tibi referam saltem donum tuum, nempe hanc ipsam Dominici Zampieri tui Tabulam, tuae concessione aere incisam / in perpetui obsequij testimonium. / Servus humilis Studiosus N. N.[9]

The print also bears an inscription stating that while the painting was by Domenichino, the print was made after a drawing by William Kent:

Dominichin pinx. Guglielmus Kent del. ('Domenichino painted it. William Kent drew it.')

It is probable that the engraving was made in Rome while Kent was still there, and also that it was made very near the date of Coke's buying the painting. Frey never went to England, while Kent returned to England in 1719; and 'N.N.', who was certainly in the Kent-Coke circle in 1714,[10] appears to be sending the engraving from Italy to Coke's home in England. There was every reason for Kent, while he was still in Rome, to make the most of the presence of his name upon an engraving of a picture sold to an important young man making the Grand Tour. The dedication of the print points to a period before Coke assumed his later titles, and the coat of arms lacks the 'supporters' which Coke was granted when he was knighted in 1725.[11]

Domenichino trained in the Carracci Academy in Bologna, and went to Rome in 1602 where he was encouraged by Annibale Carracci. Annibale involved Domenichino in his monumental fresco decoration at the Palazzo Farnese, and he was crucial in securing Domenichino several important commissions, which helped to establish him as a much sought-after artist. The earliest mention of *Lot and his daughters* is in records of the Barberini family in 1630.

The Barberini were originally from Florence, and rose to the highest point of their power in Rome with the election of Maffeo Barberini (1568-1644) as Pope Urban VIII in 1623. The new Pope's nephews, Francesco, Taddeo and Antonio, were swiftly given important and powerful positions, both secular and ecclesiastical. Francesco (1597-1679), an erudite patron of the arts, was made a cardinal in 1623, and the mention of *Lot and his daughters* appears in his household accounts. Domenichino appears to have known Cardinal Barberini well. He had painted a half-length portrait of him (now missing); the Cardinal had attended the baptism of Domenichino's third daughter; and in 1623 the Cardinal had given her 40 *scudi*. The reference to *Lot and his daughters* is as follows:

Dec 1630
A Dom.o. Zampieri d.o Deominco Bolognese Pittore sc. 60 m.ta p prezzo del quadro di Lot fatto p.S.Em.Za dalle 9.e fu donato a Mons.r. Bichi – 60.[12]

This entry states that Domenichino was paid 60 *scudi* for the 'picture of Lot' which Domenichino had made for the Cardinal, and that it was a gift from the Cardinal to a 'Mons.r Bichi'. Several members of the Sienese Bichi family had close connections with Cardinal Francesco Barberini, and there are two possible recipients of this gift, the brothers Alessandro (1596-1657) and Celio (1599-1657). A third member of the family, Antonio (1614-1691), can probably be discounted on grounds of his age.[13] A clue is the use of the abbreviation 'Mons.r'. It indicates an ecclesiastical office usually bestowed by the Pope, 'Monsignor', but in France is used by bishops, 'Monseigneur', as a matter of course. The Italian abbreviation is 'Mgr.' and 'Mons.r' would seem to indicate a French bishop, which Alessandro became in 1630.

Alessandro, the elder of the two brothers, having chosen a career in the church, became papal nuncio to Naples in 1628, and on 6 September 1630 was appointed papal nuncio to the court of Louis XIII in Paris, a key diplomatic mission. Two days later he was translated from the see of Isola and instead became bishop of Carpentras in France. These appointments would have been arranged by Francesco Barberini, who had been in charge of papal foreign affairs since 1628. His gift of the Domenichino to a Bichi family member was made in December, and it was at the beginning of that month that Alessandro Bichi arrived in Paris as papal nuncio. In view of the timing of these events, and since Francesco Barberini himself had been much involved in negotiations between France and the

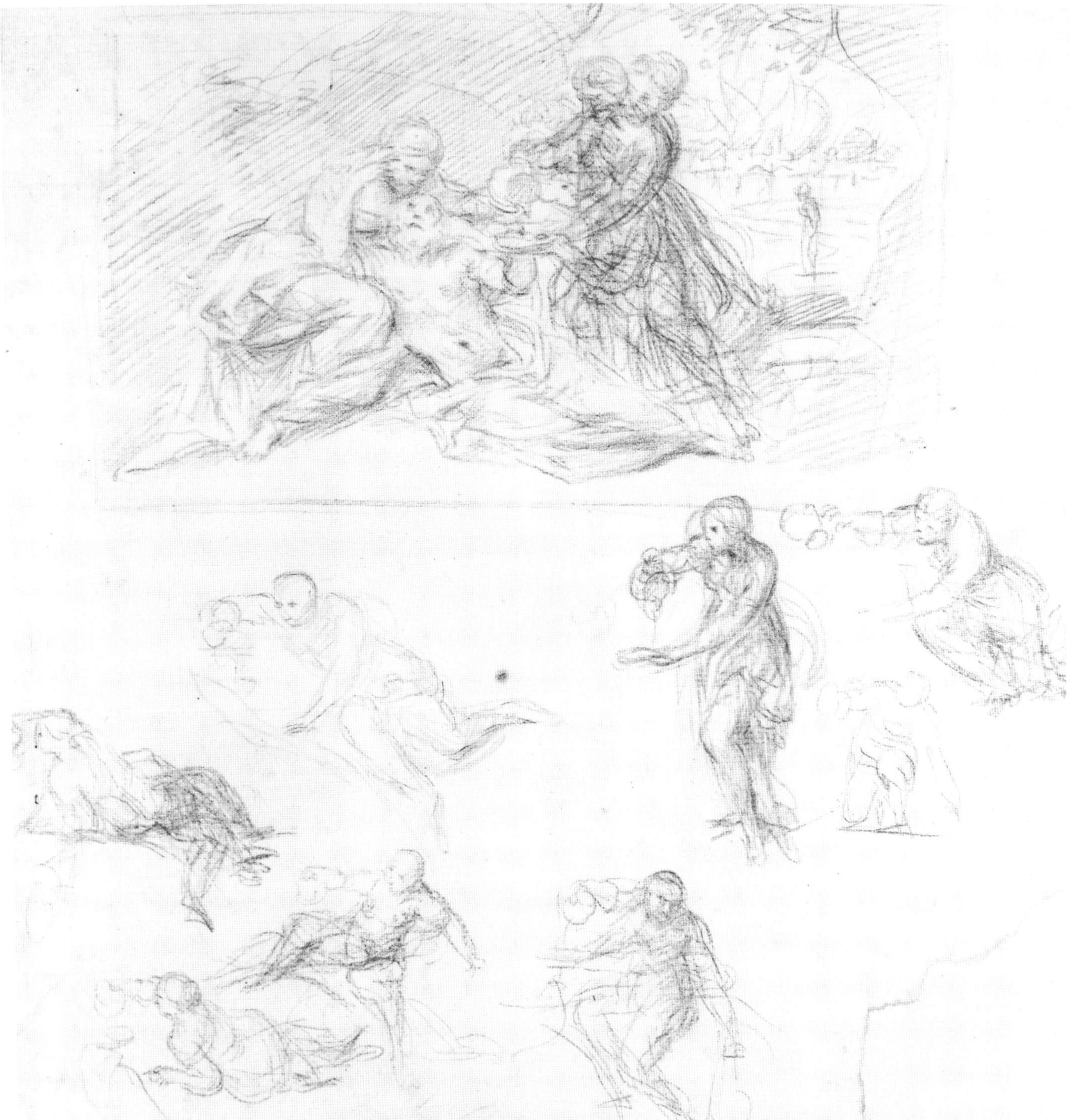

Studies for *Lot and his daughters* by Domenichino, *c.* 1630.
Red chalk on white paper, 23 × 20.7 cm.

papacy in the two years leading up to Bichi's appointment, it seems certain that the recipient of the gift was Alessandro Bichi.[14]

Alessandro Bichi was known in France more for his patronage of writers and artists than for his piety. He was also a brilliant diplomat, who received preferment at the hands of Louis XIII of France, was also trusted by the King's chief minister Cardinal Richelieu, and became especially close to Richelieu's successor Cardinal Mazarin. He himself became a cardinal in 1633. It was through Cardinal Bichi's intercession that the Barberini found refuge at the French court when they were forced to flee Rome in 1646.

The Pamphilj pope, Innocent X (*r.* 1644-55), temporarily recalled Bichi to Rome in 1654 but then refused him permission to return to France. Although he was useful to Mazarin in the election of the next (Chigi) pope, Alexander VII, in 1655, Bichi never returned to France and died in Rome on 15 May 1657. His will has not been traced and no record of the Domenichino in his collection has been found. His nearest likely heir would have been his nephew, Carlo Giacomo Bichi (1639-1718), who also became a cardinal, but again there are no records that mention such a connection.

The next definite record of a *Lot and his daughters* by Domenichino is to a picture which may well be identical with that formerly in the collection of Alessandro Bichi, and appears in a document of 18 December 1690. This is an inventory drawn up to record the three parts of the collection of the Boscoli family of Parma with a view to the donation of the entire collection in due course to the two sons of the household, Lelio and Francesco Maria.[15] The three parts are those belonging to 'Cavaliera Boscoli' (the mother, wife of Gian Simone Boscoli, née Domitilla de' Conti); the father, Gian Simone (1612-1701), Marchese di Ravarano; and their elder son, Lelio (d. 1703).[16] In the section of the inventory pertaining to Gian Simone we find:

> Un altro bislungo del sud.° Domenichino d'alt^{a} br. 2.8., larg.^{a} br. 3.7. dov'e Lot con due figliole. cornice bianca, stimato doppie ventiquattro.[17]

The measurements, which might include the frame ('cornice bianca'), reveal a large rectangular ('bislungo') picture by Domenichino of Lot 'and his two daughters' measuring 2.8 × 3.7 *braccia*, that is, 190.4 cm × 251.6 cm. Significantly, the picture is landscape-shaped: the entry identifies the measurements as height before width.[18]

It is conceivable that it was through their long-standing close connections with the great Roman family of the Farnese, rulers of Parma, that the Boscoli had come into possession of the missing Domenichino.[19] However that may be, after it was listed in 1690 among Gian Simone's works of art, the picture would have passed to his son Lelio who then died shortly after he did, on 29 January 1703. It seems possible that the painting would then have gone to Lelio's brother Francesco Maria. Whether or not it did so, or whether it passed into the possession of another Parmese family, the Sanvitale, as Campori suggests happened with much of the collection, both Thomas Coke and William Kent visited Parma at precisely the time that it is recorded as having entered Coke's possession.

In 1714 Kent and Coke left Rome to travel about northern Italy. On 14 August 1714 Kent left Coke in Padua in order to visit Parma where, on 6 September he witnessed, as he recorded in his journal,[20] the wedding of Elisabetta Farnese to Philip V of Spain in the Cathedral. Coke and his tutor, Dr. Hobart, took a more leisurely route, reaching Parma a couple of months later, from which they finally reached Turin on 3 December.[21] When Kent once again met up with Coke, at Naples in 1716, he was paid for the work he had done in collecting works of art and arranged for them to be handed over. Later that year, both Coke and Kent went together to Parma. There were therefore at least two opportunities for Kent to have acquired the Boscoli Domenichino, always supposing it to have remained in Parma, with the later occasion the more likely.

The Coke Domenichino was landscape in shape, as was the composition drawn by Domenichino in his preparatory study; and so was that recorded in the Boscoli collection. Another record of *Lot and his daughters* by Domenichino, although it, too, has disappeared, was made by his pupil Francesco Raspantino (*fl.* 1637-64) and, although smaller in size, like so many copies, it too was landscape in format. It is described in Raspantino's detailed inventory of 1664 as:

> Un quadro di Lotto da 4 e 6. con figlie, che l'imbriaca, senza cornice, mano mia, copia del Domenichino.[22]

The measurements 'da 4 e 6' (the picture is stated to be without a frame) refer to *palmi*, and are equivalent to about 92 × 138 cm. Three days before his death, Domenichino had designated Raspantino his artistic heir, leaving him the contents of his studio, and Raspantino also listed seven 'disegni di Lotto' by Domenichino in his inventory.[23]

During the years that the Domenichino remained in the Coke family after its purchase, it was first recorded in 1760, the year following Thomas Coke's death, when an inventory was made of his London residence, Thanet House, Great Russell Street, in the parish of St. Giles-in-the-Fields.[24] The picture is recorded as hanging in the drawing room, with *Apollo and Daphne* by Carlo Maratta beneath it.[25] The house partly survives, although divided into three and with a later façade (Nos. 100, 101, 102, Great Russell Street). A number of the rooms are certainly of a size that could take large pictures, while the drawing room would have been one of the two or three most important rooms in the house. The Maratta *Apollo and Daphne* survives at Holkham, and measures 68.6 × 55.2 cm. Smaller pictures such as this were hung below larger ones in the eighteenth century, and a landscape-shaped canvas of *Lot and his daughters*, even one measuring some six feet high like that recorded in the Boscoli collection, would not be out of place higher on the drawing-room wall.

Thomas Coke's widow, the Dowager Countess of Leicester, gave up the lease on the London house in the same year, 1760, and took many of the contents to Holkham Hall, although some were at this stage inherited by Wenman Coke, Lord Leicester's nephew. The Domenichino of *Lot*, however, is listed among 'The pictures brought from Russell Street to Holkham June 1760'.[26] Holkham is the great house that Coke had been building from 1734 in the Palladian style to his own designs and those of Lord Burlington, and assisted by William Kent.[27] It was not finished at Coke's death in 1759, although he did leave detailed instructions as to how it should be completed, and also where the individual pieces in his great collection should be placed within the house. On its completion, Lady Leicester made a comprehensive catalogue recording the pictures and statues at Holkham 'as they were placed in 1764/5',[28] and *Lot and his daughters* is recorded as hanging in the Drawing Room,[29] a room comfortably large enough in which to hang it (it is about 22 feet high).

In 1761, Matthew Brettingham the elder (1699-1769), who was employed by Lord Leicester from 1735 as supervisor and executive architect of the building of

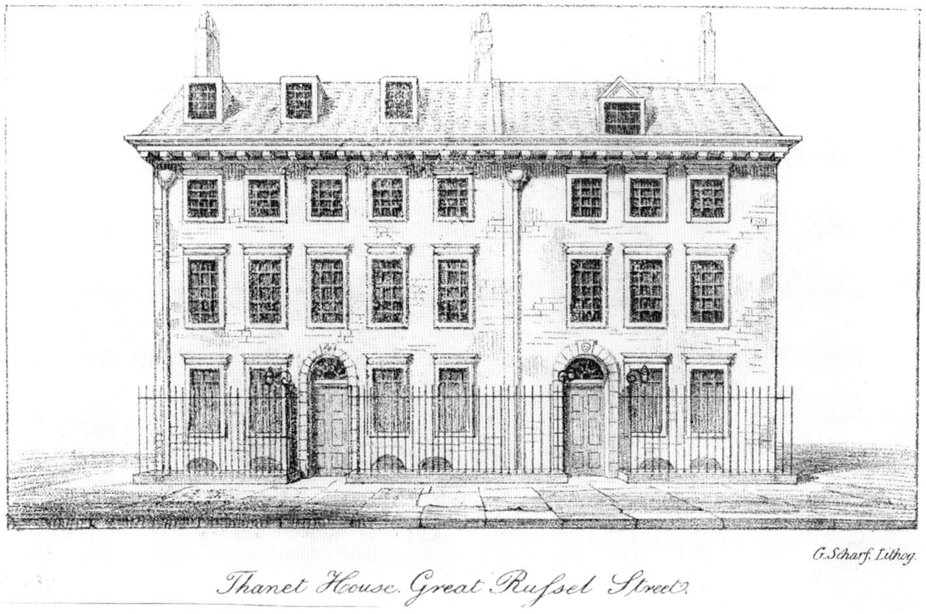

Thanet House, Great Russell Street, London.
Lithograph by George Scharf (1788-1860), *c.* 1825.
Guildhall Library and Art Gallery, London

Holkham,[30] published *The Plans and Elevations of the Late Earl of Leicester's House at Holkham*, but without giving any information about the pictures or furnishings. This was re-issued, however, in 1773 by his son, Matthew Brettingham the younger (1725-1803), now with descriptions of some of the contents of the rooms. There is now no mention of *Lot and his daughters* in the Drawing Room. Instead, hanging in the State Anti-Chamber,[31] located within the State Bed-Chamber Apartments, was:

> Lot and his two Daughters, small Life: this is a Sketch of Dominichino's Painting: the Appearance of Inebriety in the Countenance, and of Age in the Limbs and Body of the Lot, are finely delineated. There is a Print after it, by Giacomo Frey.[32]

The description clearly states that this is a small work (although the room itself is very nearly as big as the Drawing Room). The phrase 'a sketch of Dominichino's painting' also indicates that this was not the painting itself but a sketch of the painting. It was, however, evidently detailed, and probably a drawing rather than, say, an oil sketch, as is suggested by the favourable comments about the 'appearance ... finely delineated'. It seems possible, then, that this might even be the drawing by Kent which we know to have been made for the purposes of the Frey engraving, which bears, of course, the inscription '... Gulgielmus Kent del[ineavit]'.

That it is not the original painting that is being referred to here appears to be further confirmed by the end of the entry, 'There is a print after it by Giacomo Frey', because the phrase 'after it' cannot properly refer to the original painting but only to the sketch in question. This description and its details can especially be relied upon because the Brettinghams, father and son, had both been in Rome, where they would have known Frey himself, and both were closely involved with Thomas Coke and his family over many years, as architects and as agents in the acquisition of works of art.[33]

Dawson, in 1817, records the picture as being in the Stranger's Wing, in the

Blue and Yellow Bedchamber,[34] which could be either the original large painting by Domenichino or, less probably, the sketch after it. In 1826 the room contained the same pictures noted by Dawson: four (overdoor) landscapes by 'Luccatelli'; *Lot and his daughters*; St. Jerome in a landscape; and *Diana and her nymphs* by Domenichino.[35] By 1861 the *Lot* was no longer in this room,[36] but it may be that

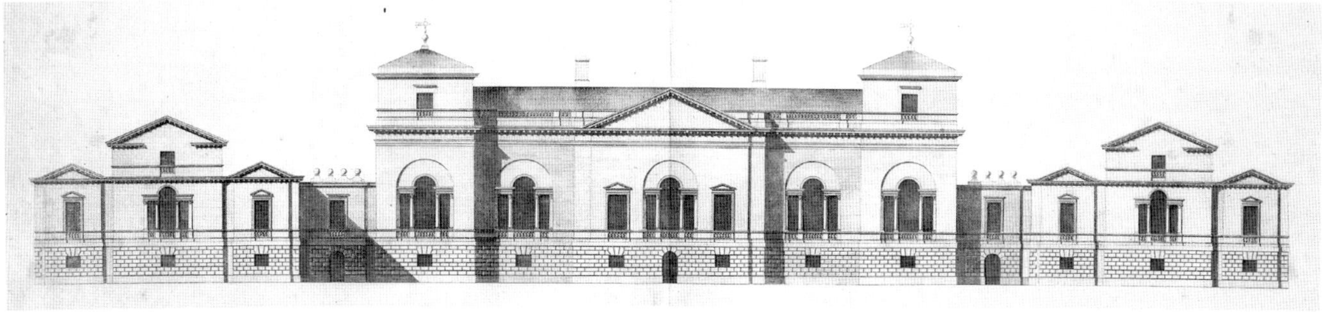

Holkham Hall,
view of the north front
from Matthew Brettingham, *The Plans, Elevations and Sections of Holkham in Norfolk*, 1773

the picture remained at Holkham until 1887, when a work of the same title was put up for sale at Foster's auction rooms in London. The picture may well have suffered from the 2nd Earl's[37] very different taste in art from that of his great-great uncle, Thomas Coke. He moved many pictures around in the house, relegating some to the attic, and in their place introduced many family portraits. He died leaving a huge inheritance but, despite this, was the seller at the 1887 auction.

By this date, Domenichino was generally not so sought after as in the eighteenth century. John Ruskin (1819-1900) commented: 'The man who painted the *Madonna del Rosario*... in the gallery of Bologna [i.e. Domenichino], is palpably incapable of doing anything good, great, or right, in any field, way or kind whatsoever... I do not recollect any instance of colour and execution so cold and feelingless.'[38] Even allowing for changes in taste, however, when *Lot and his daughters* was sold to a 'Mrs. Wheeler' for just £2 5s od in the sale of 1887, the price appears very low, especially when compared with Domenichino's *The vision of St John* which was bought in at £735 in 1884 and finally sold in 1899 for £105.[39] The suspicion must be, therefore, that what was sold under this title in 1887 was not the original painting, which may have already left the Holkham collection, but instead what had been recorded in 1773 as 'a Sketch of Dominichino's Painting', perhaps, that is to say, the drawing made by William Kent for the purposes of the Frey engraving. Whatever the truth of this tangled tale, Frey's engraving remains the chief record of this lost masterpiece.

OTHER VERSIONS OF *LOT AND HIS DAUGHTERS* BY DOMENICHINO

At least one other version of the subject by Domenichino, and perhaps more than one, existed, judging from engravings, and in a 'portrait' (vertical) format, rather than landscape. This version was engraved by Charles Grignion (1717-1810), but in the reverse sense to the composition recorded in the Coke collection. Another portrait-shaped engraving, but in the same sense as the Coke version, is by Philipp Andreas Kilian (incidentally a pupil of Frey), dated to 1758, and carrying an

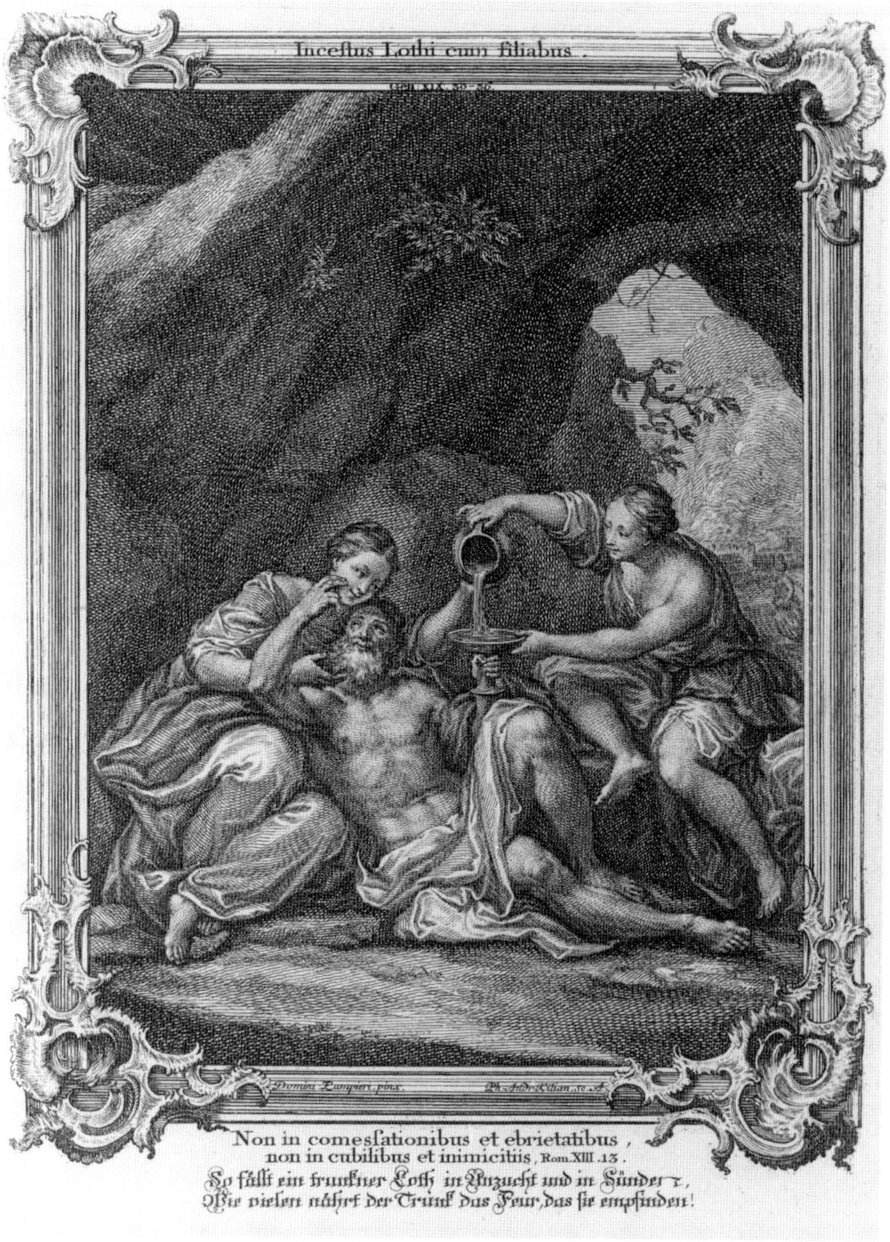

Lot and his daughters.
Engraving, 1758, by P. A. Kilian,
after a painting by Domenichino

inscription in both English and German. The figures appear very similar to those in the Frey print, but take up fully half the picture-field, and the rocky landscape dominates the top half; but the same view of the burning city of Sodom and the figure walking in the background are included.

The dedication on the engraving by Charles Grignion introduces another great English collector of the eighteenth century, Frederick Augustus Hervey (1730-1803):

To the Honourable and Reverend, Freder.[k] Hervey, this Plate is most humbly Inscribed By his most Obed.[t] Servant, W. Rider.

Hervey was ordained a priest on 26 January 1755 and the inscription therefore indicates that the engraving was made after that date but before Hervey was consecrated Bishop of Cloyne in 1767. He then became Bishop of Derry in 1768, from which wealthy diocese he received an annual income of £20,000. He subsequently inherited the title of Earl of Bristol in 1779 from his brother, the 3rd Earl, and with this inheritance came a further income of £20,000 a year, giving him a huge disposable income.[40] It is possible, although not certain, given the dedication of the print, that Hervey owned this version of the picture by Domenichino, although the supposition cannot be confirmed because of the scant surviving records of the dispersal of his collections. Part of his collection was sold in Rome after his death,[41] and there is no picture by Domenichino of *Lot and his daughters* listed in the catalogue, although there is one with the same title by Pietro Liberi,[42] a near contemporary of Domenichino, described as '7 × 5' [*palmi*, therefore approximately 161 × 115 cm], i.e. a portrait-shaped image like that recorded by Grignion and Kilian.

Another record of a Domenichino *Lot and his daughters* is to be found in the London sale of the collection of Charles Alexandre de Calonne (1734-1802) 'valuable pictures, drawings, miniatures and prints, the property of... Calonne, late Prime Minister of France' (in fact, Minister of Finance) which was held in London on 23-28 March 1795.[43] Calonne had been an avid collector of Boulle furniture, Chinese clocks, Chinese porcelain and exotic shells, as well as paintings, and had held several sales of his collection after his fall from political power in 1787. He had moved to England. Lot 46, on the fourth day of the sale in March 1795 was described as: 'Dominichino Lot, with his Daughters, *a grand composed picture*', and a figure written in pencil by the description was '47.5.0', evidently a price of £47. 5s 0d.

The date of the sale almost certainly implies that this *Lot and his daughters* is not identical with the Coke picture, because it is probable that the work of that title is documented as still hanging at Holkham Hall at this time,[44] and what the earlier provenance was of Calonne's picture remains uncertain. It might even have been the picture that had been owned by the Earl Bishop, because the paths of the two men crossed, and they moved in the same circles. After the execution of Louis XVI in 1793, Calonne remained loyal to the Bourbons, and became leader of the Counter-Revolutionary movement. In the autumn of 1789 he visited Louis XVI's two brothers, the Prince de Condé and the Comte d'Artois in Turin, and in the following year he visited Rome.[45] Bristol was also on one of his frequent visits to Rome from March to June 1790, and the two might therefore have met, conceivably introduced by the painter Madame Vigée Le Brun, who painted the Earl Bishop in Naples that year, and who was rumoured to have had an affair with Calonne. Wherever the Calonne picture of *Lot and his daughters* came from, however, it seems to have been lost after the sale of 1795.

NOTES

1 Quoted in the entry for Coke in J. Ingamells, *A Dictionary of British and Irish Travellers in Italy 1701-1800*, New Haven and London, 1997.

2 MSS 733-4, Holkham Hall, Norfolk. '... a Lot by Dominichia' appears in MS 734, p. 253. By kind permission of the Earl of Leicester and the Trustees of the Holkham Estate, and with thanks to Mr. Michael Daley, Mrs. Hiskey, and Mr. Fred Jolly for their help in examining the relevant documents at Holkham.

3 Richard E.Spear, *Domenichino*, 2 vols., New Haven and London, 1982, cat. 108, pp. 285-6.
4 John Pope-Hennessy, *The Drawings of Domenichino in the Collection of His Majesty The King at Windsor Castle*, cat. nos. 190-4; inv. no 1049. Pope-Hennessy dated the drawings to *c.* 1620-25, without knowing the Barberini account reference (see below) which shows that it was painted in 1630 or a little before.
5 Letter to Burrell Massingberd. Lincolnshire County Council, Archive Office ref. 2MM B/19A (copy in the Brinsley Ford Archive, Paul Mellon Centre for Studies in British Art, London).
6 Cinzia Maria Sicca, 'On William Kent's Roman Sources,' *Architectural History*, 29, 1986, pp. 134-47.
7 David L. Bershad, 'The Newly Discovered Testament and Inventories of Carlo Maratti and his Wife Francesca', *Antologia di Belle Arti*, 1985, p. 65.
8 The ascription to Frey appears in Matthew Brettingham the younger's *The Plans, Elevations and Sections of Holkham in Norfolk...* , 1773 (see n. 32 below). See Marie Therese Bätschmann, *Jakob Frey (1681-1752) Kupferstecher und Verleger in Rom*, Ph.D. dissertation, University of Basel, 1997, no. 115, p. 181, who states that the engraving of *Lot and his daughters* was included in the list of Frey's prints which he offered for sale at his studio in Via del Tritone.
9 'To the most noble English Lord, Thomas Coke. Most noble Lord, For all that you have acquired so many monuments of art, statues from antiquity, famous paintings and elegant engravings of pictures, may you permit, you who bring honour to your country, distinction to your family, pleasure to your friends and profit to *cognoscenti*, that I send this small token to your home, to wit the above painting by your beloved Giampiero Domenicho, engraved, by your permission, in bronze, in attestation of my enduring devotion. Your devoted humble servant, N.N.'
10 The same initials appear on William Kent's journal of 1714 which he kept while travelling with Coke and his tutor (Bodleian Library, Oxford, MSS Rawlinson D.1162: 'Remarks by way of Painting and Architecture'). The title page has several references to 'Il Sig. N.N.', apparently written by different hands, and appearing to confirm that 'N.N.' was not English: 'Il Sigre N.N. ... Roma'; 'Il Sig. Cavre N.N. .... Venezia'; 'a son eccelance My Lord N.N.'
11 Information kindly supplied by Thomas Woodcock, Norroy and Ulster King of Arms. The mode of address 'most noble Lord' in such a dedication, and especially in an Italian context, does not imply anything other than the Englishman in question bore a coat of arms. Bätschmann, loc. cit., dates the engraving to 1618/19, but her opinion that 'N.N.' might be identical with Frey is untenable.
12 Marilyn Aronberg Lavin, *Seventeenth century Barberini Documents and Inventories of Art*, New York, *c.* 1975, p. 14, doc. no. 113.
13 For the Bichi family see *Dizionario biografico degli Italiani,* Rome, 1960–.
14 Alessandro's younger brother, Celio, studied law, and in 1628 was employed by Francesco Barberini to work on political and diplomatic assignments. Celio was described as 'highly intelligent, forthcoming and shrewd', and he developed a very close relationship with Francesco, becoming his private secretary.
15 G.Campori, *Raccolta di cataloghi ed inventarii inediti...* , Modena, 1870, pp. 377ff.
16 For the Boscoli family, see G.B.Janelli, *Dizionario biografico dei parmigiani illustri o benemeriti*, 1877 (reprinted). Lelio entered the church, having trained as a lawyer and had a most distinguished career, becoming Pronotario Apostolico. He was famous for his legal writings both in the vernacular and in Latin.
17 Campori, op. cit., p. 389.
18 In practice, the term 'bislonga', oblong, appears usually to mean 'landscape' (in shape).
19 See Janelli, op. cit., for their relations with the Farnese. Gian Simone Boscoli came from an artistic family reaching back to the fifteenth century, and he himself was a distinguished military architect who also became head of the armed forces in Parma. It is highly unlikely that their attribution of *Lot and his daughters* to Domenichino can have been incorrect.
20 See n. 10 above.
21 Ingamells, op. cit.
22 'A picture of Lot of 4 × 6 [*palmi*] with daughters, who get him drunk, without a frame, by my hand, a copy after Domenichino.' For Raspantino's inventory see Spear, op. cit., p. 337-46. Many of the works that Raspantino inherited came into the possession of Carlo Maratta, thence into the collection of Pope Clement XI (*r.* 1700-21), and ultimately into the Royal Collection, among them, so it appears, five of the 'disegni di Lot'. Cardi-

nal Alessandro Albani (1692-1779), the nephew of Clement XI, the Pope who had acquired Maratta's collection of drawings in 1703, inherited the collection after his uncle's death. James Adam bought the collection from Cardinal Albani for George III: 'three hundred volumes' for 9,000 crowns. It might be imagined that Raspantino's copy of Domenichino's *Lot and his daughters* was the same as a picture which was recorded in the Staatliche Kunstsammlungen in Dresden in 1854 as a copy after Domenichino. In 1856 it was sold, and its whereabouts are now not known. It was under Augustus III, whose court was at Dresden, that a series of engravings was made by Philipp Andreas Kilian (1714-1759) of Old and New Testament stories which includes a *Lot and his daughters* inscribed as having been originally painted by Domenichino. The Kilian image at least cannot be after the Raspantino copy, however, because the print is portrait-shaped and we know that Raspantino's copy was landscape.

23 Spear, loc. cit. See Pope-Hennessy, op. cit.

24 *Survey of London.*

25 Thanet House Inventory (at Holkham), March 1760: H/Inv/4 (previously MS 765), p. 58.

26 Holkham Hall inventory : H/Inv 7, f12r.

27 But see John Kenworthy-Browne, 'Matthew Brettingham's Rome Account Book 1747-54', *Walpole Society*, XLIX (1983), pp. 37-132, p. 39.

28 Holkham Hall inventory: H/Inv/6.

29 Ibid., p. 8.

30 Kenworthy-Browne, op. cit., p. 39.

31 Now the South Dining Room.

32 Matthew Brettingham, *The Plans, Elevations and Sections of Holkham in Norfolk... To which are added, the ceilings and chimney-pieces; and also, a descriptive account of the statues, pictures, and drawings, etc.*, London, 1773, p. 6.

33 See Kenworthy-Browne, op. cit., esp. pp. 38-47.

34 J. Dawson, *The Stranger's Guide to Holkham*, Burnham, 1817, p. 46, no. 41. The room also contained four over-door landscapes by 'Luccatelli'. In a copy of this publication kept at Holkham Hall, and annotated by guests visiting the house, a derogatory comment is made by 'R' claiming the work to be 'very bad'. 'R' was apparently Richard Ramsay Reinagle, the artist.

35 *New description of Holkham...*, 1826, p. 24.

36 *Guide to Holkham, the seat of the Right Hon. The earl of Leicester...*, Norwich, 1861, p. 16. The *Diana and her nymphs* is now described as 'after' Domenichino.

37 Of the second creation (1822-1909) who succeeded in 1842.

38 John Ruskin, *Modern Painters*, in *The Works of John Ruskin*, ed. E.T. Cook and H. Wedderburn, vol. III, 1903, p. 184.

39 G. Reitlinger, *The Economics of Taste: the Rise and Fall of Picture Prices 1760-1960*, 3 vols., New York, 1982, 2, p. 300.

40 Nicola F. Figgis, 'The Roman property of Frederick Augustus Hervey, 4th Earl of Bristol and Bishop of Derry (1730-1803)', *Walpole Society*, LV (1989/90), pp. 77-88ff.

41 Ibid., p. 84. In 1794 Bristol added a codicil to his will which he had written in 1791, further benefiting his cousin the Revd. Henry Hervey-Bruce (created a baronet in 1804). All his 'pictures, Statues, Busts, Marbles, *Gesses* as well in Rome, Florence, Leghorn, to be disposed of as he judges best'. See Brian Fothergill, *The Mitred Earl*, 1974, p. 158. Hervey-Bruce also inherited Bristol's by now considerable debts, and so was forced to sell much of his inheritance. The sale catalogue of 1803/4 does not mention a Domenichino. There are various mentions of a 'Domenichino' *Lot and his daughters* in various sale catalogues in the first part of the nineteenth century. One at least of them (Christie's, 23 June 1804, lot 62) is noted to have been by Sebastiano Ricci. The details in the other sales lack dimensions and other details that might be of help. None of them can be identified as having come from any of the collections discussed here.

42 Figgis, op. cit., inventory reprinted pp. 90ff., p. 92, no. 99.

43 Calonne had mortgaged his collection to Desenfans after the French Revolution. The sale was held by the auctioneers Skinner and Dyke. Prices were not high, and many lots were bought in. See B. Scott, 'Charles Alexandre de Calonne, Economist and Collector', *Apollo*, xcvii (1973), pp. 86-91.

44 See above.

45 Scott, op. cit., p. 90.

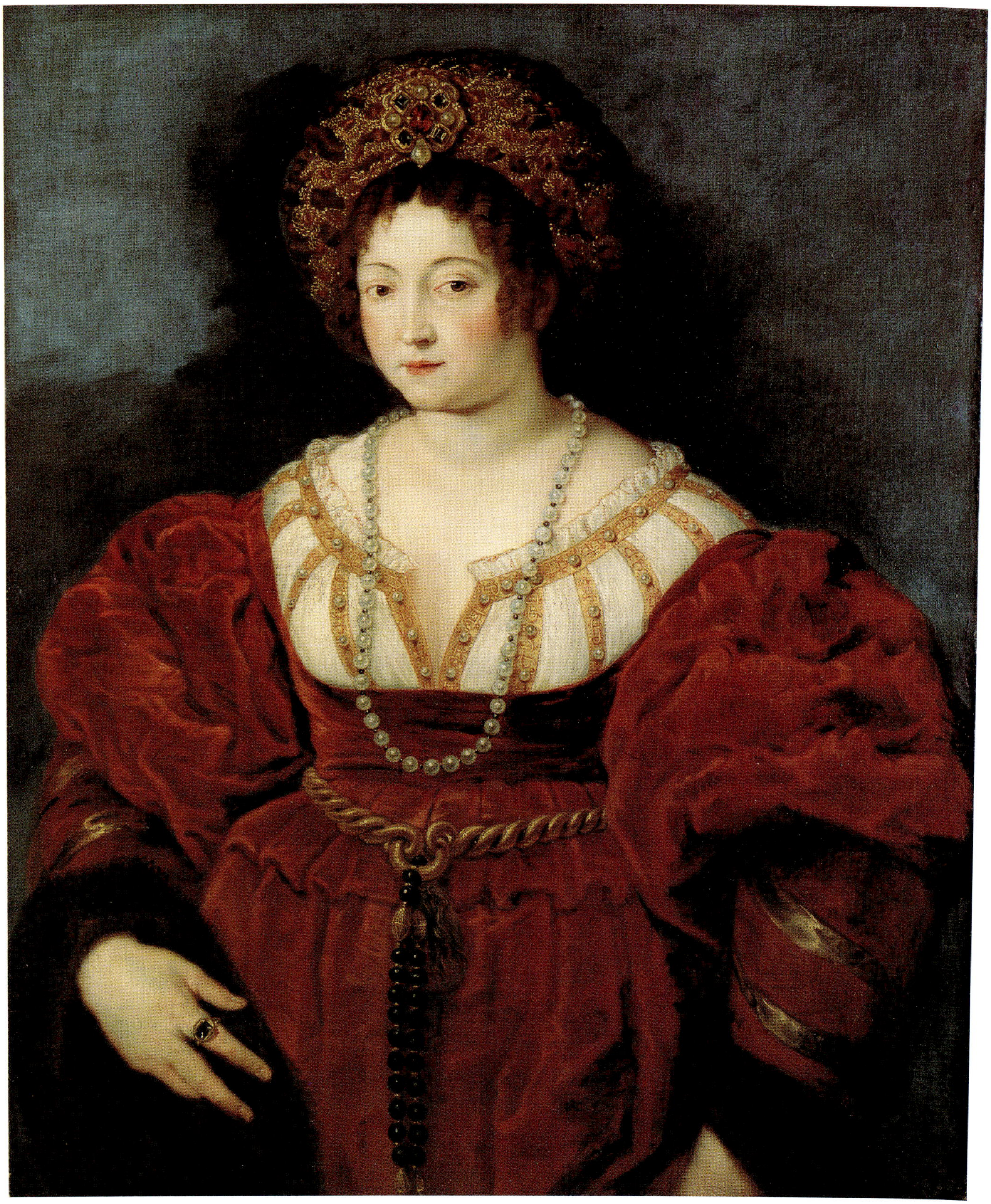

Titian (Tiziano Vecelli)

c. 1485/90-1576

Portrait of Isabella d'Este in red

Oil on canvas
91.4 × 73.7 cm

Isabella d'Este (1474-1539) was one of the most remarkable patrons of the Renaissance, who both collected antiquities and commissioned works of art from the greatest painters of her time. She was praised by such demanding critics as the humanist scholar Pietro Bembo (1470-1547), who wrote in a letter of 29 June 1537 to Cardinal Cesi, 'Today I have been to see the antiquities owned by the Illustrious Marchesa, which gave me a great deal of pleasure insofar as her Excellency has many beautiful and rare objects.'[1]

Isabella twice created a *studiolo* (a kind of study) and a *grotta* (a sort of 'grotto') in her private rooms within the Palazzo Ducale in Mantua, the first pair of rooms being situated one above the other in the tower of the Castello di S. Giorgio. The *studiolo* was decorated with a programme of classical and allegorical subjects, along lines devised with her advisers, who included the sculptor Giancristoforo Romano, her secretary Mario Equicola, who referred to her as the 'tenth Muse',[2] and the court poet Paride Ceresara. The *grotta* was directly beneath the *studiolo*, and housed her antiquities.[3] Andrea Mantegna (*c.* 1430-1506), court painter to the Gonzagas, was commissioned to paint the *Parnassus* and later *Pallas expelling the Vices from the Garden of Virtue* for the *studiolo* and the decorations were completed by three further compositions, by Lorenzo Costa and Pietro Perugino, after both Leonardo da Vinci and Giovanni Bellini had decided that either the programme or the patron might prove too demanding.[4] Shortly after her husband's death in 1519 Isabella moved to a ground-floor apartment in the Corte Vecchia of the Palazzo Ducale, where she re-created her *studiolo* and *grotta*. Correggio's *Allegory of Vice* and *Allegory of Virtue* were commissioned around 1530 to join the earlier paintings in this second *studiolo*.[5]

Isabella d'Este was brought up in Ferrara at the cultured court of her father, Ercole I d'Este (d. 1505). At the age of six she was betrothed to the *condottiere* Francesco II Gonzaga, Marquis of Mantua (1466-1519), and arrived in Mantua as his wife at the age of fifteen on 15 February 1490. Isabella was painted on many occasions: 'She changed her portrait painters in the way she changed her clothes.'[6] Some of the portraits she gave away, and some she kept. Giancristoforo Romano (*c.* 1465-1512), who had designed the entrance of the *grotta*, made a medal of her in profile, with the motto *Benemerentium Ergo* ('For those who deserve well') on the reverse.[7] She mounted a gold version of this in diamonds and enamel and kept it in her *grotta*, and she also circulated copies of it to friends and admirers. She was drawn by Leonardo da Vinci in 1499, in a cartoon that survives in the Louvre, although the drawing is cropped, and the original composition can be better appreciated in a copy of the whole in the Ashmolean Museum, Oxford.[8]

Isabella d'Este (*'Isabella in red'*) by Peter Paul Rubens (1577-1640) after Titian (Tiziano Vecelli, *c.* 1485/90-1576), *c.* 1600-1.
Oil on canvas, 102 × 82 cm.
Kunsthistorischesmuseum, Vienna

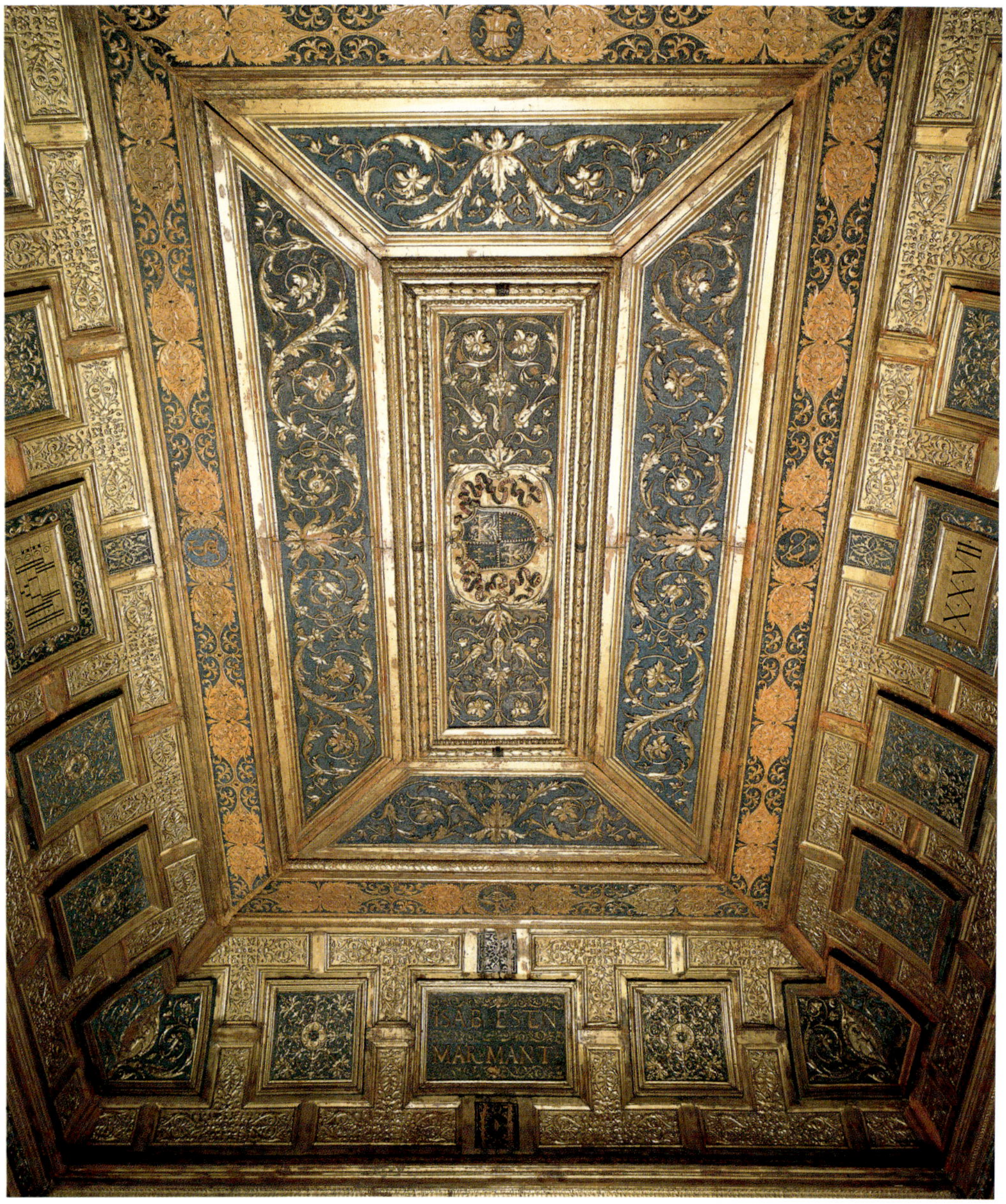

Second *grotta* of Isabella d'Este, Corte Vecchia, Palazzo Ducale, Mantua, detail of ceiling

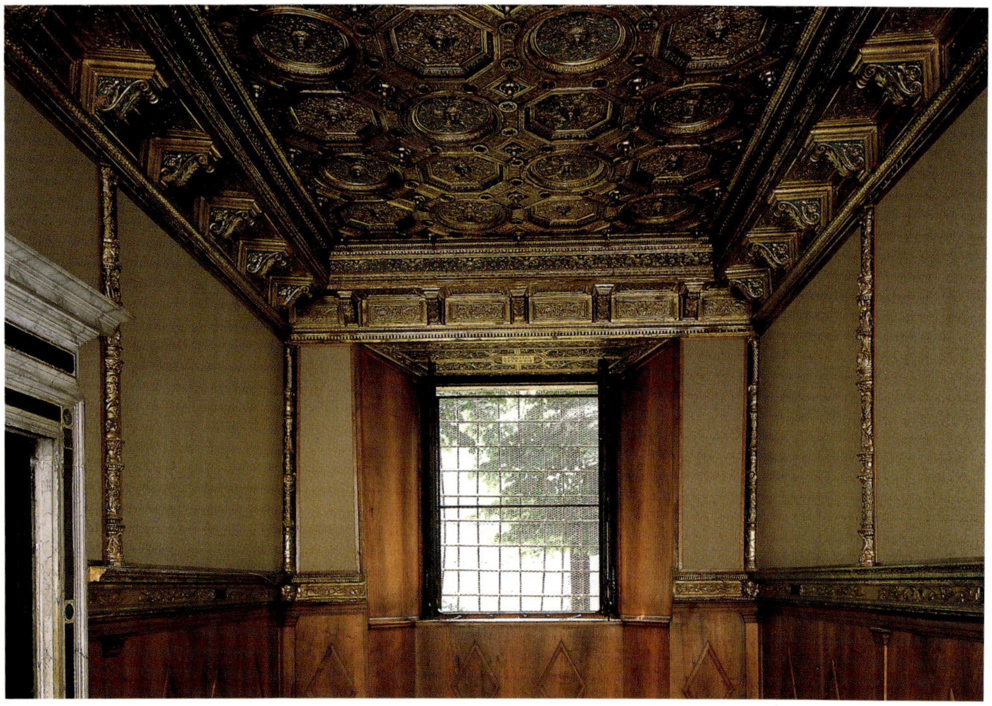

Second *studiolo* of Isabella d'Este, Corte Vecchia, Palazzo Ducale, Mantua

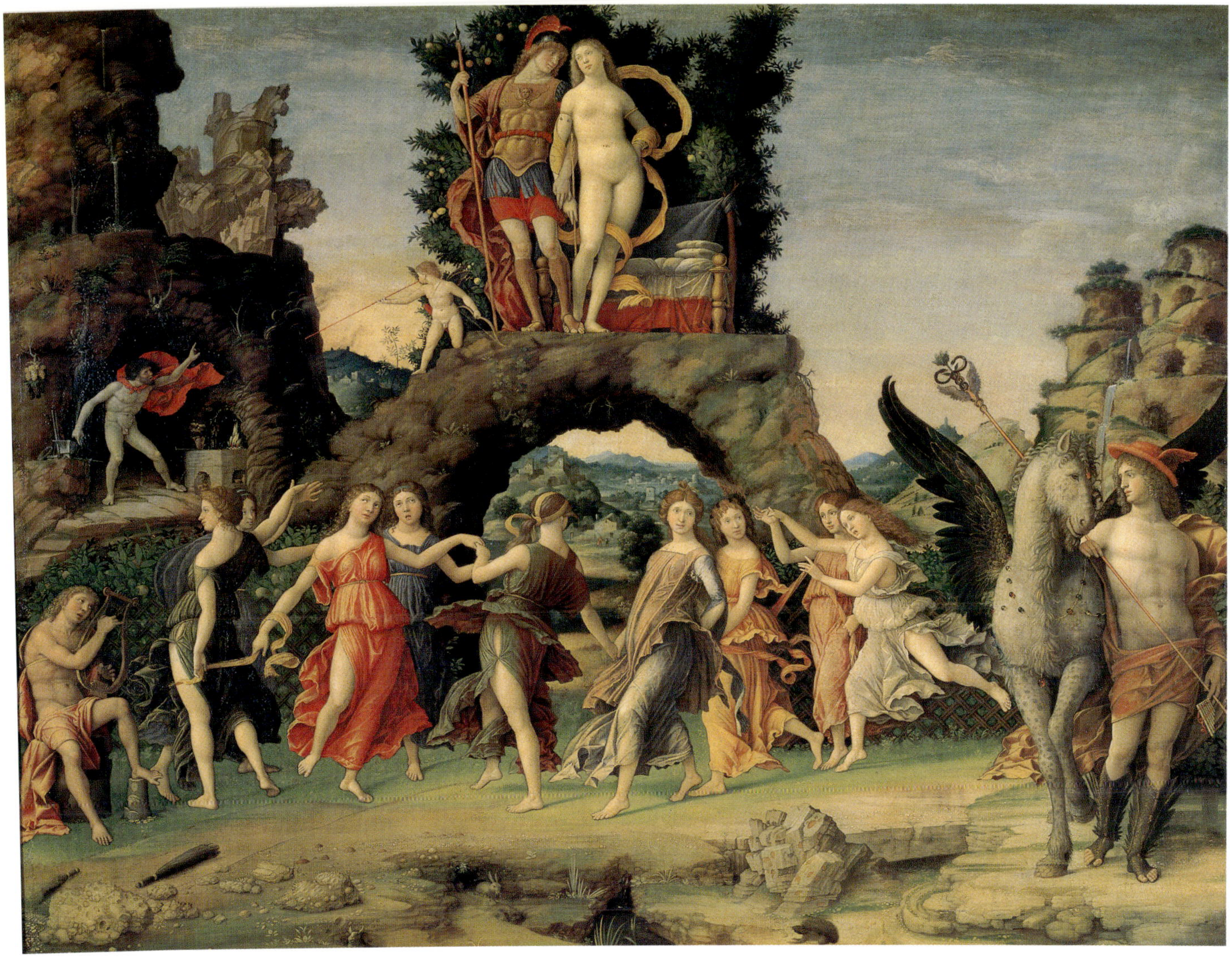

Parnassus
by Andrea Mantegna
(*c.* 1430-1506), 1497.
Tempera on canvas, 150 × 192 cm.
Musée du Louvre, Paris

Isabella was vain, however, and would often try to persuade writers to alter their descriptions of her and artists to enhance her features.[9] Some, like Titian, eventually agreed to do so. By 1516 Isabella claimed that she would no longer sit for portraits, although she continued to demand them. When she asked Titian, who was much patronised by her brother Alfonso d'Este, to paint her portrait in 1534, he had to paint it without sittings, and instead had to follow a portrait painted by Francia in 1511 when Isabella was 36, which was itself not painted from the life but 'guided only by a mediocre portrait and the description of Ludovico Bentivoglio'.[10] She acknowledged the receipt of the portrait in a letter to Agnello of 29 May 1536, remarking that Titian made her look more beautiful than she had ever actually been:

The portrait of us by the hand of Titian pleases us so much that we doubt that we were ever in that state in which he represents us with the beauty in that picture. We have indeed thought of making some remonstrations with Titian for the effort used in it, but we decided first to request the portrait of Zanninelli [i.e. the portrait of her by Francia which belonged to a member of the Zanninelli family of Ferrara] which you will understand should be returned.[11]

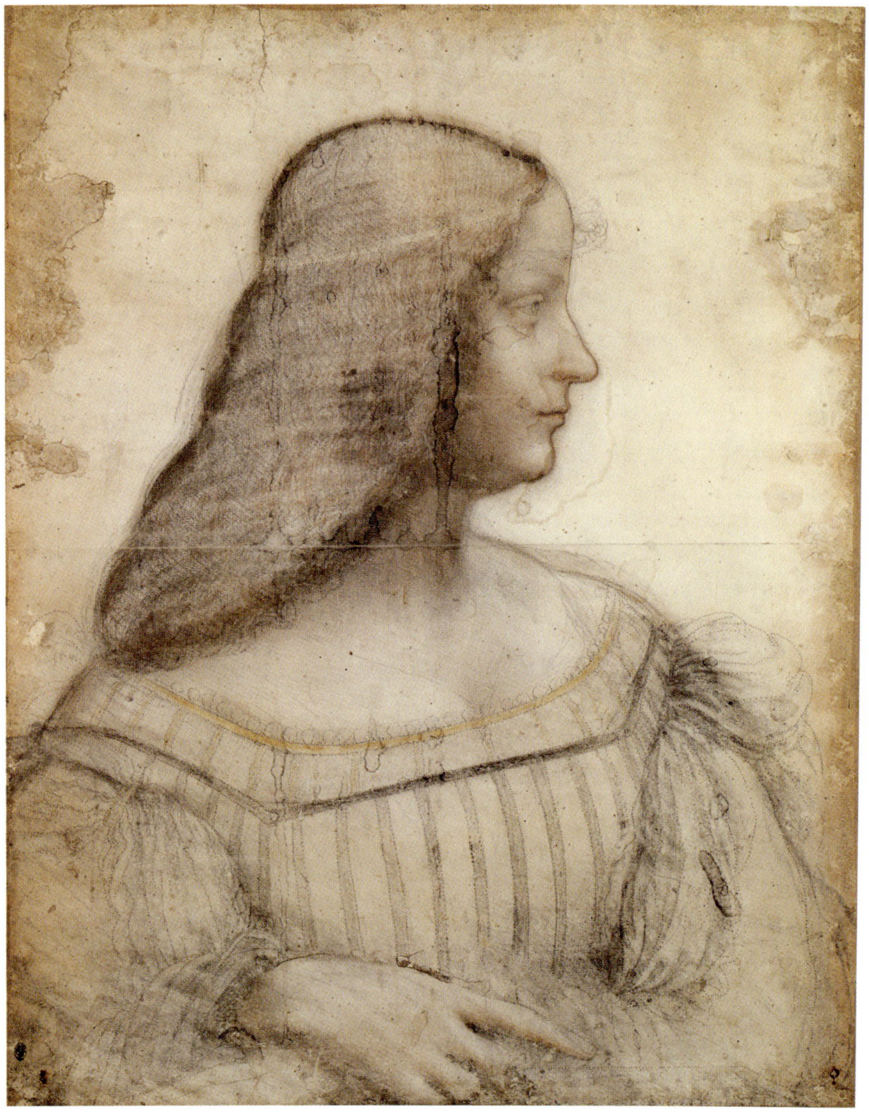

Isabella d'Este by Leonardo da Vinci (1452-1519), 1499.
Black chalk and charcoal with pastel, 63 × 46 cm.
Musée du Louvre, Paris

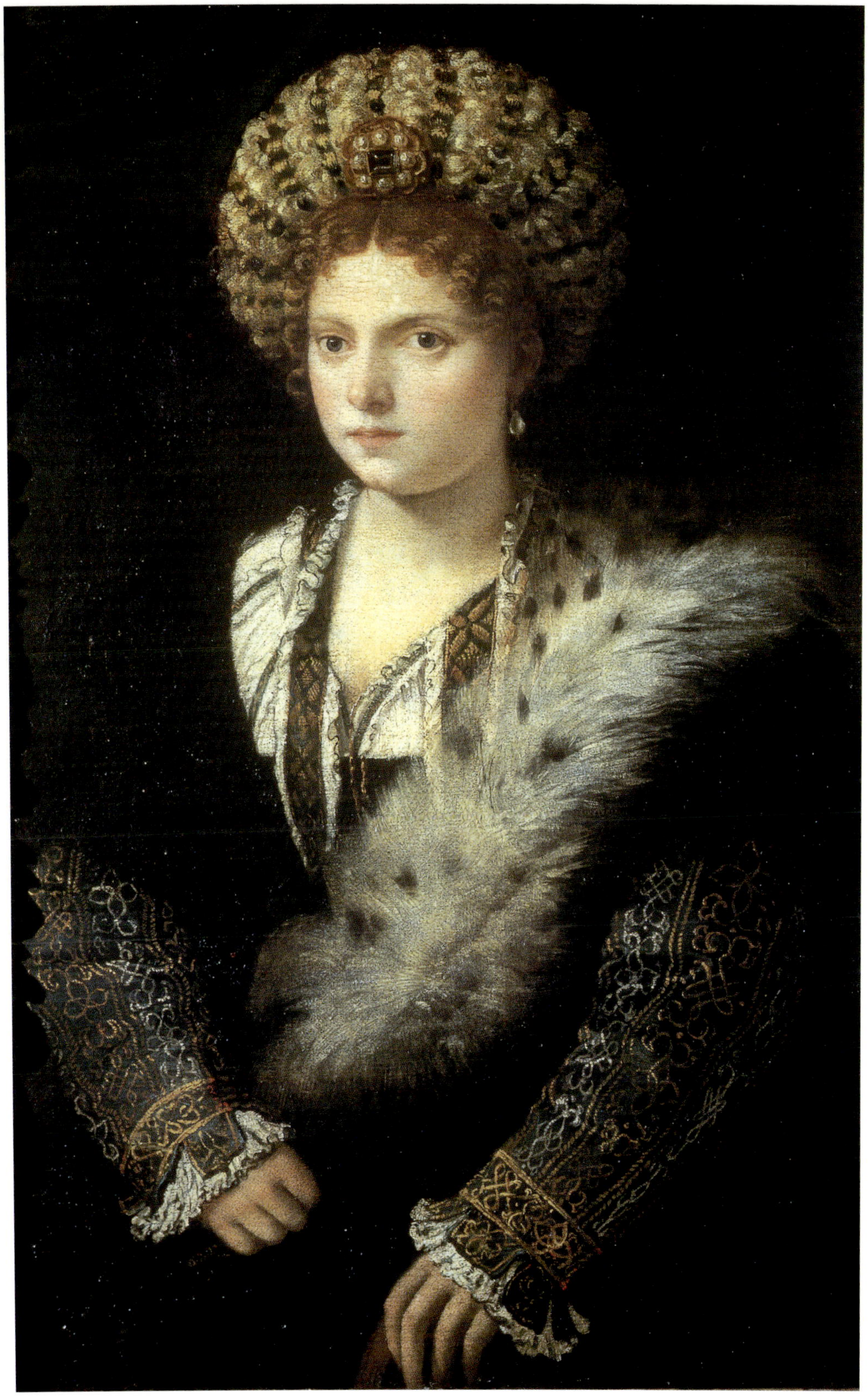

Isabella d'Este (*'Isabella in black'*) by Titian, *c.* 1536.
Oil on canvas, 102 × 64 cm.
Kunsthistorischesmuseum, Vienna

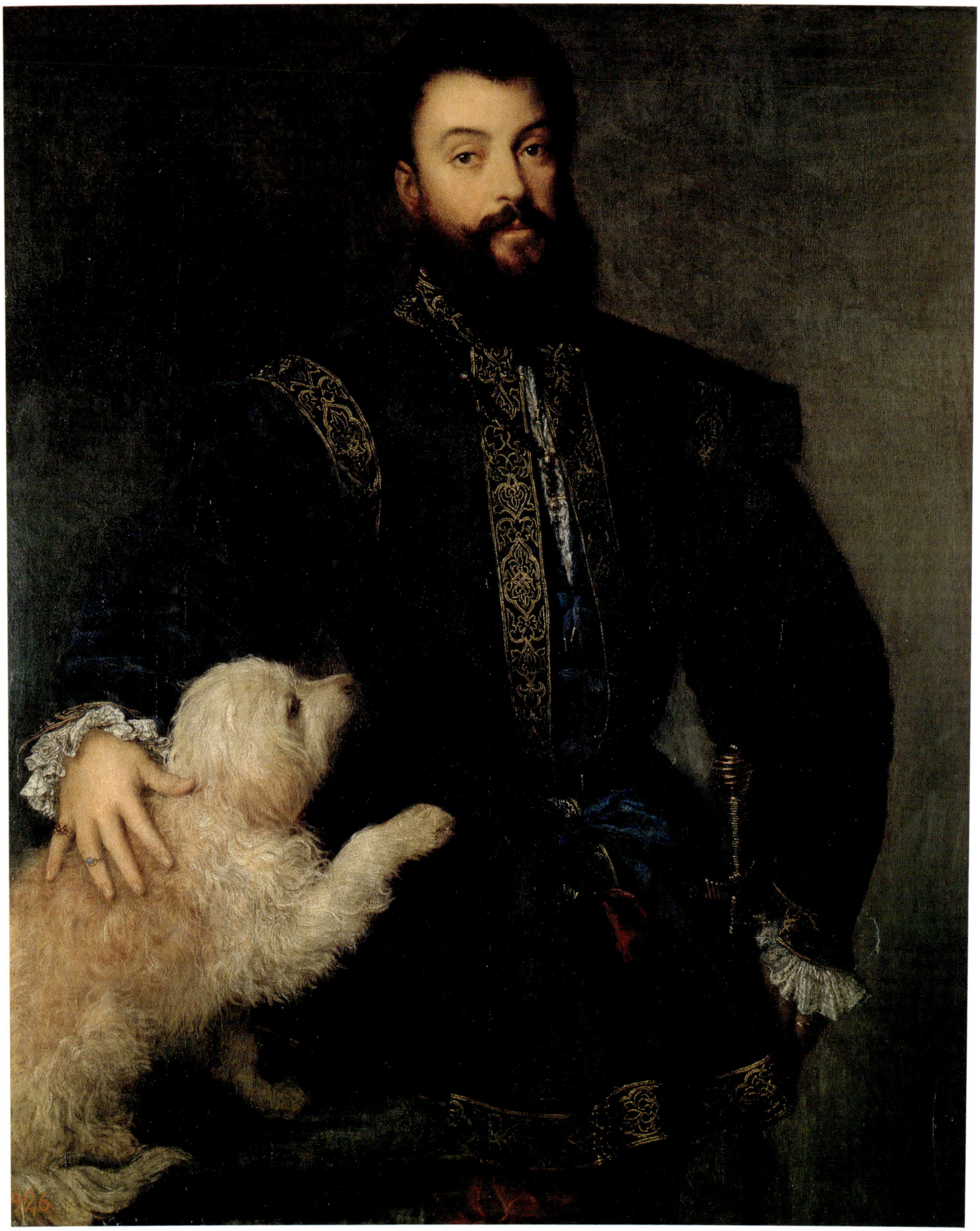

Federico II Gonzaga, Duke of Mantua by Titian.
Oil on canvas, 125 × 99 cm.
Museo del Prado, Madrid

This portrait is known as *Isabella in black* and survives in the Kunsthistorisches Museum, Vienna. Titian also portrayed her, however, much as she must have appeared in reality when in her fifties, in a portrait that, despite Isabella's announcement about not sitting after 1516, looks as if it must have been made from the life. This portrait, known as *Isabella in red*, was, paradoxically, almost certainly made earlier than *Isabella in black*, and has disappeared.[12] Its appearance is known from a copy by no less an artist than Peter Paul Rubens (1577-1640), who copied both Titian's portraits of Isabella on the occasion of his visit to Mantua in 1600/1. His copy of *Isabella in red*, like Titian's original *Isabella in black*, is in the Kunsthistorisches Museum, Vienna,[13] although, in another twist of fate, Rubens's copy of *Isabella in black* is also missing. Judging by the Rubens copy, Titian's *Isabella in red* was not very flattering, and it seems that it reflected another aspect of Isabella's character, a reluctance, despite her vanity, to disguise her actual appearance. Pietro Aretino, writing in 1534, described her, in a cruel reversal of epithets, as 'disgracefully ugly and even more deplorably un-made-up, ... (with) teeth of ebony and eyelashes of ivory'.[14]

Isabella's eldest son, Federico II Gonzaga, was created 1st Duke of Mantua in 1530, and inherited his mother's zeal for the arts, and became one of the great Gonzaga patrons. He commissioned Giulio Romano to rebuild the Palazzo Te, creating one of the greatest masterpieces of mannerist architecture and decoration. His successors continued to embellish their palaces, and to employ artists, musicians and writers. Thus Vincenzo I Gonzaga, 4th Duke of Mantua (*r.* 1587-1612), employed Rubens at the beginning of the seventeenth century to paint works for his palace and for the church of Santa Trinità, and also to make copies of paintings in collections in Rome and in Spain. It was apparently during this period that Rubens copied both the Titian portraits of Isabella d'Este, although it has been suggested, less plausibly, that he may have copied them whilst in England in 1629-1630.[15] Rubens probably painted both copies for his own collection, as they both appear in the *Specification*, a catalogue published in 1640, shortly after his death, of works by his own hand in his collection. They are listed as:

> no 56. Vn pourtrait d'Isabel d'Este Duchesse de Mantoue.
> no 57. Vn aultre pourtrait de la mesme habillée de noir.[16]

It was under the 4th Duke's son, Ferdinando (*r.* 1612-26), who was seriously short of funds, that the sale of the great Gonzaga collection was first contemplated. Approaches were made to the Countess of Arundel, wife of Thomas Howard, Earl of Arundel, the great collector, to see if there was a potential buyer at the English Court.[17] Charles I was enthusiastic, and charged Nicholas Lanier to negotiate the purchase for him, and Daniel Nys, a somewhat unscrupulous dealer who lived in Venice, to advise him. The negotiations proved protracted and complicated. Ferdinando died at a crucial point, and was succeeded by his brother, Vincenzo II (*r.* 1626-7). The new Duke became suspicious of Nys, believing him to be acting either for the Grand Duke of Tuscany or the Duke of Parma. The citizens of Mantua were distressed that the collection was being sold, and tried to reverse the decision by offering the Duke a substantial amount of money for it.[18] However, by April 1628 'the *Margaret* of London, whereof Thomas Browne is Master... did set sayle' from Venice for London with an immensely valuable cargo containing some of the great paintings from the Gonzaga collection, which had cost £15,000[19] including:

> The twelve Emperors of Titian, a large picture of Andrea del Sarto, a picture of Michelangelo

di Caravaggio; other pictures of Titian, Correggio, Giulio Romano, Tintoretto, and Guido Reni, all of the greatest beauty – in short so wonderful and glorious a collection, that the like will never again be met with; they are truly worthy of so great a king as his Majesty of Great Britain.[20]

Lanier travelled back by land: 'He doth cary with him the best pieces of paintings, namely those of Coreggio, which were in the grotta at Mantova, in regard of being in water-colours, they would not have brooked the sea.' [21]

Nys was initially proud of his achievement, and in a letter to Endymion Porter wrote:

Since I came into the world, I have made various contracts, but never a more difficult one than this and which has succeeded so happily. In the first place, the City of Mantua, and then all the Princes of Christendom, both great and small, were struck with astonishment that we could induce the Duke to dispose of them. The people of Mantua made so much noise about it.[22]

No list survives of paintings bought from the Gonzaga collection, but a 'Register' of pictures at Whitehall was compiled in about 1639 by Abraham van der Doort, appointed by the King '… Overseer or Surveyor of all our pictures of Us, Our Heires and Successors' in 1625 at an annual salary of £40.[23] He was instructed to:

Prevent and keepe them [pictures]… from being spoiled or defaced, to order marke and number them, and to keepe a Register of them, to receive and deliver them, and likewise to take order for the making and coppying of Pictures as Wee or the Lord Chamberlaine of Our Household shall directe, And to this End [we] are pleased that hee shall have Accesse at convenient Times into Our Galleries Chambers and other Roomes where our Pictures are.[24]

The descriptions are quite detailed, and often indicate where the pictures came from, including whether it was 'A Mantua Peece', although they are written in Van der Doort's idiosyncratic phonetic version of English. Listed 'In the litle *bij* roome Betwene Withdrawing roome: als called the Breakfast chamber and the longe gallorie… ' [25] was

10

26 Item the Picture *pintit opan de raeht lijeht opan* [= painted upon the right light upon] [canvas] of the Marquess of Mantua *his ladi* in an old fasshioned reed velvett apperell with her right hand *bing* [= being] done to the knees halfe figures Soe bigg as the life In a wodden guilded frame. *opan klaeht* [= upon cloth, i.e. canvas].[26]

Beside the entry is the note: '*sijd tu bi* [= said to be] done by Tichian'. The measurements are noted as being taken *Witin te frams* [= within the frames]:[27]

3 f o 2 f 5. [i.e. 3 feet × 2 feet 5 inches, about 91.4 × 73.7 cm].

This entry is of especial significance since it indicates at this date – before the death of Rubens in 1640 – that it must have been Titian's *Isabella in red* that was in Charles I's collection, because Rubens's copy of the portrait is listed in his *Specification* of that year.[28]

Van der Doort also made a list specifically of the paintings by Titian in the King's collection, in response to a request by the King:

… acording tu ju M [?directions] mak a not ar al suz ju M tizins piturs als ju haff atis tijm seffral plijsis esprst als volwing… at Wijthal…
… in de lutel bij rom ate heder end aufft long te duses auff mantu.[29]

which might be translated as:

According to your Majesty's directions make a note of all those your Majesty's pictures by

Titian as you have at this time [hanging in] several places expressed as following ... at Whitehall... in the little side room at the other end of the long [gallery], the Duchess of Mantua.

A few months after Charles I's execution, on 4 July 1649, an act was passed by Parliament '... for sale of the goods and personal estate of the late King, Queen and Prince', partly in order to raise money to pay off debts, and to maintain military and civil services.[30] Inventories were ordered to be made, with valuations, of the royal possessions in all the former palaces and houses.[31] Most of the items, except those from Hampton Court, were eventually gathered at Somerset House where what became known as the Commonwealth Sale took place, although inventories were made according to where the pictures were hanging in the various royal palaces immediately after the King's execution in January 1649.

Many of the paintings went to foreign buyers, such as Cardinal Mazarin, who was being advised by M. de Bordeaux, the French ambassador in England, and so *Isabella in Red* appears in a French transcription of the sale later published from papers in the Palais Mazarin:

193. La duchesse de Mantoue, par Tissian. Liv. o Ster. 50.[32]

De Bordeaux acquired, indirectly,[33] Correggio's *Allegory of Vice*, and Everhard Jabach, the banker, the *Allegory of Virtue*, which had been painted for Isabella d'Este's *studiolo*, and which were two of the more expensive paintings. Alonso de Cardenas, the Spanish Ambassador, was buying both for King Philip IV and for the royal minister, Luis de Haro.[34] Archduke Leopold Wilhelm did not buy directly from the Commonwealth Sale, perhaps because of the potential conflict with the Spanish buyers.[35] It is not known how he came into possession of Titian's *Isabella in black*[36] but he thus missed the chance to buy the original of *Isabella in red*, although he made sure at some point of acquiring Rubens's copy of it which, as noted above, was described in the Italian section of his 1659 inventory as No. 183:

A copy in oil and canvas of a Marchioness of Mantua in a red silk dress with a large pearl chain, with a large jewel on her head and a large golden chain around her waist, on which there hangs a black Paternoster, and in a right hand a diamond brooch. In a fully gilded flat frame, 5 spans and 4 fingers high and 3 spans and 2 fingers wide. By Rubens after the original of Titian.[37]

The fate of Titian's *Isabella in red* is obscure but is intimately connected with the particular circumstances of the Commonwealth Sale. Great though the collection was, the sale took place at a time when the art market, both in London and the Low Countries, was flooded with important pictures from other outstanding collections in England which were being sold due to recent events. Sales were for the most part slow, and money was not being raised in the quantities expected. As a result, the Trustees for the Sale of the King's Goods decided upon beginning to pay off the King's many creditors in goods as well as in cash.[38] This resulted in some of the great paintings from the Royal Collection ending up in the possession of former servants and tradesmen. John Emery, the King's Plumber, for example, bought Titian's *St. Margaret triumphing over the Devil* (now in the Prado, Madrid) for £100, and acquired another twenty-four pictures in partial settlement of his debt of £903.[39]

The complex method of disposal involved two lists of creditors being drawn up. The First List, 120 names of those most in need, 'the necessitous lyst of the late King's Servants', was put into effect on 14 March 1650. The Second List, including 970 new names, was then drawn up and allowed on 13 August 1651. These creditors could be paid 'either in ready money or by goods, according to the apprisement of the said goods...'[40] In a further complication, creditors would organize themselves in syndicates, called 'dividends', who would be allocated goods in parcels equivalent to about £5,000 which they would then divide between themselves by lot. The head of the 'dividend' might then also dispose of the goods on the open market on behalf of the new owner or owners.[41]

One of the creditors who thus acquired pictures at the Commonwealth Sale was the King's Silkman, a draper called John Geere. He was allowed the huge sum of £2,300 in the First List, although his purchases of pictures were well below that figure. He bought fourteen pictures with a total value of £230, including Van Dyck's superb portrait of *The five children of Charles I* (now in the Royal Collection, Windsor Castle). As befits an important draper, he also bought significant draperies and similar objects:

A cloth of Estate of cloth of gould wth Roses and Portcluses [portcullises] tissued–[£] 50
One other cloth of estate with the Arms of England imbroydered with twist – [£] 100.[42]

He also bought, on 3 September 1650, for £50, Titian's *Isabella in red*.:

R 193. A Dutchess of Mantua at [£] 50

the copies of the catalogue being annotated 'by Titian'. [43]

The same buyer is also listed variously as 'Geere', 'Mr Geere', and 'Captn Geere' in a surviving contemporary transcript of a manuscript record of the inventory and sales that belonged to Sir John Stanley, 'An Inventorie of the Personall Estate of the late King which was sold by Act of Parliament...', and Geere duly appears there as the buyer of Titian's *Isabella in red* under the section 'pictures at [St.] James's':

Geere A Dutchess of Mantua of Tytsian – 50 [i.e. £50].[44]

Geere was evidently in touch with the painter Emanuel de Critz (1608-65), who was head of three of the fourteen 'dividends'[45] and one of the major buyers at the Commonwealth Sale. There seems no doubt that De Critz, who was the son of John de Critz, Serjeant-Painter to the King, made serious efforts to retain items from the royal collection against the time of the Restoration, and that he stayed in contact with the exiled Charles II about them. Thus he saved Bernini's bust of Charles I, which was later to be destroyed in the Whitehall Palace fire of 1697, as he described in a supplication to the King in May 1660:

Emanuel de Critz the only Sonne left of a miserably ruined Family, by the Service of your Majesties Grand Father and Father. He hath due unto him upon Privy Seales about £4000... The said Emanuel discounted with the Parliament £800 debt, and paid above £100 ready money for the (incomparable) Statue of your Father's by Berneeno, on purpose to secure it, having used all means formerly to convey it to your majesty, but could not.[46]

A list, of the same period, survives

... of such goods of his late Majesties as are remaining in safe custody of Em: de Critz, son to the Serieant Painter, deceased, for part of whose debt they came to him in the year 1651, and haue been ever since preserved by him with great care and danger

where De Critz states that he remained in contact with Charles II about these works, '... his now Majestie hauing had oft notice from him [De Critz] of the same'.[47]

There is another record of works in de Critz's possession in 1651, where some of the same works of art appear, for example, the Bernini bust and Giulio Romano's *Rape of Europa*. This list was made by the connoisseur Richard Symonds who found '3 Rooms full of the king's pictures' in 'Austin Fryars at

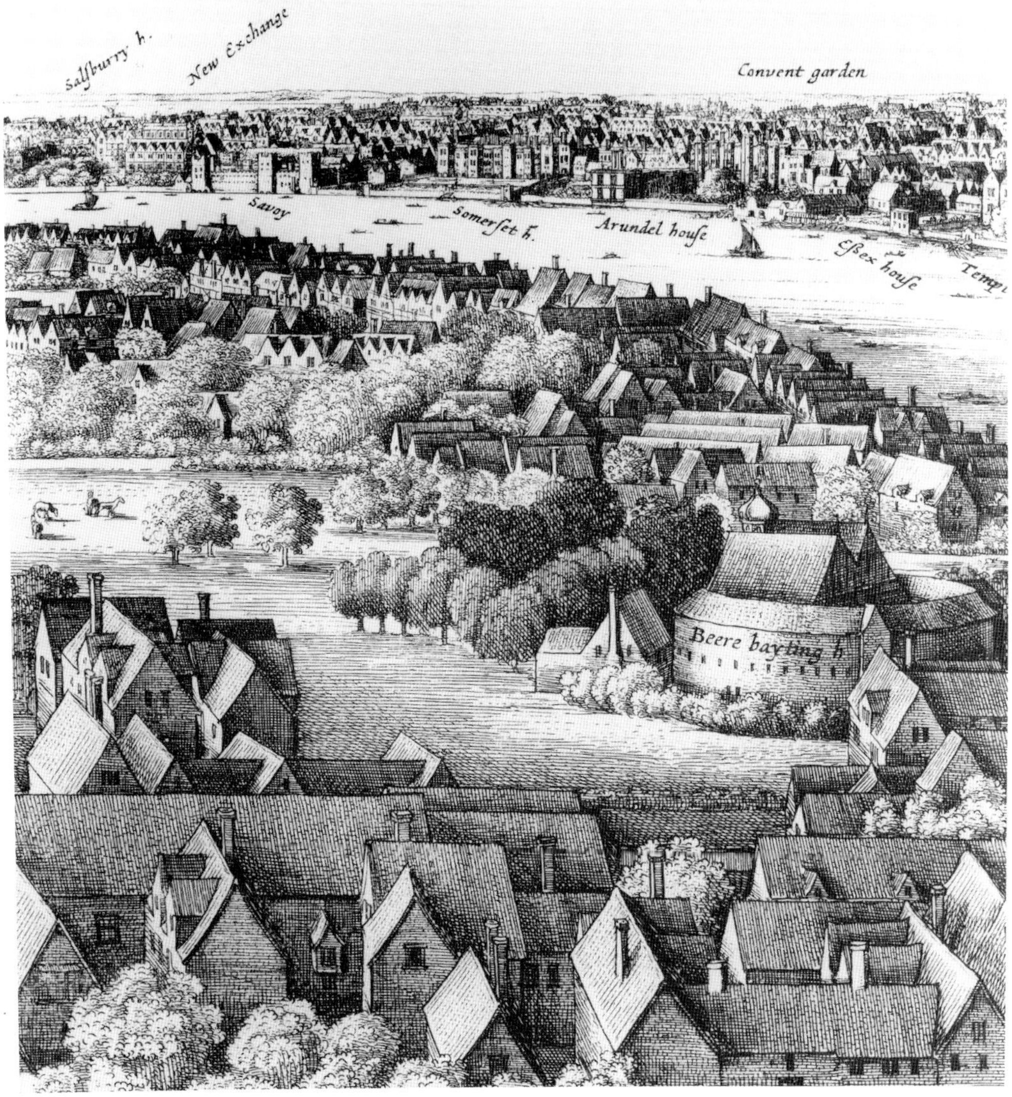

Somerset House in 1647.
Etching, detail of the '*Long View*' of London by Wenceslaus Hollar (1607-77)

Decreets house'. [48] The list includes the Van Dyck of the *Five children of Charles I* which had been bought by Geere in the previous year:

All the King's Children done together by Van Dyke.[49]

It is possible that Titian's *Isabella in red* passed to, or through the hands of, De Critz in a similar fashion. His list of May 1660 (referred to above) notes beside groups of the works of art his relative ownership:

'These came to me by lott, and I possess them solely'; 'These are mine in Partnership with others'; 'These are other men's intrusted to my hands'.[50]

There is no record of Titian's *Isabella in red*, however, in any of these lists, and 'Captain' or plain 'Mr Geere' remains the last recorded owner of this famous missing masterpiece.

NOTES

1 Clifford M. Brown, 'A Ferrarese Lady and a Mantuan Marchesa; the Art and Antiquities Collection of Isabella d'Este Gonzaga', in Cynthia Lawrence, ed., *Women and Art in Early Modern Europe*, 1997, pp. 53-71, p. 59. See especially Jennifer M. Fletcher, 'Isabella d'Este, Patron and Collector', in D. Chambers and J. Martineau, ed., *Splendours of the Gonzaga*, exh. cat., London, 1981, pp. 51-63; also S. Béguin, *Le Studiolo d'Isabelle d'Este*, exh. cat., Louvre, Paris, 1975; S. Ferino Pagden, *'La Prima Donna del Mondo': Isabella d'Este: Fürstin und Mäzenatin der Renaissance*, exh. cat., Vienna, 1994. For a discussion of Rubens's copies after Titian (but of works in the Prado, Madrid, only) see *Rubens: Copista de Tiziano*, exh. cat., Madrid, 1987.

2 Brown, op. cit., p. 59, and R. Goffen, *Titian's Women*, New Haven and London, 1997, p. 108.

3 Fletcher, op. cit., plan on pp. XXII-XXIII, pls. 3, 3a, and pls. 56-64 for views and details of the *studioli*, *grotte* and 'secret garden'.

4 See Brown, op. cit., pp. 60-1, n. 10. The five paintings from the *studiolo* are now in the Louvre. J. Martineau, ed., *Andrea Mantegna*, exh. cat., London and New York, 1991-2, 'The Studiolo of Isabella d'Este and Late Themes', pp. 418ff.

5 Fletcher, op. cit., p. 53. See also plan in Brown, op. cit., p. 62, fig. 5. Both these paintings are also in the Louvre.

6 Fletcher, op. cit., p. 57.

7 Kunsthistorisches Museum, Vienna, Chambers and Martineau, op. cit., cat. no. 109; see Fletcher, op. cit., p. 51 and pl. 49.

8 Chambers and Martineau, op. cit., cat. no. 108, and see Leonardo drawing, pl. 46.

9 The most convincing and imaginative interpretation of her character is Fletcher, op. cit., *passim*.

10 Ibid., p. 57. The recently rediscovered Francia portrait (private collection) is in Françoise Viatte, *Léonard de Vinci: Isabelle d'Este*, Paris (Louvre), n.d., p. 21, pl. 13.

11 A. Luzio, *La Galleria dei Gonzaga venduta all' Inghilterra nel 1627-8*, Milan, 1913 (reprinted Rome 1974), p. 223: 'Il ritratto nostro di man di Titiano ne piace di sorte che dubitiamo di non esser stata in quell'etade ch'egli rappresenta di quella beltá che in sè contiene. Havemo ben pensato di far qualche dimostracione con esso Titiano per la fatica usata in esso, ma habbiamo deliberato di voler prima il ritratto de Zanninelli, il quale farete intendere sollecitando che lo restituisca...' Luzio's extensive publications in the field are listed in Chambers and Martineau, op. cit., p. XIII.

12 See H. Wethey, *The Paintings of Titian*, 3 vols., 1969-75, II, *Portraits*, cat. nos. L-II, 27, respectively.

13 No. 1534.

14 '... disonestamente brutta et arcidisonestamente imbellettatta... i denti di hebano et le ciglia di avorio': Luzio, op. cit., p. 219.

15 J. Muller, *Rubens, The Artist as Collector*, Princeton, 1984, p. 107.

16 The *Specification* was to act as a sale catalogue. At his death, Rubens owned some 156 of his own works, of which about 90 were copies of works by other artists: Muller, op. cit., p. 17.

17 David Howarth, '"Mantua Peeces": Charles I and the Gonzaga Collection', Chambers and Martineau, op. cit., pp. 95-100.

18 Ibid., p. 96.

19 Ibid., p. 99.

20 Daniel Nys to Endymion Porter, 12 May 1630 [1628], W. N. Sainsbury, *Original Unpublished Papers Illustrative of the Life of Sir Peter Paul Rubens*, London, 1859, p. 326, quoted by F. Haskell, 'Charles I's Collection of Pictures', in A. MacGregor, ed., *The Late King's Goods: Collections, Possessions and Patronage of Charles I in the Light of the Commonwealth Sale Inventories*, London, 1989, pp. 203-31, p. 214.

21 Howarth, op. cit., p. 97.

22 Ibid., p. 96.

23 'Abraham van der Doort's Catalogue of the Collections of Charles I', Oliver Millar, ed., *Walpole Society*, XXXVII (1958-60), p. xiv.

24 Ibid.

25 Ibid., p. 37. The phrase means 'in the little side room between the Withdrawing Room also called the Breakfast Chamber and the Long Gallery'.

26 Ibid., p. 39. The phrase 'painted upon the right light' means painted so that the light falls from the spectator's left; painted upon the 'wrong' light means that the light falls from the spectator's right: Millar, op. cit., p. xix. (The terms are therefore used in the same sense as 'stage right' and 'stage left'.)

27 Ibid.

28 It went from there to the collection of Archduke Leopold Wilhelm, in whose possession it is listed in 1659: Wethey, op. cit., p. 197.
29 Millar, op. cit., p. 184.
30 See MacGregor, op. cit., p. 13.
31 See O. Millar, ed. (with intro.) 'The inventories and valuations of the King's goods 1649-1651', *Walpole Society*, XLIII (1970-72).
32 Gabriel Jules Cosnac, *Les Richesses du Palais Mazarin...* , Paris, 1885, p. 417.
33 Both paintings were acquired through a syndicate ('dividend'), and sold on by Emanuel De Critz and William Latham: W. L. F. Nuttall, 'King Charles I's Pictures and the Commonwealth Sale' *Apollo*, lxxxii, 1965, pp. 302-309, p. 308.
34 J. Brown, *Kings and Connoisseurs: Collecting Art in Seventeenth-Century Europe*, Princeton, 1995, p. 69. Cardenas had spent some £6,000 on behalf of Haro by mid 1651. Hilary Maddicott, 'A Collection of the Interregnum Period', *Journal of the History of Collections*, XI, no. 1 (1999), pp. 1-24.
35 Brown, op. cit., p. 160.
36 See Wethey, op. cit., p. 96, who notes that it was not in the 1627 inventory of the Gonzaga collection in Mantua. It is conceivable that it had been acquired by Daniel Nys and was among the paintings by Titian noted among the amazing treasures reported to have been discovered 'forgotten' (on purpose) in Nys's house in June 1631, and held back from the works shipped to England. Luzio, op. cit., pp. 69-86.
37 Translated from the quotation given in the catalogue of the Kunsthistorisches Museum, Vienna, *Kunsthistorische Sammlungen*, vol. II, 1884, pp. 400-01, where it notes that the picture arrived in Vienna from Brussels in 1656. Titian's *Isabella in black* was no. 367 in the 1659 inventory.
38 Nuttall, op. cit.
39 Ibid., p. 306.
40 Ibid., p. 303.
41 Ibid., p. 305.
42 V&A MS 86.GG.I2 (also catalogued as MSL/1902/613), an early copy of the inventories and sale, the original contemporary MS of which was 'in the hands of Sr John Stanley which was a present to Him from a Painter who had gott one of the pictures of Queen Elisabeth belonging to & sold again to the Crowne by Him', fol. 130/160v.
43 Millar, op. cit., 1970-2, p. 268 (the 'copies' from which such details of attribution are derived are discussed in his Introduction).
44 V&A MS 86.GG.I2, op. cit. at n. 42 above, fol. 126/156v. The whereabouts of the paintings in the Royal Collection in the various royal palaces were carefully noted in this inventory/sale record, and on 16 February 1649, when the relevant original inventory was made, Titian's picture is listed among 'pictures at [St.] James's', having evidently been moved there in the preceding years from Whitehall.
45 Nuttall, op. cit., p. 305.
46 R. Poole, 'An outline of the history of the De Critz family of painters', *Walpole Society*, II (1912-13), pp. 54ff., pp. 57-8.
47 Ibid., p. 58.
48 Ibid., p. 56.
49 Ibid., p. 57. The Stanley manuscript noted above makes no mention of Geere in this context: 'M:r de Crittz... The Great peece of Vandyke being very curiously done – [£]60/0/0'; op. cit. at n. 42 above, fol. 40/70v.
50 Ibid., p. 58.

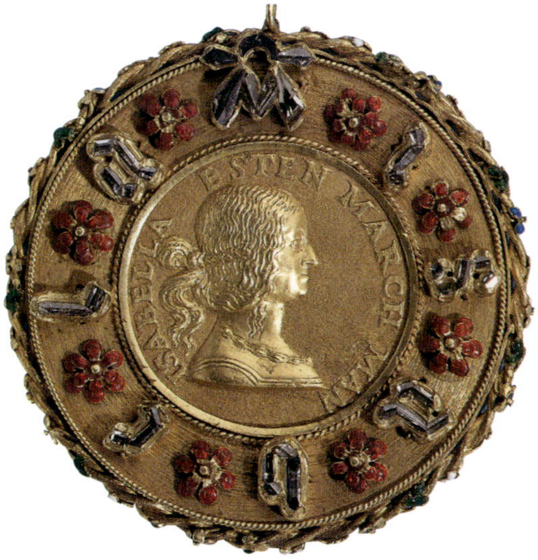

Isabella d'Este
by Giancristoforo Romano
(*c.* 1465-1512).
Medal, bronze, diam. 8.9 cm.
Kunsthistorischesmuseum, Vienna

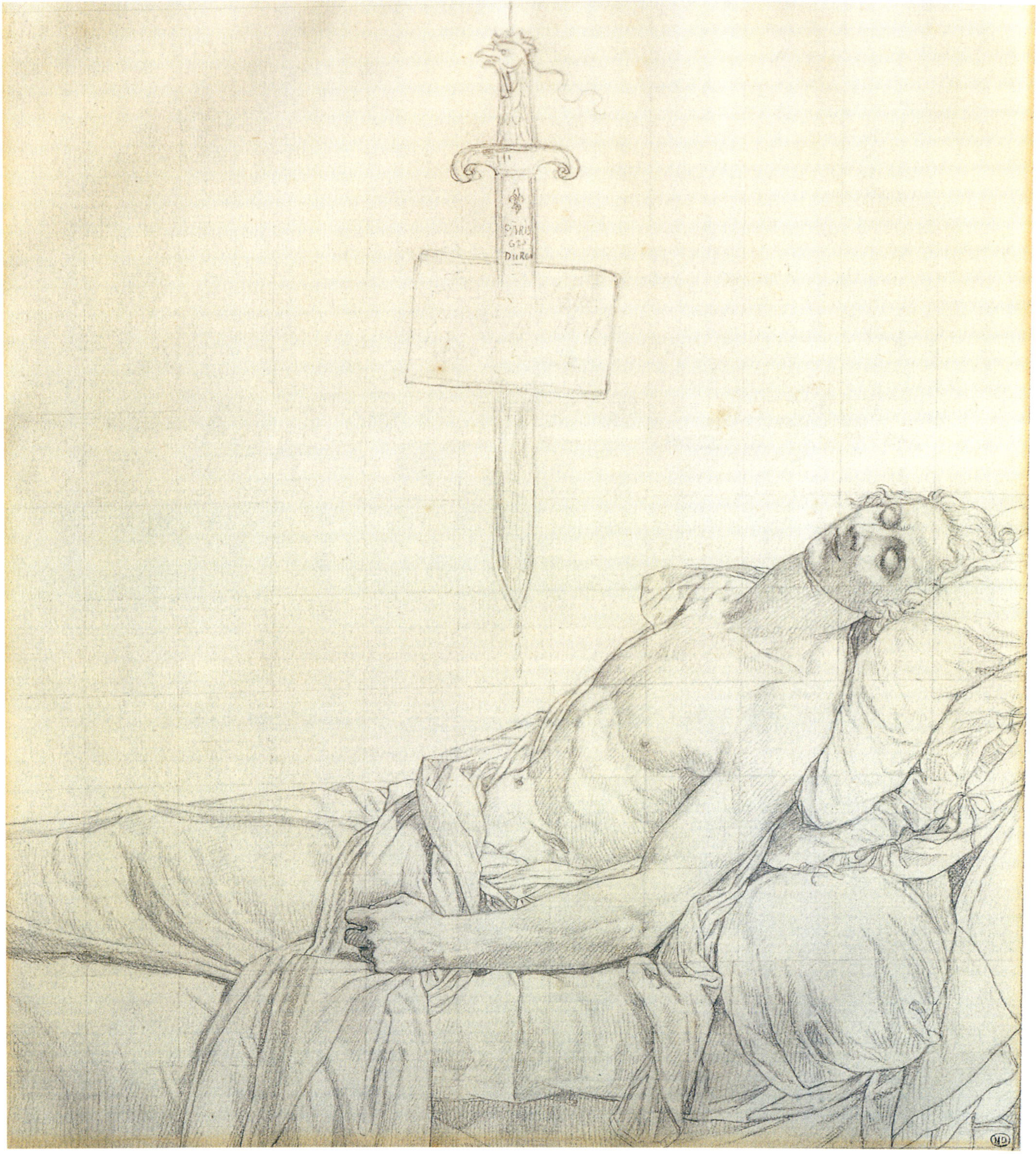

Louis-Michel Lepeletier on his death bed. Drawing by Anatole Devosge (1770-1850), 1793, of lost painting by Jacques-Louis David (1748-1825).
Black chalk, 46.7 × 40 cm.
Musée des Beaux-Arts, Dijon

Jacques-Louis David

1748-1825

Lepeletier on his death-bed

Inscribed: '*DAVID À LEPELLETIER*' and with the date '20 *Janvier* 1793'
Oil on canvas
approximately (perhaps including frame) 200 × 150 cm

On 20 January 1793, the eve of Louis XVI's execution, a former royal bodyguard named Pâris set out to assassinate the *ci-devant* aristocrat and regicide Duc d'Orléans, then known as Citizen Philippe-Egalité. Unable to find his intended victim, he came upon Michel Lepeletier[2] dining in a restaurant in the former Palais Royal. 'Are you Le Peletier de Saint-Fargeau?', he asked. 'Yes,' replied Le Peletier. 'You voted in the case of the King; what was your verdict?' continued Pâris. 'Death', replied Le Peletier, 'I found him guilty in my soul and my conscience and I judged him accordingly.' 'Villain!', Pâris cried, 'here is your punishment,' as he delivered a fatal wound to Lepeletier with his sabre before fleeing.[3]

Louis-Michel Lepeletier, Comte de Saint-Fargeau, Marquis de Montjeu, Baron de Péreuse, Seigneur de Ménilmontant, and Grand Bailli de Gien, was born on 29 May 1760.[4] As a member of the *noblesse de robe*, he was, from 1785, President of the *Parlement* of Paris, the supreme legal court of France, responsible for registering royal edicts as law. It was the aristocracy, represented by the thirteen *Parlements*, who spearheaded the revolt against the King's authority that became the French Revolution. The King was persuaded, under pressure from the *Parlements*, to summon a meeting of the Estates General in 1789, the first since 1614. This led swiftly to the abolition of the feudal system and of the nobility itself. Power moved to the Third Estate, whose members proclaimed themselves to be the National Assembly. Lepeletier, a radical, embraced the Revolution and went over to the patriots, becoming an active reformer in the Constituent Assembly.

On 19 June 1790 when the Assembly voted to abolish the *Parlements* and all noble titles, Lepeletier demanded that no citizen should bear any name other than that of his family, signing himself then, and henceforth, simply '*Louis-Michel Lepelletier*'.[5] By September 1792 the National Convention had declared a Republic. Lepeletier was among the small majority of those deputies who voted unconditionally for the death of Louis XVI on 16 January 1793.

The murder of Lepeletier provided the Convention with the first 'Martyr de la Liberté' and it was quick to exploit the propaganda potential. The regicides used Lepeletier's death to deflect criticism of their execution of the King, portraying Lepeletier as a victim of tyranny, and declaring that Pâris's sword struck not only Lepeletier but also the whole nation. In stark contrast to the sordid disposal of the King's corpse in a pit of quicklime, an elaborate state funeral[6] was planned by the poet Marie-Joseph Chénier and orchestrated by the artist and pageant-master of the Revolution, Jacques-Louis David, himself a regicide deputy of the Convention. David's production was a secular performance to equal any conventional veneration of a martyr. Displayed so as to recall both a *pietà* and a fallen hero of antiquity,

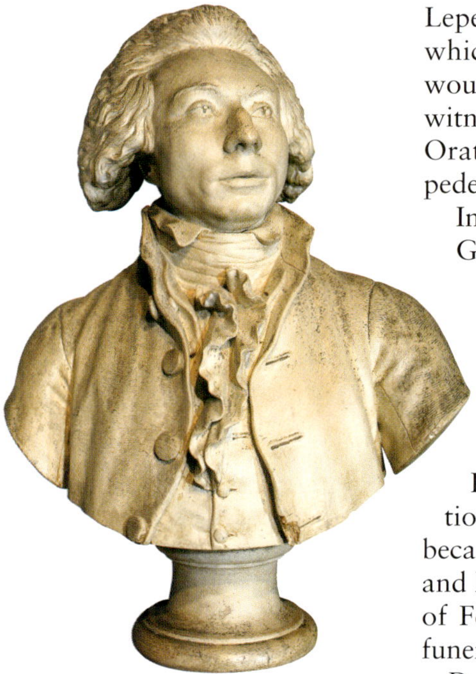

Bust of Louis-Michel Lepeletier by Claude André de Seine.
Musée des Beaux-Arts, Bourges

Lepeletier's body was placed, half-naked, on a pedestal in the Place des Piques, which had until recently borne an equestrian statue of Louis XIV.[7] The fatal wound was exposed and the murder weapon exhibited throughout the funeral. A witness reported that David sat at the foot of the monument and drew Lepeletier. Orators eulogised the martyr and the President of the Convention ascended the pedestal and placed an oak-leaf crown on the head of the corpse.[8]

In silence, save for music by the Revolution's official composer, François-Joseph Gossec (1734-1829), Lepeletier's corpse was carried in a procession to the Panthéon, where his remains were laid to rest. Grotesquely, his corpse appeared to bleed (a gourd of blood had been concealed in the drapery) and his blood-soaked clothes were carried on a pike decorated with oak and cypress leaves. Lepeletier's supposed last words were emblazoned on banners carried by citizens. Inspired by Roman example, Lepeletier's orphaned eleven-year-old daughter, Suzanne-Louise (whose mother, Marie-Adélaïde Louise de Joly, had died in 1783), was symbolically adopted by the Convention as *Mademoiselle Nation*, the first 'Orphan of the Nation'.[9] Overnight she became a celebrity and her father a cult hero, his effigy adorning countless objects and his memory honoured by revolutionaries throughout France. In the first week of February, many towns, including Auxerre and Saint-Fargeau, repeated the funeral ceremony.

During February and March 1793 David worked on a painting exalting the first martyr of the revolution, depicting Lepeletier on his death-bed beneath a

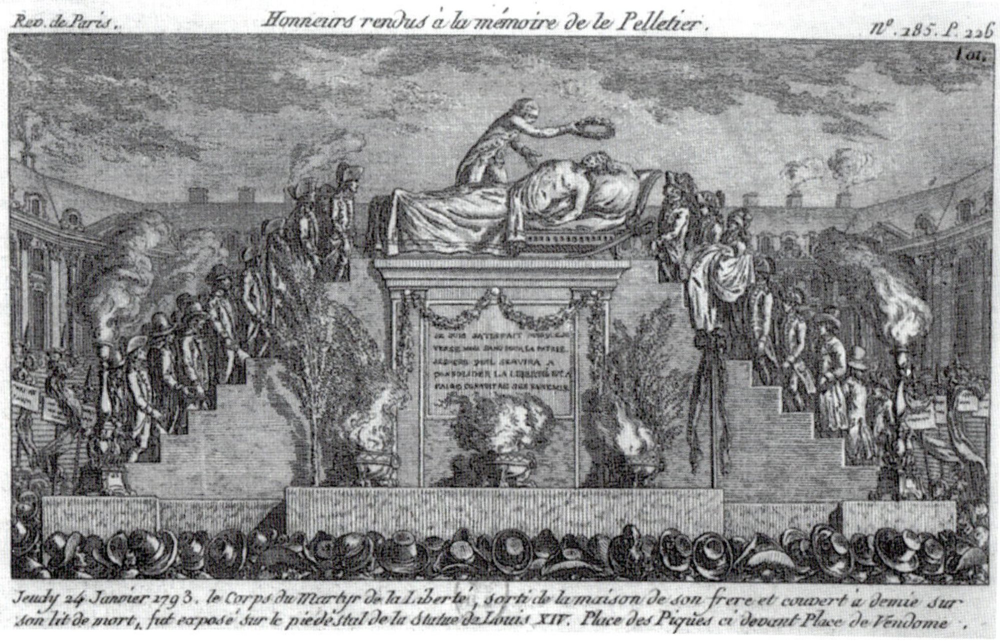

'Honneurs rendus à la mémoire de le Pelletier'.
Anonymous engraving from *Révolution de Paris*, no. 185, 1793

sword impaling a scrap of paper with the inscription '*Je vote la mort du tyran*'. This painting, and a drawing by David, possibly the one he executed at the Place des Piques, are missing. They are known only through a pupil's drawn copy, a mutilated print and some descriptions and sketches.[10]

The *Comité d'Instruction Publique* visited David's studio on 28 March 1793 at 10 o'clock 'pour voir un tableau répresentant Michel Lepeletier sur son lit de mort, dont ledit citoyen doit faire hommage à la Convention Nationale'.[11] David presented his painting to the Convention the following day. In an impassioned speech[12] David exhorted them:

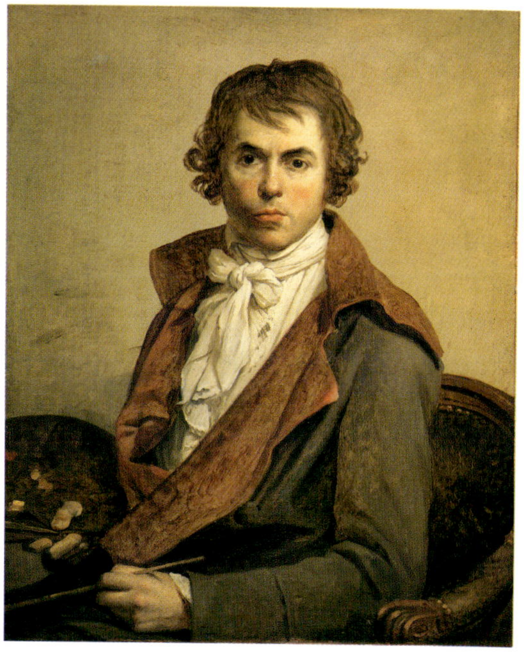

Each one of us is accountable to our country for the gifts which he has received from nature; the form may be different, but the end must be the same for all. The true patriot must seize with enthusiasm every means of enlightening his fellow citizens and of parading incessantly before their eyes the sublime features of heroism and virtue.

This is what I have tried to do in the homage which I now offer to the National Convention of a picture showing Michel Lepelletier, murdered by a coward for having voted for the death of the tyrant.

Citizens, the Supreme Being, who distributes his gifts among all his children, designed me to express my feelings and my thoughts through the instrument of painting and not by the lofty accents of that persuasive eloquence which the tireless children of Liberty cause to ring out among us. Full of respect for His immutable decrees, I am silent, and I will have discharged my duty if one day thanks to me some aged father, surrounded by his large family, will say: 'Come, my children, come and see him among your representatives who was the first to die to give you liberty; look at his face: how serene it is! It shows that if one dies for one's country there is nothing with which one can reproach oneself. Do you see that sword hanging above his head, held up

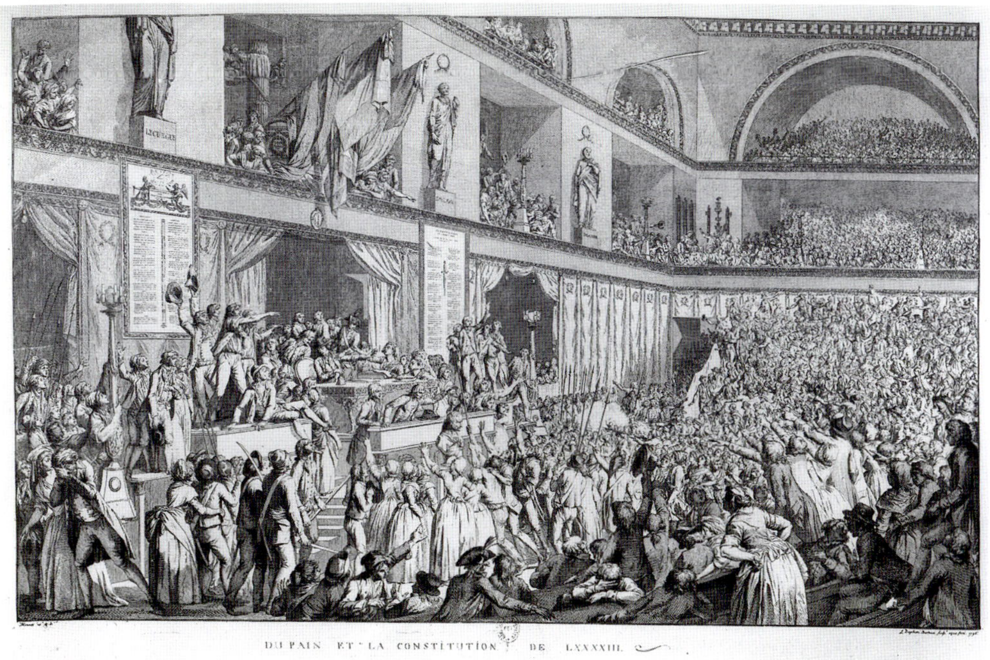

Self-portrait by Jacques-Louis David. Musée du Louvre, Paris

'Du pain et la Constitution de LXXXXIII'. Engraving of the Convention by Jean Duplessi Bertaux after Charles Monnet, 1796

only by a hair? Well, my children, this shows what courage Michel Lepelletier needed, and also his noble colleagues, to send to his punishment the notorious tyrant who had for so long been oppressing us, since, at the slightest movement, if that hair broke they would all be cruelly sacrificed! Do you see that deep wound? You weep, my children, you turn away your eyes! But notice also that crown; it is the crown of immortality. Our country holds it ready for each one of her children: learn how to deserve it – great spirits will never lack occasions to display themselves. If ever, for example, a man of ambition speaks to you of a *dictator*, a *tribune*, a *controller*, or seeks to usurp the slightest part of the sovereignty of the people, or if indeed some coward dares to suggest a king to you, fight or die like Michel Lepelletier, rather than ever agreeing; then, my children, the crown of immortality will be your reward.'

I beg the National Convention to receive the homage of my feeble talent; I would believe myself well rewarded if it should deign to accept it.

The speech was met with loud applause. In the same session the Convention decreed that an engraving of the painting should be produced at the Republic's expense under the supervision of David.[13] The engravings were to be circulated to each of the eighty-four *départements*. David commissioned his former pupil Anatole Devosge (1770-1850) to make a drawing after the painting from which Pierre-Alexandre Tardieu (1756-1844) engraved a copper plate. Only one proof of Tardieu's engraving before lettering survives, and in a mutilated state. Devosge's drawing was exhibited at the Salon on 10 August 1793 (no. 334). The inscription was later effaced and the artist bequeathed it to the Musée des Beaux-Arts in Dijon.

Within months, Jean Paul Marat – *l'ami du Peuple* – the most extreme of the regicide deputies, had been assassinated in his bath by Charlotte Corday.[14] By 23 Vendémiaire, An II (14 October 1793), David had completed his sensational painting *The death of Marat* and requested permission from the Convention to exhibit it with the Lepeletier canvas 'chez lui' at the Louvre where he had an apartment and studio.[15] After a procession through the city, the paintings were exhibited 'for several days... under a monument raised for this occasion in the courtyard of the Old Louvre', according to an anonymous note of 14 October 1793, a setting also described as 'dans un espèce de crypt funèbre, où ils furent admirés pendant six semaines'. The paintings were then taken to the Assembly where they hung as pendants, joining the bust[16] of Lepeletier, which was adorned with his oak-leaf funeral crown.

The Assembly was housed in the small Royal theatre in the Tuileries. It was a narrow room lit by windows on one long side. On the facing wall was the President's chair in the centre of a rostrum designed by David. In his novel *Quatrevingt-treize* (published 1874) Victor Hugo described 'this terrible place' where severed heads carried on the end of pikes drained blood on to the table beneath the President:

On one side of the rostrum, in a frame of black wood, there hung from a wall a nine-foot-high placard displaying on two pages separated by a kind of sceptre the Declaration of the Rights of Man; on the other side there was an empty space which was later occupied by a similar frame containing the Constitution of Year II, the two pages of which were separated by a sword. Above the rostrum, above the head of the speaker, there fluttered, emerging from a deep lodge with two compartments full of people, three immense tricolour flags, almost horizontal, supported on an altar on which could be read this word: the law. Behind this altar, like a sentinel of free speech, there was an enormous Roman *fasces*, the size of a column. Colossal statues, flush against the wall faced the representatives. The president had Lycurgus on his right and Solon on his left; above the Mountain stood Plato.

On either side of the President were to be hung, quite low, the Marat and Lepeletier canvases, where they remained until removed in 1795. Above his chair were statues alternately crowned with oak and laurel leaves. The entire composition was, wrote Hugo, 'violent, savage and geometrical. Correctness amidst barbarism'.

At this stage it appears that there was only one painting by David of Lepeletier on his death-bed. Later descriptions of the picture, however, vary so considerably that there may well have been a variant version or a copy. In January 1794 the Gobelins tapestry workers proposed that tapestries be made of the Lepeletier and Marat paintings.[17] A decree was issued by the Convention on 21 Floréal, An III (10 May 1794), that copies should be produced under the direction of David for the Gobelins tapestry factory. Whether the project was abandoned as the Terror took hold is not known, but there is no evidence that the tapestries were ever made. While it was David's practice to produce copies of his works – and copies exist of the *Marat* – the only surviving copy of the Lepeletier painting is the drawing made by Devosge for the print. This David confirmed was after his own original in a speech he made to the Convention on 24 Nivôse, An III (13 January 1794).[18]

Despite the failure of the print to be circulated, the image of *Lepeletier on his death-bed* recorded by Devosge was a familiar one. It was incorporated into a design for the decoration of a *Temple a la Felicité Publique* by Jean-Nicolas-Louis Durand (1760-1834) and Louis-Michel Thibault.[19] Their project won first prize

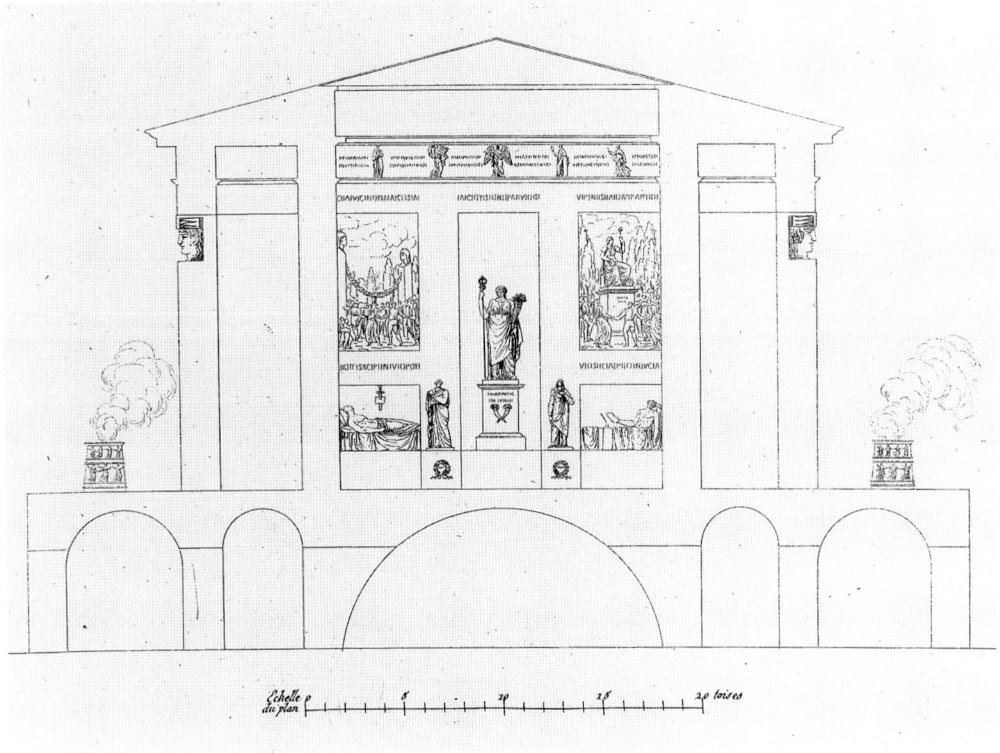

Design of 1794 for 'Temple à la Felicité Publique' by Jean-Nicolas-Louis Durand (1760-1834) and Louis-Michel Thibault.
Engraving published by L. J. Allais *et al.*, *Projets d'Architecture...*, Paris, 1806

in the public competition of 1794 for a temple to adorn the gardens of the Palais d'Elysée. The engraving of their design published in 1806 shows copies of David's paintings of Marat and Lepeletier (reversed in the engraving) hanging either side of the statue of Liberty.

The composition recorded by Devosge reflects the display of Lepeletier's corpse at his funeral. It also recalls David's work of 1783, *Andromache bewailing the death of Hector*, in which Hector wears a laurel crown.[20] But Devosge's drawing does not include the crown on which David had focused in his presentation speech of

29 March 1793: '... But notice also that crown; it is the crown of immortality.' It is of course possible that David had meant his words symbolically or had gestured towards the bust adorned with Lepeletier's actual funeral crown during his speech. Just possibly he instructed Devosges to alter the picture for the drawing from which

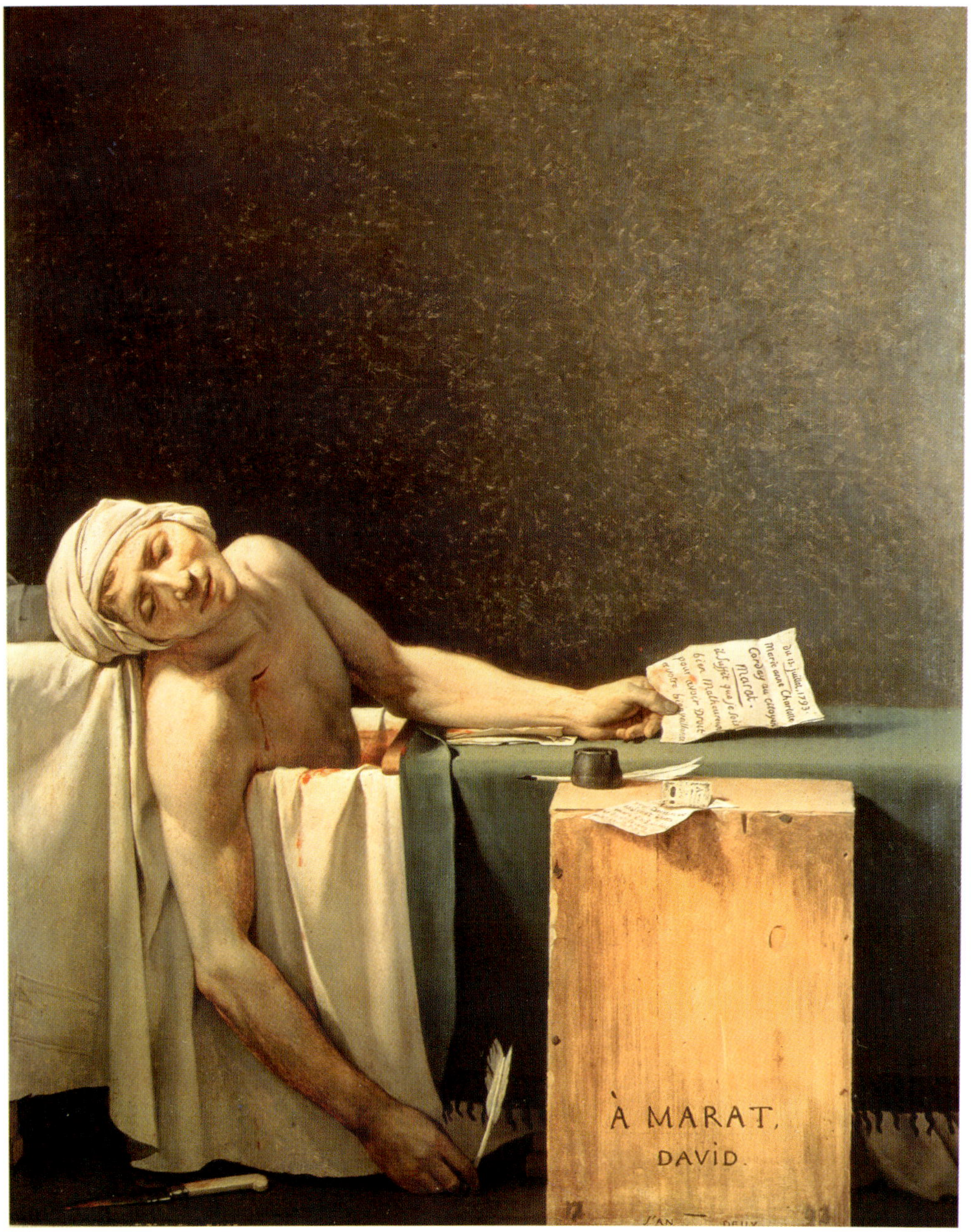

The death of Marat
by Jacques-Louis David, 1793.
Oil on canvas, 165 × 128 cm.
Brussels, Musées Royaux des Beaux-Arts

the print was made, for neither of these images shows a crown. But it is over this key detail that the various descriptions of *Lepeletier on his death-bed* differ.

Some twenty years after *Lepeletier* was painted, Etienne-Jean Delécluze (1781-1863), David's pupil and biographer, saw the canvas at the apartment of David's son, Eugène. Fearing the painting was about to be destroyed, because of its inflammatory content, Delécluze made a sketch of it which confirms the accuracy of Devosge's drawing. Delécluze described it in his journal for 23 March 1826:

Yesterday I saw in the house of Eugène David the portrait of Le Pelletier de Saint-Fargeau...The dead Le Pelletier is stretched on a bed, the body exposed down to the waist... Above the breast there hangs, like the Sword of Damocles, a sword, a sabre of the Bodyguards of the King. In the blade is inserted a slip of paper on which is written: I vote for the death of the tyrant. In the right-hand corner of the painting the words can be read: To Le Pelletier from David.[21]

However, in his later biography of David, Delécluze describes the picture somewhat differently:

The composition of the painting of Michel Lepelletier gives a pretty good idea of this combination of features which are at the same time lofty and bloody. The body lies on a bed. Its head is wreathed with a laurel crown, and its naked breast exposes a wide wound. Above the corpse, there is a sword whose form recalls that of the Bodyguards of the King, of whom Pâris was one. This sword, hanging by a string, is suspended above the breast of the dead man, and in the blade there is a slip of paper on which these words are written: I vote for the death of the tyrant. At the bottom of the painting, we also read: David to Lepelletier, and the date of the death of the latter: 20 January 1793.

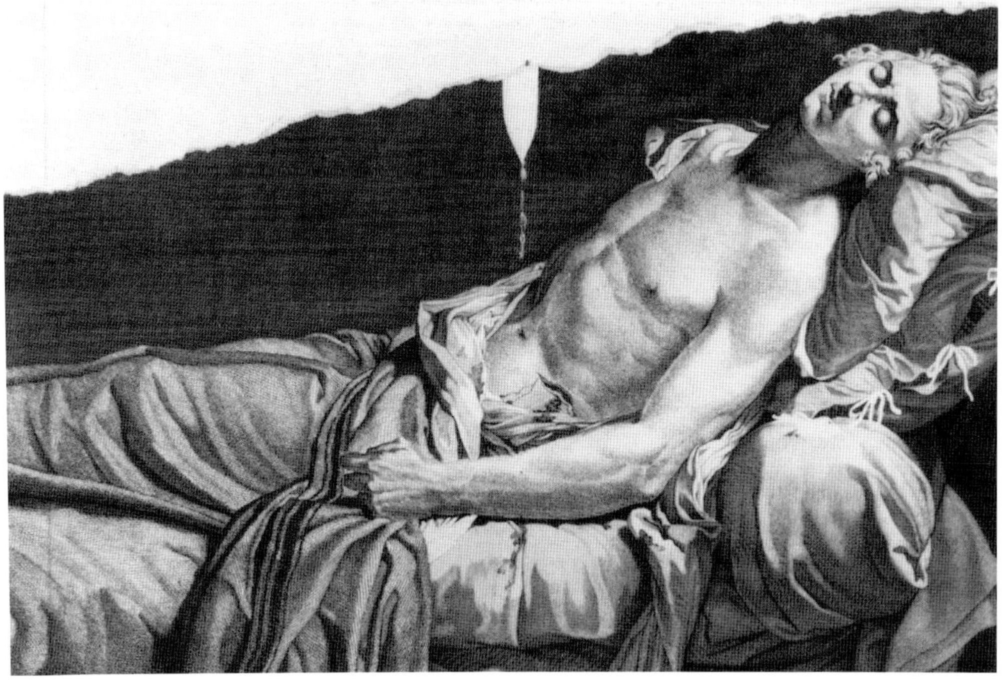

Lepeletier on his death bed.
Engraving by Pierre-Alexandre Tardieu (1756-1844) after the drawing by Devosge of David's lost painting.
Bibliothèque Nationale, Cabinet des Estampes, Paris

He also says that David only painted the head, leaving the torso to his pupil, François Gérard (1770-1837).[22] The critic August Jal, writing in 1827, made the claim that Gérard had painted the *Lepeletier*, citing a doubtless apocryphal story that David found the noble flesh of Lepeletier repulsive, preferring to paint the plebeian body of Marat.[23]

Delécluze's descriptions differ over the laurel crown and the dedication, but there is a crucial difference between the circumstances in which each account was written. His journal records an immediate impression, having been written one day after seeing the picture in 1826, whereas the second description appears in *Louis David: Son école et son temps* which was published three decades later in 1855. In the intervening years Delécluze had no opportunity to see the painting

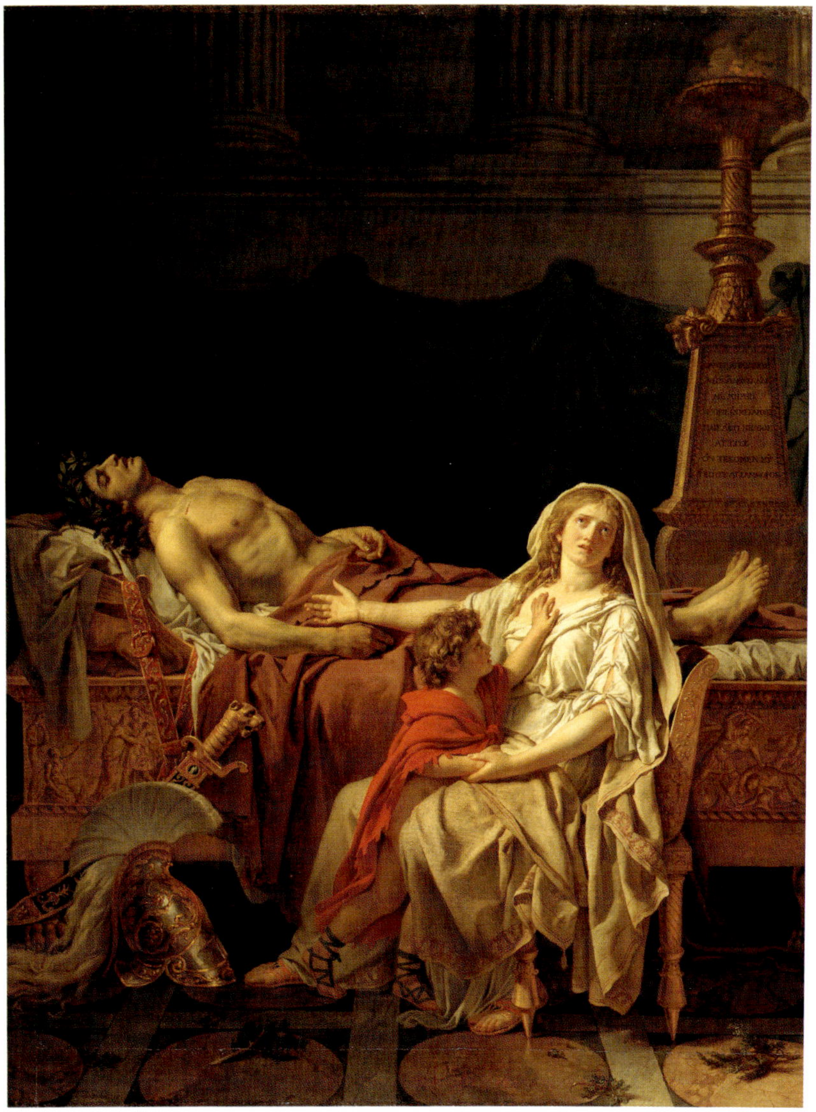

Andromache bewailing the death of Hector
by Jacques-Louis David.
Ecole nationale supérieure des Beaux-Arts, Paris

again, as it was in the possession of Lepeletier's daughter, Suzanne-Louise, by then Madame de Mortefontaine, who was obsessed with shielding it from the world, and it seems possible that by 1855 Delécluze had confused elements of the painting in his mind.

An extremely detailed description, by an anonymous artist who apparently saw the picture in 1825, was published by the historian W. Dey in 1858:

Some artists did see the painting by David in 1825... The painting might have been two metres high and one metre fifty centimetres wide. The background was in light grey, getting darker as the eye approaches the foot of the picture, showing a flat and bare wall, without any adornment. A large camp-bed covered only by a mattress with white and blue stripes crossed the entire canvas horizontally, at about half its height. On this mattress, and in the same orientation, lay the body of Lepeletier de Saint-Fargeau, his head to the right and his

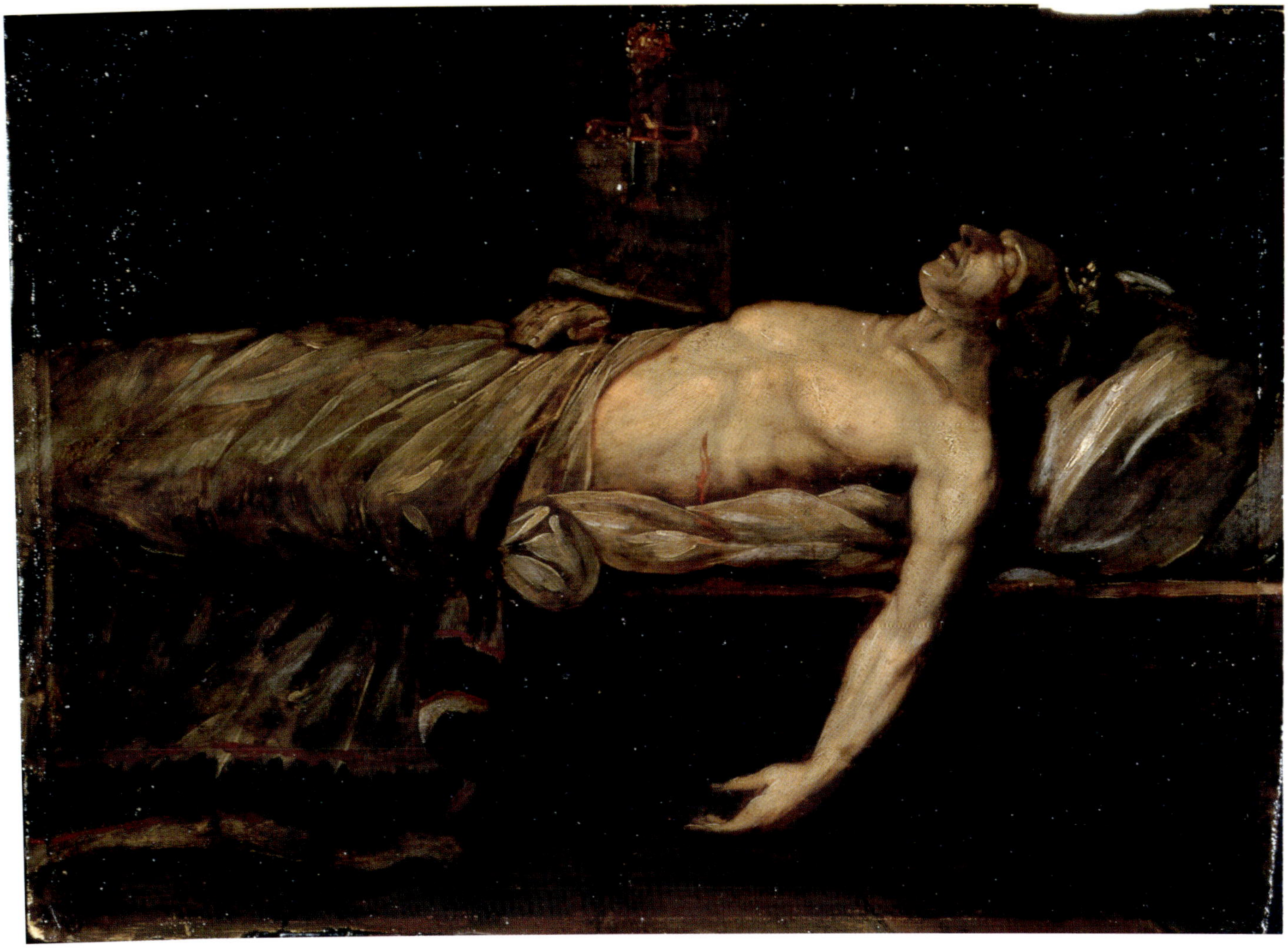

Lepeletier on his death bed.
French school, *c.* 1825-35.
Oil on panel, 25 × 32 cm.
Musée de la Révolution Francaise, Vizille

feet and part of his legs disappearing to the left of the composition. Over the corpse a dark coloured mantle had been thrown, some folds of which were falling to the ground.

His head was pale and calm. Having no support, it had fallen half way back; it was presented in profile, accompanied by a mop of dishevelled hair still showing some traces of powder; the forehead was high and the nose strongly aquiline, while the mouth and chin were sharply chiselled; the entire effect was of nobility and greatness of character.

The blood-soaked shirt, open at the breast, exposed the gaping wound to view, to which the right hand, foreshortened, was reaching back, while the left hung down out of the bed. Bright light from above shone on the face and shoulders, while the rest of the body, in any case swathed in the cloak, vanished into a diffuse half-tone.

At the back in the centre, a blood-stained sabre of the coarsest design and an oak-leaf crown hung from a hook, while on the floor below the limp left arm lay a sheet of paper on which the last vote cast by Lepeletier was written. In one of the corners of the painting the name of L. David was inscribed in large letters and the date 1793.[24]

The author states that this was the picture bought by Suzanne-Louise. Dey's article raises many questions, not least the date at which the anonymous artist could have seen the picture in Eugène's apartment. David died in Brussels on 29 December 1825. During his exile the picture was hidden in Paris. It was only exposed to (limited) public view during David's posthumous sale of April 1826. However, the description is painstaking and so different in the details from the Devosge drawing that it suggests the real possibility that another version of the painting existed. If the anonymous artist saw the picture at the same time as Delécluze in 1826, at the sale, why do their descriptions vary? Either he confused elements such as the hanging arm from the Marat painting, which was on view in the same room in 1826; or, a year earlier, at a time when the painting later bought by Suzanne-Louise was still hidden, he actually saw a different painting altogether. This possibility is perhaps strengthened by the existence of an oil sketch of the subject at the Musée de la Révolution Française in Vizille, near Grenoble. It is dated by the museum to *c.* 1825-35, and attributed to 'French School'. It is clearly not by David and, while it may record another version of the picture, the possibility must also be that it was itself painted in accordance with the description published by Dey in 1858. In any event the description could have been written from memory at any time in the thirty-two years before it was published and the anonymous artist, among other things, could have mis-remembered the date. Interestingly, however, he is specific about the crown: not laurel leaves, but the oak leaves awarded to heroic Roman citizens who saved the lives of fellow Romans in battle – which is what, in effect, Lepeletier unwittingly did by being assassinated instead of Philippe-Egalité. It was an oak-leaf crown which had adorned the corpse of Lepeletier in the Place des Piques and his bust in the National Assembly.

David managed to survive Robespierre's fall from power in 1794[25] and was imprisoned twice during 1794 and 1795. The cult of Martyrs of the Revolution was short-lived and both the Lepeletier and Marat paintings were returned to David by the Convention on 20 Pluviôse, An III (9 February 1795), and the martyrs' ashes were removed from the Panthéon.[26] Lepeletier's remains were given back to his family and finally buried at Saint-Fargeau some time between 1805-10 while, according to Joseph Farington, the ashes of Marat and Mirabeau were thrown into the public sewer.[27]

The English artist and diarist Joseph Farington (1747-1821) had taken advantage of the brief Peace of Amiens of 27 March 1802 and travelled to Paris to see Napoleon's looted works of art. On Monday 20 September 1802, he made an appointment with Mlle. Jaullie, David's Irish pupil, to visit the artist's apartment in the Louvre. There, in the first room, he

> ... saw a drawing by David; the subject Pelletier, the Republican, after He was murdered by a wound in his left side by a Sword. A Sword is suspended over him and an inscription 'Assassinated for having voted the Death of a Tyrant'.
>
> David may be supposed to have designed his subject as He was capable of, for a more violent Republican than himself did not exist during the period of the revolution.[28]

Farington makes no mention of the paintings of Marat and Lepeletier, which were presumably kept discreetly in the studio. Farington was fairly unfamiliar with (and unimpressed by) the work of David, and he may only have seen Devosge's copy. If,

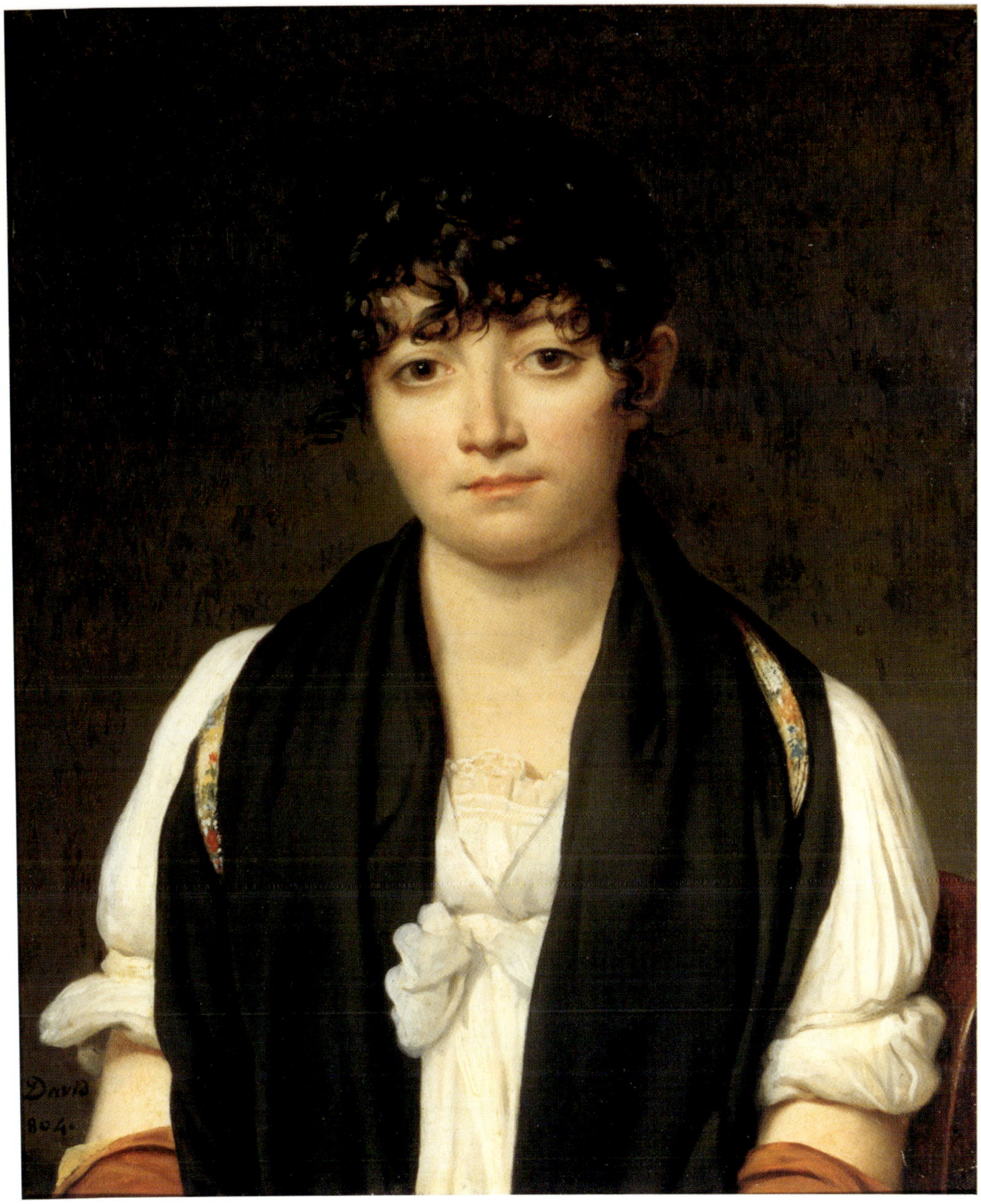

Suzanne-Louise Lepeletier de Saint-Fargeau (1782-1829) by Jacques-Louis David, 1804. Oil on canvas, 60.5 × 49.5 cm. Private collection

however, Mlle. Jaullie had acted as his guide, he was probably correctly informed that David had made the drawing. It was around this time that Suzanne-Louise bought a drawing of her father by David, which she described as 'd'après nature'.

Suzanne-Louise Lepeletier (1782-1829) had, with the death of her father, inherited his immense wealth. In 1798, aged fifteen, she married Jean François de Witt. Their two children died in infancy and by the age of twenty she had divorced. In 1804 she fell in love with her cousin, Léon Lepeletier de Mortefontaine (1771-1814), and married him two years later. He was a fervent royalist, and it was rumoured that the restoration of Louis XVIII to the throne was prepared in his house.[29] Their happy marriage was short-lived: Léon de Mortefontaine died in a riding accident in 1814, leaving his widow with two small daughters, Marguerite (1809-90) and Suzanne (1811-93).

As a motherless child, Suzanne-Louise had been brought up by her maternal grandfather, Jean Omer Joly de Fleury, until her father's half-brother, Félix Lepeletier, took over her care when her father was assassinated. Her mother's family and her future husband remained royalist throughout the Revolution. Despite this, Suzanne-Louise chose the regicide David to paint her portrait as a love-token for her fiancé in 1804.[30] At the height of his patronage by Napoleon, hers was one of the few private commissions David accepted. Although he was undoubtedly the best artist available, David was a strange choice, as Suzanne-Louise appears to have been anxious to conceal her father's revolutionary past. As we shall see, by this time she had probably already bought David's drawing and had a cabinet made in which to hide it. She subsequently tried to acquire the painting of her father, which she may have seen in David's studio while her own portrait was being painted. Did she commission her own portrait in order to have the opportunity to approach David about the painting of her father on his death-bed?

Her first attempts to buy the painting were unsuccessful. Then, at the return of the Bourbons in 1814,[31] all regicides were condemned to exile, David among them.[32] He settled in Brussels where he lived until his death on 29 December 1825. Around 1816 Suzanne-Louise turned for help to her uncle Félix, himself a vigorous supporter of the Revolution and fellow exile of David in Brussels. At the time, she believed there were two versions:

> I would pay a high price to have these two pictures back, but I would like to be completely sure that there are no copies of them hidden... Make sure that he [David] believes that it is you who are doing the deal. I would very much like to have them both for twelve thousand francs.[33]

At some stage she must have been informed that she was mistaken, as she does not mention the second picture again.

By 2 July 1825, referring only to one painting, she reassures Félix, who was concerned for the fate of the painting in her hands:

> For your part, you can trust me for the way I will treat it and you should not have supposed that I could destroy the only memorial that I have. It will be carefully conserved, not as a national monument, but out of a daughter's respect and love.[34]

But David still refused to sell, and she had to wait until after his death before trying again.

David himself was anxious to conceal the picture under the new Bourbon régime and during his exile he left his pictures in the care of his former pupil Antoine-Jean Gros (1771-1835) in Paris. Both the Lepeletier and Marat paintings were covered with a layer of white paint and hidden away from view in Gros's studio. 'Discretion,' wrote Gros to David on 5 April 1820, 'has been the watchword in their regard.'[35]

After David's death the sale of his studio was announced for 17 April 1826 in Paris.[36] Desperate to prevent her father's picture from being publicly displayed at the sale, Suzanne-Louise was at the mercy of David's family and was obliged to pay their exceptional pre-sale price of 100,000 francs, which Félix described as 'exorbitant'.[37] The inclusion in the sale of such works as *The death of Marat* was regarded by royalists, particularly the Interior Minister Corbière, as 'an affront to public morality', and stringent viewing conditions were imposed. In the event, the *Marat* proved too scandalous for sale and was withdrawn.[38]

Suzanne-Louise's private purchase of the *Lepeletier* canvas was concluded on 11 April 1826 and registered in a written agreement which casts an interesting light on the strange circumstances of the deal.[39] It was unusual to have a written contract, and in it David's heirs declare, to the best of their knowledge, that no copy, engraving or lithograph had been made other than the copper plate by Tardieu. The plate was broken up in Tardieu's presence on 13 May 1826 and the fragments were surrendered to Suzanne-Louise on 17 May.[40] The vendors stated that, without David's painting and the drawing which Suzanne-Louise already possessed, no new copies could be made. Either they did not know the whereabouts of Devosge's copy or they supressed the information.

A hazy account of the supposed negotiations is published in Dey's 1858 article. In it the author claims that during negotiations the heirs declared:

> We will only give you the painting in return for 100,000 francs and [also] a deed by which the purchaser gives an undertaking to keep it for as long as there is a descendant of David alive and to show it on request to prove that the agreement has been met.[41]

According to this source, although the heirs did not believe anyone would buy a picture for 100,000 francs and then destroy it, they refused to negotiate their demand, but the clause did not appear in the final deed of sale. Fears that Lelepetier's painting would not survive in the hands of his daughter were widespread. The rumour was persistent and was reported by Delécluze and Stendhal who wrote:

> ... the story is that she offered 100,000 francs for the famous painting of her father with the intention of burning it. The painting is one of the best canvases of David.[42]

Again, according to Dey, Suzanne-Louise had bought the painting to prove her solidarity with the royalist cause and her revulsion against her father's regicide. Her own words suggest otherwise. When the painting was first hung in her house in Paris, Suzanne-Louise was ill and wrote to Félix:

> Until I am able to climb a flight of stairs, I will not see my precious painting... When I have seen it, I will tell you what I would like rubbed out on it... Don't worry about this, but it will be necessary to find ways to ensure that there will be nothing which can one day throw me into new embarrassment and then you must give your word of honour not to let anyone at all see it.

And in another letter to him:

> This poor painting has a very bad effect, but keep it for me carefully.[43]

After the offending inscription and dedication (presumably) had been painted out, the picture was transferred to the Château de Saint-Fargeau, Yonne. Such poignant memories surrounded the house, however, that Suzanne-Louise spent little time there, living instead at her château at Verneuil-sur-Seine, near Paris, where she died on 19 August 1829.

Shortly after her death, the Marquise de Lage de Volude (1762-1842), a fervent royalist and courtier of Charles X, reported with satisfaction to her daughter that Suzanne-Louise had burnt the painting:

> 15 March 1830: Mme de Mortefontaine, whom you met at the house of Mme de Montboissier, has died. The notorious David did a portrait of her father standing up, at the moment of his assassination by M. Pâris, or, better, when he was voting for the death of the King. An ardent royalist who spent a fortune for the Allies, she bought the painting for

120,000 francs from the heirs of David, who were putting it on public exhibition, and had it burned before witnesses – the Duc de Gramont and M. de Rosanbo were present in her garden. It was this revival of the crime of her father (Pelletier de Saint-Fargeau) that brought her to her grave.[44]

The Marquise's letter is inaccurate in several details but, though clearly not a witness herself, she knew the people involved. M. de Rosanbo was Suzanne-Louise's cousin and his aunt, Mme. de Montboissier, was a friend of Volude's; while the Duc de Gramont (1755-1836) was the widower of her childhood friend Aglae de Polignac.

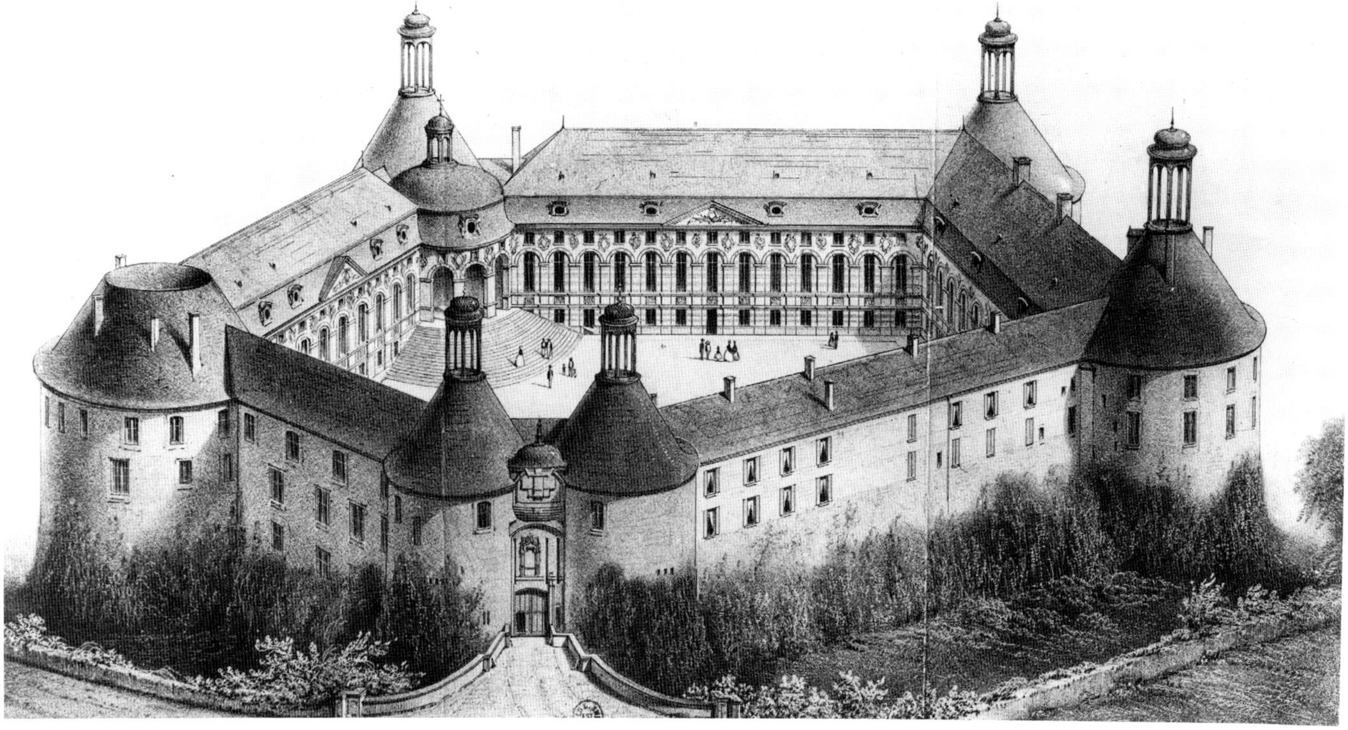

Château de Saint-Fargeau, Yonne. Nineteenth-century lithograph

Mme. de Montboissier, although also not present, was doubtless the source of the story. It would be understandable if, moving in this royalist circle in the reactionary atmosphere of the reign of Charles X, Suzanne-Louise had finally felt the need to destroy the painting which she had been at such pains to secure. But none of her previous actions show any desire to do so. The Marquise de Volude's description, which differs so markedly from the records of the lost original, suggests Suzanne-Louise could even have substituted a different picture. Perhaps, however, Suzanne-Louise initiated the bonfire rumour herself as, in her will of 1826, she stipulated that the painting should remain in the hands of the family and should not leave the Château de Saint-Fargeau.[45] Clearly, at that time, she had no intention of destroying it and, as we shall see, Félix Lepeletier at the time of his draft will certainly believed the painting still to exist at Saint-Fargeau after Suzanne-Louise's death.

The fate of the painting remained a source of speculation. Baudelaire reported in 1846 that it had disappeared in a mysterious manner.[46] But a tantalising remnant of correspondence survives between the art critic Champfleury (1821-89) – who promoted the work of the Realist painters and had rediscovered their seventeenth-century precursors the Le Nain brothers – and M.Robet from Auxerre. The letters are undated, but references to books Champfleury had written and proofs of others in progress suggest a date of around 1860 when Robet writes:

> My dear and illustrious master... The last lucky find regarding the author of the Marriage recalls to my mind a strange business which could well succeed and which would fall to the skill of a tenacious searcher, such as the Lenains have produced in you. Let me tell you that one of the two or three complete masterpieces of David, the portrait of Lepelletier de St. Fargeau, was not destroyed as is believed. Several people saw it during a fire which broke out ten years ago but did not destroy the château [1853]. However, the current owner, the Marquis de Boisgelin, husband of *la fille de Liberté*, adopted by the Convention [actually, husband of Suzanne-Louise's daughter Marguerite], is concealing the portrait from all eyes. The painting has three or four tears at the bottom, but the figure is intact. A former member of David's circle, the self-styled painter to His Majesty Charles X, now married to a neighbour in common, says that he has seen it and recognised it. In a few days' time, if you think that the business is worth the bother, I will give you some more details, since I am planning myself to go and rummage round the château of the Marquis as soon as the first cold drives him back to Paris. For greater certainty, please give me the exact dimensions of the work.

In another letter he continues:

> On the subject of pictures, do not say too much about the Lepelletier business, because the grandson of Liberty [i.e. Suzanne-Louise's son-in-law] who is very covert on this subject, would take steps which would ruin everything. I am still cherishing the hope of disarming the Cerberus who has been put in charge of guarding this daughter of Hesperus in the absence of the master. What a chance it would be for me, for art and for everyone, if a champion of your prowess could be on my side! Think about it and do what you can.[47]

The painting continued to be mentioned in family papers in such as a way as to indicate its survival. For example, a legal case brought by Suzanne-Louise's daughters after her death makes no mention of the destruction of the painting. The case concerned the inheritance of the drawing by David of Lepeletier 'd'après nature' that Suzanne-Louise had apparently bought around 1801 according to a letter she wrote to Félix:

> Fifteen years ago I purchased from the son of David the drawing which his father had done from the life, and I paid one hundred louis.[48]

The letter has been dated from its context around 1816. But various questions arise from it. Why did Suzanne-Louise buy the drawing from David's son, when the artist was still living in Paris (although the sons did work with their father)? Could she have been confused by the Revolutionary calendar, still in use until 31 December 1805, and in fact bought the drawing in 1802, perhaps the very one that was described by Joseph Farington in his journal of that year? Confusingly, Baron Chaillou des Barres reported in an article of 1849 that she bought the drawing in 1810, giving the price paid as 2,400 francs, which was the equivalent of the 100 *louis d'or* that Suzanne-Louise recalled paying. His statement was repeated by Dey in 1858.

Whatever the precise circumstances of her acquisition of the drawing, in 1828 she lent the drawing to Félix, who had returned from exile. Apparently he had repeatedly asked for a memento of his brother and agreed to Suzanne-Louise's conditions that it should be returned to her if requested and that he should keep the drawing hidden. This he did, only displaying it after her death. A clause in his undated draft will which, according to a witness, was not ratified or signed, but written in his own hand and inventoried, reveals his intentions to leave the drawing to his great-niece:

To Mme de Boisgelin, as I undertook to my niece Mme de Mortefontaine, a large volume or box enclosing the drawing by the celebrated David of his fine painting of Michel Lepeletier on his death bed, also containing four portraits of Michel. This volume must be reunited with the painting which is at Saint-Fargeau.[49]

In the actual will, however, made days before his death in January 1837, Félix omitted this clause.[50] Only after the legal judgement were the drawing and mementoes returned to Suzanne-Louise's daughters on 25 July 1837.

Much of the evidence given to Mâitre Glandaz (who acted for Mme. de Mortefontaine's heirs) came from the anonymous 'bearer to Félix of the drawing'. In a memorandum this witness describes the hiding-place in which Suzanne-Louise had kept the drawing until lending it to Félix:

Madame de Mortefontaine kept the drawing in a cupboard of her bedroom to which she had the key, to keep it from being seen by anyone in her house. It remained there until 1827 or 1828. M. Lescure, the cabinet-maker of the house, who is still alive and living at 4 rue Pont-aux-Choux, made this cupboard concealed by a curtain. He saw this painting [drawing] when it was put there. Charles, the senior butler of Madame, who is still alive, also saw this drawing in this cupboard. Finally, M. Duplan, a confidant of Mme de Mortefontaine from 1812 to 1829, when she died, was always the holder of the key of the cupboard during the absence of that Lady and was responsible for ensuring that her intention was met.[51]

From the familiar way in which the witness recalls addressing Félix ('But you promised... ') it is clear that the witness knew both Félix and Suzanne-Louise as an equal rather than a servant:

Some time after the death of Mme. de Mortefontaine, when I was in his office [Félix's] I was surprised to see the drawing and I reminded him of his promise, He replied to me: 'My niece is now dead, and there is nothing to prevent me from exhibiting it.' 'But you promised,' I told him, 'to give it back.' 'I will keep my promise,' he replied, 'and I will give it back to Mme. de Boisgelin [Suzanne-Louise's daughter] with the other memorials of my brother to be kept with the great painting.[52]

In his judgement Maître Glandaz expresses no doubt over the whereabouts of the painting, and surely Suzanne-Louise's daughters, or the anonymous confidant, would have been aware of its destruction, even if Félix had been kept in the dark.

The drawing was duly restored to Suzanne-Louise's heirs, but there is no description of it other than that it was 'd'après nature'. No description exists of the drawing David made during the funeral. In addition to the full-length drawing Farington saw, two drawings by David of Lepeletier are recorded.[53] One, of Lepeletier's un-idealised head only, after death, came to the Bibliothèque Nationale in 1863 from Michel Hennin, who bought it at the posthumous sale of the collection of Charles Meynier (1768-1832). The drawing is inscribed on the *verso* '*Dessiné par David et terminé par Meynier*'. This drawing of the head was engraved by Dominique-Vivant Denon (1747-1825), and is distinct from the drawing which had belonged to Suzanne-Louise, because that was in the possession of Félix at the time of the Meynier sale.

Another drawing, perhaps also of Lepeletier's head after death, but more probably showing him lying on the 'lit de mort', was sold in 1868 and again in 1912, when it was described:

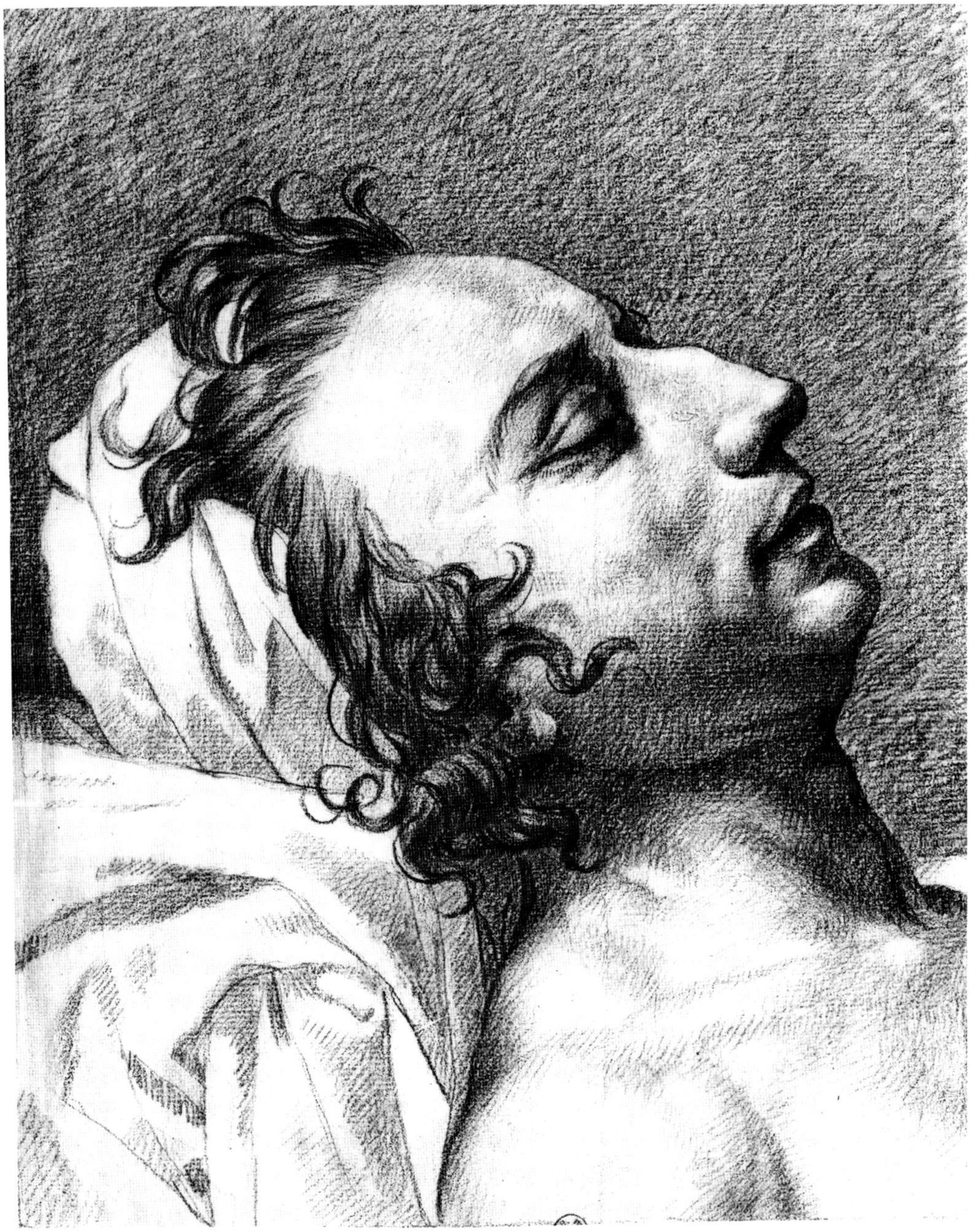

Louis-Michel Lepeletier on his death bed, attributed to Jacques-Louis David. Black chalk, 34 × 25.7 cm. Bibliothèque Nationale, Cabinet des Estampes, Paris

No. 66: David Lepelletier de Saint-Fargeau sur son lit de mort. Il est vu de profil à droite, le haut de la tête serré dans une étoffe blanche d'ou sortent les touffes de cheveux. Dessin à la plume. Haut 31 cm. Large 25 cm. 1600 Frs. Beaumont.

Given the coincidence of the dates, this drawing could well have emerged from the possession of Mme. de Boisgelin who had owned it since 1837 but who died in 1868. Whether or not that is the case, the details make it clear that it cannot have been identical with the composition of the finished painting as recorded by

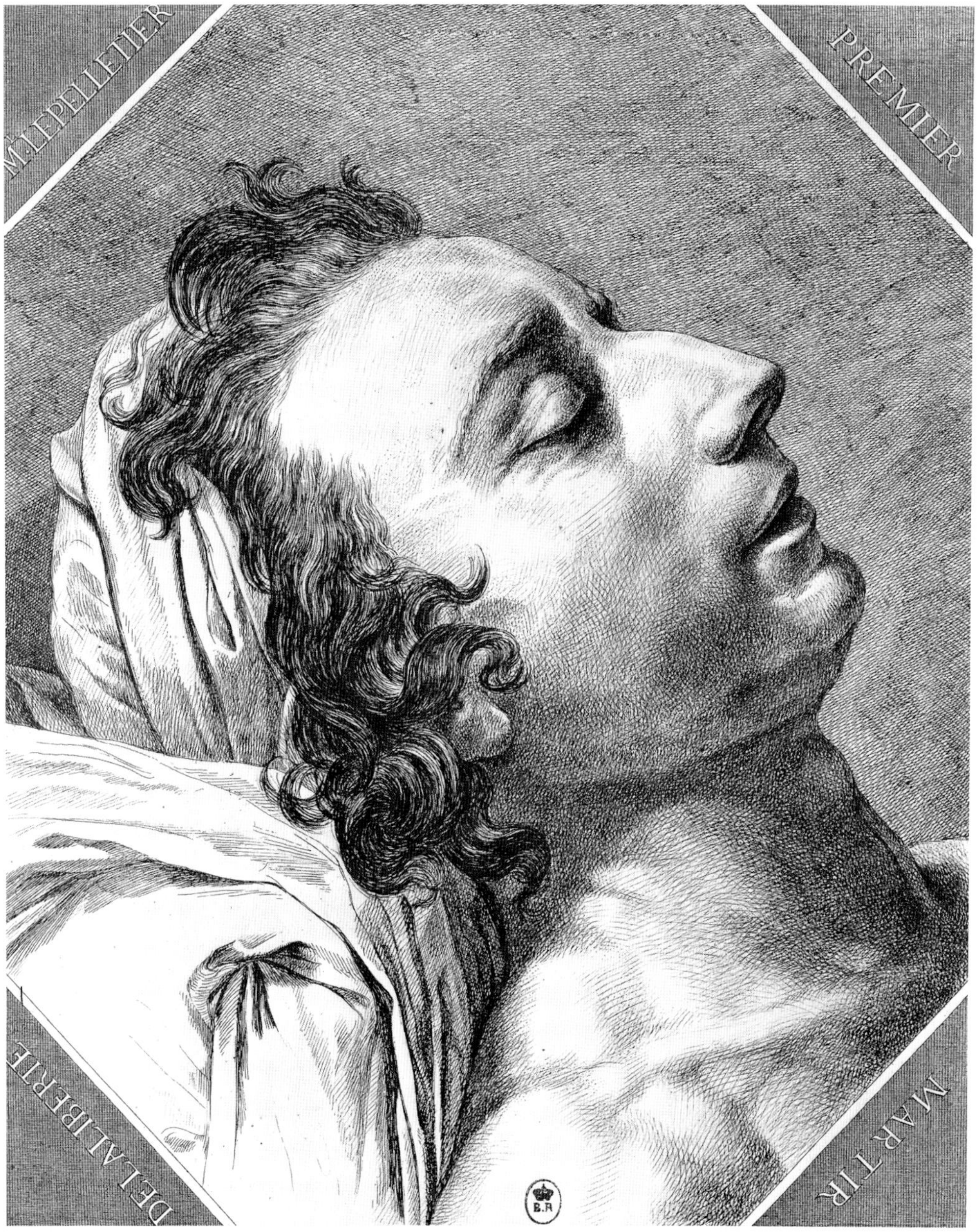

Lepeletier on his death bed.
Engraving by Baron Dominique-Vivant Denon (1747-1825)
after drawing attributed to Jacques-Louis David

Devosge: that shows the left profile of the head, not the right. The sale entry also describes a white cloth around the top of the head, from which the hair emerges. This detail is paralleled in the surviving drawing, of the head only, that entered the Bibliothèque Nationale in 1863, which is inscribed as by David but finished by Meynier, and which also shows the right profile. The drawing described in the 1868 sale, the present location of which is unknown, was probably different from the David/Meynier drawing in that, as suggested above, it apparently also showed the 'lit de mort'.[54]

This lost drawing, however, whether of the head alone or also showing the figure on the death-bed, was presumably not identical with the drawing owned by Suzanne-Louise. Her drawing was possibly that described by Farington in March 1802, and it evidently resembled the painting: the 1826 sale agreement of David's heirs declared that no engraving of the painting could be completed without using 'the drawing which has for a long time been in the possession of Mme. de Mortefontaine'. A similar phrase recurs during the judgement of 1837, which again makes it clear that Suzanne-Louise's drawing cannot have been of the head only and that it resembled the painting: '... no copy or drawing of this painting was ever made, except for the one which had been for a considerable period in the possession of Mme. de Mortefontaine;' and in his will Félix described the drawing as 'of his fine painting of Michel Lepeletier on his death bed'. As we have seen, the appearance of the painting was officially recorded by David's pupil Devosge, who retained his own drawing until 1850, and the lost drawing of the 1868 sale contains those telling details such as the cloth around the head which distinguish it from Devosge's record.

The fate of David's famous painting of Lepeletier remains uncertain. It might have been burnt before witnesses shortly before Suzanne-Louise's death without the knowledge of her family; or it might have become the property of her daughter, Mme. de Boisgelin, in whose care it was rumoured to have been *c.* 1860. Conflicting descriptions, not least David's, appear to suggest there might have been a second version or copy, which is also missing, but it is impossible to come to a firm conclusion. There are also elements of uncertainty about the drawing that Suzanne-Louise owned, in that David's drawing, executed at the funeral, may have been a study of Lepeletier's head, or a full-length compositional drawing, perhaps that seen by Farington in 1802. A drawing recording the composition of the painting was acquired by Suzanne-Louise, from David's son, around 1801-2, and subsequently kept for her by her uncle Félix Lepeletier from 1828 to 1837, when it was returned to her daughter, Mme. de Boisgelin. Certainly, during Suzanne-Louise's lifetime the whereabouts of both the drawing and the painting were closely guarded secrets, and what has happened to them remains a mystery. Attempts to find them at the château have failed.

NOTES

The spelling of Lepeletier's name follows the current usage, but original spellings are retained in all citations.

The abbreviation 'W' followed by a number refers to items found in Daniel and Guy Wildenstein, *Documents complémentaires au Catalogue de l'oeuvre de Louis David*, Paris, 1973.

Dates are given in the Revolutionary form only if the calendar was in use at the time. The French Republican calendar was adopted on 5 October 1793 and applied retrospectively from 22 September 1792; it remained in force until 31 December 1805 when Napoleon restored the Gregorian calendar.

1 P. A. Coupin, *Essai sur J. L. David*, Paris, 1827, p. 29: 'Les deux portraits de Marat et de Le Peletier, auxquels l'artiste a donné un caractère éminemment dramatique, sont de même dimension. On voit qu'ils ont été disposés pour être en regard l'un de l'autre.' W. Dey, 'Histoire de la Ville et du comté de Saint-Fargeau', *Bulletin de la Société des Sciences Historiques et naturelles de l'Yonne*, Auxerre, 1858, no. 12, pp. 600-1, quoting an anonymous painter: 'Le tableau [*Lepeletier*] pouvait avoir 2 mètres de haut sur 1m. 50c. de large... dans l'un des angles de tableau, en grosses lettres le nom de L. DAVID, avec le millésime de 1793.' According to Coupin, p. 27, the painting was inscribed at the top: '*L'An 1793, 2e République A Michel Lepelletier Assassiné pour avoir voté la mort du Tyran, J-L David, son collègue*' (W410).

2 Despite his huge fortune Lepeletier adopted an 'éminemment démocratique' lifestyle, eating in the most modest restaurants. He was an habitué of Février's restaurant in the former Palais Royal, then called the Palais de l'Egalité. Edmond Biré, *Journal d'un Bourgeois de Paris pendant la Terreur*, Paris, 1895-8, vol. II, p. 3.

3 According to the Committee of Public Safety, Pâris killed himself on 28 January 1793, but in reality he died in London in 1813. Jeannine Baticle, 'La seconde mort de Lepeletier de Saint-Fargeau. Recherches sur le sort du tableau de David', *Bulletin de la Société de l'histoire de l'art français*, 1988, p. 134.

4 Son of Michel Etienne Lepeletier (1736-78), himself President of the *Parlement* of Paris in 1764, and Louise-Suzanne Lepeletier de Beaupré, who died in 1762 leaving a large fortune. Michel's second wife was Louise Adelaïde Randon, and Félix Lepeletier (1767-1837) (see below) was one of the five children of this second marriage. On 21 June 1790 Louis-Michel Lepeletier was elected President of the National Assembly for 'quinze jours'; on 2 September 1792 he was elected deputy for Yonne at the Convention.

5 *Biographie Universelle* (Michaud, 1811-47), vol. XXIV.

6 For details of the plans for the state funeral see Baticle, op. cit., p. 141, and Biré, op. cit., vol. II, pp. 7-20. On the catafalque were written Lepeletier's supposed last words (actually composed by his colleague, Citizen Maure): 'Je suis satisfait de verser mon sang pour la patrie; j'espère qu'il servira à consolider la liberté et l'égalité et à faire reconnaitre ses ennemis.'

7 This was the Place Vendôme. The statue of Louis XIV had been torn down the day after the monarchy was abolished on 10 August 1792, Biré, op. cit., vol. II, p. 8.

8 'David avait pris place sur le piédestal avec un chevalet et une toile. Le peuple a eu ce spectacle du peintre copiant ce sanglant modèle', ibid., p. 9.

9 The convention adopts Suzanne-Louise and David proposes a monument to Lepeletier be made in marble (W409).

10 Anatole Devosge (1770-1850), *Le Peletier de Saint-Fargeau on his death-bed*, 1793, black chalk squared and indented for transfer, 46.7 × 40 cm. Exhibited at the Salon 1793, no. 334. Bequeathed by the artist to the Musée des Beaux-Arts, Dijon (1850 inv: coll. Devosge). Engraved by Pierre-Alexandre Tardieu (1756-1844). The sole example of Tardieu's print is a proof before letters were applied sold by Tardieu's widow to the Bibliothèque Nationale, Cabinet des Estampes, Paris, in 1844 (AA3 Rés). The sketch by Delécluze discussed below was formerly in the collection of Albert Vaudoyer.

11 Baticle, op. cit., n. 9.

12 David's speech is given in its entirety in Baticle, op. cit., pp. 143-4; and W427.

13 The Convention decrees that the painting be engraved and circulated to the *départements* at the expense of the Republic (W427 and W675, which gives the sum allocated to David as 2,400 livres); 24 Frimaire An II (14 December 1793), contract between David and Tardieu to engrave the plate, to be delivered by the end of December for the sum of 6,000 livres (W738); 14 Prairial An II (3 June 1794), the Commissaires de la Trésorerie

Nationale pay David the money for the engraving (W1028); 24 Nivôse An II (13 January 1794), David recommends to the Convention Devosge's drawing of the Lepeletier canvas (W777); record of payment of 400 livres received by Devosge from David for the drawing (W1047).

14 Marat gained notoriety and his sobriquet from his journal *Ami du Peuple* which he began to publish on 12 September 1789. The name of the paper was changed on 25 September 1792 to *Journal de la république française*. He was assassinated on 13 July 1793 by Charlotte Corday. She was guillotined on 17 July.

15 David requests permission to exhibit the pictures (W601); the *Journal de Paris* described the exhibition in the court of the old Louvre (W620). See also Albert Soboul, *Les Sans-culottes parisiens en l'an II*, Paris, 1958, p. 304; and Baticle, op. cit., n. 10, cites an anonymous note of 14 October 1793 in the Deloyne collection: 'Depuis plusiers jours on voit sous un monument élevé à cette occasion dans la cour du Vieux Louvre des deux tableaux ordonnés par la convention et exécutés par David.'

16 20 February 1793, David demands encouragement from the Convention for Fleuriot, who made the bust of Lepeletier, and that the bust be placed next to that of Brutus: '... et que le président pose sur la tête de ce buste la couronne qu'il a placée sur la tête de Michel Lepelletier au moment de sa pompe funèbre' (W414).

17 21 Floréal An II (10 May 1794), Thibaudeau, deputy for Vienne, decrees that copies should be made for Gobelins under David's direction (W977).

18 David declares to the Convention, '... les citoyens Wicar et Devosge ont dessiné les tableaux de Lepelletier et de Marat d'après les originaux que j'avais peints.' Wicar copied the *Marat*, and Devosge the *Lepeletier* (W777).

19 See Werner Szambien, *Jean-Nicolas-Louis Durand*, Paris, 1984, p. 44, n. 34. The idea of the monument was raised on 7 October 1793.

20 *Andromache bewailing the death of Hector*, oil on canvas, 275 × 203 cm, Ecole nationale supérieure des Beaux-Arts, Paris, on deposit at the Louvre, Inv. 8642-DL 1969 1.

21 *Etienne-Jean Delécluze, Journal 1824-28*, Robert Baschet, ed., Paris, 1948, pp. 325-8: 'Hier j'ai vu chez Eugène David le portrait de le Pelletier de Saint-Fargeau... Le Pelletier mort est étendu sur un lit, le corps découvert jusqu'a la ceinture... Au dessus de la poitrine est suspendu, comme l'épée de Damoclès, une épée, un sabre, des gardes du roi. Dans la lâme est enfilée un morceau de papier sur lequel est écrit: "Je vote la mort du tyran". Dans l'angle droit du tableau on lit: A Pelletier David... Comme ce dernier tableau... sera mutilé selon toute apparence... j'ai eu l'idée d'en faire des croquis qui en rappellant les dispositions génerale.' The drawing is reproduced in Robert Baschet, *E.J. Delécluze, témoin de son temps, 1781-1863*, Paris, 1942, p. 272.

22 Etienne-Jean Delécluze, *Louis David, son école et son temps. Souvenirs*, Paris, 1863, p. 150: 'La tête à eté peinte par David, mais le torse... est de la main de son élève Gérard.' The original of the above extended quotation runs (pp. 152-3): 'La composition du tableau de Michel Lepelletier donne une idée assez juste de ce mélange d'appareil tout à la fois fastueux et sanglant. Le personnage est couché sur un lit. Sa tête est ceinte d'une couronne de laurier, et sa poitrine nue laisse voir une large blessure. Au-dessus du cadavre est une épée dont la forme rapelle celles des gardes du roi, dont Pâris avait fait partie. Cette épée, attachée par un fil, est suspendue sur le sein du mort, et dans la lâme est passée une feuille de papier sur laquelle sont écrits ces mots: Je vote la mort du tyran. Au bas du tableau en lit encore: David à Lepelletier, et la date de la mort de ce dernier: 20 janvier 1793.'

23 Auguste Jal, in an aside to his review of the 1827 Salon, *Esquisses, croquis, pochades, ou tout ce qu'on voudra sur le Salon de 1827*, Paris, 1828, p. 385.

24 Dey, op. cit., no. 12, p. 563.

25 Robespierre was overthrown by a *coup d'état* on 9 Thermidor An II (27 July 1794), thus ending the most radical phase of the Revolution.

26 The paintings were returned to David on 20 Pluviôse An III (9 February 1795) (W1166 records the dates as 21 Pluviôse).

27 *The Diary of Joseph Farington*, ed. Kenneth Garlick and Angus Macintyre, 16 vols., New Haven and London, 1978-84, V, p. 1830.

28 Ibid., p. 1861. Farington goes on to say: 'He associated much with Robespierre, and after the death of that dreadful Character would himself have been executed for the part He acted in the days of terror while Robespierre had the rule, had not a consideration for his great ability in the art He professed operated on the minds of those who then had the power. It was signified to him why He was not further pro-

ceeded against & it was recommended to him to go home and devote the remainder of his life to the practise of his profession, his skill in which had produced so great an effect in his favor.' Mlle Jaullie, Jaullia or Julia as she is sometimes spelt, was probably the niece of the Irishman Cooper Penrose whom David had painted in An X (1802). She told Farington that her uncle had sat eighteen times for his portrait and the price was 200 guineas (16 October 1802, p. 1891). Farington arrived in France on 27 August 1802 and returned to England on 10 October.

29 The source of the rumour was Aimée de Coigny, Baticle, op. cit., n. 25. A. Wattine, *Un magistrat révolutionnaire, Michel Lepeletier de Saint-Fargeau*, Paris, 1913.

30 This portrait was recently on the market: *Portrait of Suzanne le Peletier de Saint-Fargeau*, oil on canvas, signed and dated lower left '*L. David 1804*', 60.5×49.5 cm; provenance, by descent in the sitter's family, Sotheby's, London, 11 June 1997, lot 47. See W1426.

31 Napoleon was forced to abdicate in April 1814 and Louis XVIII (1795-1824), brother of Louis XVI, re-entered Paris. Ten months later Napoleon escaped from Elba, but after the brief glory of the 'hundred days', he was defeated at the Battle of Waterloo on 18 June 1815. Louis XVIII returned in July.

32 Law of 12 January 1816 banishes all regicides. Delécluze dines with David on the eve of his departure, 26 January 1816, but David makes no mention of his exile (W1761). In about 1817 David made a list of his works and included '*La mort de Michel Pelletier*' (W1810).

33 Jean Valéry-Radot, 'Autour du portrait de Lepeletier de Saint-Fargeau. Recherches sur le sort du tableau de David', *Archives de l'art Français publiées par la Société de l'histoire de l'art Français*, vol. XXI, Paris, 1949, p. 355, n. 4, 'Je Mettrais un grand prix à ravoir les deux tableaux, mais je voudrais bien avoir être bien sûre qu'il n'en existe pas de copies... Tachés qu'il [David] croye que c'est vous qui faites le marché. Je voudrais bien avoir les deux pour douze mille francs.'

34 Ibid., p. 356, n. 1, 'J'espère que vous réussirez dans votre voyage de Bruxelles, car je ne saurais ajouter foi aux paroles d'honneur de certaines gens et je ne serai tranquille que lorsque le tableau sera hors de leurs mains. Vous pouvez vous en reposer sur moi, sur l'usage que j'en ferai et vous n'auriés pas dû supposer que je puisse détruire le seul souvenir qui me reste. Il sera soigneusement conservé non commme un monument national, mais par respect et tendresse filiale.'

35 Jules David, *Le Peintre Louis David 1748-1825*, 2 vols., Paris, 1880-2, II, p. 570: 'Les quatre toiles toujours couvertes de leur enduit n'y sont pas: la discrétion préside à tout cela.' Cf. Antoine Schnapper and Arlette Sérullaz, ed., *Jacques-Louis David 1748-1825*, exh. cat., Paris, 1989-90. Recorded in the inventory of David works dated 3 March 1826, made after his death, 'dans l'appartement rue St-Germain-des-Près no.14, occupé par M. Gros... 91 Deux originaux représentant Marat et Lepelletier après leur mort, prisés ensemble cinq mille francs ci... 5000' (W2043). In an earlier inventory by David himself *c.* 1822, and published by J. David in *Notice sur le Marat*, 1867, he described both the *Marat* and the *Lepeletier* as commissions from the Convention: '30. Le tableau de Pelletier – Par ordre de la Convention. 31. le tableau du représentant Marat – Idem.' Previously he had always described them as an 'hommage' to the Convention. Gros was ennobled by Charles X in 1824 and drowned himself in 1835.

36 The pictures went on display at 4 rue du Gros Chenet four days before the sale, while the *Marat* and *Lepeletier* were kept at Eugène David's apartment at 11 rue Cadet. For Corbière's indignation see W2053 and Bernadette Wiéner in Sotheby's catalogue, 11 June 1997, op. cit. at n. 30 above, p. 19. Corbière insisted that all visitors to the censured paintings should have a pass signed by Eugène David or Horace Vernet. See W2050–2065.

37 Félix Lepeletier recorded his reaction to the high price: 'Mme. de Mortefontaine... de crainte de voir exposer dans un encan public, un monument touchant de si près à la destinée de son père, s'est décidée... à l'acheter cent mille francs aux héritiers de M. David, qui l'avaient taxé à cette somme exorbitante, puisque dans les premiers jours de son exil, M. David, le père, n'avait vendu que quinze mille francs son beau tableau de Napoléon travaillant dans son cabinet, et six mille francs en 1824, le tableau représentant le pape Pie VII avec le cardinal Caprara.' Valéry-Radot, op. cit., p. 356. Antoine Schnapper, *David, témoin de son temps*, Fribourg, 1980, p. 151. The whole sale brought in only Ffr60,000. David's celebrated portrait of Madame Recamier fetched only Ffr6,000; the unfinished portrait of Barrat Ffr2,000; and the marvel-

lous portrait of Madame de Pastier only made Ffr400.

38 At a second sale on 10 March 1835 the *Marat* was bought back by Baroness Meunier and Eugène David (Ffr4,500). See Schnapper and Sérullaz, op. cit., p. 282. It was left to the Musées Royaux des Beaux Arts, Brussels, in 1893.

39 10 April 1826, the Préfet de Police told M. Corbière that the picture was packed to be transported to 43 rue du Faubourg Saint Honoré (W2058). The contract of sale is published in Valéry-Radot, op. cit., appendix, pp. 362-363.

40 Valéry-Radot, op. cit., pp. 357-8, and see Schnapper and Sérullaz, op. cit., p. 636.

41 Dey, op. cit., p. 563.

42 Stendhal, '... on raconte qu'elle a offert 100.000 fr. du tableau célebré de son père avec l'intention de le brûler. C'est une des meilleures toiles de David.'

43 Valéry-Radot, op. cit., p. 357, n. 1, 'Tant que je ne pourrai pas monter un escalier, je ne verrai pas mon précieux tableau... Quand je l'aurais vu, je vous dirai ce que je voudrais en effacer... Soyez tranquille: mais il faudra trouver de moyens pour que rien un jour ne puisse me jetter dans de nouveaux embarras et puis votre parole d'honneur de ne laisser voir à qui que ce soit... '; and '... Ce pauvre tableau fait bien mal: mais conservéz le moi précieusement.'

44 La Comtesse H. de Reinach-Foussemagne, *Une Fidéle: La Marquise de Lage de Volude 1764-1842 d'après des documents inédits*, Paris, 1908, p. 340: 'Dimanche, 11 avril 1830: Mme de Morfontaine que vous avez vue chez Mme de Montboissier est morte. L'infâme David a fait un portrait de son père en pied, au moment où il est tué par M. Paris, où mieux où il vote la mort du Roi. Elle, très royaliste, qui a beaucoup dépensé pour les alliés, a acheté le tableaux 120,000 francs aux héritiers de David qui le montraient publiquement; elle l'a fait brûler devant témoins; le duc de Gramont, M. de Rosanbo étaient dans son jardin. Ce renouvellement du crime de son père (Pelletier de Saint-Fargeau) l'a conduite au tombeau.' Rosanbo died at his château of St. Marcel l'Ardèche in 1858 and Antoine-Louis-Marie, Duc de Gramont, in 1836. Charles X (1757-1836) succeeded in 1824, fell in the 1830 revolution and remained in exile until his death.

45 Archives Nationales 90AP 55 and 59.

46 31 January 1846.

47 'Champfleury' was the pseudonym of Jules-François-Félix Husson. The letters quoted here are Bibliothèque d'Art et Archéologie Fondation Jacques Doucet, carton 54, dossier VII, liasse 14, 31923 and 31926.

48 Valéry-Radot, op. cit., p. 355, n. 1: 'Il y a 15 ans j'achetai au fils de David le dessin que son père avait fait d'après nature, je le payai cent louis.'

49 Ibid., p. 359, and Chaillou des Barres, 'Les Châteaux d'Ancy-le-Franc, de Saint-Fargeau', *l'Annuaire statistique de l'Yonne, 1839*, Paris, 1845, p. 294.

50 Ibid., p. 359, and des Barres op. cit., p. 295. In his last will, Félix identified his heirs as Mme. Heim, his natural daughter, and Mlle. Cazin.

51 Ibid., p. 355, extract from the anonymous memorandum accompanying the items submitted on 24 May 1837 to Maître Glandaz.

52 Ibid., p.359

53 Attributed to J.-L. David, black chalk, 34 × 25.7 cm (*recto*) *Head of Michel Lepeletier de Saint-Fargeau on his deathbed* (in the opinion of Baticle, op. cit., p. 140, this was made after a death mask, 'd'après le plâtre du masque mortuaire'); (*verso*): *Sketch of a man in profile wearing a crown* and inscribed: '*Dessiné par David et terminé par Meynier*'. Bibliothèque Nationale, Cabinet des Estampes, Paris (t. CXXX fol. 7). Provenance: Charles Meynier (1768-1832), his sale, 26 November-4 December 1832, lot no. 288 (Lugt 13129); bought Michel Hennin, who donated it to the Bibliothèque Nationale in 1863. Engraved by Baron Dominique-Vivant Denon (1747-1825). Arlette Sérullaz, *Inventaire Général des Dessins, École Française: Dessins de Jacques Louis David*, Paris, 1991, does not accept the attribution to David.

54 Marmontel sale, Paris 11-14 May 1868, lot no. 288, 31 × 25cm (Lugt 30517); Henri Rouart (1833-1912), his sale, Paris 16-18 December 1912, lot no. 66. Marguerite de Boisgelin died in Paris on 10 August 1890 and was survived by her two sons, Bruno Louis Marie Victor, Marquis de Boisgelin (1828-95), and Alexandre Marie, Comte de Boisgelin (born 1832). A sale of Boisgelin property took place on 20-21 May 1898 (Lugt 56338), but no paintings were included. Suzanne, Countess Talleyrand, died at Verneuil in 1893. She had two daughters; the younger (1832-1917) married the Prince de Ligne.

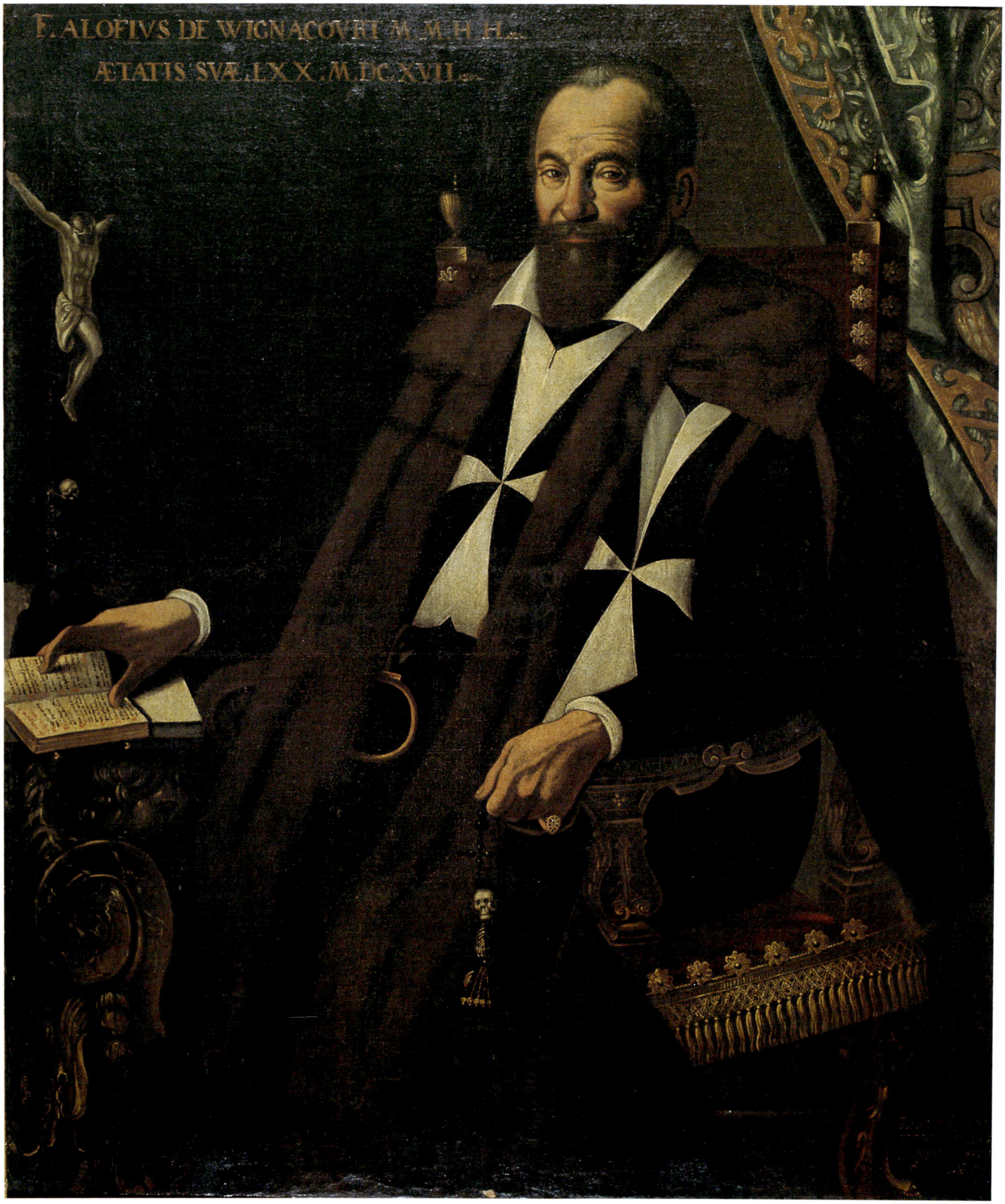
F. ALOFIVS DE WIGNACOVRT M. M. H. H.
ÆTATIS SVÆ. LXX. M. DC. XVII.

Michelangelo Merisi da Caravaggio

c. 1571-1610

Portrait of the Grand Master of the Knights of Malta, Alof de Wignacourt

1547-1622, Grand Master 1601-22

Probably oil on canvas
Probably 136 × 113 cm

Giovanni Baglione (1566-1643) first recorded, in 1642, that Caravaggio painted the portrait of Alof de Wignacourt, Grand Master of the Order of the Knights of St. John of Jerusalem:

> Poscia andossene a Malta, e introdotto a far riverenza al gran Maestro, fecegli il ritratto; onde quel principe in segno di merito dell' abito di San Giovanni il regalò e creollo cavaliere di grazia.[1]

Baglione, himself a painter, knew Caravaggio and indeed brought a libel action against him and others, including the artist Orazio Gentileschi, alleging that they had written and published scurrilous verses about him. In the court case, heard in August 1603, Caravaggio at first denied having had anything to do with these writings, but then declared that he did not think much of Baglione as a painter, and described one of his works at the centre of the dispute as 'clumsy'. Baglione gained his revenge when he wrote Caravaggio's biography, in which, among other things, he described him as 'a mocking and arrogant man', an assessment amply reflected in contemporary correspondence and literature.[2] During the libel trial, which continued into September, Caravaggio was held in prison, although he was released towards the end of the month, but a similar pattern of events, of falling foul of the law, imprisonment and release (or escape) was to be repeated throughout Caravaggio's colourful career.

Giovanni Pietro Bellori (1613-96) subsequently records two paintings by Caravaggio of Alof de Wignacourt in his biographies of artists published in 1672, and that they were executed after Caravaggio arrived in Malta, which was in July 1607:

> Caravaggio... decided to move to that island where, upon his arrival, he was introduced to the Grand Master Wignacourt, a Frenchman. He portrayed him armed and standing, and seated, without armour in the dress of the Grand Master. The first of these portraits is in the Armoury at Malta.[3]

The first, full-length, portrait can be identified with a picture in the Louvre, oil on canvas 194 × 134 cm.[4] The other portrait of Wignacourt, showing him seated 'in the dress of the Grand Master' has been missing since the seventeenth century, but is recorded in a copy in Malta, at the Collegio dei Canonici della Grotta di S. Paolo in Rabat.[5] This establishment was founded by Wignacourt himself in 1619, and so this picture can presumably be accepted as an accurate reflection of the missing original. It bears a clear inscription identifying the sitter and the date of the copy, 1617:

'F. ALOFIVS DE WIGNACOVRT M.M.H.H.
Æ TATIS SVÆ. LXX. M.DC. XVII.'

Grand Master Alof de Wignacourt in the robes of Grand Master. Copy, 1617, perhaps by Giovanni Domenico Corso, of lost portrait by Michelangelo Merisi da Caravaggio (*c.* 1571-1610) of 1608.
Oil on canvas, 136 × 113 cm.
Wignacourt Collegiate Museum, Rabat, Malta

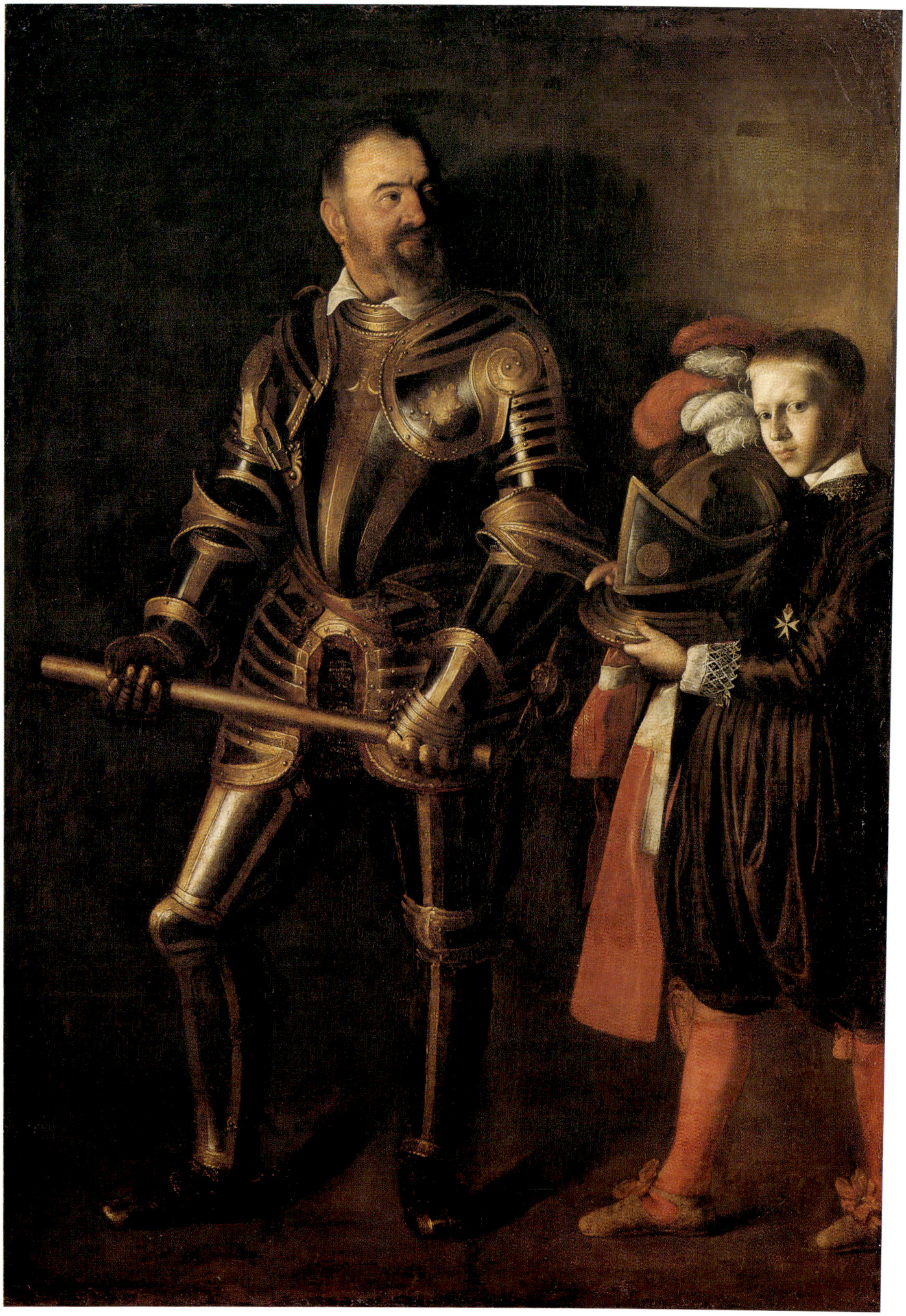

Grand Master Alof de Wignacourt in armour, with a page by Caravaggio, 1608.
Oil on canvas, 195 × 134 cm.
Musée du Louvre, Paris

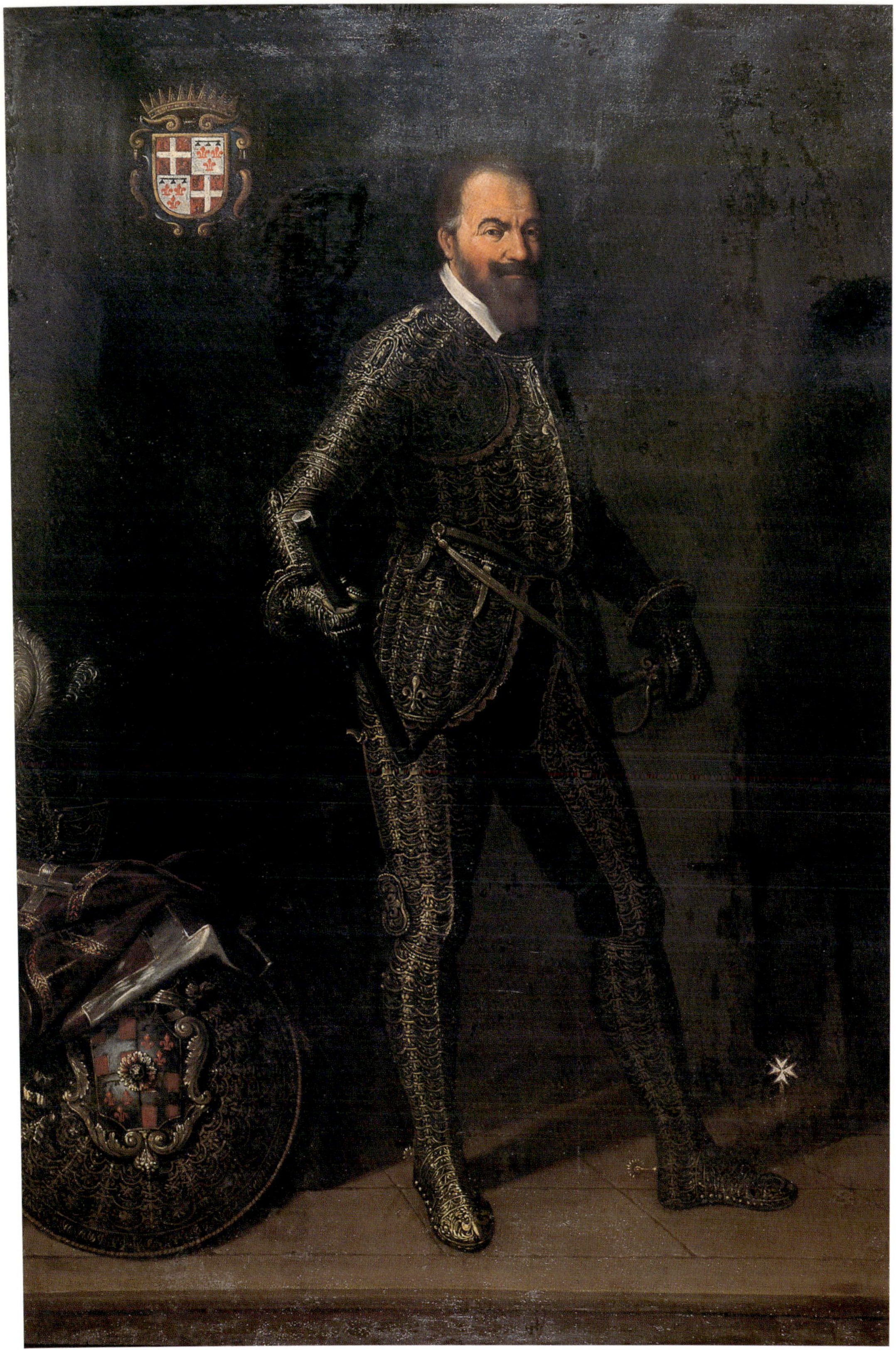

Grand Master Alof de Wignacourt in armour, formerly attributed to Cassarino, now attributed to Leonello Spada (1576-1622).
Oil on canvas. Museum of Fine Arts, Malta

The artist who made it is probably to be identified as Giovanni Domenico Corso by the letters '*G.NF. D.C.*' that also appear.[6]

The lost picture is, however, also reflected in an engraving by Philippe Thomassin as early as 1609, showing the head only, but reproduced in the same sense as the original. It bears an inscription identifying the sitter and his age and therefore, by inference, the date of the print. It appeared in the edition of that year (which is dated on the frontispiece) of the *Statuti della Sac. Religione di S.Gio.Gerosolimitano*, published in Rome by the printers Camerali.[7] The inscription reads: '*FR. ALOPHIUS DE WIGNACOVRT AET. SVAE LXII*'. This engraving was in turn the likely inspiration for another engraving, by Boyssart, of Wignacourt published in 1612 as the frontispiece of *l'Histoire des Chevaliers de l'Ordre de l'Hopital de Saint Jean de Jerusalem*, where Wignacourt is described as sixty-four years old, which suggests that this engraving was actually completed in 1611.[8]

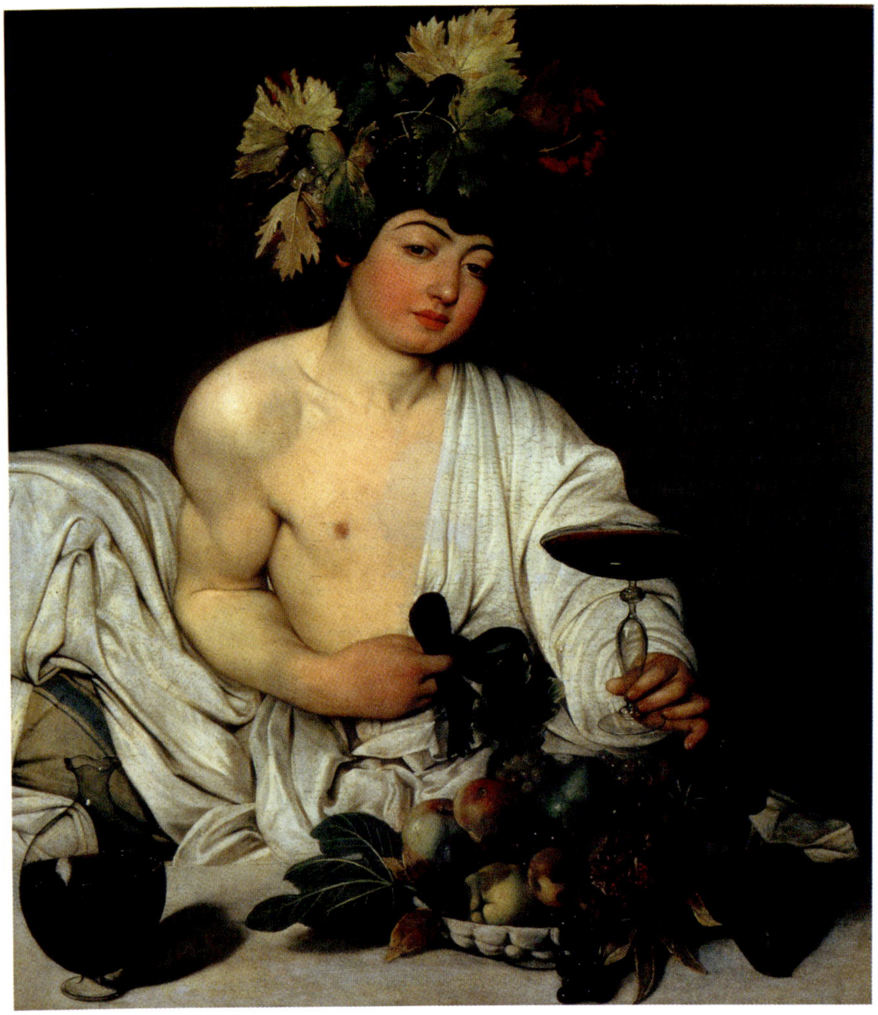

Self-portrait as Bacchus by Caravaggio, *c.* 1595. Oil on canvas, 95 × 85 cm. Uffizi, Florence

Caravaggio arrived in Malta having had to flee Rome, after killing Ranuccio Tommasoni of Terni on 26 May 1606 in a fight that had arisen over a game of tennis played in the Campo Marzio. He himself had been wounded in the head and throat by someone else in the preceding year, and he appears with alarming frequency in cases of assault and for bearing weapons without a licence. In 1601 and 1602 he was accused of armed assault; in 1604 a waiter accused him of drawing a sword and hurling a plate of artichokes at him; he was arrested for further arms offences in the same year (twice) and wounding a notary in the back of the head in 1605. On this last occasion, he had fled to Genoa, only to return after an agreement was reached out of court.

It would appear that on most, even all, of these occasions, Caravaggio received, directly or indirectly, the protection of powerful patrons who were reluctant to lose the services of such an outstanding if wayward genius.[9] On the occasion of his finally committing murder, in 1606, Caravaggio was hidden by one of these well-connected well-wishers, the Principe Marzio Colonna, on his estates to the south of Rome, before Caravaggio moved on to Naples in the autumn of that year. Here too he was initially welcomed. The Viceroy in Naples, for example, Juan Alonso Pimentel Herrera, Conde di Benevente, was himself a sophisticated art collector, and the eighteenth-century biographer Bernardo de Dominici wrote:

> Caravaggio came to Naples, where he was received with great acclaim by both painters and lovers of painting and he painted many works there.[10]

His most ambitious work was the great altarpiece, the *Madonna of Mercy*, for the church of the Confraternity of the Pio Monte della Misericordia, which showed the Seven Acts of Mercy.

The dark side of Caravaggio's character, however, continued to reveal itself at intervals, as reflected in the court hearings that offer much of the information that

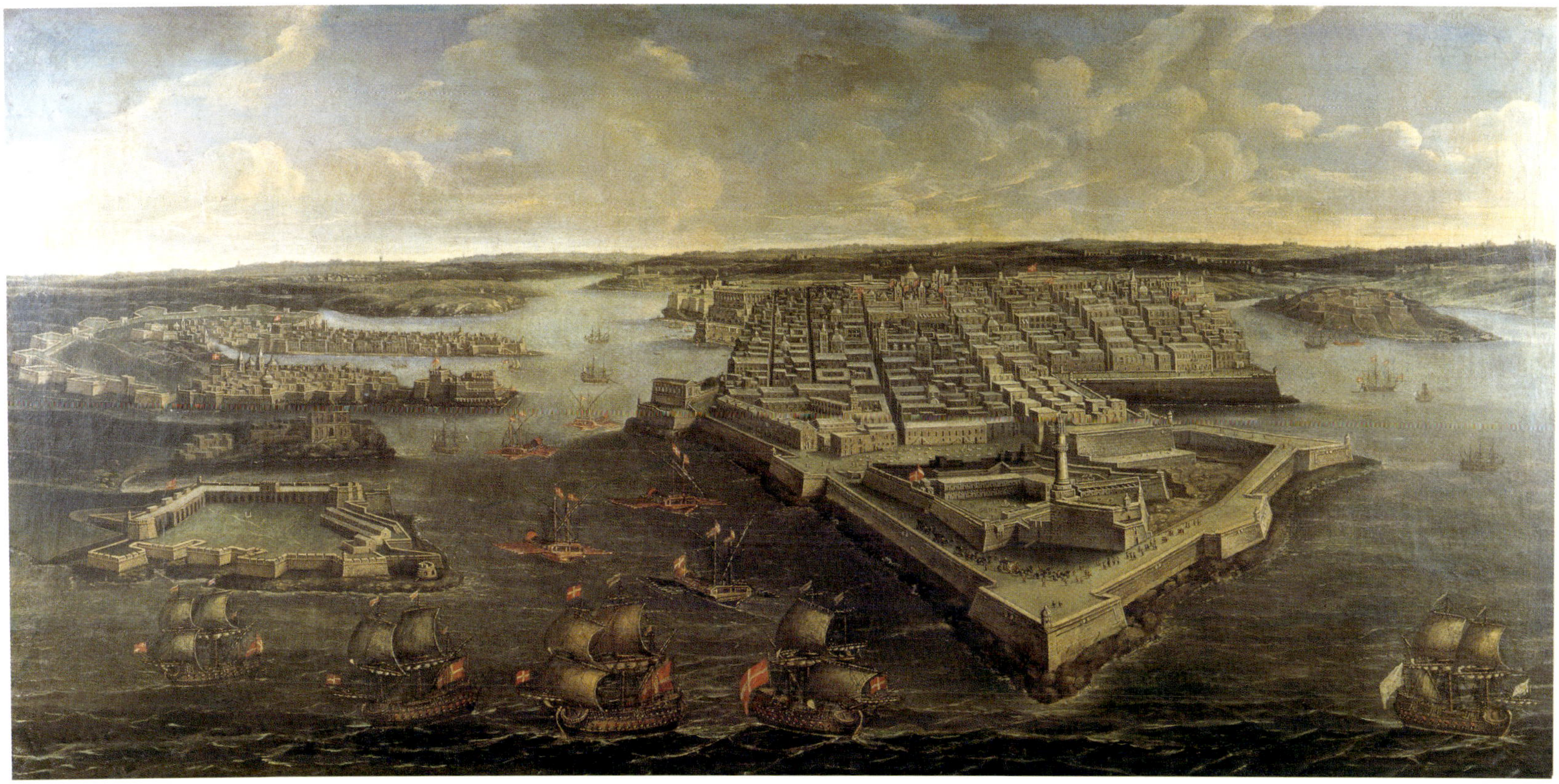

The Grand Harbour and City of Valletta, Malta, Italian school, 18th century. Oil on canvas, 106.7 × 207.6 cm. The Wallace Collection, London

is known about his life. Caravaggio's journey to Malta has to be seen in this context, and by 14 July 1607 he was already lodged with one of the Knights of St. John, Fra Giacomo Marchese, and enjoying the company of other members of the Order. Exactly one year later, he contrived to be admitted as what was formally termed a 'Knight of Obedience of the Order of the Knights of St. John of Jerusalem'.

The rules about becoming a knight were strict, and in principle there were two methods: by virtue of the possession of an unbroken noble lineage – 'di giustizia' – and through merit – 'di grazia'. Caravaggio could only take the latter route. His motives are obvious, but it is not so obvious why the Order of St. John should have so welcomed this particular new knight, who had such a bad reputation. In fact, it was the Grand Master of the Order himself, Wignacourt, who vigorously campaigned on Caravaggio's behalf. He admired Caravaggio's art and was certain that he and the Order would be immortalised through his paintings. Wignacourt corresponded with Pope Paul V, finally obtaining the Pope's permission to bestow the rank of knight on Caravaggio, and on 14 July 1608 the painter was received into the Order. In admitting Caravaggio to the Order, Wignacourt declared:

Whereas it behoves the leaders and rulers of commonweals to prove their benevolence by advancing men, not only on account of their noble birth but also on account of their art and science whatever it may be... And whereas the Honourable Michael Angelo, a native of the town Carraca in Lombardy called Caravaggio in the vernacular, having landed in this city and burning with zeal for the Order, has recently communicated to us his fervent wish to be adorned with the habit and insignia of our Knightly Order... Therefore, we wish to gratify the desire of this excellent painter, so that our Island Malta, and our Order may at last find glory in this adopted disciple and citizen with no less pride than the island of Kos (also within our jurisdiction) extols her Apelles; and that, should we compare him to more recent [artists] of our age, we may not afterwards be envious of the artistic excellence of some other man, outstanding in his art, whose name and brush are equally important.

Every new knight had to pay on admission a 'passaggio', a large sum of money, and it was also expected from him that he would leave on his death a substantial part of his wealth to the Order. It has been suggested that Caravaggio offered his now completed *The beheading of St. John the Baptist* to the Oratory of the Cathedral of St. John in Valetta in part payment or in lieu of money and that this was accepted. That may be so, although Bellori appears to say that it was the full-length portrait of Wignacourt that led to his being made a 'cavaliere di grazia', and records that in addition to this honour he was rewarded by Wignacourt with 'a precious chain of gold [a signal of courtly favour given to artists during this period, for example, to Rubens and to Van Dyck] and two slaves along with other signs of his esteem and satisfaction with his work'.

But Caravaggio was not to remain a knight for long. He fell into trouble again, for reasons that remain obscure, although both Baglione and Bellori suggest that he fell out with a notable 'cavaliere di giustizia', was jailed but escaped, and finally fled the island for Syracuse in Sicily in October 1608. Bellori records:

... all of a sudden his turbulent nature brought his prosperity to an end and caused him to lose the favour of the Grand Master [Wignacourt]; because of a very inopportune quarrel with a most noble knight he was thrown into prison and subjected to misery, fear and maltreatment.[11]

The rules stipulated that no one was allowed to leave Malta without the written permission of the Grand Master and so Caravaggio was deprived of his habit, and expelled from the Order on 1 December 1608, '... thrust forth like a rotten and fetid limb from our Order and Community'.[12] The manner of his leaving was sufficiently incorrect: he achieved a daring escape at night from the fortress prison of Castel Sant' Angelo, Vittoriosa. It is conceivable that he was allowed to escape, to avoid embarrassment all round, although Caravaggio's subsequent travails may partly have been the result of pursuing knights of the Order or their agents.

Having reached Sicily, Caravaggio moved to Messina where he worked in 1609, being still described (or still describing himself) as a 'Knight of Jerusalem'. He went to Palermo in August or September, perhaps because of wounding a schoolteacher who had objected to his unhealthy interest in his pupils,[13] and reached Naples in September or October. He was himself certainly wounded badly in the face while in Naples – having found himself surrounded by armed men 'in the doorway of the

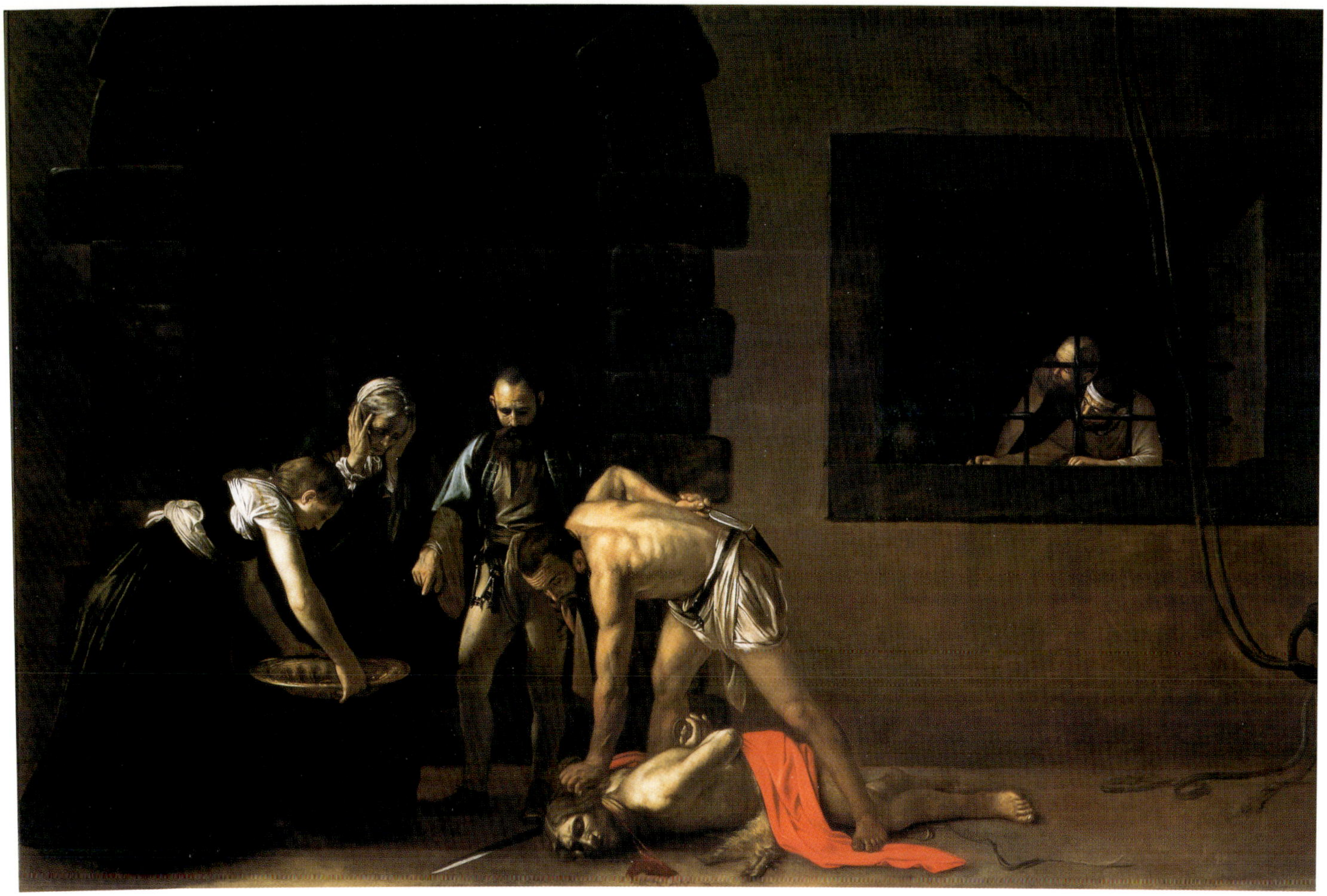

The execution of St. John the Baptist by Caravaggio, 1608.
Oil on canvas, 361 × 520 cm.
Cathedral of St. John, Malta

Osteria del Ciriglio' – and died at Porto Ercole in late July 1610. Contemporary reports show that he had still not lost the regard of his supporters, for by this date the Pope had officially pardoned him for his capital offence of murder, and he was free to return to Rome. He may not have heard about the pardon, however, and have been en route for some of his protectors in Genoa.[14] According to Bellori, he had just attempted, without success, to regain the favour of Wignacourt through the gift of a half-length showing Salome with the head of St. John the Baptist.

Caravaggio's two portraits of Alof de Wignacourt were painted between July 1607 and October 1608. The Louvre full-length shows Wignacourt clad in a splendid suit of armour accompanied by a page holding his helmet. Although Bellori refers to *Alof de Wignacourt with a page* as being 'in the Armoury at Malta' in his book published in 1672, his information was by then out of date, for this picture was in France as early as 1 March 1644. This is the date on which the English diarist, writer and collector John Evelyn (1620-1706), who had left England on the Grand Tour, saw the painting in the collection (in the rue de Seine) of Roger du Plessis, Duc de Liancourt (1598-1674):

> Cavaliero du Malta, attended by his page, said to be of Michelangelo [da Caravaggio].

Wignacourt came from a very old family in Picardy and the picture had presumably gone to France after Wignacourt's death at the age of seventy-five, which took place on 14 September 1622.

The Duc de Liancourt's collection passed after his death in 1674 to his granddaughter, who had married François, Duc de la Rochefoucauld, in 1659. In 1670, however, Louis XIV had acquired Caravaggio's painting ('un portrait d'un grandmaistre de malte faict par Michel Lange') for 14,300 livres from '[les] sieurs Vinot et Hoursel', the latter being the secretary of the Duc de Vrillière. The picture is then mentioned by André Félibien (1619-95).[15] There are, however, no sources which state that Wignacourt's other, seated, portrait had taken the same route to France. If Susinno had first-hand knowledge, the picture was still in existence in 1724 (when he referred to it), the sitter being described as 'in abito signorile di pompa', but he may simply have been adapting an earlier record such as that of Bellori.[16]

It is generally assumed that the standing portrait post-dates the lost, seated, portrait. That is not necessarily the case, and there is the possibility, rather, that it was painted by Caravaggio as a demonstration of how much better a painter he was than Cassarino (or Leonello Spada), whose two standing full-lengths of Wignacourt in armour survive in Malta. Such a demonstration of his own superiority might well have been the way in which Caravaggio won Wignacourt's good opinion, and certain factors suggest that this may have been the sequence of events. First, the portrait very obviously draws upon the grand portraits of an earlier age, specifically those of Titian and artists of the time in the Veneto, and is perhaps closest to the 1556 portrait usually attributed to Veronese of the Pase Guariento (Museo del Castelvecchio, Verona).[17] Indeed, the armour which Wignacourt wears is not of the time but of the period around 1550.[18] That it was Wignacourt's personal commission is suggested by the fact that the portrait did not remain in Malta after his death but went to France. In contrast, both the standing full-lengths by Cassarino (or Spada) of Wignacourt are still in Malta, one in the National Museum (formerly in the Armoury), the other in the Palace of the Grand Masters at Valletta, and they show the sitter wearing contemporary armour of the first years of the seventeenth century. Furthermore, these two portraits, which differ only slightly, do not reflect Caravaggio's composition, as would seem more likely if they were commissioned after his portrait, especially since Caravaggio was patronised and praised by the Grand Master himself.

The location of the original seated portrait is never recorded in the sources, which raises the possibility that quite early on it was remembered as having been painted but was no longer visible in Malta. On the other hand, since Wignacourt was specifically shown 'a sedere disarmato nell' habito di Gran Maestro' as Bellori describes it, or 'vestito in abito signorile di pompa' as Susinno puts it, it would appear that this was very much an official and public portrait, a fact also reflected in its employment as the source for the engraved portrait of Wignacourt which appeared in the *Statutes of the Order* published in Rome in 1609.[19] In contrast, the full-length portrait in armour was not engraved until the picture was in the French royal collection.[20]

The seated portrait may therefore have remained on the island so long as the Order of St. John was still established there. Its fate must be a matter of conjecture, but there would seem to be two main possibilities. From Wignacourt's death (1622) until the arrival of Napoleon (1798) the status of the Knights of Malta did not change. Their most important enemy, the Ottoman Empire, became weaker in these two centuries, especially in the eighteenth. It may be that the portrait vanished with other Napoleonic plunder on the occasion of the French invasion; but it might be that by this time it had already gone to France at some point following the death of the sitter in 1622.

NOTES

1 G.Baglione, *Le vite de' pittori, scultori e architetti...*, 1642, p. 138. 'Then he went to Malta, and being introduced in order to pay homage to the Grand Master, he painted his portrait; which is why that prince as a sign of his merit gave him the cloth of St John and made him a "cavaliere di grazia" [Knight of the Order].' The early biographies of Caravaggio are published, together with a translation into English, in W.Friedlaender, *Caravaggio Studies*, Princeton, 1955, Part III, 'Biographies and Studies', pp. 227ff., with the exception of that by Susinno (see n. 13 below).

2 See, for example, J.Gash, *Caravaggio*, London, 1988, p. 13: Caravaggio was often referred to by his acquaintances as possessed of 'un cervello stravolto' or 'stravagantissimo' – a 'highly disturbed brain'.

3 G.P.Bellori, *Le vite de' pittore, scultori, ed architetti moderni*, Rome, 1672, p. 209; see also F.Baldinucci, *Notizie dei professori del disegno...*, edn. 1845-7, vol. III, p. 686.

4 *The Age of Caravaggio*, exh. cat., New York, 1985, no. 94, pp. 328ff.; M.Marini, *Io Michelangelo da Caravaggio*, Rome, 1974, no. 74, pp. 435ff.

5 Marini, op. cit., no. 73, p. 435, where he also refers to and illustrates another copy (identified as copy E.1) showing the figure full-length, which is in the church over the Grotto of St. Paul, although it must be said that the physical resemblance between these two sitters is not entirely convincing. A third portrait hitherto supposed to be of Wignacourt, in the Palazzo Pitti, Florence, appears in Marini as no. 79, but is now generally accepted to be a portrait by Caravaggio not of Wignacourt but of Fra Antonio Martelli: M.Chiarini, 'La probabile identità del "cavaliere di Malta" di Pitti', *Antichità viva*, XXVIII, 4 (1989), pp. 15-16; J.Gash, 'The identity of Caravaggio's "Knight of Malta"', *Burlington Magazine*, CXXXIX (1997), pp. 156-60.

6 Marini, op. cit., p. 435.

7 M.Gregori, 'A new painting and some observations on Caravaggio's journey to Malta', *Burlington Magazine*, CXVI October 1974, pp. 594-603, p. 595, fig. 42.

8 Ibid., p. 597. Another portrait of Wignacourt by Caravaggio showed the head only and in an oval, and it seems logical to suppose that this portrait, which has also been lost, was directly related to the lost seated portrait of Wignacourt. This head in an oval was in the possession of Fra Francesco d'Antella , who was Secretary to, and a close friend of, the Grand Master. It was taken back to Florence by d'Antella when, in 1611, as a reward from Wignacourt, he was given the Commandery of S.Giacomo in Campo Corbolini, Florence. He kept the portrait in the manor house in the grounds of the Commandery. Caravaggio also painted for d'Antella the *Sleeping Cupid* which was in Florence by 1609 and which is still there, in Palazzo Pitti. See Helen Langdon, *Caravaggio*, London, 1998, pp. 354-5.

9 J.Gash, op. cit., pp. 16ff., discusses the various family connections of Caravaggio's protectors and patrons. A full account of Caravaggio's life is Langdon, op. cit.

10 B.de Domenici, *Vite de' pittori, scultori, ed architetti napolitani* (1742), edn. 1844, vol. III, p. 40.

11 Bellori, op. cit.

12 Quoted Gash, op. cit., p. 27.

13 Ibid., referring to F.Susinno, *Vite de' pittori messinesi* (1724), ed. V.Martinelli, Florence, 1960, who recorded Caravaggio's time in Messina.

14 Ibid., p. 16.

15 A.Félibien, *Entretiens sur les vies et les ouvrages des plus excellents peintres anciens et moderns*, 10 vols., 1666-88 (edn. 1725), III, pp. 187, 191.

16 Susinno, op. cit., p. 109.

17 See *The Age of Caravaggio*, op. cit., p. 328; the portrait is now given to Domenico Brusasorci.

18 M.Maindron, 'Le portrait du Grand-Maître Alof de Wignacourt au Musée du Louvre', *Revue de l'Art Ancien et Moderne*, XXIV (1908), pp. 241-54, who states that the armour is still in the Armoury of Malta, along with the other suit of armour that belonged to Wignacourt in which he is shown by Cassarino. It might also be observed that Caravaggio shows Wignacourt's moustache and beard cut in a manner different from their appearance in the Cassarino (or Spada) portraits, much more, in fact, in the style adopted by sitters in the earlier North Italian portraits which appear to have served as Caravaggio's model. In the Cassarino/Spada portraits Wignacourt's moustache is swept up at either end, and he appears somewhat younger.

19 See above. The official nature of this image is noted in *The Age of Caravaggio*, op. cit., p. 328.

20 Engraved by Nicholas Larmessin, in reverse, in P.Crozat, *Recueil d'estampes d'après les tableaux... dans le Cabinet du Roy...* , Paris, 1729-42, I, p. 36, pl. 92 (a print of which is in the Witt Collection at the Courtauld Institute of Art, London).

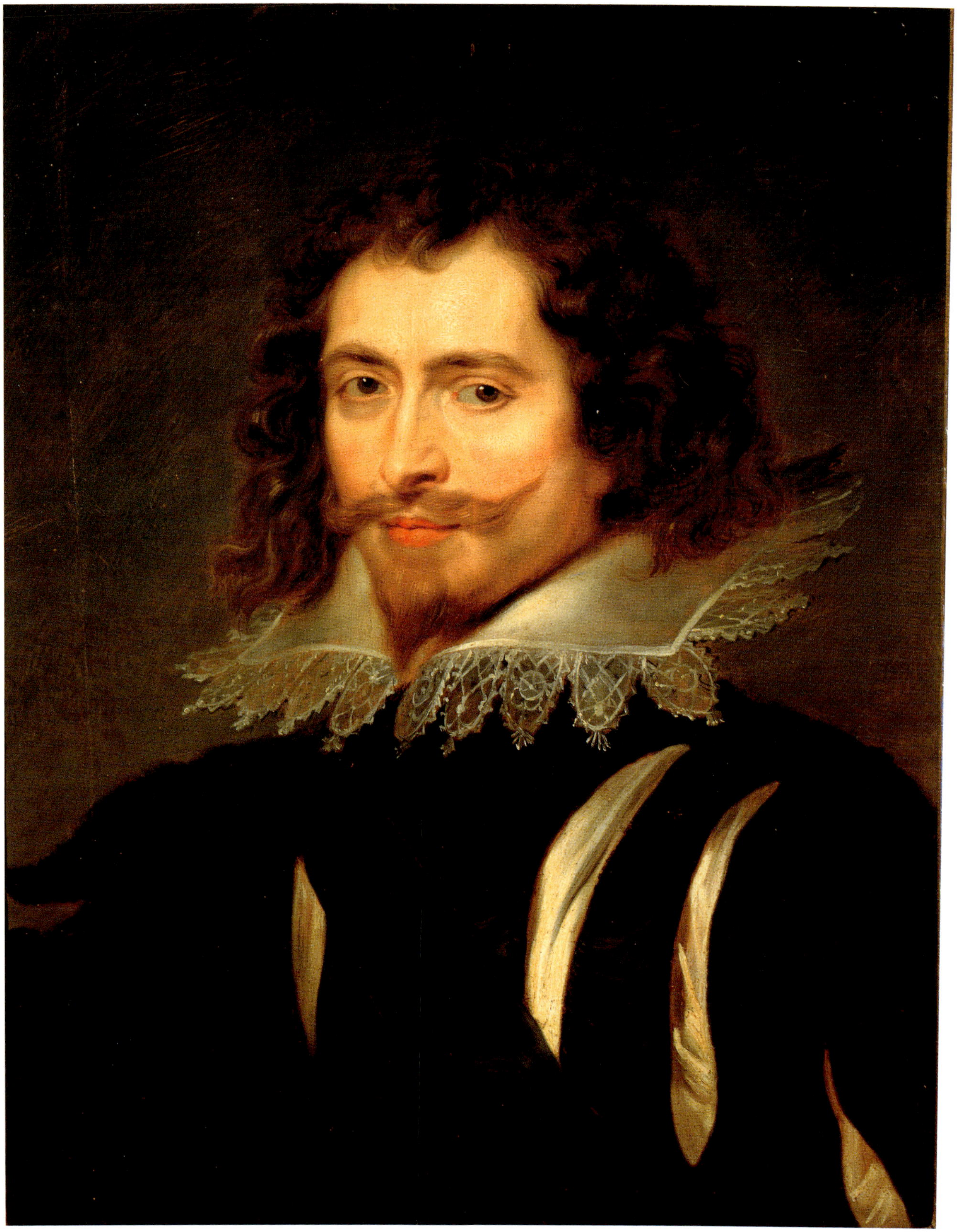

Peter Paul Rubens

1577-1640

Portrait of George Villiers, Duke of Buckingham

c. 1625

Oil on panel
c. 63 × 48 cm

On his arrival at court in 1614, the handsome George Villiers (1592-1628) soon attracted the attentions of James I. Sir John Oglander (1585-1655) wrote that James 'loved young men, his favourites, better than women, loving them beyond the love of men to women. I never saw any fond husband make so much or so great dalliance over his beautiful spouse as I have seen King James over his favourites, especially the Duke of Buckingham'.[1] This relationship with the King ensured Villiers' rapid rise at the English court, and the bestowal of many honours and titles.[2] Buckingham was also a close friend of Charles, Prince of Wales, and travelled to Madrid with him in 1623 in the abortive attempt to arrange Charles's marriage to the daughter of the Spanish king. While there he helped to encourage Charles's interest in the arts. After the Prince ascended the throne on 27 March 1625 as Charles I, Buckingham retained his position at court,[3] and became much involved in the running of the country for the next few years, although he made many enemies in so doing. He was assassinated at Portsmouth in 1628 by James Felton, who perceived him as a focus of his disaffection.

In May 1625 Buckingham went to Paris to attend the marriage by proxy of Henrietta Maria, daughter of Henry IV of France (d. 1610) and Marie de Médicis, to the young King Charles I, and to accompany her back to England. His luggage was packed with gorgeous and extravagant attire to wear on his visit:

> His Grace has for his body twenty seven rich suits embroidered and laced with silk and silver plusches, besides one rich white satten uncut velvet suit, set all over... with diamonds, the value whereof is thought to be four score thousand pounds, besides a feather made with great diamonds, with sword, girdle, hat-band and spurs with diamonds; which suit his Grace intends to enter into Paris with.[4]

Rubens was also in Paris at this time to install the great decorative scheme commissioned by the Queen for the Château de Luxembourg (the canvases are now in the Louvre), and the two were introduced, probably by Balthasar Gerbier (1591-1667), Buckingham's agent. The Duke, anxious to enlarge his rapidly growing art collection, was eager to acquire some of Rubens's paintings and antiquities, and this was probably discussed at their meeting, which possibly took place at Fontainebleau.[5] A letter written in 1625 to Buckingham by Gerbier shows the speed and single-mindedness of the Duke's collecting:

> Sometimes when I am contemplating the treasure of rarities which Your Excellency has in so short a time amassed, I cannot but feel astonished in the midst of my joy. For out of all the amateurs and princes and kings, there is not one who had collected in forty years as many pictures as Your Excellency has in five.[6]

Rubens had become court painter to Archduke Albert (d. 1621) and Archduchess

George Villiers, 1st Duke of Buckingham.
Studio of Peter Paul Rubens.
Copy of lost portrait by
Peter Paul Rubens (1577-1640).
Oil on canvas, 63 × 48 cm.
Pitti Palace, Florence

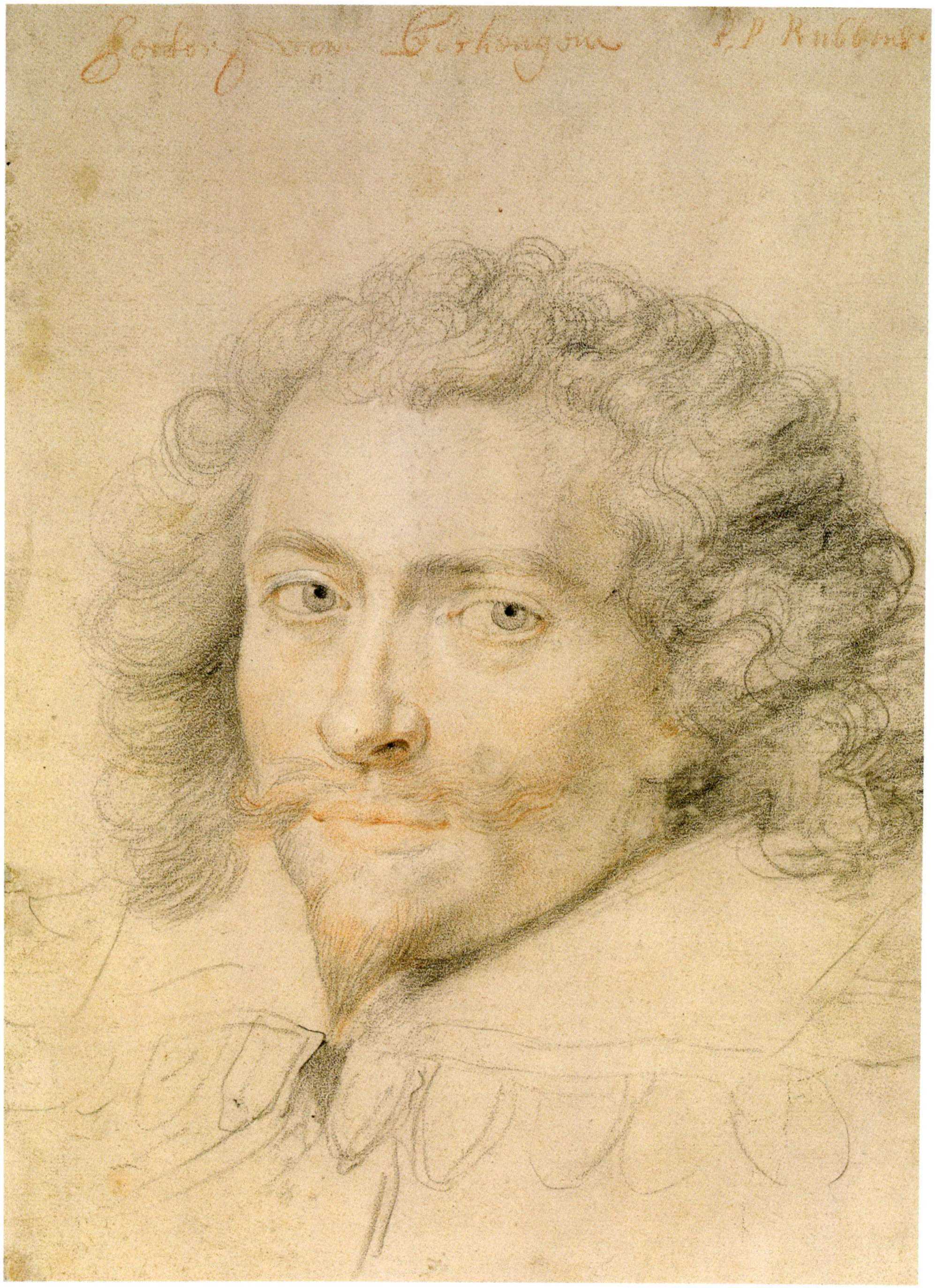

George Villiers, 1st Duke of Buckingham (1592-1628) by Peter Paul Rubens, 1625.
Black, red and white chalk, 38.3 × 26.6 cm.
Graphische Sammlung, Albertina, Vienna

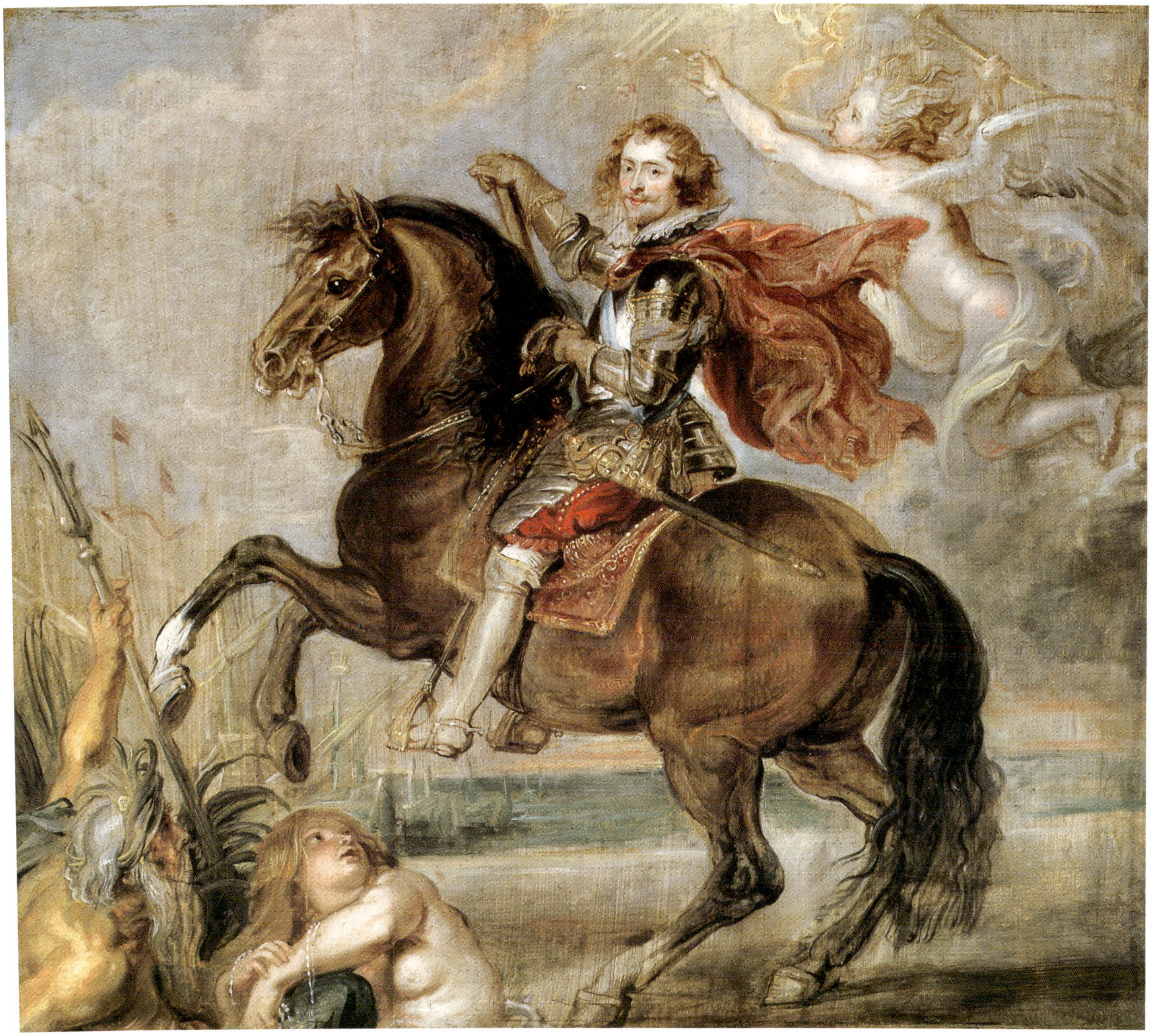

Study for *Equestrian portrait of George Villiers, 1st Duke of Buckingham* by Peter Paul Rubens, 1625.
Oil on wood, 46.6 × 51.7 cm.
Kimbell Art Museum, Fort Worth

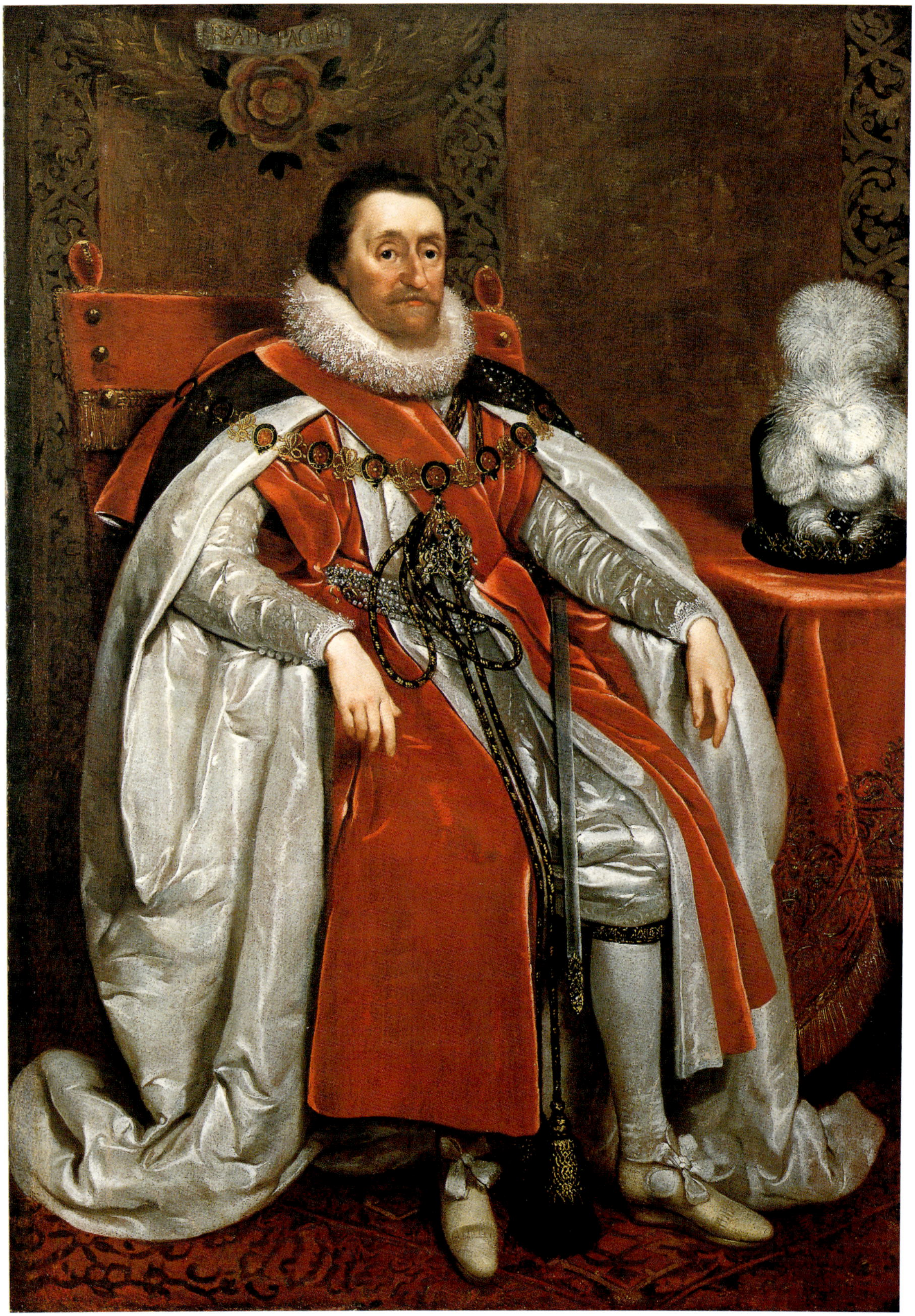

Isabella (1566-1633), rulers of the Spanish Netherlands, after his return from Italy in 1608. Since 1623 he had been involved in diplomatic affairs on behalf of the Archduchess, and was given the difficult task of trying to achieve peace between Spain and the Habsburg empire on the one hand and France and England on the other. Rubens was keen to develop his career as a diplomat, which necessitated his becoming more financially independent, and the large sum Buckingham offered him for his collection was therefore rather tempting. An even more profound motive was, of course, that Buckingham was also involved in the peace negotiations between England and Spain, and anything that could ensure his good will was desirable.

In a letter written to Signor di Valaves in Paris, Rubens gives an interesting insight into Buckingham's character:

> When I consider the caprice and arrogance of Buckingham I pity this young king who through bad counsel throws himself and his kingdom into such extremity without any need.[7]

This is a rather more realistic observation than the optimistic view of Buckingham's twentieth-century biographer, C.R.Cammell, who wrote:

> Friendship between Buckingham and Rubens was immediate: the two men were of a nature to understand and like one another, and their admiration was warm and mutual. To their meeting we owe the good fortune of being able to see the Duke through Rubens' eyes as he was when Anne of Austria saw him.[8]

Two portraits of Buckingham by Rubens, both now destroyed, are listed in the 1635 inventory of one of Buckingham's London residences, York House, as being

James I
by Daniel Mytens
(1590-1647), 1621.
Oil on canvas,
148.6 × 100.6 cm.
National Portrait Gallery,
London

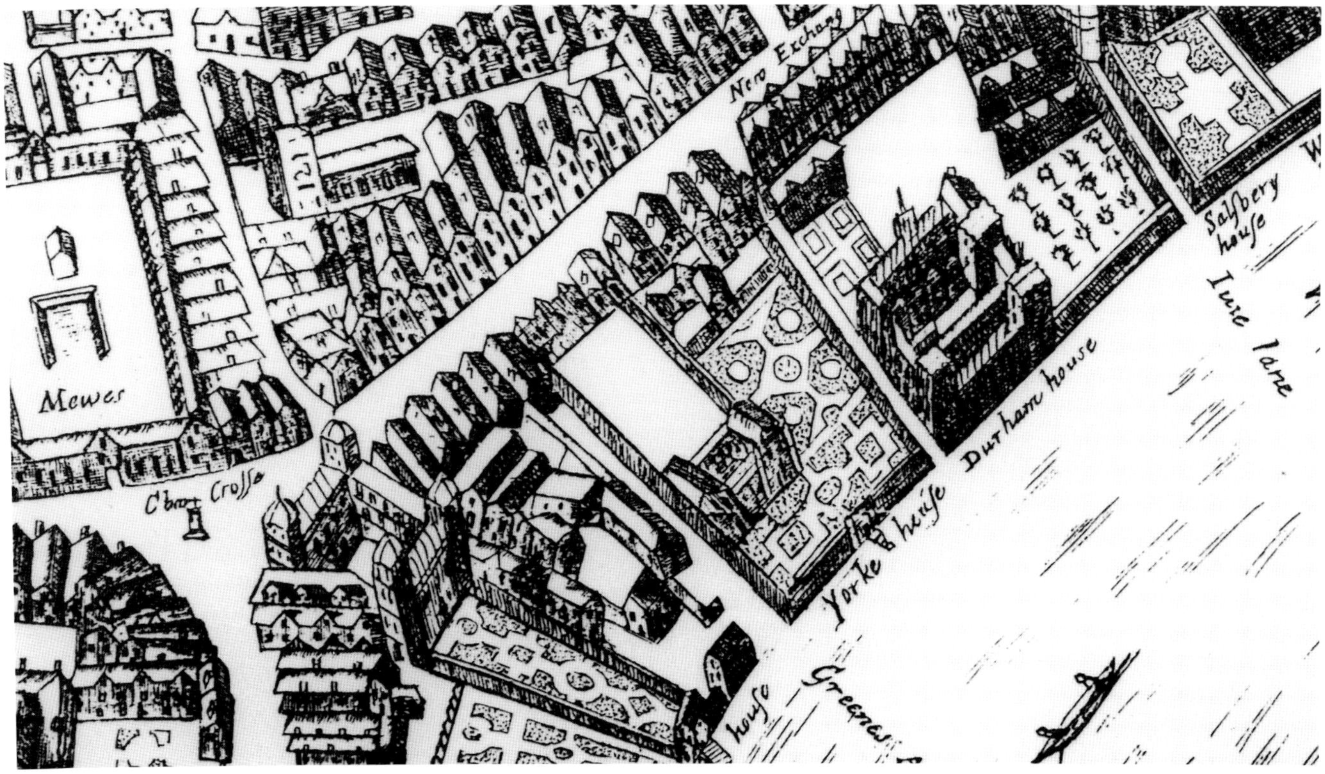

York House, London.
Detail of engraving by
Faithorne and Newcourt,
1658.
Guildhall Library
and Art Gallery, London

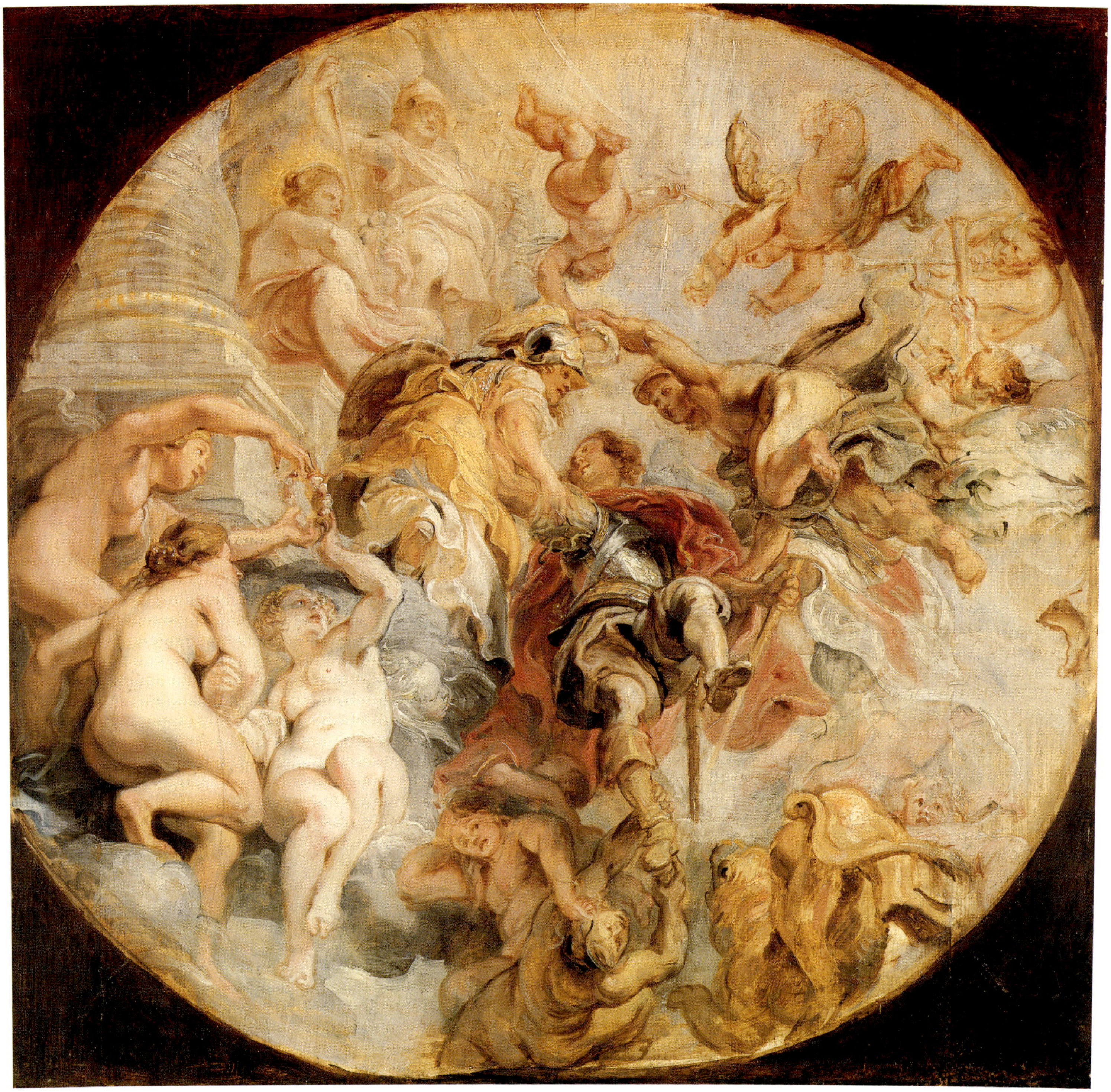

Study for *Minerva and Mercury conducting the Duke of Buckingham to the Temple of Virtue*
by Peter Paul Rubens.
Oil on wood, 64 × 63.7 cm.
National Gallery, London

'In the Great Chamber'. One of them, a large equestrian portrait of the Duke wearing armour and the Order of the Garter, and accompanied by allegorical figures, was intended to glorify the Duke in his role as Lord Admiral. Rubens was already working on it in the autumn of 1625, and a payment to the artist of £500 'for drawing his L^ps^ picture on horseback' was also made that year.[9] The equestrian portrait is described in the inventory as 'Reuben – My Lord Duke on Horseback' and a second portrait was described as by 'Reuben – A great piece for the ceiling of my Lord's Closett'.[10] The latter was the *Glorification of the Duke of Buckingham* which showed the Duke being carried upwards by Minerva and Mercury, rivalling the (later) *Apotheosis of James I* (ceiling, Banqueting House, Whitehall). Both paintings were destroyed by fire in 1949, although the oil sketches for them survive (Kimbell Museum, Fort Worth; National Gallery, London), and both may have been sent from Paris to Buckingham on 18 September 1627 when Rubens reported that several pictures painted by him for the Duke were ready to be sent off.[11] The equestrian portrait was in oil on canvas and measured 307 × 337 cm; the *Glorification of the Duke of Buckingham* was also in oil on canvas, 541 × 498 cm (formerly in the collection of the Earl of Jersey at Osterley Park).

Both these portraits would ultimately have been based upon Rubens's drawing of the Duke's head which he made when they met in Paris between 14 May and 2 June 1625,[12] but it would seem that there was also a study or, more probably, judging from later descriptions, a finished portrait in oils which would have served as the immediate model. That painting is now lost,[13] although its appearance can be assumed to be known from a Rubens studio copy (Palazzo Pitti, Florence).[14] In fact, although this painting, which shows the Duke in a lace collar and slashed doublet, would also have been available for reference in the studio, the evidence of subsequent sale descriptions suggests that the Duke was portrayed in the missing autograph work half-length in armour, in the latter respect resembling the destroyed equestrian portrait. It was, however, also in oil on panel, with dimensions very close to those of the Palazzo Pitti picture, which measures 63 × 48 cm.[15]

It is probable that the missing picture can be identified with an entry in the posthumous inventory of Rubens's own collection (the *Specification*): 'Le pourtrait du Duc de Boucquingam'.[16] Thereafter it seems that the picture can quite securely be traced in various sales. On 23 November 1691 there was a sale in London by the auctioneer Edward Davis of pictures described as '... a Collection of valuable pictures, consisting of the collections, of Cardinal Antonio Barberini, Sir James Palmer &c.'. Lot 53 was described as the 'Duke of Buckingham by P.Ruben'. It is not known why any of the collection of Barberini (1607-71) was being sold in London at this date, and it seems unlikely that he would have had a portrait of Buckingham. The other named vendor, Sir James Palmer, however, might well have had such a picture in his collection.

James Palmer would certainly have known Buckingham at the Court of James I, where he, Palmer, became a friend of Charles, Prince of Wales. In 1629 Palmer was made Keeper of the Privy Closet to King Charles, with particular reference to pictures in the royal collection, and he was also an amateur painter himself. Charles I's inventory of 1625 compiled by Abraham van der Doort listed several miniatures by Palmer in the royal collection, such as '*A Tarquin and Lucretia* Don by Sr James Paumer after Titian, given to yor Ma^ty^.'[17]

Palmer acquired pictures for the King, including the *Wilton Diptych* (National Gallery, London), and also added to his own collection. In 1640, after the death of Rubens, Sir Balthazar Gerbier sent Charles I a translation of selected items from the *Specification* of works of art found in Rubens's house at the time of his death and so either the King or Palmer could have acquired the portrait of Buckingham from Rubens's estate. Alternatively, the King might have given it to Palmer, whose collection contained many pictures which had been the King's. Although Palmer died in 1657, the sale of his collection only took place some thirty years later following the exile of his son, Roger, Earl of Castlemaine (1634-1705).[18]

It is not known who bought the portrait at the Barberini/Palmer sale but a picture that sounds similar appears in the Comte de Fraula's sale in Brussels on 21 July 1738: 'Le Portrait du Duc de Bukingam, jusqu'à la ceinture, par P.P.Rubens; haut 2 p[ieds]. 3 pou[ces]. & demi, large un pied 9 pou[ces].' These measurements correspond to 63.9 × 50.1 cm, and are therefore very close to those of the studio copy in Palazzo Pitti.[19] In the margin of the sale catalogue is the price '*162[?]-0*', but again there is no indication as to who might have purchased the picture. Thomas Fraula (1646-1738), who was born in Antwerp and died three months before this sale took place,[20] had several other pictures by Rubens in his collection, probably including a large representation of *The lion hunt*, which might be the same picture as that documented in the 1st Duke of Buckingham's collection in 1635. It eventually passed into the collection of the Duke of Richelieu (1629-1715), and is now in the Alte Pinakothek, Munich.[21]

The measurements of the Fraula portrait of Buckingham are very close to those of a picture in a later sale, that of the pictures of the deceased banker Charles Godefroy, held in Paris by Gersaint on 22 April 1748. Lot 1 is described as:

> Le Portrait du Duc de Buckingham en Buste peint sur bois, par Rubens, de vingt-trois pouces de haut sur dix-sept pouces & demi de large, dans une Bordure de bois proprement sculpté & doré.[22]

Beside it is the note in the margin '(?)*500*'.

There is an extensive discussion of Godefroy in Gersaint's catalogue. He is described as a banker and jeweller, and the sale was not only of his paintings but also 'diamonds, rings of all kinds, jewels... '. He had been assisted in his picture collecting by a painter, also called Godefroy, and also deceased (although his widow was still living), who travelled abroad on his behalf to countries such as Flanders and Holland to find 'the most beautiful pictures', on the understanding that any subsequent sales would see the profit divided equally between them. Some pictures had thus entered the French royal collection, and the same agent had also apparently assisted Robert Walpole in forming part of his collection in 1725.[23] The catalogue gives a detailed account of the relationship that existed between Buckingham and Rubens, and states:

> Rubens made several portraits of this Nobleman, who had felt friendship towards him. This picture is one of the most beautiful, and one of the finest painted, and one of the most powerful of this master. It is in perfect condition and of admirable purity.[24]

The catalogue states that Godefroy's estate was being sold in order to secure an equal amount for the 'succession' to the two separate parts of the partnership: the widow of the painter on the one hand and, presumably, the elder (or, less probably, both) of the two sons of the banker on the other. These sons were Charles-Théodose (1718-96) and Auguste-Gabriel (1728-1813), future Controller-general of the French Navy, both of whom were painted as children by Jean Baptiste Siméon Chardin (1699-1779), who was a friend of their father, the elder as *Young man with a violin* and the younger as *Boy with a top* (both Louvre, Paris).[25]

One of them acquired the Buckingham portrait at his father's sale, and although his name is not given in his own subsequent sale of pictures in 1785, where he is described only as 'M.Godefroy the son', it is probable that this was the younger of the two, Auguste-Gabriel, who became well known as a connoisseur, while his brother pursued his interests as a musician.[26] It would therefore have been Auguste-Gabriel who put his pictures up for sale in 1785: *Catalogue de tableaux italiens, flamands, hollandois et francois... provenant du cabinet de M.Godefroy*. The auction, due to be held on 23 April but postponed to 15 November, 'Direction J.B.P.Lebrun, Peintre', contained ninety-two pictures. Lot 17 was described as by P.P.Rubens:

> Bust-length portrait of the Duke of Buckingham, dressed in a cuirasse with a red sash across it; his head seen in three-quarter view and with hair in curls. Everyone knows of the close friendship that existed between these two great men; also this head is one of the most beautiful productions known by this Master... Height 45 'pouces', width 33 'pouces'... .[27]

The difference in measurements given here and those in the catalogue of the father's sale in 1748 (23 × 17½ *pouces*) must be because the measurements on this latter occasion include the frame, which was probably rococo in style with cresting at the top. There can be no question that the pictures were one and the same, because the catalogue entry for Lot 31 of a still later sale in Paris, that of the collection of the late Claude Joseph Clos by H.Delaroche on 18 November 1812, is explicit that it is the same picture that was sold in the sale of Godefroy *père* and Godefroy *fils*:

> ... [the painting] is from the collection of M.Godefroy, banker and jeweller in Paris... M.Godefroy the son, a distinguished connoisseur, and an excellent judge of beautiful things, acquired it at his father's sale, and kept it until 1785, the time of the sale of his collection by M.Lebrun, who bought it for M.Clos for the sum of 4,800 livres.[28]

These following details appear written in the margin of the 1785 sale of Godefroy *fils*, beside the Rubens (lot 17): the figure '*4800*' and '*Lebrun aîné*'.[29] The description in the 1812 sale is also very like that in the 1785 catalogue:

> Portrait of the Duke of Buckingham, minister of Charles I, King of England, show half-length, wearing a cuirasse, with a red sash, head turned three-quarters, and the hair cut in Roman fashion. This piece, worthy of the attention of true connoisseurs, is entirely by the hand of Rubens, who was a friend of this minister. The beautiful modelling of the figure, where one can recognize a character both lofty and daring, the liveliness of the flesh, the refinement of the half-tones, the ease and softness of the handling, all contribute towards what is a masterpiece of painting.[30]

These details leave no doubt that this highly prized picture showed Buckingham not in the same clothes as in the Palazzo Pitti studio image but more in the martial attire he assumes as Lord Admiral in the large equestrian portrait formerly at Osterley. Rubens was certainly working on the equestrian portrait in the autumn of 1625[31] and so it would have been the first image to be taken after the drawing that Rubens had made in the summer of that year. The painted studio 'copy' in the Pitti ought

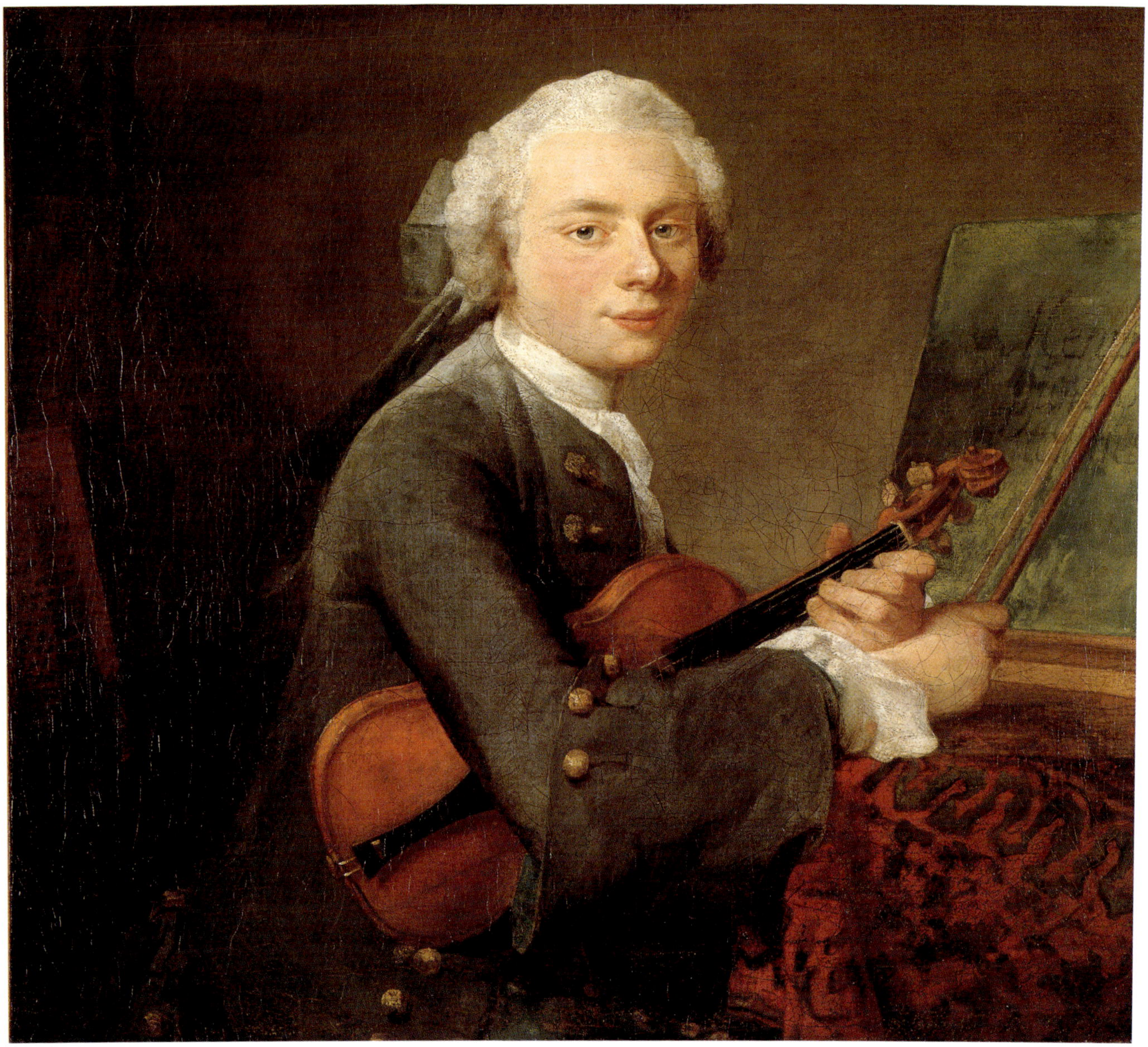

Portrait of Charles-Théodose Godefroy ('*Young man with a violin*') by Jean Baptiste Siméon Chardin, *c.* 1734-5. Oil on canvas, 67.5 × 74.5 cm. Musée du Louvre, Paris

therefore to be seen more as a version in oils made after the drawing, perhaps for use in other copies, and it seems clear that the missing portrait of Buckingham in oil on panel discussed here showed him half-length in martial attire.[32]

The 1812 auction catalogue is annotated, and next to the Rubens portrait is '*Constantin 9500*'. This refers to the price (in francs) and to the buyer of the picture, who was presumably Guillaume Constantin (1755-1816), a collector and dealer. His knowledge of the arts gave him other important opportunities in Paris. During Napoleon Bonaparte's reign, he was on the committee for reorganising the Louvre Museum, and in 1807 he became curator of Empress Josephine's picture collection. Towards the end of his life, Constantin held two sales of his collection,[33] but neither includes the portrait of Buckingham. In all probability, he had sold it shortly after he had bought it. His son Amédée took on his mantle as

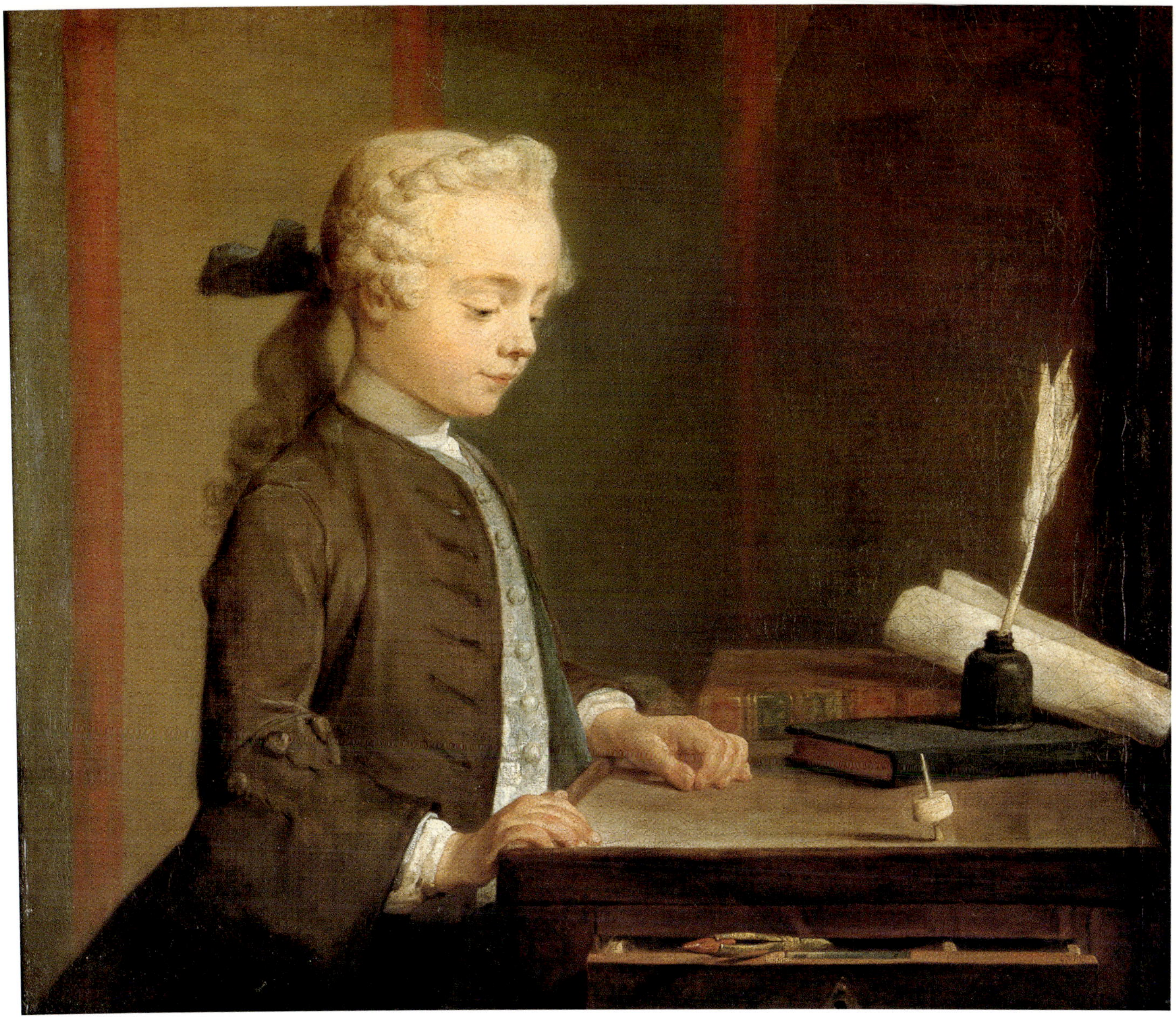

dealer, but the picture does not appear in the sale of his collection held after his death on 29 March 1840.

A picture described as 'P.P.Rubens Portrait of the Duke of Buckingham. A highly finished painting of that nobelman [*sic*]' appeared in a sale dated 29 March 1803 under the direction of Mr. Squibb of Savile Row, London. There were 152 paintings, and the seller was James Mosenau, a dealer. This cannot, however, be the same as the missing picture portraying the Duke in martial attire, because in 1803 that portrait was in the collection of Claude Joseph Clos.[34]

Portrait of Auguste-Gabriel Godefroy ('*Young man with a top*') by Jean Baptiste Siméon Chardin (1699-1779), *c.* 1738.
Oil on canvas, 67 × 76 cm.
Musée du Louvre, Paris

NOTES

1 Sir John Oglander, *A Royalist's Notebook*, Francis Bamford, ed., 1936. Quoted in C.R.Cammell, *The Great Duke of Buckingham*, London, 1939, p. 83. See also D.H.Willson, *King James VI and I*, London, 1956, for the King's relationship with Buckingham.

2 He was knighted in 1615, in 1616 was created Viscount Villiers, and by January 1617 had become Master of the Horse and a Knight of the Garter. In 1617 he was made Earl of Buckingham, in 1618 Marquess, and in 1623 Duke of Buckingham. He was Lord Admiral by 1619 and was subsequently responsible for the failed invasion of France in 1627. See, for example, Willson, op. cit., pp. 383ff.

3 See, for example, K.Sharpe, *The Personal Rule of Charles I*, New Haven and London, 1992, pp. 4ff.

4 Quoted in Cammell, op. cit., p. 255.

5 J.Brown, *Kings and Connoisseurs: Collecting Art in Seventeenth-century Europe*, Princeton, 1995, p. 31.

6 Ibid., p. 32.

7 C.Ruelens and M.Rooses, ed., *Correspondance de Rubens et documents épistolaires concernant sa vie et ses oeuvres*, 6 vols., Antwerp, 1887-1909, III, p. 412.

8 Cammell, op. cit., p. 364.

9 *Corpus Rubenianum Ludwig Burchard*, XIX, 'Portraits II' (1987), H.Vlieghe, ed., p. 66, n. 6 (hereafter *Corpus*).

10 R.Davies, 'An inventory of the Duke of Buckingham's pictures etc., at York House in 1635', *Burlington Magazine*, X (October 1906-March 1907), pp. 376ff., p. 379.

11 *Corpus*, op. cit., p. 65. Buckingham's son and heir, the 2nd Duke, sold around 200 paintings in Holland in 1648, most of which went to Archduke Leopold Wilhelm. The 1659 inventory of the Archduke's collection does not list a portrait by Rubens of the 1st Duke of Buckingham. The 2nd Duke died in 1687. For the fate of the Buckingham collection see P.McEvansoneya. 'The sequestration and dispersal of the Buckingham collection', *Journal of the History of Collections*, VIII, no. 2 (1996), pp. 133-54.

12 *Corpus*, op. cit., no. 80a, p. 63. It is not known whether Buckingham ever owned this drawing or Rubens kept it, although the latter is perhaps more likely. Later, the drawing was in the collection of Duke Albert of Sachsen-Teschen (1738-1822), and thence to the Albertina, Vienna (Inv. no. 8256).

13 *Corpus*, op. cit., no. 80, pp. 62ff.

14 Ibid., and fig. 51. It will be seen that the account given here takes a different view of the evidence from that in the *Corpus*.

15 The Pitti picture is first noted in 1675 in the possession of Leopoldo de' Medici, whence it passed continuously in Florence. *Corpus*, op. cit., p. 62.

16 J.Denucé, *De Antwerpsche 'Konstkamers', Inventarissen van de kunstverzamelingen te Antwerpen in de 16e en 17e eeuwen...*, Antwerp, 1932, p. 62. It has been suggested (*Corpus*, op. cit., p. 63, n. 2) that the same portrait may be identical with one of two 'sketches' ('2 Esquisses') recorded in the collection of Arnuld Lunden at some point after 1640 as 'Le Duc de Bucquingam', but Lunden's 'sketch' could in fact have been the drawing now in Vienna and in any case the missing picture discussed here, as will become evident, was a finished picture and not an oil sketch.

17 O.Millar, ed., 'Abraham van der Doort's Catalogue of the Collections of Charles I', *Walpole Society*, XXXVII (1958-60), p. 120.

18 Sir James Palmer's son Roger (1634-1705), diplomat and author, was famously married (in 1659) to Barbara Villiers, grand-daughter of the half-brother of the 1st Duke of Buckingham and cousin of the 2nd Duke of Buckingham. She was the mistress of the restored King Charles II by 1661 and bore him several children, while also obtaining an earldom for her husband (and thus a title for herself). Roger Palmer, however, was finally not prepared to tolerate this liaison and moved abroad after a violent quarrel with his wife. King Charles II showered Barbara Villiers with houses, pensions, jewellery and, apparently, pictures. It is possible that he gave her a picture of her relative George Villiers, 1st Duke of Buckingham, although the royal collection had been dispersed in the years following the death of King Charles I and consequently King Charles II would have had to receive the picture by gift or acquisition before he could give it away.

19 *Corpus*, op. cit., p. 63 n. 3.

20 F.-V.Goethals, *Dictionnaire des Familles Nobles du Royaume de Belgique*, 1849. We are grateful to Thomas Woodcock, Norroy and Ulster King of Arms, for bringing this reference to our attention.

21 *Corpus*, XVIII, 'Landscape and Hunting Scenes II' (1986), A.Balis, ed., p. 162.

22 The catalogue has a note at this point explaining that the measurements do not

include the frames, which could be as wide as twelve *pouces*. *Catalogue raisonné, des tableaux, diamans... et autres Effets provenant de la Succession de feu Monsieur Charles Godefroy, Banquier et Joüaillier/Par E.F. Gersaint*, Paris, 1748. The account in the *Corpus*, 'Portraits II', p. 63, n. 3, does not appear to accord with the sale records as discussed here.

23 Purchases for, or sales to, Walpole apparently included Rubens's two pictures '*Quos ego...*' which Godefroy the painter had himself put on board ship for England at Calais. The painter's widow had continued the restoration and conservation practice which she had run with her husband during his lifetime.

24 'Rubens a fait plusieurs Portraits de ce Seigneur, qui avoit de l'amitié pour lui. Celui-ci est un des plus beaux, des mieux peints, & des plus vigoureux de ce Maître. Il est d'une conservation parfaite & d'une pureté admirable.'

25 See. P. Rosenberg, *Chardin: suivi du catalogue des oeuvres*, Paris, 1999, cat. nos. 101 (Charles-Théodose, *Young man with a violin*) and 112 (Auguste-Gabriel, *Boy with a top*).

26 Ibid., and see p. 116: [Auguste-Gabriel] grand amateur de peinture, comme son père... et son nom apparaît regullèrement dans les catalogues des ventes du XVIIIe siècle.'

27 'Le Portrait en Buste du Duc de Buckingam, vêtu avec une cuirasse traversée d'une écharpe rouge; il a la tête vue de trois quarts & couverte de cheveux frisés. Tout le monde fait l'amitié étroite qui lioit ces deux grands hommes; aussi cette Tête est-elle une des plus belles productions connues de ce Maître. Hauteur 45 pouces, largeur 33 pouces. B.' The red sash (ribbon) must be that of the Order of the Bath, the other great order of chivalry beside the Garter (the Duke wore the Garter insginia or ribbon in the two large pictures at Osterley referred to above).

28 '... sort du cabinet de M Godefroy, banquier et joaillier à Paris... M. Godefroy fils, connaisseur distingué, et juste appréciateur des belles choses, en fit l'acquisition à la vente de son père, et l'a conservé jusqu'en 1785, époque de la vente qu'il a fait faire de son cabinet par M. Lebrun, qui l'acheta pour M. Clos la somme de 4,800 liv.'

29 Also included in that sale was a portrait in enamel of the Duke of Buckingham after Rubens (lot 198).

30 'Le portrait du duc de Buckingham, ministre de Charles 1er, roi d'Angleterre, représenté à mi-corps, couvert d'une cuirasse, avec écharpe rouge, la tête tournée de trois quarts, et les cheveux coupés à la romaine. Ce morceau, digne de toute l'attention des vrais connaisseurs, est entièrement de la main de Rubens, qui fut l'ami de ce ministre. Le beau modelé de cette figure, où l'on reconnoît un caractère altier et entreprenant, la vivacité de la carnation, la finesse des demi-teintes, la facilité et le moelleux de l'exécution, contribuent à l'offrir comme un chef d'oeuvre de peinture. Claude Joseph Clos, who was also selling pictures by Lorrain, Watteau, Fragonard, Rubens and Ruisdael, was described as an 'ancien conseiller d'état, lieutenant-general civil criminel et de police de prévoté de l'hôtel et grand'-prévoté de France'. 'Ami de lettres, il fut en relation avec les savants de son siècle notamment avec Voltaire qui devient son aimi particulier, il ne fut pas moins sensible aux charmes de la peinture.'

31 *Corpus*, 'Portraits', II, p. 65. Rubens wrote to Balthazar Gerbier in October or November 1625 to say that he was temporarily stopping work on the portrait because of commitments on behalf of the Infanta.

32 This account therefore modifies that to be found in *Corpus*, op. cit., pp. 62-3.

33 18-19 March, 1816, Direction Pérignon, C P: Chariot, Paris (91 pictures); 18 November– , 1816, Direction Pérignon, C P: Chariot, Paris (435 pictures).

34 The entry does indicate that there was at least one other portrait of the Duke by Rubens, although it may simply have been a copy. With such little information to go on it is impossible to make a connection between this stray reference and any of the early records.

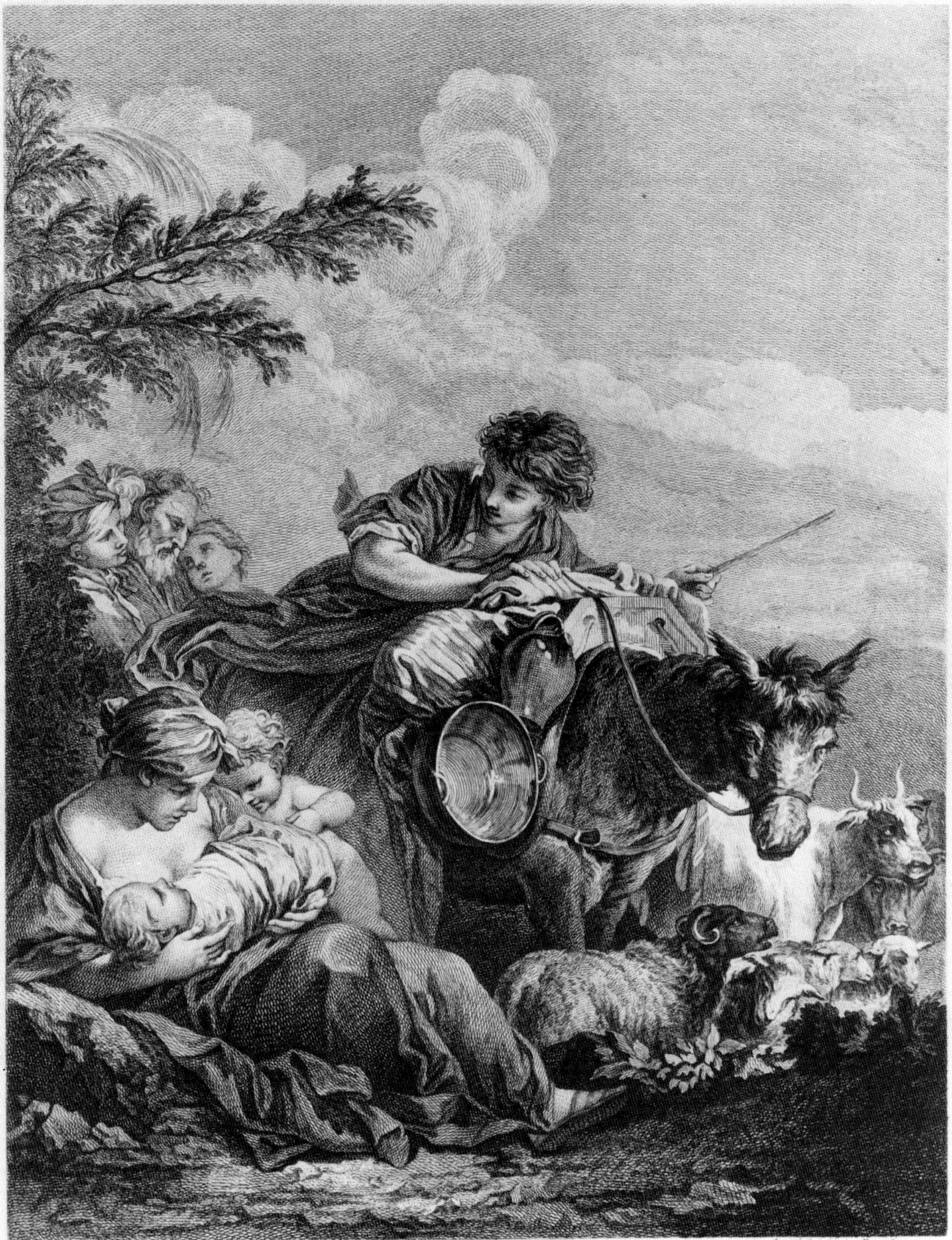

Peint par François Boucher. | *Gravé par Elisabeth Cousinet, Femme Lempereur.*

DÉPART DE JACOB.

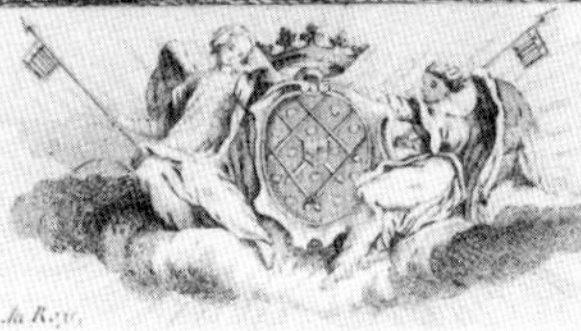

Gravé, d'après le Tableau original de François Boucher,
Tiré du Cabinet de M.r le Comte de Vence,
Maréchal de Camp des Armées du Roy.

Se vend à Paris, chez Lau. Cars, Graveur du Roy, Rue S.t Jacques vis à vis le Plessis.

François Boucher

1703-69

Le départ de Jacob

c. 1723-8

Oil on canvas
41.54 × 43.2 cm

The picture is one of several compositions by Boucher based upon the story of Jacob in the Book of Genesis. Although the original painting devoted to this episode is last heard of in 1814, it is recorded in an engraving by (Catherine) Elisabeth Cousinet which bears the title '*Départ de Jacob*'.[1] It portrays the departure of Jacob secretly from Laban (Genesis 31, vv. 3ff.), but the particular moment is perhaps more clearly depicted in Boucher's preliminary drawing, which survives.[2] In it, Jacob can be seen rousing Rachel who is suckling Joseph, his youngest son:

> And Jacob sent and called Rachel and Leah to the field and to his flock,/And said unto them, I see your father's countenance, that it is not toward me as before.
> (Genesis 31, vv. 4-5).

Another two children are to be seen behind Rachel, although these would have been sons of Jacob by Rachel's sister, Leah, i.e. Issachar and Zebulun (although one of the children might even be Leah's daughter, Dinah – Genesis 30, vv. 17-24).

The finished composition was, however, a compression of two moments of the story within one canvas. The figures in the background in the engraving are therefore Laban (the older man) and his sons who in the first verse of the same chapter are described as whispering against Jacob:

> And he [Jacob] heard the words of Laban's sons, saying, Jacob hath taken away all that was our father's; and of that which was our father's hath he gotten all this glory.

Boucher went on to depict the actual departure of Jacob secretly from Laban in another canvas that is also lost,[3] which described (including the relevant camels) the verses:

> Then Jacob rose up and set his sons and his wives upon camels;/And he carried away all his cattle, and all his goods which he had gotten… And Jacob stole away unawares to Laban the Syrian, in that he told him not that he fled./So that he fled with all that he had… ' (Genesis, 31, vv. 17-21).

Boucher portrayed other related incidents in the story, such as *The meeting of Jacob and Rachel* (engraved by Laurent Cars, the original now lost);[4] *Jacob uncovering the well for Rachel*;[5] and *Jacob deceitfully obtaining Isaac's blessing* (engraved by Daullé).[6] The popularity of this subject-matter, at first sight, might suggest an association with the court of Louis XV. After all, Mme. de Pompadour, later one of Boucher's key patrons, and the many other royal mistresses might be construed as having been in relation to the King, Louis XV, as the various wives – or servants of wives – were to Jacob: women who successively bore him sons or

Le départ de Jacob
after François Boucher (1703-93).
Engraving, 33.8 × 25.7cm.,
by Catherine Elisabeth Cousinet
Lempereur after lost painting
by François Boucher (1703-70)
of *c.* 1723-8.
Musée du Louvre, Paris

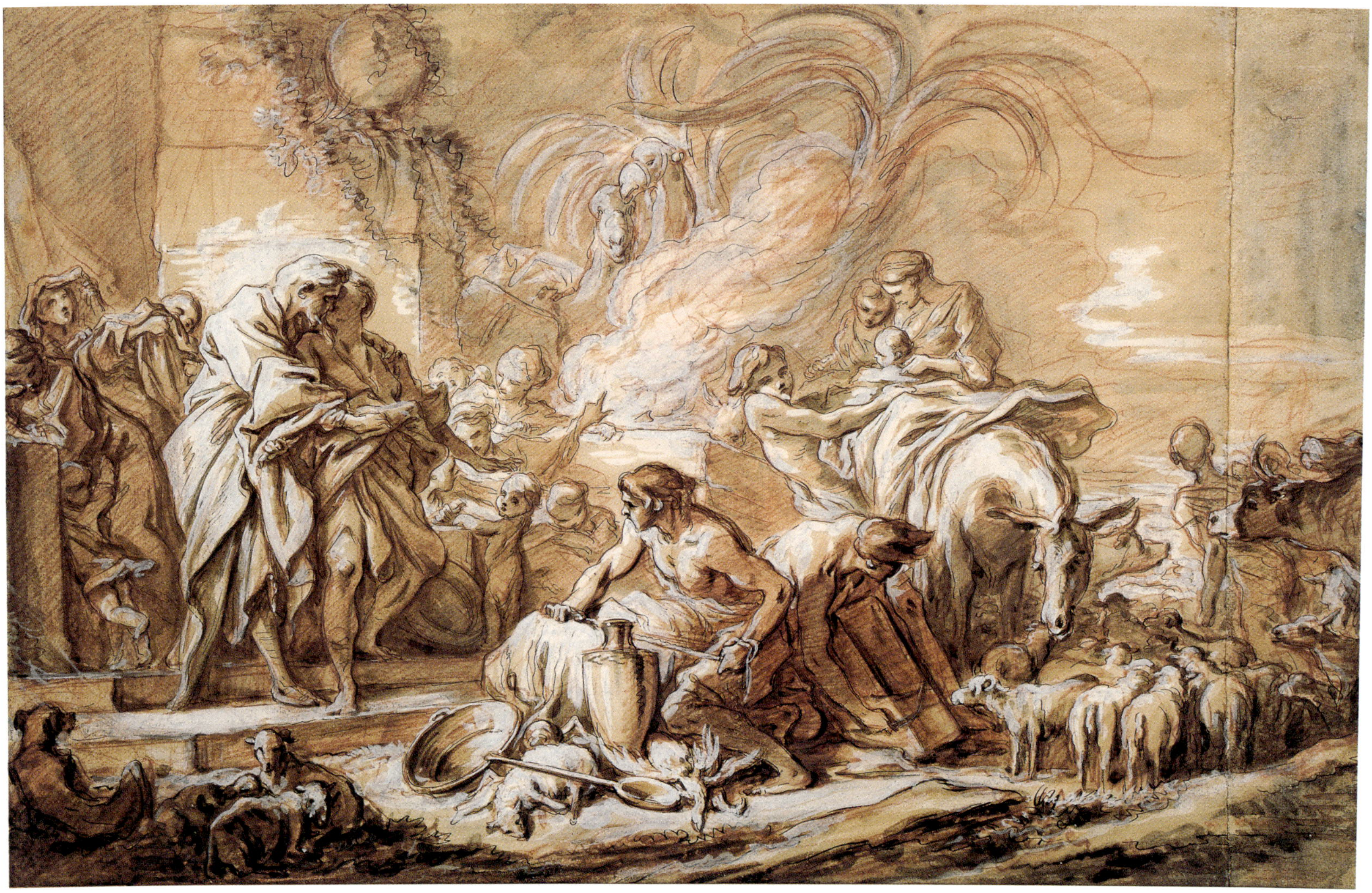

Jacob leaving Laban
by François Boucher, *c.* 1727.
Pen, wash and chalk with white gouache, 41 × 62.5 cm.
Musée du Louvre, Paris

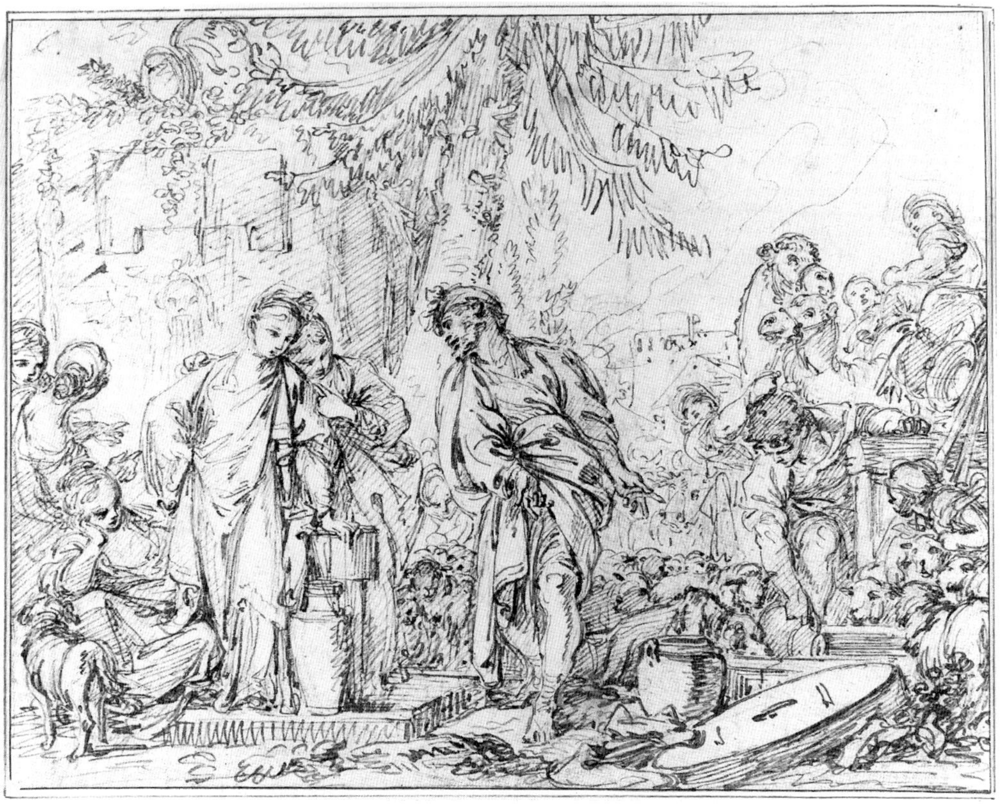

Jacob and Rachel at the well
by François Boucher.
Pen and wash over chalk, 23 × 28.9 cm.
Teyler Museum, Haarlem

were rescued from barrenness to do so through divine intervention. The early date of these pictures, however, argues against any such connection, and they appear to have been made in the years before Boucher went to Rome in 1727/8, where he remained certainly until Easter 1729, and whence he returned to Paris by 1731, or before.[7]

The principal reason at the time for the production of these predominantly Old Testament religious scenes was usually much more mundane. Boucher was foiled of his due visit to Rome after winning first prize for painting at the Académie Royale in 1723 and had to set about earning his living, which he did chiefly by working for engravers. In the years following this disappointment, Boucher was employed by Jean-François Cars at a rate of 60 *livres* per month, to provide compositions from which the engraver/publisher could create prints to accompany *précis* of the successful completion of doctoral theses, or 'thesis-plates', as they are known,[8] and for which Old Testament themes were the favoured material.

Boucher himself also worked extensively at this time as an etcher, notably in the publication by Julienne of works of Watteau. None the less, Boucher's reasons for painting such subjects was not, as has been observed, ever quite so straightforward as merely to provide fodder for the thesis-plate market. *Bethuel welcoming the servant of Abraham*, for example, which survives both as an oil sketch and as a finished painting, has prompted the observation, '... by attempting such subjects as autonomous paintings rather than merely as disposable designs for the engravers, Boucher was announcing his ambitions as a history painter.'[9]

Many of these works are now lost, and survive only in the form of engravings

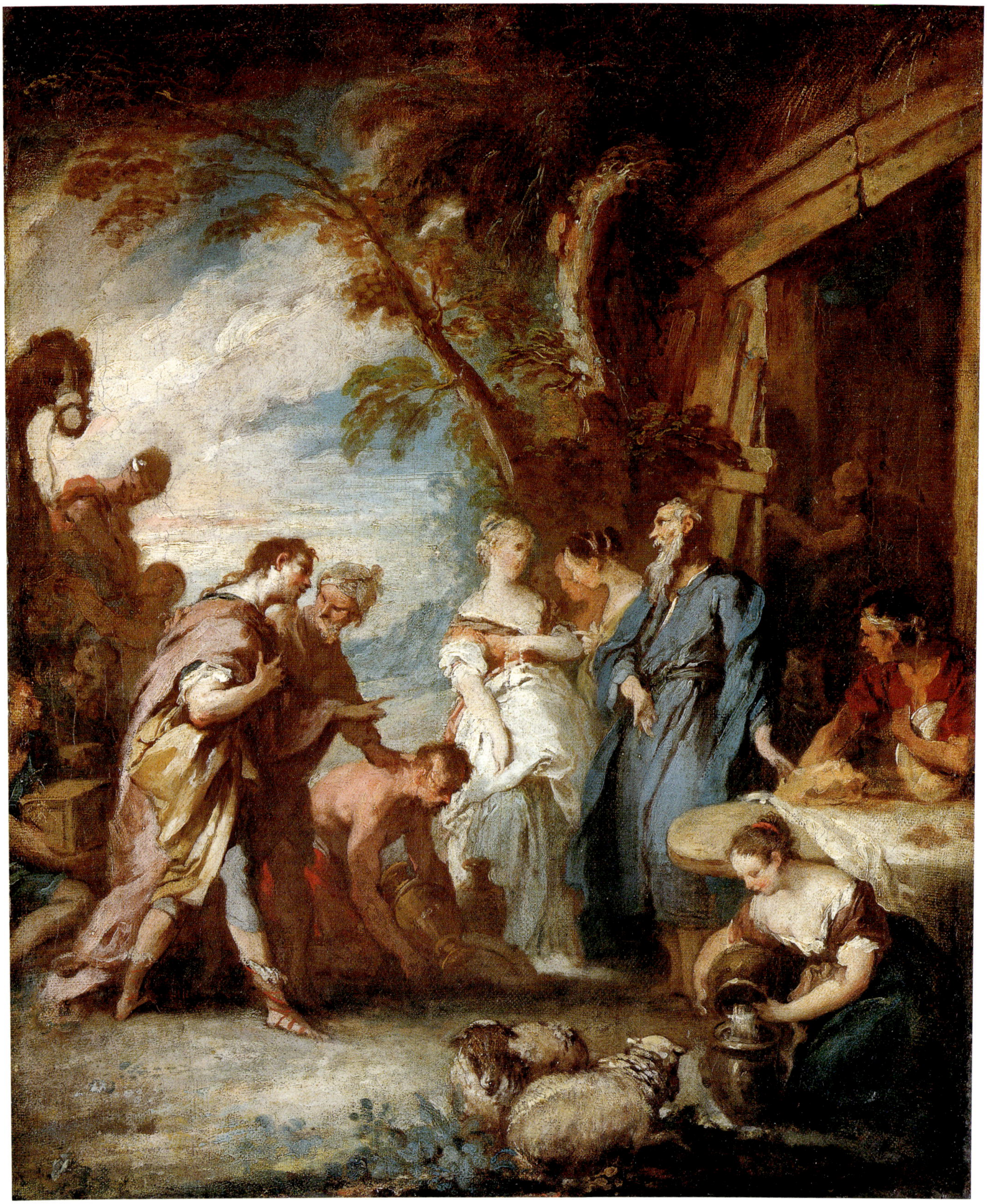

or, more rarely, related autograph drawings. What makes the *Départ de Jacob* especially interesting is that, once it was sold from the collection of the Comte de Vence, Field-Marshal of the royal army, on 9 February 1761,[10] it passed through the collections almost exclusively of distinguished engravers and artists. The painting evidently had a particular appeal for them, a fact which makes its subsequent disappearance all the more poignant. Furthermore, some of these artist-owners had worked directly with Boucher.

The first of the artists to make an appearance in the history of the *Départ de Jacob* is Pierre-Francois Basan (1723-97). He bought the picture at the Comte de Vence sale in 1761 (no. 139) for 221 *livres* where it was described (together with the next lot, no. 140, *Les bergers à la fontaine*):

> ... Boucher a peints les tableaux les deux numéros ci-dessus dans le goût italien, tant par le dessin que par rapport a la composition ingenieuse et au coloris.[11]

Basan was an engraver but more celebrated as a print-seller, as the author of a *Dictionnaire des graveurs* (1767) and in the same year as publisher of the first volume of the illustrated *Metamorphoses* of Ovid (1767-71), which included engravings after Boucher.[12] In addition, however, he was an entrepreneur of art sales, drawing up inventories and directing sales – some 112 of them between 1756 and 1792.[13]

When the picture was next sold, it was just a decade later, 1-23 July 1771, in the sale of another engraver, publisher and print-seller, the influential Gabriel Huquier (1695-1772), when it sold for 124.19 *livres*. Huquier engraved, for example, after Boucher's drawings, such as *Scènes de la vie Chinoise* and *Recueil de fontaines* (1736), as well as engraving Watteau arabesques for the *Recueil Julienne* on which Boucher also worked. In January 1736 was announced Huquier's engraving after Boucher's *Berger et bergère en conversation*.[14] Huquier's son, Jacques-Gabriel (1730-1805), was taught drawing by Boucher.[15] Huquier's extensive collections were sold in Amsterdam as well as in Paris and the 1771 Paris sale was followed by another in the November of 1772 following his death in June that year.

It would seem that Boucher's *Départ de Jacob* must have passed straight into the hands of another engraver, because it was sold again, only two years later, on 24 May 1773, for 350 *livres*, from the collection of Jean-Denis Lempereur II (1701-79), whose connection with Boucher was, if anything, even closer than Huquier's. Indeed, he probably knew this painting very well already. It was Lempereur's wife, Catherine Elisabeth Cousinet, who had engraved the painting while it was still in the collection of the Comte de Vence, and her engraving, as noted above, is the vital record of the lost painting's appearance. The De Vence sale record notes, 'Mlle Lempereur, épouse du graveur de ce nom, l'a gravé,' and the print indeed carries her name. The Lempereur sale also notes her engraving: 'Ce tableau a été gravé par Lempereur' although, interestingly, it is described only as 'Une marche d'animaux accompagnée de plusieurs figures: une femme et un enfant occupent le premier plan du tableau'.

There are further relationships here between the engravers and artists involved that shed light upon the way in which admiration for, and indeed, collaboration with, Boucher operated within a tight-knit circle. For example, Basan's cousin was the engraver Etienne Fessard (1714-77). Fessard engraved – in 1756 – the other Boucher picture in the Vence sale that was associated with the *Départ...* ,

Rebecca receiving Abraham's gifts by François Boucher.
Oil on canvas.
Musée du Louvre, Paris

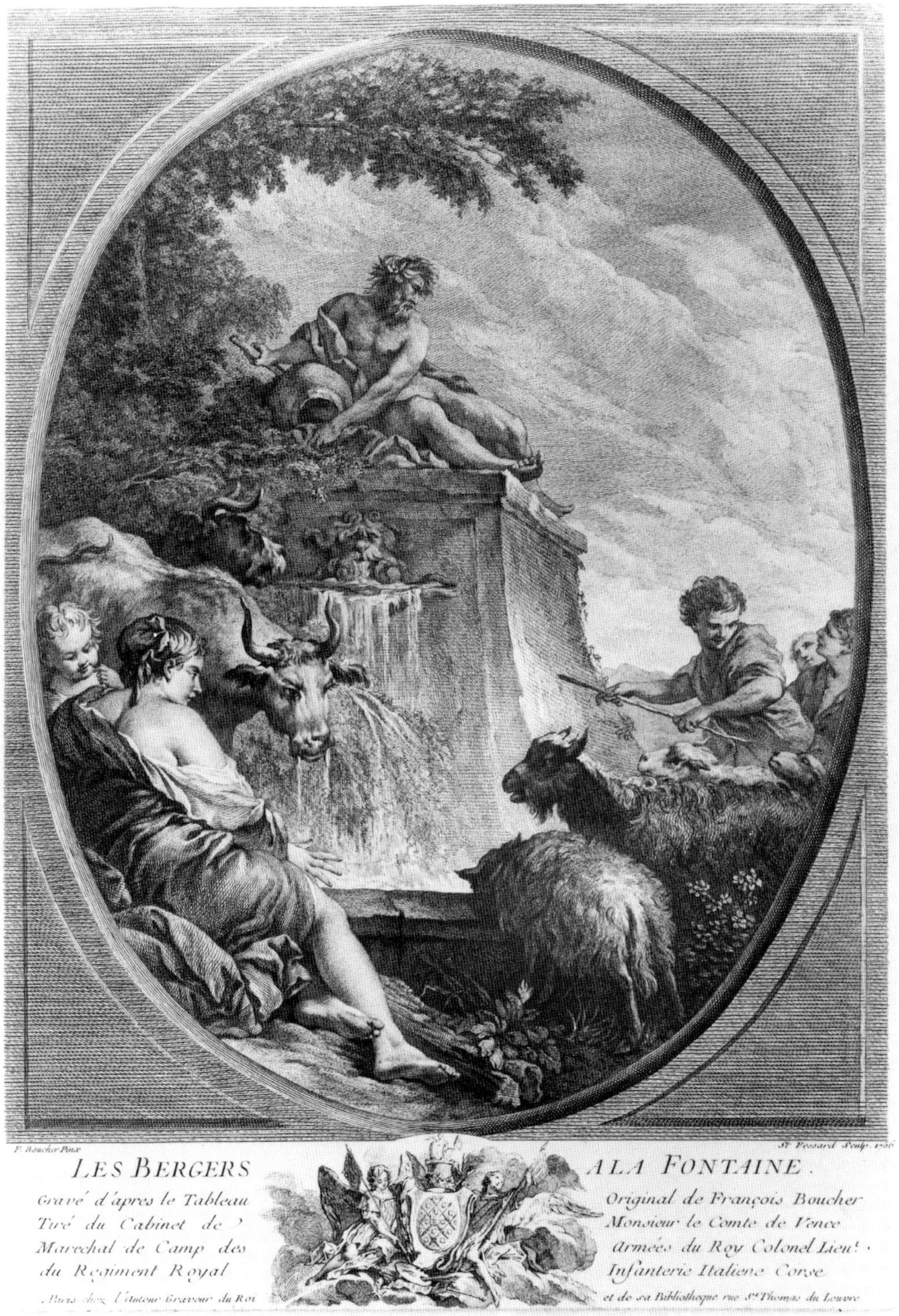

Shepherds at a fountain after François Boucher.
Engraving, 38 × 26.6 cm., by Etienne Fessard, 1756.
Musée du Louvre, Paris`

i.e. *Les bergers à la fontaine*. The actual engraver of the *Départ* was, as we have seen, Catherine Elisabeth Cousinet, the wife of the engraver Lempereur – who bought the painting of the *Départ* in the early 1770s.

At the Lempereur sale, the picture once again passed into an artist's collection, although not that of an engraver. The next recorded owner is the rather obscure sculptor Jean-Marie Nogaret. Although the facts of his life are few (he sculpted a bust of General Joubert in 1799), it is known precisely where the picture must have been between the date of the Lempereur sale and Nogaret's own disposal of it on 18 March 1782 (when it sold for 150 *livres*): he lived at 64 Faubourg Saint-Martin.[16] The description of the picture in this sale – with which, one imagines, Nogaret might have had something to do – is interesting because of the comparisons made with other artists. One of these is a reference to Boucher's picture as being in the 'genre' of 'Benedette', i.e. Benedetto Castiglione.[17] But the style is described as being like that of Lemoine, a reasonable point since this was an early work and François Lemoine was Boucher's teacher.

At this point the unbroken sequence of artist-owners of the picture is possibly interrupted, if only to be picked up again later. The purchaser at the Nogaret sale was 'Chariot' who sold it on 28 January 1788 (no. 53). Chariot was certainly committed to collecting works by Boucher, because in the same sale was a drawing by Boucher for the lost painting: '*Le Depart de Jacob*. Dans le style de Benedette. Plume... '.[18]

The painting now returned to the possession of yet another engraver, Jacques-Firmin Beauvarlet (1731-97), who in 1762 had become *Graveur du Roi*. Beauvarlet, who owned the painting until his death in 1797, trained with Laurent Cars who engraved after Boucher.[19] Beauvarlet also engraved prints after Boucher's genre subjects and became, like Boucher, an *Académicien*. Beauvarlet died in Paris on 7 December 1797 and his collection was sold on 13 March 1798 when the Boucher painting was sold (no. 29) for 69.19 *livres*. The painting then passed into the hands of a painter, Jean-Baptiste-Pierre Le Brun (1748-1813, who is perhaps better known today as the husband of the more famous Elisabeth Vigée-Le Brun but himself deserves to be remembered as one of the most important dealers in pictures of the time and as a formative influence upon modern ideas of the art gallery or museum. In addition to buying pictures for Louis XVI, Le Brun acted as curator for, among others, the Duc d'Orléans, and assisted in the purchases of Catherine the Great. He also proposed the concept of the centralised museum, familiar today but hardly dreamt of at the time in France.[20] He conducted huge numbers of sales – some 165 between 1771 and his death – and can be said to have developed the modern sale catalogue, with details of provenance, descriptions of the works in question and profiles of the collectors involved.

In Le Brun's sale of 1806, the *Départ de Jacob* was sold (for 60 *livres*) to his chief rival, Alexandre-Joseph Paillet (1743-1814), with whom, however, it seems evident, he also collaborated to some extent. Paillet had also trained as painter but is now better known as a dealer and auctioneer and one, like Le Brun, who introduced major innovations in the presentation of works of art for sale. For example, in the Hôtel de Bullion, rue Platrière, which he bought in 1779, he created top-lighting, a feature of the private gallery of J.M.W. Turner and of the Dulwich Picture Gallery in the first decades of the nineteenth century – something that had been swiftly copied by Le Brun in his competing gallery at Rue de Cléry.[21] Like Le Brun, Paillet – described by a contemporary as having 'loyalty

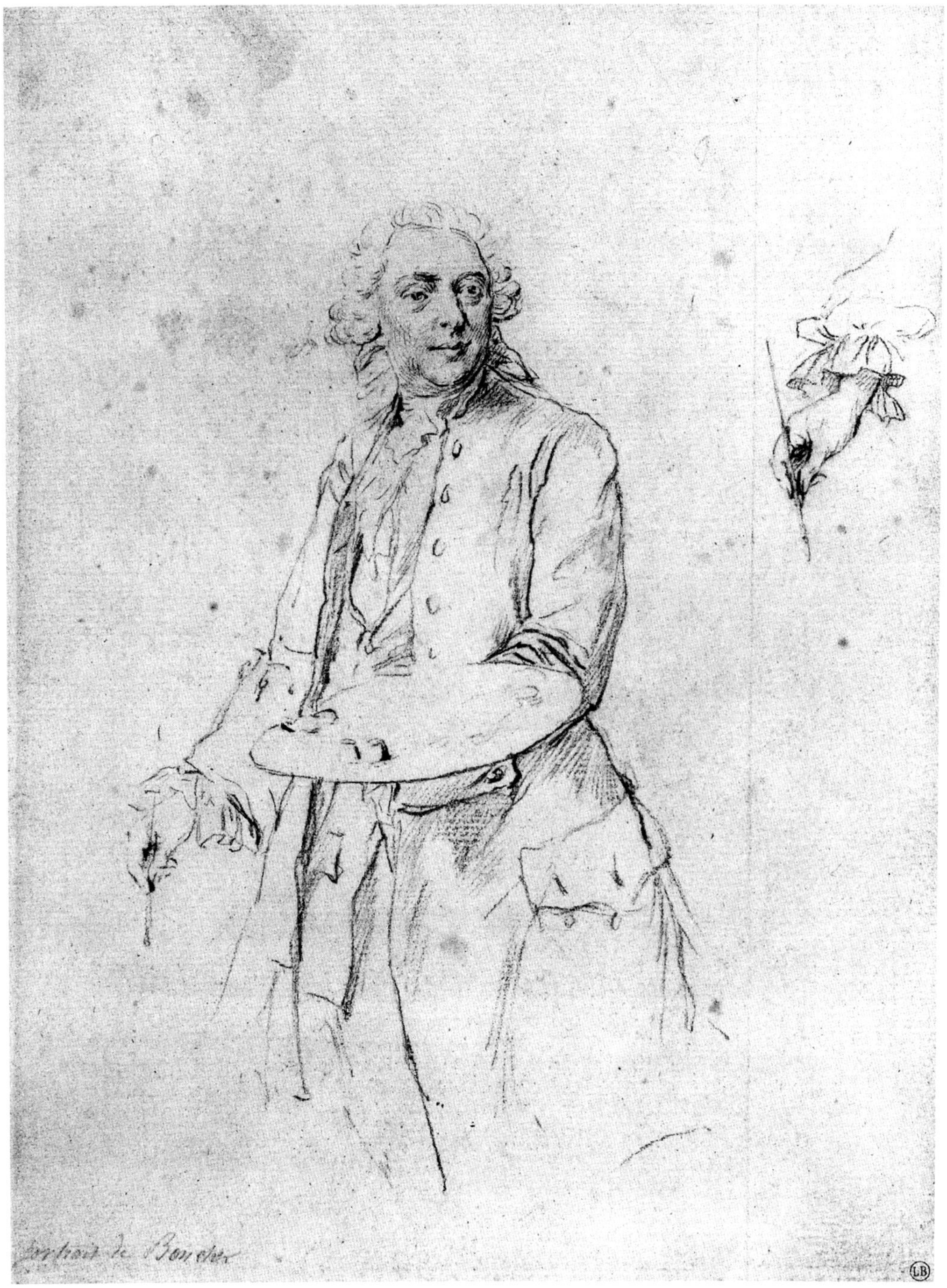

Portrait of François Boucher by Alexandre Roslin (1718-93).
Pencil on paper.
Musée Bonnat, Bayonne

and disinterestedness perhaps unknown in his profession' [22] – was also instrumental in the development of the royal collection and of the museum planned at the Louvre.

After Paillet, and presumably directly from Paillet, the picture came into the collection of 'M.Brisebarre', after whose death it is finally recorded in the posthumous sale of 6 June 1814. It was sold for 806 francs to 'Desse' (?), being described once again as 'dans le style de Benedette', and is heard of no more.[23]

The habit of engravers' keeping pictures in stock for many years, perhaps for re-use as thesis-plates, may offer a partial explanation for the eagerness with which this particular picture was snapped up by successive engravers.[24] Its later history, however, involving a sculptor and two major dealers – who were also trained as painters and were among the most discriminating connoisseurs of their day – suggests that it was also especially treasured for its own sake.

NOTES

1 A.Ananoff and D.Wildenstein, *François Boucher*, 2 vols., Lausanne and Paris, 1976 (hereafter A&W), cat. 34.
2 A&W, fig. 222; cat. 34/4.
3 A.Laing, *François Boucher*, exh. cat., 1986, Metropolitan Museum, New York, p. 16 (hereafter Laing). A&W cat. 35.
4 Laing, p. 57, fig. 36.
5 A&W cat. 32.
6 Laing, p. 16.
7 Ibid., pp. 16-17.
8 Ibid., p. 16.
9 Ibid., p. 95.
10 A&W, cat. 34.
11 Ibid., where the other picture referred to is cat. 47, and is also lost.
12 *Dictionary of Art.*
13 Ibid.
14 Laing, p. 18.
15 *Dictionary of Art.* Huquier Jnr. settled in England *c* 1779 where he worked as a portraitist in pastels.
16 S.Lami, *Dictionnaire des sculpteurs...* , edn. 1911, 2 vols., vol. 2.
17 Laing, pp. 58-9.
18 A&W, cat. 34.
19 *Dictionary of Art.*
20 Ibid.
21 Ibid.
22 Ibid., D'Angivillier to Louis XVI.
23 A&W, cat. 35.
24 Laing, pp. 95-6: 'Boucher's indebtedness to Castiglione was twofold: to his subject matter, in opening his eyes to nature, and to his technique, in liberating his facility with the brush.'

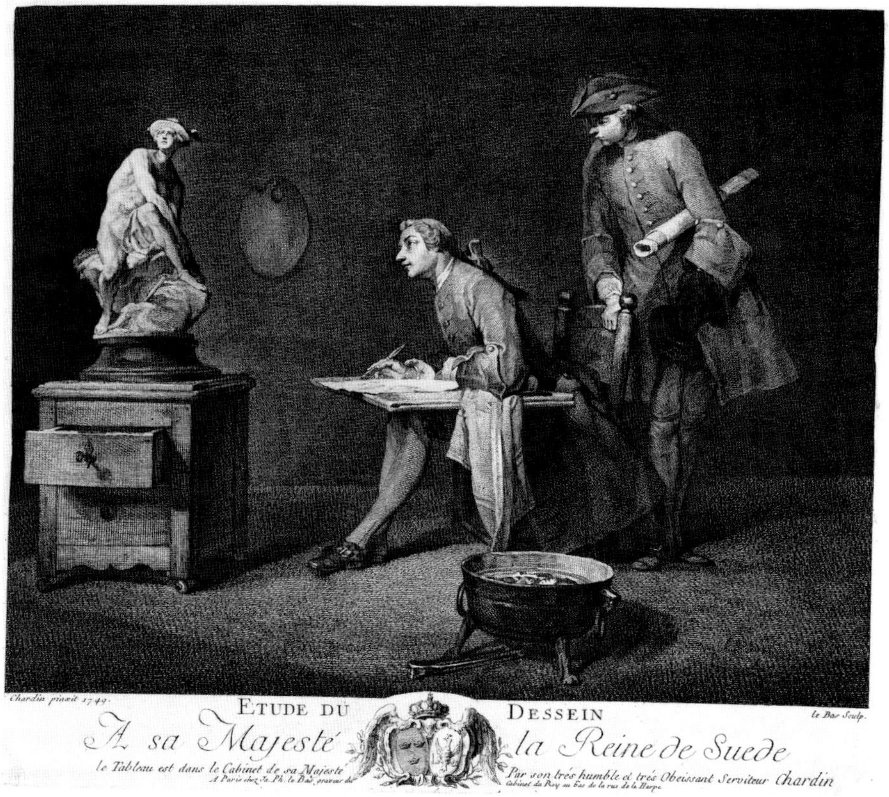
Chardin pinxit 1749.
ETUDE DU DESSEIN
le Bas Sculp.
A sa Majesté la Reine de Suede
le Tableau est dans le Cabinet de sa Majesté
Par son trés humble et trés Obeissant Serviteur Chardin
A Paris chez Ja. Ph. le Bas graveur du Cabinet du Roy au bas de la rue de la Harpe

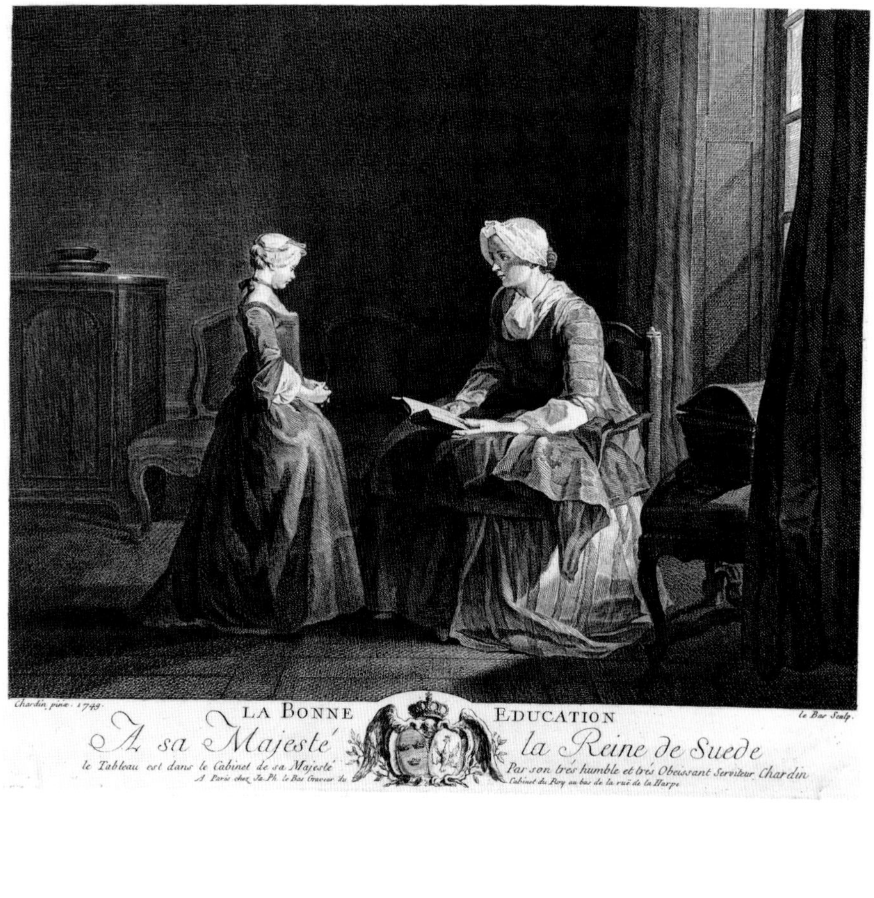
Chardin pinx. 1749.
LA BONNE EDUCATION
le Bas Sculp.
A sa Majesté la Reine de Suede
le Tableau est dans le Cabinet de sa Majesté
Par son trés humble et trés Obeissant Serviteur Chardin
A Paris chez Ja. Ph. le Bas Graveur du Cabinet du Roy au bas de la ruë de la Harpe

Jean Baptiste Siméon Chardin

1699-1779

L'étude du dessin
La bonne éducation

Oil on canvas
41 × 47 cm

This pair of pictures is known to have existed in two versions. The first pair, now lost, was painted in 1748-9 and one of them, *L'étude du dessin* (*The drawing lesson*), was exhibited at the Salon of 1748 (no. 53). Then both pictures were sent to Sweden, between September and November 1749, where they went into the collection of the then Crown Princess, later Queen Consort, Lovisa-Ulrika (or Louise-Ulrique, 1720-82), the formidable sister of Frederick the Great of Prussia, the wife of King Adolf Frederick of Sweden (*r.* 1751-71) and mother of the remarkable Gustavus III (1746-92, succeeded 1771).

This pair of pictures was subsequently engraved, in 1757, by Jacques-Philippe Le Bas (1707-83), with a dedication to the Queen and an inscription identifying them as being 'dans le Cabinet de sa Majesté'.[1] They had been commissioned by Lovisa-Ulrika in 1747, when she was Crown Princess, through Count Carl Gustaf Tessin (1695-1770), the Chancellor, who had been Ambassador in Paris, most recently in 1739-42, and who was to supervise the education of her son, the future Gustavus III. Tessin corresponded with Chardin on her behalf, immediately following the long-delayed but triumphant arrival in June 1747 at the Swedish court of Chardin's *Domestic Pleasures* and *Household Economy*:

> The pictures by Chardin are something to go on your knees before and, from one desire to another, we have come to want two more, but each with two figures; I know very well it is a matter of a year, but we shall rant, and we shall bear with patience.[2]

The price was much increased, from 600 *livres* for a 'two-figure' work for Tessin in 1741 (*La toilette du matin*, Nationalsmuseum, Stockholm)[3] to a fee now of 1,000 *livres* for each of the requested pictures. Indeed, it took two years for Chardin to complete the second of them, *A girl reciting her Gospel*, which was engraved by Le Bas as *La bonne éducation*. *L'étude du dessin* was also engraved by Le Bas at the same time, and a peculiar feature of the engravings is that *L'étude* is in the same sense as the surviving painting of that subject (Tokyo, Fuji Art Museum) while the other, *La bonne éducation*, is (as is more usual) in the reverse sense to the surviving painting (Houston, Texas, Museum of Fine Arts). *L'étude* differs in some details between the painting and the engraving, while *La bonne éducation* is identical in both. These facts may have some bearing upon the key point that, while two pairs of paintings of this subject are known to have been executed, only one pair survives.

Another confusing element in the story is the fact that while the two surviving paintings have a Swedish provenance dating back to the time of Queen Lovisa-Ulrika, they can be traced not to the royal collections – as one might expect – but

L'étude du dessin
(The drawing lesson).
Engraving, 1757,
by Jacques-Philippe le Bas
after lost painting
by Jean Baptiste Siméon Chardin
(1699-1769)

La bonne éducation
(A girl reciting her Gospel).
Engraving, 1757.
by Jacques-Philippe le Bas
after lost painting
by Jean Baptiste Siméon Chardin

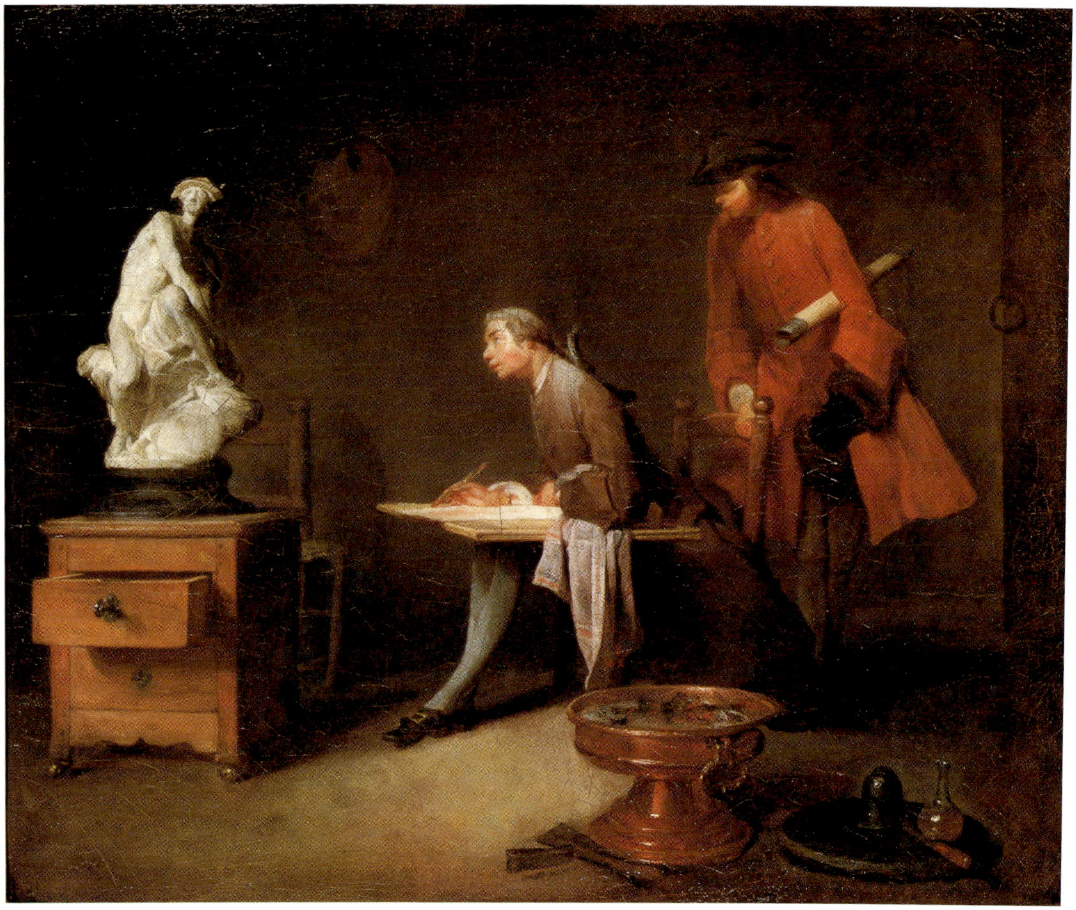

L'étude du dessin
(The drawing lesson)
by Jean Baptiste Siméon Chardin.
Oil on canvas, 41 × 47 cm.
Fuji Art Museum, Tokyo

Les amusements de la vie privée
(Domestic pleasures)
by Jean Baptiste Siméon Chardin.
Oil on canvas, 43 × 36 cm.
Nationalmuseum, Stockholm

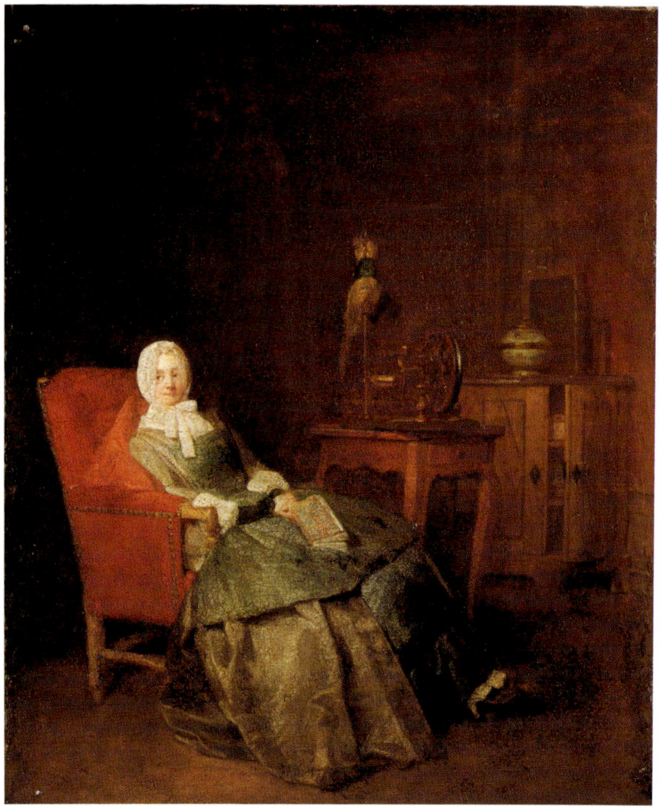

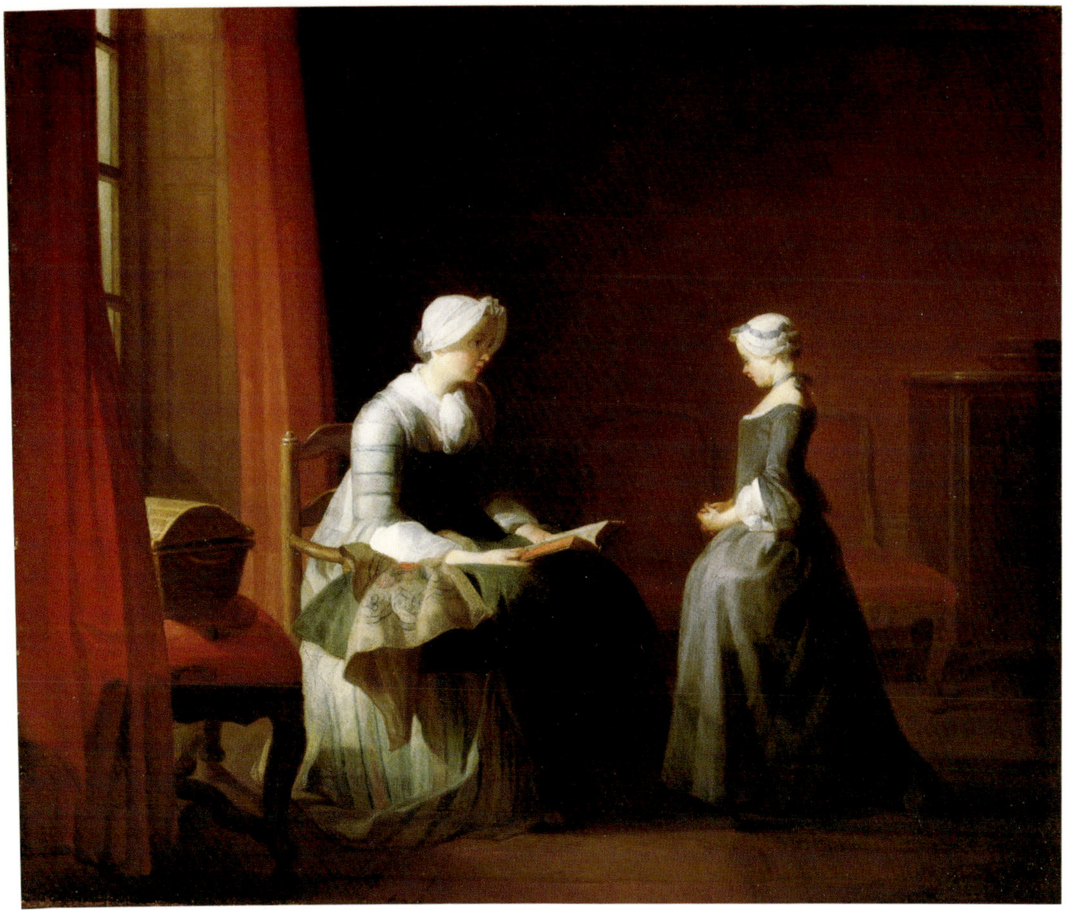

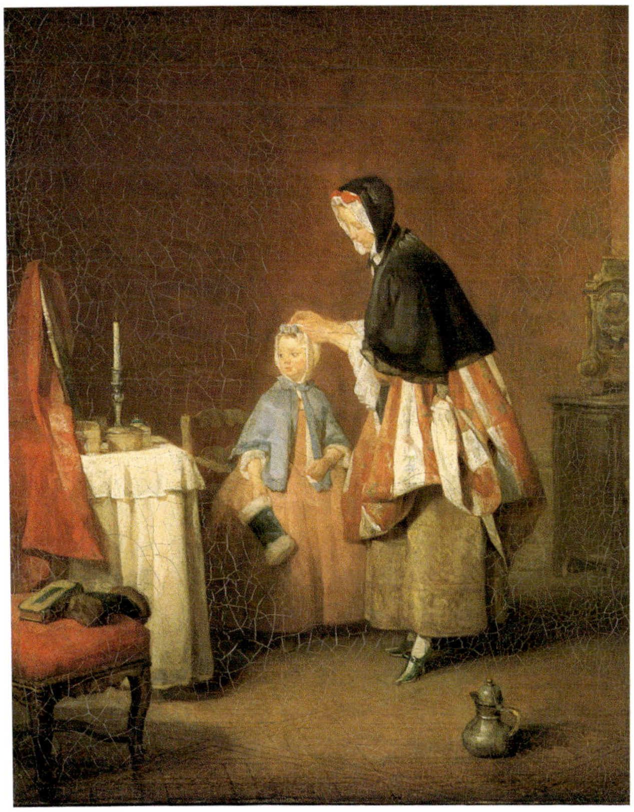

La bonne éducation
(A girl reciting her Gospel)
by Jean Baptiste Siméon Chardin.
Oil on canvas, 41.5 × 47.3 cm.
Museum of Fine Art, Houston, Texas

La toilette du matin
(The morning toilet)
by Jean Baptiste Siméon Chardin.
Oil on canvas, 49 × 39 cm.
Nationalmuseum, Stockholm

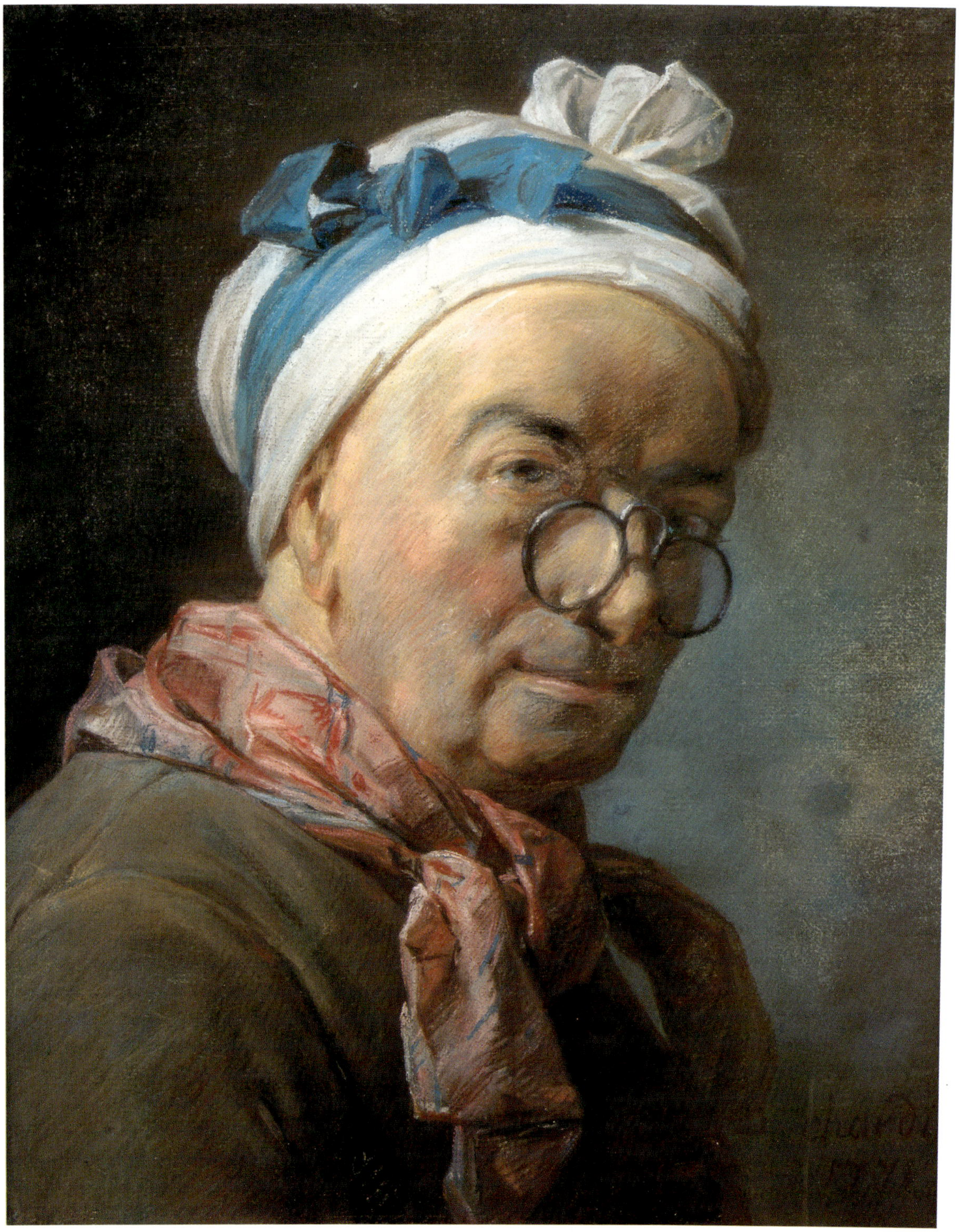

Self-portrait by Jean-Baptiste Siméon Chardin, 1771.
Pastel, 46 × 37.5 cm.
Musée du Louvre, Paris

to the family of Count Carl-Gustav Sparre (1746-94), whose collection remained largely intact in Sweden until quite recently. At first sight, it would seem logical to suppose that this surviving pair was identical with that originally recorded in the Queen's possession, and that they somehow went to Sparre, perhaps as a gift (or sale) from the Queen,[4] but that would appear not to have been the case. Both the

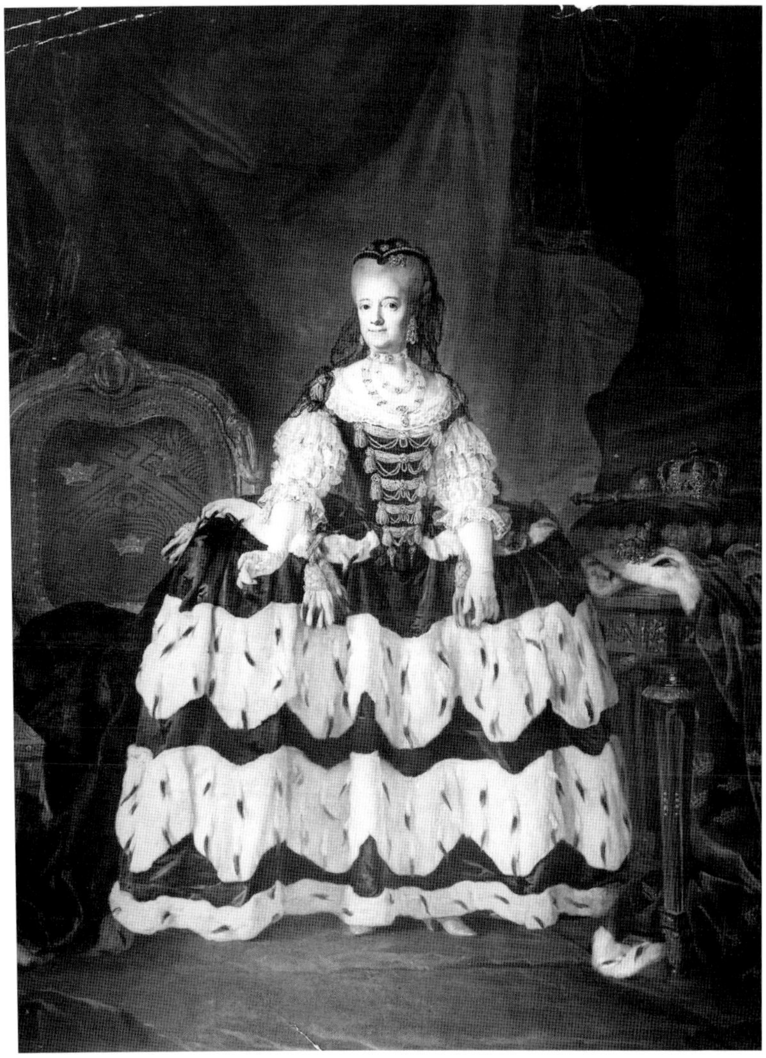

Queen Lovisa-Ulrika of Sweden (1720-80)
by Lorenz Pasch the Younger (*c.* 1733-1805), *c.* 1775.
Oil on canvas.
National Portrait Gallery, Gripsholm, Sweden

surviving pictures have a provenance from Wanås in Sweden, where the Sparre collection went in 1837,[5] and the strong probability is that Sparre bought his pair of pictures independently of the Queen. They were sold, at a price of 720 *livres* the pair, at the sale of an important collector, Ange-Laurent de La Live de Jully (1725-79), in 1770, the sale having started on 5 March and these pictures selling between 2-14 May (lot 87). They are recorded as having been sold to 'Langlier' (acting for a client).[6]

This second pair of paintings (belonging to La Live de Jully) had been exhibited at the *Salon* of 1753 (no. 59) with the explicit description that they were replicas, with certain changes made to the composition, 'répétitions avec des changements', of the paintings that had been sent to Sweden a few years previously.[7] It is conceivable that these 'changements' included the reversal of one of the original compositions on the part of Chardin. Certainly, the presence of slight but distinct differences between the engraving and surviving painting of *L'étude* suggests that the latter painting is indeed that exhibited in the 1753 Salon, and that this picture is that which, with its pair, was subsequently recorded in the sale of La Live de Jully in 1770. Prior to this sale, the pair of pictures had been listed in La Live's collection, appearing in the *Catalogue Historique du Cabinet de... M.de Lalive* of 1764. An important point is that Langlier was otherwise acting on Sparre's behalf at the 1770 sale: Sparre (who was on his Grand Tour 1768-72, most of it spent in Paris) bought a Greuze through Langlier, *La Blanchisseuse*, now in the Getty Museum, Los Angeles (Acc. 83.PA.387). The descent of the Greuze until its acquisition by the Getty in 1983 is as follows: from Count Sparre to his immediate family at Kulla Gunnarstorp, Sweden, until *c.* 1837, then by inheritance to Count C.de Geer, Leufsta, Wanås, Sweden, until 1855; and then to his granddaughter Elizabeth, Countess Wachtmeister, until 1983, having been inherited by Axel, Count Wachtmeister, still at Wanås.[8]

As noted above, the two surviving Chardin pictures in question also came from Wanås before their entry into their present collections.[9] Since they were listed in La Live's *Catalogue* and were then entered in the same sale in 1770 as *La Blanchisseuse*, where they were also sold to Langlier, it is reasonable to suppose that they were also bought there by Langlier on behalf of Count Sparre. Nor is it surprising that Count Sparre should have bought this pair of Chardin pictures at this sale: he shared in the taste for all things French that was such a feature of the Swedish court under the influence of the Queen – who, for example, insisted upon her son's speaking French (and not German) as his only foreign language.[10]

Sparre possessed a collection strong in French paintings of the period and is recorded as buying further works, including Dutch and Flemish pictures, in sales in Paris in 1780.[11] Count Tessin, also, had owned works by Chardin (including, interestingly, the only absolutely certain drawings by Chardin to survive):[12] *La toilette du matin* mentioned above, and the magnificent still-life *Hare with a caldron* (Nationalsmuseum, Stockholm). The purchase of replicas by Chardin was also entirely usual: he created compositions, as he painted, slowly and with great pains, and throughout his career made a habit of repeating successful designs, and these works were just as much sought after as the prime originals.

Lovisa-Ulrika owned an exceptionally large number of works by Chardin, which she kept, with most of her collection, at Drottningholm.[13] These works included the two paintings owned by Tessin already mentioned, which she acquired from him. All of them, apparently, as might be expected, passed to the Nationalsmuseum, Stockholm, where they remain – with the exception of the missing pair in question. The probability is therefore that these two pictures were disposed of during her lifetime. The reasons for her possibly having had to sell them – rather than giving them away, for example – are not hard to seek: she was astonishingly extravagant and continually in debt for vast sums.[14] In 1774, to take one instance, when she was Queen Dowager, her debts amounted to £16,000 and had to be paid by her son, the King (Gustavus III). She was headstrong to a fault. When involved politically, as she often was, especially in the first part of her husband's reign, it was disastrous; and she fell out with nearly everyone around her, including her eldest son, to whom she was finally reconciled (with difficulty on her part) only on her death bed.[15] Yet under her the Swedish court flourished artistically and intellectually as never before:

> Her charm, her brilliance, and her enthusiasm made her court a magnet for all that was most distinguished in the arts and sciences: Tessin, Dalin, Linnaeus, Klingenstierna, all enjoyed her patronage and her friendship... She was in her own person a link with all that was best in the intellectual life of Europe, and especially of France.[16]

The missing pair of paintings may well have been separated after leaving her collection at some unknown date – and the surviving pair has also become separated, albeit only in the 1980s. The only trace of the missing pictures – and that of only one of the pair – is the presence of a Chardin painting in a Christie's sale of 10 May 1844 (lot 40). This sale was one of works from the collection (or stock) of the brothers Rochard, who were *marchands-amateurs* (they sold works in London, Brussels and Paris between 1844-59), and in the catalogue the single painting was identified as 'The student, the engraved picture'.[17] It was not the only work by Chardin to have been sold by the Rochard brothers, for they had sold the *Still life with basket of black and white grapes* (Louvre, Paris) to Dr La Caze by 1860;[18] but this particular record of their activities is the most tantalizing.

NOTES

1 P. Connisbee, *Chardin*, 1986, pp. 172-5.
2 Tessin to Chardin, quoted ibid., p. 172.
3 P. Rosenberg, *Chardin*, exh. cat., Grand Palais, Paris, 1979, cat. no. 88.
4 This is the supposition, for example, of G. Wildenstein, *Chardin*, Zurich, 1963, cat. nos. 225, 226.
5 See below.
6 As bought by Langlier 'for Boileau', but in P. Rosenberg and R. Temperini, *Chardin, suivi du catalogue des oeuvres*, Paris, 1999, cat. 127a, 127, 128a, 128, as bought by Sparre at the La Live de Jully sale (p. 257). Sale details, Wildenstein, loc. cit.; Rosenberg, 1979, op. cit., p. 292.
7 Rosenberg and Temperini, 1999, op. cit., p. 257.
8 Getty Provenance Index. *The Dictionary of Art* states that the entire collection of Count Sparre was sold by his descendants in 1837 'to the Wachtmeister family and moved to Wanås Castle'.
9 Exhibited in Paris in 1979 (Rosenberg, 1979, op. cit.) as 'Sweden, Wanås Collection', cat. nos. 94, 95.
10 See, for example, R. Nisbet Bain, *Gustavus III and his Contemporaries*, 1894, 2 vols., I, p. 15.
11 For example, a Gerard Ter Borch, *Interior of a Stable*, now also in the Getty Museum. The family was one of the most distinguished in Sweden: for instance, the portrait of Ebba, Countess Sparre, by Sebastien Bourdon, is in the National Gallery of Art, Washington, and had formerly been in the Orléans collection. The tragic story of Count Sixtus Sparre was the subject of a famous feature film of the 1960s, *Elvira Madigan*. There is a standard work on Gustav Adolf Sparre by I. Hasselgren, *Konstsamlaren Gustav Adolf Sparre 1746-1794. Hans studieresa våning och konstsaling i Göteborg*, Göteborg, 1974.
12 Rosenberg, 1979, op. cit., p. 76, cat. nos. 1, 2, 4.
13 Rosenberg, 1979, op. cit., p. 75, notes nine in that exhibition.
14 Bain, op. cit., I, p. 249.
15 Ibid. See also Michael Roberts, *The Age of Liberty: Sweden 1719-1772*, 1986, pp. 178ff.
16 Roberts, op. cit., p. 178.
17 Rosenberg, 1979, op. cit., pp. 291-2.
18 Ibid., pp. 118-9.

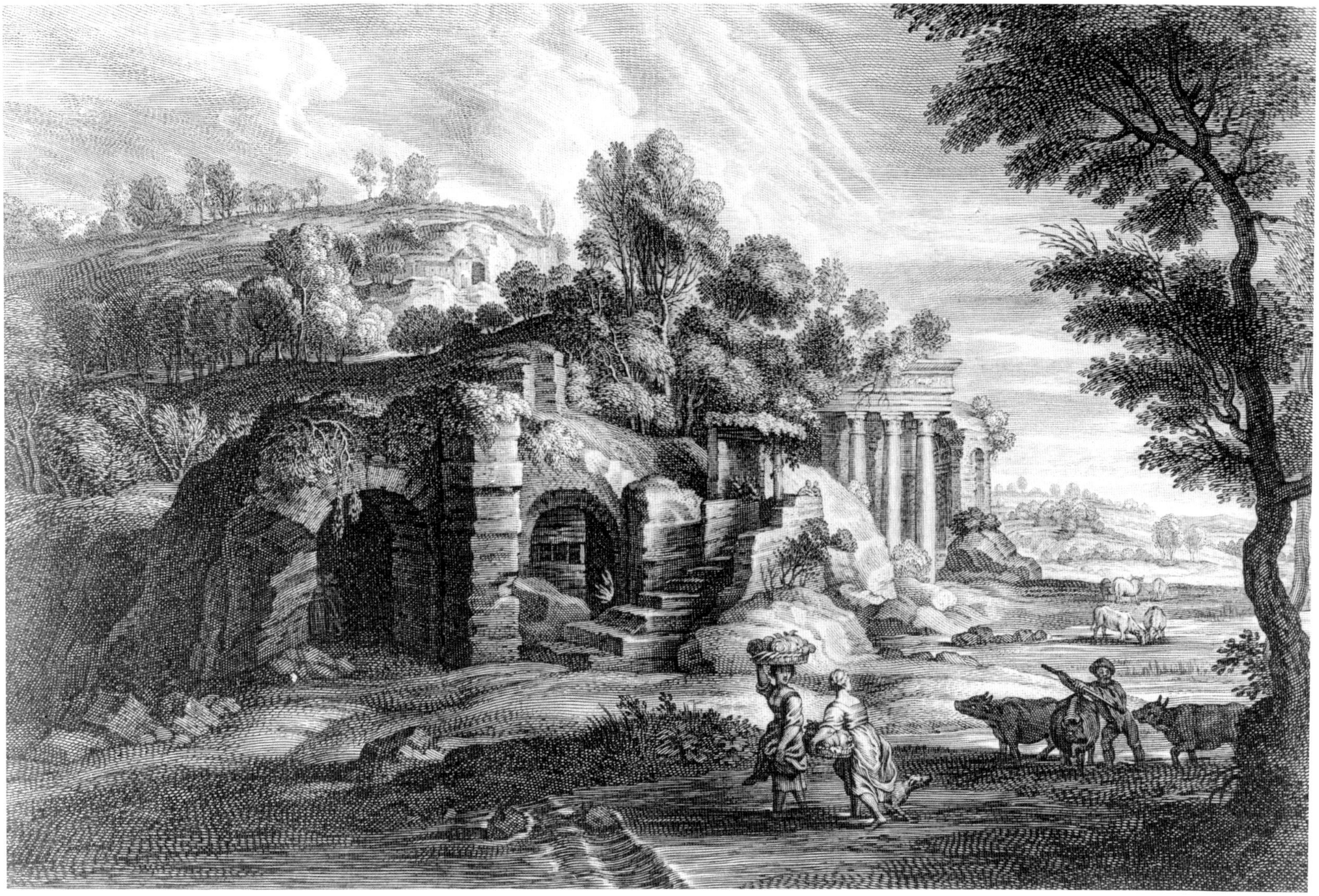

Landscape with Antique ruins.
Engraving by Schelte a Bolswert after lost painting by Peter Paul Rubens (1577-1640) of *c.* 1614, published by Gillis Hendricx, 31.9 × 45 cm

Peter Paul Rubens

1577-1640

Landscape with Antique ruins

c. 1614

Oil on canvas laid down on panel
73.5 × 107 cm

Landscape with Antique ruins has not been seen since the nineteenth century, but before that it can almost certainly be traced directly back to Rubens's own collection.[1] Its composition is known from an engraving by Schelte a Bolswert published by Gillis Hendricx,[2] which is inscribed (bottom left) '*Peter Paul Rubens pinxit/S. a Bolswert sculpsit*' and (bottom right) '*Gillis Hendricx excudit*'. It is also known from a painted copy (Musée Fabre, Montpellier), probably taken after the original in the seventeenth century, which 'well reproduces Rubens's style of colouring at the time of the *Landscape with the Ruins of the Palatine*... and *The Farm at Laken*'.[3] The composition of *Landscape with Antique ruins* is closely related to that of *Landscape with the ruins of the Palatine* and it must therefore, like that picture, have been one of the very earliest of Rubens's landscapes, and both have been dated to *c.* 1614.[4] Its disappearance is therefore especially significant.

Some elements of the composition, of both architecture and figures, are related to a sketch, perhaps dating from 1606, which Rubens made of a *trattoria* in the Baths of Diocletian in Rome,[5] where he had been most recently in 1608 towards the end of his period in Italy (which began in 1600). Further elements appear to have been derived from *Il Contento* by Adam Elsheimer (National Gallery of Scotland),[6] a painter whom Rubens much admired and who had considerable influence upon his work.

At Rubens's death in 1640 his family had an inventory taken of the many pictures in his house, transcripts of which exist in French and in English, with identical numbering but with certain differences in the details. *Landscape with Antique ruins* is generally identified with no. 105 in both versions of the inventory, and the picture is described in a similar way in both versions. The English transcript was referred to as early as July 1640 by Sir Balthazar Gerbier in a letter to William Murray: 'Brussells. ... I do send, herewith, ye register, wch I have receaved but yesterday from Antwerp,... of ye late Sr Peeter Rubens rarityes wch paper is a true translation of its original.'[7]

This 'register', headed 'An Inventory of pictures found in the Howse of the late Sr Peter Paul Rubens, Kn^{t}, after his death... ', was published by W.N.Sainsbury in 1859[8] and after listing other works it specifically states, 'Here follow the peices made by the late Sr Peter Paul Rubens... 105. A piece, an Italian Landschap, wth the ruines of a Church, which is cloth pasted upon a bord.'[9] The word 'church' is unexpected, perhaps, in this description, but the French version of the inventory is clearer about the subject-matter: 'Cy suivent les pieces faictes par feu Monsieur Rubens... 105. Une pièce collée sur du bois d'un paysage d'Italie avec la ruine

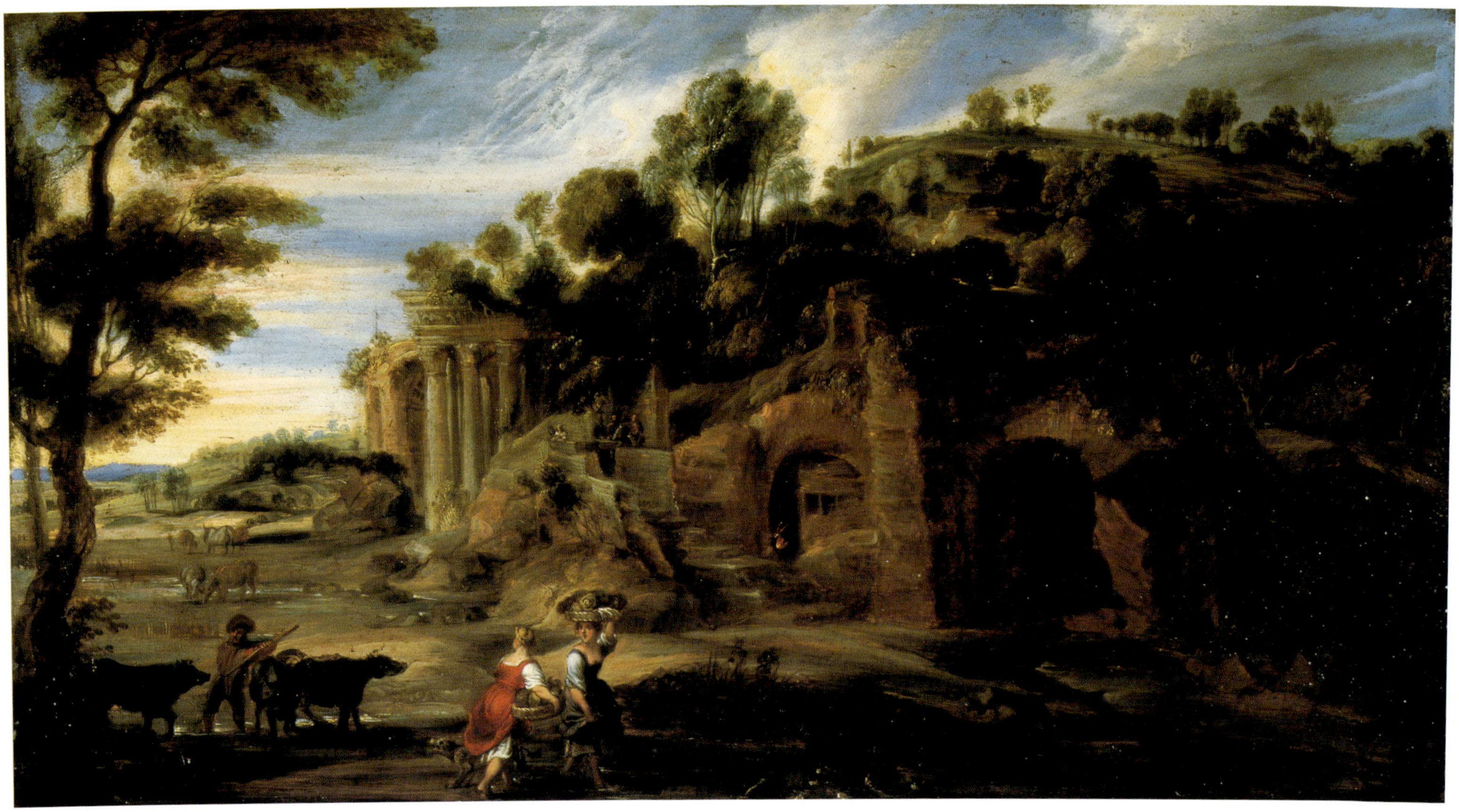

Landscape with Antique ruins.
Anonymous copy of lost painting by Peter Paul Rubens.
Oil on panel, 34.4 × 57.6 cm.
Musée Fabre, Montpellier

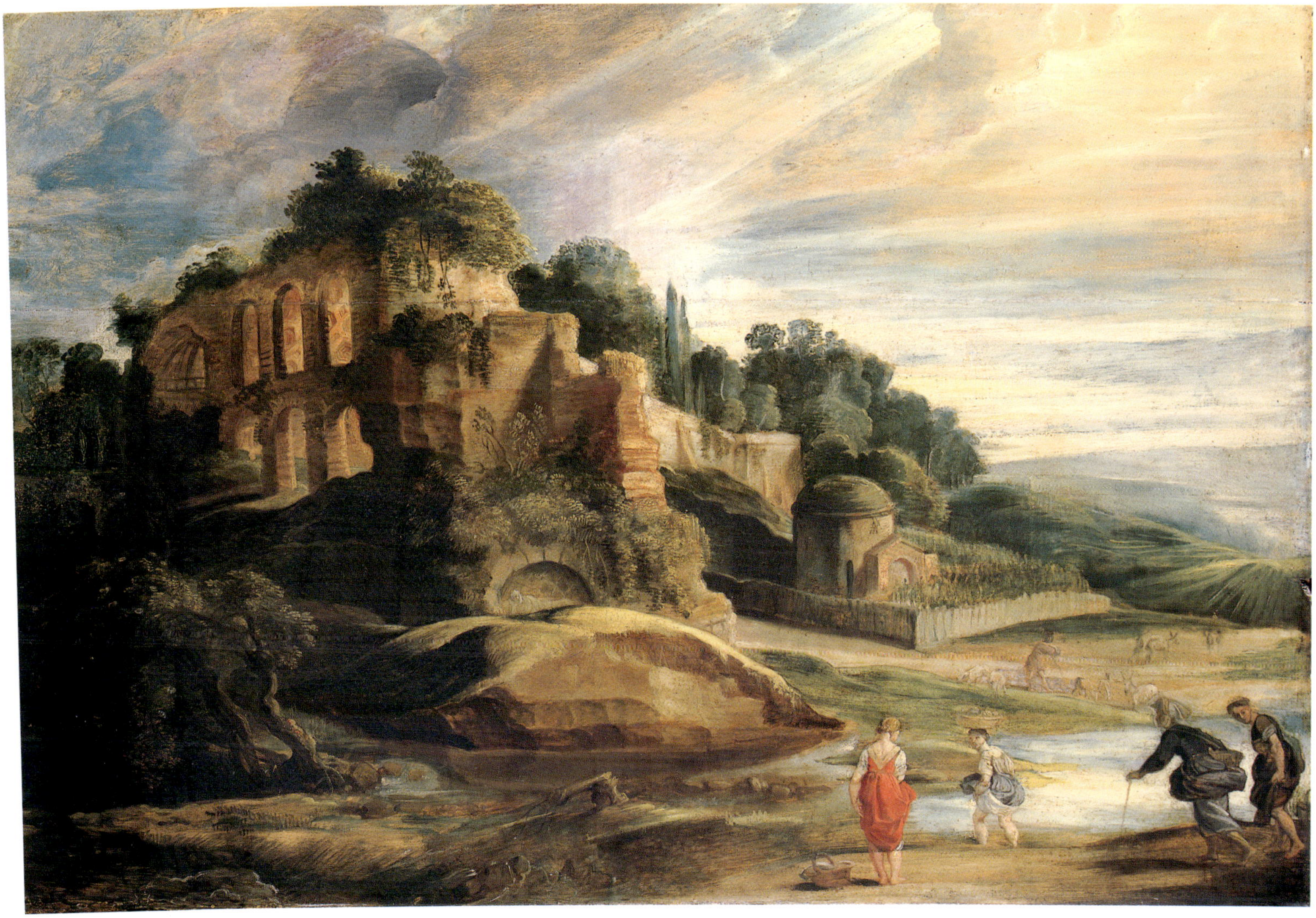

Landscape with ruins of the Palatine
by Peter Paul Rubens.
Oil on panel, 76 × 106.5 cm.
Musée du Louvre, Paris

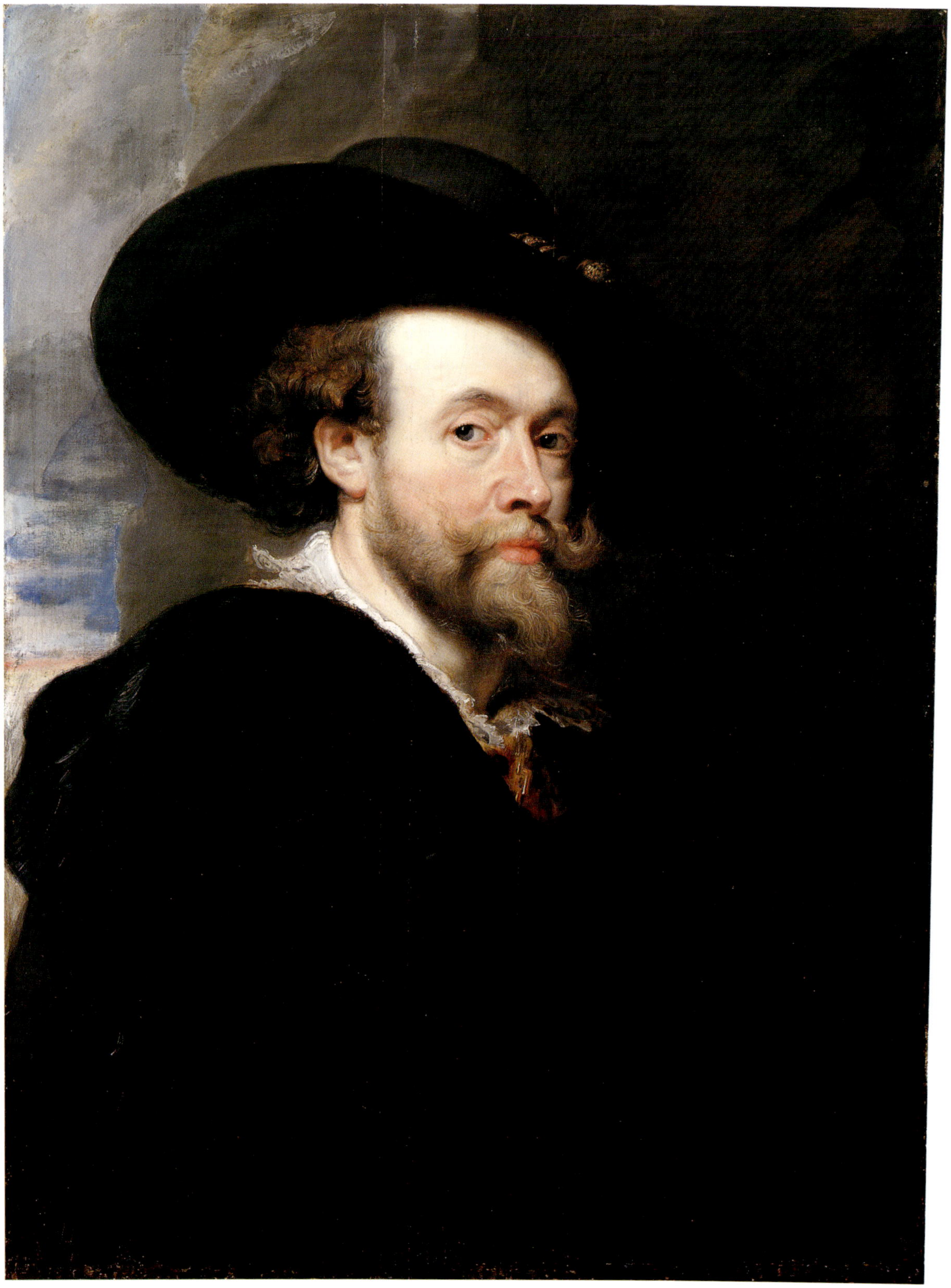

Self-portrait by Peter Paul Rubens, 1622.
Oil on panel, 85.7 × 62.2 cm.

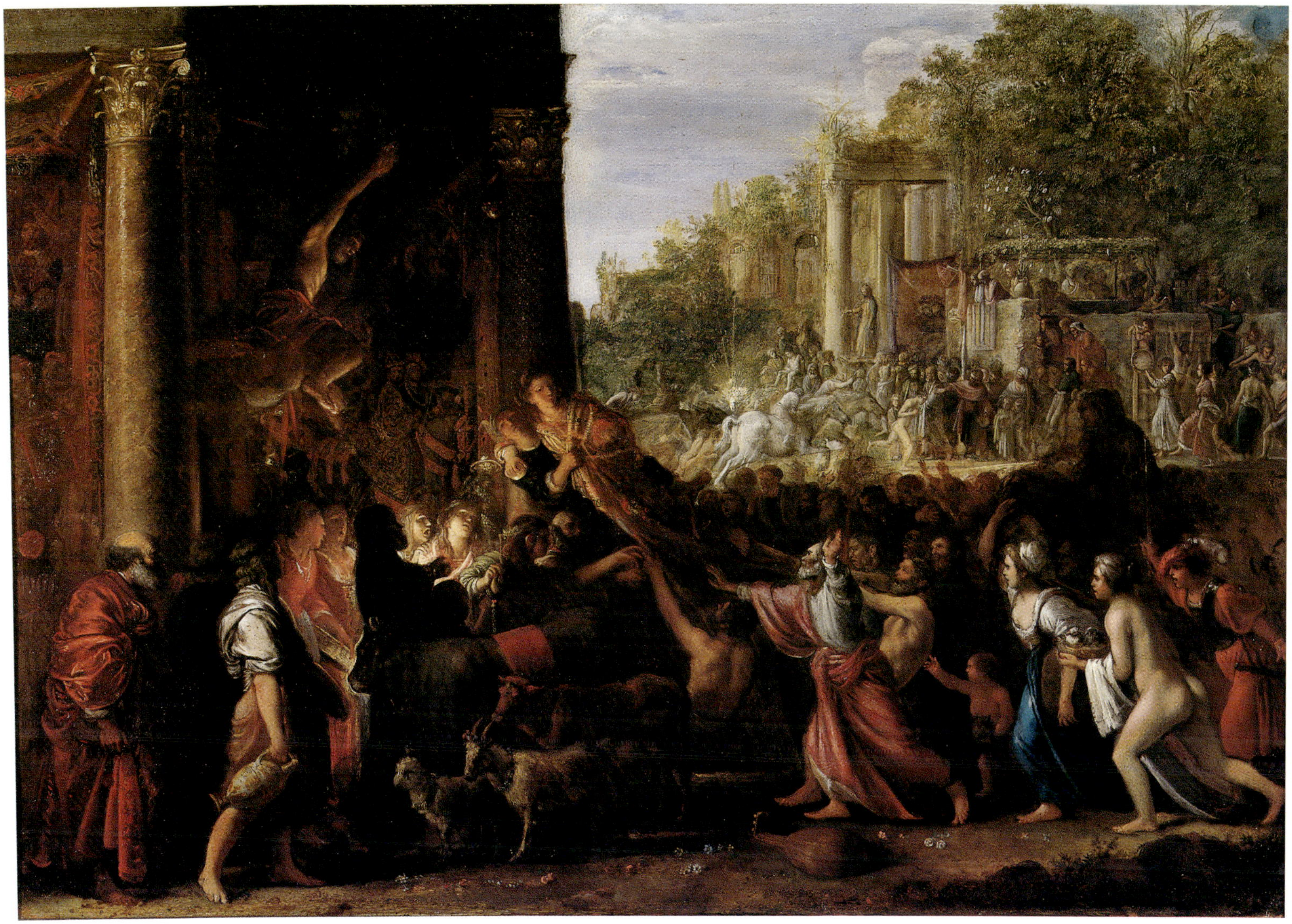

Il contento
by Adam Elsheimer
(1578-1610).
Oil on copper, 30.1 × 42 cm.
National Gallery of Scotland, Edinburgh

d'un Temple.' ('Here follow the pieces made by the late Monsieur Rubens... 105. A piece stuck down on panel with a landscape of Italy with the ruin of a temple.')[10] This inventory was described by Sainsbury as 'the printed catalogue, published in France, shortly after the death of the artist'.

It is the original purpose of the English 'register', as Balthazar Gerbier called it, which may hold the key to the early history of the lost painting. This inventory was created for the specific purpose of informing King Charles I of the contents of Rubens's collection, with a view to Gerbier's subsequently buying works of art from it for the King. If the King did in fact buy *Landscape with Antique ruins* it might explain why it is next noted by the *Corpus Rubenianum* as the picture in the collection of King James II, 'Un paysage avec figures et ruines'.[11] It is unlikely, however, that the painting could have passed by straightforward inheritance to James II, who was King Charles I's younger son, since most of Charles's collection was disposed of by the Commonwealth, following the King's beheading in 1649,

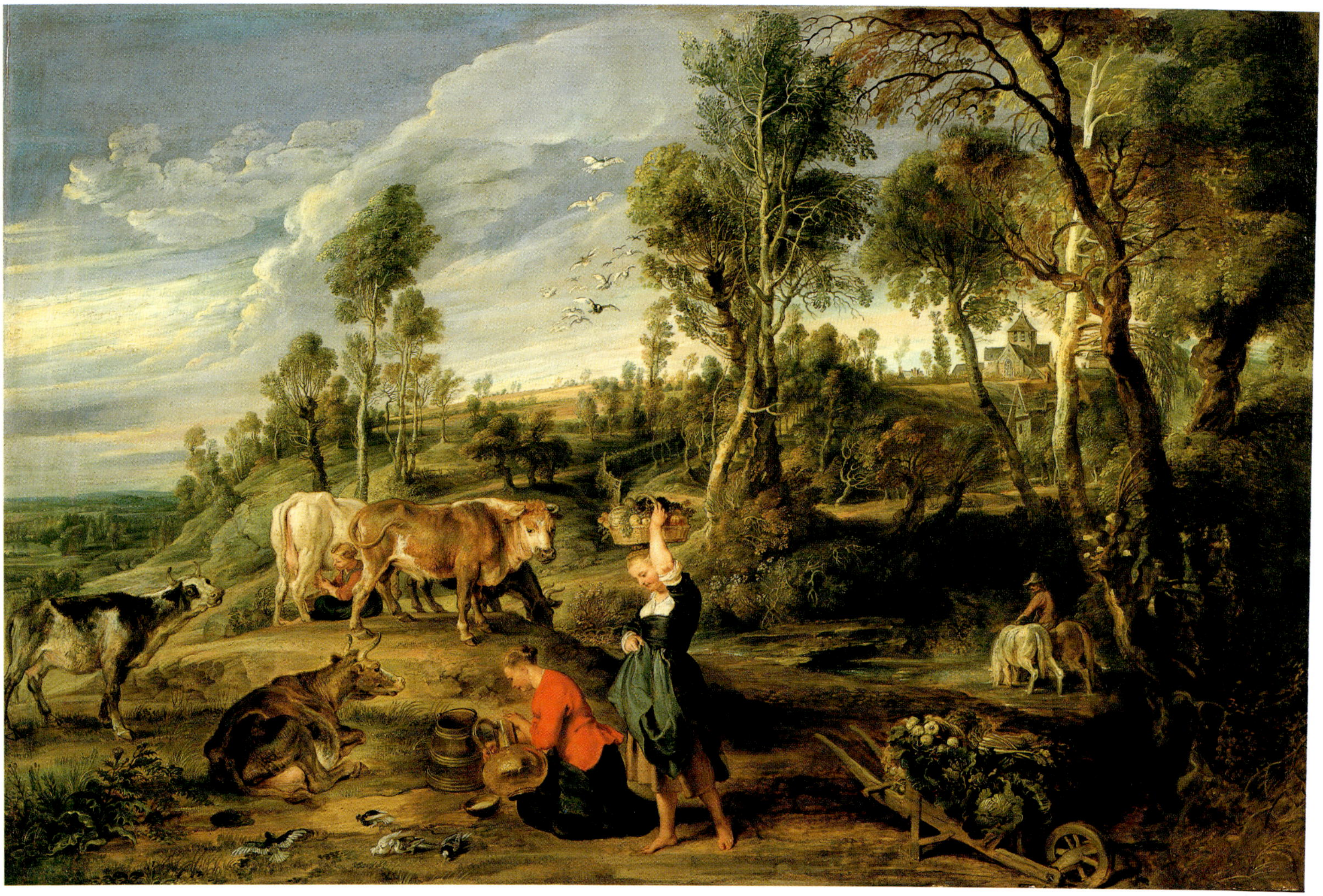

The farm at Laken
by Peter Paul Rubens, *c.* 1617.
Oil on panel, 85.7 × 125.9 cm.
The Royal Collection, © 2002
Her Majesty Queen Elizabeth II

in a series of sales around 1650.[12] On the other hand, many of the late King's pictures did find their way back in to the Royal Collection quite swiftly over the ensuing years, some through the actions of loyal courtiers, others because succeeding monarchs deliberately sought out works that had belonged to Charles's legendary collection, and some by diplomatic gifts.

Certainly, Charles's interest in purchasing works by Rubens from Rubens's own collection would have been very much in character. As King he had patronised Rubens, not least for the great ceiling of the Banqueting House at Whitehall Palace; and while still Prince of Wales he had made sure that a splendid *Self-Portrait* of the painter (1623, Collection of Her Majesty The Queen) was included in his collection of self-portraits. In return, Rubens paid Charles the compliment of calling him 'the greatest amateur of painting among the princes of the world'.[13]

Gerbier, as in other such transactions he carried out as one of the King's art agents on the Continent, urged both speed and the need for sufficient funds – not

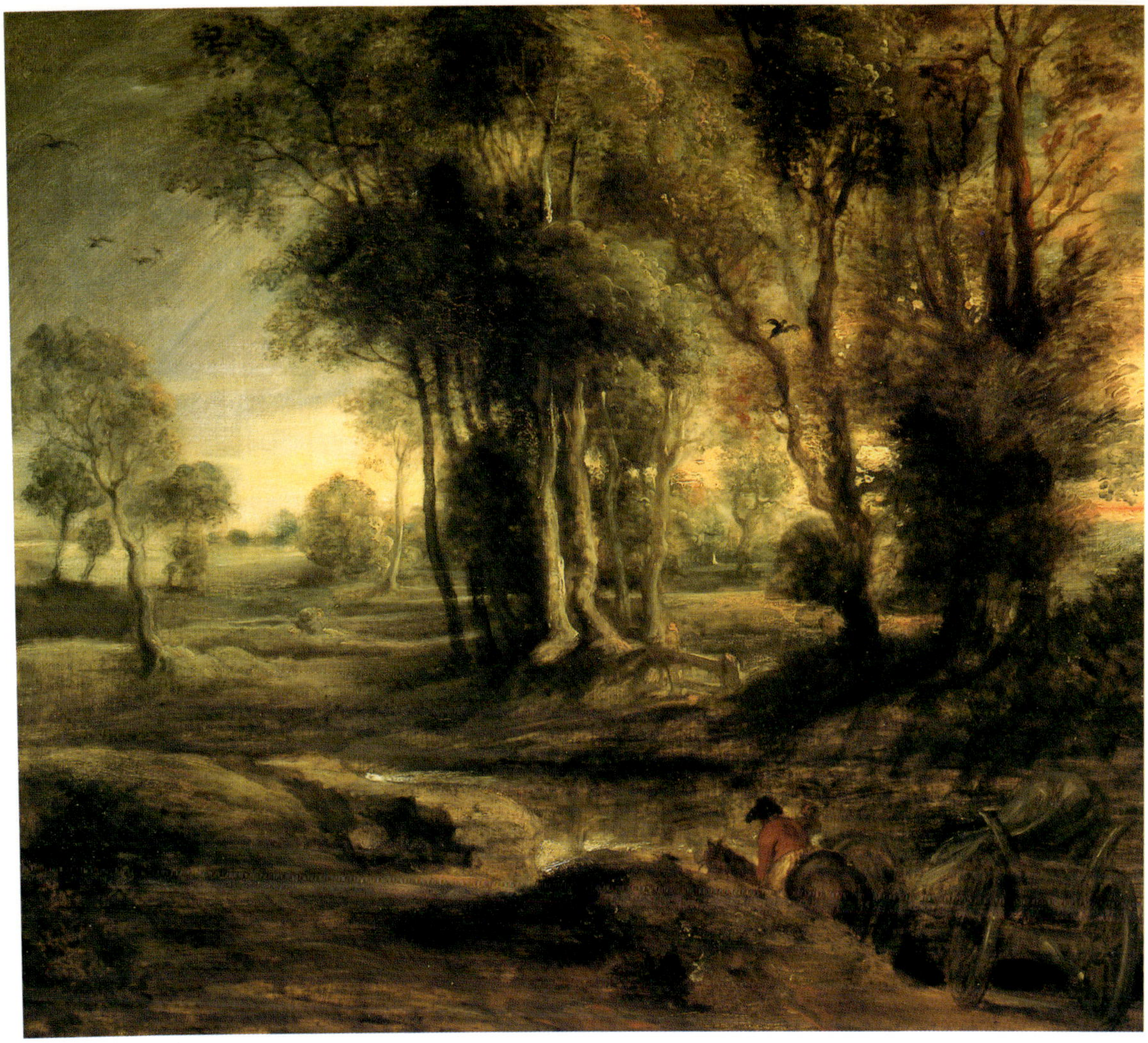

Landscape with a waggon at sunset by Rubens, *c.* 1635.
Oil on panel, 49.5 × 54.5 cm.
Museum Boymans-van Beuningen, Rotterdam

least because, as he says in the letter to Murray, his own payments were well in arrears:

Iff his Maj^{ty} and y^{r}selfe sends gelt [gold], and do cause to be pricht [priced] such parcells [lots] as I shalbe commanded to consider, I will in y^{r}, as in all other things, endeav^{r} to obey most punctually, and venter [venture] my skill for ye right choice; but gelt is my mayne matter, and soe would a favorable word in my particular helpe, to farther ye paym^{t} of my arreares, which would bee more comfort to me then shaddowes off things.[14]

The pictures alone in Rubens's collection, according to the printed catalogue in French, numbered 319 (although the English version lists 314). The initial plan had been to sell all of them by auction but instead they were valued by Snyders, Wildens and Nicholas Moermans, and were disposed of by private agreements. Charles I was not, in fact, one of the principal buyers, who are listed by Sainsbury rather as the King of Spain, the King of Poland, the Elector of Bavaria, and Cardinal Richelieu.[15]

Landscape with Antique ruins can next be traced to the collection of the 2nd

Marquess of Camden (1759-1840). It appears in his posthumous sale at Christie's 12 June 1841 (57):

57 Rubens. A Landscape, with Buildings, Cattle, and Figures. Engraved in the set of twenty landscapes, by Bolswert; most capital.

On the interleaved record of the sale appears the handwritten annotation: '*57/179.11 Fuller*'. This indicates that it sold for 171 guineas to someone called 'Fuller', about whom, however, no information is presently known, although the same 'Fuller' bought other lots at the same sale – and for similarly substantial sums.[16]

By 1847, however, the picture had evidently entered one of the most celebrated of contemporary collections, that of the poet, banker, patron of the arts, memorialist and man of taste, Samuel Rogers (1763-1855), who was painted or drawn by, among others, Sir Thomas Lawrence, John Linnell, Hoppner and Maclise, and sculpted in a bust by Dantan.[17] It was not the only landscape by Rubens which Rogers owned. One was the moonlight landscape that had belonged to Sir Joshua Reynolds (now Courtauld Institute of Art Gallery).[18] Another, significantly for the *Landscape with Antique ruins*, since it shared the same provenance, was described in the posthumous sale of Rogers's collection in 1856 (see below) as 'the Waggon landscape'. This was *Landscape with a waggon at sunset*, now in the Museum Boymans-van Beuningen, Rotterdam,[19] which had formerly been in the Marquess of Camden's collection.

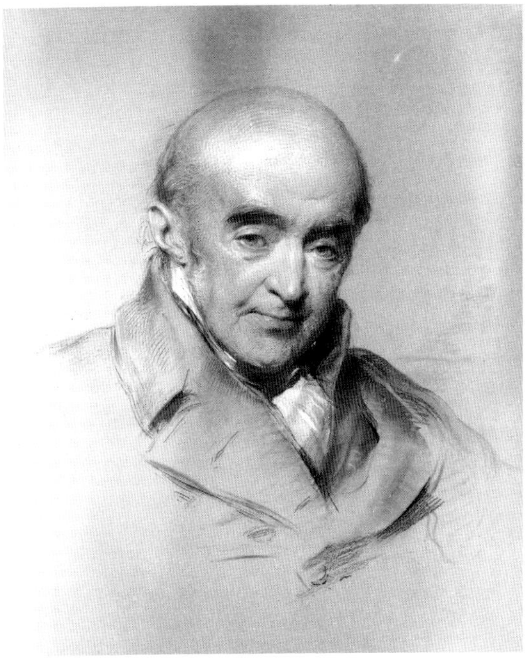

Portrait of Samuel Rogers by George Richmond (1809-96), 1848.
National Portrait Gallery, London

The *Landscape with Antique ruins* does not, however, feature in any of the posthumous sales of Rogers's collections of 1856 which, the art collection and library together, realised the huge sum of £50,000. The sales at Christie's – everything from Egyptian antiquities through books to archaic Greek vases, marbles, pictures, coins and medals – took place from 28 April 1856 and occupied the eighteen following days. The relevant sale, of the paintings proper, began on the fifth day: 'Friday May 2 1856 at one o'clock precisely... In this Catalogue is comprised the entire Collection of Pictures, with the exception of the three fine works bequeathed to the nation.'

Instead, *Landscape with Antique ruins*, as noted by the *Corpus Rubenianum*, is recorded in the collection of Samuel Rogers only during his lifetime, in 1847,[20] by *The Art-Union* magazine in its series of 'Visits to Private Galleries'. It describes 'The Collection of Samuel Rogers, Esq., F.R.S., F.S.A., St. James's-Place', where *Landscape with Antique ruins* is noted hanging in the dining-room:

'Landscape – Woody Scene with Figures.' From the collection of the Marquess of Camden.[21]

There seems to be no doubt that the picture had already left the Rogers collection by the time of his death, in view of the 1856 sale catalogue's assertion that it 'comprised the entire Collection of Pictures, with the exception of the three fine works bequeathed to the nation'. Although Rogers had no children, he was nursed in his last illness, brought on by breaking a leg in the early 1850s, by a devoted niece, and he was also close both to his brother Henry and especially his sister Sarah, 'his special friend and confidant' (*DNB*). The latter had died earlier the same year, his brother Henry some time before that. There is also a John

Rogers mentioned in the records, and each of these relations appears in provenances as having owned pictures from the Samuel Rogers collection.[22] Any of them could have been presented with the missing landscape, as could anyone among the innumerable acquaintances of Samuel Rogers, who was distinguished, according to one writer of the time, for his 'benevolence, hospitality and taste'.[23]

NOTES

1 *Corpus Rubenianum Ludwig Burchard*, Wolfgang Adler, Part XVIII, '1: Landscapes', New York, 1982, no. 15.

2 C.G.Voorhelm Schneevoogt, *Catalogue des Estampes gravées d'après P.P.Rubens*, Haarlem, 1873, p. 232, no. 53; I.G.Glück, *Die Landschaften von Peter Paul Rubens*, Vienna, 1945, no. 40 and p. 40. An impression of the engraving is in the Witt Print Collection, Courtauld Institute of Art, London.

3 Adler, *Corpus*, loc. cit.

4 See, for example, Adler, *Corpus*, op. cit., p. 68.

5 See Adler, *Corpus*, op. cit., no. 1; p. 38; and under no. 15.

6 K.Andrews, *Adam Elsheimer, Paintings, Drawings, Prints*, Oxford, 1977, no. 19, fig. 1.

7 W.Noël Sainsbury, *Original Unpublished Papers Illustrative of the Life of Sir Peter Paul Rubens, as an Artist and a Diplomatist. Preserved in H.M.State Paper Office*, London, 1859, p. 235.

8 Sainsbury says that this manuscript was first published by Dawson Turner for private circulation in 1839 and that he, Sainsbury, reprinted it by permission of Dawson Turner: Sainsbury, op. cit., p. 235.

9 Ibid., p. 239 (and not p. 105 as in Adler, *Corpus*, op. cit., and Glück, loc. cit.).

10 J.Denucé, *De Antwerpsche 'Konstkamers', Inventarissen van de kunstverzamelingen te Antwerpen in de 16e en 17e eeuwen*, Antwerp, 1932, pp. 60, 61.

11 H.Walpole, *A Catalogue of the collection of Pictures, etc., belonging to King James the Second...* , London, 1758, no. 910.

12 A.MacGregor, ed., *The Late King's Goods. Collections, Possessions and Patronage of Charles I in the Light of the Commonwealth Sale Inventories*, London and Oxford, 1989.

13 R.S.Magurn, ed., *The Letters of Peter Paul Rubens*, Cambridge, Mass., 1955, p. 101.

14 Sainsbury, op. cit., p. 235.

15 Ibid., p. 235, n. 295.

16 The sale and price are also recorded, with a full description of the picture ('... 2ft 5 by 3ft 7.–c. Collection of the late Marquis of Camden, [sold by] Christie and Manson, 1841, 171 gs.'), by John Smith, *A Catalogue Raisonné of the works of the most eminent Dutch, Flemish and French Painters...* , IX (Supplement), 1842, p. 331, no. 321.

17 Adler, *Corpus*, op. cit., no. 15, p. 64. For Rogers, see *DNB*.

18 This was lot 593.

19 Adler, *Corpus*, op. cit., no. 58. The Christie's record in the catalogue of Rogers's sale beginning 2 May 1856 shows that it was sold to 'Bentley' for the considerable sum of 610 guineas ('Bentley' is also recorded as having bought for £210, lot 608, Rubens's *Horrors of War*, acting for the National Gallery).

20 Adler, *Corpus*, no. 15, p. 64.

21 *The Art-Union*, 'Monthly journal of the Fine Arts, and the Arts, decorative and ornamental,' vol. 9, 1847, p. 85.

22 Getty Provenance Index.

23 This was Edward Everett: see *DNB*.

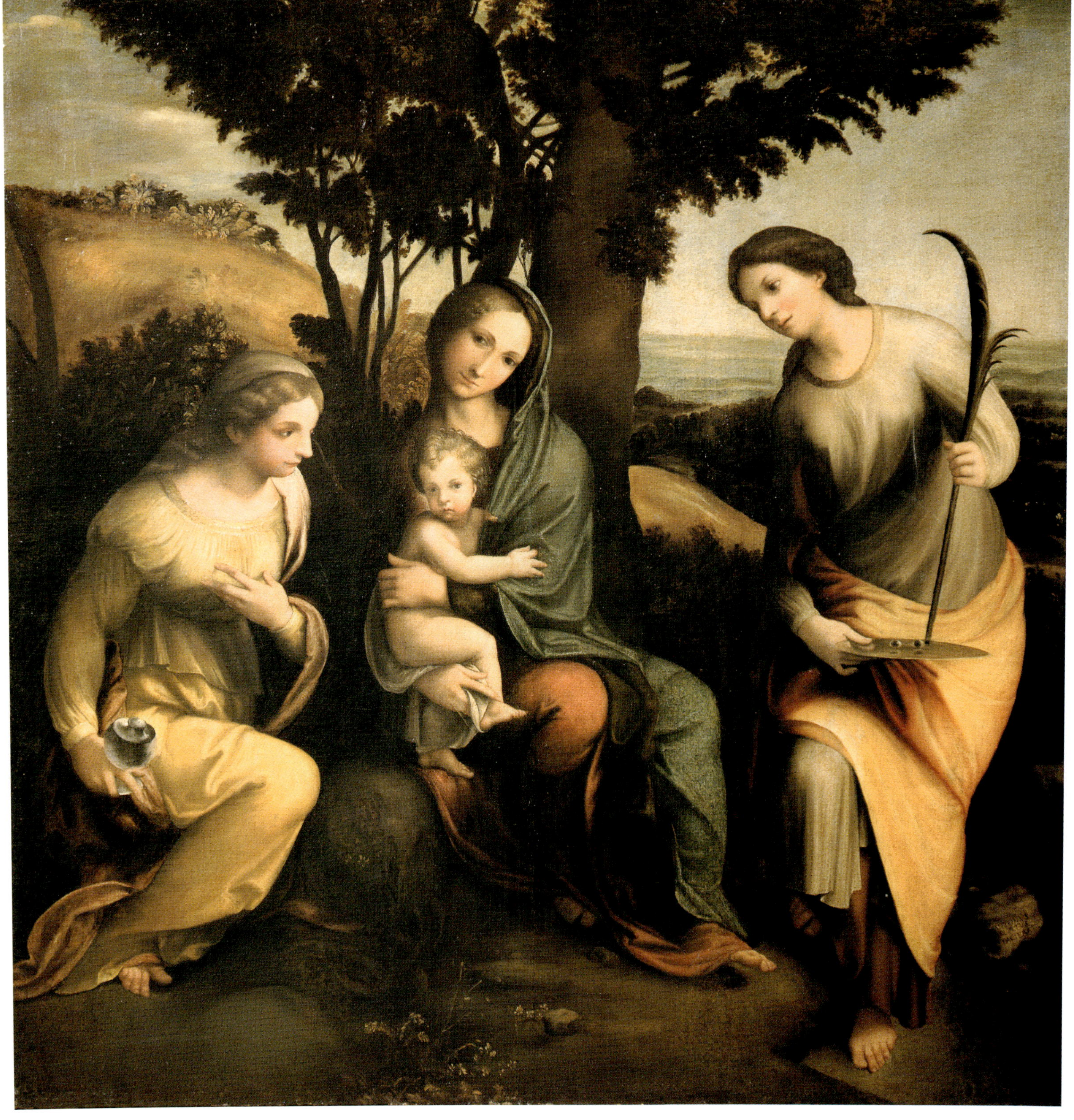

Antonio Allegri, called Correggio

1494-1534

Madonna and Child with St. Mary Magdalen and St. Lucy (‘The Albinea Madonna’)

1517-19

Probably oil on panel
Probably 160 × 152 cm

This early work by Correggio was paid for jointly by the Arciprete Giovanni Guidotti di Roncopò and his parishioners for the church of S. Prospero at Albinea, near Reggio in Emilia, usually known as the ‘Pieve’ (parish church), in or shortly before 1517.[1] In a letter of 12 May in that year the priest asked Alessandro de’ Malaguzzi to contact the artist and, if the work was not too far advanced, to make an effort, along the lines of their own previous discussion, to ensure the greater durability of the ‘ancona’ (altarpiece) in question. The initial contract had evidently been drawn up between the Arciprete and the artist directly, without the intervention of a notary, as is made clear by the document which records the final payment to the artist on 14 October 1519.[2] The altarpiece cost 50 ducats, exactly half that of Correggio’s earlier *Madonna of St. Francis* (Dresden, Gemäldegalerie) of 1514-15, an altarpiece in oil on panel (as the *Albinea Madonna* is likely to have been) measuring 299 × 245.5 cm.

Another document shows that the Albinea altarpiece was installed on 18 December 1519.[3] In the preceding year, on 14 June, the Vicar General of the Bishop of Reggio had authorized Fra Erberto de Caranctino of Correggio to travel about the diocese collecting money to pay for the high altar of S.Prospero at Albinea, which was dedicated to the Blessed Virgin Mary. This document makes it clear that, as was quite often the case in Italy, an already existing and much revered altarpiece was to be ‘updated’, on this occasion by Correggio’s, and the fact that the earlier altarpiece was held to be miracle-working may well have led to the unusual efforts that were made to pay for the new picture. These included the diversion, for two separate years, 1518-19 and 1520-21, of funds from monies available for the fabric of St Peter’s in Rome.[4]

The picture was forcibly removed from the church in 1647, just over a century after it had been installed, on the orders of Francesco I d’Este, Duke of Modena (1610-58, *r.* from 1629).[5] It vanished thereafter and the composition is now known only from copies. One, apparently by Giovanni (or Jean) Boulanger (1606-60), who was Francesco’s court painter, is still in the church at Albinea. This copy measures 160 × 152 cm, which may be assumed to to be very close to the dimensions of the original, and was presented by Francesco to the church in substitution for the panel he had carried off,[6] something which he did on other occasions, even to the extent of substituting a Boulanger copy without any warning that he was about to take the original. This is what happened, for example, with Correggio’s *Rest on the flight into Egypt* and his *Madonna of St. Francis* in the convent of

Madonna with Sts. Mary Magdalen and Lucy, copy after lost painting by Antonio Allegri, called Correggio (1494-1534).
Oil on canvas, 161.5 × 153.4 cm.
Galleria Nazionale, Parma

S. Francesco in the artist's home town of Correggio, and reflects the ruthlessness of Francesco in acquiring works of art and pictures by Correggio in particular.

In his attempts at obtaining these latter two works, Francesco at first opened secret negotiations with the Prior of the convent and made some headway, but it became clear that the citizens of Correggio would be extremely unwilling to part with either of the pictures, and especially the *Rest on the flight into Egypt*. In March

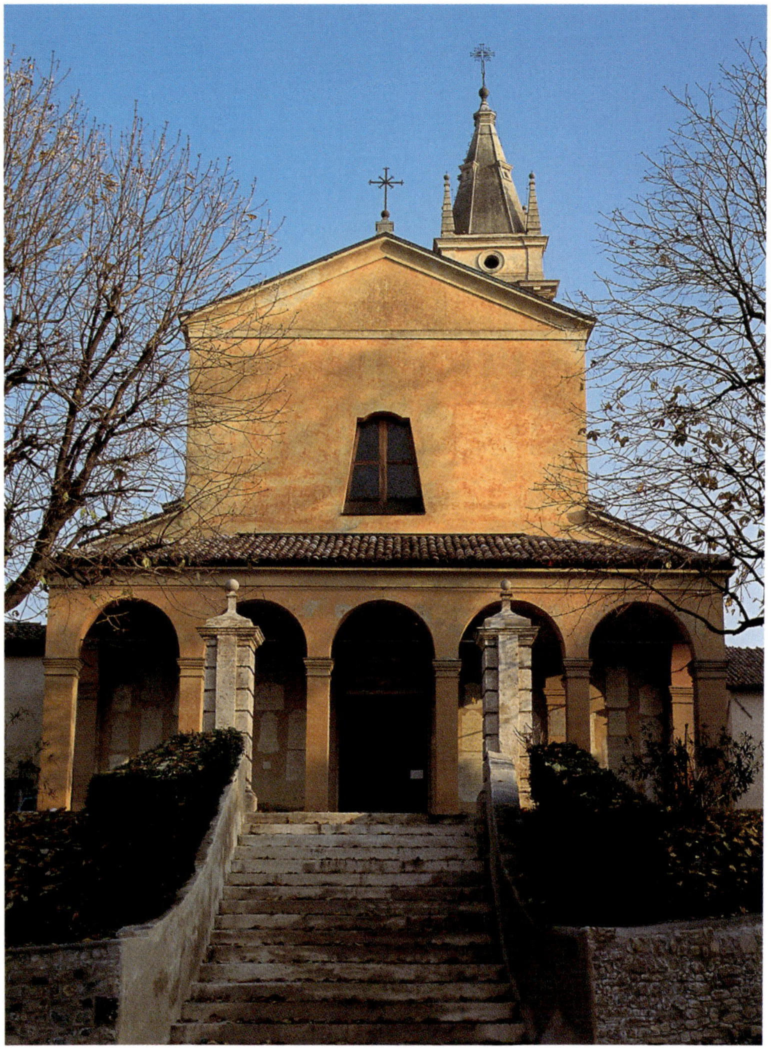

Church of S. Prospero, Albinea, Reggio Emilia

1638, therefore, the Duke conceived a plan: Boulanger appeared with letters to Francesco's governor of the city, Annibale Molza, requesting permission to make a copy of the *Rest on the flight into Egypt*. On the morning of 12 April the Prior discovered that the *Rest* had been replaced with Boulanger's copy: both the original pictures had been spirited away overnight. Appeals were fruitless, and the Duke blandly waved away protests with the spurious explanation that the friars had already been rewarded with land and that, anyway, the previous ruler of the city,

Don Siro da Correggio, had earlier purchased two pictures from the same church.[7]

Another, even more famous, Correggio was similarly removed by the Duke under cover of darkness, the *Night-time Nativity* ('*La Notte*'), which he took in 1640 from the chapel of the Pratoneri in the church of S.Prospero in Reggio Emilia. The Duke was not ready with his customary copy on this occasion. The church had to wait two years until the painter and picture-restorer Gabriele

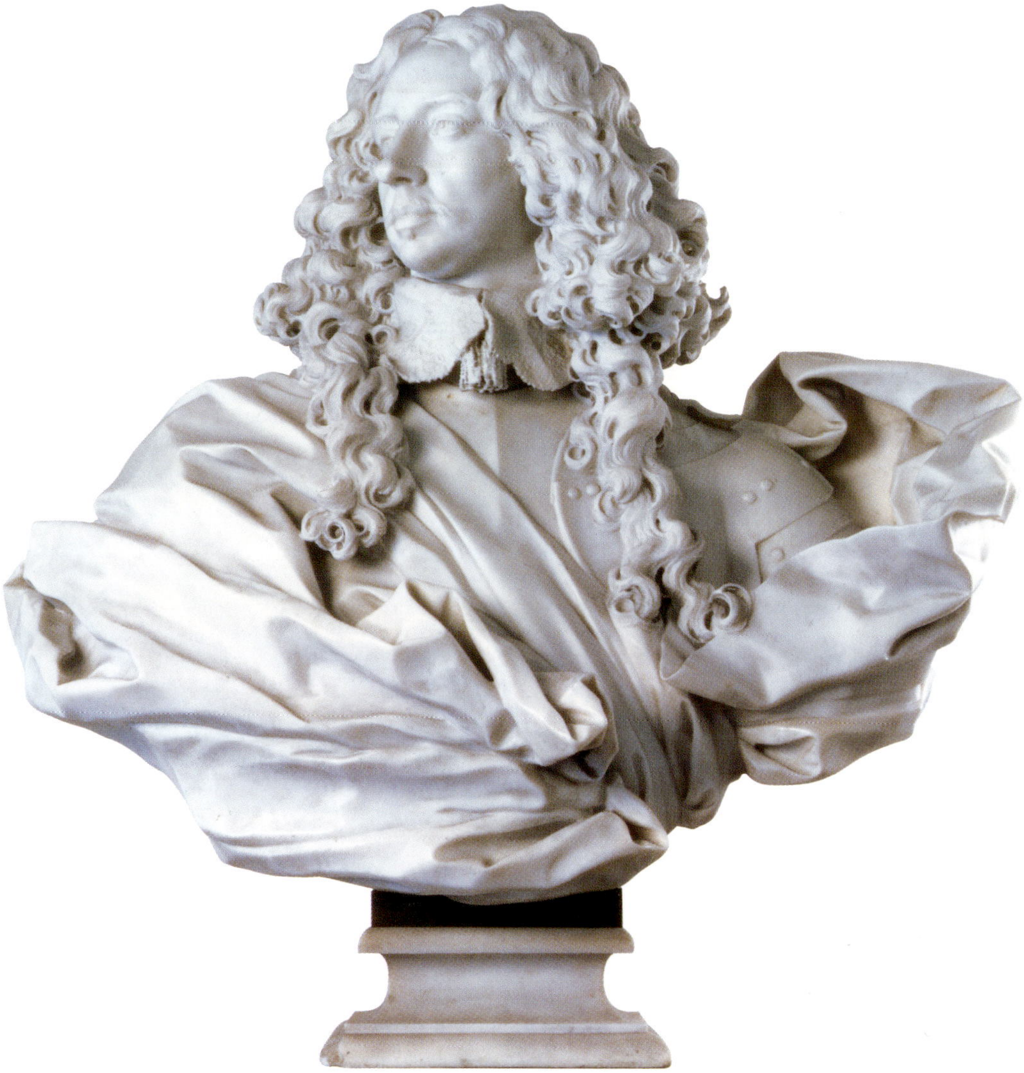

Francesco I d'Este
by Gianlorenzo Bernini (1598-1680), 1650-1.
Marble, ht. 100 cm.
Galleria Estense, Modena

Balestrieri (d. 1648) took them a copy of *La Notte* created on Francesco's orders by way of inadequate compensation.[8] The outstanding example of this pattern of behaviour, in the sense of the value of the replacement work provided, was Francesco's removal of Correggio's *Madonna of St. George* (Dresden, Gemäldegalerie) in 1649 from the oratory of S.Pietro Martire, Modena: on that occasion the copy presented 'in exchange' was by none other than Guercino.[9]

The *Albinea Madonna* and its copying by Boulanger therefore fits into a series

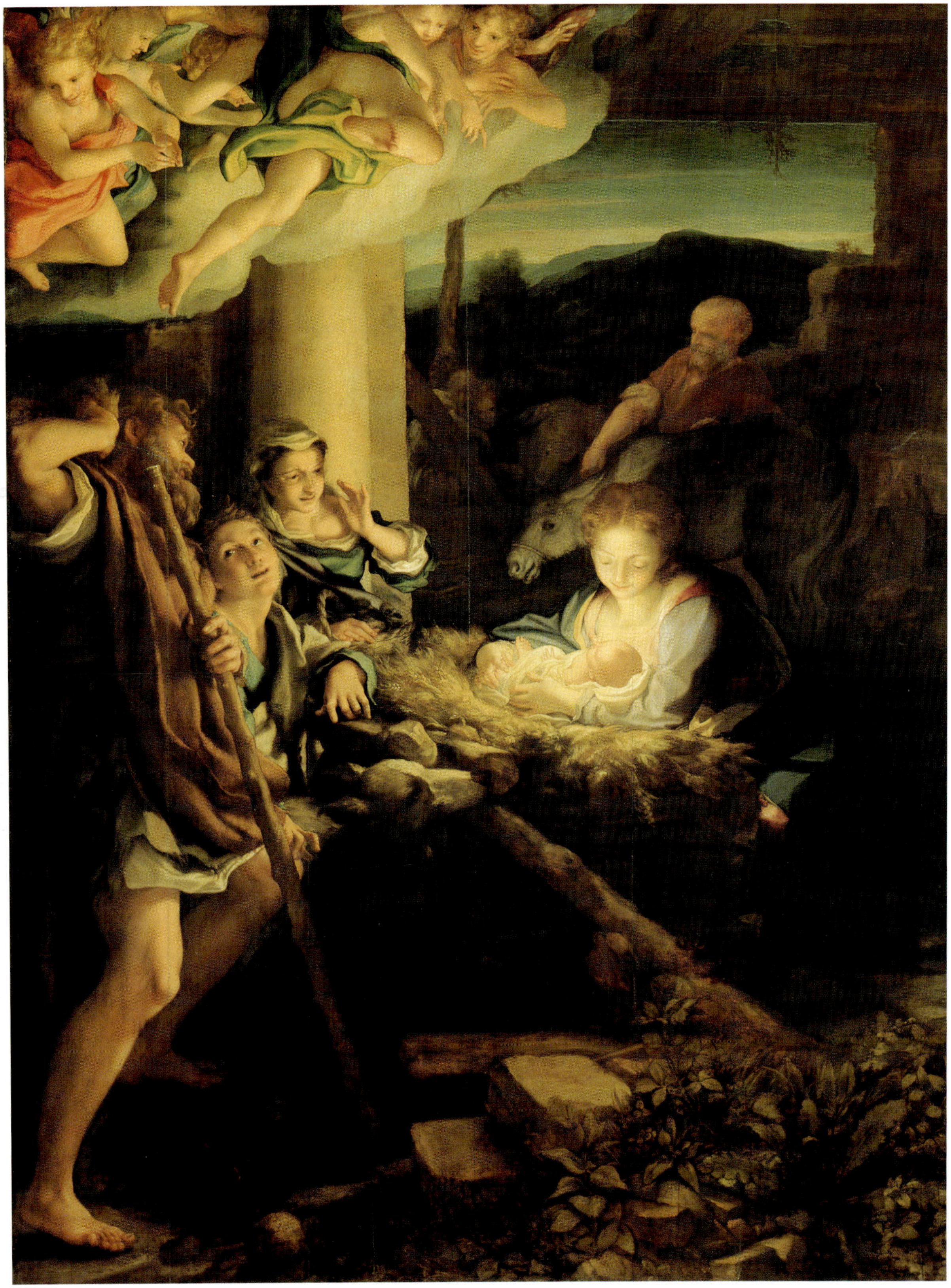

La Notte (Night-time Nativity) by Correggio.
Oil on panel, 256 × 188 cm.
Gemäldegalerie, Dresden

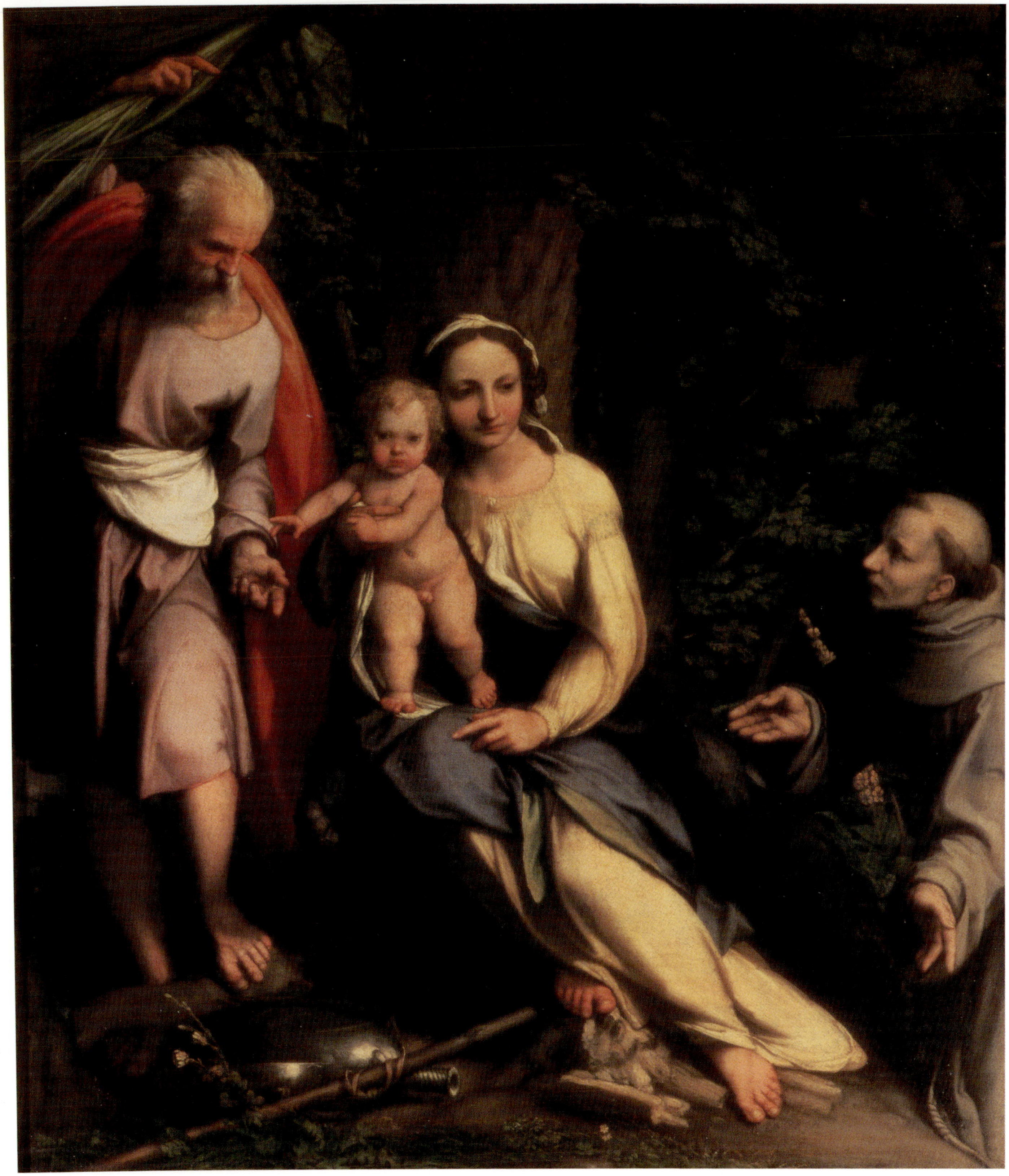

Rest on the flight into Egypt, with St. Francis by Correggio.
Oil on canvas, 146.2 × 136.4 cm.
Uffizi, Florence

of rapacious acquisitions of works of art by Francesco I d'Este. He was not, however, merely an avid and unscrupulous collector. He was determined throughout his reign to elevate the status of the d'Este family to its former glory, in particular hoping once more to gain possession of the family's ancient seat at Ferrara.[10] He proved himself to be a brilliant general in the field, notably in the campaign against the Spanish in 1658 when in command of the allied armies, where he met his death. Earlier in life, however, he had been an ally of Spain, through which he gained the city of Correggio as a reward in 1635, and a visit to Madrid in 1638

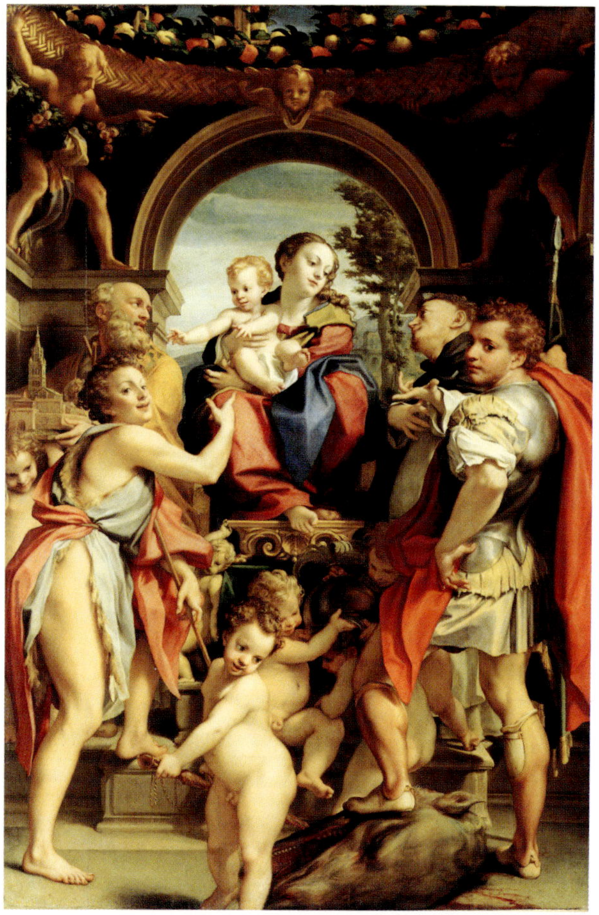

Madonna of St. George by Correggio.
Oil on panel, 285 × 190 cm.
Gemäldegalerie, Dresden

was decisive in forming his determination to rebuild and extend the splendid d'Este art collections. He proved himself a discerning patron, too, and was painted by Velázquez (1639) and sculpted in a magnificent marble by Bernini in 1651 (Galleria Estense, Modena). He also favoured Guercino.

Francesco's main efforts, however, were directed towards acquiring works by the great masters of the previous century, and on his behalf Balestrieri 'scoured Northern Italy for pictures from 1638 to 1649'.[11] It was, no doubt, during one of these 'raids' that the Duke's attention was brought to the Correggio masterpiece hidden away in humble Albinea, a small town on the foothills of the Apennines above Reggio in the Po valley. In addition to the copy made for the church by

Boulanger on the Duke's orders, other copies of the lost picture exist, including one in the Galleria Nazionale, Parma (on loan from the Brera, Milan), which records, on the stone by the foot of St. Lucy at the right of the composition, what must have been the original appearance of the signature, '*Antonus* [=*Antonius*] *Laetus faciebat*';[12] and there is another in the Museo Capitolino, Rome. In addition to having the copy made for the original parish church, Francesco also arranged to pay some money to the *comune* of Albinea, representatives of which had in some way connived at the removal of the altarpiece; but the method by

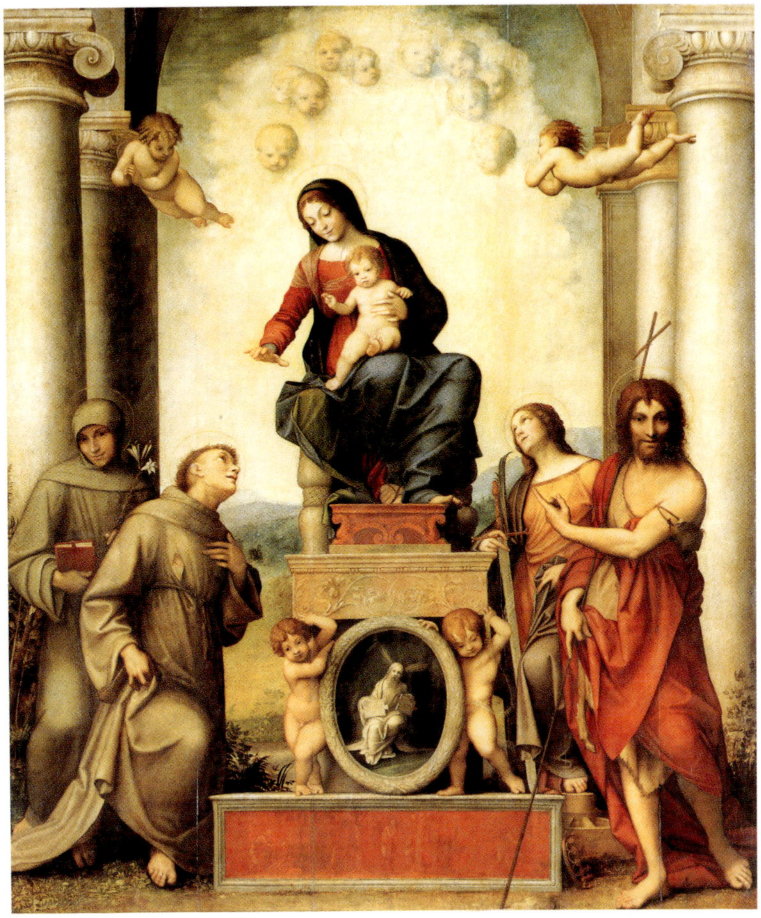

Madonna of St. Francis by Correggio.
Oil on panel, 299 × 245 cm.
Gemäldegalerie, Dresden

which they were to receive money was so byzantine that the subsequent disagreement over it continued for over a century.[13]

The fate of the missing picture is not known, although certain possibilities suggest themselves. In some ways, it is surprising that it does not survive among the other famous pictures still in Dresden, including works by Correggio, which found their way there from the collections of the Dukes of Modena during the reign of Augustus III (1696-1763, *r.* from 1733), King of Poland and Elector of Saxony (the latter as Frederick Augustus II), who succeeded his remarkable father, Augustus the Strong, in 1733: 'Until the disaster of the Seven Years War [1756-63] nearly a quarter of a century later the collecting activities of this man

[Augustus III] and his dictatorial minister Count Brühl were among the most outstanding in Europe.'[14] These activities included the purchase of one hundred choice pictures from the collection of the Dukes of Modena.[15]

Heinrich Graf von Brühl (1700-63), who masterminded most of the acquisitions of Augustus III – and indeed his every act – and who soon built his own splendid art gallery, had risen rapidly under Augustus the Strong. The son, Frederick Augustus II of Saxony, was elected to the throne of Poland, as Augustus III, in succession to his father at the end of 1733. In Dresden, the capital of Saxony, Brühl was immediately appointed Director of the Art Collections and collecting intensified, with the assistance of agents spread throughout Europe: in Vienna, Madrid, Paris, Rome and the Netherlands, activities which involved the curious figure of Count Francesco Algarotti (1712-64). Brühl became ever more powerful, and in 1746 was made Prime Minister of Saxony, a position hitherto unknown within the Electorate. So many were the paintings brought to Dresden that they could not all be hung, and many remained propped up on the floor in the galleries against the skirting-boards.[16] The result was the building of new galleries to house them.

The one hundred pictures from the collections of the Dukes of Modena were bought *en bloc* for one hundred thousand *zecchini*, a purchase finally settled in 1746 after negotiations had begin in 1743.[17] It so happened that this was the time when the finances of Francesco III of Modena (*r.* 1737-80) were at their most stretched.[18] This was partly the result of his having to bear the costs of his position in charge of the Spanish troops in the War of Austrian Succession (1740-48). Correggio's *La Notte* had been the first object of the Saxon enquiries in 1743. In an act of extreme irony, in view of the manner of its acquisition by his ancestor Francesco I, Francesco III specifically requested a copy of this, his most treasured possession, which was duly provided by its new owner. By the following year one hundred works were identified for purchase. The pictures were in Padua by the end of November 1745 and then on 6 July 1746 left Venice in five carriages bound for Dresden.[19]

In none of the manuscripts relating to this extraordinary story does there appear to be any reference to the *Albinea Madonna*, although it should be noted that the 1744 inventory of the pictures in the collections of the Duke of Modena was not exhaustive, and appears to have been confined to the principal state rooms in the palace at Modena.[20] It is possible that it was in another of Francesco III's residences, or that it had already left the family during the reign of one of his predecessors. Of these, Alfonso IV (*r.* 1658-62), who succeeded Francesco I, is generally celebrated with him as the founder of the Galleria Estense in Modena.[21] He was succeeded by his son Francesco II, at the age of fourteen in 1674, after a period of regency by Alfonso's widow, Laura Martinozzi. Francesco II died in 1694, succeeded by his uncle Rinaldo I (d. 1737), who abandoned his life as a religious in order to take over the state; and then followed Francesco III.

It has been noted that the reign of Francesco II in particular led inadvertently to the loss of many works of art from the scattered family collections.[22] Even supposing that the *Albinea Madonna* remained with the family past this date, however, the subsequent history of the d'Este family and of Modena after the reign of Francesco III was full of vicissitudes during which the picture could have been lost. These difficulties included the family's abandonment of the city after its occupation by the French revolutionary army in 1796, an exile which was not concluded until the return of the dynasty to Modena in the shape of Francesco IV (d. 1846) in 1814.

NOTES

1 C. Gould, *The Paintings of Correggio*, London, 1976, pp. 56-7, 278-9; D. Ekserdjian, *Correggio*, New Haven and London, 1997, pp. 66-8; see also C. Ricci, *Antonio Allegri da Correggio: His Life, his Friends, and his Time*, London, 1896; idem., *Correggio*, Rome, 1930; J. Bentini, *Sovrane passioni: le raccolte d'arte della Ducale Galleria Estense*, exh. cat., Modena, 1998, no. 155, pp. 404-5, and ill. (copy after Correggio of the *Madonna di Albinea*, Parma, Galleria Nazionale, oil on panel, 161.5 × 153.4 cm).

2 Ekserdjian, op. cit., p. 66. These documents might suggest that, contrary to local legend recorded in earlier literature, Correggio worked on the picture at home and not at Albinea: his address is given as his father's house in Correggio; see, e.g., Ricci, op. cit. (1930), pp. 42ff. Bentini concludes, however, that the inclusion of living and accommodation expenses in the contract suggests that Correggio worked on site: op. cit., 1998, p. 404.

3 See Ekserdjian, op. cit., p. 66, and Bentini, op. cit., 1998, p. 404.

4 Ibid.

5 Ricci, op. cit. (1896), pp. 132ff., recounts the early history of the picture (repeating a legend about the artist's having actually worked in Albinea which appears to conflict with the known documents), and the events surrounding its removal by Francesco and its sequel. For Francesco's methods of collecting, including his taking of the *Albinea Madonna*, see R. W. Lightbown, 'Princely Pressures: 2. Francesco I d'Este and Correggio', *Apollo*, xix (1963), pp. 193-9; A. Venturi, *La R. Galleria Estense in Modena*, Modena, 1883, pp. 199-259.

6 Lightbown, op. cit., p. 199; Ricci, op. cit. (1896), p. 132. The measurements are very close to those of the copy in the Galleria Nazionale, Parma, on loan from the Brera, Milan: see n. 1 above. According to Bentini, loc. cit., this copy may be attributable to Giovanni Giaroli (or Giarola) di Correggio (*fl.* 1529-57) and date from around the mid-sixteenth century.

7 Lightbown, op. cit., pp. 197-8, who makes the point that the pictures, in the case of Don Siro, had not left the city after his purchase of them.

8 Ibid., p. 198.

9 Ibid., p. 199. See D. Mahon, *Il Guercino: Catalogo critico dei dipinti*, Bologna, 1968, pp. 199-201.

10 See Lightbown, op. cit., pp. 193ff. for an account of Francesco's political and aesthetic concerns.

11 Ibid., p. 197.

12 Gould, op. cit., p. 279. The form 'laetus' is a Latin form of the Italian 'lieto' ('cheerful') which Correggio used in two legal documents: Ekserdjian, p. 305, n. 133; both forms are related to the artist's surname Allegri ('allegro'=cheerful). The copy is illustrated in colour in Ekserdjian, op. cit., pl. 64.

13 Ricci, op. cit. (1896), pp. 132ff.

14 F. Haskell, *Painters and Patrons*, London, 1963, p. 294.

15 See J. Winkler, ed., *La Vendita di Dresda*, Modena, 1989, especially G. Bonsanti, 'La Galleria Estense: Storia di una collezione', pp. 13-26; J. Winkler, 'Storia di un acquisto straordinario', pp. 27-57; also *La Vendita di Dresda. Notizie storiche*, Modena, *Aedes Muratoriana*, 1982, pp. 36ff. (O. B. Giovanardi's transcription of the relevant documents); and also P. E. Gherardi, *Descrizione di cento pezzi di Pitture, passati nell'anno 1746 dalla Galleria Estense in Modena a quella di Federigo Augusto III. Re di Polonia ed elector di Sassonia pel valore e prezzo di Zecchini Veneziani Cento-mila* (MS, Reggio Emilia, 1752), ed. G. Bonsanti, transcribed by O. B. Giovanardi, Modena, 1986. See the inventory of pictures in the collections of Francesco I in Gherardi's earlier MS of 1744: Pietro Ercole Gherardi, *Descrizione delle pitture esistenti in Modena nell'Estense Ducal Galleria*, ed. G. Bonsanti, transcribed and researched by O. Baracchi, Modena, 1986, which includes the list of the one hundred pictures sold to Dresden on pp. 246-9.

16 G. Rudloff-Hille (trans. K. M. Leake), *Dresden Gemäldegalerie*, London, 1960, p. 6.

17 See Winkler, op. cit., pp. 34ff.

18 Ibid., pp. 30ff.

19 G. Bonsanti, 'La Galleria Estense: Storia di una Collezione', in Winkler (ed.), op. cit., pp. 13-26, p. 22. The Dukes had a summer residence in the Euganean Hills near Padua and a winter residence in Venice.

20 See n. 15 above.

21 Ibid., p. 20; *passim* for the history summarised here. See also A. Venturi, *La R. Galleria Estense in Modena*, Modena, 1883.

22 Ibid., p. 21.

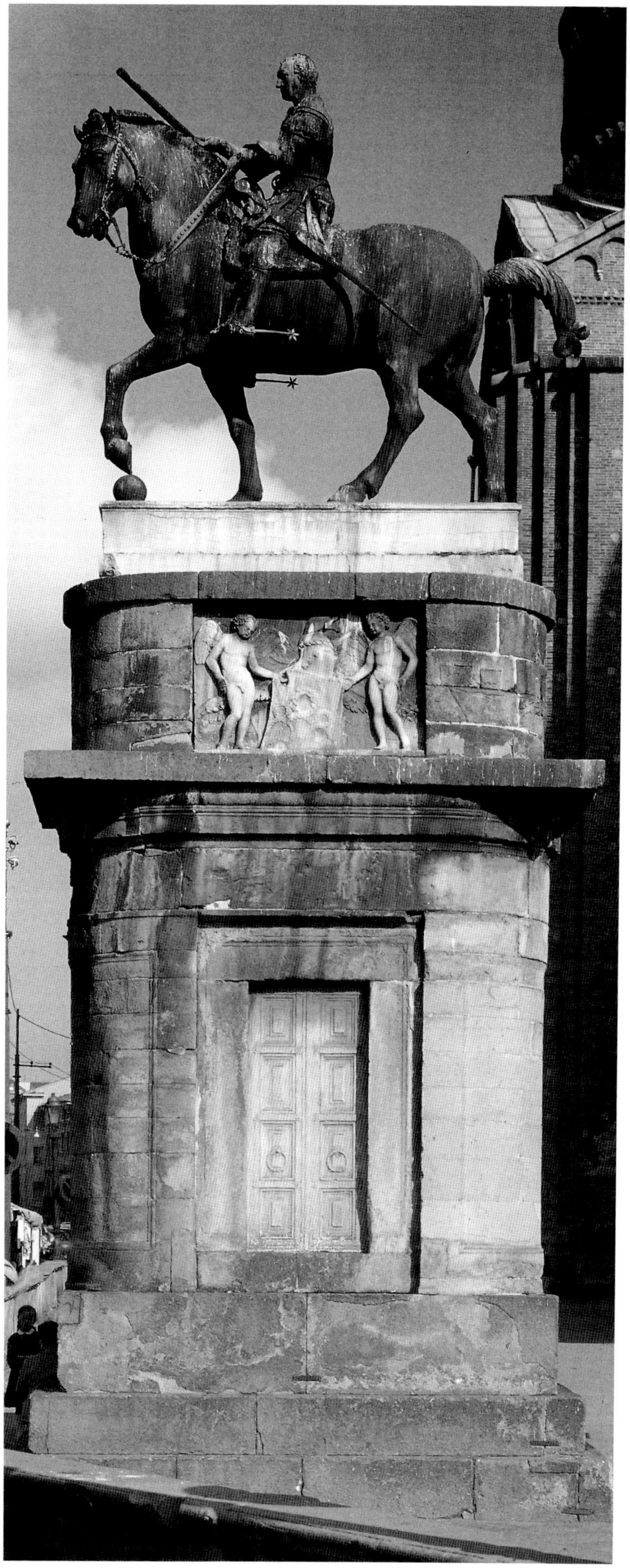

Jacopo Bellini (*c.* 1400-70/1)
with his sons
Gentile (*c.* 1435-1507) and Giovanni (*c.* 1438-1516)
Gattamelata Altarpiece
1459/60

Tempera on panel

Chapel of Sts. Francis and Bernardino, Basilica di S. Antonio ('Il Santo'), Padua
Triptych with predella, each main panel *c.* 110 × 57 cm
(central and right-hand panels missing); lunette above (missing) *c.* 59 × 168 cm

Erasmo da Narni, called 'Gattamelata' ('honeyed cat') (d. 1443), was one of the greatest '*condottieri*', those highly specialised international warrior-knights who flourished for well over two-and-a-half centuries from the thirteenth century onwards. They could be hired ('condotta' – a contract) to fight for a city or state, at a time when warfare was more or less continuous on one or more fronts. A *condottiere* could depend upon being in a position to supply a constant demand in one country or another across Europe, and the most prominent of these hired 'war machines' would often be entrusted with the conduct of an entire campaign. Their expertise in the art of waging war was at a high premium; they were hugely expensive but almost essential to employ; and their loyalty thus purchased was often rewarded by their employers after death.

Sudden death, after all, was their trade. It was a fate always before them, more so even than for most people at the time. The prospect concentrated the mind wonderfully, both individually and collectively, upon the after-life. And so the age of the *condottieri* was also the age of the chantry chapel, where those whose lives had so often been abruptly curtailed could employ spiritual armies on their behalf: priests to pray for their souls 'in perpetuity' (which in practice might mean a few generations).

In addition to these careful insurance policies taken out by the deceased and their families, grateful employers would pay for public celebrations of the Mass and erect magnificent monuments in the most prominent places. Thus the English *condottiere* Sir John Hawkwood is commemorated by a life-size fresco by Uccello in the nave of the Cathedral at Florence, as is Niccoló da Tolentino in a pendant fresco by Andrea del Castagno. Verrocchio's bronze equestrian monument to Bartolommeo Colleoni outside the church of SS. Giovanni e Paolo is still one of the most imposing sights of Venice. The inspiration for *Colleoni* was the even finer bronze equestrian statue of Gattamelata by Donatello erected by the Venetian dependency of Padua outside the massive pilgrimage church of S. Antonio in Padua (the 'Santo').

The Gattamelata monument now dominates the exterior of the Santo to an even greater extent than it would originally have done, because when it was built it was surrounded by tombs which were subsequently swept away. The stone illusionistic

Erasmo da Narni, called Gattamelata (d. 1443) by Donatello (*c.* 1388-1466), 1443-7.
Bronze on marble base,
height of statue 340 cm.
Basilica del Santo, Padua (piazza)

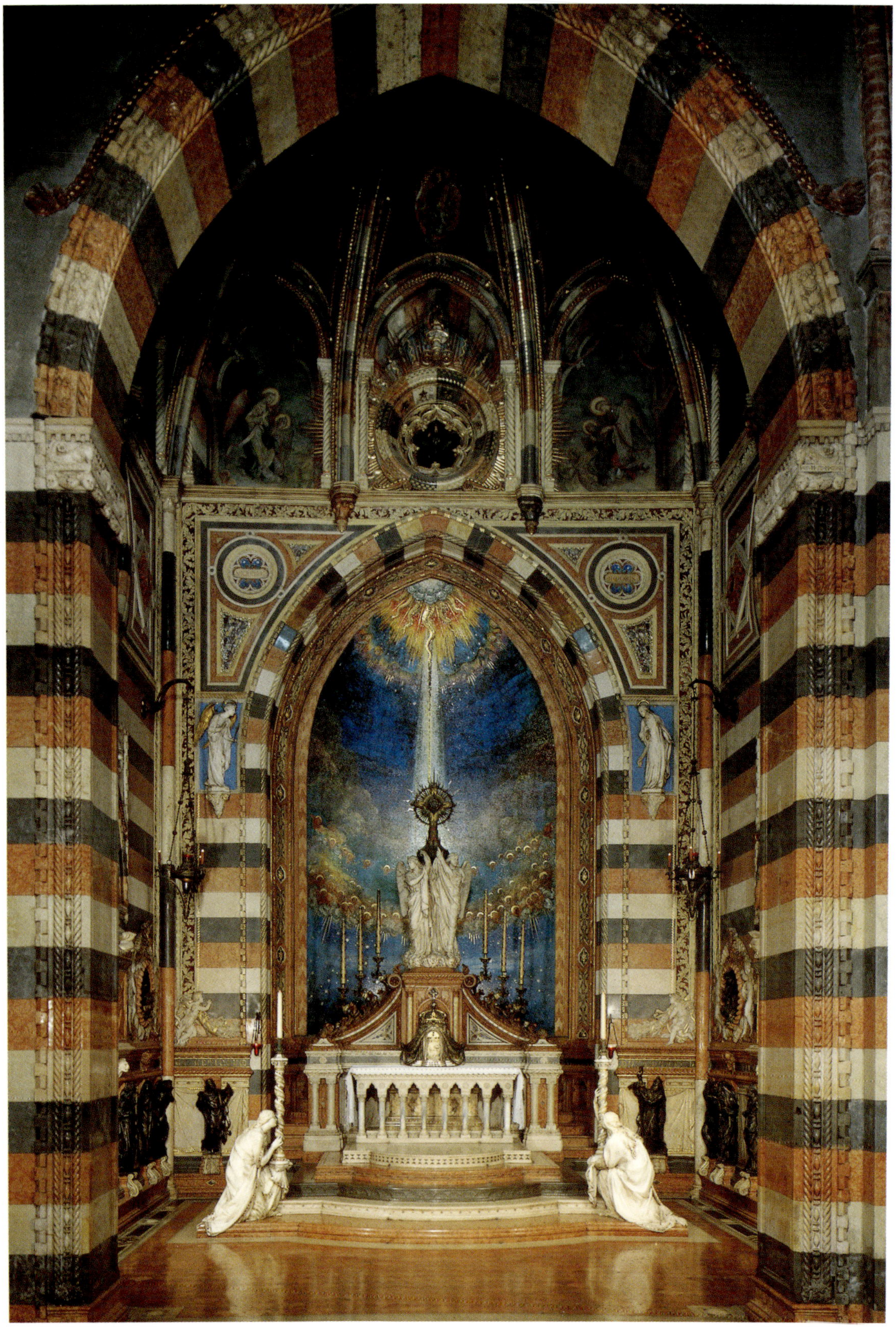

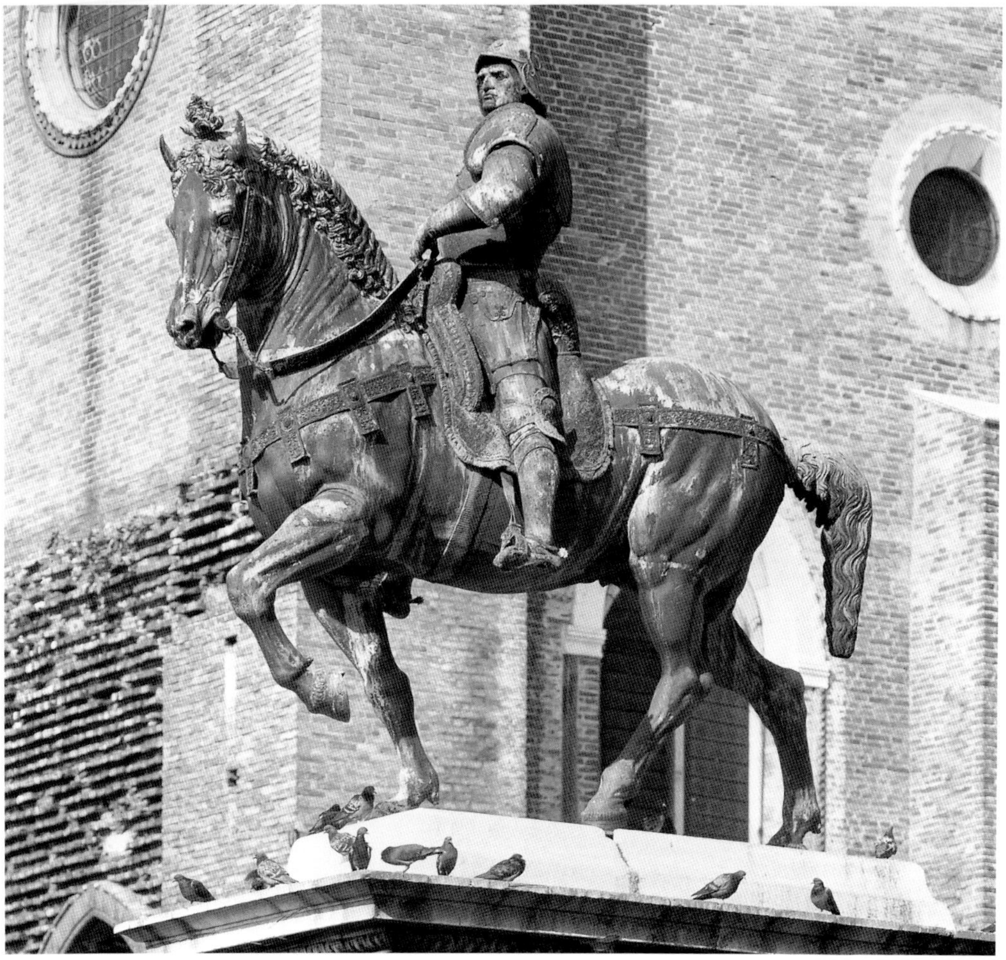

Bartolommeo Colleoni (d. 1475) by Andrea del Verrocchio (*c.* 1435-88), 1481-8/96. Gilded bronze, height of statue 395 cm. Campo di SS. Giovanni e Paolo, Venice

Chapel of the Holy Sacrament (formerly of Sts. Francis and Bernardino), Basilica del Santo, Padua

doorways on either side of the base of the statue suggest that it is a tomb monument, but Gattamelata's actual tomb was inside the basilica, and was always intended to be so, in a specially built chantry chapel on the south side of the nave, commissioned by his widow, Giacoma da Leonessa. His will of 1441 stated that it was to be paid for from his estate and dedicated to Sts. Francis and Bernardino. The fact that St. Bernardino was not actually canonized until 1450 was not something that would have hindered his being invoked on such an occasion, and the presence of St. Francis would have acted as an official dedication. In the event, by the time that Giacoma was petitioning to erect the chapel, 15 November 1456, Bernardino's canonisation had taken place, and the chapel was now officially 'sub vocabulo et nomine sancti Bernardini'.[1] Permission was duly granted to Giacoma, on 15 December 1456, to break through the nave wall in the third bay and to intrude, at a point near some family tombs, into the cloister which had been built a little earlier by Cristoforo and Giovanni da Bolzano. The event which led to this belated building was the death in 1455 of the son of Gattamelata and Giacoma, Giannantonio, also a *condottiere*, who had died at Montagana of wounds received at Castiglione delle Stivere.

One of the architects of the new cloister, Giovanni da Bolzano, was commissioned (the business was undertaken by by Giacoma's son-in-law, Lancelotto da

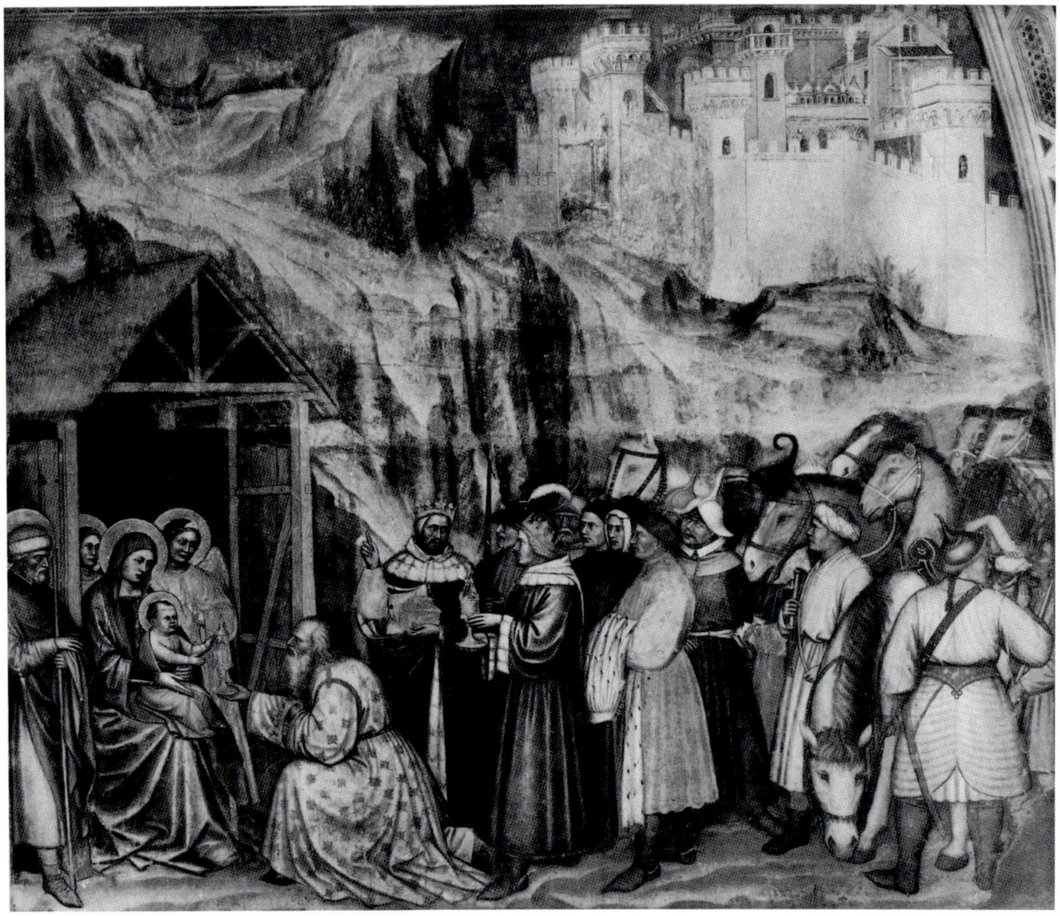

Adoration of the Magi
by Altichiero (*c.* 1340-93), 1379-84.
Fresco.
Oratory of St. George, Padua

Partial reconstruction of the
Gattamelata Altarpiece
by Jacopo Bellini
(*c.* 1400-70/1)
and his sons Gentile
(*c.*? 1435-1507)
and Giovanni
(*c.*? 1438-1516),
showing the four
surviving panels.
Above, *Sts. Anthony Abbot and Bernardino*;
below, the three
predella panels

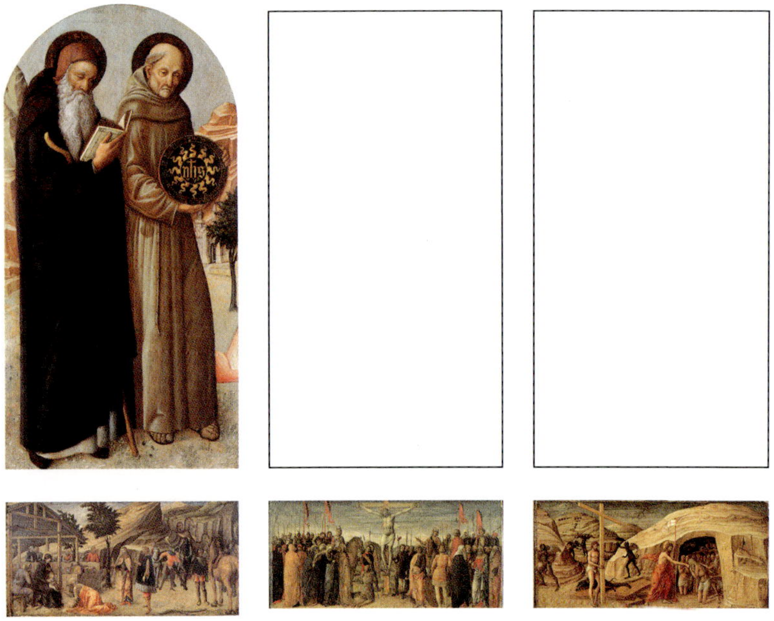

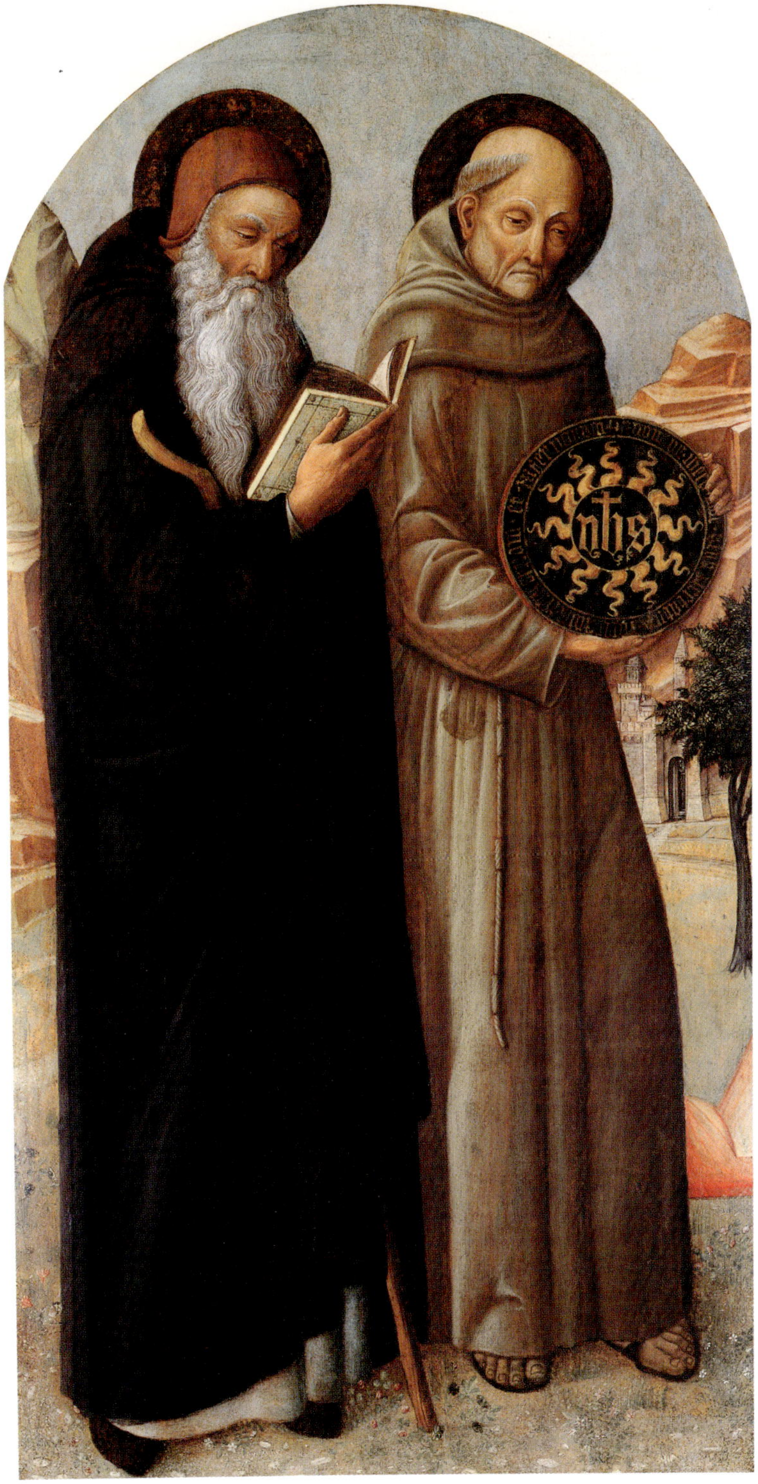

Sts. Anthony Abbot and Bernardino by Jacopo Bellini and his sons.
Tempera on panel, 110 × 57 cm.
National Gallery of Art,
Washington, D.C.

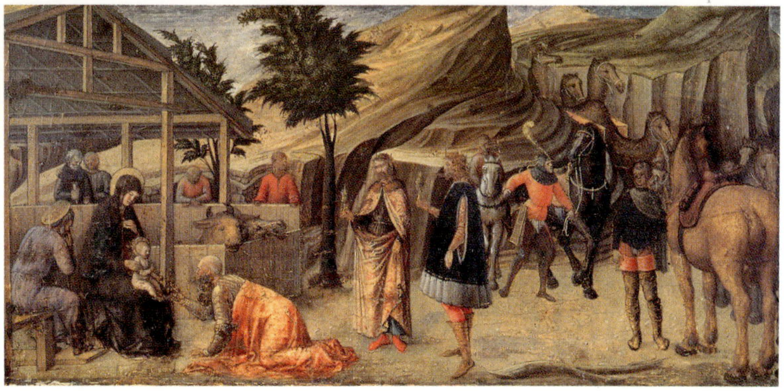

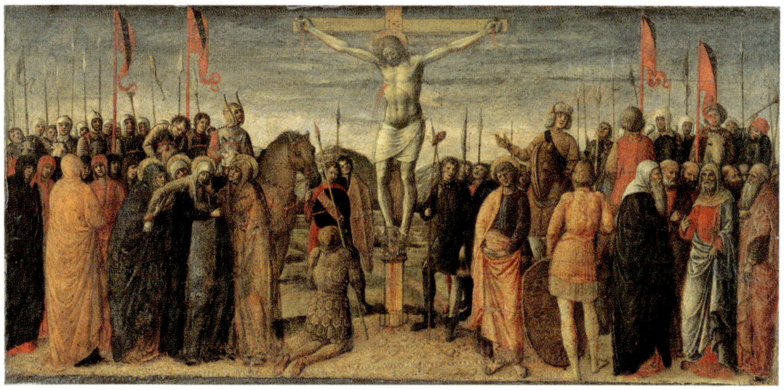

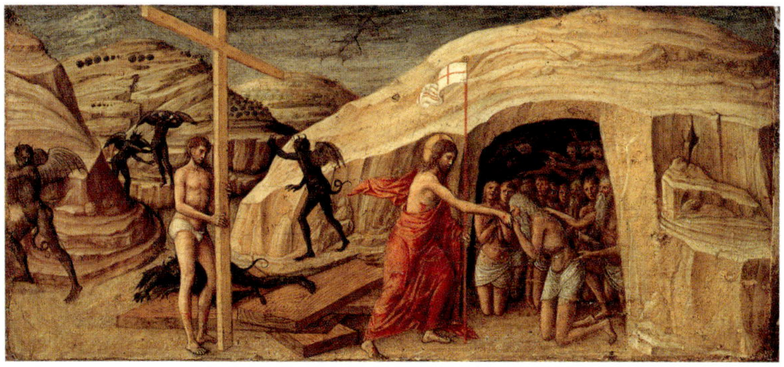

Adoration of the Magi by Jacopo Bellini and his sons.
Tempera on panel, 28.5 × 57 cm. Pinacoteca Nazionale, Ferrara,

Crucifixion by Jacopo Bellini and his sons.
Tempera on panel, 28.6 × 57 cm. Museo Correr, Venice

Descent into Limbo by Jacopo Bellini and his sons.
Tempera on panel, 28.5 × 58 cm. Museo Civico, Padua

Narni) to carry out the work on the chapel in a meeting on 17 December 1456 when the sculptor Gregorio d'Allegretto, who was to create the two tombs, of Gattamelata and his son, was also present.[2] The design was then deposited in the 'sacristy', which suggests that the whole project must already have been well advanced before permission was sought and given. The two tombs, which are on either side wall of the chapel, were finished on 19 September 1458, and the building of the chapel finished by 29 May 1459, at which point it had already cost the very substantial sum of 2,500 ducats, in contrast with the 500-700 ducats which Gattamelata had stipulated in his will. The pictorial decoration of the walls was still to do, and the intention to carry this out was confirmed in a codicil of that year to Giacoma's earlier will of 1457. In it she states that the chapel is to be painted with 'a sky with gold stars and other figures for which should be spent a sum up to the value of three hundred gold ducats'.[3]

This detailed will and codicil makes no mention of an altarpiece, but we know from early records that there was one, signed by Jacopo Bellini and his sons Gentile and Giovanni. It must already have been paid for, and is almost certainly accounted for within the large sum noted on 29 May 1459. It is of great significance in the history of altarpiece design in the Renaissance, but its main elements have disappeared, although fragments of it have been identified in recent years, from which it has been possible to reconstruct it and to speculate with a high degree of probability about its iconography.[4] The altarpiece must have taken the form of a triptych with a predella, having on the left-hand side a surviving panel showing Sts. Anthony Abbot and Bernardino (private collection, New York), and, presumably, on the right-hand side St. Francis (who was also depicted in the fresco decoration of the walls) with St. Anthony of Padua, the titular saint of the basilica. The predella panels survive with, on the left, *The adoration of the Magi* (Ferrara, Pinacoteca Nazionale); in the centre, *The Crucifixion* (Museo Correr, Venice); and on the right *The descent into Limbo* (Padua, Museo Civico).[5]

The choice of Jacopo Bellini as the artist of the altarpiece would have been influenced by the fact that Giacoma da Leonessa had already come across him, because he had painted one for the church of S.Alessandro, Brescia, where her brother Gentile da Leonessa had been buried in 1453. She evidently had a special devotion to St. Bernardino, too, because she went on to found another chapel dedicated to him in that church, in 1460.[6] The panel of Sts. Anthony Abbot and Bernardino of Siena is now accepted as by Jacopo Bellini (there have been suggestions that the figure of St. Bernardino may also show the assistance of Gentile).[7] Humfrey also suggests that the panel is reflected in a now-dismembered triptych of Giorgio Schiavone for S.Francesco Grande, Padua.[8] *The adoration of the Magi* is identical in width with the surviving panel of *Sts. Anthony Abbot and Bernardino of Siena*. This fact argues that the three panels were indeed the predella of the missing triptych and, as Eisler has suggested, it is also probable that these two panels in particular – *Sts Anthony Abbot and Bernardino of Siena*, and *The adoration of the Magi* – were originally set directly one above the other. The hand of the young Giovanni Bellini has been identified both in the *Adoration* and in the *Crucifixion*.

There must remain speculation about the subject of the central panel, although, as we shall see, the probability is that it was a *Resurrection*. Drawings by Jacopo Bellini exist which hint at its content, and comparisons can also be made with works of art in or close to the Santo. The Gattamelata altarpiece is therefore included in this book as something of an exception to the usual rules. Only parts of the work are still missing, although in its totality the whole can be said to have been lost. The triptych is not fully recorded in a single visual record but, at the same time, it is possible to suggest accurately what the missing parts of the whole might consist of, by reference to the existing parts of the same complex work and to comparable works.

One of the key records of the lost altarpiece is that of Fra Valerio Polidoro in 1609, who recorded, not without a tantalising element of apparent inaccuracy, the inscription as follows:

JACOBI BELLINI VENETI PATRIS AC GENTILIS ET JOANNIS NATORUM OPVS M. CCCC. IX.[9]

Clearly, '1409', as suggested by the Roman numerals as they stand, is impossible for a work by the Bellini, father and sons. It may be that one of the numeral letters was already rubbed out; there is a faint possibility that the 'IX' was mistranscribed and should be 'LX', and thus represent the number '60'.[10] If, on the other hand, the letters are correctly recorded, and a letter obliterated, there could well have been an 'L' before the 'IX' giving the number '59', and therefore the date 1459, which is that of the chapel's completion. Either of the likely dates, however, within a year of each other, makes no difference to the fact that the missing altarpiece is, by common consent, one of the crucial works in the evolution of the *Sacra Conversazione* in Venetian art. It stands (in its conjectural reconstruction) before a series of four triptychs now reckoned to be the inspiration of Jacopo, rather than Giovanni Bellini, for the church of the Carità in Venice between 1460 and 1464, and so also before the large altarpieces by Giovanni Bellini that date from the mid-1460s onwards.[11]

When Polidoro recorded the inscription, Michiel had already described the chapel and its altarpiece in the early 1530s, in the 'Anonimo':

> La prima capella a man dextra intrando in chiesia instituida per Gatta mellata, fu dipinta da Jacomo da Montagnana Padoano, et da Piero Calzetta suo cugnato; ma la palla iui fu de mano de Jacomo Bellino, Zuane et Gentil suoi figli, come apar per la sottoscriptione. Iui sono li sepulchri di Gatta mellata et de Zuanantonio, suo fiol, che morse conduttier, e giovane.[12]

It may be observed here that there is some internal evidence to suggest that the *Adoration of the Magi* must have a Paduan connection, rather than being associated, for example, with a quite separate lost altarpiece by Jacopo Bellini for the Scuola di S.Giovanni Evangelista, Venice, as has been suggested. [13] This evidence is the reflection in the *Adoration* panel of the fresco of the same subject in the Oratory of St. George at the Santo by Altichiero, dating from 1379-84.[14] In 1459-60, that frescoed *Adoration* was (as it remains) prominently on view, immediately to the left of the entrance inside the Oratory, and its influence upon the Bellini predella may be seen in the form of the stable, the configuration of the hills and the positioning of some of the key figures.

So far as the identification of the subject of the missing central panel is concerned, the discussion can be widened again by reference to the surviving frescoes of Altichiero, this time in what is now the Chapel of S.Felice (originally St. James) which is situated in the Santo on the right-hand side of the nave, i.e. the same side as the Gattamelata chapel, and very prominently so, since it occupies the whole of

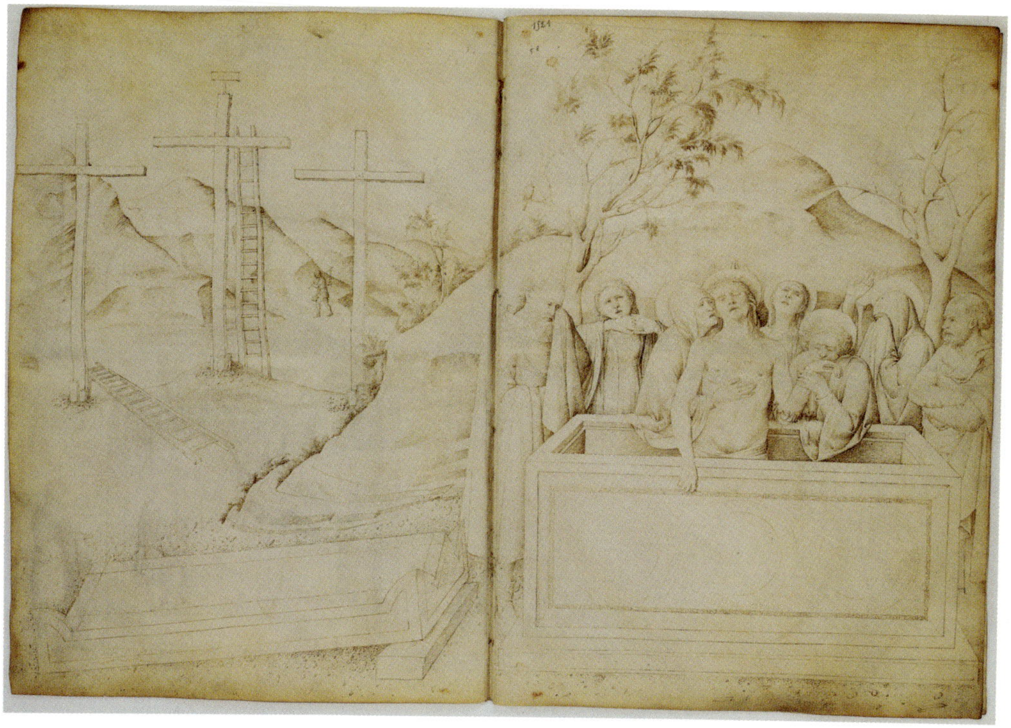

Lamentation in a landscape by Jacopo Bellini.
Drawing, *Book of Drawings*, fols. 32v, 33r.
Musée du Louvre, Paris

the right transept. It too was a funerary chapel and also features two tombs, one to either side of the altar (although admittedly, they are situated on the altar wall in the S. Felice chapel, but on the side walls of the Gattamelata chapel). Each of these S. Felice tombs is decorated with a fresco directly above it, illusionistically painted to suggest, at the left, the *Entombment*, and, at the right, the *Resurrection*. These are specifically the two subjects which have been suggested as likely for the missing central Bellini panel: the *Man of Sorrows/Lamentation* and *Resurrection/Resurrected Christ*.[15]

Reconstructions of the Bellini altarpiece have taken into account the lid of a sarcophagus clearly visible at the right of the panel showing Sts. Anthony Abbot and Bernardino of Siena, with the supposition that this lid was then shown in the central panel as part of an illusion of continuous space across the whole triptych. This fact, that the landscape would have been continuous, is one the factors that give this missing altarpiece its historical significance. The lid is distinguished by having acroteria, almost like 'ears' at the corners, a feature which could be seen in the fifteenth century on many classical examples surviving in Padua and which were also frequently to be found in the city upon the many consciously classicising tombs of the fourteenth century.

The missing subject is rather more likely, on iconographical grounds, to have been a *Resurrection* or *Resurrected Christ* because that is where the lid of the tomb is usually depicted, which it is not in the *Lamentation* or *Man of Sorrows*. The reason is that, at the Resurrection, Christ emerges from the tomb, casting the lid aside; in the *Lamentation*, the lid usually plays no role and is not normally shown. An exception, surviving in the form of a drawing only (and with no knowledge of what the finished painted work might have been), is to be found in

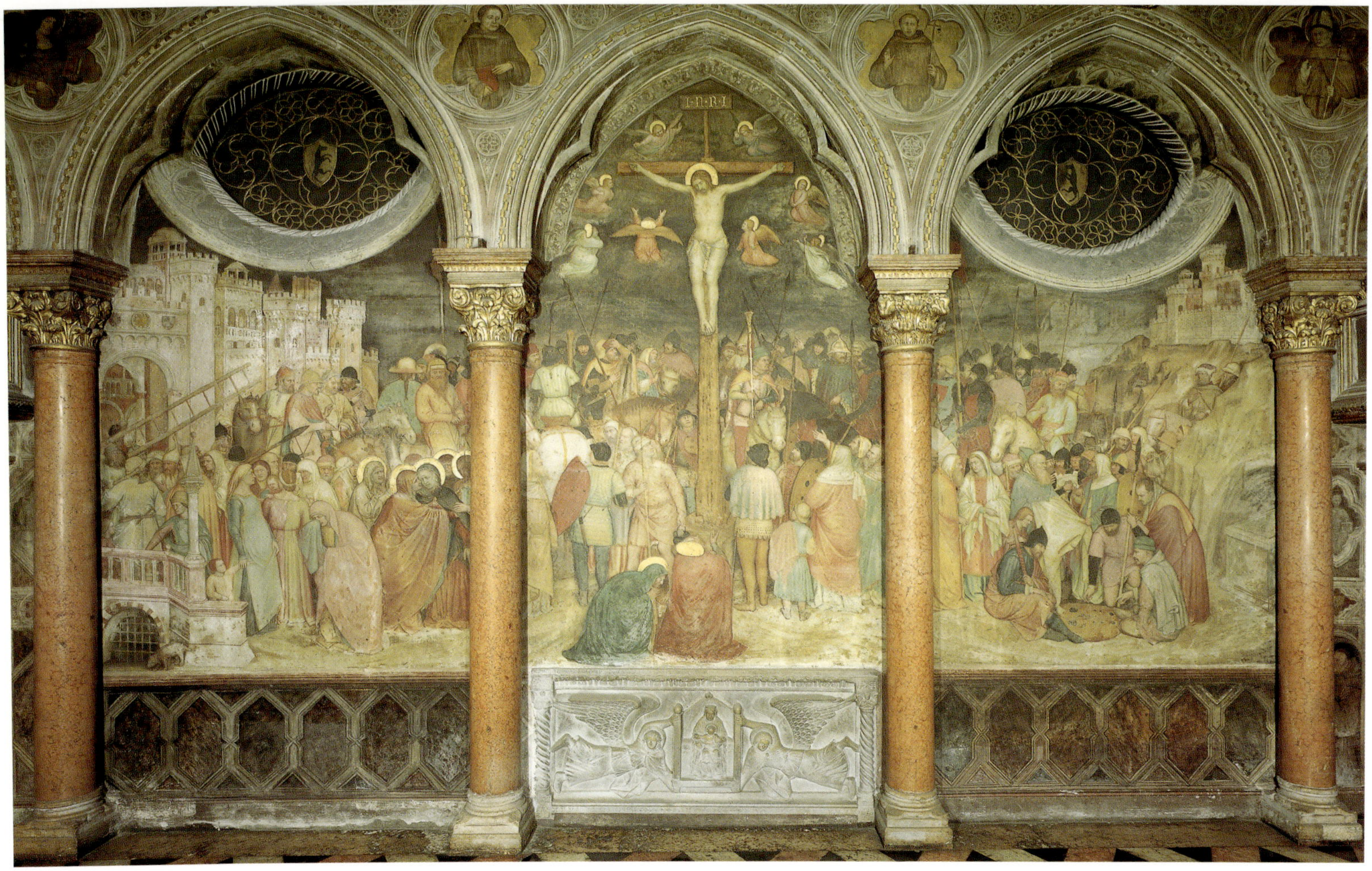

two drawings of Jacopo Bellini (Paris, Louvre, Book of Drawings, ff. 32v-33r), where the lid is to the left of a *Lamentation*, itself depicted as part of a *Deposition* (note the ladder at left), and the two scenes are clearly united in a continuous space (note the drapery detail of the standing man). This design, however, is most unlikely to have been for an altarpiece, since the left-hand panel of such an altar would have been devoid of figures, and an unlikely horizontal (landscape) shape for such a function would be created.

Altichiero's fresco of the *Resurrection* referred to above may provide the more likely iconographical model for the missing Bellini altarpiece. When the probable predella is taken into account, this likelihood is further increased. At the left of the presumed predella is an *Adoration*, a key early scene in the Life of Christ. The iconography of the version here is suggestive of the several compositions showing the intercessory supplications of rulers and *condottieri* kneeling before the Virgin and Child that are frequently to be found in Padua in the two generations or so before the commissioning of the Gattamelata chapel, notably in the tomb of the Dotti[16] in the Eremitani and also in the Oratory of St. George. The predella continues, to the right, with the *Crucifixion*, the key event of the Passion. It ends with

Crucifixion by Altichiero, 1377-9, altar wall of Chapel of S. Felice, Basilica del Santo, Padua (for frescoes over the tombs to either side of the *Crucifixion* see illustrations on pp. 304-5)

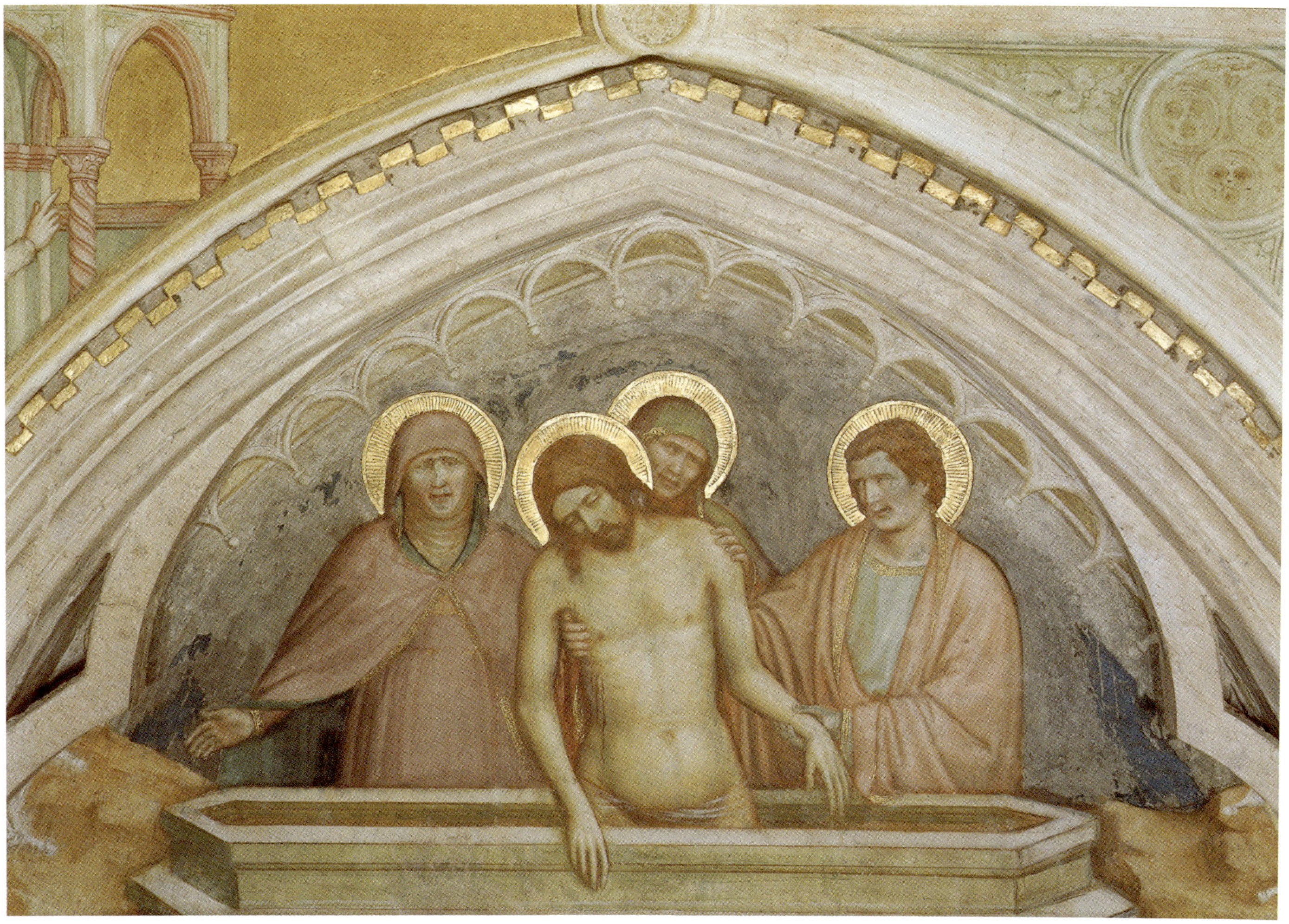

Pietà by Altichiero, 1377-9.
Fresco over tomb in Chapel of S. Felice, Basilica del Santo, Padua

the *Descent into Limbo*, which immediately follows the *Crucifixion* ('He descended into hell...') but immediately precedes the *Resurrection* ('on the third day He rose again from the dead...'). The *Resurrection* in a central position in the triptych would therefore have formed a logical narrative conclusion.

Another point in favour of this argument is that the overriding theme of funerary chapels is usually the Resurrection: even the positioning of tombs within chapels took into account such things as the immediate contiguity of the altar, and the Real Presence in the form of the reserved Sacrament. The deceased were positioned conveniently for the Last Day, as are the two Gattamelata *condottieri* in sculpted effigy upon their tombs, with their feet towards the altar (the position in which they would have been interred). Conversely, it is also true that major altarpieces showing the *Man of Sorrows/Lamentation* as the central event are few, although one of them was carried out by Jacopo Bellini – the missing altarpiece for the Scuola di S. Giovanni Evangelista, Venice. This was not, however, painted for a funerary chapel but for devotional and meditational purposes.

The *Man of Sorrows* is generally shown in a minor but complementary position relative to the main scene in major altarpieces; and is appropriate for smaller

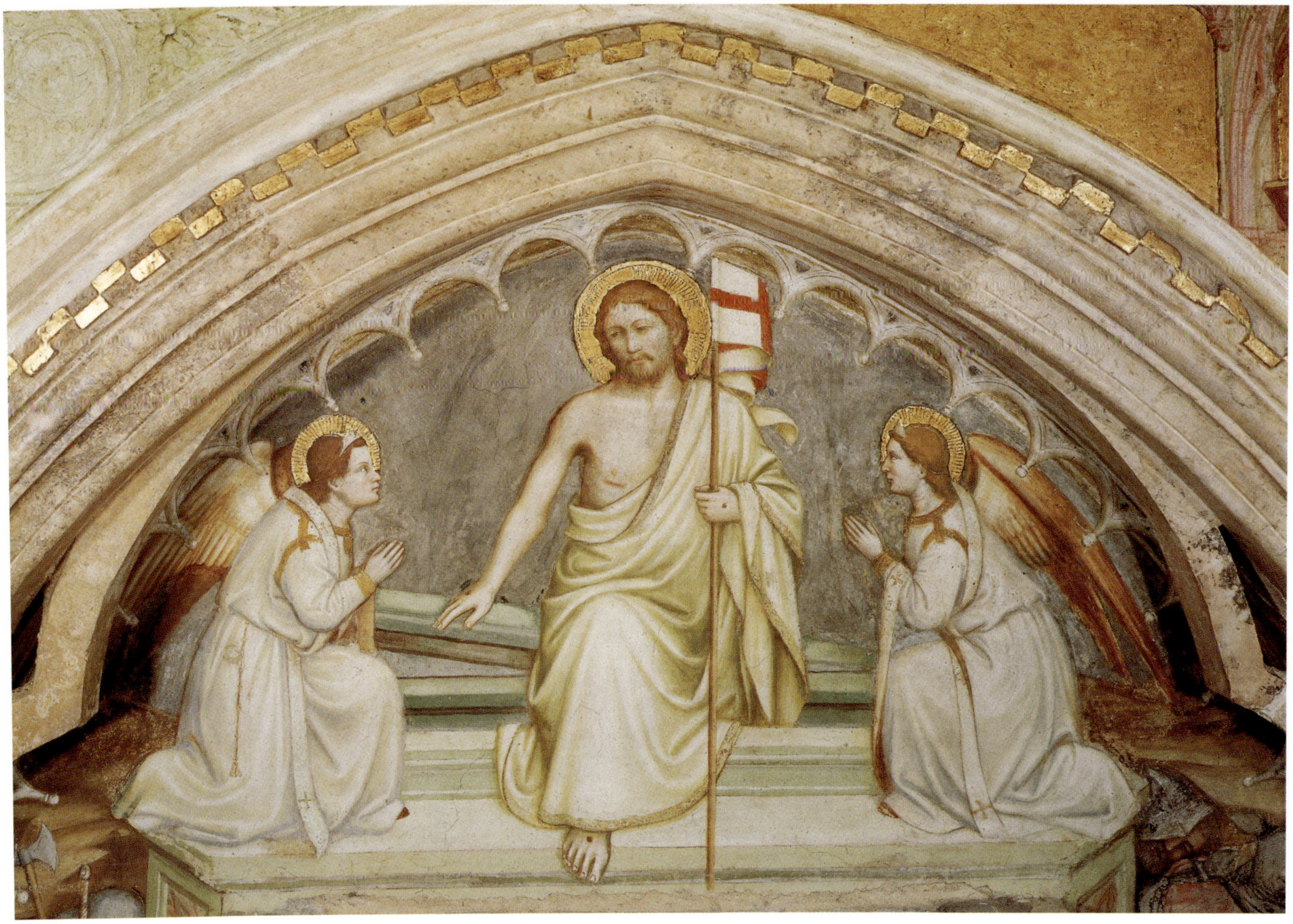

Resurrection by Altichiero, 1377-9.
Fresco over tomb in Chapel of S. Felice, Basilica del Santo, Padua

works of private devotion.[17] There are examples within the known work of the Bellini which support this point, notably the St. Vincent Ferrer triptych in SS. Giovanni e Paolo, Venice, where the *Man of Sorrows* is to be seen above the main central panel. It is conceivable, therefore, that a *Man of Sorrows* was to be seen above the central scene of the lost Gattamelata altarpiece, within an arched top[18] that would have been set over all three panels of the triptych (compare the position of the *Man of Sorrows* in the St. Vincent Ferrer altarpiece).

Shortly after Polidoro recorded it, however, the triptych was removed from the chapel in a remodelling of 1651, when Gattamelata's funerary chapel was turned into the chapel of the Holy Sacrament.[19] The rights in the family chapel had descended to the Counts of Sanguineto, whose agreement to these changes was necessary, as it was also for further developments in 1741.[20] The chapel was then altered again after a decision of 1901 to make the chapel yet more 'dignified' for the Sacrament, work beginning in 1921 and continuing until 1936. In the baroque remodelling of 1651 when the altarpiece was removed, an apse was created: until that time it had been flat-ended, like the contiguous chapel of S.Felice.[21] Although one part of the predella, the *Descent into Limbo*, has apparently remained in Padua ever since, the other parts were dispersed, some of them

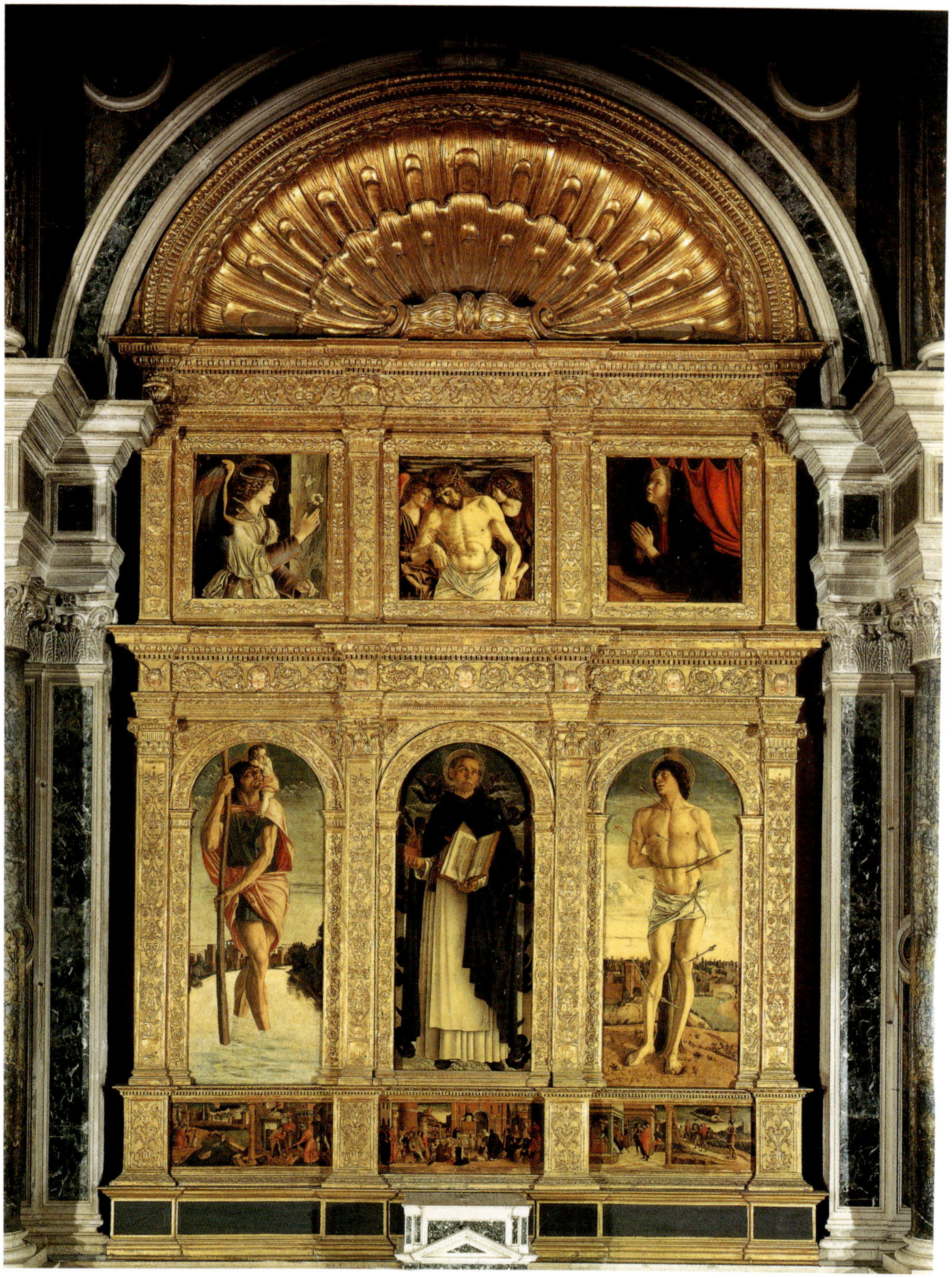

St Vincent Ferrer Altarpiece
by Giovanni Bellini
(*c.* 1438-1516), *c.* 1470.
Each main panel 60 x 36 cm.
SS. Giovanni e Paolo, Venice

surviving in various museums. There is as yet no record of how that 'diaspora' happened, nor of where the missing parts of the altarpiece might now be, and so its evident significance in the history of altarpiece design and of Venetian art generally remains tantalisingly incomplete.

NOTES

1 V. Lazzarini, 'Gli autori della cappella e dei monumenti Gattamelata al Santo', *Il Santo*, IV, 1932, pp. 228-33, p. 228. See A. Sartori, *Documenti per la storia dell'arte a padova*, C. Fillarini, ed., Vicenza, 1976, pp. 80ff.; B. Gonzati, *La basilica di Sant'Antonio di Padova, descritta ed illustrata*, 2 vols., Padua, 1852-3 (includes plans, etc.); A. Sartori, 'La cappella del Sacramento al Santo decorata da Ludovico Pogliaghi', *Il Santo*, X, 1970, pp. 183-204; C. Semenzato, *Fonti e Studi per la Storia del Santo a Padova IX*, Studi 5, Vicenza, 1984.

2 Lazzarini, op. cit., p. 228.

3 For these documents, ibid., and G. Lorenzoni, ed., *Fonti e Studi per la storia del Santo a Padova III: l'Edificio del Santo a Padova*, Vicenza, 1981, pp. 108ff.; Gonzati, op. cit., esp. docs. XXXIII, XXXVIII.

4 C. Eisler, 'Saints Anthony Abbot and Bernardino of Siena designed by Jacopo and painted by Gentile Bellini', *Arte Veneta*, 39 (1985), pp. 32-40; M. Boskovits, 'Giovanni Bellini: quelques suggestions sur ses débuts', *Revue du Louvre et des Musées de France*, 36 (1986), pp. 386-93; *idem*, 'Per Jacopo Bellini Pittore (Postilla ad Un Colloquio)', *Paragone*, xxxvi, 419-421-423 (1985), pp. 111-23; K. Christiansen, 'Venetian Painting of the Early Quattrocento', *Apollo*, March, 1987, pp. 166-77; P. Humfrey, 'Jacopo Bellini: Sts. Anthony Abbot and Bernardine of Siena' in D. Garstang, ed., *Gothic to Renaissance: European Painting 1300-1600*, exh. cat., Colnaghi (London and New York), 1988-9, pp. 18-26; P. Humfrey, 'The Bellini and the Vivarini in Venice', in E. Borsook and F. S. Gioffredi, ed., *Italian Altarpieces 1250-1550, Function and Design*, Oxford, 1994, pp. 139-74 (hereafter Humfrey, 1994).

5 See C. Eisler, *The Genius of Giovanni Bellini. The Complete Paintings and Drawings*, New York, 1989, pp. 60ff., figs. 47-51; Humfrey, 1994, pp. 148ff. and illustrations; P. Humfrey, *The Altarpiece in Renaissance Venice*, New Haven and London, 1993; R. Goffen, *Giovanni Bellini*, New Haven and London, 1989, pp. 8ff.; B. Degenhart and A. Schmitt, *Corpus der Italienischen Zeichnungen 1300-1450*, 5 vols., II, *Venedig: Jacopo Bellini*, v, text (Berlin, 1990). See also R. Goffen and G. N. Sciré, *Il colore rittrovato: Bellini a Venezia*, exh. cat., Venice, 2000, pp. 122 ff. ('I quattro trittici della Chiesa della Carità').

6 See Humfrey, 1994, p. 151. Giacoma was also a patron of Mantegna who might conceivably have been her first choice for the Gattamelata altarpiece (ibid., p. 150).

7 C. Eisler, op. cit. at n. 4 above.

8 Humfrey, 1994, p. 148.

9 V. Polidoro, *Le religiose memorie...* , Venice, 1590, fol. 25r.

10 This is the date given in the footnote to the English translation of the 'Anonimo' of Marcantonio Michiel edited by G. C. Williamson (text translated by P. Mussi), London, 1903, p. 7 (for the original text see n. 12 below).

11 See Goffen and Sciré, op. cit. at n. 5 above. It is also significant in that it raises the question of the actual date of birth of Giovanni Bellini and his emergence as an independent master. The probability is that Giovanni was born rather later than *c.* 1427 (the date preferred by some scholars).

12 Th. Frimmel, ed., *Der Anonimo Morelliano (Marcantonio Michiel's Notizia d'Opere del Disegno)*, Vienna, 1888, p. 4. 'The first chapel on the right as you go in was founded by Gattamelata, and was painted by Jacopo da Montagnana and his brother-in-law Piero Calzetto; but the altarpiece is from the hand of Giacomo Bellini and Giovanni and Gentile, his sons, as is clear from the inscription. Here [also] are the tombs of Gattamelata and of his son Giannantonio, who was [also] a condottiere, and died young.'

13 Humfrey, 1994, pp. 148-9.

14 See J. Richards, *Altichiero: An Artist and his Patrons in the Italian Trecento*, Cambridge, 2000, pl. 79.

15 Humfrey, 1994, p. 149.

16 Destroyed in the Second World War; see Richards, op. cit., pl. 118.

17 As noted by Humfrey, 1994, p. 142.

18 The shape suggested by Humfrey, 1994, pp. 149-50.

19 Gonzati, op. cit., also states that the frescoes perished at this time.

20 A. Bigoni, *Il forestiere istruto...* , Padua, 1876, p. 59.

21 G. Lorenzoni, op. cit., pl. 135 (eighteenth-century drawing), pp. 108ff.

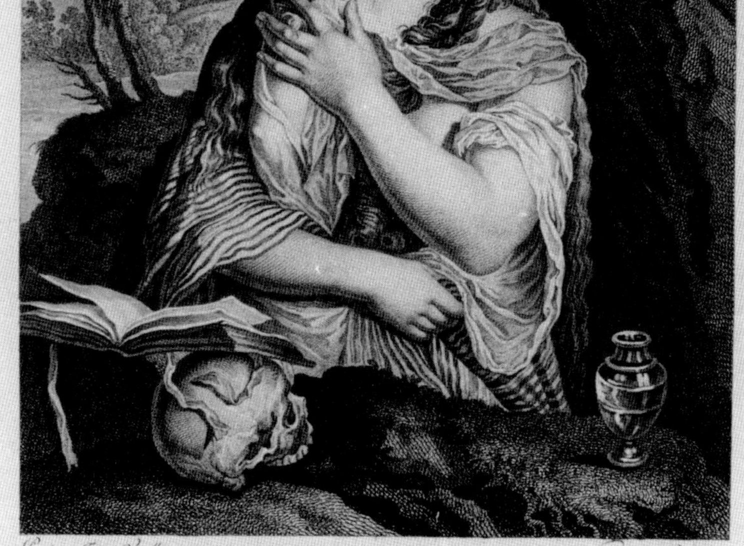

Peint par Titien Vecelli — Gravé par Romanet

LA MADELEINE

De la Galerie du Palais d'Orléans

ÉCOLE VENITIENNE.

XIVme TABLEAU DE TITIEN VECELLI.

Peint sur Toile, ayant de hauteur 3 Pieds 7 Pouces, sur 3 Pieds de Large.

Cette Pénitente est de bout entre des Rochers, les yeux levés vers le Ciel, une main sur son sein, et exprimant dans toute son attitude la douleur et le repentir.

Ce Morceau est regardé comme une des plus admirables productions du Titien, autant pour la beauté et la force du Coloris, que pour la délicatesse du Pinceau, le fini précieux, et l'expression la plus touchante.

Titian (Tiziano Vecelli)

c. 1485/90-1576

Mary Magdalen in penitence

Possibly 1560

Oil on canvas

104.2 × 91.5 cm[1] or 106 × 86.8 m[2]

Titian first treated the subject of Mary Magdalen in penitence around 1530 and returned to the subject at least twelve times over the next thirty-five years. The early versions depict the sinner saint as a voluptuous nude, the later clothed. The principal versions hang now in the Pitti Palace, Florence (1530); Museo di Capodimonte, Naples (1550); Hermitage Museum, St. Petersburg (1560); and another, now destroyed, hung in the Monastery of San Lorenzo, Escorial (1561). Studio variants and copies exist of each type.[3] One of the autograph depictions of the *Magdalen*, similar to the one in the Hermitage, but distinguished by showing the skull (upon which the saint rests her book), has not been seen since the nineteenth century. It passed through the hands of some of Europe's greatest collectors, including Queen Christina of Sweden and the Duc d' Orléans, and is now known through a print by A.-L. Romanet, in reverse, made in the eighteenth century.[4]

The numerous versions testify to the immediate appeal of the image. A version of, or copy after, that now in the Pitti Palace inspired a eulogy by the poet Giambattista Marino (1569-1625) in his *Galeria* of 1619, a collection of poems celebrating his love for the arts and admiration for artists:

> But nature and truth cede
> To that which the learned artificer has imaged,
> For he painted her here, as beautiful and alive
> As he conceived her in his soul and thought.
> Oh, celestial semblance, oh, masterly craft,
> For in his work he outdoes himself;
> Eternal ornament of cloth and paper,
> Marvel of the world, honor of art![5]

Another was recommended by Philip II's envoy in Venice, García Hernández, who reported in a letter of 20 November 1561, 'Good judges in art say that this [Magdalen] is the best thing Titian has done.'[6] Philip acquired it and the picture hung in the Escorial.[7] Vasari describes Titian working on Philip's picture:

> Tiziano afterwards painted, for sending to the Catholic King, a figure of St. Mary Magdalene from the middle of the thighs upwards, all dishevelled; that is, with the hair falling over the shoulders, about the throat, and over the breast, the while that, raising the head with the eyes fixed on Heaven, she reveals remorse in the redness of the eyes, and in her tears repentance for her sins. Wherefore the picture moves mightily all who behold it; and what is more, although she is very beautiful, it moves not to lust but to compassion. This picture, when it was finished, so pleased Silvio [Badoer], a Venetian gentleman, that in order to have it, being one who takes supreme delight in painting, he gave Tiziano a hundred

Mary Magdalen in penitence. Engraving by A.L. Romanet after lost original by Titian (Tiziano Vecelli, *c.* 1485/90-1576), published as plate 14 in J. Couché, *Galerie des Tableaux du Palais Royal*, 1786-1808

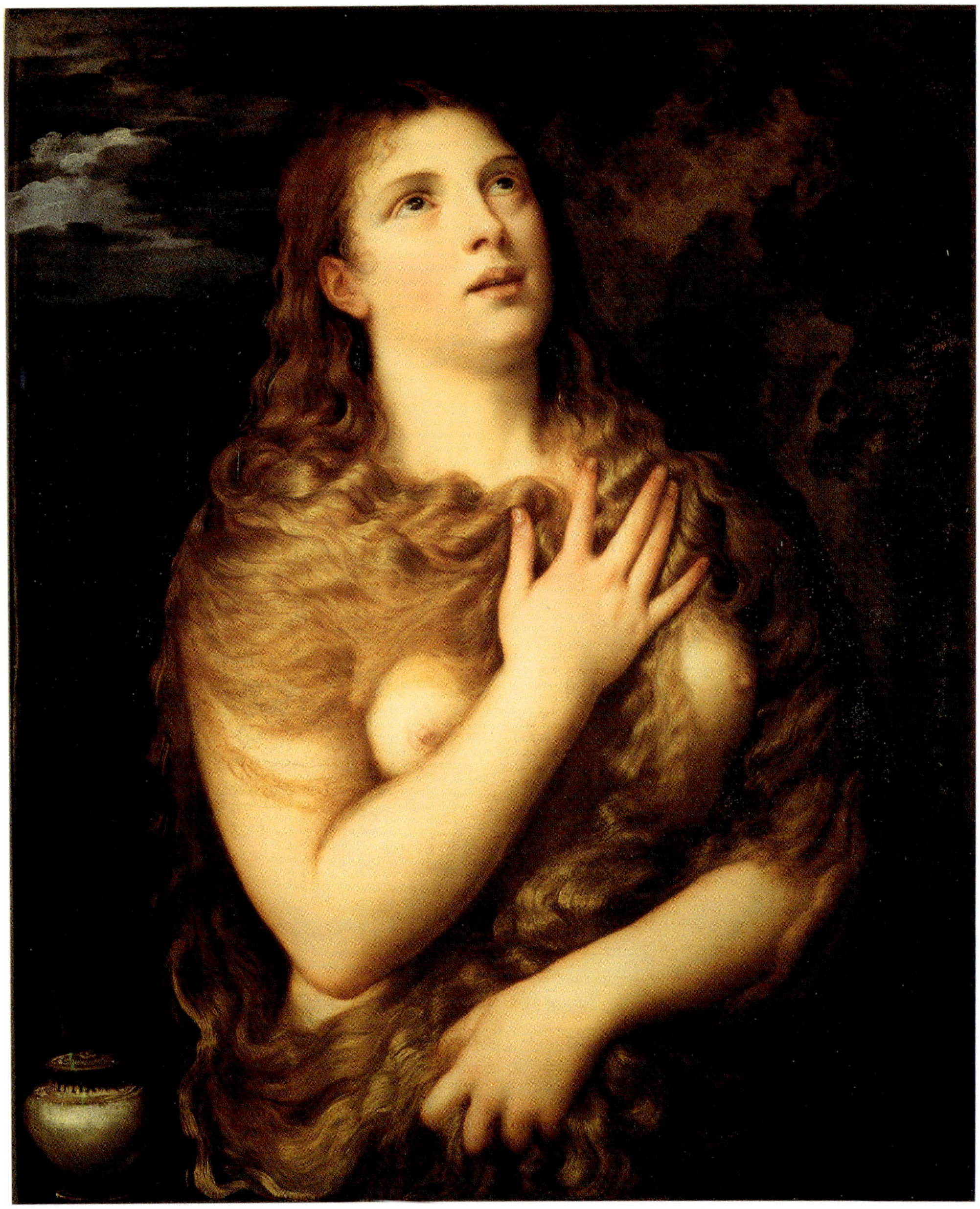

Mary Magdalen in penitence by Titian *c.* 1535.
Oil on panel, 84 × 69 cm.
Pitti Palace, Florence

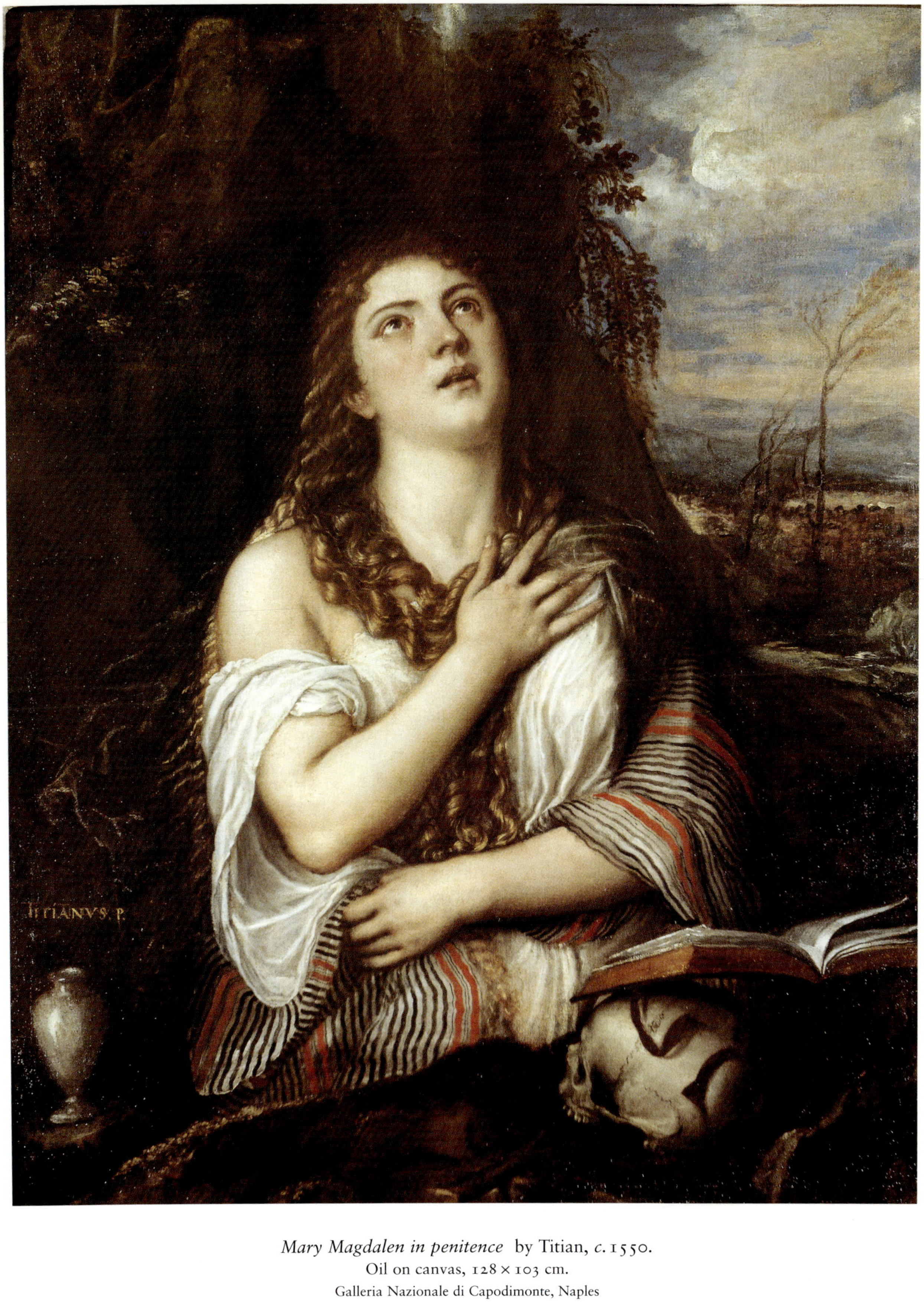

Mary Magdalen in penitence by Titian, *c.* 1550.
Oil on canvas, 128 × 103 cm.
Galleria Nazionale di Capodimonte, Naples

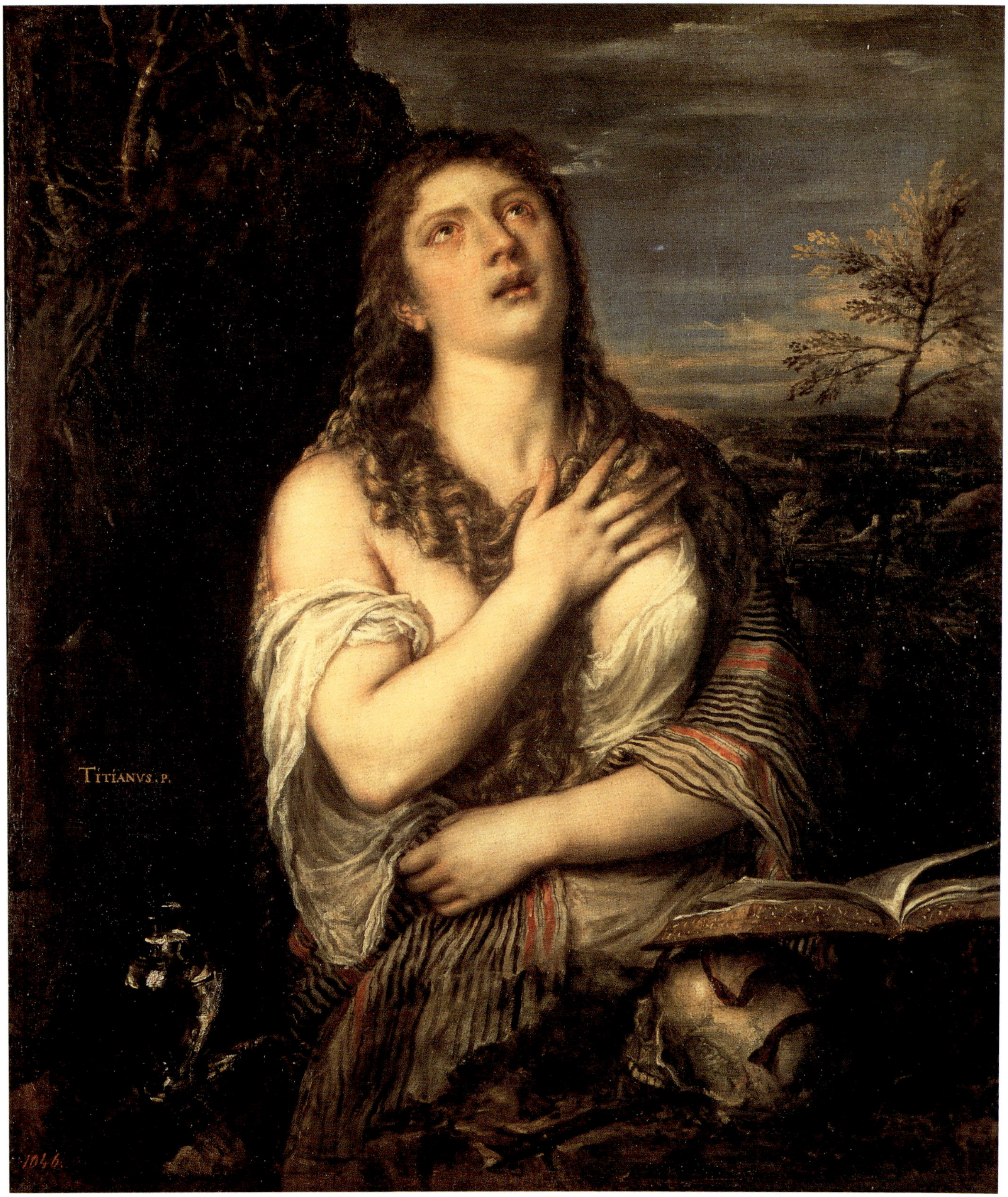

Mary Magdalen in penitence by Titian, *c.* 1560.
Oil on canvas, 118 × 97 cm.
State Hermitage Museum, St. Petersburg

crowns: wherefore Tiziano was forced to paint another, which was not less beautiful, for sending to the above-named Catholic King [of Spain].[8]

According to Ridolfi, Titian initially took the pose from an antique statue but, 'in order to observe certain natural effects he used a beautiful young neighbour of his who, standing in this posture with great dedication, shed copious tears and showed, as though she was in grief, that aspect of the face which he marvellously expresses'.[9]

The signed *Magdalen* now in the Hermitage (inventory no. 117) was found in Titian's house at his death and sold to Russia from the Barbarigo collection in the nineteenth century.[10] The missing picture, with its own distinct, and distinguished, provenance is similar to the Hermitage version in that the saint is represented clothed, seen before a Bible resting upon a skull. There is also a prominent tree in the background. To the saint's right is her attribute of a jar of ointment. The Magdalen is the archetypal repentant female sinner, absolved from her sins through her love of Christ. According to medieval *Golden Legend* of Jacobus da Voragine, she retired to the desert where she spent thirty years in penitence, refreshed by celestial food and transported daily to Heaven by angels.

A 'Maria Magdalena, von Titian', which can be identified as the missing painting, is recorded in an inventory around 1600 of the collection of Rudolf II (1552-1612), twenty-four years after his inauguration as Holy Roman Emperor.[11] How or when it entered the Imperial Collection is not known, but Rudolf's great-uncle, Charles V (1500-58), had commissioned paintings from Titian, most of which are now in the Prado Museum in Madrid. When he abdicated in 1556, which predates the probable date of the execution of the missing *Magdalen*, his dominions were divided between his son Philip, later Philip II of Spain, and his brother Ferdinand, who succeeded him as Holy Roman Emperor. Ferdinand I continued to patronise the arts, mainly in order to glorify the Habsburg dynasty, and it is also said that he was the first ruler who kept his collections in specially designed rooms which he called a *Kunstkammer*. He was succeeded by his grandson, Rudolf II.

Having spent his formative years amongst the Habsburg treasures at the Spanish Court, Rudolf established himself as one of the greatest patron and collectors of all time. He transferred the Imperial Court from Vienna to Prague in about 1583, and in 1590-96 he added a new gallery to Prague Castle. He subsequently created a 'Spanish Hall' in 1604-6 for the exhibition of paintings and sculptures. The 1607-11 inventory compiled by his miniature painter and antiquary, David Froschl, divides the contents of the *Kunstkammer* into three categories: Naturalia (natural objects), Artificialia (works of art) and Scientifica (scientific objects, books). Paintings and regalia did not belong to any of these categories and were therefore not listed in this inventory.[12]

Rudolf's mental health, precarious at the best of times, was already deteriorating by 1598, and the Emperor became a virtual recluse. After 1600 his fortune and position declined dramatically. He was not married, thus throwing the question of succession wide open, and his power-hungry brother Matthias openly undermined Rudolf's authority. In 1608 Matthias forced Rudolf to hand him the crown of Hungary, which was followed in 1611 by that of Bohemia, leaving Rudolf with only the imperial title and no effective power.[13] Finally, there was the constant threat of warfare with an invigorated and menacing neighbour, the Ottoman Empire.

Rudolf died on 20 January 1612 and an inventory was drawn up of his possessions, but it has not yet been found. He was succeeded by his brother Matthias,

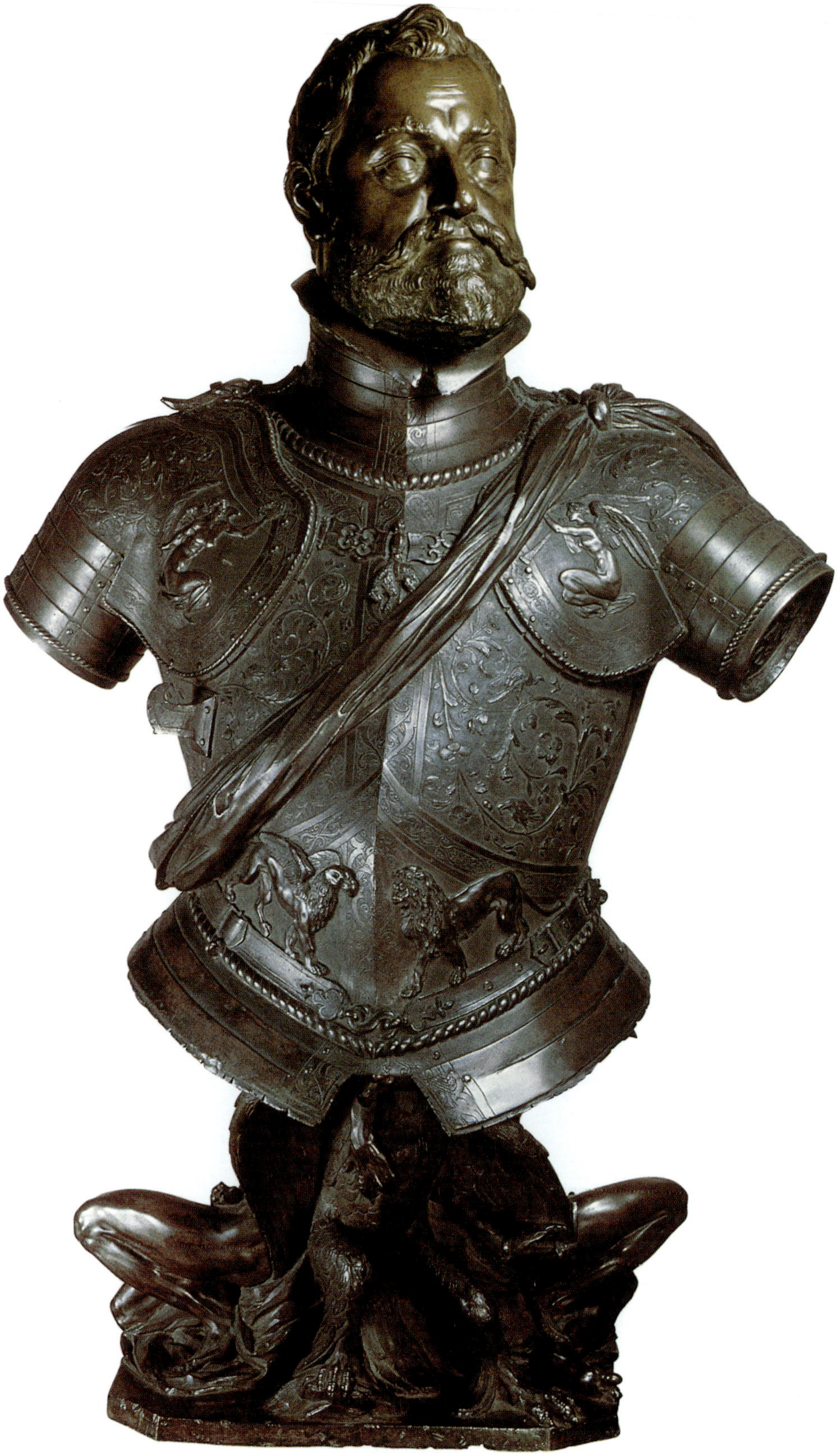

whereupon the new Emperor moved the Court and part of the collection back to Vienna. Matthias was intent upon uniting in one place those extremely valuable elements of the collection appropriate to a *Schatzkammer* (treasury), which is what he now called the new Viennese centrepiece of the Habsburg collections.[14] As a consequence, most of the paintings, numbering some 3,000, thus remained behind in Prague, including many major examples and, despite various dispersals,[15] many subsequently fell into the hands of the invading Swedes, which is how Titian's missing *Magdalen* must have passed into the possession of Queen Christina of Sweden. Paintings only regained a central place in the Habsburg collections when Archduke Leopold Wilhelm moved his huge collection into the Stallburg in Vienna in 1659.

In 1619 the childless Emperor Matthias died and Ferdinand II succeeded him. The Crown of Bohemia was now contested, as the rebellious Bohemian Estates had elected a Protestant, Frederick V of the Palatine, as King. In the Battle of the White Mountain (1620) Frederick was beaten decisively. The following execution of the rebels, the confiscation of their properties, the imposition of religious orthodoxy, and the suppression of the Czech language had dramatic effects: the population of Bohemia roughly halved between 1621 and 1629, a gruesome reminder of Ferdinand II's words that he preferred 'no population to a population of heretics'.

In 1619, when war between the Emperor and the Bohemian Estates became a certainty, the Estates compiled a list of objects from Rudolf's collections which they wanted to sell in order to raise money for the war effort, but the speed with which events unfolded made the list obsolete, and anyway it contained no paintings. There could, of course, have been a second list containing paintings, but this, like the inventory taken upon Rudolf's death, has not yet been discovered.

In December 1621 another inventory of Rudolf's collections in Prague (or what was left of them) was compiled under the direction of Ferdinand II's trusted advisor, the Duke of Liechtenstein.[16] No. 859 of this inventory lists 'Ein Maria Magdalen vom Tician (Orig.)' and this is in all probability the now-missing *Magdalen* which was later owned by Queen Christina of Sweden.

In 1648, the final year of the Thirty Years War, Queen Christina of Sweden's troops under General Johan Christoph, Count von Königsmark, entered Prague and stormed and looted the Castle. Miseroni, the Keeper of the Collection, was forced to hand over the keys and inventories and was only able to save a few items. A brief inventory of the captured treasures was compiled 31 August-10 September 1648, probably on the orders of Königsmark, and among the 764 paintings listed were four depicting Mary Magdalen, but without descriptions or the names of artists. None the less, only one of the three is specified as a half-length, and so it is likely to be the missing Titian: '... 398: Maria Magdalene brust Bilt'.[17] This loot eventually arrived in Stockholm in late May 1649, and in a letter written in May 1653 to the Duke of Bracciano in Italy, the Queen tells him that the Prague gallery has arrived in Stockholm. She continues:

> It is really enormous and beautiful. There is an infinite range of items, but apart from some thirty or forty Italian originals, I discount them all. There are works by Albrecht Dürer and other German masters whose names I do not know but who would arouse the profound admiration of anyone apart from myself. But I do declare that I would exchange them all for two Raphaels, and I think that even this would be doing them too much honour.[18]

In 1652, the Marquis du Fresne (1611-61), appointed *garde des tableaux* by the Queen, catalogued the collection, which comprised 750 paintings, 470 of which

Rudolf II by Adriaen de Vries (*c.* 1560-1626), 1603.
Bronze, ht. 112 cm.
Kunsthistorischesmuseum, Vienna

had come from Prague.[19] Again, no artists' names were given, although Du Fresne included a more detailed description, as well as indicating the provenance of the paintings. No. 236 in the lists reads:

... de Prague. Dito [un tableau de moyen grandeur] qui represente une femme avec un liure et une robbe des Indes, sur de la toile.

The reference is to a half-length female 'with a book' and with an 'Indian' drapery, which reasonably identifies Titian's length of rich striped stuff that is intended to suggest the Magdalen's former finery.

Queen Christina, lauded as the 'Minerva of the North', craved knowledge and intellectual society. She invited Descartes to Sweden, and devoted as much time as she was able to spare from her tedious court duties to the philosopher. He played an influential role in encouraging Christina's ambivalence towards her Lutheran faith in favour of a conversion to Catholicism, but he succumbed to the icy climate and died before she was able to put her secret plan of abdication and voluntary exile into action. By the summer of 1653 she had begun to ship treasures to Antwerp including 'les plus belles tapisseries de sa maison, le meilleur de sa bibliothèque et le plus pretieux de son cabinet'.[20]

On 6 June 1654 she abdicated in the Great Hall of Uppsala Castle, to the consternation and astonishment of her Swedish subjects, and began her journey south *incognito*. On her arrival in Antwerp, she stayed at the palace of her Minister-Resident, the Portuguese-Jewish banker Don García de Yllán. It was there that an inventory of her possessions was later drawn up, in May 1656, by the *notaire* J. S. Le Rousseau which lists two paintings of Mary Magdalen by Titian, although with no details in the brief descriptions: 'Une pièce, une Magdaleine, de Titian... Encores une pièce, Marie Magdalene, de Titian.'[21] In view of her critical remarks quoted above about Dürer, is is significant that Queen Christina left almost all her works by northern masters behind in Stockholm Castle. In contrast, she evidently prized the missing *Magdalen* among her best pictures, because, as we shall see, it was listed among her possessions in Rome, where she only brought about twenty portraits and forty other works by Italian artists, which became the nucleus of an ever-expanding collection.[22]

Christina reached Brussels on 23 December 1654 where she was rapturously greeted by Archduke Leopold Wilhelm, Governor of the Spanish Netherlands. He was witness to her secret reception into the Roman Catholic faith on Christmas Eve, and while staying with him she acquired his Titian of *Diana and Actaeon*. During these months Christina planned her future life in Rome, finally arriving in the Eternal City on 19 December 1655. During her journey through Italy, Christina was greeted with a thunderous reception, which probably exceeded even her expectations. Her official entry into Rome on 23 December 1655 was through the Porta del Popolo, which Bernini had redesigned for the occasion. A triumphal arch was constructed at the Via Giulia, St. Peter's was decorated with allegorical figures, and a false façade was erected at her temporary address, the Palazzo Farnese; and Pope Alexander VII presented her with a sedan chair designed by Bernini, together with a carriage and litter, which was entered using a small silver ladder carried by a servant walking alongside. Her permanent residence became the Palazzo Riario on the Via della Lungara, where Christina soon assembled the intellectual lights of the city around her.

Christina did not have her treasures from the north unpacked until 1662, at which time another inventory was drawn up by the master of her household, Sebastiano Bevilacqua, and that contains references to two paintings of the Magdalen by Titian, where it is clear that no. 22, specified as a half-length on the scale of life ('grande al Naturale') and with a landscape, must be the picture in question:

No 22. Una Madalena mezza figura grande al Naturale, con Paese in Tela impiedi con cornice liscia indorata, alta palmi cinque e mezzo, e larga palmi cinque. DI TITIANO.

No 23. Altra Madalena della medema grandezza et effegie, Mezza figura grande al naturale; ma diversa nel paese nel velo, ne capelli; e quasi in tutto il resto in Tela inpiedi con cornice liscia indorata, alta palmi cinque e mezzo, e larga palmi cinque – DI TITIANO.[23]

While in Rome, Christina added considerably to the collection which she had brought with her, and was advised in her purchases by her antiquary, the art-historian Giovanni Pietro Bellori, as well as by Bernini. She also assembled a large collection of Antique sculptures and busts, including statues of eight muses from the Villa Adriana, which were displayed in the Stanza delle Muse at the Palazzo Riario. Count Nicodemus Tessin, later architect of the Royal Palace in Stockholm, visited Queen Christina's collection during his second stay in Rome from 1687-9. He noted her seventeen pictures by Titian, remarking on two Magdalens:

Vom Titien wahren darin 17 Quadri, dheren das eine schoner alss dass andere wahr. Erstens wahr dass menschliche alter von ihme vorgestelt durch 2 kinder...; darnach... , zweij gleiche Magdalenen.[24]

Christina died in Rome on 19 April 1689 and a *post-mortem* inventory was compiled. Like Bevilacqua's 1662 inventory, it lists two paintings of the Magdalen by Titian, the first of which can be identified as the missing picture:

32 Un quadro di una Maddalena piangente, più di mezza figura di buon naturale ignuda con le braccia e poca parte del petto con capelli sciolti, e vanti di se una testa di morto con un libro aperto in bel paese, di *Tiziano*, in tela in piedi, alta p.^{mi} quattro e trequarti, larga p.^{mi} quattro meno un quarto con cornice dorata liscia alla romana.

33 Un altro quadro di una Madalena simile quanto all'idea del viso, ma diversa in tutto il rimanente, dell'istesso *Tiziano*, in tela piedi alta p.^{mi} quattro, larga p.^{mi} quattro meno un 1/4, cornice liscia dorata all romana...[25]

According to Christina's will of 1673, which was confirmed in early 1689, the collection went to her sole heir and trusted friend Cardinal Decio Azzolino and, upon his death, which took place very shortly afterwards, in June 1689, the collection passed to his nephew, Marchese Pompeo Azzolino.

The Marchese was not a man of great fortune and in 1692 he sold the greater part of Queen Christina's collections for 123,000 Roman *scudi* to the immensely rich Don Livio Odescalchi, later Duca di Bracciano (1652-1713).[26] The 7,000 objects and works of art in the collection included tapestries, statues, furniture, medals, weapons and 240 pictures. The Odescalchi inventory of 1692, however, includes not two but only one painting of the Magdalen by Titian,[27] and, since the later provenance of this picture can be followed, subsequent descriptions make it evident that this *Magdalen* still in the Odescalchi collection in 1692 was the picture that is now missing.[28]

Don Livio, a bachelor, died on 7 September 1713, leaving the collections to his adopted nephew and heir Baldassare d'Erba Odescalchi, Duke of Bracciano, and Cardinal Benedetto Odescalchi, Archbishop of Milan. An Odescalchi inventory of 1714 lists a *Magdalen* by Titian, and gives the provenance as the Queen of Sweden:

[fol. 321] 1170 Un Quadro in tela alta palmi quattro, e tre quarti larga palmi quattro rappresenta S. Maria Maddalena piangente in mezza figura originale di Tiziano con cornice liscia dorata proviene dall sud.[a] Regina di Svezia.[29]

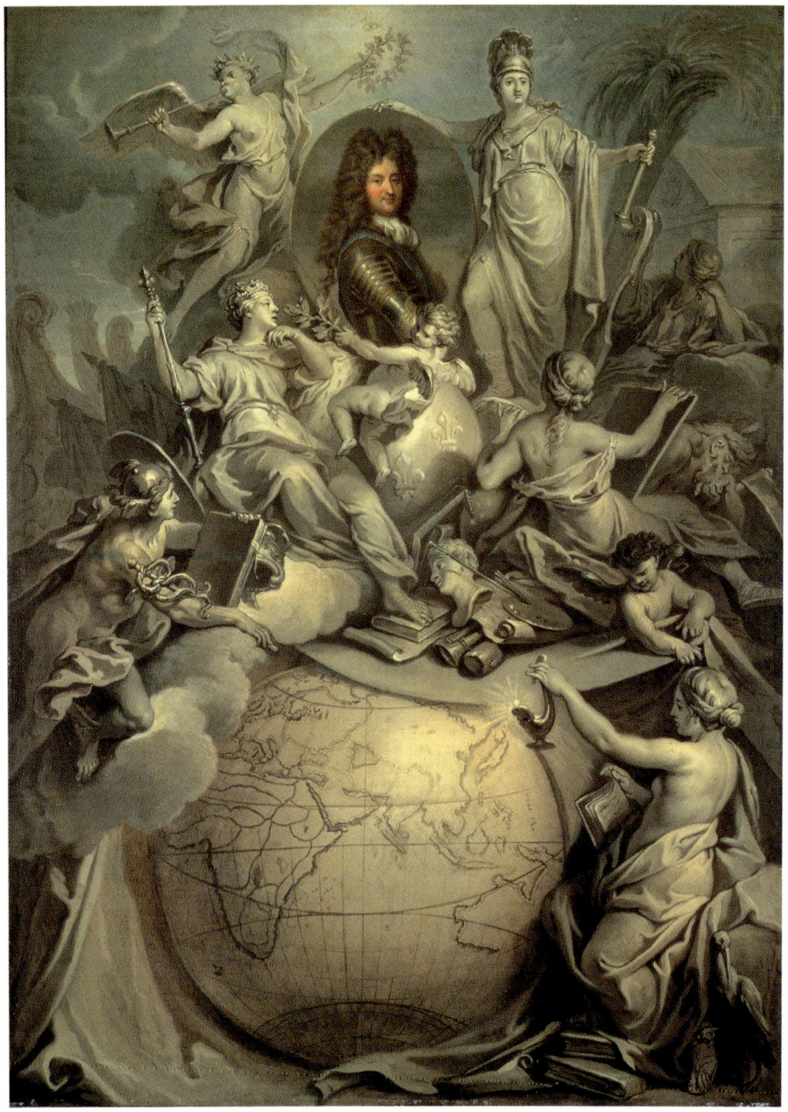

Allegorical portrait of Philippe, Duc d'Orléans (1674-1723), Regent of France by Antoine Dieu (1662-1727), 1718.
Oil on canvas.
Château de Versailles

In the same year, Pierre Crozat (1665-1740), the banker, connoisseur and collector of drawings, travelled to Rome on behalf of Philippe, Duc d'Orléans, who was then the Regent of France, to make his first offer of 110,000 Roman *scudi* for the collection. The family wanted 200,000, and it was to be seven years before the sale of the pictures alone was finalised at 93,000 *écus*. An inventory of 1721 lists as no. 8 'Una Madalena' by Titian, and by 1722 the collection of Old Masters, including the *Magdalen*, had arrived in Paris and was displayed at the Palais Royal. The *Description des tableaux du Palais Royal...* by Du Bois de Saint Gelais, published in 1727, includes the *Magdalen*, giving the provenance as the Queen of Sweden.[30] Many of the Orléans pictures were shortly thereafter reproduced in Pierre Crozat's monumental volume of engravings, *Recueil d'estampes*

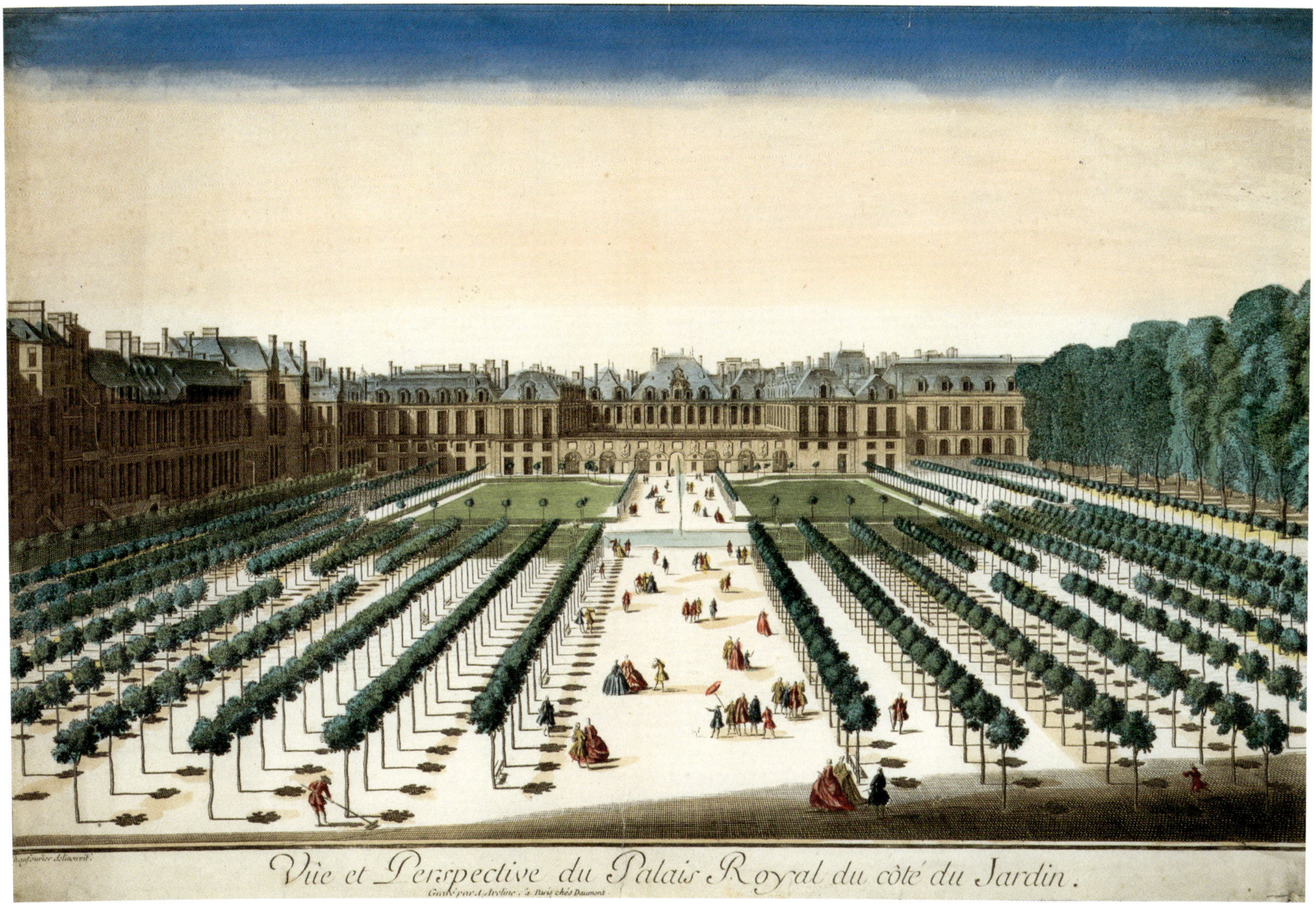

d'après les plus beaux tableaux ... qui sont en France (1729), and throughout the eighteenth century the picture gallery of the Palais Royal was regarded as the most splendid and most important collection in Europe, second possibly only to the royal collection in Spain. In 1786 the publisher Couché began to print the engravings of 355 of the more significant of the works in the Orléans gallery and Titian's *Magdalen*, as noted above, appears in his publication as plate 14. The last

View and perspective of the Palais Royal, Paris, from the garden side.
Engraving by Antoine Aveline (1691-1743) after Jean Chaufourier (1679-1757).
Private collection

owner of the collection of the House of Orléans was Louis Philippe Joseph, 5th Duc d'Orléans, born on 13 April 1747, known as Philippe Egalité on account of his revolutionary activities. He was guillotined in 1793. Early in life he developed an unquenchable desire to gamble, both at the tables and politically, and he was thus permanently in debt, despite his huge fortune and income. He finally sold 295 Italian and French paintings of the Orléans collection to the Brussels banker Vicomte Edouard de Walckiers, who sold them to his cousin, the French financier Laborde de Méréville, who was unable to return to revolutionary France, where his father had already been guillotined. Eventually this part of the Orléans collection was acquired by a triumvirate of noblemen, the Duke of Bridgewater, Lord Gower and the Earl of Carlisle, who quietly selected the best works for themselves.[31] All the Orléans pictures were exhibited in the rooms of the dealer Michael Bryan at 88 Pall Mall and at the Lyceum in the Strand, London, while Bryan organised a sale on behalf of the syndicate. The six-month selling exhibition opened to the public at a charge of half-a-crown on 26 December 1798 to great acclaim. William Buchanan recorded in his *Memoirs of Art* that a 'Mr. Maitland' was among the 'early and considerable purchasers from the collection'. He can be identified as John Maitland (*c.*1754-1831), a merchant, and M.P. for Chippenham, who bought Titian's *Magdalen* which hung at the Lyceum (no. 231) for 350 guineas.[32]

Shortly after his death, Maitland's entire collection was sold by Christie's on 30 July 1831, where the legendary collector Lord Northwick (1770-1859) bought the *Magdalen* (lot 101) for £126.[33] At first, the picture hung in the gallery of Northwick's London house at Connaught Place, until he sold the house and its 'magnificent and celebrated Gallery of Pictures' through Christie's on 24 May 1838. The *Magdalen* was included as lot 60 with a huge reserve of £600, but failed to sell at 370 guineas, and so remained with the rest of Northwick's extensive collection, in his country house, Northwick Park, Gloucestershire.

Lord Northwick was a passionate collector who described the pleasure of his lifelong admiration for the Italian masters as '... the seduction amusements of my youth: they have clung to me through a long life, and they are now the solace of my old age'. Northwick Park, however, proved too small for the collection, and so Lord Northwick bought Thirlestaine House in Cheltenham, Gloucestershire, to which he added a gallery which was open all year, free, to the public. The *Morning Post* reported that Thirlestaine House's '... liberal owner had no greater pleasure than that of knowing that his pictures drew visitors by the hundred'. In 1854 Henry Davies published an account of the collection entitled *Hours in Lord Northwick's Picture Galleries, being a catalogue with critical and descriptive notices of the Principal Paintings contained in the Thirlestane House Collection* where Titian's *Magdalen* is recorded hanging in the 80-foot principal gallery (no. 167):

> The character of the head, the drawing of the hands, the cast of the draperies, and the general colouring of the whole are excellent. It was formerly considered among the most precious of Titian's paintings in the Orléans Gallery.

In 1859 Lord Northwick died unmarried and intestate and the property had to be divided between his three next of kin. The entire collection was sold by Phillips at Thirlestaine House in a mammoth twenty-two-day sale from 26 July 1859. In eighteen days Northwick's 1,430 pictures and 83 miniatures, engraved gems and bronzes raised a total of £94,722 18s. The *Morning Post* (30 August 1859) reported indignantly:

These splendid collections are now scattered to the winds. They were brought together in the course of a very long life, they cost immense sums of money, and repaid their owner by the gratification they afforded to his own refined taste and the pleasure they afforded to

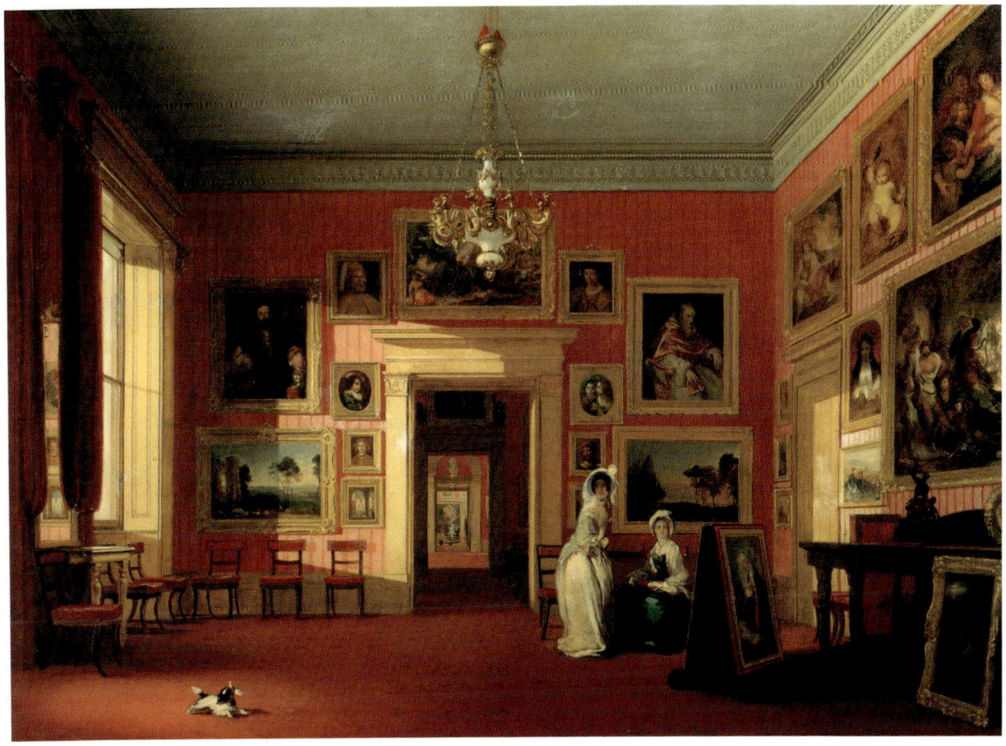

Lord Northwick's Picture Gallery at Thirlestaine House by Robert Huskisson (1820-61), *c.* 1846-7.
Oil on canvas, 81.4 × 108.5 cm.
Yale Center for British Art, New Haven, Paul Mellon Collection

others. But they are scattered, and it may be a whole generation before another collection at all approaching to it in number, value, and public usefulness shall be formed... To collect pictures at great cost and then sell them by auction is to throw to the winds a large amount of money... Next to the mischief of making an unfair will is that of making none at all... A gallery of pictures left to a family or to the public is an offering at the shrine of art; but, sold by auction, and dispersed among innumerable private purchasers, is sheer vanity and labour lost.

Titian's *Magdalen* was lot 1506, and in the sale catalogue 'David Marks' is listed as the buyer for 69 guineas.[34] David Marks has not as yet been identified. As *The Times* reported on 19 September 1859, 'So much doubt and mystery attended the sale of this collection, in consequence of a majority of the purchases having been made "on commission", that it is really a matter of interest to know with certainty into whose hands these treasures have fallen.' Among the purchasers identified by *The Times* were the Duc d'Aumale and the Dukes of Cleveland, Wellington, Newcastle, Hamilton and Buccleuch, who all bought works through agents. Other major buyers were the Marquess of Hertford, Baron de Rothschild, Mr. Holford, Mr. Baring, Mr. Davenport Bromley, the Marquess of Lansdowne and, the largest purchaser of all, Mr. Erle Drax. With so many of the buyers using agents to osbcure their identity, 'David Marks' might well have been acting in this capacity, although he could conceivably have been a dealer himself. He is only recorded as buying on one day of the twenty-two-day sale, chiefly religious pictures, and for relatively small amounts. It is also quite possible that he did not exist, and was merely the code name used by the auctioneer for bought-in pictures that day.

The ever-decreasing prices that the *Mary Magdalen* fetched at auction, when it sold at all, may well reflect a change of taste where this type of painting was concerned. Admittedly Ruskin may not have been voicing a widespread opinion when he used the term 'disgusting' of Titian's related version of the *Magdalen* in the Pitti Palace, Florence, remarking upon Titian's '... often treating base subjects, or elevated subjects basely, as in the disgusting *Magdalen* of the Pitti Palace'.[35] None the less, Lord Northwick's distinctive and hitherto highly prized *Magdalen* by Titian, that had graced so many famous collections throughout Europe, now vanished from sight.

NOTES

1 Measurements given in H. Wethey, *The Paintings of Titian*, 3 vols., London, 1969-75, I, *The Religious Pictures*, p. 147, cat. no. 126.

2 G. Campori, *Raccolta di cataloghi ed inventarii inediti*, Modena, 1870, p. 343, Queen Christina's *post-mortem* inventory in Rome, 1689: '... alta palmi quattro e tre quarti, larga palmi quattro meno un quarto con cornice dorata liscia all romana', interpreted as 106 × 86.8 cm by Wethey, loc. cit. Couché (see below, n. 4) has 'trois pieds sept pouces large de trois pieds', the French 'pied' being equivalent to about one foot and three-quarters of an inch, English measure. See also E. K. Waterhouse, 'Queen Christina's Italian Pictures in England' *in Queen Christina of Sweden, Documents and Studies*, Stockholm, 1966, pp. 372-5, p. 374, no. 64, citing Olof Granberg, *Drottning Kristinas Tafvelgalleri på Stockholms slott och i Rom*, Stockholm, 1896.

3 Wethey, op. cit., pp. 143ff., cat. nos. 120-29.

4 Print by A.-L. Romanet published in J. Couché, *Galerie des Tableaux du Palais Royal*, Paris, 1786-1808, pl. 14. See Wethey, op. cit., cat. no. 128. There is a drawing by Borel for Romanet's engraving (Bibliothèque Doucet, Institut d'Art et d'Archéologie, Paris), illustrated with the other relevant images in Granberg, op. cit., cat. no. 33.

5 'Ma ceda la natura e ceda il vero
A quel che dotto artefice ne finse,
Che, qual l'avea ne l'alma e nel pensiero,
Tal bella e viva ancor qui la dipinse.
Oh celeste sembianza, oh magistero,
Ove ne l'opra sua se stesso ei vinse;
Fregio eterno de' lini e de le carte.
Meraviglia del mondo, onor de l'arte!'
James V. Mirollo, *The Poet of the Marvelous: Giambattista Marino*, 1963, pp. 292, 293. See Wethey, op. cit., cat. no. 120, p. 143.

6 J. A. Crowe & G. B. Cavalcaselle, *Life and Times of Titian*, 2 vols., London, 1877, II, p. 312.

7 Wethey, op. cit., cat. no. 127 (destroyed in London in 1873).

8 Vasari, *The Lives* ... , 2 vols. (Everyman Library), London, 1996, II, p. 795.

9 C. Ridolfi, *Le Maraviglie dell'Arte* (1648), 2nd. edn., Padua, 1835, p. 171. Ridolfi here talks of the picture's going to the King of Spain (i.e. the destroyed Escorial version) although, as noted by Wethey, op. cit., p. 143, the details of the poem by Marino suggest that he was inspired by a picture of the Pitti type.

10 Wethey, op. cit., p. 146, cat. no. 123.

11 A. Ritter von Perger, 'Studien zur Geschichte der K. K. Gemäldegalerie im Belvedere zu Wien', *Berichte und Mittheilungen des Altertums-vereins zu Wien*, VII (1864), pp. 101-68, p. 105. For an outline of the provenance, see Wethey, op. cit., p. 148.

12 Thus the reference to a Magdalen in the 1607-11 inventory is to a wax model in a shrine: 'No. 257. Ein Maria *Magdalena* in

einer *grotta…* '. R. Bauer and H. Haupt, 'Das Kunstkammerinventar Kaiser Rudolf II. 1607-1611', *Jahrbuch der Kunsthistorischen Sammlungen in Wien*, 72 (1976), p. 106.

13 E. Fučikova, 'Prague Castle under Rudolf II, His Predecessors and Successors', *in Rudolf II and Prague, The Court and the City*, exh. cat. (Prague), London, 1997, pp. 2-71, p. 63.

14 R. Distelberger, 'The Habsburg Collections in Vienna', in *The Origins of Museums: the cabinet of curiosities in sixteenth and seventeenth century Europe*, O. Impey and A. MacGregor, ed., Oxford, 1985, pp. 39-46, p. 40. The nature of the exhibits in the *Schatzkammer* is described pp. 41-4.

15 Fučikova, op. cit., pp. 64-5.

16 H. Zimmerman, 'Das Inventar der Prager Schatz- und Kunstkammer vom 6. Dezember 1621', *Jahrbuch der Kunsthistorischen Sammlungen in Wien*, XXV/2 (1905), pp. xiii-lxxv.

17 O. Granberg, *La Galérie de tableaux de la reine Christine de Suède ayant appartenus à l'empereur Rudolphe II plus tard aux ducs d'Orleans* (abridged French trans. of Granberg, op. cit., 1896), Stockholm, 1897, Appendix I. See also Granberg, op. cit., 1896, p. 15.

18 *Christina: A Personality in European Culture*, Council of Europe, exh. cat., 1966, p. 419. Christina's criticism of Dürer is of interest since anything by him, but countless more things claimed erroneously to be by him, had been a central part of Matthias's *Schatzkammer*: Distelberger, op. cit., pp. 40-1.

19 Granberg, op. cit., 1897, Appendix II.

20 Curt Weibull, *Christina of Sweden*, Gothenburg, 1966, p. 96.

21 J. Denucé, *Les galeries d'art à Anvers aux 16e et 17e siècles. Inventaires*, s'Gravenhage, 1932, pp. 176-179.

22 See, for example, the entry in *The Dictionary of Art*.

23 Kindly supplied by Görel Cavalli-Björkman, Nationalmuseum, Stockholm, where the measurements are translated as equivalent to 122.6 x 112 cm. It seems clear in view of the other record (see n. 25 below) that the frame is here included.

24 O Sirén, ed., *Nicodemus Tessin d.Y:s studieresor*, Stockholm, 1914, p. 184.

25 Granberg, op. cit., 1897, Appendix III; Campori, op. cit. at n. 2 above, pp. 343. '32 A painting of a penitent Magdalen, more in half-length, very life-like with the arms and a small part of the breast exposed, and with dishevelled hair and before her a death's head with an open book against a beautiful landscape, by *Titian*, on canvas, $4^{3}/4$ palmi high and $3^{3}/4$ wide, with a plain gold Roman frame… 33 Another painting of a Magdalen similar in respect of the face but different in all other respects, also by *Titian*, on canvas, 4 palmi high and $3^{3}/4$ wide, with a plain gold Roman frame.' The copy of this inventory at the Nationalmuseum, Stockholm, differs in the measurements, which are translated in the archive notes respectively as 105.9 x 83.6 cm and 89 x 72.5 cm. Compare n. 23 above.

26 He bought the title in 1693.

27 Titian's *Magdalen* is noted in the Odescalchi Archives of 1692, 'Nota', fol. 57, *Inventario*, fol. 466v, no. 32 (Wethey, op. cit., p. 148).

28 In a reply from the Nationalmuseum, Stockholm, to a letter of 12 December 1964 from Carl Nordenfalk it is noted that Pompeo Azzolino must have sold the other *Magdalen* to Cardinal Pietro Ottoboni. Information kindly suppplied by Henry Avar.

29 Records in the Nationalmuseum, Stockholm, kindly communicated by Henry Avar.

30 An enlarged and revised edition of this book was published in 1737.

31 For more details of the Orléans sale in London see the chapter on Pordenone's *Hercules and Achelous* elsewhere in this volume, and J. Pomeroy, 'The Orléans Collection: its impact on the British art world', *Apollo*, February, 1997, pp. 26 ff.; D. Sutton, 'The Orléans Collection', *Apollo*, May 1984, pp. 362 ff. See also F. Haskell, *The Ephemeral Museum: Old Master Paintings and the Art Exhibition*, 2000.

32 Wethey, loc. cit.

33 See Waterhouse, op. cit., p. 374, no. 64.

34 Ibid., and see Wethey, loc. cit.

35 *The Works of John Ruskin*, E. T. Cook and Alexander Wedderburn, ed., 1903, vol. IV, p. 195.

Bibliography

Andresen, A., *Nicolaus Poussin, Verzeichniss der nach seinen Gemälden gefertigten gleichzeitingen und spätern Kupferstiche*, Leipzig, 1863, abridged and illus. French trans. by G. Wildenstein, *Gazette des Beaux-Arts*, LX (2), 1962, pp. 139ff

Andrews, K., *Adam Elsheimer, Paintings, Drawings, Prints*, Oxford, 1977

Baglione, G., *Le vite de' pittori, scultori e architetti...* , 1642

Bain, R. Nisbet, *Gustavus III and his Contemporaries*, 2 vols., 1894

Baldinucci, F., *Notizie dei professori del disegno dal Cimabue in qua* (Florence, 1681), edn. 1845-7

Barres, Baron Chaillou des, 'Les Châteaux d'Ancy-le-Franc, de Saint-Fargeau', *l'Annuaire statistique de l'Yonne, 1839*, Paris, 1845

Baschet, R., *E.J.Delécluze, témoin de son temps, 1781-1863*, Paris, 1942

Baticle, J., 'La seconde mort de Lepeletier de Saint-Fargeau. Recherches sur le sort du tableau de David', *Bulletin de la Société de l'histoire de l'art français*, 1988

Bätschmann, M.T., *Jakob Frey (1681-1752) Kupferstecher und Verleger in Rom*, Ph.D., University of Basel, 1997

Bauer, R., and H. Haupt, 'Das Kunstkammerinventar Kaiser Rudolf II. 1607-1611', *Jahrbuch der Kunsthistorischen Sammlungen in Wien*, 72 (1976)

Baumeister, W., 'On the history of the portrait of the Jabach family by Le Brun', *Wallraf-Richartz Jahrbuch*, vols. III and IV, 1926-7, pp. 211-21

Beard, G., 'Batoni and Mengs', *Leeds Art Calendar*, no. 44, 1960, pp. 23-4

Béguin, S., *Le Studiolo d'Isabelle d'Este*, exh. cat., Louvre, Paris, 1975

Bellori, G.P., *Le vite de' pittore, scultori, ed architetti moderni*, Rome, 1672

Bellori, G.P., *Nota Delli Musei, Librerie, Galerie, et Ornamenti di Statue e Pitture ne'Palazzi, nelle café, e ne'Giardini di Roma*, 1664

Belvisi, F., *Elogio Storico del Pittore Lodovico Caracci*, Bologna, 1825

Bentini, J., ed., *Quadri Rinomatissimi – Il Collezionismo dei Pio di Savoia*, 1994

Bentini, J., *Sovrane passioni: le raccolte d'arte della Ducale Galleria Estense*, exh. cat., Modena, 1998

Beresford, R., *A Dance to the Music of Time*, exh. cat., Wallace Collection, London, 1995

Bershad, D.L., 'The Newly Discovered Testament and Inventories of Carlo Maratti and his Wife Francesca', *Antologia di Belle Arti*, 1985

Bertele, T., *Il palazzo degli ambasciatori di Venezia a Constantinopoli*, Bologna, 1932

Bertolotti, A., 'Esportazione di oggetti di belli arti da Roma nel secolo XVIII', F. Gori, *Archivio Storico Artistico Archeologico e Letterario della Città e provincia di Roma*, vol. IV [1880]

Bigoni, A., *Il forestiere istruto...* , Padua, 1876

Biographie Universelle (Michaud), 45 vols., Paris, 1811-47

Biré, E., *Journal d'un Bourgeois de Paris pendant la Terreur*, Paris, 1895-8

Blanchot, P. *et al.*, *Mennecy sous la Révolution ou la Révolution de Jean Michel*, Le Mée-sur-Seine, 1989

Block, J.C., *Jeremias Falck, sein Leben und seine Werke*, Danzig, Leipzig and Vienna, 1890

Blunt, A., *Nicholas Poussin, The A. W. Mellon Lectures in Fine Art, 1958*, National Gallery of Art, Washington, D.C., 3 vols., New York and London, 1967

Bodart, D., *Tiziano e Federico II Gonzaga: Storia di un rapporto di committenza*, Rome, 1998

Bonsanti, G., 'La Galleria Estense: Storia di una Collezione', in J. Winkler, ed., *La Vendita di Dresda*, Modena, 1989, pp. 13-26

Boskovits, M., 'Giovanni Bellini: quelques suggestions sur ses débuts', *Revue du Louvre et des Musées de France*, 36 (1986), pp. 386-93

Boskovits, M., 'Per Jacopo Bellini Pittore (Postilla ad Un Colloquio)', *Paragone*, xxxvi, 419-421-423 (1985), pp. 111-23

Branca, S. Savini, *Il collezionismo veneziano del '600*, Padua, 1964

Bredius, A., and O. Hirschmann, *Kunstler Inventare: Urkunden zur Geschichte der Holländischen Kunst des XVIten, XVIIten, und XVIIIten Jahrhunderts*, 8 vols., The Hague, 1915-22

Brettingham, M., *The Plans, Elevations and Sections of Holkham in Norfolk... To which are added, the ceilings and chimney-pieces; and also, a descriptive account of the statues, pictures, and drawings, etc.*, London, 1773

Brigstocke, H., *William Buchanan and the Nineteenth-Century Art Trade* [London], 1982

Britton, J., and E. Wedlake Brayley, *The Beauties of England and Wales...* , 1801

Brown, C., J. Kelch and P. van Thiel, *Rembrandt: the Master & his Workshop – Paintings*, exh. cat., New Haven and London, 1992

Brown, C. M., '"Une nostre-Dame de pitié... de la main du grand Miquel-Ange"; A lost painting attributed to Michelangelo in the 1532 inventory of the Château de Bury', in *Bibliothèque d'Humanisme et Renaissance*, 53 (1981), pp. 159-63

Brown, C. M., 'A Ferrarese Lady and a Mantuan Marchesa; the Art and Antiquities Collection of Isabella d'Este Gonzaga', in C. Lawrence, ed., *Women and Art in Early Modern Europe*, 1997, pp. 53-71

Brown, J., *Kings and Connoisseurs: Collecting Art in Seventeenth-Century Europe* (The A. W. Mellon Lectures in the Fine Arts, 1994), Princeton, 1995

Bruyn, J., B. Haak, S. H. Levie, P. J. J. van Thiel and E. van de Wetering, *A Corpus of Rembrandt Paintings. By the Stichtung Foundation Rembrandt Project*, The Hague, 1982– [3 vols., up to 1642]

Buchanan, W., *Memoirs of Painting with a Chronological List of the Importation of Pictures by the Great Masters into England since the French Revolution*, 2 vols., 1824

Burgheres, J., *Wenceslaus Hollar, Seventeenth-century Prints from the Museum Boymans-Van Beuningen, Rotterdam*, exh. cat., 1994

Burney, C., *Music, Men and Manners in France and Italy*, 1770

Caglioti, F., 'Donatello, i Medici e Gentile de' Becchi: un po' d'ordine intorno alla Giuditta (e al 'David') in Via Larga – III', *Prospettiva*, 80 (October 1995), pp. 15-58

Caglioti, F., 'Il David bronzeo di Michelangelo (e Benedetto da Rovezzano): il problema dei pagamenti', in F. Caglioti *et al.*, *Ad Alessandro Conti (1946-1994)*, Pisa, 1996

Cammell, C. R., *The Great Duke of Buckingham*, London, 1939

Campori, G., *Raccolta di cataloghi ed inventarii inediti*, Modena, 1870

Catalogue des tableaux composant la Galerie de feu son Eminence le cardinal Fesch, Rome, 1841 (Salviucci et Fils)

Chambers, D., and J. Martineau, ed., *Splendours of the Gonzaga*, exh. cat., London, 1981

Chapman, H. Perry, *Rembrandt's Self-Portraits: A Study in Seventeenth-Century Identity*, Princeton, 1990

Chiarini, M., 'La probabile identità del "cavaliere di Malta" di Pitti', *Antichità viva*, XXVIII, 4 (1989), pp. 15-16

Christiansen, K., 'Venetian Painting of the Early Quattrocento', *Apollo*, March 1987, pp. 166-77

Christina: A Personality in European Culture, exh. cat., Council of Europe, 1966

Clark, A. M., ed. E. P. Bowron, *Pompeo Batoni: Complete Catalogue*, New York and Oxford, 1985

Cohen, C. E., *The Art of Giovanni Antonio da Pordenone: Between Dialect and Language*, 2 vols., Cambridge, 1996

Condivi, A., *Vita di Michelangelo Buonarroti*, ed. G. Nencioni, with contributions by M. Hirst and C. Elam, Florence, 1998

Connisbee, P., *Chardin*, 1986

Constable, W. G., 'Rubens in the Museum of Fine Arts, Boston', *in Miscellanea Leo Van Puyvelde*, Brussels, 1949

Corpus Rubenianum Ludwig Burchard, XVIII, W. Adler, '1: Landscapes' (1982)

Corpus Rubenianum Ludwig Burchard, XIX, H. Vlieghe, ed., 'Portraits II' (1987)

Correspondance des Directeurs de l'Académie de France à Rome, nouvelle série, II, *Directorat de Suvée 1795-1807*, G. Brunel and I. Julia, ed., 1984

Cosnac, G. J., *Les Richesses du Palais Mazarin...* , Paris, 1885

Couché, J., *Galerie du Palais Royal gravée d'après les tableaux des différentes Ecoles qui la composent...* , 3 vols., Paris, 1786-1808

Coupin, P. A., *Essai sur J. L. David*, Paris, 1827

Cousin, J. V., 'De divers tableaux du Poussin qui sont en Angleterre et particulièrement de l'Inspiration du Poète, *Archives de l'Art français*, III (1853-5)

Cox, M. L., 'Inventory of the Arundel Collection', *Burlington Magazine*, XIX (1911), pp. 282-6

Cox-Rearick, J., *The Collection of Francis I*, New York, 1996

Crowe, J. A., & G.B. Cavalcaselle, *Life and Times of Titian*, 2 vols., London, 1877

Crozat, P., *Recueil d'estampes d'après les tableaux... dans le Cabinet du Roy...* , Paris, 1729-42

Dan, Père P., *Le trésor des merveilles de la maison royale de Fontainebleu*, Paris, 1642

D'Argenville, A. N. Dezallier, *Voyage Pittoresque des Environs de Paris ou Description des Maisons Royales, Châteaux et autres Lieux de Plaisance, situés a quinze lieues aux environs de cette ville*, Paris, 1755

David, J., *Le Peintre Louis David 1748-1825*, 2 vols., Paris 1880-2

David, J., *Notice sur le Marat*, 1867

Davies, R., 'An inventory of the Duke of Buckingham's pictures etc., at York House in 1635', *Burlington Magazine*, X (October 1906-March 1907), pp. 376ff

Dawson, J., *The Stranger's Guide to Holkham*, Burnham, 1817

Degenhart, B., and A. Schmitt, *Corpus der Italienischen Zeichnungen 1300-1450*, II, 'Venedig: Jacopo Bellini', Berlin, 1990

Delécluze, E.-J., *Etienne-Jean Delécluze, Journal 1824-28*, ed. R. Baschet, Paris, 1948

Delécluze, E.-J., *Louis David, son école et son temps. Souvenirs*, Paris, 1863

Denucé, J., *De Antwerpsche 'Konstkamers', Inventarissen van de kunstverzamelingen te Antwerpen in de 16e en 17e eeuwen...* , Antwerp, 1932

Denucé, J., *Les galeries d'art à Anvers aux 16e et 17e siècles. Inventaires*, s'Gravenhage, 1932

Der Glanz der Farnese, exh. cat., Munich, 1995

Desjardons, A., *Ambassade diplomatique de la France avec la Toscane*, 6 vols., Paris, 1869-86

Dey, W., 'Histoire de la Ville et du comté de Saint-Fargeau', *Bulletin de la Société des Sciences Historiques et naturelles de l'Yonne*, Auxerre, 1858

Dictionary of Art, see Turner, J. Shoaf

Dictionary of National Biography, 1885–

Distelberger, R., 'The Habsburg Collections in Vienna', in *The Origins of Museums: the cabinet of curiosities in sixteenth and seventeenth century Europe*, O. Impey and A. MacGregor, ed., Oxford, 1985, pp. 39-46

Dizionario biografico degli Italiani , Rome, 1960–

Domenici, B. de, *Vite de' pittori, scultori, ed architetti napolitani* (1742), edn. 1844

Donati, L., 'Due immagini ignote di Solimano I (1494-1566)', in *Studi orientalistici in onore di Giorgio Levi della Vida*, Rome, 1956, vol. I, pp. 219-33

Dorez, L., *La Cour du pape Paul III*, 2 vols., Paris, 1932

Drei, G., *I Farnese: Grandezza e Decadenza di una Dinastia Italiana*, Rome, 1954

Dussler, L., *Die Zeichnungen des Michelangelo: kritischer Katalog*, 2 vols., Berlin, 1959

Dussler, L., *Sebastiano del Piombo*, Basel, 1942

Eisler, C., 'Saints Anthony Abbot and Bernardino of Siena designed by Jacopo and painted by Gentile Bellini', *Arte Veneta*, 39 (1985), pp. 32-40

Eisler, C., *The Genius of Giovanni Bellini. The Complete Paintings and Drawings*, New York, 1989

Ekserdjian, D., *Correggio*, New Haven and London, 1997

Farington, J., *The Diary of Joseph Farington*, ed. K. Garlick and A. Macintyre, 16 vols., New Haven and London, 1978-84

Feigenbaum, G., *Lodovico Carracci: A Study of His Late Career and a Catalogue of his Paintings*, Ph.D., Princeton, 1984

Félibien, A., *Entretiens sur les vies et les ouvrages des plus excellents peintres anciens et moderns*, 10 vols. (1666-88), edn. 1725

Figgis, N. F., 'The Roman property of Frederick Augustus Hervey, 4th Earl of Bristol and Bishop of Derry (1730-1803)', *Walpole Society*, LV (1989/90), pp. 77-88ff

Fletcher, J. M., 'Isabella d'Este, Patron and Collector', in D. Chambers and J. Martineau, ed., *Splendours of the Gonzaga*, exh. cat., London, 1981

Fonti per la Storia della Pittura, I-III, Serie Documentaria, 'Lettere e Altri Documenti intorno alla Storia dell Pittura. Giovanni Benedetto Castiglione detto il Grecchetto. Giovanni Francesco Castiglione. Salvatore Castiglione', Genoa, 1971-5 [Part III, Monzambona]

Fothergill, B., *Sir William Hamilton, Envoy Extraordinary*, 1969

Fothergill, B., *The Mitred Earl*, 1974

Fraser, F., *Beloved Emma*, 1986

Friedlaender, W., and A. Blunt, *The Drawings of Nicholas Poussin. A Catalogue Raisonné*, 5 vols., London, 1939-74

Friedlaender, W., *Caravaggio Studies*, Princeton, 1955

Frimmel, Th., ed., *Der Anonimo Morelliano (Marcantonio Michiel's Notizia d'Opere del Disegno)*, Vienna, 1888

Fučikova E., 'Prague Castle under Rudolf II, His Predecessors and Successors', in *Rudolf II and Prague, The Court and the City*, exh. cat. (Prague), London, 1997

Garas, K., 'Die Entstehung der Galerie des Erzherzogs Leopold Wilhelm', *Jahrbuch der Kunstsammlungen in Wien*, N.F., XXVII (1967), pp. 39-80

Gash, J., 'The identity of Caravaggio's "Knight of Malta"', *Burlington Magazine*, CXXXIX (1997), pp. 156-160

Gash, J., *Caravaggio*, London, 1988

Gasparoni, F. and B., ed., *Arti e Lettere*, Rome, 1865

Gatti, L., '"Delle cose de' pictori et Sculptori si può mal promettere cosa certa"; la diplomazia Fiorentina presso la corte del Re di Francia e il David bronzeo di Michelangelo Buonarotti' in *Mélanges de l'école Française de Rome: Italie et Mediterranée*, vol. 106, 2 (1994), pp. 433-472

Gaye, G., *Carteggio inedito d'artisti dei secoli XIV, XV, XVI pubblicato ed illustrato con documenti pure inediti dal dott. G. Gaye*, ed. J. W. Gaye, 3 vols., Florence, 1839-40

Gelder J. G. van, 'Jan de Bisschop', *Oud Holland*, LXXXXVI (1971)

Gersaint, E. F., *Catalogue raisonné, des tableaux, diamans... et autres Effets provenant de la Succession de feu Monsieur Charles Godefroy, Banquier et Joüaillier/Par E. F. Gersaint*, Paris, 1748

Gerson, H., *Seven Letters by Rembrandt* [translated into English by Yda D. Ovink], The Hague, 1961

Getty Provenance Index. B. Frederickson, *The Index of paintings sold in the British Isles during the nineteenth century*, London, New York, Paris, 1993; and on line

Gherardi, P. E., *Descrizione delle pitture esistenti in Modena nell'Estense Ducal Galleria* (MS, 1744), ed. G. Bonsanti, transcribed and researched by O. Baracchi, Modena, 1986

Gherardi, P. E., *Descrizione di cento pezzi di Pitture, passati nell'anno 1746 dalla Galleria Estense in Modena a quella di Federigo Augusto III. Re di Polonia ed elector di Sassonia pel valore e prezzo di Zecchini Veneziani Cento-mila* (MS, Reggio Emilia, 1752), ed. G. Bonsanti, transcribed by O. B. Giovanardi, Modena, 1986

Gibbon, E., *Gibbon's journey from Geneva to Rome. His Journal from 20 April to 2 October 1764*, ed. Georges A. Bonnard, *c.* 1961

Giovanardi, O.B., *La Vendita di Dresda. Notizie storiche*, in *Aedes Muratoriana*, Modena, 1982

Glück, I. G., *Die Landschaften von Peter Paul Rubens*, Vienna, 1945

Goethals, F.-V., *Dictionnaire des Familles Nobles du Royaume de Belgique*, 1849

Goffen, R., and G. N. Sciré, *Il colore rittrovato: Bellini a Venezia*, exh. cat., Venice, 2000

Goffen, R., *Giovanni Bellini*, New Haven and London, 1989

Goffen, R., *Titian's Women*, New Haven and London, 1997

Gonzati, B., *La basilica di Sant'Antonio di Padova, descritta ed illustrata*, 2 vols., Padua, 1852-3

Gould, C., *The Paintings of Correggio*, London, 1976

Granberg, O., *Drottning Kristinas Tavelgalleri på Stockholms slott och i Rom*, Stockholm, 1896

Granberg, O., *La Galérie de tableaux de la reine Christine de Suède ayant appartenus à l'empereur Rudolphe II plus tard aux ducs d'Orleans*, Stockholm, 1897

Gregori, M., 'A new painting and some observations on Caravaggio's journey to Malta', *Burlington Magazine*, CXVI (October 1974), pp. 594-603

Grésy, F., 'Inventaire des objets d'art composant la succession de Florimond Robertet', in *Mémoires de la Société Imperiale des Antiquaires de France*, ser. 3, X, 1868

Gronau, G., 'Die Kunstbestrebungen der Herzöge von Urbino', *Jahrbuch d. Kgl. Preuss. Kunstsammlungen*, XXV, 1904

Grossman, F., 'Holbein, Flemish Paintings and Everhard Jabach', *Burlington Magazine*, XCIII (1951), pp. 16-25

Grouchy, Vicomte de, 'Everhard Jabach, collectionneur parisien 1695', *Mémoires de la Society de l'Histoire de Paris et de l'Ile-de-France*, vol. XXI, Paris, 1894, pp. 217-92

Gualandi, M., *Nuova raccolta di lettere*, 3 vols., Bologna, 1844-56

Guarino, S., '"Qualche Quadro per Nostro Servizio": i dipinti Pio di Savoia inventariati, venduti e dispersi', in J. Bentini, *Quadri Rinomatissimi: Il Collezionismo dei Pio di Savoia*, Modena, 1994

Guide to Holkham, the seat of the Right Hon. The earl of Leicester... , Norwich, 1861

Haskell, F., 'Charles I's Collection of Pictures' in A. MacGregor, ed., *The Late King's Goods: Collections, Possessions and Patronage of Charles I in the Light of the Commonwealth Sale Inventories*, London, 1989, pp. 203-31

Haskell, F., 'Art Exhibitions in XVII Century Rome', *Biblioteca dell'Archivum Romanicum. Studi Secenteschi*, vol. 1, 1960

Haskell, F., *Painters and Patrons*, London, 1963

Haskell, F., *The Ephemeral Museum: Old Master Paintings and the Art Exhibition*, 2000

Hasselgren, I., *Konstsamlaren Gustav Adolf Sparre 1746-1794. Hans studieresa våning och konstsaling i Göteborg*, Göteborg, 1974

Haynes, D. E. L., *The Arundel Marbles*, Oxford, 1975

Held, J., 'Rubens' "King of Tunis" and Vermeyen's Portrait of Mulay Ahmad', *Art Quarterly*, III (1940), pp. 173-81

Held, J., *Rubens-Studien*, Leipzig, 1987

Hervey, M.F.S., *The Life, Correspondence & Collections of Thomas Howard Earl of Arundel*, Cambridge, 1921,

Hibbert, C., *Rome, Portrait of a City*, 1985

Hirst, M., 'Sebastiano del Piombo's Pietà for the Commendador Mayor', *Burlington Magazine*, CXIV (1972), pp. 585ff

Hirst, M., *Sebastiano del Piombo*, Oxford, 1981

Hollingsworth, M., *Patronage in Sixteenth-century Italy*, London, 1996

Hope, C., *Titian*, London, 1980

Horn, J., *Jan Cornelisz Vermeyen: Painter of Charles V and His Conquest of Tunis*, 2 vols., Doornspijk, 1989

Howarth, D., '"Mantua Peeces": Charles I and the Gonzaga Collection', in D. Chambers and J. Martineau, ed., *Splendours of the Gonzaga*, exh. cat., London, 1981, pp. 95-100

Howarth, D., 'The Patronage and Collecting of Aletheia, Countess of Arundel 1606-54', *Journal of the History of Collections*, 10, no. 2 (1998), pp. 125-37

Howarth, D., *Lord Arundel and his Circle*, New Haven and London, 1985

Humfrey, P., 'The Bellini and the Vivarini in Venice', in E. Borsook and F.S. Gioffredi, ed., *Italian Altarpieces 1250-1550, Function and Design*, Oxford, 1994, pp. 139-74

Humfrey, P., 'Drawing and Collaboration in the Carracci Academy', in *Essays in Honor of Irving Lavin on his Sixtieth Birthday*, M. Lavin, ed., New York, 1990

Humfrey, P., 'Jacopo Bellini: Sts. Anthony Abbot and Bernardine of Siena' in D. Garstang, ed., *Gothic to Renaissance: European Painting 1300-1600*, exh. cat. Colnaghi (London and New York), 1988-9, pp. 18-26

Humfrey, P., *Lorenzo Lotto*, New Haven and London, 1997

Humfrey, P., *The Altarpiece in Renaissance Venice*, New Haven and London, 1993

Ilchester, Lord, *Chronicles of Holland House, 1820-1900*, 1937

Ingamells, J., *A Dictionary of British and Irish Travellers in Italy 1701-1800*, New Haven and London, 1997

Inventaire des Tableaux du Roy restez au Cabinet des Peintures du château de Fontainebleau (D'Estrechy), 1692

Irwin, D. & F., *Scottish Painters at Home and Abroad 1700-1900*, 1975

Jaffé, D., *et al.*, 'The Earl and Countess of Arundel: Renaissance Collectors', *Apollo*, August, 1996

Jal, A., *Esquisses, croquis, pochades, ou tout ce qu'on voudra sur le Salon de 1827*, Paris, 1828

Janelli, G.B., *Dizionario biografico dei parmigiani illustri o benemeriti*, 1877 (reprinted)

Jenkins, I., and K. Sloan, *Vases and Volcanoes*, exh. cat., London, 1996

Jestaz, B., *Le Palais Farnèse III, 3, L'inventaire du Palais et des Propriétés Farnèse à Rome en 1644*, Ecole Française de Rome, 1994

Judith, J., *Mennecy, son Histoire, sa Vie*, 1973

Kenworthy Browne, J., 'Matthew Brettingham's Rome Account Book 1747-54', *Walpole Society*, XLIX (1983), pp. 37-132

Klibansky, R., and H.J. Paton, ed., *Philosophy and History. Essays presented to E. Cassirer*, Oxford, 1936

L'officina della maniera: varietà e fierezza nell'arte fiorentina del Cinquecento fra le due repubbliche (1494-1530), exh. cat., Florence (Uffizi), 1994

La Galerie Electorale de Dusseldorff ou Catalogue Raisonné et Figuré de ses Tableaux... par Chrétien de Mechel &c, Basel, 1778

Labande-Mailfert, Y., *Charles VIII et son milieu (1470-1498)*, Paris, 1975

Landucci, L., *Diario Fiorentino dal 1450 al 1516, di L. Landucci continuato da un anonimo fino al 1542... con annotazioni da Iodoco del Badia*, ed. J. del Badia, Florence, 1883

Langdon, H., *Caravaggio*, London, 1998

Lavin, M. A., *Seventeenth century Barberini Documents and Inventories of Art*, New York, *c.* 1975

Lawrence, C., ed., *Women and Art in Early Modern Europe*, 1997

Lazzarini, V., 'Gli autori della cappella e dei monumenti Gattamelata al Santo', *Il Santo*, IV, 1932, pp. 228-33

Le Siècle de Titien, exh. cat., Paris, 1993

Levine, S., 'Michelangelo's marble David and the lost bronze David: the drawings', *Artibus et Historiae*, 9, 1984

Lightbown, R. W., 'Princely Pressures: 2. Francesco I d'Este and Correggio', *Apollo*, xix (1963), pp. 193-99

Logan, A.-M. S., *The 'Cabinet' of the Brothers Gerard and Jan Reynst*, Amsterdam, Oxford and New York, 1979

Lorenzoni, G., ed., *Fonti e Studi per la storia del Santo a Padova III: l'Edificio del Santo a Padova*, Vicenza, 1981

Lotto, Lorenzo, *Libro di Spese Diverse (1538-1556)*, ed. P. Zampetti, Florence, 1969

Lugt, F., 'Italiaanische kunstwerken in Nederlandsche verzamelingen van vroeger tijden', *Oud Holland*, LIII (1936)

Luzio, A., *La Galleria dei Gonzaga venduta all' Inghilterra nel 1627-8*, Milan, 1913 (reprinted Rome 1974)

MacGregor, A., ed., *The Late King's Goods. Collections, Possessions and Patronage of Charles I in the Light of the Commonwealth Sale Inventories*, London and Oxford, 1989

Macmillan, D., *Scottish Painting; The Golden Age*, exh. cat., London and Edinburgh, 1986

Maddicott, H., 'A Collection of the Interregnum Period', *Journal of the History of Collections*, II, no. 1 (1999), pp. 1-24

Magurn, R. S., ed., *The Letters of Peter Paul Rubens*, Cambridge, Mass., 1955

Mahon, D., 'Notes on the "Dutch Gift" to Charles II', *Burlington Magazine*: part I, XCI (November 1949), pp. 303-5; part II (December 1949, pp. 349-50); and part III, vol. XCII (January 1950), pp. 12-18

Mahon, D., *Il Guercino: Catalogo critico dei dipinti*, Bologna, 1968

Maindron, M., 'Le portrait du Grand-Maître Alof de Wignacourt au Musée du Louvre', *Revue de l'Art Ancien et Moderne*, XXIV (1908), pp. 241-54

Malvasia, C. C., *La Felsina pittrice: Vite de' pittori bolognesi*, 2 vols., Bologna, 1678

Manazzale, A., *Rome et ses environs. Dernière edition augmentée et corrigée par l'antiquaire*, 2 vols., Rome, 1802

Mander, K. van, *Het schilder-boeck*, Haarlem, 1603-4

Marchi, G. de, *Mostre di Quadri a S. Salvatore in Lauro (1682-1725)*, Rome, 1987

Mariette, P. J., *Abecedario*, ed. P. de Chennevières and A. de Montaiglon, 6 vols., Paris, 1851-60

Marini, M., *Io Michelangelo da Caravaggio*, Rome, 1974

Marshall, R. K., *The house of Hamilton in its Anglo-Scottish setting in the Seventeenth Century: with a calendar of the correspondence in the Hamilton Archives at Lennoxlove, to 1712*, Ph.D., Edinburgh University, 1970

Martineau, J., 'The Studiolo of Isabella d'Este and Late Themes', in J. Martineau, ed., *Andrea Mantegna*, exh. cat., London and New York, 1991-2, pp. 418ff

Martineau, J., ed., *Andrea Mantegna*, exh. cat., London and New York, 1991-2

Martinoni, R., *Gian Vincenzo Imperiale, politico, letterato e collezionista genovese del Seicento*, Padua, 1983

Mayer, C.-A., and D. Bentley-Cranch, *Florimond Robertet (?-1527): Homme d'Etat français*, Paris, 1994

McEvansoneya, P., 'The sequestration and dispersal of the Buckingham collection', *Journal of the History of Collecting*, VIII, no. 2 (1986), pp. 133-54

McEwan, P. J. M., *Dictionary of Scottish Art & Architecture*, Woodbridge, 1994

Michiel, M., *Notizia d'opere di disegno... scritta da un anonimo...* , ed. J. Morelli, Bassano, 1880

Millar, O., ed. (with intro.) 'The inventories and valuations of the King's goods 1649-1651', *Walpole Society*, XLIII (1970-72)

Millar, O., ed., 'Abraham van der Doort's Catalogue of the Collections of Charles I', *Walpole Society*, XXXVII (1958-1960)

Mirollo, J.V., *The Poet of the Marvelous: Giambattista Marino*, 1963

Muller, J., *Rubens, The Artist as Collector*, Princeton, 1984

New description of Holkham... , 1826

Nolhac, P. de, 'Une galerie de peinture au XVIe siècle. La collection de Fulvio Orsini', *Gazette des Beaux-Arts*, 1884, pp. 427-436

Nouaillac, J., *Villeroy, Secrétaire d'Etat et Ministre*, Paris, 1909

Nulli, S.A., *Giulia Gonzaga*, Milan, 1938

Nuttall, W.L.F., 'King Charles I's Pictures and the Commonwealth Sale' *Apollo*, lxxxii, 1965, pp. 302-309

Oglander, Sir J., *A Royalist's Notebook*, ed. F. Bamford, 1936

Oliva, M., *Giulia Gonzaga Colonna tra Rinascimento e Controriforma*, Mursia, 1985

Pagden, S. Ferino, *'La Prima Donna del Mondo': Isabella d'Este: Fürstin und Mäzenatin der Renaissance*, exh. cat., Vienna, 1994

Panofsky, E., 'Et in Arcadia Ego', in *Philosophy and History. Essays presented to E. Cassirer*, R. Klibansky and H.J. Paton, ed., Oxford, 1936, pp. 222-54

Parronchi, A., *Opere giovanili di Michelangelo*, Florence, 1968

Perger, A. Ritter von, 'Studien zur Geschichte der K.K. Gemäldegalerie im Belvedere zu Wien', *Berichte und Mittheilungen des Altertums-vereins zu Wien*, VII (1864)

Planiscig, L., *Die Estensische Kunstsammlung, Bd. I, Skulpturen und Plastike des Mittelalters und der Renaissance*, Vienna, 1919

Pomeroy, J., 'The Orléans Collection: its impact on the British art world', *Apollo*, February 1997, pp. 26ff

Ponz, A., *Viage de España...* (13 vols., Madrid, 1776-84), edn. Madrid, 1947

Poole, R., 'An outline of the history of the De Critz family of painters', *Walpole Society*, II (1912-13), pp. 54ff

Pope-Hennessy, J., *The Drawings of Domenichino in the Collection of His Majesty The King at Windsor Castle*, 1948

Postle, M., 'Driven by Passion', *The Royal Academy Magazine*, no. 45, Winter 1994, pp. 34-5

Pressouyre, S., 'Les Stucs', in *La Galerie François Ier à Fontainebleau, Revue de l'Art*, 16-17 (1972)

Ramage, N., 'A list of Sir William Hamilton's property', *Burlington Magazine*, CXXXI (October 1989), pp. 704-6

Ramsden, E.H., *Come, Take this Lute, A Quest for Identities in Italian Renaissance Portraiture*, 1983

Reinach-Foussemagne, La Comtesse H. de, *Une Fidéle: La Marquise de Lage de Volude 1764-1842 d'après des documents inédits*, Paris, 1908

Reiset, M., 'Un bronze de Michel-Ange', in *Athenaeum française*, 1853

Reitlinger, G., *The Economics of Taste: the Rise and Fall of Picture Prices 1760-1960*, 3 vols., New York, 1982

Rembrandt, *The Rembrandt Documents, compiled by W.L. Strauss and M. van der Meulen...* , New York, 1979

Répaci-Courtois, G., 'A propos du David en bronze de Michel-Ange', *La Revue du Louvre et des Musées*, 1976, pp. 250-54

Reports of the Royal Commission on Historical Manuscripts, 1st-9th, 1870-83 (reprinted 1979)

Revitt, C., *The Man who would be King: The Life of Philippe d'Orléans, Regent of France*, London, 1997

Ricci, C., *Antonio Allegri da Correggio: His Life, his Friends, and his Time*, London, 1896

Ricci, C., *Correggio*, Rome, 1930

Richards, J., *Altichiero: An Artist and his Patrons in the Italian Trecento*, Cambridge, 2000

Ridolfi, C., *Le Maraviglie dell'Arte* (1648), 2nd edn., corrected with notes, 2 vols., Padua, 1835; and D. von Hadeln, ed., 2 vols., Berlin, 1914-24

Ristori, R., *Il Carteggio di Michelangelo*, 5 vols., Florence, 1973

Roberts, M., *The Age of Liberty: Sweden 1719-1772*, 1986

Robertson, C., and C. Whistler, *Drawings by the Carracci from British Collections*, exh. cat., 1996/7

Robertson, C., 'Osservazioni sul mecenatismo del cardinale Odoardo Farnese', in *I Farnese: Arte e collezionismo. Studi*, Milan, 1995

Robertson, C., ed., *Lodovico Carracci*, exh. cat., Bologna, 1993

Robertson, C., *Il Gran Cardinale: Alessandro Farnese, Patron of the Arts*, New Haven and London, 1992

Robinson, J. M., *The Dukes of Norfolk*, Oxford and New York, 1982

Rogers, J. M., and R. M. Ward, *Suleyman the Magnificent*, exh. cat., British Museum, 1988

Rosenberg, P., and R. Temperini, *Chardin, suivi du catalogue des oeuvres*, Paris, 1999

Rosenberg, P., *Chardin*, exh. cat., Grand Palais, Paris, 1979

Rowlands, J., *Holbein: The Paintings of Hans Holbein the Younger, Complete Edition*, Oxford, 1985

Rubens: Copista de Tiziano, exh. cat., Madrid, 1987

Rudloff-Hille, G. (trans K.M. Leake), *Dresden Gemäldegalerie*, London, 1960

Rudolph, S., *Niccolò Maria Pallavicini: L'ascesa al Tempio della Virtù attraverso il Mecenatisimo*, Rome, 1995

Ruelens, C., and M. Rooses, ed., *Correspondance de Rubens et documents épistolaires concernant sa vie et ses oeuvres*, 6 vols., Antwerp, 1887-1909

Ruskin, J., *The Works of John Ruskin*, ed. E. T. Cook and A. Wedderburn, 1903

Sainsbury, W. N., *Original Unpublished Papers Illustrative of the Life of Sir Peter Paul Rubens, as an Artist and a Diplomatist. Preserved in H. M. State Paper Office*, London, 1859

Saint-Gelais, Du Bois de, *Description des tableaux du Palais Royal*, Paris, 1727

Sartori, A., 'La cappella del Sacramento al Santo decorata da Luovico Pogliaghi', *Il Santo*, X, 1970, pp. 183-204

Sartori, A., *Documenti per la storia dell'arte a Padova*, ed. C. Fillarini, Vicenza, 1976

Sass, E. Kai, *Comments on Rembrandt's Passion Paintings and Constantijn Huygens's Iconography*, Copenhagen, 1971

Saxl, F., 'Veritas filia Temporis' in *Philosophy and History. Essays presented to E. Cassirer*, R. Klibansky and H. J. Paton, ed., Oxford, 1936

Schama, S., *Rembrandt's Eyes*, 1999

Schnapper, A., and A. Sérullaz, ed., *Jacques-Louis David 1748-1825*, exh. cat., Paris, 1989-90

Schnapper, A., *David, témoin de son temps*, Fribourg, 1980

Schneevoogt, C. G. Voorhelm, *Catalogue des Estampes gravées d'après P. P. Rubens*, Haarlem, 1873

Schwarz, G., *Rembrandt: His life, His Paintings* [1984], London, 1991

Scott, B., 'Charles Alexandre de Calonne, Economist and Collector', *Apollo*, xcvii (1973), pp. 86-91

Semenzato, C., *Fonti e Studi per la Storia del Santo a Padova IX*, Studi 5, Vicenza, 1984

Serassi, P., ed., *Delle Poesie Volgari e Latine di F. M. Molza*, Bergamo, 1747

Sérullaz, A., *Inventaire Général des Dessins, École Française: Dessins de Jacques Louis David*, Paris, 1991

Seymour, C., *Michelangelo's David: A Search for Identity*, Pittsburgh, 1967

Shakeshaft, P., 'Documents for the history of Collecting: I. The Correspondence of Hamilton and Feilding', *Burlington Magazine*, CXXVIII (February 1986), pp. 114-132

Sharpe, K., *The Personal Rule of Charles I*, New Haven and London, 1992

Sicca, C.M., 'On William Kent's Roman Sources,' *Architectural History*, 29 (1986), pp. 134-147

Simon, R., *The Portrait in Britain and America*, London and Boston, 1987

Sirén, O., ed., *Nicodemus Tessin d.Y:s studieresor*, Stockholm, 1914

Smith, J., *A Catalogue Raisonné of the works of the most eminent Dutch, Flemish and French Painters...* , IX (Supplement), 1842

Soboul, A., *Les Sans-culottes parisiens en l'an II*, Paris, 1958

Spear, R.E., *Domenichino*, 2 vols., New Haven and London, 1982

Springell, F.C., *Connoisseur & Diplomat... The Earl of Arundel's Embassy...* , London, 1963

Sumerscale, A., *Malvasia and the Carracci*, Pennsylvania, 2000

Survey of London, F.H.W.Shephard, ed., 1900–

Susinno, F., *Vite de' pittori messinesi* (1724), ed. V.Martinelli, Florence, 1960

Sutton, D., 'The Orléans Collection', *Apollo*, May 1984, pp. 362 ff

Sutton, P.C., *et al.*, *The Age of Rubens*, exh. cat., Boston, 1993

Szambien, W., *Jean-Nicolas-Louis Durand*, Paris, 1984

The Age of Caravaggio, exh. cat., New York, 1985

The Anonimo [Marcantonio Michiel]: notes on pictures and works of art in Italy made by an anonymous writer in the sixteenth century, translated by P.Mussi, G.C.Williamson, ed., London, 1903

The Complete Peerage, V.Gibbs *et al.*, ed., 1910-59

Tischbein, J.H.W., *Collection of Engravings from Ancient Vases Discovered in the Kingdom of the Two Sicilies between 1789-90*, 5 vols., Naples, 1793–

Titian Prince of Painters, exh. cat., Venice and Washington, 1990-1

Tiziano nelle gallerie Fiorentine, exh. cat., Florence, 1978

Tolnay, C.de, *The youth of Michelangelo*, Princeton, 1943, and 2nd edn. in *Michelangelo*, Princeton, 1947, vol. I

Turner, J.Shoaf, ed., *The Dictionary of Art*, 34 vols., London, 1996

Valéry-Radot, J., 'Autour du portrait de Lepeletier de Saint-Fargeau. Recherches sur le sort du tableau de David', *Archives de l'art Français publiées par la Société de l'histoire de l'art Français*, vol. XXI, 1949

Varchi, B., *Orazione Funerale di M. Benedetto Varchi. Fatta, e recitata da Lui pubblicamente nell'essequie di Michelangelo Buonarroti in Firenze, nella chiese di San Lorenzo*, Florence, 1564

Varchi, B., *Storia Fiorentina*, Florence, edn. 1838-1841

Vasari G., *Lives of the Painters, Sculptors and Architects*, 2 vols. (Everyman Library), London, 1996

Vasari, G., *Le vite...* , ed. R.Bettarini and P.Barocchi, 6 vols., Florence, 1966–

Venturi A., *La R.Galleria Estense in Modena*, Modena, 1883

Vertue, G., 'Vertue Notebooks', I, *Walpole Society*, XVIII (1930)

Waagen, G.F., *Treasures of Art in Great Britain*, 3 vols., London, 1854

Walpole, H., *A Catalogue of the collection of Pictures, etc., belonging to King James the Second...* , London, 1758

Walpole, H., *Anecdotes of Painting in England... volume the fifth and last*, ed. F.W.Hilles and P.B.Daghlian, 1937

Walpole, H., ed. W.S.Lewis *et al.*, *Horace Walpole's Correspondence*, 48 vols., 1937-83

Waterhouse, E.K., 'Paintings from Venice for Seventeenth Century England', *Italian Studies*, VII (1952), pp. 1-23

Waterhouse, E.K., 'Queen Christina's Italian Pictures in England' in *Queen Christina of Sweden, Documents and Studies*, Stockholm, 1966

Waterhouse, E.K., 'The British Contribution to the Neo-Classical Style of Painting', *Proceedings of the British Academy*, XL (1954)

Wattine, A., *Un magistrat révolutionnaire, Michel Lepeletier de Saint-Fargeau*, Paris, 1913

Weibull, C., *Christina of Sweden*, Gothenburg, 1966

Weijtens, F.H.C., *De Arundel-Collectie, Commencement de la Fin, Amersfoort, 1655*, Utrecht, 1971

Wethey, H., *The Paintings of Titian*, 3 vols., London, 1969-75

Wheelock, A.K., Jr., *Dutch Paintings of the Seventeenth Century, The Collections of the National Gallery of Art [Washington, D.C.]*, Washington, D.C., 1995

Wildenstein, D. and G., *Documents complémentaires au Catalogue de l'oeuvre de Louis David*, Paris, 1973

Willson, D.H., *King James VI and I*, London, 1956

Winkler, J., ed., *La Vendita di Dresda*, Modena, 1989

Wuthrich, L., *Zürcher Kunst nach der Reformation. Hans Asper und seine Zeit*, exh. cat., Zürich, 1981

Zeri, F., *La Galleria Pallavicini*, Florence, 1959

Zimmerman, H., 'Das Inventar der Prager Schatz- und Kunstkammer vom 6. Dezember 1621', *Jahrbuch der Kunsthistorischen Sammlungen in Wien*, XXV/2 (1905), pp. xiii-lxxv

Acknowledgements and photographic credits

The author is grateful to the following people and institutions for their kind permission to reproduce these illustrations:

Agnew's, London 104
AKG, London (Swedish National Portrait Gallery) 271
Albertina, Vienna 244, 266 *(both)*
Alte Pinakothek, Munich, photo Artothek 126, 128, 129
Ashmolean Museum, Oxford 55, 146 *(top)*

Bayerische Staatsgemäldesammlung, Munich 68 *(top)*
Bibliothèque Nationale, Paris 210 *(bottom)*, 211 *(bottom)*, 215, 226
Bridgeman Art Library (Museo del Prado, Madrid) 32, 56, (Yale Center for British Art) 76 *(both)*, (Musée de la Chartreuse, Douai) 86, (Musée Condé, Chantilly) 89, (British Library) 94, (Wallace Collection, London) 117, (Château de Versailles) 119, (Musée du Louvre) 137, (Kunsthistorisches Museum, Vienna) 140/1, (Petworth House, National Trust) 142, (Ackerman & Johnson Ltd.) 148, 164, (Collection of the Earl of Leicester, Holkham Hall) 182, (Museo del Prado) 200, (Musée Royaux des Beaux-Art, Brussels) 214, (Musée de la Révolution Francaise, Vizille) 217, (Uffizi, Florence) 236, (Wallace Collection, London) 237, (Cathedral of St. John, Malta) 239, (Musée Bonnat, Bayonne) 264, (Musée du Louvre) 270, (Galleria Estense, Modena) 287, (Uffizi, Florence) 289, 306
British Library 134, 146 *(bottom)*, 172,
British Museum 13, 97, 102 *(both)*, 156, 168, 173, 174

Christie's Images 132
Courtauld Institute of Art, Witt Library 36, 78 *(both)*, 79 *(both)*, 82, 105, 112, 115, 131, 180, 183, 190, 274
Courtauld Gallery of Art, London 109

David & Alfred Smart Museum of Art, University of Chicago 84,

Fotomas (British Museum) 139,
Fuji Art Museum, Tokyo 268 *(top)*

Galleria Nazionale, Parma (on loan from Brera, Milan) 284
Gemäldegalerie, Dresden 288, 290, 291
Guildhall Library, London 70, 188, 205, 247

Herzog Anton-Ulrich Museum, Brunswick, photo B.P.Kelser 122
His Grace, the Duke of Norfolk 21
Historisch Museum, Amsterdam 158
Hunterian Art Gallery, University of Glasgow 74

Index, Florence, photo Vasari 43, 196 *(both)*, 286, 294, 296, 297 *(top)*, 303, 304, 305

J.Paul Getty Museum, Los Angeles 176/7
John and Mable Ringling Museum, Florida 107

Kimbell Museum, Fort Worth, photo Michael Bodycomb 245
Kunsthistorischesmuseum, Vienna 101, 194, 199, 207

Len Golding Photography 10

Mauritshuis, The Hague 130
Musée des Beaux-Arts et d'Archéologie, Besançon, photo Charles Choffet 68 *(bottom)*
Musée des Beaux-Arts, Bourges 210 *(top)*
Musée des Beaux-Arts, Dijon 208
Museum Boymans-Van Beuningen, Rotterdam 30, 281
Musée Fabre, Montpellier 276
Museum of Fine Arts, Boston 28
Museum of Fine Art, Houston, Texas 269 *(top)*
Museum of Fine Arts, Malta, photo Patrick Fenech 235

National Gallery of Art, Washington (Widener Collection) 87, (partial gift of an Anonymous Donor) 299 *(left)*
National Gallery, London 248
National Gallery, Prague 12
National Gallery of Scotland 75, 77 *(both)*, 279,
National Portrait Gallery, London, 14, 15, 171, 246, 282
Nationalmuseum, Stockholm *(bottom)* 268, 269 *(bottom)*

Öffentliche Kunstsammlung Basel, Kunstmuseum, photo Martin Buhler 19

Pinacoteca Nazionale, Bologna, photo Balducci Gabrieli 151
Pinacoteca Nazionale, Ferrara *(top right)* 299
Pinacoteca Vaticana, Rome 113

Pitti Palace, Florence, photo Rabatti Domingue 242

Réunion des Musées Nationaux (all from the Musée du Louvre, Paris) 50, 114, 197, 198, 211 *(top)*, (on loan from the Ecole des Beaux-Arts, Paris) 216, 234, 256, 258, 260, 262, 277, 302
RIBA, London 46, 57, 58, 90, 189, 213
Rijksmuseum, Amsterdam 35
Roger-Viollet, Paris 222, (Bibliothèque Nationale, Paris) 225

The Royal Collection, © 2002, Her Majesty Queen Elizabeth II 116, 185, 278, 280

Scala (Uffizi, Florence) 40, (Pitti, Florence) 41, (Galleria Nazionale di Capodimonte, Naples) 42, (Museo Nazionale, Florence) 52, (Accademia, Florence) 53, (Uffizi, Florence) 108, (Pinacoteca Nazionale, Siena) 160, (Pinacoteca Civica, Brescia) 161, 297, (Museo Correr, Venice) *(centre right)* 299, (Museo Civico, Padua) *(bottom right)* 299
Scottish National Portrait Gallery 136, 149,
Sotheby & Co. 71, 219
Staatliche Museen zu Berlin, photo Preussische Kulturbesitz 138
State Hermitage Museum, St. Petersburg 23
Syndics of the Fitzwilliam Museum, Cambridge 33, 64

Teyler Museum, Haarlem 259

Wallraf-Richartz-Museum, Cologne, photo Rheinisches Bildarchiv 24
Wiesbaden Museum 38,
Wignacourt Collegiate Museum, Rabat, photo Daniel Cilia 232

Index

Subjects of illustrations are shown in italics; major entries are shown in bold type.